Artificial Intelligence
A New Synthesis

Artificial Intelligence
A New Synthesis

 **Nils J. Nilsson**

Stanford University

 Morgan Kaufmann Publishers, Inc.
San Francisco, California

Sponsoring Editor   Michael B. Morgan
Director of Production and Manufacturing   Yonie Overton
Production Editor   Cheri Palmer
Assistant Editor   Marilyn Alan
Cover Design   Carrie English, canary studios
Text Design   Detta Penna, Penna Design & Production
Composition and Illustrations   Windfall Software, using ZzTEX
Copyeditor   Robert Fiske
Proofreader   Jennifer McClain
Indexer   Valerie Robbins
Printer   Courier Corporation

Morgan Kaufmann Publishers, Inc.
Editorial and Sales Office
340 Pine Street, Sixth Floor
San Francisco, CA 94104-3205
USA
Telephone   415 / 392-2665
Facsimile   415 / 982-2665
Email   mkp@mkp.com
WWW   www.mkp.com
Order toll free   800 / 745-7323

Advice, Praise, Errors: Any correspondence related to this publication or intended for the author should be addressed to the Editorial and Sales Office of Morgan Kaufmann Publishers, Inc., Dept. AI APE. Please report any errors by email to *aibugs@mkp.com*. Please check the errata page at *http://www.mkp.com/nils/clarified* to see if the bug has already been reported and fixed.

02 01 00   5 4 3

Library of Congress Cataloging-in-Publication Data
Nilsson, Nils J., (date)
    Artificial Intelligence : a new synthesis / Nils J. Nilsson.
        p.   cm.
    Includes bibliographical references and index.
    ISBN 1-55860-467-7 (cloth). — ISBN 1-55860-535-5 (paper)
    1. Artificial intelligence.   I. Title.
Q335.N495 1998
006.3–dc21   97-47159
                                                                 CIP

For Scott and Ryan

Contents

Preface   xix

1 *Introduction*   1

  1.1 What Is AI?   1

  1.2 Approaches to Artificial Intelligence   6

  1.3 Brief History of AI   8

  1.4 Plan of the Book   11

  1.5 Additional Readings and Discussion   14

  Exercises   17

I Reactive Machines   19

2 *Stimulus-Response Agents*   21

  2.1 Perception and Action   21

    2.1.1 Perception   24

    2.1.2 Action   24

    2.1.3 Boolean Algebra   25

    2.1.4 Classes and Forms of Boolean Functions   26

vii

2.2   Representing and Implementing Action Functions   27

   2.2.1   Production Systems   27

   2.2.2   Networks   29

   2.2.3   The Subsumption Architecture   32

2.3   Additional Readings and Discussion   33

Exercises   34

3   *Neural Networks*   **37**

3.1   Introduction   37

3.2   Training Single TLUs   38

   3.2.1   TLU Geometry   38

   3.2.2   Augmented Vectors   39

   3.2.3   Gradient Descent Methods   39

   3.2.4   The Widrow–Hoff Procedure   41

   3.2.5   The Generalized Delta Procedure   41

   3.2.6   The Error–Correction Procedure   43

3.3   Neural Networks   44

   3.3.1   Motivation   44

   3.3.2   Notation   45

   3.3.3   The Backpropagation Method   46

   3.3.4   Computing Weight Changes in the Final Layer   48

   3.3.5   Computing Changes to the Weights in Intermediate Layers   48

3.4   Generalization, Accuracy, and Overfitting   51

3.5   Additional Readings and Discussion   54

Exercises   55

4   *Machine Evolution*   **59**

4.1   Evolutionary Computation   59

4.2   Genetic Programming   60

   4.2.1   Program Representation in GP   60

4.2.2   The GP Process   62

4.2.3   Evolving a Wall–Following Robot   65

4.3   Additional Readings and Discussion   69

Exercises   69

5   *State Machines*   **71**

5.1   Representing the Environment by Feature Vectors   71

5.2   Elman Networks   73

5.3   Iconic Representations   74

5.4   Blackboard Systems   77

5.5   Additional Readings and Discussion   80

Exercises   80

6   *Robot Vision*   **85**

6.1   Introduction   85

6.2   Steering an Automobile   86

6.3   Two Stages of Robot Vision   88

6.4   Image Processing   91

6.4.1   Averaging   91

6.4.2   Edge Enhancement   93

6.4.3   Combining Edge Enhancement with Averaging   96

6.4.4   Region Finding   97

6.4.5   Using Image Attributes Other Than Intensity   101

6.5   Scene Analysis   102

6.5.1   Interpreting Lines and Curves in the Image   103

6.5.2   Model–Based Vision   106

6.6   Stereo Vision and Depth Information   108

6.7   Additional Readings and Discussion   110

Exercises   111

II   Search in State Spaces   115

7   *Agents That Plan*   117

7.1   **Memory Versus Computation**   117

7.2   **State–Space Graphs**   118

7.3   **Searching Explicit State Spaces**   121

7.4   **Feature–Based State Spaces**   122

7.5   **Graph Notation**   124

7.6   **Additional Readings and Discussion**   125

    Exercises   126

8   *Uninformed Search*   129

8.1   **Formulating the State Space**   129

8.2   **Components of Implicit State–Space Graphs** 130

8.3   **Breadth–First Search**   131

8.4   **Depth–First or Backtracking Search**   133

8.5   **Iterative Deepening**   135

8.6   **Additional Readings and Discussion**   136

    Exercises   137

9   *Heuristic Search*   139

9.1   **Using Evaluation Functions**   139

9.2   **A General Graph–Searching Algorithm**   141

9.2.1   Algorithm A*   142

9.2.2   Admissibility of A*   145

9.2.3   The Consistency (or Monotone) Condition   150

9.2.4   Iterative-Deepening A*   153

9.2.5   Recursive Best-First Search   154

9.3 **Heuristic Functions and Search Efficiency** 155

9.4 **Additional Readings and Discussion** 160

Exercises 160

10   *Planning, Acting, and Learning*   163

10.1 **The Sense/Plan/Act Cycle** 163

10.2 **Approximate Search** 165

     10.2.1   Island–Driven Search 166

     10.2.2   Hierarchical Search 167

     10.2.3   Limited–Horizon Search 169

     10.2.4   Cycles 170

     10.2.5   Building Reactive Procedures 170

10.3 **Learning Heuristic Functions** 172

     10.3.1   Explicit Graphs 172

     10.3.2   Implicit Graphs 173

10.4 **Rewards Instead of Goals** 175

10.5 **Additional Readings and Discussion** 177

Exercises 178

11   *Alternative Search Formulations and Applications*   181

11.1 **Assignment Problems** 181

11.2 **Constructive Methods** 183

11.3 **Heuristic Repair** 187

11.4 **Function Optimization** 189

Exercises 192

12   *Adversarial Search*   195

12.1 **Two–Agent Games** 195

12.2 **The Minimax Procedure** 197

12.3	**The Alpha–Beta Procedure**	202
12.4	**The Search Efficiency of the Alpha–Beta Procedure**	207
12.5	**Other Important Matters**	208
12.6	**Games of Chance**	208
12.7	**Learning Evaluation Functions**	210
12.8	**Additional Readings and Discussion**	212
	Exercises	213

III Knowledge Representation and Reasoning 215

13 *The Propositional Calculus* 217

13.1	**Using Constraints on Feature Values**	217
13.2	**The Language**	219
13.3	**Rules of Inference**	220
13.4	**Definition of Proof**	221
13.5	**Semantics**	222
	13.5.1 Interpretations	222
	13.5.2 The Propositional Truth Table	223
	13.5.3 Satisfiability and Models	224
	13.5.4 Validity	224
	13.5.5 Equivalence	225
	13.5.6 Entailment	225
13.6	**Soundness and Completeness**	226
13.7	**The PSAT Problem**	227
13.8	**Other Important Topics**	228
	13.8.1 Language Distinctions	228
	13.8.2 Metatheorems	228
	13.8.3 Associative Laws	229

13.8.4   Distributive Laws   229

Exercises   229

14   *Resolution in the Propositional Calculus*   **231**

14.1   A New Rule of Inference: Resolution   231

14.1.1   Clauses as wffs   231

14.1.2   Resolution on Clauses   231

14.1.3   Soundness of Resolution   232

14.2   Converting Arbitrary wffs to Conjunctions of Clauses   232

14.3   Resolution Refutations   233

14.4   Resolution Refutation Search Strategies   235

14.4.1   Ordering Strategies   235

14.4.2   Refinement Strategies   236

14.5   Horn Clauses   237

Exercises   238

15   *The Predicate Calculus*   **239**

15.1   Motivation   239

15.2   The Language and Its Syntax   240

15.3   Semantics   241

15.3.1   Worlds   241

15.3.2   Interpretations   242

15.3.3   Models and Related Notions   243

15.3.4   Knowledge   244

15.4   Quantification   245

15.5   Semantics of Quantifiers   246

15.5.1   Universal Quantifiers   246

15.5.2   Existential Quantifiers   247

15.5.3   Useful Equivalences   247

15.5.4   Rules of Inference   247

15.6 **Predicate Calculus as a Language for Representing Knowledge** 248

15.6.1 Conceptualizations 248

15.6.2 Examples 248

15.7 **Additional Readings and Discussion** 250

Exercises 250

16 **Resolution in the Predicate Calculus** 253

16.1 **Unification** 253

16.2 **Predicate–Calculus Resolution** 256

16.3 **Completeness and Soundness** 257

16.4 **Converting Arbitrary wffs to Clause Form** 257

16.5 **Using Resolution to Prove Theorems** 260

16.6 **Answer Extraction** 261

16.7 **The Equality Predicate** 262

16.8 **Additional Readings and Discussion** 265

Exercises 265

17 **Knowledge-Based Systems** 269

17.1 **Confronting the Real World** 269

17.2 **Reasoning Using Horn Clauses** 270

17.3 **Maintenance in Dynamic Knowledge Bases** 275

17.4 **Rule–Based Expert Systems** 280

17.5 **Rule Learning** 286

17.5.1 Learning Propositional Calculus Rules 286

17.5.2 Learning First-Order Logic Rules 291

17.5.3 Explanation-Based Generalization 295

17.6 **Additional Readings and Discussion** 297

Exercises 298

18   *Representing Commonsense Knowledge*   **301**

18.1   **The Commonsense World**   301

     18.1.1   What Is Commonsense Knowledge?   301

     18.1.2   Difficulties in Representing Commonsense Knowledge   303

     18.1.3   The Importance of Commonsense Knowledge   304

     18.1.4   Research Areas   305

18.2   **Time**   306

18.3   **Knowledge Representation by Networks**   308

     18.3.1   Taxonomic Knowledge   308

     18.3.2   Semantic Networks   309

     18.3.3   Nonmonotonic Reasoning in Semantic Networks   309

     18.3.4   Frames   312

18.4   **Additional Readings and Discussion**   313

     Exercises   314

19   *Reasoning with Uncertain Information*   **317**

19.1   **Review of Probability Theory**   317

     19.1.1   Fundamental Ideas   317

     19.1.2   Conditional Probabilities   320

19.2   **Probabilistic Inference**   323

     19.2.1   A General Method   323

     19.2.2   Conditional Independence   324

19.3   **Bayes Networks**   325

19.4   **Patterns of Inference in Bayes Networks**   328

19.5   **Uncertain Evidence**   329

19.6   **D–Separation**   330

19.7   **Probabilistic Inference in Polytrees**   332

     19.7.1   Evidence Above   332

     19.7.2   Evidence Below   334

19.7.3	Evidence Above and Below	336
19.7.4	A Numerical Example	336
19.8	**Additional Readings and Discussion**	338
	Exercises	339

20   Learning and Acting with Bayes Nets   **343**

20.1	**Learning Bayes Nets**	343
20.1.1	Known Network Structure	343
20.1.2	Learning Network Structure	346
20.2	**Probabilistic Inference and Action**	351
20.2.1	The General Setting	351
20.2.2	An Extended Example	352
20.2.3	Generalizing the Example	356
20.3	**Additional Readings and Discussion**	358
	Exercises	358

IV   Planning Methods Based on Logic   **361**

21   The Situation Calculus   **363**

21.1	**Reasoning about States and Actions**	363
21.2	**Some Difficulties**	367
21.2.1	Frame Axioms	367
21.2.2	Qualifications	369
21.2.3	Ramifications	369
21.3	**Generating Plans**	369
21.4	**Additional Readings and Discussion**	370
	Exercises	371

22 *Planning* 373

22.1 STRIPS **Planning Systems** 373

22.1.1 Describing States and Goals 373

22.1.2 Forward Search Methods 374

22.1.3 Recursive STRIPS 376

22.1.4 Plans with Run–Time Conditionals 379

22.1.5 The Sussman Anomaly 380

22.1.6 Backward Search Methods 381

22.2 Plan Spaces and Partial–Order Planning 385

22.3 Hierarchical Planning 393

22.3.1 ABSTRIPS 393

22.3.2 Combining Hierarchical and Partial–Order Planning 395

22.4 Learning Plans 396

22.5 Additional Readings and Discussion 398

Exercises 400

V Communication and Integration 405

23 *Multiple Agents* 407

23.1 Interacting Agents 407

23.2 Models of Other Agents 408

23.2.1 Varieties of Models 408

23.2.2 Simulation Strategies 410

23.2.3 Simulated Databases 410

23.2.4 The Intentional Stance 411

23.3 A Modal Logic of Knowledge 412

23.3.1 Modal Operators 412

23.3.2 Knowledge Axioms 413

23.3.3 Reasoning about Other Agents' Knowledge   415

23.3.4 Predicting Actions of Other Agents   417

23.4 Additional Readings and Discussion   417

Exercises   418

24   ***Communication among Agents***   **421**

24.1 Speech Acts   421

24.1.1 Planning Speech Acts   423

24.1.2 Implementing Speech Acts   423

24.2 Understanding Language Strings   425

24.2.1 Phrase–Structure Grammars   425

24.2.2 Semantic Analysis   428

24.2.3 Expanding the Grammar   432

24.3 Efficient Communication   435

24.3.1 Use of Context   435

24.3.2 Use of Knowledge to Resolve Ambiguities   436

24.4 Natural Language Processing   437

24.5 Additional Readings and Discussion   440

Exercises   440

25   ***Agent Architectures***   **443**

25.1 Three–Level Architectures   444

25.2 Goal Arbitration   446

25.3 The Triple–Tower Architecture   448

25.4 Bootstrapping   449

25.5 Additional Readings and Discussion   450

Exercises   450

Bibliography   453

Index   493

Preface

This introductory textbook employs a novel perspective from which to view topics in artificial intelligence (AI). I will consider a progression of AI systems or "agents," each slightly more complex than its predecessor. I begin with elementary agents that react to sensed properties of their environments. Even such simple machines allow me to treat topics in machine vision, machine learning, and machine evolution. Then, by stages, I introduce techniques that allow agents to exploit information about the task environment that cannot be immediately sensed. Such knowledge can take the form of descriptive information about the state of the environment, iconic models of the environment, state–space graphs, and logical representations. Because the progression follows what plausibly might have been milestones in the evolution of animals, I have called this approach *evolutionary artificial intelligence*. I intend the book to be as much a proposal about how to think about AI as it is a description of AI techniques. Examples will be used to provide motivation and grounding.

Although I use agents to motivate and illustrate AI techniques, the techniques themselves have much broader application. Many ideas invented by AI researchers have been assimilated into computer science generally for applications in expert systems, natural language processing, human–machine interaction, information retrieval, graphics and image processing, data mining, and robotics (to name some examples). The agents theme serves to unify what might otherwise seem to be a collection of disparate topics.

Regarding coverage, my intention is to treat the middle ground between theory and applications. This middle ground is rich in important AI *ideas*, and in this book I try to motivate and explain the ideas that I think have lasting value in AI. (Being subject to the usual human frailties, I admit to possible errors of omission and commission in selecting topics for inclusion.) Also, some subjects are treated in more depth than others—both because I thought some subjects more important and because I wanted to provide at least some examples of greater depth of exposition. Although some pseudocode algorithms are presented, the book is not an AI programming and implementation book. (Some "AI techniques" books are [Shoham 1994, Norvig 1992, Tracy & Bouthoorn 1997].) I do not give proofs of all of the important theoretical results, but I try to give intuitive arguments and citations to formal proofs. My goals are to present a modest-sized textbook for a one-semester introductory college course, to give the student and reader sufficient motivation and preparation to go on to more advanced AI courses, and to make the extensive literature on AI accessible.

A somewhat unconventional feature of the book is that machine learning is not treated as a separate topic; instead, various aspects of learning arise throughout the book. Neural nets and fundamental ideas about supervised learning are presented early; techniques for learning search heuristics and action policies are discussed in the chapters on search; rule learning, inductive logic programming, and explanation–based learning are treated toward the end of the chapters on logic; and learning plans is presented after discussing logic–based planning.

In my previous books, I included a "bibliographic and historical remarks" section at the end of each chapter. (Some readers may find those sections of some interest still.) I have not done so in the present book, both because AI history has now accumulated to such a great extent and because the longer text by [Russell & Norvig 1995] has already done such a thorough job in that regard. Instead, I include remarks and citations as appropriate throughout the text and provide some additional ones in discussion sections at the end of most chapters. The serious student who intends to specialize in AI research will want to consult many of the references. I hope the casual reader is not bothered by the many citations.

Sample exercises are included at the end of each chapter. They vary in difficulty from routine application of ideas presented in the book to mildly challenging. I expect that instructors will want to augment these problems with favorite ones of their own, including computer exercises and projects. (In keeping with my decision to concentrate on ideas instead of programs, I have not included any computer exercises or projects. Several good programming and project ideas can be found in texts devoted to AI programming techniques.)

The following typographical conventions are used in this book. Sans serif font is used for the names of actions and for "proto–English" sentences communicated among agents. SANS SERIF capitals are used for the names of computer languages, algorithms, and AI systems. Boldface capital letters, such as $\mathbf{W}$ and $\mathbf{X}$, are used for vectors, matrices, and modal operators. Typewriter font is used for genetic programs, for expressions and subexpressions in the predicate calculus, and for

STRIPS rules and operators. Lowercase Greek letters are used for metavariables ranging over predicate–calculus expressions, subexpressions, and occasionally for substitutions. Uppercase Greek letters are used to denote sets of predicate-calculus formulas. Lowercase p's are used to denote probabilities.

Students and researchers will find much helpful material about AI on the World Wide Web. I do not provide URLs here; any list written today would be incomplete and inaccurate within months. Use of one of the web search engines will quickly steer the reader to sites with sample applications, frequently asked questions, extensive bibliographies, research papers, programs, interactive demonstrations, announcements of workshops and conferences, homepages of researchers, and much more.

Material specifically in support of this book is provided on a Web page on the publisher's Web site at *www.mkp.com/nils*. If you discover any errors, please email them to the publisher at *aibugs@mkp.com*. Errata and clarifications can be found at *http://www.mkp.com/nils/clarified*.

My previous AI textbook, *Principles of Artificial Intelligence* (Morgan Kaufmann, 1980), is by now quite out of date, but some of the material in that book is still useful, and I have borrowed freely from it in preparing the present volume. Cross-checking against other AI textbooks (particularly [Russell & Norvig 1995, Rich & Knight 1991, Stefik 1995]) was also very helpful.

Students and teaching assistants in my Stanford courses on artificial intelligence and machine learning have already made several useful suggestions. I hope the following list includes most of them: Eyal Amir, David Andre, Scott Benson, George John, Steve Ketchpel, Ron Kohavi, Andrew Kosoresow, Ofer Matan, Karl Pfleger, and Charles Richards. Colleagues and reviewers at Stanford and elsewhere helped me learn what they already knew. Thanks to Helder Coelho, Oscar Firschein, Carolyn Hayes, Giorgio Ingargiola, Leslie Kaelbling, Daphne Koller, John Koza, Richard Korf, Pat Langley, John McCarthy, Bart Selman, Yoav Shoham, Devika Subramanian, Gheorghe Tecuci, and Michael Wellman. Special thanks go to Cheri Palmer, my production editor at Morgan Kaufmann, who kept me on schedule, cheerfully accepted my endless changes, and worked extra hard to meet a difficult publication date. Work on this book was carried on in the Robotics Laboratory of Stanford's Department of Computer Science and at the Santa Fe Institute. Continuing research support by the National Science Foundation is gratefully acknowledged.

1 Introduction

I believe that understanding intelligence involves understanding how knowledge is acquired, represented, and stored; how intelligent behavior is generated and learned; how motives, and emotions, and priorities are developed and used; how sensory signals are transformed into symbols; how symbols are manipulated to perform logic, to reason about the past, and plan for the future; and how the mechanisms of intelligence produce the phenomena of illusion, belief, hope, fear, and dreams—and yes even kindness and love. To understand these functions at a fundamental level, I believe, would be a scientific achievement on the scale of nuclear physics, relativity, and molecular genetics.

> —James Albus, Response to Henry Hexmoor, from URL:
> *http://tommy.jsc.nasa.gov/er/er6/mrl/papers/symposium/albus.txt*
> February 13, 1995

1.1 What Is AI?

Artificial Intelligence (*AI*), broadly (and somewhat circularly) defined, is concerned with intelligent behavior in artifacts. Intelligent behavior, in turn, involves perception, reasoning, learning, communicating, and acting in complex environments. AI has as one of its long-term goals the development of machines that can do these things as well as humans can, or possibly even better. Another goal

1

of AI is to understand this kind of behavior whether it occurs in machines or in humans or other animals. Thus, AI has both engineering and scientific goals. In this book, I will largely be concerned with AI as engineering, focussing on the important concepts and ideas underlying the design of intelligent machines.

AI has always been surrounded by controversy. The question *Can machines think?* has interested philosophers as well as scientists and engineers. In a famous article, Alan Turing, one of the founders of computer science, rephrased that question in terms more amenable to an empirical test, which has come to be called the *Turing test* [Turing 1950]. I will describe that test shortly, but Turing also noted that the answer to the question "Can machines think?" depends on how we define the words *machine* and *think*. He might also have added that it depends on how we define *can*.

Let's consider the word *can* first. Do we mean can machines think someday or can they now? Do we mean that in principle they might be able to think (even if we could never build ones that do), or are we asking for an actual demonstration? These are important questions since no artifact yet possesses broad thinking skills.

Some people believe that thinking machines might have to be so complex and have such complex experiences (interacting with their environment and with other thinking machines, for example) that we could never actually design or build them. The processes that generate global weather provide a good analogy. Even if we knew everything of importance about the weather, that knowledge wouldn't necessarily allow us to duplicate weather phenomena artificially in all of its richness. No system less complex than the actual earth's surface, atmosphere, and seas—embedded in space, warmed by the sun, and influenced by the tides—would be able to duplicate weather phenomena in all of their details. Similarly, full-scale, human-level intelligence may be too complex, or at least too dependent on the precise physiology of humans, to exist apart from its *embodiment* in humans situated in their environment. (For a discussion of the importance of this notion of embodiment see, for example, [Lakoff 1987, Winograd & Flores 1986, Harnad 1990, Mataric 1997].) The matter of whether or not we could ever build human-level thinking machines is still undecided, and AI progress toward that goal has been steady, albeit slower than some early pioneers predicted. I am optimistic about our eventual success.

Next, we come to the word *machine*. To many people, a machine is a rather stolid thing. The word evokes images of gears grinding, steam hissing, and steel parts clanking. How could such a thing think? Nowadays, however, the computer has greatly expanded our notion of what a machine can be. Our growing understanding of biological mechanisms is expanding it even further. Consider, for example, the simple virus called *E6 Bacteriophage* shown schematically in Figure 1.1. Its head contains viral DNA. The virus attaches itself to the cell wall of a bacterium with its tail fibers, punctures the wall, and squirts its DNA into the bacterium. The DNA then directs the bacterium to manufacture thousands of

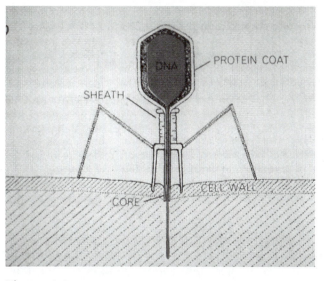

Figure 1.1

Schematic Illustration of E6 Bacteriophage

copies of all of the viral parts. These parts then automatically assemble themselves into new viruses that explode out of the bacterium to repeat the process. The complete assembly looks and operates very much like a machine, and we might as well call it a machine—one made of proteins.

What about other biological processes and organisms? The complete genome of the bacterium *Haemophilus influenzae* Rd has recently been sequenced [Fleischmann, et al. 1995]. This genome has 1,830,137 base pairs (consisting of the "letters" A, G, C, and T). That's roughly 3.6×10^6 bits or one-half a megabyte. Although the function of all of its 1743 genes is not yet known, scientists are beginning to explain the development and functioning of such organisms in the same way that they would explain machines—very complex machines, of course. In fact, techniques quite familiar to computer scientists, namely, the use of timing diagrams for logic circuits, are proving useful for understanding the regulation by genes of the complex biochemistry of a bacteria-infecting virus [McAdams & Shapiro 1995]. Sequencing the complete genomes of other organisms, including humans, is proceeding. Once we know these "blueprints," will we think of these organisms—bacteria, worms, fruit flies, mice, dolphins, humans—as machines? If humans are machines, then machines *can* think! We have an existence proof. We "simply" don't know yet how the human machine works.

Yet, even should we agree about what a machine is, there are some additional twists to this argument. Even if machines made of proteins can think, perhaps ones made of silicon wouldn't be able to. A well-known philosopher, John Searle, believes that what we are made of is fundamental to our intelligence [Searle 1980, Searle 1992]. For him, thinking can occur only in very special machines—living ones made of proteins.

Directly opposed to Searle's belief (and to the notion of embodiment mentioned earlier) is the *physical symbol system hypothesis* of Newell and Simon [Newell & Simon 1976]. That hypothesis states that a physical symbol system has the necessary and sufficient means for general intelligent action. According to Newell and Simon, a physical symbol system is a machine, like a digital computer, that is capable of manipulating symbolic data—adding numbers, rearranging lists of symbols (such as alphabetizing a list of names), replacing some symbols by others, and so on. An important aspect of this hypothesis is that it doesn't matter what the physical symbol system is made of! Newell and Simon's hypothesis is "substrate neutral." An intelligent entity could be made of protein, mechanical relays, transistors, or anything else, so long as it can process symbols.[1]

Still others believe that it isn't whether or not machines are made of silicon or protein that is important; these people think that much intelligent behavior is the result of what they call *subsymbolic* processing—processing of *signals*, not symbols. Take the recognition of familiar faces, for example. Humans do that effortlessly, and although we don't know how they do it, it is suspected that the best explanation for the process would involve treating images or parts of them as multidimensional signals, not as symbols.

I could list many other points of view about what sorts of machines might be capable of humanlike thought. Some of the claims one often hears are

- The brain processes information in parallel, whereas conventional computers do it serially. We'll have to build new varieties of parallel computers to make progress in AI.
- Conventional computing machinery is based on true–or–false (binary) logic. Truly intelligent systems will have to use some sort of "fuzzy" logic.
- Animal neurons are much more complex than switches—the basic building blocks of computers. We'll need to use quite realistic artificial neurons in intelligent machines.

Perhaps it is still too early for the field of AI to reach a consensus about what sort of machinery is required, although many AI researchers accept the physical symbol system hypothesis.

Finally, we come to the most difficult word, *think*. Rather than attempt to define this word, Turing proposed a test, the Turing test, by which it could be

---

1. Of course, some building materials will be better than others if we take into account such practical matters as speed, permanence, reliability, suitability for parallel processing, temperature sensitivity, and so on.

decided whether or not a particular machine was intelligent or not. The test was originally described as a game. I quote from Turing's article [Turing 1950]:

> It is played with three people, a man (A), a woman (B), and an interrogator (C) who may be of either sex. The interrogator stays in a room apart from the other two [communicating with them via teletype]. The object of the game for the interrogator is to determine which of the other two is the man and which is the woman. He knows them by labels X and Y, and at the end of the game he says either "X is A and Y is B" or "X is B and Y is A." The interrogator is allowed to put questions to A and B thus:
>
> C: Will X please tell me the length of his or her hair?
>
> Now suppose X is actually A, then A must answer. It is A's object in the game to try and cause C to make the wrong identification.
>
> . . .
>
> The object of the game for the third player (B) is to help the interrogator.
>
> . . .
>
> We now ask the question, "What will happen when a machine takes the part of A in this game?" Will the interrogator decide wrongly as often when the game is played like this as he does when the game is played between a man and a woman? These questions replace our original, "Can a machine think?"

The Turing test is often simplified to one in which a machine attempts to convince a human interrogator that it is a human. Various versions of this simpler test have been staged, and because it is possible for even some rather trivial machines to fool human interrogators for a while, the simple version is not usually considered to be a very useful test of a machine's intelligence. For example, Joseph Weizenbaum's ELIZA program uses some very simple tricks but appears to the tolerant user to be able to carry on a rather realistic, if inane, dialog [Weizenbaum 1965]. Mauldin's JULIA program is a more recent and sophisticated dialog program [Mauldin 1994].[2]

Aside from the Turing test, it does seem worthwhile to attempt to ask what abilities should we require of a machine before we label it intelligent. Already, there are many computer programs that accomplish marvelous things, including planning optimal, fuel–efficient airplane routes, simulating global meteorological conditions, scheduling the use of machines in a factory, and so on. Are these programs intelligent? Should they be considered part of the subject matter of AI? I begin this book by describing machines that hardly anyone would

---

2. In 1991, Hugh Loebner started the Loebner Prize competition, offering a $100,000 prize to the author of the first computer program to pass an unrestricted Turing test. Annual competitions are held each year with smaller prizes for the best program on a restricted Turing test.

call intelligent. As I increase their complexity, do they gradually become more and more intelligent? I think so, but others will, no doubt, have their own opinions.

1.2   *Approaches to Artificial Intelligence*

Even though AI has already produced some practically useful systems, it is generally conceded that the ultimate goal of achieving human–level intelligence is still distant. That being so, there is much discussion and argument about what are the best approaches for AI—best in the sense of laying the core foundations for achieving long–term goals as well as best in the sense of producing shorter–term results. Thus, a number of different paradigms have emerged over the past 40 years or so. Each has its ardent advocates, and some have produced sufficiently many interesting results so as not to be dismissable out of hand. Perhaps combinations of these approaches will be required. In any case, their advocates often feel that theirs is the "breakthrough" methodology that deserves special attention. The several paradigms can be clustered into two major groups.

The first group includes what I will call the symbol–processing approaches. These are based on Newell and Simon's physical symbol system hypothesis, and although that hypothesis is not yet universally accepted, much of what might be called "classical" AI (what the philosopher John Haugeland calls "good–old–fashioned–AI" or GOFAI) is guided by it. A prominent member of this family of approaches is one that uses logical operations applied to declarative knowledge bases. Inspired originally by John McCarthy's "advice–taker" memos [McCarthy 1958], this style of AI represents "knowledge" about a problem domain by declarative sentences, often based on or substantially equivalent to sentences in first–order logic. Logical reasoning methods are used to deduce consequences of this knowledge. This method has many variants, including ones emphasizing the role of formal axiomatization of domains in logical languages. When applied to "real" problems, the approach requires substantial knowledge of the domain and is then often called a *knowledge-based* approach. Many systems have been built using these methods, and I will be referring to some of them later in the book.

In most of the symbol–processing approaches, analysis of desired behavior and the synthesis of machines to achieve it extend through several levels. At the top is the *knowledge level* [Newell 1982] where the knowledge needed by the machine is specified. Next comes the *symbol level*, where this knowledge is represented in symbolic structures, such as lists written in the programming language LISP, and operations on these structures are specified. Then, there are the lower levels in which symbol–processing operations are actually implemented. Most symbol–processing approaches use a "top–down" design method; they begin at the knowledge level and proceed downward through the symbol and implementation levels.

The second group of approaches to AI includes what are called the "subsymbolic" ones. These usually proceed in "bottom–up" style, starting at the lowest level and working upward. At the lowest levels, the concept of *symbol* is not as appropriate as is the concept of *signal*. Prominent among the subsymbolic approaches is what some have called the "animat approach." People partial to this style [Wilson 1991, Brooks 1990] point out that human intelligence evolved only after a billion or more years of life on earth. In order to make intelligent machines, they claim, we'll have to follow many of the same evolutionary steps. So we ought to concentrate first on duplicating the signal–processing abilities and control systems of simpler animals—insects, for example—and proceed in steps up the evolutionary ladder. Not only will this strategy lead in the short term to useful artifacts, but it will develop the substrata upon which higher levels of intelligence must necessarily build.

This second group of approaches also emphasizes *symbol grounding*. [Brooks 1990] contrasts the physical symbol system hypothesis with his *physical grounding* hypothesis in which various behavior modules of an agent interact with the environment to produce complex behavior without using centralized models. (However, he concedes that achieving human–level AI might require integration of the two approaches.)

Interaction between the machine and the environment leads to what is called *emergent behavior*. In the words of one researcher [Maes 1990b, p. 1]:

> The functionality of an agent is viewed as an emergent property of the intensive interaction of the system with its dynamic environment. The specification of the behavior of the agent alone does not explain the functionality that is displayed when the agent is operating. Instead the functionality to a large degree is founded on the properties of the environment. The environment is not only taken into account dynamically, but its characteristics are exploited to serve the functioning of the system.

Well–known examples of machines coming from the subsymbolic school include the so–called *neural networks*. These systems, inspired by biological models, are interesting mainly for their ability to learn. Interesting machines have also been produced by processes that simulate certain aspects of biological evolution—including sexual crossover, mutation, and fitness–proportional reproduction. Other bottom–up, animat–style approaches are based on control theory and on the analysis of dynamic systems (see, for example, [Beer 1995, Port & van Gelder 1995]).

Intermediate between the top–down and bottom–up approaches is one based on *situated automata* [Kaelbling & Rosenschein 1990, Rosenschein & Kaelbling 1995]. Kaelbling and Rosenschein propose a programming language for specifying desired agent behavior at a high level and a compiler for creating action-evoking circuitry from programs written in the language.

1.3   *Brief History of AI*

When digital computers were first being developed in the 1940s and 1950s, several researchers wrote programs that could perform elementary reasoning tasks. Prominent among these were papers describing the first computer programs that could play chess [Shannon 1950, Newell, Shaw, & Simon 1958] and checkers [Samuel 1959, Samuel 1967] and prove theorems in plane geometry [Gelernter 1959]. In 1956, John McCarthy and Claude Shannon coedited a volume entitled *Automata Studies* [Shannon & McCarthy 1956]. Disappointed that the papers dealt mainly with the mathematical theory of automata, McCarthy decided to use the phrase *Artificial Intelligence* as the title of a 1956 Dartmouth conference. Several important early papers were delivered at that conference, including one by Allen Newell, Cliff Shaw, and Herbert Simon on a program called the Logic Theorist [Newell, Shaw, & Simon 1957], which could prove theorems in propositional logic. Even though many other names for the field were tried, including *complex information processing, machine intelligence, heuristic programming,* and *cognology,* the name *artificial intelligence* has persisted, no doubt because a progression of textbooks, college courses, conferences, and journals used that name.

The first of many steps toward artificial intelligence was taken long ago by Aristotle (384–322 B.C.) when he set about to explain and codify certain styles of deductive reasoning that he called *syllogisms.* Some efforts to automate intelligence would seem quixotic to us today. Ramon Llull (ca 1235–1316), a Catalan mystic and poet, built a set of wheels, called the *Ars Magna* (Great Art), that was supposed to be a machine capable of answering all questions. But the quest to bottle reason was pursued by scientists and mathematicians also. Martin Gardner [Gardner 1982, p. 3] attributes to Gottfried Leibniz (1646–1716) the dream of "a universal algebra by which all knowledge, including moral and metaphysical truths, can some day be brought within a single deductive system." Leibniz called his system a *calculus philosophicus* or *ratiocinator*; it was, of course, a dream that could not be fulfilled with the technical apparatus of the time. Substantial progress did not begin until George Boole [Boole 1854] developed the foundations of propositional logic. Boole's purpose was (among other things) "to collect . . . some probable intimations concerning the nature and constitution of the human mind." Toward the end of the nineteenth century, Gottlieb Frege proposed a notational system for mechanical reasoning and in doing so invented much of what we now know as the predicate calculus [Frege 1879]. He called his language *Begriffsschrift*, which can be translated as "concept writing."

In 1958, John McCarthy proposed using the predicate calculus as a language for representing and using knowledge in a system he called the "advice taker" [McCarthy 1958]. This system was to be told what it needed to know rather than programmed. A modest but influential implementation of these ideas was undertaken by Cordell Green in his system called QA3 [Green 1969a]. Surviving much controversy among AI researchers, the predicate calculus and several of its variants constitute the foundation for knowledge representation in AI.

Twentieth–century logicians, including Kurt Gödel, Stephen Kleene, Emil Post, Alonzo Church, and Alan Turing, formalized and clarified much of what could and could not be done with logical and computational systems. More recently, computer scientists, including Stephen Cook and Richard Karp, identified classes of computations that, while possible in principle, might require utterly impractical amounts of time and memory.

Many of these results from logic and computer science were about "truths that could not be deduced" and "computations that could not be performed." Possibly cheered by these negative findings, some philosophers and others [Lucas 1961, Penrose 1989, Penrose 1994] interpreted them as confirmation that human intelligence would never be mechanized. They imagined that humans were somehow immune from the computational limitations inherent in machines. Most logicians and computer scientists, however, believe that these negative results in no way imply that machines have any limits that don't also apply to humans.

The first modern article dealing with the possibility of mechanizing human-style intelligence was the one by Alan Turing that I have already cited [Turing 1950]. During this same period, Warren McCulloch and Walter Pitts theorized about the relationships between simple computing elements and biological neurons [McCulloch & Pitts 1943]. They showed that it was possible to compute any computable function by networks of logical gates. (See [Minsky 1967] for a very readable treatment of the computational aspects of "McCulloch-Pitts neurons.") Other work by Frank Rosenblatt [Rosenblatt 1962] explored the use of networks, called *perceptrons*, of neuronlike elements for learning and for pattern recognition. Several other streams of work, among them cybernetics [Wiener 1948], cognitive psychology, computational linguistics [Chomsky 1965], and adaptive control theory [Widrow & Hoff 1960], also contributed to the intellectual matrix within which AI developed.

Much of the early AI work (during the 1960s and early 1970s) explored a variety of problem representations, search techniques, and general heuristics—employing them in computer programs that could solve simple puzzles, play games, and retrieve information. One of the influential programs was the General Problem Solver (GPS) of Allen Newell, Cliff Shaw, and Herbert Simon [Newell, Shaw, & Simon 1959, Newell & Simon 1963]. Some sample problems solved by these early systems included symbolic integration [Slagle 1963], algebra word problems [Bobrow 1968], analogy puzzles [Evans 1968], and control of a mobile robot [Nilsson 1984b]. Many of these systems are the subjects of papers in the volume *Computers and Thought* [Feigenbaum & Feldman 1963].

Attempts to "scale up" these programs and their techniques to cope with applications of practical importance revealed that they could solve only "toy problems."

More powerful systems required much more built-in knowledge about the domain of application. The late 1970s and early 1980s saw the development of more capable programs that contained the knowledge required to mimic expert human performance at several tasks, including diagnosis, design, and analysis. Several methods of representing problem–specific knowledge were explored and developed. The program that is credited with first demonstrating the importance of large amounts of domain–specific knowledge is DENDRAL, a system for predicting the structure of organic molecules given their chemical formula and mass spectrogram analyses [Feigenbaum, Buchanan, & Lederberg 1971, Lindsay, et al. 1980]. Several other "expert systems" followed, including ones that performed medical diagnoses [Shortliffe 1976, Miller, Pople, & Myers 1982], configured computer systems [McDermott 1982], and evaluated potential ore deposits [Campbell, et al. 1982, Duda, Gaschnig, & Hart 1979]. A good account of the history of AI work and workers up through this period has been written by [McCorduck 1979].

Game playing is one area in which substantial progress has been made in scaling up toy problems. On May 11, 1997, an IBM program named DEEP BLUE beat the reigning world chess champion, Garry Kasparov, by 3.5 to 2.5 in a six-game match. Championship performance has been achieved by sophisticated search algorithms, high–speed computers, and chess–specific hardware.

Human intelligence encompasses many abilities, including the ability to perceive and analyze a visual scene and the ability to understand and generate language. These specific topics have received much attention. Larry Roberts developed one of the first scene analysis programs [Roberts 1963]. This work was followed by extensive work on machine vision ([Nalwa 1993] is a good general textbook) and was informed by scientific studies of animal vision systems [Letvinn, et al. 1959, Hubel 1988, Marr 1982]. An early natural language understanding system was developed by Terry Winograd [Winograd 1972]. A multisite project during the 1970s developed prototype continuous speech understanding systems; the LUNAR system [Woods 1973], developed by William Woods, was able to answer spoken English questions about rock samples collected from the moon by the NASA missions. Although several natural language understanding systems now exist, their competence is restricted to specialized topic areas and vocabularies. Broad coverage awaits further advances in the representation of large amounts of general, commonsense knowledge. The CYC project [Guha & Lenat 1990, Lenat & Guha 1990, Lenat 1995] has as one of its goals the collection and representation of much of this needed knowledge.

Although interest in neural networks sagged a bit after the pioneering work by Frank Rosenblatt in the late 1950s, it resumed energetically in the 1980s. Networks of nonlinear elements with adjustable–strength interconnections are now recognized as an important class of nonlinear modeling tools. There are now several important applications of neural networks. Along with neural nets, the animat approach has helped to focus AI research on the problems of connecting

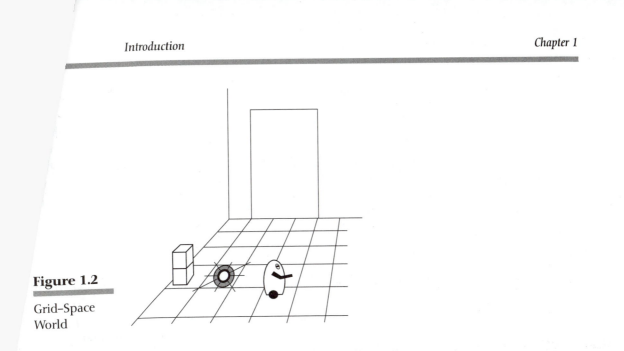

Figure 1.2

Grid–Space
World

properties and to store internal models of the world. In all cases, the actions taken by *reactive* agents are functions of the current and past states of their worlds—as they are sensed and remembered. Reactive agents can have quite complex perceptual and motor processes. Although I do treat the subject of visual perception in some detail (in Chapter 6), space does not permit including topics related to the low–level control of robot motion.

Most AI systems use some sort of model or representation of their world and task. I take a "model" broadly to be any symbolic structure and set of computations on it that correlate sufficiently with the world that the computations yield information about the world useful to the agent. This information may be about the agent's present world state or about possible future world states. As I move along the spectrum of simple to more complex AI agents, I also travel back and forth across a major divide separating one class of AI system from another. One type uses models that I term *iconic*. These involve data structures and computations that *simulate* aspects of an agent's environment and the effects of agent actions upon that environment. Representing the state of play in chess by an eight–by–eight array of cells occupied by chess pieces is an example of an iconic representation. An iconic chess model is "complete" in the sense that it contains information about the location of *all* of the pieces.

The other type of model I call "feature based." This kind of model uses declarative *descriptions* of the environment. In chess, for example, two (of many) features might be whether or not a rook and king have "castled" and how many times the king has been put in check. A set of descriptive features is generally incomplete—a virtue of feature–based representations because they can tolerate the inevitable gaps in an agent's knowledge about complex worlds.

symbolic processes to the sensors and effectors of robots ⸜
ments.

Projecting present trends into the future, I think there will
on integrated, autonomous systems—robots and "softbots." So⸝
Weld 1994] are software agents that roam the Internet, findiⱱ
they think will be of interest to their users. The constant pressuⱱ
the capabilities of robot and software agents will motivate and gⱱ
intelligence research for many years to come.

1.4   *Plan of the Book*

Many ideas and techniques relevant to mechanizing intelligence havⱱ
developed by AI researchers. I will be describing these in the context of a seⱱ
ever more capable and complex "agents." There are many different kinds of aⱱ
and environments that we might consider. For example, we could imagine robⱱ
that function in the zero–gravity conditions of outer space, in the dark watersⱱ
the ocean floor, in office buildings or factories, or in the symbolic "data–worlds
of the Internet. But such "real–world," practical agents are often too complex
to transparently illustrate the AI concepts that give them intelligence. Instead, I
will use a series of "toy" agents in a fictional environment I call *grid-space world*.
Although the basic world is easy to describe, a variety of enhancements makes
it sufficiently rich to demand "intelligence" of its inhabiting agents.

Grid–space world is a three–dimensional space demarcated by a two–
dimensional grid of cells called the "floor." Cells may contain objects having
various properties, and there may be wall–like boundaries between sets of cells.
The agents are confined to the floor and may move from cell to cell. Objects
must either be on the floor or supported by a stack of other objects resting on
the floor. Sometimes I will use just a two–dimensional subspace consisting of
the floor alone. I show a typical grid–space world in Figure 1.2. Two robots are
shown. A primitive, two–dimensional robot has sensors that can sense whether
or not adjacent cells are free for it to move to; a more complex one has an arm
that can manipulate objects.

Readers already familiar with some of the AI literature will recognize that
grid–space world can be customized to many of the "worlds" used in AI research,
including the blocks world, tile world [Pollack & Ringuette 1990], wumpus world
[Russell & Norvig 1995, pp. 153ff], and ant world [Koza 1992, pp. 54ff]. All of these
are discrete in the sense that there are a countable number of locations, agents,
objects, and time points. Most of the AI techniques that I will be describing
apply in discrete worlds and will require subsymbolic processes to connect them
to continuous worlds.

I start with "reactive" agents that have various means of sensing their worlds
and acting in them. The more complex ones will also have the ability to remember

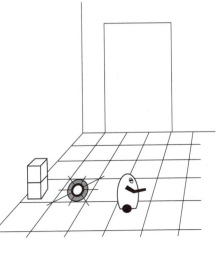

Figure 1.2

Grid–Space
World

properties and to store internal models of the world. In all cases, the actions taken by *reactive* agents are functions of the current and past states of their worlds—as they are sensed and remembered. Reactive agents can have quite complex perceptual and motor processes. Although I do treat the subject of visual perception in some detail (in Chapter 6), space does not permit including topics related to the low–level control of robot motion.

Most AI systems use some sort of model or representation of their world and task. I take a "model" broadly to be any symbolic structure and set of computations on it that correlate sufficiently with the world that the computations yield information about the world useful to the agent. This information may be about the agent's present world state or about possible future world states. As I move along the spectrum of simple to more complex AI agents, I also travel back and forth across a major divide separating one class of AI system from another. One type uses models that I term *iconic*. These involve data structures and computations that *simulate* aspects of an agent's environment and the effects of agent actions upon that environment. Representing the state of play in chess by an eight–by–eight array of cells occupied by chess pieces is an example of an iconic representation. An iconic chess model is "complete" in the sense that it contains information about the location of *all* of the pieces.

The other type of model I call "feature based." This kind of model uses declarative *descriptions* of the environment. In chess, for example, two (of many) features might be whether or not a rook and king have "castled" and how many times the king has been put in check. A set of descriptive features is generally incomplete—a virtue of feature–based representations because they can tolerate the inevitable gaps in an agent's knowledge about complex worlds.

symbolic processes to the sensors and effectors of robots in physical environments.

Projecting present trends into the future, I think there will be new emphasis on integrated, autonomous systems—robots and "softbots." Softbots [Etzioni & Weld 1994] are software agents that roam the Internet, finding information they think will be of interest to their users. The constant pressure to improve the capabilities of robot and software agents will motivate and guide artificial intelligence research for many years to come.

1.4 *Plan of the Book*

Many ideas and techniques relevant to mechanizing intelligence have been developed by AI researchers. I will be describing these in the context of a series of ever more capable and complex "agents." There are many different kinds of agents and environments that we might consider. For example, we could imagine robots that function in the zero-gravity conditions of outer space, in the dark waters of the ocean floor, in office buildings or factories, or in the symbolic "data-worlds" of the Internet. But such "real-world," practical agents are often too complex to transparently illustrate the AI concepts that give them intelligence. Instead, I will use a series of "toy" agents in a fictional environment I call *grid-space world*. Although the basic world is easy to describe, a variety of enhancements makes it sufficiently rich to demand "intelligence" of its inhabiting agents.

Grid-space world is a three-dimensional space demarcated by a two-dimensional grid of cells called the "floor." Cells may contain objects having various properties, and there may be wall-like boundaries between sets of cells. The agents are confined to the floor and may move from cell to cell. Objects must either be on the floor or supported by a stack of other objects resting on the floor. Sometimes I will use just a two-dimensional subspace consisting of the floor alone. I show a typical grid-space world in Figure 1.2. Two robots are shown. A primitive, two-dimensional robot has sensors that can sense whether or not adjacent cells are free for it to move to; a more complex one has an arm that can manipulate objects.

Readers already familiar with some of the AI literature will recognize that grid-space world can be customized to many of the "worlds" used in AI research, including the blocks world, tile world [Pollack & Ringuette 1990], wumpus world [Russell & Norvig 1995, pp. 153ff], and ant world [Koza 1992, pp. 54ff]. All of these are discrete in the sense that there are a countable number of locations, agents, objects, and time points. Most of the AI techniques that I will be describing apply in discrete worlds and will require subsymbolic processes to connect them to continuous worlds.

I start with "reactive" agents that have various means of sensing their worlds and acting in them. The more complex ones will also have the ability to remember

My next series of agents will have the ability to anticipate the effects of their actions and take those that are expected to lead toward their *goals*. Such agents can be said to make *plans*. For some researchers, this ability is criterial for intelligence; for them, it is where AI begins. Agents acting in worlds that cannot be perfectly sensed and modeled will need also to keep track of whether or not their actions have their anticipated effects.

Most grid-space worlds will have implicit constraints that are analogous to properties of real worlds. For example, if an object is at one location, it cannot, at the same time, be at another location. Agents that are able to take these constraints into account will usually be more effective. My next series of agents are able to "reason"; they can "deduce" properties of their worlds that are only implicit in the constraints.

Finally, I consider agents that exist in worlds inhabited by other agents. Effective performance then sometimes requires anticipating and influencing what other agents might do. Communication among agents then becomes an important action in itself.

Everywhere along the spectrum of increasing agent complexity, I also consider methods by which agents can learn about their environments. Along with the ability to plan, the ability to learn is thought to be one of the hallmarks of an intelligent system. I agree fully with [Russell & Wefald 1991, p. 18], who write

> Learning is an important part of *autonomy*. A system is autonomous to the extent that its behaviour is determined by its immediate inputs and past experience, rather than by its designer's. Agents are usually designed for a *class* of environments, where each member of the class is consistent with what the designer knows about what the real environment might hold in store for the agent. But a system that operates on the basis of built-in assumptions will only operate successfuly when those assumptions hold, and thus lacks flexibility. A truly autonomous system should be able to operate successfully in any environment, given sufficient time to adapt. The system's internal knowledge structures should therefore be constructible, in principle, from its experience of the world. One should not equate autonomous systems with *tabula rasa* systems. A reasonable half-way point is to design systems whose behaviour is determined in large part, at least initially, by the designer's knowledge of the world, but where all such assumptions are as far as possible made explicit and amenable to change by the agent. This sense of autonomy seems also to fit in reasonably well with our intuitive notions of intelligence.

In addition to the grid-space illustrations of AI techniques, which I use to unify and focus my treatment, I will mention along the way several important applications to realistic problems.

1.5 *Additional Readings and Discussion*

For an argument against using the Turing test (which, sadly, also seems to be an argument for abandoning AI's grand goal of achieving human–level intelligence), see [Hayes & Ford 1995]. The Turing test plays an interesting role in the novel *Galetea 2.2* [Powers 1995].

Both the bottom–up and top–down approaches to AI have been inspired and informed by studies of animal and human behavior. The bottom–up people tend to focus on (usually simple) behavior that can be achieved by assemblages of neuronlike computational elements or logic gates. They have used and helped to create various computational models of animal behavior, as studied by ethologists. Much of the so–called behavior–based and animat approaches to AI mentioned in this chapter derive from animal models. For exemplary discussions of the parallels between animals and robots, see [Anderson & Donath 1990, Beer, Chiel, & Sterling 1990].

Bottom–up researchers and neuroscientists have also developed neural-network models that purport to explain certain human perceptual and motor phenomena, as studied by psychologists. Examples are networks that learn to pronounce words from written text [Sejnowski & Rosenberg 1987]; networks that recognize alphanumeric characters that vary in size, orientation, and position [Minnix, McVey, & Iñigo 1991]; and networks that are sensitive to context effects in letter perception [McClelland & Rumelhart 1981, McClelland & Rumelhart 1982].

When top–down researchers draw inspiration from animal and human behavior, they tend to focus on those aspects that are best modeled by symbol-processing operations. These include various problem–solving, language, and memory tasks, as studied by cognitive psychologists. Two pioneers in developing computer models of human problem solving are Herbert Simon and Allen Newell. (See [Newell & Simon 1972, Newell 1991]. For reviews of the latter book and a response by Newell, see *Artificial Intelligence*, vol. 59, 1993.) For more on the relationship between cognitive science and computer science, see [Johnson-Laird 1988].

Of course, one can also take the view that whichever way animals and humans achieve intelligent behavior may well be irrelevant to the engineering problem of designing intelligent artifacts. Just as airplanes don't fly like birds or insects, well-engineered intelligent machines, able even to surpass human performance, may differ substantially from naturally occurring intelligences. Citing the success of "brute–force" (and therefore presumably nonhuman) search methods in several domains, including game playing, scheduling, and planning, [Ginsberg 1996] speculates that the superior thinking methods of machines may end up being quite different from that of humans. On the other hand, some think that computer architectures (as presently conceived) are so different from the brains of humans and animals that artificial intelligences based on these constrained architectures will not be able to duplicate human behavior [Dreyfus 1979, Dreyfus 1992, Dreyfus & Dreyfus 1986].

The influence of other scientific disciplines on AI cannot always be characterized as oriented toward either a bottom–up or top–down approach. For example, [McFarland & Bösser 1993] discuss many examples of computation as it occurs in animals, but their ideas are closely tied to economics and utility theory. According to them, an animal is an economic agent. Chapter 3 of their book concentrates especially on the role of utility theory in animal models. Michael Wellman, an AI researcher, has developed an approach he calls "market–oriented programming" [Wellman 1996], and [Shoham 1996] presents a related point of view.

Also cutting across the top–down and bottom–up approaches is the matter of how intelligent behavior is to be defined. Should behavior be judged as intelligent independently of how it is computed so long as it is the "right" behavior? There are two somewhat contrasting views. According to [McFarland & Bösser 1993, p. 6], "Intelligent behavior is the behavior that comes up with the right answer, irrespective of how the answer is arrived at." But, in the opinion of [Russell & Wefald 1991, p. 1], ". . . inescapable constraints on the reasoning capabilities of any physical system make it impossible to do the right thing in all instances. A designer of intelligent systems therefore needs to forget about doing the right thing, per se, and think instead about designing the right system . . . ." This view leads Russell and Wefald to describe an approach based on "bounded rationality." They maintain that an intelligent agent must always be deciding between two kinds of actions, action in the world and computational action directed at improving the estimate of what action in the world would be best. (See also [Russell 1997].)

Computational concerns do indeed limit what can be achieved by intelligent systems. Much has been made of focussing on those computations that are "tractable" (that is, achievable in polynomial space and time) according to the dictates of complexity analysis [Garey & Johnson 1979]. But complexity analysis usually is concerned with "worst–case" (instead of "average–case") results. Many of the computations of interest in AI have worst-case exponential complexity. Thus, I think the proper way to respond to those who worry about the intractibility of many AI algorithms is to say that we seek algorithms with good average-case performance and that we are also willing to settle for approximate and nonoptimal solutions in many situations.

Specifying a progression of increasingly versatile agents that might correlate with some of the steps in the evolution of intelligence in animals is not new with me. [Dennett 1995, pp. 373ff] proposes a similar evolutionary sequence of agents that he terms *Darwinian, Skinnerian, Popperian,* and *Gregorian.*

Although we are still far from creating systems of general human-level intelligence, it is important to ask what would be the consequences of doing so.

Obviously, inexpensive robots, softbots, natural language systems, and expert systems will have major economic effects. Will the use of these systems lead to massive unemployment, or will they, like earlier technologies, create more jobs than they eliminate? What happens if most of the very jobs they create can themselves be performed by intelligent machines? (For some of my earlier thoughts about this problem, see [Nilsson 1984a].) Joseph Weizenbaum [Weizenbaum 1976] has worried about a somewhat different problem, namely, the dangers of using AI systems for tasks for which he thinks they are inappropriate, such as counseling, teaching, and judging. Since automated systems sometimes create the illusion of being able to perform tasks that they really cannot, there is also the danger of premature reliance on AI systems. But compensating for that danger is the risk of not using an automatic system that is able to perform with fewer errors than can any human. For a collection of essays about the various impacts of AI, see [Trappl 1986].

Perhaps the most profound impact of AI will be the effects that artificial intelligences will have on our understanding of ourselves. Copernicus and later astronomers moved us from the center of the universe to a small planet in one of countless galaxies. Darwin and later evolutionists moved us from the center of creation to our present place among countless DNA-based life forms. These changes of perspective were difficult for some of us to accept. What changes await us if we are successful in building machines as intelligent as we?

I close this section with a short list of general source materials for AI. This list will be augmented by sources related to various AI subtopics as these are presented in other chapters of the book. Some important journals are *Artificial Intelligence*, the online *Journal of Artificial Intelligence Research*, *Computational Intelligence*, and the *Journal of Experimental and Theoretical Artificial Intelligence*. The major conferences are the annual National Conferences on Artificial Intelligence (sponsored by the American Association for Artificial Intelligence, AAAI) and the biennial International Joint Conferences on Artificial Intelligence, IJCAI. Several countries and regions hold conferences with published proceedings also—for example, the European Conferences on Artificial Intelligence (ECAI). The AAAI holds annual Spring Symposia and Fall Workshops in which ongoing research ideas are reported and discussed. The Association for Computing Machinery (ACM) has a special interest group on AI (SIGART), which publishes a newsletter, and the AAAI publishes the *AI Magazine*.

The magazine *PC AI* publishes articles about applications of AI techniques—concentrating on decision support and expert systems. The journal *Engineering Applications of Artificial Intelligence (EAAI)* contains articles focussing on real-time systems. A series of articles in *IEEE Expert* on "Intelligent Systems and their Applications" features AI labs from around the world that are devoted to applied research and technology transition.

Good summaries of various AI topics can be found in *The Encyclopedia of Artificial Intelligence* [Shapiro 1992], the several volumes of *The Handbook of Artificial Intelligence* [Barr & Feigenbaum 1981, Barr & Feigenbaum 1982, Cohen & Feigenbaum 1982, Barr, Cohen, & Feigenbaum 1989], and *Exploring Artificial Intelligence* [Shrobe 1988]. Important papers in several subfields of AI are reprinted in volumes entitled *Readings in X* (for various instantiations of *X*).

Exercises

1.1 Give your definition of the word *machine*. Do you believe that humans are machines? Whatever your belief (perhaps it is either yes, no, maybe, or not entirely), use your definition and evidence about the various abilities of humans to support your belief.

1.2 Can you think of any practical advantages for making thinking machines of protein (rather than of silicon)?

1.3 Suppose you were the interrogator in a Turing test. Compose five questions that you would ask of *X* and/or *Y* to determine which is a human and which is not.

1.4 Comment critically on whether or not you think the Turing test is appropriate for deciding whether or not nonhuman machines can "think." Propose at least one alternative.

1.5 Some AI researchers have argued that the goal of AI should be to build machines that *help* people in their intellectual tasks rather than to *do* those tasks. Loosely speaking, "helping" is sometimes called *weak AI*, and "doing" is sometimes called *strong AI*. What is your opinion and why?

Part I
Reactive Machines

When you think on the field, you've automatically lost that down. The time you should be thinking is during the course of the week in practice. That's when the light should go on. When you get in the game, it's all about reacting to what you see.

> —Albert Lewis, cornerback of the Oakland Raiders, as quoted by Sam Farmer in the *San Jose Mercury News*, page 1D, August 30, 1996.

2 Stimulus–Response Agents

2.1 Perception and Action

In this chapter, I consider machines that have no internal state and that simply react to immediate stimuli in their environments. We'll call these machines *stimulus-response* (S-R) agents. A variety of robots can be built that exhibit surprisingly interesting behavior based on motor responses to rather simple functions of immediate sensory inputs. One of the earliest examples of this kind of robot was Grey Walter's *Machina speculatrix*—a wheeled device with motors, photocells, and two vacuum tubes [Walter 1953] that moved toward light of moderate intensity and avoided bright light. Similar machines are described by Braitenberg [Braitenberg 1984].

I begin my discussion with an illustrative example. Consider the robot in the two–dimensional grid–space world shown in Figure 2.1. This robot's world is completely enclosed by boundaries and may contain other large, unmovable objects, as shown. The world has no "tight spaces" (spaces between objects and boundaries that are only one cell wide), and the design of our robot will take advantage of that fact.

We want this robot to execute the following behavior: go to a cell adjacent to a boundary or object and then follow that boundary along its perimeter forever. To be capable of such boundary–following behavior, the robot must be able to sense whether or not certain cells are free for it to occupy, and it must be able to perform certain primitive actions.

The robot is able to sense whether or not the eight cells surrounding it are free. These sensory inputs are denoted by the binary-valued variables $s_1, s_2, s_3, s_4, s_5, s_6, s_7$, and s_8. They have value 0 whenever the corresponding cell (relative to the robot, as shown in Figure 2.1) can be occupied by the robot; otherwise, they have

Note: For elaboration of the no–tight–space condition, see *www.mkp.com/nils/clarified*.

21

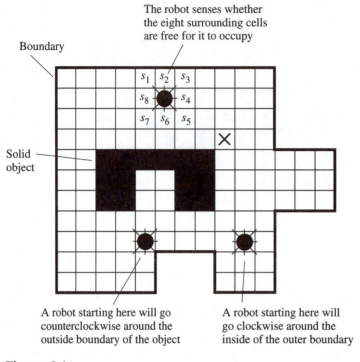

Boundary

The robot senses whether
the eight surrounding cells
are free for it to occupy

Solid
object

A robot starting here will go
counterclockwise around the
outside boundary of the object

A robot starting here will
go clockwise around the
inside of the outer boundary

Figure 2.1

A Robot in a Two–Dimensional Grid World

value 1. If the robot were in the position marked by an X, the values of the sensory inputs (starting with s_1 and proceeding clockwise) would be (0,0,0,0,0,0,1,0).

The robot can move to a (free) adjacent cell in its column or row. There are four such actions:

1. north moves the robot one cell up in the cellular grid
2. east moves the robot one cell to the right
3. south moves the robot one cell down
4. west moves the robot one cell to the left

All of the actions have their indicated effects unless the robot attempts to move into a cell that is not free; in that case, the action has no effect.

Given the properties of the kinds of worlds that a robot might inhabit (Figure 2.1, for example), the task that the robot is to perform (following a boundary), and the robot's sensory and motor abilities, the designer's job is to specify a function of the sensory inputs ($s_1, \ldots, s_8$, in our example) that selects actions appropriate for the task. It is common to divide the processes

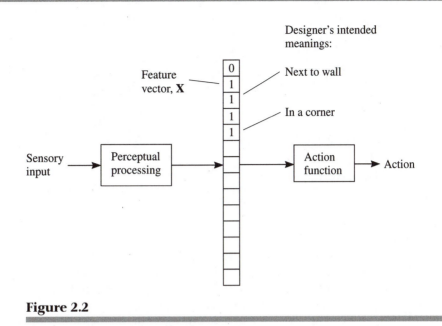

Figure 2.2

Perception and Action Components

of computing an action from the sensory signals into two separate phases, as illustrated in Figure 2.2. A perceptual processing phase produces a vector, $\mathbf{X}$, of *features*, $(x_1, \ldots, x_i, \ldots, x_n)$, and an action computation phase selects an action based on the feature vector. The values of the features can be either real numbers (*numeric features*) or categories (*categorical features*). (A categorical feature is one whose value is a name or a property. For example, the value of the feature "color" might be "red," "blue," or "green.") The special case of binary–valued features can be regarded as either numeric (0,1) or categorical (T, *True*, and F, *False*). The features are selected by the designer to correlate with those properties of the robot's environment that are relevant to which action should be performed in the state described by the features.

Of course, the split between perception and action is completely arbitrary. I could have lumped the whole process as either perception (the world is perceived to be in a state in which action north is appropriate) or as action (action north is computed to be appropriate based on the raw sensory data). Usually, the split is made in such a way that the same features would be used repeatedly in a variety of tasks to be performed. Different tasks would have the same feature vector but different action functions. Viewed as computer programs, the computation of features from sensory signals can be regarded as often used library routines—needed by many different action computations. Deciding how

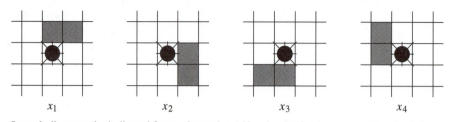

In each diagram, the indicated feature has value 1 if and only if at least one of the shaded cells is *not* free.

Figure 2.3

Features for Boundary Following

to split into the two processes is part of the art of the design of these machines, and I will not have very much to say about that art here.

After deciding how to split, we are left with two problems: (1) converting raw sensory data into a feature vector, and (2) specifying an action function. I will discuss each of these problems briefly in the context of our example.

2.1.1   Perception

The sensory input for our boundary–following robot consists of the values of $s_1, \ldots, s_8$. There are $2^8 = 256$ different combinations of these values. In our environment, some of the combinations are ruled out because of my restriction against tight spaces. For the task at hand, it happens that there are four binary-valued features of the sensory values that are useful for computing an appropriate action. I denote these features by x_1, x_2, x_3, and x_4. Their definitions are given in Figure 2.3. For example, $x_1 = 1$ if and only if $s_2 = 1$ or $s_3 = 1$.

For this example, perceptual processing consists of relatively simple computations. For more complex worlds, and for robots with more complex sensors and tasks, designing appropriate perceptual processing can be challenging. Also, in many real tasks, perceptual processing might occasionally give erroneous, ambiguous, or incomplete information about the robot's environment. Such errors might evoke inappropriate actions, although depending on the task and on the environment, poorly selected actions may not cause too much harm if they are infrequent. I will return to the subject of perception in Chapter 6.

2.1.2   Action

Given the four features, we must now specify a function of them that selects the appropriate boundary–following action. We note first that if *none* of the features has value 1 (that is, if the robot senses that all of its surrounding cells are free), the robot can move in *any* direction until it encounters a boundary. Let's have it move north. Whenever at least one of the other features has value 1, boundary-following behavior is achieved by the following rules for action:

if $x_1 = 1$ and $x_2 = 0$, move east

if $x_2 = 1$ and $x_3 = 0$, move south

if $x_3 = 1$ and $x_4 = 0$, move west

if $x_4 = 1$ and $x_1 = 0$, move north

The conditions under which the robot should take these various actions happen, in this case, to be Boolean combinations of the features. The features themselves are also Boolean combinations of the sensory inputs. Since several important perceptual and action selection methods involve Boolean functions, it will be helpful to digress briefly here to discuss them before continuing with our example.

2.1.3   Boolean Algebra

A Boolean function, $f(x_1, x_2, \ldots, x_n)$ maps an n tuple of $(0,1)$ values to $\{0, 1\}$. *Boolean algebra* is a convenient notation for representing Boolean functions. Boolean algebra uses the connectives $\cdot$, $+$, and $^-$. For example, the *and* function of two variables is written $x_1 \cdot x_2$. By convention, the connective $\cdot$ is usually suppressed, and the *and* function is written $x_1 x_2$. The function $x_1 x_2$ has value 1 if and only if *both* x_1 and x_2 have value 1; otherwise, it has value 0. The (inclusive) *or* function of two variables is written $x_1 + x_2$. $x_1 + x_2$ has value 1 if and only if either or both of x_1 or x_2 has value 1; otherwise, it has value 0. The *complement* or *negation* of a variable, x, is written $\bar{x}$. $\bar{x}$ has value 1 if and only if x has value 0; otherwise, it has value 0.

These definitions are compactly given by the following rules for Boolean algebra:

$$1 + 1 = 1, \ 1 + 0 = 1, \ 0 + 0 = 0$$

$$1 \cdot 1 = 1, \ 1 \cdot 0 = 0, \ 0 \cdot 0 = 0$$

$$\bar{1} = 0, \ \bar{0} = 1$$

As an example, the condition under which our boundary-following robot should move north is given by the expression $\bar{x_1}\,\bar{x_2}\,\bar{x_3}\,\bar{x_4} + x_4\bar{x_1}$. The functions that compute features from sensory signals also happen to be Boolean in this case. For example, $x_4 = s_1 + s_8$. The other features and action rules are given by similar functions.

Sometimes the arguments and values of Boolean functions are expressed in terms of the constants T (*True*) and F (*False*) instead of 1 and 0, respectively.

The connectives $\cdot$ and $+$ are commutative. Thus, $x_1 x_2 = x_2 x_1$ and $x_1 + x_2 = x_2 + x_1$. They are also associative; thus $x_1(x_2 x_3) = (x_1 x_2)x_3$ and $x_1 + (x_2 + x_3) = (x_1 + x_2) + x_3$. Therefore, we can drop the parentheses and write expressions like $x_1 x_2 x_3$ and $x_1 + x_2 + x_3$ without ambiguity.

A Boolean formula consisting of a single variable, such as x_1, is called an *atom*. One consisting of either a single variable or its complement, such as $\overline{x_1}$, is called a *literal*.

We cannot interchange the order of the connectives $\cdot$ and $+$ in complex expressions. Instead, we have DeMorgan's laws (which can be verified by using the preceding definitions):

$$\overline{f_1 f_2} = \overline{f_1} + \overline{f_2}$$

$$\overline{f_1 + f_2} = \overline{f_1} \overline{f_2}$$

DeMorgan's laws can often be used to simplify Boolean functions. For example, $x_1 \overline{x_2} = (s_2 + s_3)\overline{(s_4 + s_5)} = (s_2 + s_3)\overline{s_4}\,\overline{s_5}$.

Another important law is the *distributive law*:

$$f_1(f_2 + f_3) = f_1 f_2 + f_1 f_3$$

2.1.4   Classes and Forms of Boolean Functions

Boolean functions come in a variety of forms. An important form is $\lambda_1 \lambda_2 \cdots \lambda_k$, where the λ_i are literals. A function written in this way is called a *conjunction* of literals or a *monomial*. The conjunction itself is called a *term*. Some example terms are $x_1 x_7$ and $x_1 x_2 \overline{x_4}$. The *size* of a term is the number of literals it contains. The examples are of sizes 2 and 3, respectively.

It is easy to show that there are exactly 3^n possible monomials of n variables (see Exercise 2.4). The number of monomials of size k or less is bounded from above by

$$\sum_{i=0}^{k} C(2n, i) = O(n^k),$$

where

$$C(i, j) = \frac{i!}{(i-j)!j!}$$

is the binomial coefficient.

A *clause* is any expression of the form $\lambda_1 + \lambda_2 + \cdots + \lambda_k$, where the λ_i are literals. Such a form is called a *disjunction* of literals. Some example clauses are $x_3 + x_5 + x_6$ and $x_1 + \overline{x_4}$. The *size* of a clause is the number of literals it contains. There are 3^n possible clauses and fewer than $\sum_{i=0}^{k} C(2n, i)$ clauses of size k or less. If f is a term, then (by DeMorgan's laws) $\overline{f}$ is a clause, and vice versa. Thus, terms and clauses are duals of each other.

A Boolean function is said to be in *disjunctive normal form* (DNF) if it can be written as a *disjunction* of terms. Some examples in DNF are $f = x_1 x_2 + x_2 x_3 x_4$ and $f = x_1 \overline{x_3} + \overline{x_2}\,\overline{x_3} + x_1 x_2 \overline{x_3}$. Any Boolean function can be written in DNF. A DNF expression is called a k–term DNF expression if it is a disjunction of k terms; it is in the class k–DNF if the size of its largest term is k. The preceding examples are 2–term and 3–term expressions, respectively. Both expressions are in the class 3–DNF.

Disjunctive normal form has a dual: *conjunctive normal form (CNF)*. A Boolean function is said to be in CNF if it can be written as a *conjunction* of clauses. An example in CNF is $f = (x_1 + x_2)(x_2 + x_3 + x_4)$. All Boolean functions also have a CNF form. A CNF expression is called a k–clause CNF expression if it is a conjunction of k clauses; it is in the class k–CNF if the size of its largest clause is k. The example is a 2–clause expression in 3–CNF. If f is written in DNF, an application of DeMorgan's law renders $\bar{f}$ in CNF, and vice versa.

2.2   *Representing and Implementing Action Functions*

If there are R possible actions, then we must find an appropriate R–valued function of the feature vector to compute an action. Various ways of representing and implementing action functions have been investigated, and I describe some of them next.

2.2.1   Production Systems

One convenient representational form for an action function is a *production system*. A production system comprises an ordered list of rules called *production rules* or, simply, *productions*. Each rule is written in the form $c_i \longrightarrow a_i$, where c_i is the *condition part*, and a_i is the *action part*. A production system consists of a list of such rules:

$$c_1 \longrightarrow a_1$$
$$c_2 \longrightarrow a_2$$
$$\vdots$$
$$c_i \longrightarrow a_i$$
$$\vdots$$
$$c_m \longrightarrow a_m$$

In general, the condition part of a rule can be any binary–valued (0,1) function of the features resulting from perceptual processing of the sensory inputs. Often, it is a monomial—a conjunction of Boolean literals. To select an action, the rules are processed as follows: starting with the first rule, namely, $c_1 \longrightarrow a_1$, we look for the first rule in the ordering whose condition part evaluates to 1 and select the action part of that rule. The action part can be either a primitive action, a call to another production system, or a set of actions to be executed simultaneously. Usually, the last rule in the ordering has 1 as its condition part; if no rule above it has a condition part equal to 1, then the action associated with the last rule is executed by default. As actions are executed, sensory inputs and the values of features based on them change. We assume that the conditions are continuously being checked so that the action being executed at any time corresponds to the first rule whose condition (at that precise time) has value 1.

Using Boolean algebra and the feature literals defined earlier for the boundary-following robot, here is a production system representation of the boundary-following routine:

$$x_4\overline{x_1} \longrightarrow \text{north}$$
$$x_3\overline{x_4} \longrightarrow \text{west}$$
$$x_2\overline{x_3} \longrightarrow \text{south}$$
$$x_1\overline{x_2} \longrightarrow \text{east}$$
$$1 \longrightarrow \text{north}$$

Boundary-following behavior is an example of a *durative* procedure—one that never ends. The robot continues to execute actions forever. In contrast, some tasks require acting only until some specific *goal* condition is achieved and then ceasing activity. The goal is usually expressed as a Boolean condition on the features. As an example, instead of having our robot follow a boundary forever, we might want it to go to a (concave) corner and stay there. Given a corner-detecting feature, say, c, whose value is 1 if and only if the robot is in a corner, the following production system will get the robot to a corner (if there is one to be found):

$$c \longrightarrow \text{nil}$$
$$1 \longrightarrow \text{b-f}$$

Here, nil is the null or do-nothing action, and b-f is the boundary-following procedure, which we have just defined.

In goal-achieving production systems, c_1, the condition part of the rule at the top of the list, specifies the overall goal that we want the action program to achieve. Whenever it is satisfied, the agent performs no action. Condition c_2 and action a_2 are usually chosen so that if c_1 is not satisfied, and c_2 is, then the execution of action a_2 will eventually achieve c_1. And so on down the list. This style of production system forms the basis of a formalism called *teleo-reactive (T-R) programs* [Nilsson 1994]. In a T-R program, each properly executed action in the ordering works toward achieving a condition higher in the list. Production systems with this property are usually easy to write, given an overall goal for an agent (stated as a condition on the features). T-R programs are also quite robust; actions proceed inexorably toward the goal. Occasional setbacks, caused perhaps by faulty perception, improperly executed actions, or exogenous processes in the environment, are recouped so long as perception is reasonably accurate and

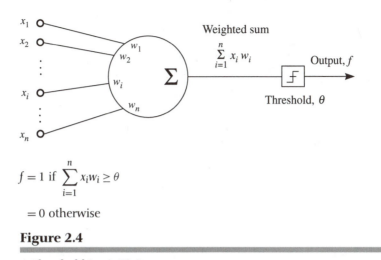

$$f = 1 \text{ if } \sum_{i=1}^{n} x_i w_i \geq \theta$$

$$= 0 \text{ otherwise}$$

Figure 2.4

A Threshold Logic Unit

the actions usually achieve their designed effects.[1] Besides these features, T-R programs can have parameters that are bound when the programs are called, and they can call other T-R programs and themselves recursively.

2.2.2 Networks

Boolean functions and production systems can easily be implemented by computer programs. Alternatively, they can be implemented directly as electronic circuits.[2] The inputs to the circuitry can be the sensory signals themselves. In logic circuits, Boolean functions are usually implemented by networks of logical gates (AND, NAND, OR, etc.). A popular type of circuit consists of networks of threshold elements or other elements that compute a nonlinear function of a weighted sum of their inputs. An example of such an element is the *threshold logic unit (TLU)* shown in Figure 2.4. It computes a weighted sum of its inputs, compares this sum to a threshold value, and outputs a 1 if the threshold is exceeded. Otherwise, it outputs a 0.

The Boolean functions implementable by a TLU are called the *linearly separable functions*. (A TLU separates the space of input vectors yielding an above–threshold response from those yielding a below–threshold response by a linear

---

1. T-R programs are ones that are both "pulled" toward their goals and react to their situations. The prefix *teleo* is derived from the Greek word for "end" or "purpose."

2. Even so, the behavior of the circuit is often simulated by some type of circuit-simulation program running on a computer. Nevertheless, thinking of the behavior as being generated by a circuit instead of by a program helps us to understand the dynamic dependence of appropriate action on immediate sensory inputs.

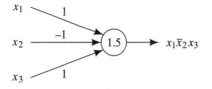

Figure 2.5

Implementation of a Monomial with a TLU

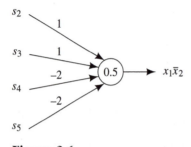

Figure 2.6

Implementing a Function for Boundary Following

surface—called a *hyperplane* in n dimensions.) Many, but far from all, Boolean functions are linearly separable. For example, any monomial (a conjunction of literals) or any clause (a disjunction of literals) is linearly separable. I show a TLU implementation of a monomial in Figure 2.5. The TLU weights are shown drawn next to their corresponding input lines, and the threshold is drawn inside the circle representing the TLU. The exclusive-or function of two variables ($f = x_1\overline{x_2} + \overline{x_1}x_2$), however, is an example of a function that is not linearly separable.

The functions used by the boundary-following robot can be implemented by TLUs. As an example, an implementation of $x_1\overline{x_2} = (s_2 + s_3)\overline{(s_4 + s_5)} = (s_2 + s_3)\overline{s_4}\,\overline{s_5}$ by a single TLU is shown in Figure 2.6.

In applications in which there are only two possible actions, it may be that a single TLU can compute the proper action, given a coded representation of the feature vector as input. For more complex problems, a network of such elements is needed. Such circuits are called *neural networks* because the TLUs are thought to be simple models of biological neurons, which fire or not depending on the summed strength of their inputs across synapses of various strengths. We study neural networks in more detail in the next chapter.

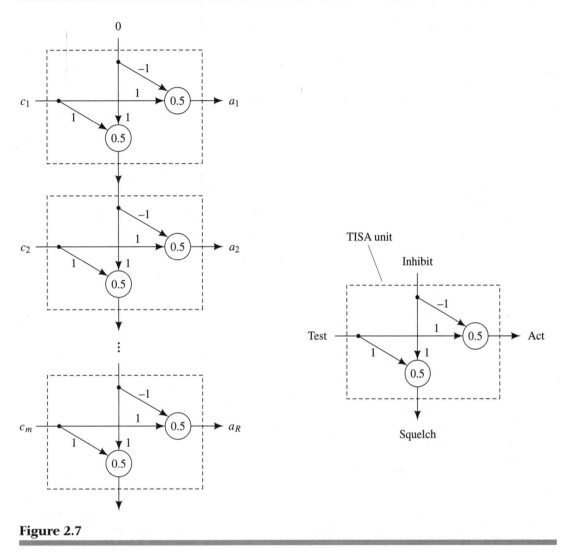

Figure 2.7

A Network of TISA Units

Katz[3] has suggested that a simple network structure with repeated combinations of inverters and **AND** gates (which can be implemented by TLUs) can be used to implement any T–R program. I show my version of such a network in Figure 2.7. The inputs to the network are the binary (0,1) values of the conditions,

---

3. Edward Katz, private communication, April 1996.

c_i; the outputs of the network energize the corresponding actions, a_i. (Not shown here are the computations that produce the c_i; since the c_i are often conjunctions of literals, they too might be computed by TLUs.) Each rule in the T–R program is implemented by a subcircuit (called a TISA, *Test, Inhibit, Squelch, Act*) with two inputs and two outputs. One TLU in the TISA computes the conjunction of one of its inputs with the complement of the other input; the other TLU computes the disjunction of its two inputs. The inhibit input is 0 when *none* of the rules above has a true condition; the test input is 1 only if the condition, c_i, corresponding to this rule is satisfied. If the test input is 1 and the inhibit input is 0, the act output is 1 (energizing the corresponding action, a_i). If either the test input or the inhibit input is 1, the squelch output is 1 (inhibiting all units below). Using programmable gate arrays or some equivalent form of dynamic circuit building, it can be arranged that calling a T–R program dynamically builds the run–time circuit.

2.2.3 The Subsumption Architecture

There have been several other formalisms that have been proposed for converting immediate sensory inputs into actions. Among these is the *subsumption architecture* of Rodney Brooks [Brooks 1986, Brooks 1990, Connell 1990]. Although there seems to be no precise definition of what constitutes such an architecture, the general idea is that an agent's behavior is controlled by a number of "behavior modules." Each module receives sensory information directly from the world. If the sensory inputs satisfy a precondition specific to that module, then a certain behavior program, also specific to that module, is executed. One behavior module can subsume another. In Figure 2.8, each upper module can subsume the one below it. When module *i* subsumes module *j*, then if module *i*'s precondition is met, then module *i*'s program replaces that of module *j*. Brooks terms this a *horizontal* architecture as contrasted with a *vertical* one. Brooks and his students have demonstrated that surprisingly complex behaviors can emerge from the interaction of a relatively simple reactive machine with a complex environment [Mataric 1990, Connell 1990]. As contrasted with much other work in artificial intelligence, Brooks's machines do not depend on complex internal representations of their environments or on reasoning about them [Brooks 1991a, Brooks 1991b].[4] But, of course, one must recognize that all S–R machines, although capable of perhaps very interesting behavior, are nevertheless quite limited. ([Kirsh 1991] has written an interesting commentary on Brooks's approach.)

---

4. Because many of Brooks's subsumption machines do have small amounts of internal state, it might have been more appropriate to mention them in Chapter 5. We include them here because of their close relationship to T–R programs.

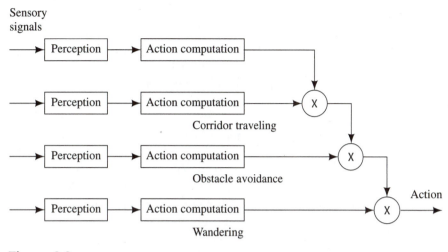

Figure 2.8

Subsumption Modules

2.3 *Additional Readings and Discussion*

S–R agents are ubiquitous in our modern, electronic world. Thermostats for maintaining temperature, cruise control for maintaining automobile speed, interrupt-driven components of a computer operating system, and thousands of different automatic devices in factories are all S–R agents. Ordinarily, these kinds of systems and devices would not be considered part of the subject matter of artificial intelligence, but I include them in my treatment because they inhabit the territory at the beginning of our journey toward more intelligent systems.

In some laboratory courses in robotics and AI, students begin by building S–R robots using Lego components. (See, for example, [Resnick 1993].) AI researchers exploring behavior–based control strategies have experimented with sonar–guided S–R robots capable of wandering, obstacle avoidance, and wall following [Mataric 1990, Connell 1990].

Our proposed split between perception and action is common in agent design. Following [Kaelbling & Rosenschein 1990], we assign to perceptual processing the task of computing a feature vector from raw sensory input, and we assign to the action function the task of selecting an action based on this feature vector. Kaelbling and Rosenschein think of this architectural style as vertical in contrast to Brooks's horizontal structure. Comparing these two styles, they say [Kaelbling & Rosenschein 1990, pp. 36–37]

> Horizontal decompositions that cut across perception and action have been advocated by Brooks as a practical way of approaching agent design. . . .

The horizontal approach allows the designer to consider simultaneously those limited aspects of perception and action needed to support specific behaviors. . . . The alternative is a vertical strategy based on having separate system modules that recover broadly useful information from multiple sources [i.e., perception] and others that exploit it for multiple purposes [i.e., action]. The inherent combinatorics of information extraction and behavior generation make the vertical approach attractive as a way of making efficient use of a programmer's effort.

Actually, the split between perception and action can accommodate the horizontal approach also. The feature vector can be divided into separate fields—each field computed by specialized perceptual apparatus and evoking separate actions or behaviors, as in the subsumption architecture.

T–R programs and other reactive systems bear a close relationship to various ethological models of animal behavior [McFarland 1987]. In some of these models, a goal–achieving sequence of animal actions is elicited by arranging that the result of one action acts as a stimulus or trigger that "releases" the next one in the sequence. The conditions and actions of a T–R program are selected so that the program works in this manner. My work on T–R programs was inspired partly by a book by [Deutsch 1960].

Animals that seek out and move toward certain stimuli exhibit what are called *tropisms*. Phototropic animals move toward light, for example. [Genesereth & Nilsson 1987] term the kinds of agents discussed in this chapter *tropistic agents*.

Some experimental research uses simulated S–R robots rather than physical ones. Simulations are sometimes criticized as "doomed to succeed" [Brooks & Mataric 1993, p. 209], but those that do not succeed well enough help us refine perceptual and action strategies. And sometimes the simulation is actually the "real thing." For example, in computer–based education, entertainment, and dramatic art, animated characters interact with their simulated environments and with a user [Bates 1994, Blumberg 1996]. (Blumberg's ALIVE system is another example of one that uses principles from ethology to build interactive characters.)

For more on Boolean functions, see [Unger 1989]. Production systems can be thought of as a generalization of Boolean functions called *decision lists* [Rivest 1987].

Exercises

2.1 Write the following Boolean function in DNF:

$$f = (x_1 + x_2)(x_3 + x_4)$$

2.2 Show that $x_1x_2x_3 + \overline{x_1}x_2x_3 = x_2x_3$.

2.3 Indicate which of the following Boolean functions of three input variables can be realized by a single threshold element with weighted connections to the inputs. You do *not* need to calculate the weight and threshold values:

1. x_1

2. $x_1 x_2 x_3$

3. $x_1 + x_2 + x_3$

4. $(x_1 x_2 x_3) + (\overline{x_1}\, \overline{x_2}\, \overline{x_3})$

5. 1

2.4 Prove that there are exactly 3^n monomials of n dimensions and 3^n clauses of n dimensions.

2.5 Refer to the definitions of the features, x_1, x_2, x_3, x_4 on page 24 and to the rules for action on page 25. Show that the assumption that there are no "tight spaces" in the two–dimensional grid world implies that no two of the action rules can be satisified simultaneously.

2.6 Design (by hand) a neural network that accepts as inputs the sensory signals $s_1, s_2, \ldots, s_8$ and produces as outputs the conditions needed by a network of TISA units to implement the action rules on page 25 for the wall–following robot.

2.7 In this chapter, I stated that the actions prescribed by T–R programs "proceed inexorably toward the goal." Is this statement strictly true? Can you think of situations in which a T–R program does not terminate with the top condition becoming true?

3 Neural Networks

3.1 Introduction

At different points in this book, I will be discussing methods by which machines can *learn*. In this chapter, I show how the action–selecting computations performed by S–R machines can be learned through exposure to a set of samples of inputs paired with the action that would be appropriate for each input. Although there are many different computational structures that might be used, I concentrate here on networks of TLUs with adjustable weights. Learning is achieved by adjusting the weights in the network until its action–computing performance is acceptable. As mentioned in the last chapter, TLU networks are called *neural networks* because they model some of the properties of biological neurons. I won't be speculating here about the relationships between neural networks and how brains or parts of brains might function; instead, I will consider the networks strictly as interesting and useful engineering devices.

I consider the following learning problem: we are given a set, Ξ, of n–dimensional vectors, $\mathbf{X}$, with components x_i, $i = 1, \ldots, n$. These vectors might be the feature vectors computed by the perceptual processing component of a reactive agent. The values of the components can be real numbers or Boolean values, as I mentioned earlier. For each $\mathbf{X}$ in Ξ, we also know what the appropriate action, a, would be. Perhaps these actions are those that the learner observes performed by a teacher in response to a set of inputs. These associated actions are sometimes called the *labels* or the *classes* of the vectors. The set Ξ and the associated labels constitute what is called the *training set*. The machine learning problem is to find a function, say, $f(\mathbf{X})$, that responds "acceptably" to the members of the training set. Usually, we want the action computed by f to agree with the label for as many vectors in Ξ as possible. Because the labels are given along with the input vectors, we say that the learning process is *supervised*.

Even if we find a function that responds appropriately to the training set, what grounds do we have for believing that it will respond appropriately to inputs that it has not seen during training? Besides the experimental evidence supporting the belief that it will, there is a body of theory that shows (under certain conditions) that if the training set is "typical" of the kinds of other inputs likely to be encountered, then these other inputs "probably" will evoke "approximately correct" outputs. For more on this topic, refer to the literature on *probably approximately correct (PAC)* learning theory [Kearns & Vazirani 1994, Haussler 1988, Haussler 1990]. In practice, there are various methods for estimating what the accuracy of a learned function, f, is likely to be on similar (but so–far unseen) inputs. I will present some of these methods later in the chapter.

3.2   *Training Single TLUs*

3.2.1   TLU Geometry

I will begin by considering how the weights of a single TLU can be adjusted or *trained* so that it produces appropriate outputs for certain training sets. If a TLU is to be used to compute an action, its inputs must be numeric (so that a weighted sum can be computed); if the perceptual processing system produces categorical features, these will have to be coded as numbers in some way. Of course, a reactive machine that uses a single TLU to compute its actions will be capable of only two actions, corresponding to the two possible outputs of the TLU. A single TLU has also been called a *Perceptron* and an *Adaline* (for *adaptive linear element*). Their use was extensively explored by Rosenblatt and by Widrow [Rosenblatt 1962, Widrow 1962]. Training a TLU is accomplished by adjusting its variable weights. A geometric explanation of how a TLU responds to its inputs will aid our intuitive understanding of TLU training methods.

A TLU is defined by its weights and threshold. The weights, $(w_1, \ldots, w_i, \ldots, w_n)$, can be represented by a weight vector $\mathbf{W}$. I denote the TLU threshold by θ. Here we assume that the input vector $\mathbf{X}$ has numeric components (so that a weighted sum of them can be computed). A TLU has an output of 1 if the vector dot product, $s = \mathbf{X} \cdot \mathbf{W}$, is greater than θ, and has an output of 0 otherwise. A TLU divides the space of input vectors by a linear boundary as sketched in Figure 3.1. In two dimensions, the boundary is a line, and in three it is a plane. In higher–dimensional spaces, a linear boundary is called a *hyperplane*. The hyperplane separates the vectors for which $\mathbf{X} \cdot \mathbf{W} - \theta > 0$ from the vectors for which $\mathbf{X} \cdot \mathbf{W} - \theta < 0$. The equation of the hyperplane itself is $\mathbf{X} \cdot \mathbf{W} - \theta = 0$. We can change the position of the hyperplane boundary (with respect to the origin)

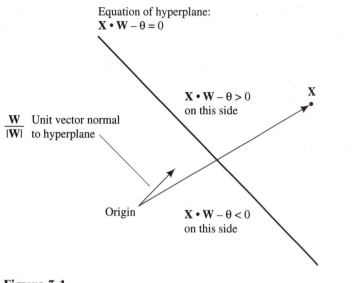

Equation of hyperplane:
$\mathbf{X} \cdot \mathbf{W} - \theta = 0$

$\mathbf{X} \cdot \mathbf{W} - \theta > 0$
on this side

X

$\dfrac{\mathbf{W}}{|\mathbf{W}|}$ Unit vector normal to hyperplane

Origin

$\mathbf{X} \cdot \mathbf{W} - \theta < 0$
on this side

Figure 3.1

TLU Geometry

by adjusting the threshold θ, and we can adjust the orientation of the hyperplane by adjusting the weights.

3.2.2   Augmented Vectors

There are several procedures that have been proposed for adjusting the weights of a TLU. My explanation of these is simplified if I adopt the convention that the threshold of the TLU is always equal to 0. Arbitrary thresholds are achieved by using $(n + 1)$-dimensional "augmented" vectors instead. The $(n + 1)$-th component of the augmented input vector always has value 1; the $(n + 1)$-th component, w_{n+1}, of the augmented weight vector is set equal to the negative of the desired threshold value, θ. Hereafter, when I use the $\mathbf{X}$-$\mathbf{W}$ notation, I will be assuming $(n + 1)$-dimensional augmented vectors. The output of a TLU, then, has value 1 when $\mathbf{X} \cdot \mathbf{W} \geq 0$, and has value 0 otherwise.

3.2.3   Gradient Descent Methods

One way to approach the problem of training a TLU so that it responds appropriately to the training vectors is to define an *error function* that can be minimized by adjusting weight values. A commonly used error function is squared error:

$$\varepsilon = \sum_{X_i \in \Xi} (d_i - f_i)^2$$

where f_i is the actual response of the TLU for input $\mathbf{X}_i$, d_i is the desired response, and we sum over all vectors in the training set. For fixed Ξ, we see that ε depends on the weight values (through f_i). We can find a minimum of ε by performing a *gradient descent* process. To do gradient descent, we calculate the gradient of ε in "weight space" and move the weight vector along the negative gradient (downhill). One problem with calculating the gradient of ε (as defined) is that ε depends on *all* the input vectors in Ξ. Often, it is preferable to try the TLU on one member of Ξ at a time, make an adjustment to the weights, and then try another member of Ξ—an incremental training process using a sequence, Σ, of labeled input vectors. Of course, the results of incremental training can only approximate those of the so–called batch version, but the approximation is usually quite effective. I will be describing the incremental version here.

The squared error for a single input vector, $\mathbf{X}$, evoking an output of f when the desired output is d is

$$\varepsilon = (d - f)^2$$

The *gradient* of ε with respect to the weights is

$$\frac{\partial \varepsilon}{\partial \mathbf{W}} \stackrel{\text{def}}{=} \left[\frac{\partial \varepsilon}{\partial w_1}, \ldots, \frac{\partial \varepsilon}{\partial w_i}, \ldots, \frac{\partial \varepsilon}{\partial w_{n+1}} \right]$$

(The gradient of a quantity ϕ with respect to a vector $\mathbf{W}$ is sometimes denoted by $\nabla_{\mathbf{W}}\phi$.)

Since ε's dependence on $\mathbf{W}$ is entirely through the dot product, $s = \mathbf{X} \cdot \mathbf{W}$, we can use the chain rule to write

$$\frac{\partial \varepsilon}{\partial \mathbf{W}} = \frac{\partial \varepsilon}{\partial s} \frac{\partial s}{\partial \mathbf{W}}$$

Then, because $\frac{\partial s}{\partial \mathbf{W}} = \mathbf{X}$,

$$\frac{\partial \varepsilon}{\partial \mathbf{W}} = \frac{\partial \varepsilon}{\partial s} \mathbf{X}$$

Note that $\frac{\partial \varepsilon}{\partial s} = -2(d - f)\frac{\partial f}{\partial s}$. Thus,

$$\frac{\partial \varepsilon}{\partial \mathbf{W}} = -2(d - f)\frac{\partial f}{\partial s}\mathbf{X}$$

We have a problem, however, in attempting to carry out the partial derivative of f with respect to s. The TLU output, f, is not continuously differentiable with respect to s because of the presence of the threshold function. Most small changes in the dot product do not change f at all, and when f does change, it changes abruptly from 1 to 0 or vice versa. I will consider two approaches to dealing with this problem. In one, we ignore the threshold function and let $f = s$. In the other, we replace the threshold function with another nonlinear function that is differentiable.

3.2.4   The Widrow–Hoff Procedure

Suppose we attempt to adjust the weights so that every training vector labeled with a 1 produces a dot product of exactly 1, and every vector labeled with a 0 produces a dot product of exactly -1. In that case, with $f = s$, the incremental squared error, $\varepsilon = (d - f)^2 = (d - s)^2$, and $\frac{\partial f}{\partial s} = 1$. Now, the gradient is

$$\frac{\partial \varepsilon}{\partial \mathbf{W}} = -2(d - f)\mathbf{X}$$

Moving the weight vector along the negative gradient, and incorporating the factor 2 into a *learning rate parameter*, c, the new value of the weight vector is given by

$$\mathbf{W} \longleftarrow \mathbf{W} + c(d - f)\mathbf{X}$$

Whenever $(d - f)$ is positive, we add a fraction of the input vector into the weight vector. This addition makes the dot product larger and $(d - f)$ smaller. Whenever $(d - f)$ is negative, we subtract a fraction of the input vector from the weight vector—yielding the opposite effect. This procedure is known as the *Widrow-Hoff* or *Delta* rule [Widrow & Hoff 1960].[1] Of course, after finding a set of weights that minimizes the squared error (using $f = s$), we are free to reinsert the threshold function to produce f values of 0 or 1.

3.2.5   The Generalized Delta Procedure

Another way of dealing with the nondifferentiable threshold function was proposed by Werbos [Werbos 1974] and independently pursued by several other researchers, for example, [Rumelhart, et al. 1986]. The trick involves replacing the threshold function by an S-shaped differentiable function called a *sigmoid*.[2] Usually, the sigmoid function used is $f(s) = \frac{1}{1+e^{-s}}$, where s is the input and f is the output. The output of a sigmoid function, superimposed on that of a threshold function, is shown in Figure 3.2.

This choice for the sigmoid function gives us the following partial derivative:

$$\frac{\partial f}{\partial s} = f(1 - f)$$

Substitution of this expression into $\frac{\partial \varepsilon}{\partial \mathbf{W}} = -2(d - f)\frac{\partial f}{\partial s}\mathbf{X}$ yields

$$\frac{\partial \varepsilon}{\partial \mathbf{W}} = -2(d - f)f(1 - f)\mathbf{X}$$

---

1. Anyone familiar with numerical methods will recognize the Widrow–Hoff procedure as an instance of a *relaxation method* for solving linear equalities.

2. [Russell & Norvig 1995, p. 595] attribute the use of this idea to [Bryson & Ho 1969].

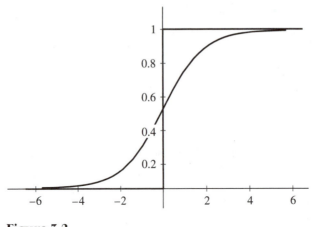

Figure 3.2

A Sigmoid Function

giving us the following weight–change rule, known as the *generalized Delta procedure*:

$$\mathbf{W} \longleftarrow \mathbf{W} + c(d - f)f(1 - f)\mathbf{X}$$

Comparing Widrow–Hoff with generalized Delta reveals these differences:

1. In Widrow–Hoff, the desired output, d, is either 1 or -1, whereas in generalized Delta it is 1 or 0.
2. In Widrow–Hoff, the actual output, f, equals s, the dot product, whereas in generalized Delta, it is the output of the sigmoid function.
3. In generalized Delta, there is the added term $f(1 - f)$ due to the presence of the sigmoid function. With the sigmoid function, $f(1 - f)$ can vary in value from 0 to 1. When f is 0, $f(1 - f)$ is also 0; when f is 1, $f(1 - f)$ is 0; $f(1 - f)$ obtains its maximum value of 1/4 when f is 1/2 (that is, when the input to the sigmoid is 0). The sigmoid function can be thought of as implementing a "fuzzy" hyperplane. For an input vector far away from this fuzzy hyperplane, $f(1 - f)$ has value close to 0, and the generalized Delta rule makes little or no change to the weight values regardless of the desired output. Weight changes are made only within the region of "fuzz" surrounding the hyperplane (the only place where changes have much effect on f), and these changes are in the direction of correcting the error.

After the generalized Delta procedure finds a set of weights, the sigmoid function can be replaced with a threshold function if desired.

3.2.6   The Error–Correction Procedure

In the next method, we keep the threshold element (instead of replacing it by a sigmoid) and make an adjustment to the weight vector only when the TLU responds in error, that is, when $(d - f)$ has value 1 or -1. It is called an *error-correction* procedure. The weight change rule is

$$\mathbf{W} \longleftarrow \mathbf{W} + c(d - f)\mathbf{X}$$

Again, the change is in the direction that helps correct the error (and might actually correct it, depending on the value of the learning rate parameter, c). One difference between this rule and Widrow–Hoff is that in error correction both d and f are either 0 or 1, whereas in Widrow–Hoff, d is $+1$ or -1, and $f = s$ is the value of the dot product.

It can be proved that if there is some weight vector, $\mathbf{W}$, that produces a correct output for all of the input vectors in Ξ, then after a finite number of input vector presentations, the error-correction procedure will find such a weight vector and thus make no more weight changes. (The proof requires that each input vector appear in the training sequence, Σ, an infinite number of times, even though the procedure is guaranteed to terminate after only a finite number of examples from Σ are presented.) For nonlinearly separable sets of input vectors, the error-correction procedure will never terminate and thus cannot be used to find a "best" weight vector judged against some error criterion. The Widrow–Hoff and generalized Delta procedures, however, will find minimum squared-error solutions even when the minimum error is not zero.

We saw examples of linearly separable functions in Chapter 2. Recall the production rules for the actions of the boundary-following robot. One of these, for example, was

$$x_1 \overline{x_2} \longrightarrow \text{east}$$

Expressed in terms of the sensory inputs, $x_1 \overline{x_2} = (s_2 + s_3)\overline{s_4}\,\overline{s_5}$. This function is linearly separable and can be implemented by the TLU shown in Figure 2.6. Thus, we can expect that error-correction training on a sufficiently large set of appropriately labeled sensory vectors would terminate with a TLU that correctly discriminates between inputs for which the robot should move east and those for which it should not. We could assemble a set of training vectors, such as those shown in Figure 3.3. You might want to try the error-correction procedure using these and additional labeled input vectors. (Don't forget to include the $s_9 \equiv 1$ input and the w_9 weight component!) How does the trained TLU perform on inputs that it has not been trained on? How many input vectors are needed in the training set before the TLU performs acceptably?

For additional background, citations, proofs, and examples of error-correction procedures, see [Nilsson 1965].

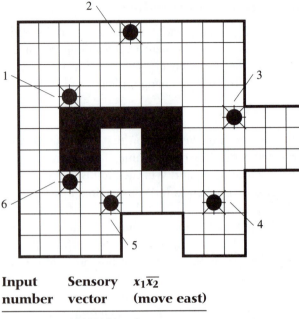

Input number	Sensory vector	$x_1 \overline{x_2}$ (move east)
1	00001100	0
2	11100000	1
3	00100000	1
4	00000000	0
5	00001000	0
6	01100000	1

Figure 3.3

A Training Set for Learning When to Move East

3.3   *Neural Networks*

3.3.1   **Motivation**

It often happens that there are sets of stimuli and responses that cannot be learned by a single TLU. (The training set may not be linearly separable.) In that case, it is possible that a network of TLUs can give correct responses. The function implemented by a network of TLUs depends on its topology as well as on the weights of the individual TLUs. *Feedforward networks* have no cycles: in a feedforward network, no TLU's input depends (through 0 or more intermediate TLUs) on that TLU's output. (Networks that are not feedforward are called *recurrent networks*. We'll study an instance of a recurrent network in a later chapter.) If the TLUs of a feedforward network are arranged in layers, with the elements of layer j

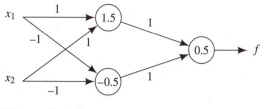

Figure 3.4

A Network of TLUs That Implements the Even–Parity Function

receiving inputs only from TLUs in layer $j-1$, then we say that the network is a *layered, feedforward network*. The network in Figure 3.4, which implements the function $f = x_1 x_2 + \overline{x_1}\,\overline{x_2}$ (called the *even-parity function*), is a layered, feedforward network having two layers (of weights). (Some people count the layers of TLUs and include the inputs as a layer also; they would call the network of Figure 3.4 a three–layer network.)

In the following sections, I describe a general procedure for training a multilayer, feedforward network. It is called the *backpropagation procedure* and uses gradient descent. Since we will be taking partial derivatives of an error function with respect to weight vectors, we replace all threshold functions in the network with sigmoid functions. (After training, threshold functions can be substituted back in for the sigmoid functions.)

3.3.2   Notation

I show a general, k–layer, feedforward network of sigmoid units in Figure 3.5. The sigmoid units in all but the last layer are called *hidden units* since their outputs only indirectly affect the final output. The network of Figure 3.5 has only one output unit; several output units would be used when there are more than two actions or categories of inputs. (With several output units, a decoding scheme is needed to transform the output vector into a category. [Brain, et al. 1962] used codes based on maximal shift–register sequences, and [Dietterich & Bakiri 1991, Dietterich & Bakiri 1995] have investigated the use of similar error–correcting codes.)

I use Figure 3.5 to introduce some useful notation. Each of the layers of sigmoid units will have outputs that we take to be the components of vectors, just as the input features are components of an input vector. The j-th layer of sigmoids ($1 \leq j < k$) will have as their outputs the vector $\mathbf{X}^{(j)}$. This vector is then the input vector to each of the $(j+1)$-th layer of sigmoids. The input vector is denoted by $\mathbf{X}^{(0)}$, and the final output (of the k-th layer TLU) is f. Each sigmoid in each layer has a weight vector (connecting it to its inputs); the i-th sigmoid unit in the j-th layer has a weight vector denoted by $\mathbf{W}_i^{(j)}$. As before, we will assume that

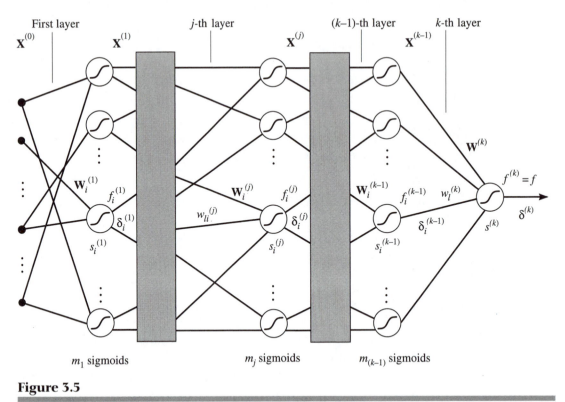

Figure 3.5

A *k*-layer Network of Sigmoid Units

the "threshold weight" is the last component of the associated weight vector. We denote the weighted sum input to the *i*-th sigmoid unit in the *j*-th layer by $s_i^{(j)}$. The input to a sigmoid unit is called its *activation* and is given by

$$s_i^{(j)} = \mathbf{X}^{(j-1)} \cdot \mathbf{W}_i^{(j)}$$

The number of sigmoid units in the *j*-th layer is denoted by m_j. The vector $\mathbf{W}_i^{(j)}$ has components $w_{l,i}^{(j)}$ for $l = 1, m_{(j-1)} + 1$.

3.3.3   The Backpropagation Method

We will compute the gradient of the squared–error function, $\varepsilon = (d - f)^2$. In this case, the weight vector over which the gradient is computed should be a vector consisting of *all* of the weights in the network. It is convenient, however, to take the partial derivatives of ε with respect to the various weights in groups corresponding to the weight vectors of the individual sigmoids. The partial derivative of ε with respect to a weight vector, $\mathbf{W}_i^{(j)}$, is

$$\frac{\partial \varepsilon}{\partial \mathbf{W}_i^{(j)}} \overset{\text{def}}{=} \left[\frac{\partial \varepsilon}{\partial w_{1i}^{(j)}}, \cdots, \frac{\partial \varepsilon}{\partial w_{li}^{(j)}}, \cdots, \frac{\partial \varepsilon}{\partial w_{m_{j-1}+1,i}^{(j)}} \right]$$

where $w_{li}^{(j)}$ is the l-th component of $\mathbf{W}_i^{(j)}$.

Just as before, since ε's dependence on $\mathbf{W}_i^{(j)}$ is entirely through $s_i^{(j)}$, we can use the chain rule to write

$$\frac{\partial \varepsilon}{\partial \mathbf{W}_i^{(j)}} = \frac{\partial \varepsilon}{\partial s_i^{(j)}} \frac{\partial s_i^{(j)}}{\partial \mathbf{W}_i^{(j)}}$$

Again, because $s_i^{(j)} = \mathbf{X}^{(j-1)} \cdot \mathbf{W}_i^{(j)}$, $\frac{\partial s_i^{(j)}}{\partial \mathbf{W}_i^{(j)}} = \mathbf{X}^{(j-1)}$. Substituting yields

$$\frac{\partial \varepsilon}{\partial \mathbf{W}_i^{(j)}} = \frac{\partial \varepsilon}{\partial s_i^{(j)}} \mathbf{X}^{(j-1)}$$

Now, $\frac{\partial \varepsilon}{\partial s_i^{(j)}} = \frac{\partial (d-f)^2}{\partial s_i^{(j)}} = -2(d-f) \frac{\partial f}{\partial s_i^{(j)}}$, so

$$\frac{\partial \varepsilon}{\partial \mathbf{W}_i^{(j)}} = -2(d-f) \frac{\partial f}{\partial s_i^{(j)}} \mathbf{X}^{(j-1)}$$

The quantity $(d-f) \frac{\partial f}{\partial s_i^{(j)}} = -\frac{1}{2} \frac{\partial \varepsilon}{\partial s_i^{(j)}}$ plays an important role in our calculations; I shall denote it by $\delta_i^{(j)}$. Each of the $\delta_i^{(j)}$'s tells us how sensitive the squared error of the network output is to changes in the input of the corresponding sigmoid function. The gradient of ϵ can be written using the δ's as

$$\frac{\partial \varepsilon}{\partial \mathbf{W}_i^{(j)}} = -2\delta_i^{(j)} \mathbf{X}^{(j-1)}$$

Since we will be changing weight vectors in directions along their negative gradients, our fundamental rule for weight changes throughout the network will be

$$\mathbf{W}_i^{(j)} \leftarrow \mathbf{W}_i^{(j)} + c_i^{(j)} \delta_i^{(j)} \mathbf{X}^{(j-1)}$$

where $c_i^{(j)}$ is the learning rate constant for this weight vector. (Usually, the learning rate constants for all weight vectors in the network are the same.) We see that this rule is quite similar to that used in the procedures for a single TLU or sigmoid unit. A weight vector is changed by the addition of a factor times its vector of (unweighted) inputs.

3.3.4   Computing Weight Changes in the Final Layer

Now, we turn our attention to the calculation of the $\delta_i^{(j)}$'s. Using the definition, we have

$$\delta_i^{(j)} = (d-f)\frac{\partial f}{\partial s_i^{(j)}}$$

We first calculate $\delta^{(k)}$ in order to compute the weight change for the final sigmoid unit:

$$\delta^{(k)} = (d-f)\frac{\partial f}{\partial s^{(k)}}$$

Since f is the sigmoid function, and $s^{(k)}$ is its input, we have (as before) $\frac{\partial f}{\partial s^{(k)}} = f(1-f)$. Thus,

$$\delta^{(k)} = (d-f)f(1-f)$$

And the backpropagation weight adjustment for the single element in the final layer can be written as

$$\mathbf{W}^{(k)} \leftarrow \mathbf{W}^{(k)} + c^{(k)}(d-f)f(1-f)\mathbf{X}^{(k-1)}$$

which is the same rule as the generalized Delta procedure would have given us if the final sigmoid unit were the only one in the network and if $\mathbf{X}^{(k-1)} = \mathbf{X}$.

3.3.5   Computing Changes to the Weights in Intermediate Layers

Using our expression for the δ's, we can similarly compute how to change each of the weight vectors in the network. Recall

$$\delta_i^{(j)} = (d-f)\frac{\partial f}{\partial s_i^{(j)}}$$

Again we use a chain rule. The final output, f, depends on $s_i^{(j)}$ through each of the summed inputs to the sigmoids in the $(j+1)$-th layer. So

$$\delta_i^{(j)} = (d-f)\left[\frac{\partial f}{\partial s_1^{(j+1)}}\frac{\partial s_1^{(j+1)}}{\partial s_i^{(j)}} + \cdots + \frac{\partial f}{\partial s_l^{(j+1)}}\frac{\partial s_l^{(j+1)}}{\partial s_i^{(j)}} + \cdots + \frac{\partial f}{\partial s_{m_{j+1}}^{(j+1)}}\frac{\partial s_{m_{j+1}}^{(j+1)}}{\partial s_i^{(j)}}\right]$$

$$= \sum_{l=1}^{m_{j+1}}(d-f)\frac{\partial f}{\partial s_l^{(j+1)}}\frac{\partial s_l^{(j+1)}}{\partial s_i^{(j)}} = \sum_{l=1}^{m_{j+1}}\delta_l^{(j+1)}\frac{\partial s_l^{(j+1)}}{\partial s_i^{(j)}}$$

It remains to compute the $\frac{\partial s_l^{(j+1)}}{\partial s_i^{(j)}}$'s. To do that, we first write

$$s_l^{(j+1)} = \mathbf{X}^{(j)} \cdot \mathbf{W}_l^{(j+1)}$$

$$= \sum_{\nu=1}^{m_j+1} f_\nu^{(j)} w_{\nu l}^{(j+1)}$$

And then, since the weights do not depend on the s's,

$$\frac{\partial s_l^{(j+1)}}{\partial s_i^{(j)}} = \frac{\partial \left[\sum_{\nu=1}^{m_j+1} f_\nu^{(j)} w_{\nu l}^{(j+1)} \right]}{\partial s_i^{(j)}} = \sum_{\nu=1}^{m_j+1} w_{\nu l}^{(j+1)} \frac{\partial f_\nu^{(j)}}{\partial s_i^{(j)}}$$

Now, we note that $\frac{\partial f_\nu^{(j)}}{\partial s_i^{(j)}} = 0$ unless $\nu = i$, in which case $\frac{\partial f_\nu^{(j)}}{\partial s_\nu^{(j)}} = f_\nu^{(j)}(1 - f_\nu^{(j)})$. Therefore,

$$\frac{\partial s_l^{(j+1)}}{\partial s_i^{(j)}} = w_{il}^{(j+1)} f_i^{(j)}(1 - f_i^{(j)})$$

We use this result in our expression for $\delta_i^{(j)}$ to give

$$\delta_i^{(j)} = f_i^{(j)}(1 - f_i^{(j)}) \sum_{l=1}^{m_j+1} \delta_l^{(j+1)} w_{il}^{(j+1)}.$$

The preceding equation is recursive in the δ's. (It is interesting to note that this expression is independent of the error function; the error function explicitly affects only the computation of $\delta^{(k)}$.) Having computed the $\delta_i^{(j+1)}$'s for layer $j + 1$, we can use this equation to compute the $\delta_i^{(j)}$'s. The base case is $\delta^{(k)}$, which we have already computed:

$$\delta^{(k)} = (d - f)f(1 - f)$$

We use this expression for the δ's in our generic weight changing rule, namely,

$$\mathbf{W}_i^{(j)} \leftarrow \mathbf{W}_i^{(j)} + c_i^{(j)} \delta_i^{(j)} \mathbf{X}^{(j-1)}$$

Although this rule appears complex, it has an intuitively reasonable explanation. The quantity $\delta^{(k)} = (d - f)f(1 - f)$ controls the overall amount and sign of *all* weight adjustments in the network. (Adjustments diminish as the final output, f, approaches either 0 or 1, because they have vanishing effect on f then.) As the recursion equation for the δ's shows, the adjustments for the weights going *in* to a sigmoid unit in the j-th layer are proportional to the effect that such adjustments have on that sigmoid unit's output (its $f^{(j)}(1 - f^{(j)})$ factor). They are

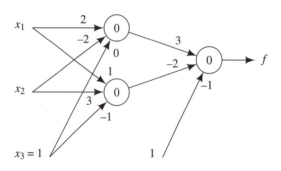

Figure 3.6

A Network to
Be Trained by
Backprop

also proportional to a kind of "average" effect that any change in the output of that sigmoid unit will have on the final output. This average effect depends on the weights going *out* of the sigmoid unit in the j-th layer (small weights produce little downstream effect) and the effects that changes in the outputs of $(j+1)$-th layer sigmoid units will have on the final output (as measured by the $\delta^{(j+1)}$'s). These calculations can be simply implemented by "backpropagating" the δ's through the weights in reverse direction (thus, the name *backprop* for this algorithm). For additional information about backprop and its applications, see [Chauvin & Rumelhart 1995].

As an example of the backpropagation process, let's go through one step of training the neural network of Figure 3.6—starting with the random weights shown. (I use our standard network notation here in order to make it easier to follow my use of the backprop equations.) Our target function is the even–parity function of two binary variables. The inputs (including the "threshold input") and the desired labels are

1. $x_1^{(0)} = 1, x_2^{(0)} = 0, x_3^{(0)} = 1, d = 0$
2. $x_1^{(0)} = 0, x_2^{(0)} = 0, x_3^{(0)} = 1, d = 1$
3. $x_1^{(0)} = 0, x_2^{(0)} = 1, x_3^{(0)} = 1, d = 0$
4. $x_1^{(0)} = 1, x_2^{(0)} = 1, x_3^{(0)} = 1, d = 1$

The first input vector is $(1,0,1)$, which evokes first-layer outputs of $f_1^{(1)} = 0.881$ and $f_2^{(1)} = 0.500$ and a final output of $f = 0.665$. Using the equation for the base case, we calculate $\delta^{(2)} = -0.148$. Backpropagating this δ through the weights in the second layer produces $\delta_1^{(1)} = -0.047$ and $\delta_2^{(1)} = 0.074$. Then, using the weight-adjusting equations (and a learning rate constant $c = 1$), the new weights are calculated to be

$$\mathbf{W}_1^{(1)} = (1.953, -2.000, -0.047)$$

$$\mathbf{W}_2^{(1)} = (1.074, 3.000, -0.926)$$

$$\mathbf{W}^{(2)} = (2.870, -2.074, -1.148)$$

Note that (even though $f_2^{(1)} = 0.500$—just where maximum sensitivity to adjust-ments occurs) no adjustment is made to $w_{2,2}^{(1)}$ or $w_{1,2}^{(1)}$ since $x_2^{(0)} = 0$. The adjustments to the first layer of weights act to decrease the values of both $f_1^{(1)}$ and $f_2^{(1)}$, which in turn, together with the adjustments to the second layer of weights, act to de-crease f and the error for this input vector. It would be instructive for you to write a program (or use a spreadsheet) to continue this training process.

<h2>3.4   Generalization, Accuracy, and Overfitting</h2>

The neural–network training example just presented is quite atypical. Because of its low dimensionality, we are able to train on *all* possible (only four) input vectors. According to Figure 3.4, there exists a set of weights that classifies all of them correctly. In most applications, the dimensionality is much greater, often around 100 or more. With 100 binary components, there are 2^{100} possible input vectors. We could use only a tiny fraction of these for training. And, even if the network were to classify the entire training set correctly (which would be unlikely[3]), we would have no guarantee that it would classify other input vectors the way we would want it to. A network is said to *generalize* when it appropriately classifies vectors not in the training set. Generalization ability is measured by the *accuracy* with which it makes these classifications. I show shortly how to estimate generalization accuracy.

Why would we expect a neural network to be able to generalize at all? The situation is somewhat analogous to curve fitting. When we try to fit a straight line or a low–degree polynomial curve, say, to data, we have confidence that we have captured some underlying relationship in the data if the fit to the data is very good and if there is a lot of data. The fitted curve can then be used to estimate (with reasonable reliability) values for new data points not used earlier in the fitting process. If a straight line does not fit the data well, then perhaps we might try a second–degree curve, and so on. A similar story can be told for neural networks. A neural network computes a complex, nonlinear function of its inputs. If the classification of these inputs is in fact some function that is close to some member of the set of functions implementable by the network, and if the fit by a trained network on the training data is very good—for a large number of inputs, then most likely the training process has captured an underlying functional relationship between inputs and classification. In that case, generalization to new inputs should be good.

It is important that the number of training input vectors be greater than the number of degrees of freedom (the number of variable weights) of the network.

---

3. Performance is always limited by noise. Some components of an input vector might be noisy, as would be the case, for example, if they were derived from noisy sensors. Or an input vector in the training set might occasionally be mislabeled. The first type of noise is called *attribute noise*, the second *classification noise*.

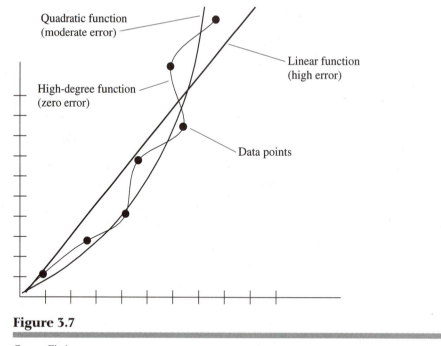

Quadratic function
(moderate error)

Linear function
(high error)

High-degree function
(zero error)

Data points

Figure 3.7

Curve Fitting

Again, an analogy with curve fitting is helpful. Even if a straight line does not fit the data, and if there are m data points, then certainly some $(m-1)$-degree polynomial can be found to fit the data perfectly. But since such a fit is possible regardless of the disposition of the m data points, it is unlikely that it captures anything special about the data. Instead, we have *overfitted* the data. If the data is noisy (perhaps a straight line could have fit the nonnoisy data), then our extra degrees of freedom are essentially just fitting the noise. As is well known in curve fitting, the number of data points should be significantly greater than the degree of the polynomial used for fitting. And, given sufficient data, the *Occam's Razor* principle dictates a choice of the lowest–degree polynomial that adequately fits the data.[4] We illustrate some of these ideas for curve fitting in Figure 3.7. The quadratic function provides a better fit than does the linear one without overfitting the data as does the high–degree function. Similar principles apply to neural networks.

Consider a two–layer, feedforward, neural network with n inputs, h hidden-layer units, and one output. Such a network has approximately (not counting the

---

4. William of Occam, 1285–1349, was an English philosopher who is claimed to have said: "*non sunt multiplicanda entia praeter necessitatem,*" which means "entities should not be multiplied unnecessarily."

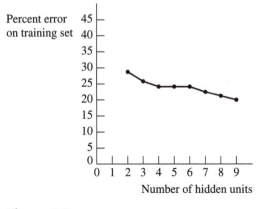

Figure 3.8

Error Versus Number of Hidden Units (Adapted from [Duda, Hart, & Stork 1998])

threshold weights) $nh + h = (n + 1)h$ variable weights. For fixed input dimension, the degrees of freedom are essentially controlled by the number of hidden units. We would expect the percentage classification error on the training set to decrease as the number of hidden units increases—until some minimal error percentage is reached. (Of course, if the training set is linearly separable, we can get zero error on the training set with just one hidden unit.) I show a typical example of training set error as a function of the number of hidden units in Figure 3.8. However, as discussed earlier, to avoid overfitting, we would not want so many hidden units that $(n + 1)h$ begins to approach the number of training input vectors.

Even if the training set error is low, generalization might not be good. There are various ways to estimate what the error rate would be for inputs not in the training set but drawn from the same underlying distribution as the training set. This error rate is called in statistics the *out-of-sample-set error rate*. Perhaps the simplest technique is to divide the input vectors available for training into two disjoint sets and use just one of these, which we will call the *training set*, for training. Then, after training is finished, we use the other set, which we will call the *validation set*, for estimating the out-of-sample error rate. If the number of vectors in both sets is large, the error rate on the validation set is a reasonable estimate of generalization accuracy. (Of course, it usually overestimates the true out-of-sample error rate. Why?) Experienced designers usually include about 2/3 of the available vectors in the training set and the remainder in the validation set.

Another popular method of estimating generalization accuracy is called *cross validation*. There, we divide the vectors available for training into k (usually 10) disjoint subsets, called *folds*. We select one of these folds as a validation set and use the other $k − 1$ (combined) as a training set. We do this k times, each time selecting a different fold as a validation set and its complement as the training set. We compute the error rate for each validation set (after training on its complement)

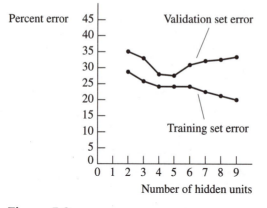

Figure 3.9

Estimate of Generalization Error Versus Number of Hidden Units (Adapted from [Duda, Hart, & Stork 1998])

and take the average of these error rates as the estimate of the out–of–sample error. For the special case of $k = m$, where m is the number of labeled vectors available, we have what is called *leave-one-out* cross validation. Experimental results suggest that 10–fold cross validation gives reasonable estimates (slightly pessimistic) of generalization accuracy. In Figure 3.9, I show how the estimate of out–of–sample error rate as measured by a validation set varies with the number of hidden units for a typical classification problem. Note how validation set error begins to increase due to overfitting as the number of hidden units increases.

3.5   *Additional Readings and Discussion*

Neural networks have been applied to several problems in pattern recognition, automatic control, and brain–function modeling. Typical examples are hand–written (ZIP code) character recognition [LeCun, et al. 1989], speech recognition [Waibel, et al. 1988], and learning to pronounce words presented as written text [Sejnowski & Rosenberg 1987]. However, it must be stressed that designing and training neural networks for these applications is still an art requiring experience and experiments. Some of the best research results and applications of neural networks are presented at the annual conferences on Neural Information Processing Systems (NIPS) whose published proceedings are entitled *Advances in Neural Information Processing Systems*.

As mentioned, the basic component of a neural network, the TLU, divides the space of input vectors by a hyperplane. If the convex hulls of two subsets of training inputs do not intersect, a hyperplane can perform the separation. A separating hyperplane can be obtained either by the training procedures mentioned in this chapter or by linear programming methods (which are known to be of polynomial complexity) [Karmarkar 1984].

I dealt here only with layered, feedforward networks. The analysis of the behavior of recurrent networks is more complex but is explained clearly in [Hertz, Krogh, & Palmer 1991], using analogies with the physics of dynamical systems. The backpropagation algorithm has been generalized (independently by [Pineda 1987, Almeida 1987, Rohwer & Forrest 1987]) to cover the case of recurrent networks (when such networks converge to stable states). (A readable presentation of the algorithm is given in [Hertz, Krogh, & Palmer 1991, pp. 172–176].)

Neural networks are but one of the many structures used in machine learning. Another is the decision tree—favored by some people because the functions that trees implement (such as DNF Boolean functions) are more easily understood than are those of neural networks. In AI, Ross Quinlan pioneered decision-tree learning methods with ID3 [Quinlan 1979] and C4.5 [Quinlan 1993]. (Similar techniques were developed independently by statisticians [Breiman, et al. 1984].)

I will present other machine learning techniques at various points in the book, but I mention here some of the sources for information about the topic. The major annual conference is the International Conference on Machine Learning (ICML), whose proceedings are published. Papers on computational learning theory appear in the Proceedings of the Workshops on Computational Learning Theory (COLT). The major journal is *Machine Learning*. Important textbooks are [Mitchell, T. 1997, Langley 1996, Weiss & Kulikowski 1991]. [Fu 1994, Haykin 1994, Hertz, Krogh, & Palmer 1991] are books about neural networks. [Shavlik & Dietterich 1990] is a collection of papers, and [Dietterich 1990] is an excellent survey of the field of machine learning.

Exercises

3.1 A TLU with weight vector $\mathbf{W}$ and threshold θ implements a hyperplane boundary. Derive an expression for the Euclidean distance of the hyperplane from the origin. From an arbitrary point $\mathbf{X}$. (Refer to Figure 3.1.)

3.2 The following training set is linearly separable:

input	output
1 0 0	1
0 1 1	0
1 1 0	1
1 1 1	0
0 0 1	0
1 0 1	1

Train (by hand) a linear threshold element on this training set. Your unit will have four inputs counting the one that implements the threshold. Assume that the initial values of all weights are zero. Train your unit with the *fixed increment error-correction procedure* until it converges with a solution. Show the set of weights at the end of each pass through a training cycle. Draw a sketch of a 3–D cube with the preceding inputs as vertices, and sketch in the separating plane corresponding to the final weight set.

3.3 You are to classify a set of n–dimensional input vectors with a TLU. But suppose, for technological reasons, you can use only nonnegative weights. How would you arrange to perform this classification?

3.4 Design (don't train) a feedforward network to implement the exclusive–or function of two inputs. Your network should have (1) a hidden layer consisting of linear threshold elements receiving inputs x_1 and x_2, and (2) a final output unit receiving inputs from the outputs of the hidden layer (but not inputs from x_1 and x_2).

3.5 Prove that it is possible to implement *any* Boolean function of n inputs with a network of threshold elements consisting of just one hidden layer.

3.6 Consider the nonlinear unit shown in the figure:

$$\mathbf{X} \cdot \mathbf{W} \longrightarrow \boxed{\int} \longrightarrow f(\mathbf{X})$$

$f(\mathbf{X}) = 0$ if $\mathbf{X} \cdot \mathbf{W} < -b$

$\qquad = 1$ if $\mathbf{X} \cdot \mathbf{W} > b$

$\qquad = (1/2b)(\mathbf{X} \cdot \mathbf{W} + b)$ otherwise

Instead of the usual threshold or sigmoid nonlinearity, we have a "ramp" function as defined in the figure. Derive the weight-adjusting rule for the weight vector, $\mathbf{W}$, resulting from a steepest-descent procedure applied incrementally at each input vector presentation to minimize the squared error, ε, between the actual output, f, and the desired output, d. Comment on your result.

3.7 Consider the *cascade* network shown in the following figure. There are three inputs to the network, namely, x_1, x_2, and x_3. Sigmoid unit number 1 receives all of these inputs (as well as a "threshold input," $x_4 \equiv 1$). Sigmoid unit number 2 has as its inputs the output of sigmoid 1 and x_1, x_2, x_3, and x_4. All inputs to the sigmoid units are weighted with adjustable weights. Derive an appropriately instantiated backpropagation–style incremental weight-adjustment procedure for this network based on minimizing the squared error between the network's output and the labels of a set of training input vectors. Assume a learning–rate factor of c for all weight vector adjustments. Your answer may use vector notation; that is, you don't have to instantiate down to the level of the components, x_i, of the input vectors.

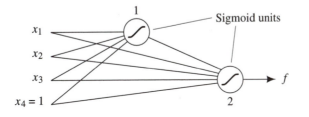

3.8 A *dot product unit (DPU)* computes the vector dot product of an input vector **X** with a weight vector **W**. It has no threshold; its output can be written simply as the matrix equation **WX**, where **W** is a row vector and **X** is a column vector. Consider the network of DPUs shown here. Prove that the entire network is equivalent to a single DPU. What is the weight vector for this DPU?

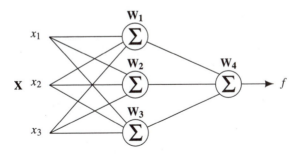

3.9

1. Develop an incremental, gradient descent weight change rule for a single sigmoid unit in which the error function is $\varepsilon = |d - f|$, where d is the desired output, $f = 1/(1 - e^{-s})$, $s = \mathbf{X} \cdot \mathbf{W}$, **X** is an $(n + 1)$–dimensional input vector, and **W** is the $(n + 1)$–dimensional weight vector being changed.

2. Explain how your rule differs from the one that uses a squared–error criterion.

3. What changes must be made to the backprop rule for a multilayer, feedforward network if this new error criterion is used?

4 Machine Evolution

4.1 Evolutionary Computation

The systems we studied in the last chapter adapt their behaviors so that they conform to a set of training instances. This type of learning mimics some aspects of learning in biological systems. Another way in which biological systems adapt is by *evolution*: generations of descendants are produced that perform better than do their ancestors. Can we use processes similar to evolution to produce useful programs? In this chapter, I examine a technique that attempts to do just that.

Biological evolution proceeds by the production of descendants *changed* from their parents and by the *selective survival* of some of these descendants to produce more descendants. These two aspects, change through reproduction and selective survival, are sufficient to produce generations of individuals that are better and better at doing whatever contributes to their ability to reproduce. The following geometric analogy portrays a simplified version of the process: imagine a mathematical "landscape" of peaks, valleys, and flat terrain populated by a set of individuals located at random places on the landscape. The height of an individual on this landscape is a measure of how well that individual performs its task relative to the performance of the other individuals. Those individuals at low elevations cease to exist, with a probability that increases with decreasing height. Those individuals at high elevations "reproduce" with a probability that increases with increasing height. Reproduction involves the production of new individuals whose location on the landscape is related to, but different from, that of the parent(s). The most interesting and efficacious kind of reproduction involves the production of new individuals jointly by two parents. The location(s) of the offspring on the landscape is a function of the locations of the parents. In some instantiations of the evolutionary process, the location of an offspring is somewhere "between" (in some sense) the locations of the parents.

We can regard this process as one of searching for high peaks in the landscape. Newly generated individuals sample new terrain, and those at the low elevations die off. After a while, some individuals will be located on peaks. The efficiency of the exploration process depends on the way in which an individual differs from its parent and on the nature of the landscape. Offspring might have elevations lower than their parents, but some might occasionally be higher.

Evolutionary search processes have been used in computer science for two major purposes. The most straightforward application is in function optimization. There, we attempt to find the maximum (say) of a function, $f(x_1, \ldots, x_n)$. The arguments $(x_1, \ldots, x_n)$ specify the location of individuals, and the value f is the height. John Holland [Holland 1975] proposed a class of *genetic algorithms (GAs)* for solving problems of this sort. GAs are well described in various textbooks and articles. (See, for example, [Goldberg 1989, Mitchell, M. 1996, Michalewicz 1992].)

The other application is to evolve programs to solve specific problems—for example, programs to control reactive agents. This is the application that concerns us here. Elaborations on GAs called *classifier systems* [Holland 1986], [Holland 1975, pp. 171ff, 2nd ed.] have been used successfully for this purpose. Another technique, called *genetic programming (GP)* [Koza 1992, Koza 1994], evolves programs in a somewhat more direct manner than do GAs. In the next section, I will illustrate the GP process with an example.

4.2   *Genetic Programming*

4.2.1   **Program Representation in GP**

In GP, we evolve *functional programs* such as LISP functions. Such programs can be expressed as rooted trees with labeled nodes. Internal nodes are functions, predicates, or actions that take one or more arguments. Leaf nodes are program constants, actions, or functions that take no arguments. I show an example of how a program for computing $3 + (5 \times 4)/7$ is expressed as a tree in Figure 4.1. In this case, the leaf nodes are the constants 3, 4, 5, and 7, and the internal nodes are the functions $+$, $\times$, and $/$.

Here, I show how GP can be used to evolve a wall–following robot whose task is the same as that considered in Chapter 2. Suppose the world for this robot is the two–dimensional grid world shown in Figure 4.2. We want to evolve a program that takes as inputs the robot's current sensory data and computes a single action. The robot is controlled by repeated execution of this program, and we want repeated execution to move the robot from an arbitrary initial position to a cell adjacent to the wall and then to follow the wall around forever.

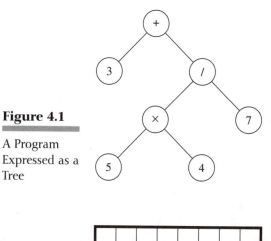

Figure 4.1

A Program
Expressed as a
Tree

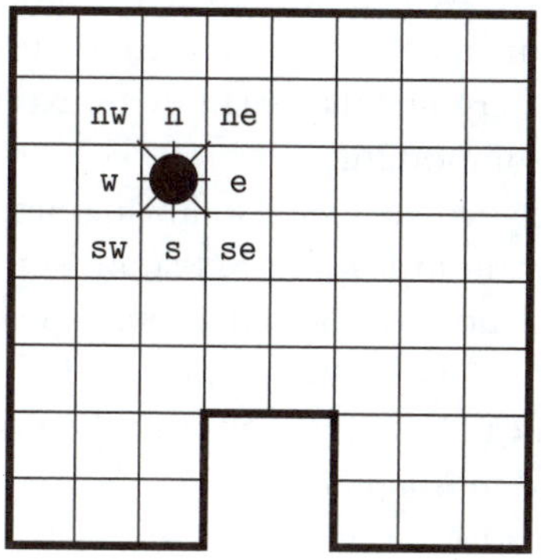

Figure 4.2

A Robot in a
Grid World

The primitive functions to be used in the program include four Boolean functions, `AND`, `OR`, `NOT`, and `IF`; and four actions, north, east, south, and west. The Boolean functions have their usual definitions:

1. `AND(x,y)` = 0 if x = 0; else y
2. `OR(x,y)` = 1 if x = 1; else y
3. `NOT(x)` = 0 if x = 1; else 1
4. `IF(x,y,z)` = y if x = 1; else z

The actions are defined as before:

1. north moves the robot one cell up in the cellular grid
2. east moves the robot one cell to the right
3. south moves the robot one cell down
4. west moves the robot one cell to the left

The action functions themselves have effects but no values; the evaluation of any of them terminates the program so that there is no need to pass a value up the tree. All of the action functions have their indicated effects unless the robot attempts to move into the wall; in that case, the action has no effect except to terminate the program. Of course, repeating the execution of a program that terminates with no effect will also have no effect.

We use the same sensory inputs as before. Here, rather than using the $s_1, \ldots, s_8$ notation, I use the more mnemonic n, ne, e, se, s, sw, w, and nw. These inputs have value 0 whenever the corresponding cell is free for the robot to occupy; otherwise, they have value 1. Figure 4.2 shows the locations of the cells being sensed relative to the robot.

For GP, we must ensure that all expressions and subexpressions used in a program have values for all possible arguments (unless execution of an expression terminates the program). For example, if we were to use the function *Divides*(x, y) to denote the value of x divided by y, we will need to give it some value (perhaps 0) when y is 0. In this way, we ensure that any tree constructed so that each function has its proper number of arguments describes an executable program. We will see later why this point is important.

Before proceeding to use GP to evolve a wall–following program, I show an example of a wall–following program in Figure 4.3; I show both the tree representation and the equivalent list–structure representation. Repeated execution of the program will cause the robot to go north to the wall and follow it around in a clockwise direction. This program can be compared with the production system for boundary following developed in Chapter 2.

4.2.2   The GP Process

In genetic programming, we start with a population of random programs, using functions, constants, and sensory inputs that we think may be the ones that will be needed by programs if they are to be effective in the domain of interest. These initial programs are said to constitute *generation 0*. The size of the population of programs in generation 0 is one of the parameters of a GP run. In my illustration of how GP works, we are going to start with 5000 random programs and attempt to evolve a wall–following robot. We produce these initial random programs from the primitive functions AND, OR, NOT, and IF, the actions north, east, south, and west, the sensory functions n, ne, e, se, s, sw, w, nw, and the constants 0 and 1. Programs in each generation are evaluated, and a new generation is produced until a program is produced that performs acceptably well.

A program is evaluated by running it to see how well it does on the task we set for it. In our case, we run a program 60 times and count the number of cells next to the wall that are visited during these 60 steps. (There are 32 cells next to the wall, so a program that never gets to the wall would have a count of 0, and a perfect program would have a count of 32.) Then we do ten of these runs with the robot starting in ten randomly chosen starting positions. The total count of

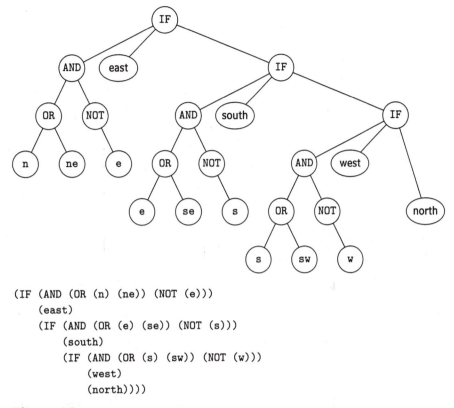

```
(IF (AND (OR (n) (ne)) (NOT (e)))
    (east)
    (IF (AND (OR (e) (se)) (NOT (s)))
        (south)
        (IF (AND (OR (s) (sw)) (NOT (w)))
            (west)
            (north))))
```

Figure 4.3

A Wall–Following Program

next–to-the–wall cells visited during these ten runs is then taken as the *fitness* of the program. The highest possible fitness value will be 320—achievable only by a robot that on each of its ten fitness runs visits all of the next–to-the–wall cells within 60 steps.

The $(i + 1)$-th generation is constructed from the i-th one in the following manner:

1. Five hundred programs (10%) from generation i are copied directly into generation $i + 1$. Individuals are chosen for copying by the following *tournament selection* process: seven programs are randomly selected (with replacement) from the population of 5000. Then the most fit of these seven programs is chosen. (Tournament selection has been found to be an efficient method for selecting fit individuals. The number 7 and the percentage of programs to be copied are additional parameters of the GP process.)

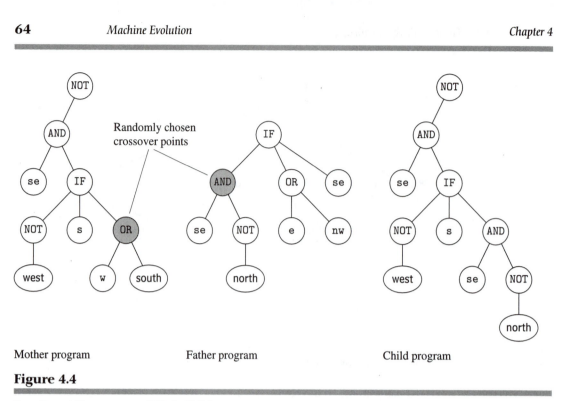

Mother program   Father program   Child program

Figure 4.4

Two Parent Programs and Their Child

2. Forty–five hundred new *child* programs (90%) are put into generation $i + 1$. Each child program is produced from a *mother* and a *father* program by a *crossover* operation as follows: a mother and a father are each chosen from generation i by tournament selection (as before). Then a randomly chosen subtree from the father replaces a randomly selected subtree from the mother. The result is the child program. (Executability of the child is guaranteed by the requirement that all functions used in the programs be executable for all possible values of their arguments.) I show an illustration of the crossover operation in Figure 4.4. The shaded node in each parent has been selected as a crossover point. The child program may or may not have higher fitness than its parents. The motivation for the possible effectiveness of the crossover operation is that a main program and a subexpression of fit parents are incorporated into their child.

3. Sometimes a *mutation operator* is also used in constructing individuals for the next generation. When used, it is used sparingly (perhaps at a 1% rate). The mutation operator selects a single parent from generation i by tournament selection (as before). A randomly chosen subtree is deleted from this parent and replaced by a newly grown random subtree (created

in the same manner as individuals are created for generation 0). My illustrative example does not use mutation.

Note that several rather arbitrary parameters must be set in constructing the next generation. These include the number of individuals to be copied, the number to be produced by crossover, the number used in tournament selection, and the mutation percentage. The parameters used here in my illustrative experiment are based on the recommendations of experts in the technique of genetic programming.

4.2.3   Evolving a Wall–Following Robot

Starting with our population of 5000 random programs, and using the techniques just described, we start the GP process for evolving a wall-following robot.[1] Many of the random, generation 0 programs do nothing at all: for example, (AND (sw)(ne)) (with fitness = 0) evaluates its first argument, terminates if the result is 0, and otherwise evaluates its second argument and terminates. Some programs move in one direction only regardless of their inputs. For example, when program (OR (e)(west)) evaluates west, it moves west and terminates. That program had a fitness of 5 (some of its random runs happened to traverse cells next to the wall). The 5000 programs in generation 0 can be regarded as an uninformed search of the space of computer programs using ingredients chosen for this particular problem class.

The list–structure form of the most fit program of generation 0 (fitness = 92) and two of its fitness runs are shown in Figure 4.5. As is usual with GP, the program is rather difficult to read and has many redundant operations. (Some of these might be removed by a postprocessing translator.) Starting in any cell, this program moves east until it reaches a cell next to the wall; then it moves north until it can move east again or it moves west and gets trapped in the upper–left cell.

The best program of generation 2 has a fitness of 117. The program and its performance on two typical fitness cases are shown in Figure 4.6. The program is smaller than the best one of generation 0, but it does get stuck in the lower–right corner.

By generation 6, performance has improved to a best fitness of 163. The best program follows the wall perfectly but still gets stuck in the bottom–right corner, as shown in Figure 4.7.

Finally, by generation 10, the process has evolved a program that follows the wall perfectly. This program and two of the paths it takes from different starting

---

1. I thank David Andre for programming this illustrative example.

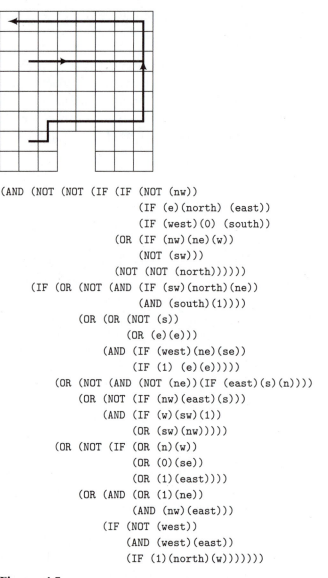

```
(AND (NOT (NOT (IF (IF (NOT (nw))
                        (IF (e)(north) (east))
                        (IF (west)(0) (south)))
                   (OR (IF (nw)(ne)(w))
                       (NOT (sw)))
                   (NOT (NOT (north)))))))
     (IF (OR (NOT (AND (IF (sw)(north)(ne))
                       (AND (south)(1))))
             (OR (OR (NOT (s))
                     (OR (e)(e)))
                 (AND (IF (west)(ne)(se))
                      (IF (1) (e)(e)))))
         (OR (NOT (AND (NOT (ne))(IF (east)(s)(n))))
             (OR (NOT (IF (nw)(east)(s)))
                 (AND (IF (w)(sw)(1))
                      (OR (sw)(nw)))))
         (OR (NOT (IF (OR (n)(w))
                      (OR (0)(se))
                      (OR (1)(east))))
             (OR (AND (OR (1)(ne))
                      (AND (nw)(east)))
                 (IF (NOT (west))
                     (AND (west)(east))
                     (IF (1)(north)(w)))))))
```

Figure 4.5

The Most Fit Individual in Generation 0

positions are shown in Figure 4.8. The program follows the wall around clockwise and moves south to the wall if it doesn't start next to it.

I show in Figure 4.9 a curve of the fitness of the most fit individual in each generation. Note the progressive (but often small) improvement from generation to generation.

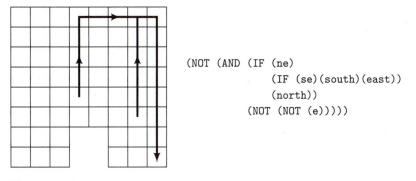

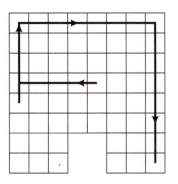

```
(NOT (AND (IF (ne)
              (IF (se)(south)(east))
              (north))
         (NOT (NOT (e)))))
```

Figure 4.6

The Most Fit Individual in Generation 2

```
(IF (AND (NOT (e))
         (IF (e)(s)(nw)))
    (OR (IF (1)(e)(south))
        (IF (north)(east)(nw)))
    (IF (OR (AND (0)(north))
            (AND (e)(IF (e)
                        (IF (se)(south)(east))
                        (north))))
        (AND (e)
             (NOT (IF (s)(sw)(e))))
        (OR (OR (AND (nw)(east))
                (west))
            (nw))))
```

Figure 4.7

The Most Fit Individual in Generation 6

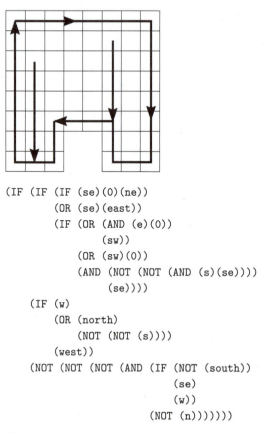

```
(IF (IF (IF (se)(0)(ne))
        (OR (se)(east))
        (IF (OR (AND (e)(0))
                (sw))
            (OR (sw)(0))
            (AND (NOT (NOT (AND (s)(se))))
                (se))))
    (IF (w)
        (OR (north)
            (NOT (NOT (s))))
        (west))
    (NOT (NOT (NOT (AND (IF (NOT (south))
                            (se)
                            (w))
                        (NOT (n)))))))
```

Figure 4.8

The Most Fit Individual in Generation 10

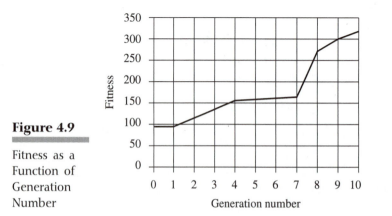

Figure 4.9

Fitness as a
Function of
Generation
Number

4.3 *Additional Readings and Discussion*

Genetic algorithms and genetic programming have been applied in a variety of settings. GP methods have successfully evolved reactive agents similar to those studied by other AI researchers. These include box pushing, ant trail following, truck trailer backing, and inverted pendulum balancing. These and other demonstrations of the versatility of the technique are described in [Koza 1992]. Added power is gained when the method is extended to allow the evolution of subroutines that can subsequently be used by the coevolving main program just as if they were primitive functions. This feature and its applications are presented in [Koza 1994]. Perhaps the most complex and successful applications of GP are in synthesizing electronic filters, amplifiers, and other circuits [Koza, et al. 1996]. Some preliminary work has also been done on GP methods for evolving programs that create and use memory structures, that search, and that employ recursion [Andre 1995, Teller 1994, Brave 1996].

Genetic programming and genetic algorithms research papers appear in Proceedings of the Conferences on Genetic Programming, the *IEEE Transactions on Evolutionary Computation*, and the Proceedings of the International Conferences on Genetic Algorithms.

Exercises

4.1 Specify fitness functions for use in evolving agents that

1. Control an elevator
2. Control stop lights on a city main street

4.2 Determine what the words *genotype* and *phenotype* mean in (biological) evolutionary theory. How might these words be used to describe GP?

4.3 How might the GP crossover process be changed to allow GP to relax the requirement that the execution of every subtree return a value?

4.4 The crossover operation used in GP selects a random subtree in both parents. Comment on what you think the effects would be of biasing the random selection according to

1. Preferring those subtrees that were highly active during the fitness trials
2. Preferring larger subtrees to smaller ones, and vice versa

4.5 How could an evolutionary process, like GP, be used to evolve

1. Neural networks?
2. Production systems?

Describe in some detail. In particular, how would the crossover operation be implemented? Comment on whether or not you allow Lamarckian evolution in the evolution of neural networks.

4.6 Why do you think mutation might or might not be helpful in evolutionary processes that use crossover?

5 State Machines

5.1 *Representing the Environment by Feature Vectors*

The feature vector used by an S–R agent can be thought of as representing the state of the environment so far as that agent is concerned. From this feature vector, the S–R agent computes an action appropriate for that environmental state. As I have mentioned, sensory limitations of the agent preclude completely accurate representation of environmental state by feature vectors—especially feature vectors that are computed from *immediate* sensory stimuli. The accuracy can be improved, however, by taking into account previous sensory history. Important aspects of the environment that cannot be sensed at the moment might have been sensed before. Suppose the agent does have an initial representation of the environment at some time $t = 0$. (This initial representation might be preloaded by the designer, for example.) We then assume that the representation of environmental state at any subsequent time step, $t + 1$, is a function of the sensory input at $t + 1$, the representation of environmental state at the previous time step, t, and the action taken at time t. We call machines that track their environment in this way *state machines*. Besides immediate sensory inputs, state machines must have *memory* in which to store a model of the environment.

This model can take many forms. Perhaps the simplest representation is a vector of features—just as is used by S–R machines. But now, the feature vector, $\mathbf{X}_{t+1}$, depends on a remembered feature vector, $\mathbf{X}_t$. Figure 5.1 illustrates this type of state machine.

Because agent environments might be arbitrarily complex, it is always the case that the agent can only imperfectly represent its environment by a feature vector. But it is also the case that agents designed for specific tasks can afford to conflate many environmental states. The agent designer must arrange for a

71

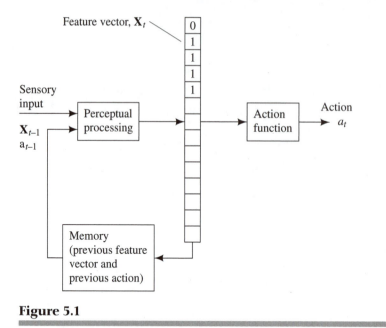

Figure 5.1

A State Machine

feature vector that is an *adequate* representation of the state of the environment—at least insofar as the agent's tasks are concerned.

As an example of a state machine, let's consider our boundary-following robot from Chapter 2. Recall that it modeled its environment by the values of features computed from eight sensory inputs that informed the agent whether or not the eight surrounding cells were free. Let's consider a somewhat sensory-impaired version of the boundary-following robot. Assume that this robot can sense only the cells immediately to its north, east, south, and west. That is, it cannot sense the four diagonally adjacent cells. Its sensory inputs are (s_2, s_4, s_6, s_8), and these inputs have value 1 only if the cells to the north, east, south, and west, respectively, are *not* free. Otherwise, these inputs have value 0. Even with this impairment, this robot can still perform boundary-following behavior if it computes the needed feature vector from its immediate sensory inputs, the previous feature vector, and the just-performed action. (Again, I assume there are no tight spaces in the environment.)

To follow our practice of making action dependent on a feature vector, we use features $w_i = s_i$, for $i = 2, 4, 6, 8$. In place of the four sensory inputs that are absent, we substitute four features, namely, w_1, w_3, w_5, and w_7. w_1 has value 1 if and only if at the previous time step w_2 had value 1 and the robot moved east. Similarly, w_3 has value 1 if and only if at the previous time step w_4 had value 1 and the robot moved south, and so on. (Otherwise, the w_i have value 0.)

Using these features, the following production system gives wall-following behavior (in worlds without tight spaces):

$w_2\overline{w_4} \longrightarrow$ east

$w_4\overline{w_6} \longrightarrow$ south

$w_6\overline{w_8} \longrightarrow$ west

$w_8\overline{w_2} \longrightarrow$ north

$w_1 \longrightarrow$ north

$w_3 \longrightarrow$ east

$w_5 \longrightarrow$ south

$w_7 \longrightarrow$ west

$1 \longrightarrow$ north

Note that the boundary-following robot of Chapter 2 (without the sensory impairment) managed without memory of previous inputs, features, or actions. If all of the important aspects of the environment can be sensed at the time the agent needs to know them, there is no reason to retain a model of the environment in memory. But sensory abilities are always limited in some way, and thus agents equipped with stored models of the environment will usually be able to perform tasks that memoryless agents cannot.

5.2 Elman Networks

An agent can use a special type of recurrent neural network (called an *Elman network* [Elman 1990]) to learn how to compute a feature vector and an action from a previous feature vector and sensory inputs. I illustrate how this might be done for the wall-following robot that senses only those four cells to the north, east, south, and west. The network learns to store those properties of previously sensed data that are appropriate to the task at hand. I show such an Elman network in Figure 5.2. The network has eight hidden units, one for each feature needed by the robot just considered.[1] The input to the network consists of the four immediate sensory inputs (s_2, s_4, s_6, s_8) plus the values of the eight hidden units one time step earlier. These extra inputs, called *context units*, allow the network to base its actions on learned properties of data previously sensed—that is, on the context in which the robot currently finds itself. As previously mentioned, there are various ways to arrange for multiple network outputs. In this case, we need four distinguishable outputs, corresponding to the actions north, east, south, and west. The network of Figure 5.2 has four output units, one for each action. Each output unit computes

---

1. Of course, in a typical learning situation, we won't know how many hidden units (or how many layers) are needed.

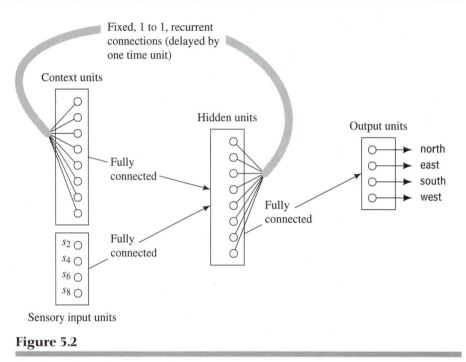

Figure 5.2

An Elman Network

its action from the same set of hidden units (features). We train so that only one output unit has a desired output of 1; the others have desired outputs of 0. Training is accomplished by presenting a sequence of sensory inputs, labeled by the appropriate corresponding actions, that would occur in a typical run of an expert wall–following teacher. In actual operation (after training), we select that action corresponding to the output unit with the largest output. Although an Elman network is a special case of the recurrent neural networks mentioned in Chapter 3, training can be accomplished by ordinary backpropagation because the backward–directed weights (from hidden units to context units) are fixed, and the context units are treated as just another set of inputs.

5.3 *Iconic Representations*

Feature vectors are just one way of representing the environment. Other data structures may also be used. For example, our boundary–following robot might use an array to store a map of free and nonfree cells as it senses them. These two possibilities, representing the world either by features or by data structures, foreshadow a profound division in artificial intelligence. On one side, we have what I call a *feature-based* representation of the world—a vector of features or

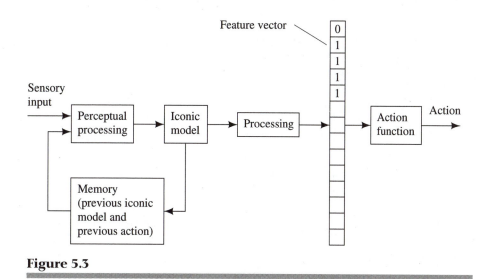

Figure 5.3

An Agent That Computes Features from an Iconic Representation

attributes. On the other side, we have what I call an *iconic* representation—data structures such as maps, which can usually be thought of as simulations of important aspects of the environment. (Iconic representations are sometimes also called *analogical representations*.) A crisp and precise distinction between iconic and feature–based representations is difficult to make, but it is a distinction that we will encounter throughout this book.

When an agent uses an iconic representation, it must still compute actions appropriate to its task and to the present (modeled) state of the environment. Reactive agents react to the data structure in much the same way that agents without memory react to sensory stimuli: they compute features of the data structure. One way to organize such an agent is illustrated in Figure 5.3. The sensory information is first used to update the iconic model as appropriate. Then, operations similar to perceptual processing are used to extract features needed by the action computation subsystem. The actions include those that change the iconic model as well as those that affect the actual environment. The features derived from the iconic model must represent the environment in a manner that is adequate for the kinds of actions the robot must take.

When the iconic representation of a grid–space robot is a matrix of free and nonfree cells, it is as if the robot had sensors that could sense whether or not any of the cells in the grid were free. For example, consider a robot whose representation of its local environment is as shown in Figure 5.4. Free cells are represented by 0's in the corresponding array element; nonfree cells

1	1	1	1	1	1	1	1	?
1	0	0	0	0	0	0	0	?
1	0	0	0	0	0	0	0	?
1	0	0	0	0	0	0	0	?
1	0	0	0	0	0	0	0	?
1	0	0	R	0	0	0	0	?
1	0	0	0	0	0	0	0	?
1	0	0	0	0	0	0	0	?
1	0	0	0	0	0	0	0	?
1	?	?	?	?	?	?	?	
?	?	?	?	?	?	?	?	?

Figure 5.4

A Maplike Iconic Representation

are represented by 1's; unknown cells are represented by ?'s; and the robot's
own location relative to the surrounding cells is represented by the letter *R*. The
environmental situation represented by the array in Figure 5.4 should evoke the
action west in a wall–following robot designed to go to the closest wall and then
begin wall following. Of course, after taking the action, the robot must update
its model to change its own position and to take into account new sensory data.

Another type of action computation mechanism uses a model in the form of
an *artificial potential field*. This technique is used extensively in controlling robot
motion [Latombe 1991, Ch. 7]. The robot's environment is represented as a two-
dimensional potential field.[2] The potential field is the sum of an "attractive"
and a "repulsive" component. An attractive field is associated with the goal
location—the place that the robot is ordered to go. A typical attractive function
is $p_a(\mathbf{X}) = k_1 d(\mathbf{X})^2$, where $d(\mathbf{X})$ is the Euclidean distance from a point, $\mathbf{X}$, to the
goal. Such a function has minimum value 0 at the goal location. Obstacles in the
environment evoke a repulsive field. A typical repulsive function is $p_r(\mathbf{X}) = \frac{k_2}{d_o(\mathbf{X})^2}$,
where $d_o(\mathbf{X})$ is the Euclidean distance from $\mathbf{X}$ to the closest obstacle point.

The total potential is the sum, $p = p_a + p_r$. Motion of the robot is then directed
along the gradient of the potential field—sliding downhill, so to speak. Either the
potential field can be precomputed and stored in memory as an aspect of the
world model or it can be computed incrementally at the robot's location just
before the robot needs to decide on a move. An example of a potential field is
shown in Figure 5.5. The robot is at the position marked with an *R*, and the goal
location is marked with a *G* in Figure 5.5a. The attractive, repulsive, and total

2. Higher–dimensional fields are used when there are many degrees of freedom to be
controlled.

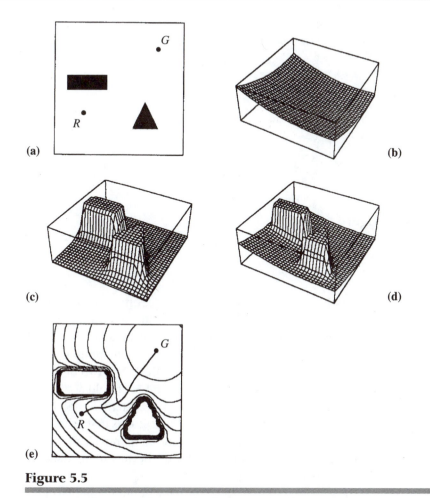

Figure 5.5

Equipotential Curves of an Artificial Potential Field (Adapted from [Latombe 1991])

potentials are shown in Figures 5.5b, c, and d, respectively. Equipotential curves and the path to be followed by the robot are shown in Figure 5.5e. The method suffers from the fact that there can be potential minima that would trap the robot. Several methods have been explored to avoid this problem [Latombe 1991].

5.4   *Blackboard Systems*

Data structures used to model the world do not necessarily have to be iconic, although they often are. An important style of AI machine is based on a *blackboard* architecture [Hayes–Roth 1985, Nii 1986a, Nii 1986b], which uses a data structure called a *blackboard*. The blackboard is read and changed by programs called *knowledge sources* (*KSs*). Blackboard systems are elaborations of the production

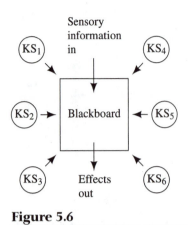

Figure 5.6

A Blackboard System

systems I have already described. Each KS has a condition part and an action part. The condition part computes the value of a feature; it can be any condition about the blackboard data structure that evaluates to 1 or 0 (or *True* or *False*, if that notation is preferred). The action part can be any program that changes the data structure or takes external action (or both). When two or more KSs evaluate to 1, a *conflict resolution* program decides which KSs should act. In addition to changing the blackboard, KS actions can also have external effects. And the blackboard might also be changed by perceptual subsystems that process sensory data. Often, the blackboard data structure is organized hierarchically, with subordinate data structures occupying various levels of the hierarchy. I show a schematic of a blackboard system in Figure 5.6.

The KSs are supposed to be "experts" about the part(s) of the blackboard that they watch. When they detect some particular aspect of their part(s) of the blackboard, they propose changes to the blackboard, which, if selected, may evoke other KSs, and so on. Blackboard systems are designed so that as computation proceeds in this manner, the blackboard ultimately becomes a data structure that contains the solution to some particular problem and/or the associated external effects change the world in some desired way. The blackboard architecture has been used in several applications ranging from speech understanding [Erman, et al. 1980], to signal interpretation [Nii 1986b], and medical patient–care monitoring [Hayes–Roth, et al. 1992].

For an example, I return to a robot in grid world—this time our robot can sense all eight cells immediately surrounding it. However, this robot's sensors (like all real sensors) sometimes give erroneous information. The robot also keeps a partial map of its world—similar to the map shown in Figure 5.4. Because of previous sensor errors, the map can be incomplete and incorrect. The data structure representing the map and a data structure containing sensory data

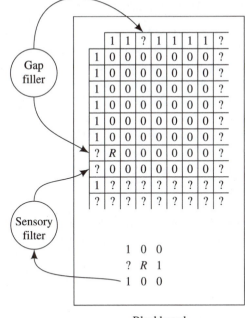

Blackboard

Figure 5.7

A Robot's Blackboard and KSs

compose the blackboard. I show the blackboard as it appears at one instant of the robot's experience in Figure 5.7.

To help the robot correct blackboard errors, it has two KSs, namely, a *gap filler* and a *sensory filter*. The gap filler looks for tight spaces in the map, and (knowing that there can be no tight spaces) either fills them in with 1's or expands them with additional adjacent 0's. (I leave it to you to speculate about the basis for filling or expanding.) For example, the gap filler decides to fill the tight space at the top of the map in Figure 5.7.

The sensory filter looks at both the sensory data and the map and attempts to reconcile any discrepancies. In Figure 5.7, the sensory filter notes that s_7 is a strong "cell–occupied" signal but that the corresponding cell in the map was questionable. It decides to reconcile the difference by replacing that ? in the map with a 1. Similarly, it decides that, based on the map data, the $s_4 = 1$ signal is in error and therefore does not alter the map based on this signal. After these actions, the gap filler can replace the lone ? in the left-hand column of the map by a 1.

Depending on the task set for the robot, some other KS (reacting to the adjusted map) can propose a robot action.

5.5 *Additional Readings and Discussion*

State machines are even more ubiquitous than S–R agents. And much of what I said at the end of Chapter 2 about the relationship between S–R agents and ethological models of animal behavior applies also to state machines. Many animals maintain at least partial information about features of their external and internal worlds that cannot be immediately sensed. (See Exercise 5.4.) Production systems that respond to memory as well as to perception have been used to model certain psychological phenomena [Newell 1973].

Elman networks are one example of learning finite–state automata. This problem has also been studied by [Rivest & Schapire 1993].

Many researchers [Kuipers, et al. 1993, Kuipers & Byun 1991] have studied the problem of learning spatial maps, which are examples of iconic representations. When there is uncertainty about the current state and about the effects of actions, map learning is more difficult. This case has been studied by [Dean, Basye, & Kaelbling 1993].

[Genesereth & Nilsson 1987] term agents whose behavior depends on past history *hysteretic agents*.

Exercises

5.1 A discrete elevator can sense the following information about its world:

1. What floor the elevator is stopped at.

2. What floors passengers in the elevator want to go to.

3. What floors passengers outside of the elevator want rides from and whether they want to go up or down.

4. The status of the elevator door (open or closed).

The elevator is capable of performing the following actions:

1. Go up exactly one floor (unless it is already at the top floor).

2. Go down exactly one floor (unless it is already at the bottom floor).

3. Open the elevator door.

4. Close the elevator door.

5. Wait Δ seconds (a fixed time sufficient for all in the elevator to get off and for all outside the elevator to get in).

Design a production system to control the elevator in an efficient manner. (It is not efficient, for example, to reverse the elevator direction from going up to going down either if there is someone still inside the elevator who wants to go to a higher floor or if there is someone outside the elevator who wants to get on from a higher floor.)

5.2 An "artificial ant" lives in a two–dimensional grid world and is able to follow a continuous "pheromone trail" (one cell wide) of marked cells. The ant occupies a single cell and faces either up, left, down, or right. It is capable of five actions, namely, move one cell ahead (m), turn to the left while remaining in the same cell (l), turn to the right while remaining in the same cell (r), set a state bit "on" (on), and set the state bit "off" (off). The ant can sense whether or not there is a pheromone trace in the cell immediately ahead of it (in the direction it is facing), and whether or not the state bit is on. (Assume that the state bit is off initially.) Specify a production system for controlling the ant such that it follows the trail. Assume that it starts in a cell where it can sense a pheromone trace. (Recall that a production system consists of an ordered set of condition–action rules; the action executed is the one that corresponds to the first satisfied condition. A rule might have more than one action on its right–hand side.) Make sure your ant doesn't turn around and retrace its steps backward!

5.3 The three–disc Tower–of–Hanoi puzzle has three pegs, A, B, and C, on which can be placed three discs (labeled D_3, D_2, and D_1) with holes in their centers to fit on the pegs. Disc D_3 is larger than disc D_2, which is larger than disc D_1. Ordinarily, the puzzle has the three pegs in a line, but let's suppose we position them on a circle. We start with the three discs on peg A and want to move them to one of the other pegs. (See the figure.) The rules are that you can move any disc to any peg except that only the top disc on a peg can be moved, and you cannot place a disc on top of a smaller disc. You might be familiar with a recursive algorithm for solving this problem.

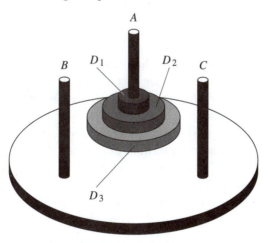

Note: For a simpler algo–rithm, see www.mkp.com /nils/clarified.

Interestingly, there is another, nonrecursive, algorithm, which can be stated as follows in English: we will *always* move the largest disc that can be moved, but we will *never* move it in a direction that undoes the move just previously made. Whenever possible, we move clockwise (CW) on odd–numbered moves and counterclockwise (CCW) on even–numbered moves. When adhering to this CW/CCW schedule is not possible (because there is no such move of the biggest disc that won't reverse a move just made), we move in the nonpreferred direction instead and then resume the original schedule.

We are going to specify a production system to implement this algorithm. Assume the following six disc–moving actions: move(num, dir), where num can be D_3, D_2, or D_1, and dir can be CW (clockwise) or CCW (counterclockwise). We also assume sensors that can determine the truth or falsity of the following conditions: B_1, B_2, and B_3, where B_i means that disc D_i is the largest disc that can be moved. In addition, we will have the following "state" conditions that will be set and unset by the production system: CW (meaning that the last move was clockwise); and M_1, M_2, and M_3, where M_i means that the last disc moved was disc D_i. The state-changing actions are toggle, which toggles the state CW (that is, when toggle is executed, CW changes from 1 to 0 or from 0 to 1), and moved(D_3), moved(D_2), and moved(D_1), where moved(D_i) sets M_i to true and M_j to false for $j \neq i$.

Using these sensory and state conditions and these actions, specify a production system that implements this algorithm. Don't forget to specify the initial values of the state conditions! Assume that the production system is of the sort in which the production rules are ordered and the action to be executed is the action associated with the highest rule whose condition is satisfied. The action part of a production rule can contain both disc–moving and state–changing actions, which can be executed simultaneously.

5.4 The female solitary wasp, *Sphex*, lays her eggs in a cricket that she has paralyzed and brought to her burrow nest. The wasp grubs hatch and then feed on this cricket. According to [Wooldridge 1968, p. 70], the wasp exhibits the following interesting behavior:

> . . . the wasp's routine is to bring the paralyzed cricket to the burrow, leave it on the threshold, go inside to see that all is well, emerge, and then drag the cricket in. If the cricket is moved a few inches away while the wasp is inside making her preliminary inspection, the wasp, on emerging from the burrow, will bring the cricket back to the threshold, but not inside, and will then repeat the preparatory procedure of entering the burrow to see that everything is all right. If again the cricket is removed a few inches while the wasp is inside, once again she will move the cricket up to the threshold and reenter the burrow for a final check. . . . On one occasion this procedure was repeated forty times, always with the same result.

Invent features, actions, and a production system that this wasp might be using in behaving this way.

5.5 Invent an artificial potential function (with attractive and repulsive compo-nents) that can be used to guide a robot from any cell in the two–dimensional grid world shown here to the goal cell marked by a 0. (Assume that the robot's possible actions are moves to the north, east, south, and west.) Does the sum of the attractive and repulsive components have local minima? If so, where? Invent a particular overall potential function for this grid world that has no local minima and whose use guarantees shortest paths to the goal.

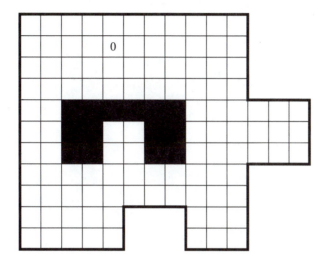

6 Robot Vision

6.1 Introduction

Most of the examples I have used so far to describe S–R and state machines used quite limited sensory inputs, which provided information only about adjacent cells in their grid worlds. There are many other sensory modalities that can reveal important information about an agent's world—acoustic, temperature, pressure, and so on. Sensory transducers are used in many different kinds of machines whose functions must be responsive to their environments.

In animals, the sense of vision is able to provide a large amount of distal information about the world with each glance. Endowing machines with the means to "see" is one of the concerns of a subject called *computer vision*. The field is very broad and consists of both general techniques and ones specialized for its many applications, which include alphanumeric character recognition, photograph interpretation, face recognition, fingerprint identification, and robot control.

Although vision is apparently effortless for humans, it has proved to be a very difficult problem for machines. Major sources of difficulty include variable and uncontrolled illumination, shadows, complex and hard–to–describe objects such as those that occur in outdoor scenes and nonrigid objects, and objects occluding other objects. Some of these difficulties are lessened in man–made environments, such as the interior of buildings, and computer vision has generally been more successful in those environments. I have space here only for a representative sampling of some of the major ideas, focussing on robot vision.

The first step in computer vision is to create an image of a scene on an array of photosensitive devices, such as the photocells of a TV camera. (For stereo vision, two or more images are formed. I discuss stereo vision later in the chapter.) The image is formed by a camera through a lens that produces a *perspective projection* of

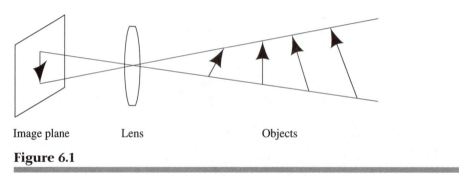

Image plane   Lens   Objects

Figure 6.1

The Many–to–One Nature of the Imaging Process

the scene within the camera's field of view. The photocells convert the image into a two–dimensional, time–varying matrix of image intensity values, $I(x, y, t)$, where x and y range over the photocell locations in the array, and t ranges over time. (In color vision, three such matrices are formed—one for each of three primary colors. I deal only with the monochromatic case here. I also simplify by eliminating the time variable—presuming a static scene.) A vision–guided reactive agent must then process this matrix to create either an iconic model of the scene surrounding it or a set of features from which the agent can directly compute an action.

As illustrated in Figure 6.1, perspective projection is a many–to–one transformation. Several different scenes can produce identical images. To complicate matters, the image can also be noisy due to low ambient light levels and other factors. Thus, we cannot directly "invert" the image to reconstruct the scene. Instead information useful to the agent is extracted from the image(s) by using specific knowledge about the likely objects in the scene and general knowledge about the properties of surfaces in the scene and about how ambient illumination is reflected from these surfaces back toward the camera.

The kinds of information to be extracted depend on the purposes and tasks of the agent. To navigate safely through a cluttered environment, an agent needs to know about the locations of objects, boundaries, and openings and about the surface properties of its path. To manipulate objects, it needs to know about their locations, sizes, shapes, compositions, and textures. For other purposes, it may need to know about their color and to be able to recognize them as belonging to certain classes. Based on how all of this information has changed over an observed time interval, an agent might need to be able to predict probable future changes. Extracting such information from one or more images is a tall order, and, as previously mentioned, I can only give a general overview of some of the techniques.

6.2   *Steering an Automobile*

In certain applications involving S-R agents, neural networks can be used to convert the image intensity matrix directly into actions. A prominent example is

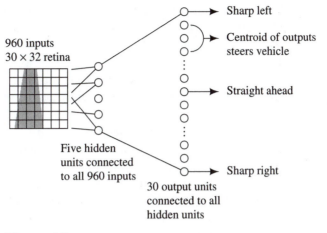

Figure 6.2

The ALVINN Network

the ALVINN[1] system for steering an automobile [Pomerleau 1991, Pomerleau 1993]. I discuss this system before dealing with more general processes for robot vision. The input to the network is derived from a low–resolution (30 × 32) television image. The TV camera is mounted on the automobile and looks at the road straight ahead. This image is sampled and produces a stream of 960–dimensional input vectors to the neural network. The network is shown in Figure 6.2.

The network has five hidden units in its first layer and 30 output units in the second layer; all are sigmoid units. The output units are arranged in a linear order and control the automobile's steering angle. If a unit near the top of the array of output units has a higher output than most of the other units, the car is steered to the left; if a unit near the bottom of the array has a high output, the car is steered to the right. The "centroid" of the responses of all of the output units is computed, and the car's steering angle is set at a corresponding value between hard left and hard right.

The system is trained by a modified "on-the-fly" training regime. A human driver drives the car, and his actual steering angles are taken as the correct labels for the corresponding inputs. The network is trained incrementally by backprop to produce the driver–specified steering angles in response to each visual pattern as it occurs in real time while driving. Training takes about five minutes of driving time.

This simple procedure has been augmented to avoid two potential problems. First, since the driver is usually driving well, the network would never get

---

1. Autonomous Land Vehicle In a Neural Network.

any experience with far–from–center vehicle positions and/or incorrect vehicle orientations. Also, on long, straight stretches of road, the network would be trained for a long time only to produce straight-ahead steering angles; this training would overwhelm earlier training involving following a curved road. We wouldn't want to try to avoid these problems by instructing the driver to drive erratically occasionally, because the system would learn to mimic this erratic behavior.

Instead, each original image is shifted and rotated in software to create 14 additional images in which the vehicle appears to be situated differently relative to the road. Using a model that tells the system what steering angle ought to be used for each of these shifted images, given the driver–specified steering angle for the original image, the system constructs an additional 14 labeled training vectors to add to each of those encountered during ordinary driver training.

After training, ALVINN has successfully steered various testbed vehicles on unlined paved paths, jeep trails, lined city streets, and interstate highways. On highways, ALVINN has driven for 120 consecutive kilometers at speeds up to 100 km/hr.

6.3   *Two Stages of Robot Vision*

Although ALVINN's performance is impressive, more sophisticated processing of higher–resolution images is required for many robot tasks. Since many robot tasks involve the need to know about objects in the scene, I focus my discussion on techniques relevant to finding out about objects. First, what is an object? In man–made environments such as the interiors of buildings, objects can be doorways, furniture, other agents, humans, walls, floors, and so on. In exterior natural environments, objects can be animals, plants, man–made structures, automobiles, roads, and so on. Man–made environments are usually easier for robot vision because most of the objects tend to have regular edges and surfaces.

Two computer vision techniques are useful for delineating the parts of images that relate to objects in the scene. One technique looks for "edges" in the image. An image edge is a part of the image across which the image intensity or some other property of the image changes abruptly. Another technique attempts to segment the image into *regions*. A region is a part of the image in which the image intensity or some other property of the image changes only gradually. Often, but not always, edges in the image and boundaries between regions in the image correspond to important object-related discontinuities in the scene that produced the image. Some examples of discontinuities are illustrated in Figure 6.3.[2] Depending on illumination levels, surface properties, and camera

---

2. Adapted from [Nalwa 1993, p. 77].

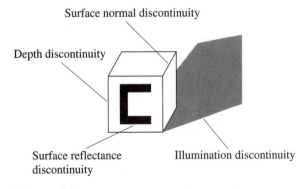

Figure 6.3

Scene Discontinuities

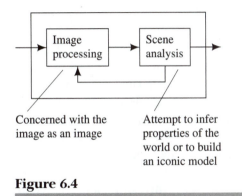

Figure 6.4

The Two Stages of Robot Vision

angle, these discontinuities might all be represented by image edges or image region boundaries. Thus, extracting these image features is an important task for robot vision.

I divide my discussion of visual processing into two major stages, as shown in Figure 6.4. The image processing stage is concerned with transforming the original image into one that is more amenable to the scene analysis stage. Image processing involves various filtering operations that help reduce noise, accentuate edges, and find regions in the image. Scene analysis routines attempt to create from the processed image either an iconic or a feature–based description of the original scene—providing the task–specific information about it that the agent needs. My division of robot vision into these two stages is a simplification; actual robot vision programs often involve more stages, and usually the stages interact.

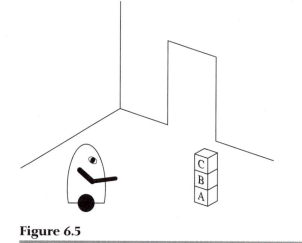

Figure 6.5

A Robot in a Room with Toy Blocks

I will discuss the two stages in more detail later, but to give the general idea, consider the grid–space robot depicted in Figure 6.5. In view of the robot are three toy blocks with labels *A*, *B*, and *C*, a doorway, and a corner of the room. First, image processing eliminates spurious noise and accentuates the edges of objects and other discontinuities. Next, knowing that the world comprises objects and forms with rectilinear boundaries, the scene analysis component might produce an iconic representation of the visible world—similar, say, to the sort of models used in computer graphics. Typically, this iconic model is used to update the more comprehensive model of the environment stored in memory, and then actions appropriate to this presumed state of the environment are computed.

Depending on the task, iconic models do not have to portray all the detail that a computer graphics model does. If the task at hand deals only with the toy blocks, then the location of the room corner and the doorway may be irrelevant. Suppose further that only the disposition of the blocks is important. Then the appropriate iconic model might be the list structure ((C B A FLOOR)), which is meant to represent that *C* is on top of *B*, which is on top of *A*, which is on the floor. If *C* were moved to the floor, the appropriate iconic model would be ((C FLOOR) (B A FLOOR)). (It could also be ((B A FLOOR) (C FLOOR)), but assuming that the relative horizontal locations of the blocks are also unimportant, the order of the first–level elements of the list structure need not have representational significance.) Since the last element of each component list is always *FLOOR*, we can shorten our lists by excluding this term.

For robots that do not use iconic models at all, scene analysis might alter-natively convert the processed image directly into features appropriate to the task for which the robot is designed. If it is important, for example, to determine whether or not there is another block on top of the block labeled C, then an adequate description of the environment might include the value of a feature, say, CLEAR_C. This feature has value 1 if block C is clear; otherwise, it has value 0. (Here, I use mnenomic names for the features instead of the usual x_i. We must remember though that the names are mnenomic just to help us; they are not mnenomic for the robot.) In this case, scene analysis has only to compute the value of this feature from the processed image. We see from these examples that the process of scene analysis is highly dependent on the design of the robot doing it and the tasks that it is to perform.

6.4   *Image Processing*

6.4.1   Averaging

We assume that the original image is represented as an $m \times n$ array, $I(x, y)$, of numbers, called the *image intensity array*, that divides the image plane into cells called *pixels*. The numbers represent the light intensities at corresponding points in the image. Certain irregularities in the image can be smoothed by an averaging operation. This operation involves sliding an *averaging window* all over the image array. The averaging window is centered at each pixel, and the weighted sum of all the pixel numbers within the averaging window is computed. This sum then replaces the original value at that pixel. The sliding and summing operation is called *convolution*. If we want the resulting array to contain only binary numbers (say, 0 and 1), then the sum is compared with a threshold. Averaging tends to suppress isolated noise specks but also reduces the crispness of the image and loses small image components.

Convolution is an operation that derives from signal processing. It is often explained as a one–dimensional operation on waveforms (sliding over the time axis). If we slide or convolve a function $w(t)$ over a signal, $s(t)$, we get the averaged signal, $s^\star(t)$:

$$s^\star(t) = \int s(u)w(u - t)du = s(t) \star w(t)$$

I use the operator $\star$ to denote convolution.

In image processing, the two–dimensional, discrete version of convolution is

$$I^\star(x, y) = I(x, y) \star W(x, y) = \sum_{u=-\infty}^{\infty} \sum_{v=-\infty}^{\infty} I(u, v)W(u - x, v - y)$$

where $I(x, y)$ is the original image array, and $W(u, v)$ is the convolution weighting function. I assume that $I(x, y) = 0$ for $x < 0$ or $x \geq n$ and $y < 0$ or $y \geq m$. (Thus, the convolution operation will have some "edge effects" near the boundaries of the image.)

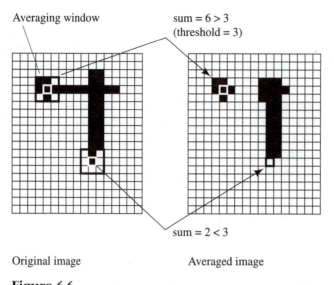

Averaging window   sum = 6 > 3
                     (threshold = 3)

sum = 2 < 3

Original image   Averaged image

Figure 6.6

Elements of the Averaging Operation

Sometimes, the value of the weighting function $W(x, y)$ is taken to be 1 over a rectangular range of x and y and zero outside of this range. The size of the rectangle determines the degree of smoothing, with larger rectangles achieving more smoothing. I show an example of what the averaging operation does for a binary image smoothed by a rectangular smoothing function and then thresholded in Figure 6.6. (In this figure, I assume that black pixels have a high intensity value and that white pixels have a low or zero intensity value. This convention may seem reversed, but it makes this illustration a bit simpler.) Notice that the smoothing operation thickens broad lines and eliminates thin lines and small details.

A very common function used for smoothing is a Gaussian of two dimensions:

$$W(x, y) = G(x, y) = \frac{1}{2\pi\sigma^2} e^{-\frac{x^2+y^2}{2\sigma^2}}$$

The surface described by this function is bell–shaped, as shown in Figure 6.7. (I have displaced the axes in this figure in order to display the Gaussian surface more clearly.) The standard deviation, σ, of the Gaussian determines the "width" of the surface and, thus, the degree of smoothing. $G(x, y)$ has a unit integral over x and y. Three Gaussian–smoothed versions of a grid–space scene containing blocks and a robot, using different smoothing factors, are shown along with the

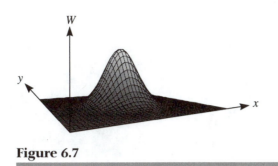

Figure 6.7

The Gaussian Smoothing Function

original image in Figure 6.8.[3] (Discrete versions of image smoothing and filtering operations usually interpolate between discrete values to enhance performance.)

You will note that the sequence of images in Figure 6.8 is increasingly blurred. One way to think about this blurring is to imagine that the image intensity function $I(x, y)$ represents an initial temperature field over a rectangular, heat-conducting plate. As time passes, heat diffuses isotropically on the plate causing high temperatures to blend with lower ones. According to this view, the sequence of images in Figure 6.8 represents temperature fields at later and later points of time. Koenderink [Koenderink 1984] has noted that convolving an image with a Gaussian with standard deviation σ is, in fact, equivalent to finding the solution to a diffusion equation at time proportional to σ when the initial condition is given by the image intensity field.

6.4.2   Edge Enhancement

As previously mentioned, computer vision techniques frequently involve extracting image edges. These edges are then used to convert the image to a line drawing of some sort. The outlines in the converted image can then be compared against prototypical (model) outlines characteristic of the sorts of objects that the scene might contain. One method of extracting outlines begins by enhancing boundaries or edges in the image. An *edge* is any boundary between parts of the image with markedly different values of some property, such as intensity. Such edges are often related to important object properties as illustrated in Figure 6.3.

I motivate my discussion by first considering images that are only "one-dimensional" in the sense that $I(x, y)$ varies only along the x dimension, not along the y dimension. Then, I will generalize to the two-dimensional case. We can

---

3. I thank Charles Richards for creating the images and programming the image processing operations illustrated in this chapter.

(a) Original image

(b) Width of Gaussian = 2 pixels

(c) Width of Gaussian = 4 pixels

(d) Width of Gaussian = 8 pixels

Figure 6.8

Image Smoothing with a Gaussian Filter

enhance intensity edges in one–dimensional images by convolving a vertically oriented, partly negative, partly positive window over the image. Such a window is shown in Figure 6.9. The window sum is zero over uniform parts of the image.

If the window shown in Figure 6.9 is convolved in the x direction over an image, a peak will result at positions where an edge is aligned with the y direction. This operation is approximately like taking the first derivative, dI/dx, of the image intensity function with respect to x. An even more pronounced effect would occur if we were to take the second derivative of the image intensity. In that case, we would get a positive band on one side of the edge, crossing through zero at the edge, and a negative band on the other side of the edge. These effects, illustrated for one dimension, are shown in Figure 6.10, in which the intensity changes smoothly (and thus differentiably) instead of abruptly as in Figure 6.9. Of course, the steeper the change in image intensity, the narrower will be the peak in dI/dx. Edges in the image occur at places where $d^2I/dx^2 = 0$, that is, at the "zero–crossings" of the twice–differentiated image.

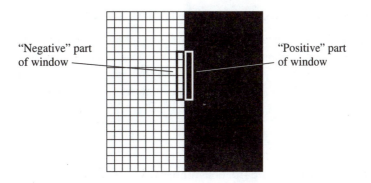

Figure 6.9

Edge Enhancement

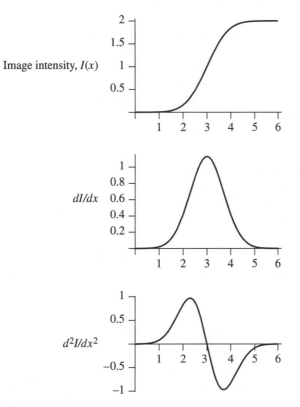

Figure 6.10

Taking Derivatives of Image Intensity

6.4.3   Combining Edge Enhancement with Averaging

Edge enhancement alone would tend to emphasize spurious noise elements of the image along with enhancing edges. To be less sensitive to noise, we can combine the two operations, first averaging and then edge enhancing. In the continuous, one–dimensional case, we use a one–dimensional Gaussian for smoothing. It is given by

$$G(x) = \frac{1}{\sqrt{2\pi}\sigma}e^{-\frac{x^2}{2\sigma^2}}$$

where σ is the standard deviation, which is a measure of the width of the smoothing function. Smoothing with a Gaussian gives the filtered image

$$I^\star(x) = I(x) \star G(x) = \int I(u)G(u-x)\,du$$

Subsequent edge enhancement yields

$$d^2[I^\star(x)]/dx^2 = d^2[I(x) \star G(x)]/dx^2 = d^2\left[\int I(u)G(u-x)\,du\right]/dx^2$$

which is equivalent to $I(x) \star d^2G(x)/dx^2$ because the order of differentiation and integration can be interchanged. That is, to combine smoothing with edge enhancement, we can convolve the one–dimensional image with the second derivative of a Gaussian curve instead of having to take the second derivative of a convolved image.

Moving now to two dimensions, we need a second–derivative–type operation that enhances edges of any orientation. The *Laplacian* is such an operation. The Laplacian of $I(x,y)$ is defined as

$$\nabla^2 I(x,y) = \partial^2 I(x,y)/\partial x^2 + \partial^2 I(x,y)/\partial y^2$$

If we want to combine edge enhancement with Gaussian smoothing in two dimensions, we can interchange the order of differentiation and convolution (as in the one–dimensional case), yielding

$$I(x,y) \star [\partial^2 G(x,y)/\partial x^2 + \partial^2 G(x,y)/\partial y^2]$$

The Laplacian of the two–dimensional Gaussian function looks a little bit like an upside–down hat, as shown in Figure 6.11. (Again, I have translated the origin of the coordinate space.) It is often called a *sombrero* function. The width of the hat determines the degree of smoothing.

The entire averaging/edge–finding operation, then, can be achieved by convolving the image with the sombrero function. This operation is called *Laplacian filtering*; it produces an image called the Laplacian filtered image. It has been remarked that early visual processing in the retinas of vertebrates seems to resemble Laplacian filtering. The zero–crossings of the Laplacian filtered image can

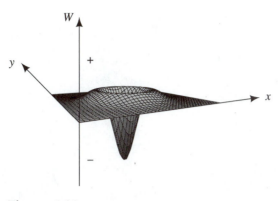

Figure 6.11

The Sombrero Function Used in Laplacian Filtering

then be used to create a rough outline drawing. The entire process, Laplacian filtering and zero–crossing marking, constitutes what is called the *Marr-Hildreth* operator [Marr & Hildreth 1980]. (The output of the Marr–Hildreth operator is a component of what Marr called the *primal sketch*.) I show the results of these operations on the image of the grid–space scene in Figure 6.12.[4] Note that the Marr–Hildreth operator provides a reasonable basis for an outline sketch for those parts of the scene with simple boundaries. The more complex robot in front of the doorway, however, is not well delineated.

There are several other edge–enhancing and line–finding operations, some of which produce better results than does the easy–to–explain and popular Marr–Hildreth operator. Among the prominent ones are the Canny operator ([Canny 1986]), the Sobel operator (attributed to Irwin Sobel by [Pingle 1969]), the Hueckel operator ([Hueckel 1973]), and the Nalwa–Binford operator ([Nalwa & Binford 1986]). It should be noted that the Marr–Hildreth and other edge–enhancing operators label pixels as candidates that might be on an image edge or line. The candidate pixels must then be linked to form lines or other simple curves.

6.4.4   Region Finding

Another method for processing an image attempts to find "regions" in the image within which intensity or some other property, such as texture, does not change abruptly. In a sense, finding regions is a process that is dual to finding outlines; both techniques segment the image into, we hope, scene–relevant portions. But

4. In calculating the image of Figure 6.12, I used "band" crossings instead of zero–crossings. The image intensity had to cross a band around zero in order to be displayed.

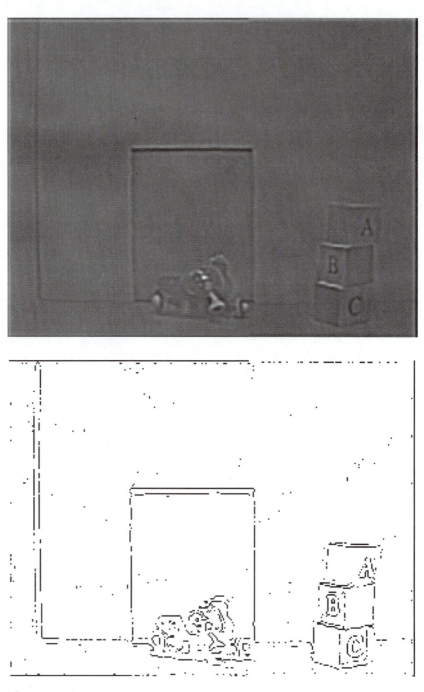

Figure 6.12

Laplacian Filtering and the Marr–Hildreth Operator (width of Laplacian = 1 pixel)

since finding outlines and finding regions are both subject to idiosyncrasies due to noise, the two techniques are often used to complement each other.

First, I must define what is meant by a *region* of the image. A region is a set of connected pixels satisfying two main properties:

1. A region is *homogeneous*. Examples of commonly used homogeneity properties are as follows:

   (a) The difference in intensity values of pixels in the region is no more than some ϵ.

   (b) A polynomial surface of degree k (for some low, preassigned value of k) can be fitted to the intensity values of pixels in the region with largest error (between the surface and an intensity value in the region) less than ϵ.

2. For no two adjacent regions is it the case that the union of all the pixels in these two regions satisfies the homogeneity property.

Usually, there is more than one possible partition of an image into regions, but, often, each region corresponds to a world object or to a meaningful part of one.

As with edge enhancement and line finding, there are many different techniques for segmenting a scene into regions. I will describe one of these, called the *split-and-merge* method [Horowitz & Pavlidis 1976]. In a version that is rather easy to describe, the algorithm begins with just one candidate region, namely, the whole image. For ease of illustration, let's assume the image is square and consists of a $2^l \times 2^l$ array of pixels. Obviously, this candidate region will not meet the definition of a region because the set of all the pixels in an image will not satisfy the homogeneity property (except for an image of uniform intensity). For all candidate regions that do not satisfy the homogeneity property, those candidate regions are each split into four equal–sized candidate regions. These splits continue until no more splits need be made. In Figure 6.13, I illustrate the splitting process for an artificial 8×8 image using a homogeneity property in which intensities may not vary by more than 1 unit. After no more splits can be made, adjacent candidate regions are merged if their pixels satisfy the homogeneity property. Merges can be done in different orders—resulting in different final regions. In fact, some merges could have been performed before the splitting process finished. To simplify my illustration of the process in Figure 6.13, all of the merges take place in the last step.

I used the low–resolution image of Figure 6.13 to illustrate the region-finding process. I show results for a higher–resolution image in Figure 6.14. Just as in Figure 6.13, we see some small regions and many irregularities in the region boundaries. The regions found by the split–merge algorithm can often be "cleaned up" by eliminating very small regions (some of which are transitions between larger regions), straightening bounding lines, and taking into account the known

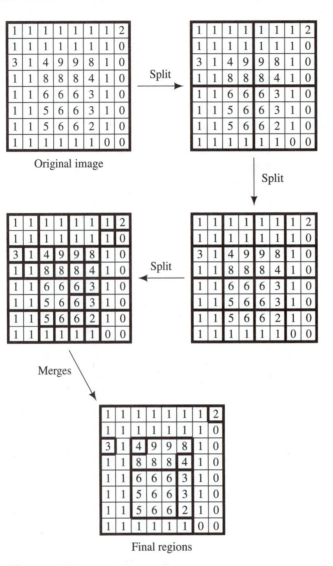

Figure 6.13

Splitting and Merging Candidate Regions

shapes of objects likely to be in the scene. Intensity gradients along the wall of the grid–world scene produce many regions in the image of Figure 6.14.

Recall that in my discussion of image smoothing with a Gaussian, I mentioned that the process was related to isotropic heat diffusion. Perona and Malik [Perona & Malik 1990] have proposed a process of anisotropic diffusion that can be used to create regions. The process encourages smoothing in directions of small intensity

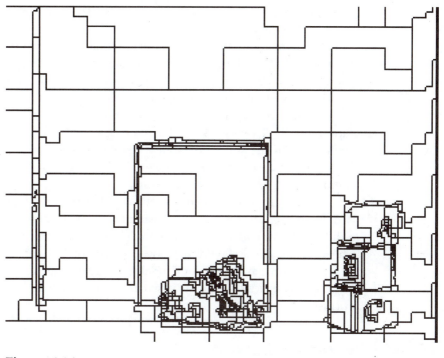

Figure 6.14

Regions Found by Split Merge for a Grid–World Scene

change and resists smoothing in directions of large intensity change. As described by [Nalwa 1993, p. 96], the result is "the formation of uniform–intensity regions that have boundaries across which the intensity gradient is high."

6.4.5   Using Image Attributes Other Than Intensity

Edge enhancement and region finding can be based on image attributes other than the homogeneity of image intensity. Visual texture is one such attribute. The surface reflectivity of many objects in the world has fine–grained variation, which we call visual texture. Examples are a field of grass, a section of carpet, foliage in trees, the fur of animals, and so on. These reflectivity variations in objects cause similar fine–grained structure in image intensity.

Computer vision researchers have identified many varieties of texture and have developed various tools for analyzing texture. Among these are structural and statistical methods. The methods are applied either to classify parts of the image as having textures of a certain sort or to segment the image into regions such that each region has its own special texture. The structural methods attempt to represent regions in the image by a tessellation of primitive "texels"—small shapes comprising black and white parts. (See [Ballard & Brown 1982, Ch. 6] for a thorough discussion.)

Statistical methods are based on the idea that image texture is best described by a probability distribution for the intensity values over regions of the image. As a rough example, an image of a grassy field in which the blades of grass are oriented vertically in the image would have a probability distribution that peaks for thin, vertically oriented regions of high intensity, separated by regions of low intensity. Recent work by Zhu and colleagues [Zhu, Wu, & Mumford 1998] involves estimating these probability distributions for various types of visual textures. Once the distributions are known, they can be used to classify textures and to segment images based on texture.

In addition to texture, there are other attributes of the image that might be used. If we had a direct way to measure the range from the camera to objects in the scene (say, with a laser range finder), we could produce a "range image" (where each pixel value represents the distance from the corresponding point in the scene to the camera) and look for abrupt range differences. Motion and color are other properties that might be sensed or computed and subjected to image processing operations.

6.5   *Scene Analysis*

After the image has been processed by techniques such as those just discussed, we can attempt to extract from it the needed information about the scene. This phase of computer vision is called *scene analysis*. Since the scene–to–image transformation is many–to–one, the scene analysis phase requires either additional images or general information about the kinds of scenes to be encountered (or both). I will discuss the use of additional images later when I describe stereo vision; here I mention various methods in which knowledge about the scene can be used to extract information about it.

The required extra knowledge can be very general (such as the surface reflectivity properties of objects) or quite specific (such as the scene is likely to contain some stacked boxes near a doorway). It can also be explicit or implicit. For example, a line–finding algorithm might have implicit knowledge about what constitutes a line built into its operation. Between these extremes are other pieces of information about the scene, such as camera location, locations of illumination sources, and whether the scene is indoors in an office building or outdoors. My discussion below samples some points along these spectra. Again, please see computer vision textbooks for detailed treatments.

Knowledge of surface reflectivity characteristics and shading of intensity in the image can often be used to give information about the shape of smooth objects in the scene. Specifically, we can use image shading to help compute surface normals of objects. Methods for inferring shape from shading have been developed by Horn and colleagues (see [Horn 1986] for descriptions). The fact that textural elements as represented in the image are perspective projections of elements in the scene also facilitates shape and qualitative depth recovery from texture.

As already mentioned, sometimes an iconic model of the scene is desired, and sometimes certain features of the scene suffice. Iconic scene analysis usually attempts to build a model of the scene or of parts of the scene. Feature–based scene analysis extracts features of the scene needed by the task at hand. So–called *task-oriented* or *purposive* vision (see, for example, [Ballard 1991, Aloimonos 1993]) typically employs feature–based scene analysis.

6.5.1   Interpreting Lines and Curves in the Image

For scenes that are known to contain rectilinear objects (such as the scenes confronted inside of buildings and scenes in grid–space world), an important step in scene analysis is to postulate lines in the image (which later can be associated with key components of the scene). Lines in the image can be created by various techniques that fit segments of straight lines to edges or to boundaries of regions. For scenes with curved objects, curves in the image can be created by attempting to fit conic sections (such as ellipses, parabolas, and hyperbolas) to the primal sketch or to boundaries of regions. (See, for example, [Nalwa & Pauchon 1987].) These fitting operations, followed by various techniques for eliminating small lines and joining line and curve segments at their extremes, convert the image into a *line drawing*, ready for further interpretation.

Various strategies exist for associating scene properties with the components of a line drawing. Such an association is called *interpreting* the line drawing. By way of example, I mention here one strategy for interpreting a line drawing if the scene is known to contain only planar surfaces such that no more than three surfaces intersect in a point. (Such combinations of surfaces are called *trihedral vertex polyhedra.*) I show a typical example of such a scene in Figure 6.15. Illustrated there is an interior scene with bounding walls, floor, and ceiling, with a cube on the floor. For such scenes, there are only three kinds of ways in which two planes can intersect in a scene edge. One kind of edge is formed by two planes, with one of them occluding the other (that is, only one of the planes is visible in the scene). Such an edge is called an *occlude*. The occludes are labeled in Figure 6.15 with arrows ($\rightarrow$), with the arrowhead pointing along the edge such that the surface doing the occluding is to the right of the arrow. Alternatively, two planes can intersect such that both planes are visible in the scene. In one such intersection, called a *blade*, the two surfaces form a convex edge. These edges are labeled with pluses (+). In another type of intersection, called a *fold*, the edge is concave. These edges are labeled with minuses (−).

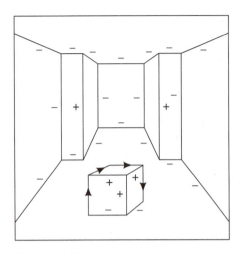

Figure 6.15

A Room Scene

Suppose an image is captured from such a scene and suppose that the image can be converted into a line drawing—much like the one shown in Figure 6.15. Can we label the lines in the *image* in such a way that they accurately describe the types of edges in the *scene*? Under certain conditions, we can. First the image of the scene must be taken from a *general viewpoint*, one in which no two edges in the scene line up to produce just one line in the image. The method for attempting to label lines in the image is based on the fact that (under our assumption about trihedral vertex polyhedra) there can only be certain kinds of labelings of junctions of lines in the image. The different kinds of labelings are shown in Figure 6.16. Even though there are many more ways to label the lines at image junctions, these are the only labelings possible for our polyhedral scenes.

Line–labeling scene analysis proceeds by first labeling all of the junctions in the image as V, W, Y, or T junctions according to the shape of the junctions in the image. I have done that for the image of our room scene in Figure 6.17. (Note that there are no T junctions in this image.) Next, we attempt to assign +, −, or → labels to the lines in the image. But we must do that in one of the ways illustrated in Figure 6.16. Also, an image line that connects two junctions must have a consistent labeling. These constraints often (but not always) force a unique labeling. If there is no consistent labeling, then there must have been some error in converting the image into a line drawing, or the scene must not have been one of trihedral polyhedra. The problem of assigning labels to the image lines, subject to these constraints, is an instance of what in AI is called a *constraint satisfaction problem*. I will discuss methods for solving this general class of problem later, but in the meantime, you might experiment with methods for

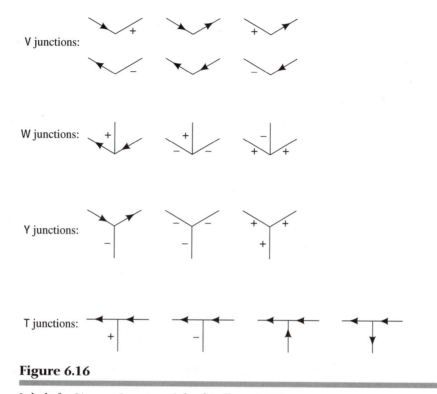

Figure 6.16

Labels for Lines at Junctions (after [Huffman 1971])

coming up with a consistent labeling for the image of Figure 6.17. (Of course, a labeling of the image corresponding to the labeled scene in Figure 6.15 is one such consistent labeling, but the scene was stipulated to have those labels. Can you think of an automatic way to find a consistent labeling for the image lines?)

Scene analysis techniques that label junctions and lines in images of trihedral vertex polyhedra began with [Guzman 1968, Huffman 1971, Clowes 1971] and were extended by [Waltz 1975] and others. Some success has also been achieved at performing similar analyses for scenes containing nonplanar surfaces. For a more complete exposition (with citations) of work on interpreting line drawings, see [Nalwa 1993, Ch. 4].

Interpretation of the lines and curves of a line drawing yields a great deal of useful information about a scene. For example, a robot could predict that heading toward a vertically oriented fold (a concave edge in the scene) would eventually land it in a corner. Navigating around polyhedral obstacles could be performed by skirting vertically oriented blades (convex edges). With sufficient general knowledge about the class of scenes, either the needed features or iconic models can be obtained directly from an interpreted line drawing.

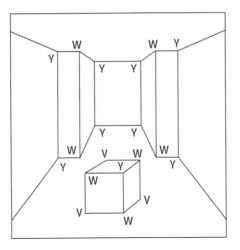

Figure 6.17

Labeling Image Junctions According to Type

6.5.2   Model–Based Vision

Progressing further along the spectrum of using increasing knowledge about the scene, I now turn to the use of models of objects that might appear in the scene. If, for example, we knew that the scene consisted of industrial parts and components used in robot assembly, then geometric models of the shapes of these parts could be used to help interpret images. I give a brief overview of some of the methods used in model-based vision; see [Binford 1982, Grimson 1990, Shirai 1987] for further reading.

Just as lines and curves can be fitted to boundary sections of regions in the image, so can perspective projections of models and parts of models. If, for example, we knew that the scene contained a parallelepiped (as does the scene in Figure 6.15), we could attempt to fit a projection of a parallelepiped to components of an image of this scene. The parallelepiped would have parameters specifying its size, position, and orientation. These would be adjusted until a set of parameters is found that allowed a good fit to an appropriate set of lines in the image.

Researchers have also used *generalized cylinders* [Binford 1987] as building blocks for model construction. A generalized cylinder is shown in Figure 6.18. Each cylinder has nine parameters as shown in the figure. An example rough scene reconstruction of a human figure is shown in Figure 6.19. The method can be adapted to hierarchical representations, because each cylinder in the model can be articulated into a set of smaller cylinders that more accurately represent the figure. Representing objects in a scene by a hierarchy of generalized cylinders

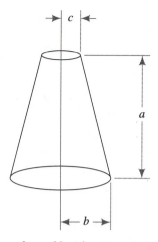

a, b, c + 6 location parameters

Figure 6.18

A Generalized Cylinder

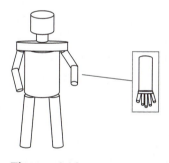

Figure 6.19

A Scene Model Using Generalized Cylinders

is, as Nalwa says, "easier said than done" [Nalwa 1993, p. 293], but the method has been used for certain object–recognition applications [Brooks 1981]. For more discussion on the use of models in representing three–dimensional structures, see [Ballard & Brown 1982, Ch. 9].

Using a variety of model components, model fitting can be employed until either an iconic model of the entire scene is produced or sufficient information about the scene is obtained to allow the extraction of features needed for the task at hand. Model-based methods can test their accuracy by comparing the actual image with a simulated image constructed from the iconic model produced by scene analysis. The simulated image must be rendered from the model using parameters similar to those used by the imaging process (camera angle, etc.). To do so requires good models of illumination, surface reflectance characteristics, and all of the other aspects of the rendering processes of computer graphics.

6.6   *Stereo Vision and Depth Information*

Under perspective projection, a large, distant object might produce the same image as does a similar but smaller and closer one. Thus, the estimation of the distance to objects from single images is problematical. Depth information can be obtained using *stereo vision*, which is based on triangulation calculations using two (or more) images.

Before discussing stereo vision, however, I point out that under some circumstances, and with appropriate prior knowledge, some depth information can be extracted from a single image. For example, the analysis of texture in the image (taking into account the perspective transformation of scene texture) can indicate that some elements in the scene are closer than are others. Even more precise depth information can be obtained from single images in certain situations. In an office scene, for example, if we know that a perceived object is on the floor, and if we know the camera height above the (same) floor, then, using the angle from the camera lens center to the appropriate point on the image, we can calculate the distance to the object. An example of such a calculation is shown in Figure 6.20. (The angle α can be calculated in terms of the camera focal length and image dimensions.) Similar calculations can be used to calculate distances to doorways, sizes of objects, and so on.

Stereo vision also uses triangulation. The basic idea is very simple. Consider the two-dimensional setup shown in Figure 6.21. There we have two lenses whose centers are separated by a *baseline, b*. The image points of a scene point, at distance *d*, created by these lenses are as illustrated. The angles of these image points from the lens centers can then be used to calculate *d*, as shown. For given precision in the measurements of angles and baseline, higher accuracies are obtained for larger baselines and smaller object distances. Figure 6.21 oversimplifies the situation somewhat in that the optical axes are parallel, the image planes are coplanar, and the scene point is in the same plane as that formed by the two parallel optical axes. When these conditions are generalized, the geometry is more complex, but the general idea of triangulation is the same. (In animals and in some robots, the optical axes can be rotated to point at an object of interest in the scene.)

The main complication in stereo vision, however, is not the triangulation calculations. In scenes containing more than one point (the usual case!), it must be established which pair of points in the two images correspond to the same scene point (in order to calculate the distance to that scene point). Put another way, for any scene point whose image falls on a given pixel in one image, we

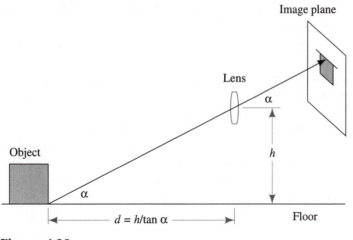

Figure 6.20

Depth Calculation from a Single Image

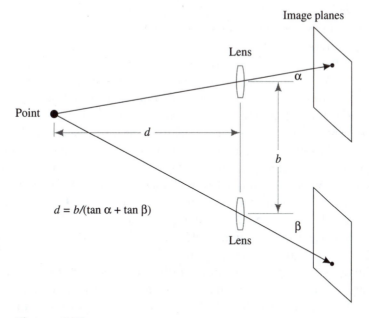

Figure 6.21

Triangulation in Stereo Vision

must be able to identify a corresponding pixel in the other image. Doing so is known as the *correspondence problem*. Space does not permit detailed discussion of techniques for dealing with the correspondence problem, but I will make a few observations.

First, given a pixel in one image, geometric analysis reveals that we need only search along one dimension (rather than two) for a corresponding pixel in the other image. This one dimension is called an *epipolar line*. One–dimensional searches can be implemented by cross–correlation of two image intensity profiles along corresponding epipolar lines. Second, in many applications, we do not have to find correspondences between individual pairs of image points but can do so between pairs of larger image components, such as lines.[5] Scene analysis of each image can provide clues as to which pairs of lines correspond. For an excellent review of computational methods in stereo vision, see [Nalwa 1993, Ch. 7].

6.7   *Additional Readings and Discussion*

The team that developed ALVINN continues to develop other autonomous driving systems, some of which use techniques related to those I discussed in this chapter ([Thorpe, et al. 1992]). In a related effort, [Hebert, et al. 1997] describes mobility software for an autonomous vehicle driving in open terrain using both stereo and infrared sensors.

Although there are applications in which a three–dimensional model of an entire scene is required from a computer vision system, usually robots require only information sufficient to guide action. Reacting to early work in vision directed at computing complete scene models, some researchers have concentrated on what they consider to be the more relevant task of *purposive vision*. [Horswill 1993] gives an interesting example of a simple, task–oriented robotic vision system. These task–oriented systems often suffice for robust mobile robot navigation. See also [Churchland, Ramachandran, & Sejnowski 1994].

Much about the process of visual perception has been learned by studying the psychology and neurophysiology of human and animal vision. [Gibson 1950, Gibson 1979] studied, among other phenomena, how the changing visual field informed a moving subject about its surroundings. [Julesz 1971] discovered that humans can exploit discontinuities in the statistics of random dots to perceive depth. [Marr & Poggio 1979] developed a plausible neural model of stereo vision.

Experiments with frogs [Letvinn, et al. 1959] revealed that their visual system notices only changes in overall illumination (such as would be caused by the shadow of a large approaching animal) and rapid movement of small, dark objects (such as flies). Experiments with monkeys [Hubel & Wiesel 1968] revealed

---

5. Or we can find correspondences between the image points where lines intersect.

that neurons in their visual cortex were excited by short, oriented line segments in their visual field. Experiments with horseshoe crabs revealed that adjacent neurons in their visual system inhibit each other (*lateral inhibition*), achieving an effect much like what later came to be known as Laplacian filtering [Reichardt 1965]. For more on biological vision, see [Marr 1982, Hubel 1988].

[Bhanu & Lee 1994] employed genetic techniques for image segmentation.

The major computer vision conferences are the International Conference on Computer Vision (ICCV), the European Conference on Computer Vision (ECCV), and Computer Vision and Pattern Recognition (CVPR). The *International Journal of Computer Vision* is a leading journal.

Textbooks on computer vision include [Nalwa 1993, Horn 1986, Ballard & Brown 1982, Jain, Kasturi, & Schunck 1995, Faugeras 1993]. [Fischler & Firschein 1987] is a collection of some of the important papers. A book devoted to outdoor scenes is [Strat 1992]. [Gregory 1966] is a popular account of how we see.

Exercises

6.1 You are to design a visual system for detecting small black objects against a light background. Assume that the image of one of these objects is a square that is 5 pixels wide. Your system is to be used to create a Boolean feature that has value 1 whenever a *single* such image appears anywhere in a 100×100 image array and has value 0 for any other image. Describe how you would design such a system, first using a neural network (with one hidden layer) and second, using convolution with a specially designed weighting function.

6.2 A one–dimensional image function, $I(x)$, and a one–dimensional weighting function, $W(x)$, are shown below. Draw a plot of $I(x) \star W(x)$.

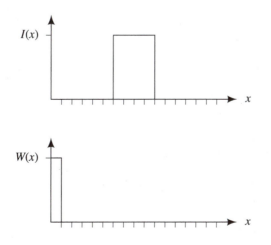

6.3 A very simple edge finder (the so–called *Roberts cross*) computes an image $I^*(x, y)$ from an image $I(x, y)$ according to the following definition:

$$I^*(x, y) = \sqrt{(I(x, y) - I(x + \Delta, y + \Delta))^2 + (I(x, y + \Delta) - I(x + \Delta, y))^2}$$

where Δ is a one-pixel offset, and the positive root is taken. Use differential calculus to approximate this definition for small pixel sizes, and then use your approximation to compute $I^*(x, y)$ when $I(x, y)$ is given in polar coordinates by

$I(r, \theta) = 1$ for $r < 9$

$I(r, \theta) = 0$ for $r > 10$

$I(r, \theta) = 10 - r$ for $9 < r < 10$

Assume a circular image field of radius 20. (Note: Expressing the image in polar coordinates is a hint that will be useful toward the end of your solution!) A rough sketch of the image intensity is shown here:

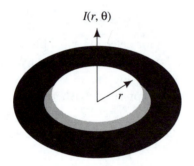

6.4 Copy the following drawing, and label the lines using the vertex classes and line labels discussed in Section 6.5.1. If there is more than one consistent labeling, show as many as you can think of, and describe a physical interpretation of each.

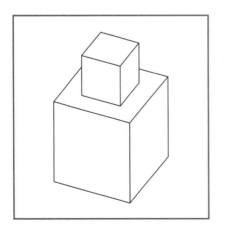

6.5 Can you find a consistent labeling for the lines in the image of the famous impossible figure called the Penrose triangle shown here? Assume the figure is suspended in empty space. Discuss the relationship between what might be called "local consistency" and "global consistency."

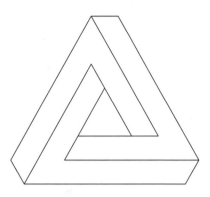

Part II

Search in State Spaces

A man who does not plan long ahead will find trouble right at his door.
—Confucius

... [the ant] knew that a certain arrangement had to be made, but it could not figure how to make it. It was like a man with a tea-cup in one hand and a sandwich in the other, who wants to light a cigarette with a match. But, where the man would invent the idea of putting down the cup and sandwich—before picking up the cigarette and the match—this ant would have put down the sandwich and picked up the match, then it would have been down with the match and up with the cigarette, then down with the cigarette and up with the sandwich, then down with the cup and up with the cigarette, until finally it had put down the sandwich and picked up the match. It was inclined to rely on a series of accidents to achieve its object. It was patient and did not think. ... Wart watched the arrangements with a surprise which turned into vexation and then into dislike. He felt like asking why it did not think things out in advance ...
—T. H. White, *The Once and Future King*, Chapter 13.

7 Agents That Plan

Memory Versus Computation

The action functions of reactive agents (Figures 2.2, 5.1, and 5.3) do very little computation. Essentially, these agents have their actions selected for them—either by their designers, by learning, by evolutionary processes, or by some combination of these sources. The action functions themselves can be implemented by tables, production rules, or combinational logic circuits that prescribe actions given a feature vector. Such implementations lie toward the "space" end of the classic space–time tradeoff in computer science. They are space- or memory–based implementations—compilations of the designer's knowledge.

A broadly competent reactive machine, able to perform complex tasks in complex environments would require large amounts (perhaps unattainable amounts) of memory. In addition, a designer of such a reactive machine would require superhuman foresight in anticipating appropriate reactions for all possible situations. We are thus led to consider trading time for space and adaptation instead of explicit design. As a start, let's bring inside the action function some of the computations that a designer of a reactive machine would have had to do. These computations will take time, of course, but they will reduce the agent's memory requirements and the burden on the designer.

Some of the computations we might consider are those that predict the consequences of the actions possible in any given situation. Surely, a designer of a competent reactive machine would have had to base the design on these anticipated consequences. The designer (or evolutionary or learning processes) still has to specify what these computations are, but the programs for doing the computations (at the time they are needed) will typically require much less space than would all of their results. And it will be easier for the designer to specify the

117

computations than to carry them out for all possible situations. Perhaps the most important point is that if these consequence-predicting computations could be automatically learned or evolved, the agent using them would be able to select appropriate actions even in those environments that a designer might not have been able to foresee.

To predict the consequences of an action, an agent must have a model of the world it inhabits and models of the effects of its actions on its model of the world. Actual actions, then, need not be taken until their simulations showed them to be safe and effective.

7.2   *State-Space Graphs*

As an example, consider a grid-space world containing three toy blocks, *A*, *B*, and *C*, all initially on the floor. Suppose the task for our robot is to stack them so that *A* is on top of *B* and *B* is on top of *C* and *C* is on the floor. While it is obvious for us what actions should be performed, it is not so obvious for a robot. Suppose the robot were able to model the effects of each of its actions on its environment. It might do this by a pair of world models—one that represents the world state before the action is taken and one that represents the world state after the action is taken. For the purposes of this example, suppose the robot is capable of moving any block, *x*, that has no other block on top of it, to another place *y*, either the floor or on top of a block that doesn't already have another block on top of it. We model these actions by instances of a *schema*, move(x, y), where *x* can be either A, B, or C, and *y* can be either A, B, C, or Floor, and we understand that some instances of this schema (for example, move(A, A)) do not name executable actions. Instances of the schema, such as move(A, C), are called *operators*. Thus, operators are models of actions.

Using list-structure iconic models, I show in Figure 7.1 the modeled effects of all of those actions that can be taken when all of the blocks are on the floor.[1] (For clarity, I have included a pictorial sketch of each situation. Pictures are iconic for us, whereas lists can be iconic for list-processing agents.) Two of these effects, namely, ((AB)(C)) and ((A)(BC)), seem to be "closer" in some respects to the goal ((ABC)) than do the others. Thus, considering just the predicted effects of a single action, the robot might prefer the actions modeled by move(A, B) and move(B, C) to the others. And, of course, the robot has not taken a real action yet.

Looking ahead just one step in a simulation can often produce useful predictions, but looking ahead more steps, perhaps all the way to task completion, can find shortcuts and avoid blind alleys. A most useful structure for keeping track of

---

1. For simplicity, I continue to use an abstract representation in which the horizontal positions of the blocks are not relevant and therefore are not represented.

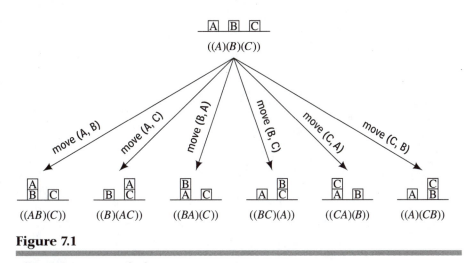

Figure 7.1

Effects of Moving a Block

the effects of several alternative sequences of actions is a directed graph. The set of worlds that an agent might produce through its actions can be represented by a directed graph whose nodes are labeled by representations of the individual worlds and whose arcs are labeled by operators. (I begin by using graph–theory terminology somewhat informally; later in the chapter, I will present relevant formal definitions of the graph–theory concepts that we will be using.) The representations at the nodes can be either iconic or feature based. Although I will be considering both types, I begin with iconic representations.

If the number of different distinguishable world situations is sufficiently small, a graph representing all of the possible actions and situations can be stored explicitly. For example, the graph illustrated in Figure 7.2 shows all the situations and moves relevant to manipulating three blocks. Such a graph of world models and actions is called a *state-space graph*. Note that each of the actions is reversible, although to make the picture less cluttered I label only one of each pair of reciprocal moves between configurations. It is easy to see from the graph that if the initial situation is given by the world model $((A)(B)(C))$, and if the task is to achieve the situation described by $((ABC))$, then the robot should execute the following sequence of actions: {move(B, C), move(A, B)}.

One of the advantages of representing the possible worlds in a graph structure is that any of the nodes in the graph can be taken to represent a goal situation—perhaps a goal specified by some external source such as a human. This flexibility in tasks is to be contrasted with the single–purpose agents that we have studied up to now. To find a set of actions that will achieve a specified goal, the robot needs simply to find a path in the graph from a node representing its initial world state (the *start node*) to a node representing the specified goal state (the

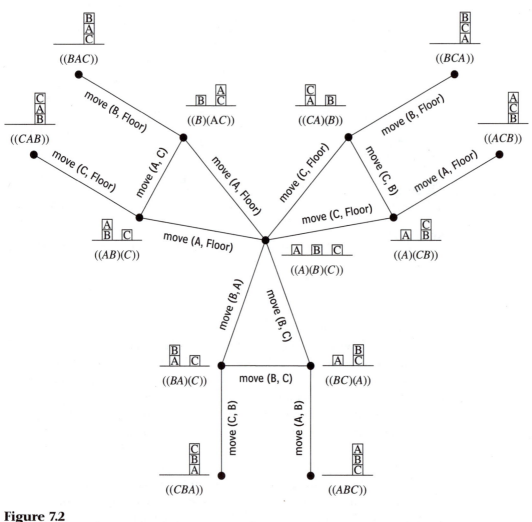

Figure 7.2

A State–Space Graph

goal node). The actions that will achieve that goal can then be read out as the labels on the arcs in this path. For example, if the task for our block–stacking robot was to stack blocks *C* on *B* on *A* on the floor, and if the initial state was *A* on *B* on *C* on the floor, the action sequence would be {move(A, Floor), move(B, A), move(C, B)}. For the graph shown in Figure 7.2, it is easy (for us!) to find paths by visual inspection; however, computational agents will need to use various graph–searching processes in order to find paths.

The operators labeling the arcs along a path to a goal can be assembled into a sequence called a *plan*, and searching for such a sequence is called *planning*.

The process of predicting a sequence of world states resulting from a sequence of actions is called *projecting*. Of course, for the execution of a sequence of actions found in this manner to achieve the goal depends upon a number of assumptions. The agent must be able to represent all of the relevant world situations by nodes in a graph, and it must have accurate models of how actions take it between pairs of world states. The actions must always have their modeled effects—there can be no slipups or uncertainty in the agent's effector system. The agent's perceptual system must accurately identify the start node. And there can be no other agents or dynamic processes that change the world. If all of these assumptions are met, and if the time allowed for the task permits search to a goal state, then an entire sequence of actions can be planned and then executed (ballistically, as it were) without need for sensory feedback from the environment.

Even though these assumptions do not hold in most real–world applications, graph–search planning is an extremely useful and important idealization. Either it can often be generalized to accommodate settings with less restrictive assumptions or it can be embedded as a component of architectures adapted to such settings. I return to this topic in Chapter 10. In this chapter, I begin my treatment of searching for paths in graphs by describing a particularly simple search procedure, appropriate when the graph to be searched can be stored explicitly. Usually, in that case, the graph is reasonably small, so we don't necessarily have to be too concerned with efficient search methods. In the following two chapters, I will discuss graph–searching methods applicable to graphs so large that they can only be represented implicitly and must be searched efficiently.

7.3   *Searching Explicit State Spaces*

Search methods for explicit graphs involve propagating "markers" over the nodes of the graph. We start by labeling the start node with a 0, and then we propagate successively larger integers out in waves along the arcs until an integer hits the goal node. Then, we trace a path back from the goal to the start along a decreasing sequence of numbers. The actions along this path, from start to goal, are the actions that should be taken to achieve the goal. This method requires $O(n)$ steps, where n is the number of nodes in the graph. (If there is a single goal node, the process could also be implemented in the reverse direction—starting with the goal node and ending when an integer hits the start node.) The integers put on the nodes by this process can be thought of as a kind of artificial potential function over the nodes, with a global minimum at the start node. The reverse path (from goal to start) then falls along the "gradient" of this function.

The stages of marker propagation for the problem of transforming $((BAC))$ into $((ABC))$ are shown in Figure 7.3. This method corresponds to what is called a *breadth-first search* and was first proposed by [Moore 1959].

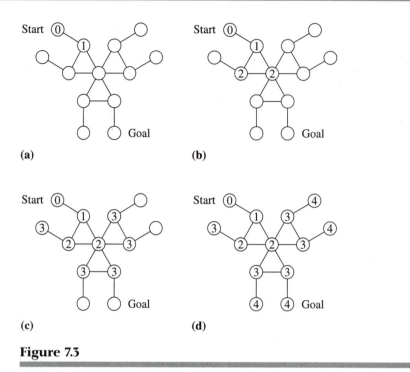

Figure 7.3

Stages of Search

We call the process of marking the successors of a node *expansion*. Expansion puts marks on all of the marked node's unmarked neighbors. An important efficiency question is which marked (but unexpanded) node should be expanded next? In breadth–first search, we expand next any unexpanded node labeled by a number no larger than that of any other unexpanded node. That is, we expand all of the nodes labeled by a number i before expanding those labeled by a number j for $i < j$. Other search methods make other choices about node expansion; these will be described in detail later.

7.4 *Feature-Based State Spaces*

It was rather straightforward to explain state spaces when using iconic models to label the nodes—we could easily visualize the effects of actions on the states. It is also possible to define graphs whose nodes are labeled by features, but to do so we need a way to describe how an action affects features. One technique for describing such effects was introduced in a system called STRIPS [Fikes & Nilsson 1971, Fikes, Hart, & Nilsson 1972]. The basic idea is to define an operator by three lists. The first, called the *precondition list*, specifies those features that must have

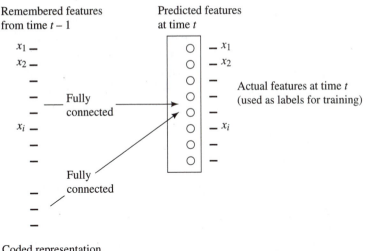

Remembered features
from time $t - 1$

Predicted features
at time t

Actual features at time t
(used as labels for training)

Fully
connected

Fully
connected

Coded representation
of action taken at time $t - 1$

Figure 7.4

Predicting a Feature Vector with a Neural Network

value 1 and those that must have value 0 in order that the action can be applied at all. The second, called the *delete list*, specifies those features that will have their values changed from 1 to 0. The third, called the *add list*, specifies those features that will have their values changed from 0 to 1. The values of the features not explicitly mentioned in the delete and add lists are unchanged. These three lists compose a STRIPS operator—a model of the effects of an action. I defer discussion of using STRIPS operators in feature-based spaces until later in the book after I have introduced more powerful techniques for computations involving features.

We might also be able to train a neural network to learn to predict the value of a feature vector at time t from its value at time $t - 1$ and the action taken at time $t - 1$ [Jordan & Rumelhart 1992]. Such a network is shown in Figure 7.4. Although I have shown a network of only one layer, intermediate layers of hidden units might also be used. After training, the prediction network can be used to compute the feature vectors that would result from various actions. These in turn could be used as new inputs to the network to predict the feature vector two steps ahead, and so on. A similar process (based on statistical clustering techniques) was used for controlling a mobile robot by [Mahadevan 1992, Connell & Mahadevan 1993a]. Because of unavoidable errors in the prediction process, it proved futile to attempt to plan more than a very few moves ahead using this method.

7.5   *Graph Notation*

Before moving on in the next chapters to present techniques for dealing with very large state spaces, it will be helpful to define some of the accepted terminology that is used in discussions of graphs and graph search. In Figure 7.5, I use a sample graph and tree to illustrate the terms I will be defining.

A *graph* consists of a (not necessarily finite) set of *nodes*. Certain pairs of nodes are connected by *arcs*, and these arcs are *directed* from one member of the pair to the other. Such a graph is called a *directed graph*. For our purposes, the nodes are labeled by models of world states, and the arcs are labeled by names of actions. If an arc is directed from node n_i to node n_j, then node n_j is said to be a *successor* (or *child*) of node n_i, and node n_i is said to be a *parent* of node n_j. In the graphs that are of interest to us, a node can have only a finite number of successors. A pair of nodes may be successors of each other; in this case, we replace the pair of arcs by an *edge*. Graphs that contain only edges are called *undirected graphs*. In my subsequent diagrams of graphs, arcs will have arrows, and edges will not.

A (rooted) *directed tree* is a special case of a directed graph in which each node (except one) has exactly one parent. The node with no parent is called the *root node*. A node in the tree having no successors is called a *tip node* or *leaf node*. We say that the root node is of *depth* zero. The depth of any other node in the tree is defined to be the depth of its parent plus 1. A (rooted) *undirected tree* (with edges instead of arcs) is an undirected graph in which there is precisely one and only one path along edges between any pair of nodes.

Certain trees, useful in theoretical analyses, have the property that all nodes except the tip nodes have the same number, b, of successors. In this case, b is called the *branching factor* of the tree.

A sequence of nodes $(n_1, n_2, \ldots, n_k)$, with each n_{i+1} a successor of n_i for $i = 1, \ldots, k - 1$, is called a *path* of *length k* from node n_1 to node n_k. (Alternatively, we could define a path as the sequence of arcs connecting the nodes.) If a path exists from node n_i to node n_j, then node n_j is said to be *accessible* from node n_i. Node n_j is then a *descendant* of node n_i, and node n_i is an *ancestor* of node n_j.

Often it is convenient to assign positive *costs* to arcs, to represent the cost of performing the corresponding action. I use the notation $c(n_i, n_j)$ (or, sometimes $c(a)$) to denote the cost of an arc, a, directed from node n_i to successor node n_j. It will be important in some of my later arguments to assume that these costs are all greater than some arbitrarily small positive number, ϵ. The cost of a path between two nodes is then the sum of the costs of all of the arcs connecting the nodes on the path. In some problems, we want to find that path having *minimal* cost between two nodes. Such a path is called an *optimal path*.

In the simplest type of problem, we desire to find a path (perhaps having minimal cost) between a given node n_0, representing the initial state, and another

Graph notation   Tree notation

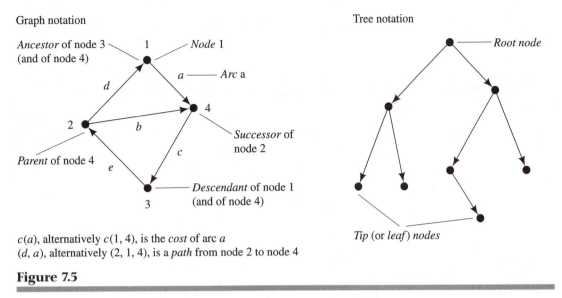

$c(a)$, alternatively $c(1, 4)$, is the *cost* of arc a

(d, a), alternatively $(2, 1, 4)$, is a *path* from node 2 to node 4

Figure 7.5

Graph and Tree Notation

given node n_g, representing some other state. The more usual situation, though, involves finding a path between a node n_0 and *any* member of a set of nodes that represent states satisfying some goal condition. We call this set the *goal set*, and each node in it is a *goal node*.

Given an explicit graph, we might sometimes want to find a path to some node, n_0, from each of the other nodes in the graph. Such a collection of paths constitutes a *spanning tree* of the graph—a tree rooted at n_0. (Note that my definition of a *tree* has to be changed a bit in order for a spanning tree to be a tree. See Exercise 7.2.)

Since I am representing state spaces as graphs, I sometimes use the word *node* interchangeably to mean a node in the graph, the world state that it represents, and the representation of that state (either a data structure or a set of features) that labels the node. Similarly, I will use the word *arc* to represent an arc in the graph, the action that it represents, and the operator (on state descriptions) that models that action.

7.6   *Additional Readings and Discussion*

For more on the computational aspects of graphs and on graph algorithms, see [Cormen, Leiserson, & Rivest 1990, Ch. VI]. Many problems can be posed as the task of finding a path (or paths) in graphs, and thus the methods described in this and the following chapters find application in several areas beyond that of agent planning.

Exercises

7.1 A robot must find the shortest path between a starting point, *s*, and a goal location, *g*, in the two–dimensional space populated by polygonal obstacles shown here. Assume the robot is of infinitesimal size. The path can be adjacent to (touching) the obstacles, but it may not intersect any.

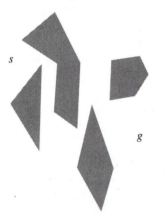

1. Copy the diagram, and draw the shortest path between *s* and *g*.
2. Although there are an infinite number of points in this 2–D space, what is the minimal set of points that must be considered in searching for a shortest path between an arbitrary *s* point and an arbitrary *g* point?
3. Given one of the points in the minimal set you just found, describe a method for generating the successors of this point in the corresponding search graph. What are the successor points for point *s* in the figure?

7.2 Spanning trees: Given a node *n* in a directed graph, $\mathcal{G}$, for which there is at least one path from every node in $\mathcal{G}$ to *n*, state a precise definition for a spanning tree of $\mathcal{G}$ rooted at *n*. Then, think of what might be meant by a *minimum spanning tree*.

7.3 The "Missionary and Cannibals" problem has a famous history in AI. Here is one statement of the problem:

> Three missionaries and three cannibals come to a river. There is a boat on their side of the river that can be used by either one or two persons. How should they use this boat to cross the river in such a way that cannibals never outnumber missionaries on either side of the river?

Specify the form of state descriptions, the starting state, and the goal state for this problem. Draw the entire state description graph, and label its nodes. (You need include only those states that are "legal"—that is, states in which cannibals do not outnumber missionaries on either side of the river.)

7.4 Refer to the three–disc Tower–of–Hanoi puzzle defined in Exercise 5.3. Suppose we do not know about the CW/CCW method of moving discs but must search for a solution. Let the operators that describe actions be given by the schema move(x,y,z), where x can be any of the three discs D_1, D_2, or D_3, and y and z can be any pair of distinct pegs A, B, or C. Define state descriptions for this puzzle, identify the start state and a goal state, and draw the complete search space containing all possible states of the puzzle. Label the arcs by the appropriate operators. (Each move is reversible; you need label only one of each pair of reversible moves.)

8 Uninformed Search

Formulating the State Space

Many problems of practical interest have search spaces so large that they cannot be represented by explicit graphs. Elaborations of the basic search procedure described in the last chapter are then required. First, we need to be especially careful about how we formulate such problems for search; second, we have to have methods for representing large search graphs implicitly; and, third, we need to use efficient methods for searching such large graphs.

In some planning problems, like the one about block stacking, it is not too difficult to conceive of data structures for representing the different world states and the actions that change them. Typically though, finding representations that result in manageable state–space graphs is difficult. Doing so requires careful analysis of the problem—taking into account symmetries, ignoring irrelevant details, and finding appropriate abstractions. Unfortunately, the task of setting up problems for search is largely an art that still requires human participation.

In addition to problems involving agents stacking blocks, sliding tile problems are often used to illustrate how state–space search is used to plan action sequences. For variety, I will use problems of this sort in this and the next chapter. A typical example is the Fifteen-puzzle, which consists of fifteen tiles set in a four-by-four array—leaving one empty or blank cell into which an adjacent tile can be slid. The task is to find a sequence of tile movements that transforms an initial disposition of tiles into some particular arrangement. The Eight-puzzle is a reduced version, with eight tiles in a three-by-three array. Suppose the object of the puzzle is to slide tiles from the starting configuration until the goal configuration is reached, as shown in Figure 8.1.

Figure 8.1

Start and Goal Configurations for the Eight–Puzzle

In this problem, an obvious iconic state description would be a three–by–three array in which each cell contains one of the numbers 1 through 8 or a symbol representing the blank space. A goal state is the array representing the configuration on the right side of Figure 8.1. The moves between states correspond to sliding a tile into the blank cell. As mentioned, we often have representational choices in setting up the state space of a problem. In the Eight–puzzle, we might imagine that we have 8×4 different moves, namely, move 1 up, move 1 down, move 1 left, move 1 right, move 2 up, . . . , and so on. (Of course, not all of these moves are possible in any given state.) A more compact formulation involves only four different moves, namely, move blank left, move blank up, move blank right, move blank down. A given start state and the set of possible moves implicitly define the graph of states accessible from the start. The number of nodes in the state–space graph for this representation of the Eight–puzzle is 9! = 362,880. (It happens that the state space for the Eight–puzzle is divided into two separate graphs; a tile configuration in one graph cannot be reached from one in the other graph.)

8.2   *Components of Implicit State-Space Graphs*

That part of a state–space graph reachable by actions from the start state is represented implicitly by a description of the start state and by descriptions of the effects of actions that can be taken in any state. Thus, it is possible in principle to transform an implicit representation of a graph into an explicit one. To do so, one generates all of the nodes that are successors of the start node (by applying all possible operators at that node), then generates all of their successors, and so on. For graphs that are too large to represent explicitly, the search process need render explicit only so much of the state space as is required to find a path to the goal. The process terminates when an acceptable path to a goal node has been found.

More formally, there are three basic components to an implicit representation of a state–space graph:

1. A description with which to label the *start node*. This description is some data structure modeling the initial state of the environment.

2. Functions that transform a state description representing one state of the environment into one that represents the state resulting after an action.

These functions are usually called *operators*. In our agent problems, they are models of the effects of actions. When an operator is applied to a node, it generates one of that node's successors.

3. A *goal condition*, which can be either a *True-False*-valued function on state descriptions or a list of actual instances of state descriptions that correspond to goal states.

We will study two broad classes of search processes. In one, we have no problem–specific reason to prefer one part of the search space to any other, insofar as finding a path to the goal is concerned. Such processes are called *uninformed*. In the other, we do have problem–specific information to help focus the search. Such processes are called *heuristic*.[1] I begin with the uninformed ones and will discuss heuristic processes in the next chapter.

8.3 *Breadth-First Search*

Uninformed search procedures apply operators to nodes without using any special knowledge about the problem domain (other than knowledge about what actions are legal ones). Perhaps the simplest uninformed search procedure is *breadth-first search*. That procedure generates an explicit state-space graph by applying all possible operators to the start node, then applying all possible operators to all the direct successors of the start node, then to their successors, and so on. Search proceeds uniformly outward from the start node. Since we apply all possible operators to a node at each step, it is convenient to group them into a function called the *successor function*. The successor function, when applied to a node, produces the entire set of nodes that can be produced by applying all of the operators that can be applied to that node. Each application of a successor function to a node is called *expanding* the node.

Figure 8.2 shows the nodes created in a breadth-first search for a solution to the Eight-puzzle problem. The start and goal nodes are labeled, and the order of node expansions is shown by a numeral next to each node. Nodes of the same depth are expanded according to some fixed order. In expanding a node, I applied operators in the order: move blank left, up, right, down. Even though each move is reversible, I omit the arcs from successors back to their parents. The solution path is shown by the dark line. As we shall see, breadth–first search has the property that when a goal node is found, we have found a path of minimal length to the goal. A disadvantage of breadth–first search, however, is that it requires the generation and storage of a tree whose size is exponential in the depth of the shallowest goal node.

---

1. The word *heuristic* comes from the Greek *heuriskein*, meaning "to discover." The borrowed phrase *Eureka*! ("I have found it!") comes from the same source.

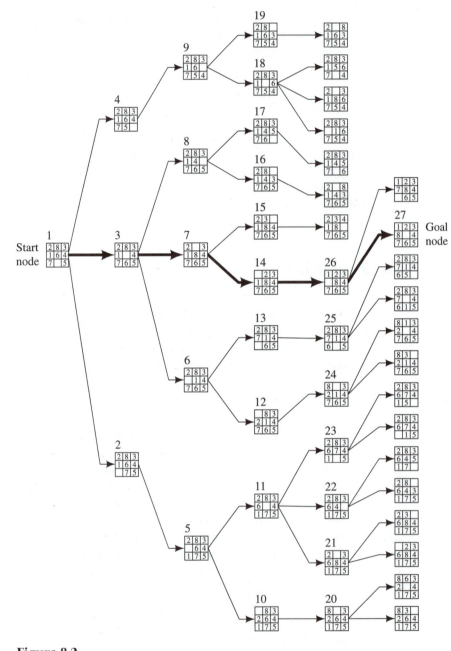

Figure 8.2

Breadth–First Search of the Eight–Puzzle

Uniform-cost search [Dijkstra 1959] is a variant of breadth–first search in which nodes are expanded outward from the start node along "contours" of equal cost rather than along contours of equal depth. If the costs of all arcs in the graph are identical (equal to 1, say), then uniform–cost search is the same as breadth–first search. Uniform-cost search, in turn, can be considered to be a special case of a heuristic search procedure, which I will describe in the next chapter. The brief presentations just given of breadth–first and uniform–cost search methods give the main idea, but they need technical elaboration to cover those cases in which node expansion produces nodes already reached previously by the search process. I defer discussion of these finer points until I deal with the more general algorithm in the next chapter.

8.4 *Depth-First or Backtracking Search*

Depth–first search generates the successors of a node just one at a time by applying individual operators. A trace is left at each node to indicate that additional operators can eventually be applied there if needed. At each node, a decision must be made about which operator to apply first, which next, and so on. As soon as a successor is generated, one of its successors is generated and so on. To prevent the search process from running away toward nodes of unbounded depth from the start node, a *depth bound* is used. No successor is generated whose depth is greater than the depth bound. (It is presumed that not all goal nodes lie beyond the depth bound.) This bound allows us to ignore parts of the search graph that have been determined not to contain a sufficiently close goal node.

I illustrate the process using the Eight–puzzle and a depth bound of 5. Again, we apply operators in the order move blank left, up, right, down, and we omit arcs from successors back to their parents. In Figure 8.3a, I show the first few node generations. The number at the left of each node shows the order in which the node is generated; I also show arcs leaving nodes that are not yet fully expanded. At node 5, we reach the depth bound without having reached the goal, so we consider the next most recently generated, but not yet fully expanded node, node 4, and generate the other of its successors, node 6. (See Figure 8.3b.) At this point, we can throw away node 5, since we are not going to generate nodes below it. Node 6 is also at the depth bound and is not a goal node, so we consider the next most recently generated but not fully expanded node, node 2, and generate node 7—throwing away node 3 and its successors since we are not going to generate any more nodes below them. Going back to node 2 is an example of what is called *chronological backtracking*. When the depth bound is reached again, we have the graph shown in Figure 8.3c. At this point, not having reached a goal node, we generate the other successor of node 8, which is not a goal node either. So, we throw away node 8 and its successors and backtrack to generate another successor of node 7. Continuing this process finally results in the graph shown in Figure 8.4.

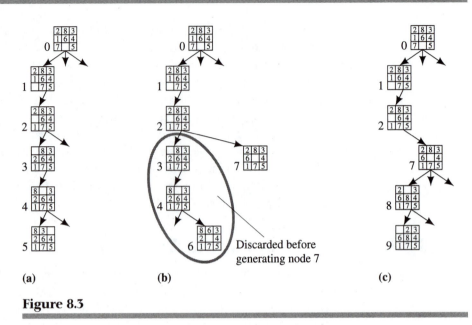

(a)   **(b)**   **(c)**

Figure 8.3

Generation of the First Few Nodes in a Depth–First Search

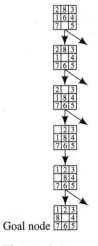

Figure 8.4

The Graph When the Goal Is Reached in Depth–First Search

Note that depth–first search obliges us to save only that part of the search tree consisting of the path currently being explored plus traces at the not yet fully expanded nodes along that path. The memory requirements of depth–first search are thus linear in the depth bound. A disadvantage of depth–first search is that when a goal is found, we are not guaranteed to have found a path to a goal having minimal length. Another problem is that we may have to explore a large part of the search space even to find a shallow goal if it is the only goal and a descendant of a shallow node expanded late in the process.

8.5   *Iterative Deepening*

A technique called *iterative deepening* [Korf 1985, Stickel & Tyson 1985] enjoys the linear memory requirements of depth–first search while guaranteeing that a goal node of minimal depth will be found (if a goal can be found at all). In iterative deepening, successive depth–first searches are conducted—each with depth bounds increasing by 1—until a goal node is found. I illustrate how iterative deepening works on a sample tree in Figure 8.5.

Surprisingly, the number of nodes expanded by iterative-deepening search is not many more than would be expanded by breadth-first search. Let's calculate this number for the (worst) case of searching a tree with uniform branching factor of b in which the shallowest goal node is at depth d and is the last node to be generated at that depth. The number of nodes expanded by a breadth-first search could be as high as

$$N_{\mathrm{bf}} = 1 + b + b^2 + \cdots + b^d = \frac{b^{d+1} - 1}{b - 1}$$

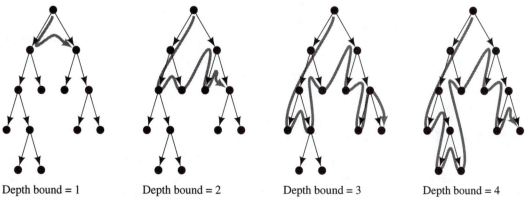

Depth bound = 1   Depth bound = 2   Depth bound = 3   Depth bound = 4

Figure 8.5

Stages in Iterative-Deepening Search

To calculate the number of nodes expanded by iterative deepening, we first note that the number of nodes expanded by a complete depth–first search down to level j is

$$N_{\text{df}_j} = \frac{b^{j+1} - 1}{b - 1}$$

In the worst case, iterative–deepening search for a goal at depth d has to conduct separate, complete depth–first searches for depths up to d. The sum of the number of nodes expanded for all of these searches is

$$N_{\text{id}} = \sum_{j=0}^{d} \frac{b^{j+1} - 1}{b - 1}$$

$$= \frac{1}{b - 1} \left[b \left(\sum_{j=0}^{d} b^j \right) - \sum_{j=0}^{d} 1 \right]$$

$$= \frac{1}{b - 1} \left[b \left(\frac{b^{d+1} - 1}{b - 1} \right) - (d + 1) \right]$$

Simplifying yields the total number of nodes that might be expanded by an iterative–deepening search for a goal of depth d:

$$N_{\text{id}} = \frac{b^{d+2} - 2b - bd + d + 1}{(b - 1)^2}$$

For large d, the ratio $N_{\text{id}}/N_{\text{bf}}$ is $b/(b - 1)$. For a branching factor of 10 and deep goals, we expand only about 11% more nodes in an iterative–deepening search than we would in a breadth–first search.

Another, related technique called *iterative broadening* is useful under certain circumstances when there are many goal nodes. I refer you to [Ginsberg & Harvey 1992, Harvey 1994] for descriptions of this method.

8.6   *Additional Readings and Discussion*

Various improvements can be made to chronological backtracking. These include *dependency-directed backtracking* [Stallman & Sussman 1977], *backjumping* [Gaschnig 1979], and *dynamic backtracking* [Ginsberg 1993]. The last–cited paper compares these methods and shows the advantages of dynamic backtracking. These en-hanced backtracking techniques are usually employed in constraint–satisfaction problems (which will be described in Chapter 11).

Exercises

8.1 In the water–jug puzzle, we are given a 3–liter jug, named *Three*, and a 4–liter jug, named *Four*. Initially, *Three* and *Four* are empty. Either jug can be filled with water from a tap, *T*, and we can discard water from either jug down a drain, *D*. Water may be poured from one jug into the other. There is no additional measuring device. We want to find a set of operations that will leave precisely two liters of water in *Four*. [Don't worry! Here's a solution: (a) fill *Three* from the tap, (b) pour *Three* into *Four*, (c) fill *Three* from the tap, (d) pour as much from *Three* into *Four* as will fill it, (e) discard *Four*, (f) pour *Three* into *Four*.]

1. Set up a state–space search formulation of the water–jug puzzle:
    (a) Give the initial iconic state description as a data structure.
    (b) Give a goal condition on states as some test on data structures.
    (c) Name the operators on states and give precise descriptions of what each operator does to a state description.

2. Draw a graph of all of the *distinct* state–space nodes that are within three moves of the start node, label each node by its state description, and show at least one path to each node in the graph—labeling each arc by the name of the appropriate operator. In addition to these nodes, show also all of the nodes and arcs (properly labeled) on a path to the solution.

8.2 List the order in which nodes are visited in the tree below for each of the following three search strategies (choosing leftmost branches first in all cases):

1. Depth–first search

2. Depth–first iterative-deepening search (increasing the depth by 1 each iteration)

3. Breadth–first search

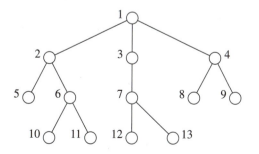

8.3 Consider a finite tree of depth *d* and branching factor *b*. (A tree consisting of only a root node has depth zero; a tree consisting of a root node and its *b* successors has depth 1; etc.) Suppose the shallowest goal node is at depth $g \leq d$.

1. What is the *minimum* and *maximum* number of nodes that might be generated by a *depth-first* search with depth bound equal to d?

2. What is the *minimum* and *maximum* number of nodes that might be generated by a *breadth-first* search?

3. What is the *minimum* and *maximum* number of nodes that might be generated by a *depth-first iterative-deepening* search? (Assume that you start with an initial depth limit of 1 and increment the depth limit by 1 each time no goal is found within the current limit.)

8.4 Assume that 10,000 nodes per second can be generated in a breadth–first search. Suppose also that 100 bytes are needed to store each node. What are the memory and time requirements for a complete breadth–first search of a tree of depth d and branching factor of 5? Show these in a table. (You can use approximate numbers when time is better expressed in hours, days, months, years, etc.)

8.5 Assume we are searching a tree with branching factor b. However, we do not know that we are really searching a tree, so we are considering checking each state description generated to see if it matches a previously generated state description. How many such checks would have to be made in a search of the tree to depth d?

9 Heuristic Search

Using Evaluation Functions

The search processes that I describe in this chapter are something like breadth-first search, except that search does not proceed uniformly outward from the start node; instead, it proceeds preferentially through nodes that heuristic, problem-specific information indicates might be on the best path to a goal. We call such processes *best-first* or *heuristic* search. Here is the basic idea.

1. We assume that we have a heuristic (evaluation) function, $\hat{f}$, to help decide which node is the best one to expand next. (The reason for the "hat" over the f will become apparent later. We pronounce $\hat{f}$ "f-hat.") We adopt the convention that small values of $\hat{f}$ indicate the best nodes. This function is based on information specific to the problem domain. It is a real-valued function of state descriptions.

2. Expand next that node, n, having the smallest value of $\hat{f}(n)$. Resolve ties arbitrarily. (I assume in this chapter that node expansion produces all of the successors of a node.)

3. Terminate when the node to be expanded next is a goal node.

People are often able to specify good evaluation functions for best-first search. In the Eight-puzzle, for example, we might try using the number of tiles out of place as a measure of the goodness of a state description:

$$\hat{f}(n) = \text{number of tiles out of place (compared with goal)}$$

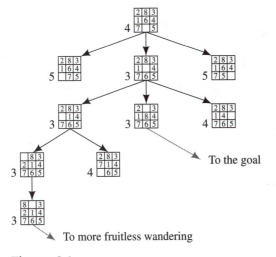

Figure 9.1

A Possible Result of a Heuristic Search Procedure

Using this heuristic function in the search procedure just described produces the graph shown in Figure 9.1. The numeral next to each node is the value of $\hat{f}$ for that node.

This example shows that we need to bias the search in favor of going back to explore early paths (in order to prevent being led "down a garden path" by an overly optimistic heuristic). So, we add a "depth factor" to $\hat{f}$: $\hat{f}(n) = \hat{g}(n) + \hat{h}(n)$, where $\hat{g}(n)$ is an estimate of the "depth" of n in the graph (that is, the length of the shortest path from the start to n), and $\hat{h}(n)$ is a heuristic evaluation of node n. If, as before, we let $\hat{h}(n)$ = number of tiles out of place (compared with the goal) and take $\hat{g}(n)$ = the depth of node n in the search graph, we get the graph shown in Figure 9.2. In this figure, I have written the values of $\hat{g}(n) + \hat{h}(n)$ next to each node. We see that search proceeds rather directly toward the goal in this case (with the exception of the circled node).

These examples raise two important questions. First, how do we settle on evaluation functions for guiding best–first search? Second, what are some properties of best–first search? Does it always result in finding good paths to a goal node? Some guidance about evaluation–function selection will be offered toward the end of the chapter, and some methods for automatically learning evaluation functions will be explained in Chapter 10. But most of the chapter will be devoted to a presentation of the formal aspects of best–first search. I begin by developing a general graph search algorithm that includes versions of best–first search as special cases. (For more details about heuristic search than a single chapter or

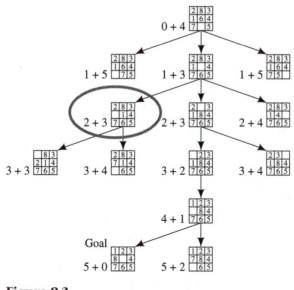

Figure 9.2

Heuristic Search Using $\hat{f}(n) = \hat{g}(n) + \hat{h}(n)$

two can provide, refer to the articles cited and to the excellent book by Pearl [Pearl 1984].)

9.2   *A General Graph-Searching Algorithm*

To be more precise about the heuristic procedures to be explained in this chapter, I need to present a general graph–searching algorithm that permits any kind of ordering the user might prefer—heuristic or uninformed. I call this algorithm GRAPHSEARCH. Here is (a first version of) its definition.

GRAPHSEARCH

1. Create a search tree, *Tr*, consisting solely of the start node, n_0. Put n_0 on an ordered list called *OPEN*.

2. Create a list called *CLOSED* that is initially empty.

3. If *OPEN* is empty, exit with failure.

4. Select the first node on *OPEN*, remove it from *OPEN*, and put it on *CLOSED*. Call this node *n*.

5. If *n* is a goal node, exit successfully with the solution obtained by tracing a path backward along the arcs in *Tr* from *n* to n_0. (Arcs are created in step 6.)

6. Expand node n, generating a set, $\mathcal{M}$, of successors. Install $\mathcal{M}$ as successors of n in Tr by creating arcs from n to each member of $\mathcal{M}$. Put these members of $\mathcal{M}$ on *OPEN*.

7. Reorder the list *OPEN*, either according to some arbitrary scheme or according to heuristic merit.

8. Go to step 3.

This algorithm can be used to perform best–first search, breadth–first search, or depth–first search. In breadth–first search, new nodes are simply put at the end of *OPEN* (first in, first out, or FIFO), and the nodes are not reordered. In depth–first-style search, new nodes are put at the beginning of *OPEN* (last in, first out, or LIFO). In best–first (also called heuristic) search, *OPEN* is reordered according to the heuristic merit of the nodes.

9.2.1   Algorithm A*

I will particularize GRAPHSEARCH to a best–first search algorithm that reorders (in step 7) the nodes on *OPEN* according to increasing values of a function $\hat{f}$, as in the Eight-puzzle illustration. I will call this version of GRAPHSEARCH, algorithm A*. As we shall see, it will be possible to define $\hat{f}$ functions that will make A* perform either breadth–first or uniform–cost search. In order to specify the family of $\hat{f}$ functions to be used, I must first introduce some additional notation.

Let $h(n) =$ the *actual* cost of the minimal cost path between node n and a goal node (over all possible goal nodes and over all possible paths from n to them).

Let $g(n) =$ the cost of a minimal cost path from the start node, n_0, to node n.

Then $f(n) = g(n) + h(n)$ is the cost of a minimal cost path from n_0 to a goal node over all paths that are constrained to go through node n. Note that $f(n_0) = h(n_0)$ is then the cost of an (unconstrained) minimal cost path from n_0 to a goal node.

For each node, n, let $\hat{h}(n)$ (the heuristic factor) be some estimate of $h(n)$, and let $\hat{g}(n)$ (the depth factor) be the cost of the lowest–cost path found by A* so far to node n. In algorithm A* we use $\hat{f} = \hat{g} + \hat{h}$. Note that algorithm A* with $\hat{h}$ identically 0 gives uniform–cost search. These definitions are illustrated in Figure 9.3.

The search process for the Eight-puzzle illustrated in Figure 9.2 is an example of an application of A*. There, I assumed unit arc costs, so $g(n)$ is simply the depth of node n in the graph. There is a slight complication, though, which I have overlooked in the definition of algorithm A*. What happens if the implicit graph being searched is not a tree? That is, suppose there is more than one sequence of actions that can lead to the same world state from the starting state. For example, the implicit graph of the Eight-puzzle is obviously not a tree because the actions are reversible—each of the successors of any node, n, has n as one of its successors. I ignored these loops in creating the Eight-puzzle search tree. They

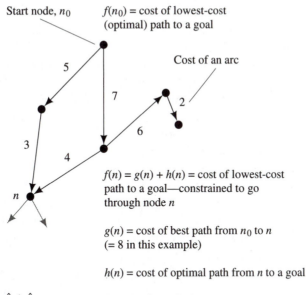

Start node, n_0 $f(n_0)$ = cost of lowest-cost
(optimal) path to a goal

Cost of an arc

5

7

2

3

6

4

$f(n) = g(n) + h(n)$ = cost of lowest-cost
path to a goal—constrained to go
through node n

n

$g(n)$ = cost of best path from n_0 to n
(= 8 in this example)

$h(n)$ = cost of optimal path from n to a goal

$\hat{f}, \hat{g}, \hat{h}$ are estimates of f, g, h, respectively

$\hat{f} = \hat{g} + \hat{h}$

Figure 9.3

Heuristic Search Notation

were easy to ignore in that case; I simply did not include the parent of a node among its successors. Instead of step 6 as written in GRAPHSEARCH, I actually used

6. Expand node n, generating a set, $\mathcal{M}$, of successors that are not already parents of n in Tr. Install $\mathcal{M}$ as successors of n in Tr by creating arcs from n to each member of $\mathcal{M}$. Put these members of $\mathcal{M}$ on *OPEN*.

To take care of longer loops, we replace step 6 by

6. Expand node n, generating a set, $\mathcal{M}$, of successors that are not already ancestors of n in Tr. Install $\mathcal{M}$ as successors of n in Tr by creating arcs from n to each member of $\mathcal{M}$. Put these members of $\mathcal{M}$ on *OPEN*.

Of course, to check for these longer loops, we need to see if the data structure labeling each successor of node n is equal to the data structure labeling any of node n's ancestors. For complex data structures, this step can add to the complexity of the algorithm.

The modified step 6 prevents the algorithm from going around in circles in its search for a path to the goal. But there is still the possibility of visiting the same world state via different paths. One way to deal with this problem is simply to ignore it. That is, the algorithm doesn't check to see if a node in $\mathcal{M}$ is already on *OPEN* or *CLOSED*. The algorithm is then oblivious to the possibility that it might reach the same node via different paths. This "same node" might then be repeated in *Tr* as many times as the algorithm discovers different paths to it. If two nodes in *Tr* are labeled by the same data structure, they will have identical subtrees hanging below them. That is, the algorithm will duplicate search effort that it need not have repeated. We will see later that under very reasonable conditions on $\hat{f}$, when A* first expands a node n in *Tr*, it has already discovered a path to node n having the smallest value of $\hat{f}$.

To prevent duplicated search effort when these yet–to–be–mentioned conditions on $\hat{f}$ do not prevail requires some modification to algorithm A*. Because search might reach the same node along different paths, algorithm A* generates a search graph, which we call G. G is the structure of nodes and arcs generated by A* as it expands the start node, its successors, and so on. A* also maintains a search tree, *Tr*. *Tr*, a subgraph of G, is the tree of best (minimal cost) paths produced so far to all of the nodes in the search graph. I show examples for a graph having unit arc costs in Figure 9.4. An early stage of search is shown in Figure 9.4a. The search–tree part of the search graph is indicated by the dark arcs; gray arcs are in the search graph but not the search tree. The dark arcs indicate the least costly paths found so far to the nodes in the search graph. Note that node 4 in Figure 9.4a has been reached by two paths; both paths are in the search graph, but only one is in the search tree. We keep the search graph because subsequent search may find shorter paths that use some of the arcs in the earlier search graph that were not in the earlier search tree. For example, in Figure 9.4b, expanding node 1 finds shorter paths to node 2 and its descendants (including node 4), so the search tree is changed accordingly.

For completeness, I state the version of A* that maintains the search graph. We note, however, that this version is seldom needed because we can usually impose conditions on $\hat{f}$ that guarantee that when algorithm A* expands a node, it has already found the least costly path to that node.

Algorithm A*

1. Create a search graph, G, consisting solely of the start node, n_0. Put n_0 on a list called *OPEN*.

2. Create a list called *CLOSED* that is initially empty.

3. If *OPEN* is empty, exit with failure.

4. Select the first node on *OPEN*, remove it from *OPEN*, and put it on *CLOSED*. Call this node n.

5. If n is a goal node, exit successfully with the solution obtained by tracing a path along the pointers from n to n_0 in G. (The pointers define a search tree and are established in step 7.)

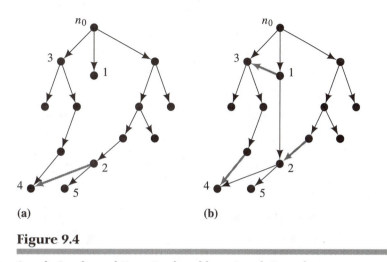

Figure 9.4

Search Graphs and Trees Produced by a Search Procedure

6. Expand node n, generating the set, M, of its successors that are not already ancestors of n in G. Install these members of M as successors of n in G.

7. Establish a pointer to n from each of those members of M that were not already in G (i.e., not already on either *OPEN* or *CLOSED*). Add these members of M to *OPEN*. For each member, m, of M that was already on *OPEN* or *CLOSED*, redirect its pointer to n if the best path to m found so far is through n. For each member of M already on *CLOSED*, redirect the pointers of each of its descendants in G so that they point backward along the best paths found so far to these descendants.

8. Reorder the list *OPEN* in order of increasing $\hat{f}$ values. (Ties among minimal $\hat{f}$ values are resolved in favor of the deepest node in the search tree.)

9. Go to step 3.

In step 7, we redirect pointers from a node if the search process discovers a path to that node having lower cost than the one indicated by the existing pointers. Redirecting pointers of descendants of nodes already on *CLOSED* saves subsequent search effort but at the possible expense of an exponential amount of computation. Hence this part of step 7 is often not implemented. Some of these pointers will ultimately be redirected in any case as the search progresses.

9.2.2   **Admissibility of** A*

There are conditions on graphs and on $\hat{h}$ that guarantee that algorithm A* applied to these graphs always finds minimal cost paths. The conditions on the graphs are

1. Each node in the graph has a finite number of successors (if any).

2. All arcs in the graph have costs greater than some positive amount, ϵ.

The condition on $\hat{h}$ is

3. For all nodes n in the search graph, $\hat{h}(n) \le h(n)$. That is, $\hat{h}$ never over-estimates the actual value, h. (Such an $\hat{h}$ function is sometimes called an *optimistic estimator*.)

Often, it is not difficult to find an $\hat{h}$ function that satisfies this lower bound condition. For example, in route–finding problems over a graph whose nodes consist of cities, the straight–line distance from a city, n, to a goal city is a lower bound on the distance of an optimal route from n to the goal node. In the Eight–puzzle, the number of tiles out of place is a lower bound on the number of steps remaining to the goal.

With these three conditions, algorithm A* is guaranteed to find an optimal path to a goal, if any path to a goal exists. I can state this result as a theorem. (I give a new version of a proof of this theorem next; for the original proof, see [Hart, Nilsson, & Raphael 1968].)

Theorem 9.1

Under the conditions on graphs and on $\hat{h}$ stated earlier, and providing there is a path with finite cost from the start node, n_0, to a goal node, algorithm A is guaranteed to terminate with a minimal-cost path to a goal.*

Proof: The main component of the proof is the following important lemma. It is important to understand this lemma thoroughly in order to gain intuition about why A* is guaranteed to find optimal paths.

Lemma 9.1

At every step before termination of A, there is always a node, say, n^*, on OPEN with the following properties:*

1. *n^* is on an optimal path to a goal.*

2. *A* has found an optimal path to n^*.*

3. *$\hat{f}(n^*) \le f(n_0)$.*

Proof of Lemma: To prove that the conclusions of the lemma hold at every step of A*, it suffices to prove that (1) they hold at the beginning of the algorithm and (2) if they hold before a node expansion, they will continue to hold after a node expansion. We call this kind of proof, proof by *mathematical induction*. Here is how it goes.

Base case: At the beginning of search (when just node n_0 has been selected for expansion), node n_0 is on *OPEN*, it is on an optimal path to the goal, and A*

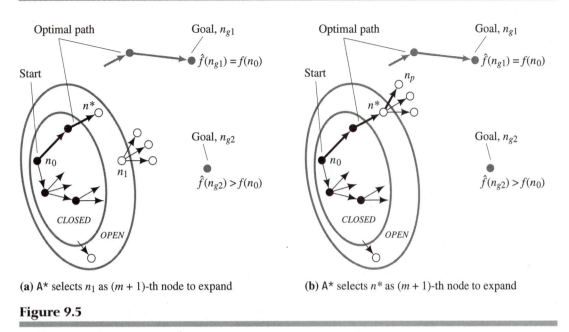

(a) A* selects n_1 as $(m + 1)$-th node to expand   **(b)** A* selects n^* as $(m + 1)$-th node to expand

Figure 9.5

The Situation When the $(m + 1)$-th Node Is Selected for Expansion

has found this path. Also $\hat{f}(n_0) \le f(n_0)$ because $\hat{f}(n_0) = \hat{h}(n_0) \le f(n_0)$. Thus, node n_0 can be the node n^* of the lemma at this stage.

Induction step: We assume the conclusions of the lemma at the time m nodes have been expanded ($m \ge 0$) and (using this assumption) prove them true at the time $m + 1$ nodes have been expanded. It may be helpful to refer to Figure 9.5 as we prove the induction step.

We let n^* be the hypothesized node on *OPEN*, which is on an optimal path found by A* after it has expanded m nodes. Now, if n^* is not selected for expansion on the $(m + 1)$-th step (Figure 9.5a), n^* has the same properties as before, thus proving the induction step for that case. If n^* is selected for expansion (Figure 9.5b), all of its new successors will be put on *OPEN*, and at least one of them, say, n_p, will be on an optimal path to a goal (since an optimal path is hypothesized to go through n^* and it must continue through one of its successors). And A* has found an optimal path to n_p because, if there were a better path to n_p, that better path would also be a better path to a goal (contradicting our hypothesis that there is no better path to the goal than the one A* has found through n^*). So, in this case, we let n_p be the new n^* for the $(m + 1)$-th step, and we have proved the induction step except for the property that $\hat{f}(n^*) \le f(n_0)$.

We prove that property now for all steps m before termination. For any node, n^*, on an optimal path and to which A* has found an optimal path, we have

$\hat{f}(n^*) = \hat{g}(n^*) + \hat{h}(n^*)$ by definition

$\leq g(n^*) + h(n^*)$ because $\hat{g}(n^*) = g(n^*)$ and $\hat{h}(n^*) \leq h(n^*)$

$\leq f(n^*)$ since $g(n^*) + h(n^*) = f(n^*)$ by definition

$\leq f(n_0)$ because $f(n^*) = f(n_0)$ since n^* is on an optimal path

which completes a proof of the lemma.   ▣

Continuing now with the proof of the theorem, we prove first that A* must terminate if there is an accessible goal, and then that it terminates by finding an optimal path to a goal.

- A* must terminate: Suppose it does not terminate. In that case, A* continues to expand nodes on *OPEN* forever and would eventually expand nodes deeper in the search tree than any preset finite depth bound—since we have assumed that the graph being searched has finite branching factor. Since the cost of each arc is larger than $\epsilon > 0$, the $\hat{g}$ (and thus the $\hat{f}$) values of all nodes on *OPEN* will eventually exceed $f(n_0)$. But that would contradict the lemma.

- A* terminates in an optimal path: A* can terminate only in step 3 (if *OPEN* is empty) or in step 5 (in a goal node). A step 3 termination can occur only for finite graphs containing no goal node, and the theorem claims to find an optimal path to a goal only if there is a goal node. Therefore, A* terminates by finding a goal node. Suppose it terminates by finding a nonoptimal goal, say, n_{g2} with $f(n_{g2}) > f(n_0)$ when there is an optimal goal, say, $n_{g1} \neq n_{g2}$ with $f(n_{g1}) = f(n_0)$ (see Figure 9.5 again). At termination in n_{g2}, $\hat{f}(n_{g2}) \geq f(n_{g2}) > f(n_0)$. But just before A* selected n_{g2} for expansion, by the lemma there was a node n^* on *OPEN* and on an optimal path with $\hat{f}(n^*) \leq f(n_0)$. Thus, A* could not have selected n_{g2} for expansion because A* always selects that node having the smallest value of $\hat{f}$ and $\hat{f}(n^*) \leq f(n_0) < f(n_{g2})$.   ▣

This completes the proof of the theorem. We say that any algorithm that is guaranteed to find an optimal path to the goal is *admissible*. Thus, with the three conditions of the theorem, A* is admissible. By extension, we say that any $\hat{h}$ function that does not overestimate h is admissible. From now on, when I talk about applying A*, I assume that the three conditions of the theorem are satisfied.

If two versions of A*, namely, A_1^* and A_2^*, differ only in that $\hat{h}_1 < \hat{h}_2$ for all nongoal nodes, we will say that A_2^* is *more informed* than A_1^*. I state the following result without proof (see [Hart, Nilsson, & Raphael 1968, Hart, Nilsson, & Raphael 1972, Nilsson 1980]).

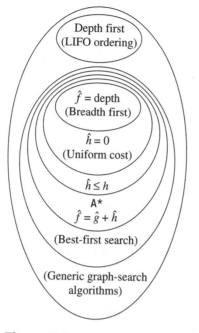

Figure 9.6

Relationships Among Search Algorithms

Theorem 9.2

If A_2^* is more informed than A_1^*, then at the termination of their searches on any graph having a path from n_0 to a goal node, every node expanded by A_2^* is also expanded by A_1^*.

It follows that A_1^* expands at least as many nodes as does A_2^*, and thus A_2^*, the more informed algorithm, is typically more efficient. Thus, we seek an $\hat{h}$ function whose values are as close as possible to those of the actual h function (for search efficiency), while still not exceeding them (for admissibility). Of course, in measuring *total* search efficiency, we should also take into account the cost of computing $\hat{h}$. The most informed algorithm would have $\hat{h} \equiv h$, but, typically, such an $\hat{h}$ function could be obtained only at high cost by completing the very search we are attempting!

Figure 9.6 summarizes relationships among some of the search algorithms we have discussed. When $\hat{h} \equiv 0$ for all nodes, we have a uniform–cost algorithm. (The search spreads out along contours of equal cost.) When $\hat{f}(n) = \hat{g}(n) = \text{depth}(n)$, we have breadth–first search, which spreads out along contours of equal depth. Both the uniform–cost and breadth–first algorithms are special cases of A^* (with $\hat{h} \equiv 0$), so, of course, they are both admissible.

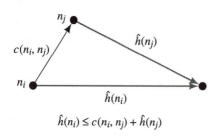

$$\hat{h}(n_i) \leq c(n_i, n_j) + \hat{h}(n_j)$$

Figure 9.7

The Consistency Condition

9.2.3   The Consistency (or Monotone) Condition

Consider a pair of nodes such that n_j is a successor of n_i. We say that $\hat{h}$ obeys the *consistency condition* if, for all such pairs in the search graph,

$$\hat{h}(n_i) - \hat{h}(n_j) \leq c(n_i, n_j)$$

where $c(n_i, n_j)$ is the cost of the arc from n_i to n_j. We could also write

$$\hat{h}(n_i) \leq \hat{h}(n_j) + c(n_i, n_j)$$

and

$$\hat{h}(n_j) \geq \hat{h}(n_i) - c(n_i, n_j)$$

This condition states that along any path in the search graph, our estimate of the optimal (remaining) cost to the goal cannot decrease by more than the arc cost along that path. That is, the heuristic function is locally consistent taking into account the known cost of an arc.[1] The consistency condition can also be thought of as a type of triangle inequality as shown in Figure 9.7.

The consistency condition also implies that the $\hat{f}$ values of the nodes in the search tree are monotonically nondecreasing as we move away from the start node. Let n_i and n_j be two nodes in the search tree generated by **A*** with n_j a successor of n_i. Then, if the consistency condition is satisfied, $\hat{f}(n_j) \geq \hat{f}(n_i)$. To prove this fact, we start with the consistency condition:

$$\hat{h}(n_j) \geq \hat{h}(n_i) - c(n_i, n_j)$$

We then add $\hat{g}(n_j)$ to both sides:

$$\hat{h}(n_j) + \hat{g}(n_j) \geq \hat{h}(n_i) + \hat{g}(n_j) - c(n_i, n_j)$$

---

1. Pearl [Pearl 1984, pp. 82–83] defines a notion of *global* consistency of the heuristic function and shows that it is equivalent to our definition of (local) consistency.

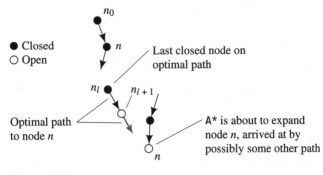

Figure 9.8

Graph Used in Proof of Theorem 9.3

But $\hat{g}(n_j) = \hat{g}(n_i) + c(n_i, n_j)$. (We might worry that $\hat{g}(n_j)$ might be lower than this value because we might have arrived at n_j along some path less costly than that through n_i. But then n_j would not be a successor of n_i in the search *tree*.) Thus,

$$\hat{f}(n_j) \geq \hat{f}(n_i)$$

For this reason, the consistency condition (on $\hat{h}$) is often called the monotone condition (on $\hat{f}$).

We have an important theorem involving the consistency condition ([Hart, Nilsson, & Raphael 1968]).

Theorem 9.3

If the consistency condition on $\hat{h}$ is satisfied, then when A* expands a node n, it has already found an optimal path to n.

Proof: Suppose A* is about to expand an open node, n, in a search for an optimal path from a start node, n_0, to a goal node in an implicit graph, G. Let $\xi = (n_0, n_1, \ldots, n_l, n_{l+1}, \ldots, n = n_k)$ be a sequence of nodes in G constituting an optimal path from n_0 to n. Let n_l be the last node on ξ expanded by A*. (See Figure 9.8.) Because n_l is the last closed node on ξ, we know that n_{l+1} is on *OPEN* and thus a candidate for expansion.

For any node, n_i, and its successor, n_{i+1}, in ξ (an optimal path to n), we have

$$g(n_{i+1}) + \hat{h}(n_{i+1}) = g(n_i) + c(n_i, n_{i+1}) + \hat{h}(n_{i+1})$$

$$\geq g(n_i) + \hat{h}(n_i) \text{ when the consistency condition is satisfied}$$

Transitivity of the $\geq$ relation gives us

$$g(n_j) + \hat{h}(n_j) \geq g(n_i) + \hat{h}(n_i) \text{ for any } n_i \text{ and } n_j \text{ on } \xi \text{ if } i < j$$

In particular,

$$g(n) + \hat{h}(n) \geq g(n_{l+1}) + \hat{h}(n_{l+1}) = \hat{f}(n_{l+1}) \text{ because A* has found an}$$

optimal path to n_{l+1}, making $\hat{g}(n_{l+1}) = g(n_{l+1})$

But since A* is about to expand node n instead of node n_{l+1}, it must be the case that

$$\hat{f}(n) = \hat{g}(n) + \hat{h}(n) \leq \hat{f}(n_{l+1})$$

But we have already established that

$$\hat{f}(n_{l+1}) \leq g(n) + \hat{h}(n)$$

Therefore,

$$\hat{g}(n) \leq g(n)$$

But since our method for computing the $\hat{g}$'s implies that $\hat{g}(n) \geq g(n)$, it must be the case that

$$\hat{g}(n) = g(n)$$

which completes the proof, showing either that $n_{l+1} = n$ or that we must already have found some other optimal path to node n. ■

The consistency condition is important because when it is satisfied, A* never has to redirect pointers (in step 7). Searching a graph is then no different from searching a tree.

With the consistency condition satisfied, we can give a simple, intuitive argument for the admissibility of A*. It goes like this:

1. Monotonicity of $\hat{f}$ implies that search expands outward along contours of increasing $\hat{f}$ values.

2. Thus, the first goal node selected will be a goal node having a minimal $\hat{f}$ value.

3. For any goal node, n_g, $\hat{f}(n_g) = \hat{g}(n_g)$. (Here, we use the fact that if the $\hat{h}$ function is consistent it will also never be greater than the true h function [Pearl 1984, p. 83].)

4. Thus, the first goal node selected will be one having minimal $\hat{g}$ value.

5. As a consequence of Theorem 9.3, whenever (in particular) a goal node, n_g, is selected for expansion, we have found an optimal path to that goal node. That is, $\hat{g}(n_g) = g(n_g)$.

6. Thus, the first goal node selected will be one for which the algorithm has found an optimal path.

Many heuristic functions satisfy the consistency condition. For example, the "tiles–out–of–place" function in the Eight–puzzle does. When a heuristic function does not satisfy the consistency condition, but is otherwise admissible, then (using an idea proposed by Mérõ [Mérõ 1984]) we can adjust it (during search) to one that does satisfy the consistency condition. Suppose, at every step of A* we check the $\hat{h}$ values of the successors of the node, say, n, just expanded. Any of these whose $\hat{h}$ values are smaller than $\hat{h}(n)$ minus the arc cost from n to that successor will have their $\hat{h}$ values adjusted (during search) so that they are exactly equal to $\hat{h}(n)$ minus that arc cost. (But it is possible that a node on *CLOSED* that has its $\hat{h}$ value adjusted in this way may have to be moved back to *OPEN*.) I leave it to you to verify that this adjustment leaves the algorithm admissible.

9.2.4   Iterative–Deepening A*

In Chapter 8, I stated that the memory requirements of breadth–first search grew exponentially with the depth of the goal in the search space. Heuristic search has the same disadvantage although good heuristics do reduce the branching factor. Iterative–deepening search, introduced in Chapter 8, allows us to find minimal–cost paths with memory that grows only linearly with the depth of the goal. A method called *iterative-deepening* A* (IDA*), proposed by [Korf 1985], can achieve a similar benefit for heuristic search. Further efficiencies can be gained by using a parallel implementation of IDA* (see [Powley, Ferguson, & Korf 1993]).

The method works in a manner similar to ordinary iterative deepening. We execute a series of depth–first searches. In the first search, we establish a "cost cut–off" equal to $\hat{f}(n_0) = \hat{g}(n_0) + \hat{h}(n_0) = \hat{h}(n_0)$, where n_0 is the start node. For all we know, the cost of an optimal path to a goal may equal this cut–off value. (It will if $h(n_0) = \hat{h}(n_0)$; it cannot be less because $h(n_0) \geq \hat{h}(n_0)$.) We expand nodes in depth–first fashion—backtracking whenever the $\hat{f}$ value of a successor of an expanded node exceeds the cut–off value. If this depth–first search terminates at a goal node, it obviously has found a minimal–cost path to a goal. If it does not, then the cost of an optimal path must be greater than the cut–off value. So, we increase the cut–off value and start another depth–first search. What is the next possibility for the cost of an optimal path? It might be as low as the lowest of the $\hat{f}$ values of the nodes visited (but not expanded) in the previous depth–first search. The node having this lowest $\hat{f}$ value might be on an optimal path (now that we know that no optimal path exists having cost equal to the previous cut–off value). This lowest $\hat{f}$ value is used as the new cut–off value in the next depth–first search. And so on. Intuitively, it is easy to see that IDA* is guaranteed to find a minimal–cost path to a goal. ([Korf 1985] presents a proof of this result, as does [Korf 1993]. The latter work also discusses limitations of iterative deepening in the case in which the monotone condition is not satisfied and presents an alternative algorithm called *recursive best-first search*.)

IDA* does have to repeat node expansions, but (as with ordinary iterative deepening) there are potential tradeoffs involving the reduced memory requirements and the implementational efficiencies of depth–first search (as compared with breadth–first search). But note what happens in the case in which all of the $\hat{f}$ values are different for each node in the search space—the number of iterations can equal the number of nodes having $\hat{f}$ values less than the cost of an optimal path! (There are ways to ameliorate this problem at the price of giving up admissibility. I leave it to you to invent how this might be done.)

9.2.5   Recursive Best–First Search

A search method proposed by Korf called *recursive best-first search*, RBFS ([Korf 1993]), uses slightly more memory than does IDA* but generates fewer nodes than does IDA*. When a node, say, n, is expanded, RBFS computes the $\hat{f}$ values of the successors of n and recomputes the $\hat{f}$ values of n and all of n's ancestors in the search tree. This recomputation process is called *backing up* the $\hat{f}$ values. Backing up is done as follows: The backed–up value of a successor of the node just expanded is simply the $\hat{f}$ value of that successor. The backed–up value, $\hat{f}(m)$, of node m in the search tree with successors m_i is

$$\hat{f}(m) = \min_{m_i} \hat{f}(m_i)$$

where $\hat{f}(m_i)$ is the backed–up value of node m_i.

If one of those successors of node n (which was just expanded) has the smallest value of $\hat{f}$ over all *OPEN* nodes, it is expanded in turn, and so on. But suppose some other *OPEN* node, say, n'—not a successor of n—has the lowest value of $\hat{f}$. In that case, the algorithm backtracks to the lowest common ancestor, say, node k, of nodes n' and n. Let node k_n be the successor of node k on the path to n. RBFS removes the subtree rooted at k_n, k_n becomes an *OPEN* node with $\hat{f}$ value equal to its backed–up value, and search continues below that *OPEN* node, namely, n', with the lowest value of $\hat{f}$.

I illustrate the main idea of this algorithm in Figure 9.9. At all times, the search tree consists of a single path of nodes plus the siblings of all nodes on the path. Thus, the storage requirements are still linear in the length of the best path explored so far. The tip nodes are all on *OPEN*, and all nodes in the search tree have associated backed–up $\hat{f}$ values.

For a review of and citations to other space–efficient search algorithms, see [Korf 1996].

Start node   Backed-up $\hat{f}$ values

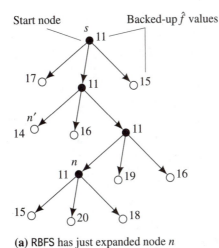

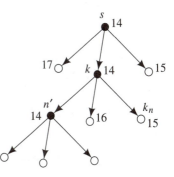

(a) RBFS has just expanded node n but has not yet backed up the $\hat{f}$ values of its successors

(b) $\hat{f}$ values have been backed up, the subtree below k_n has been discarded, and search continues below n'

Figure 9.9

Recursive Best–First Search

9.3   *Heuristic Functions and Search Efficiency*

The selection of the heuristic function is crucial in determining the efficiency of A*. Using $\hat{h} \equiv 0$ assures admissibility but results in a uniform–cost search and is thus usually inefficient. Setting $\hat{h}$ equal to the highest possible lower bound on h expands the fewest nodes consistent with maintaining admissibility. In the Eight–puzzle, for example, the function $\hat{h}(n) = W(n)$ (where $W(n)$ is the number of tiles in the wrong place) is a lower bound on $h(n)$, but it does not provide a very good estimate of the difficulty (in terms of number of steps to the goal) of a tile configuration. A better estimate is the function $\hat{h}(n) = P(n)$, where $P(n)$ is the sum of the (Manhattan) distances that each tile is from "home" (ignoring intervening pieces).

Early in the history of AI, [Newell, Shaw, & Simon 1959, Newell 1964] suggested using a simplified model to form a "plan" to guide search. Similar ideas, applied to the problem of finding a good heuristic function, are described by [Gaschnig 1979] and by [Pearl 1984, Ch. 4]. For example, we can relax the conditions of the Eight–puzzle by allowing less restrictive tile movements. If we allow a tile to move directly (in one step) to its goal square, then the number of steps to the goal is just the sum of the number of tiles in the wrong place, $W(n)$. A less relaxed (and therefore better) model allows tiles to move to an adjacent square even though there may already be a tile there. The number of steps to a goal for this model is the sum of the distances that each tile is from its goal square, $P(n)$. These models show how an agent might automatically calculate the $\hat{h}$ functions we intuitively guessed. Pearl points out that we might have calculated an $\hat{h}$ function that is slightly better than $W(n)$ by using a model in which any tile can be swapped with the blank position in one move. Another less relaxed model would be one in which tiles can move only to the position of the blank cell along a path of adjacent cells—counting each position along the path as a move.

The use of Euclidean (straight-line) distances as $\hat{h}$ functions in road–map navigation problems can also be explained by relaxed models. Instead of having to travel over existing roads, a traveler in a relaxed model can "tele–transport" directly to any city using a straight-line distance. Since solutions in relaxed models are never more costly than solutions in the original problem, the $\hat{h}$ functions so selected are always admissible! It turns out that they are also consistent, so algorithms using them do not have to revisit previously expanded nodes.

In selecting an $\hat{h}$ function, we must take into consideration the amount of effort involved in calculating it. The less relaxed the model, the better will be the heuristic function—although typically the more difficult it will be to calculate. The absolute minimum number of node expansions is achieved if one uses a heuristic function identically equal to h, but the calculation of such an $\hat{h}$ would require solving the original problem. There is usually a tradeoff between the benefits gained by an accurate $\hat{h}$ function and the cost of computing it.

Often, search efficiency can be gained at the expense of admissibility by using some function for $\hat{h}$ that is not a lower bound on h. That is, a possibly nonoptimal path might be easier to find than would be a guaranteed optimal one. And an $\hat{h}$ function that is not a lower bound on h might be easier to compute than one that is a lower bound. In these cases, efficiency might be doubly improved—because the total number of nodes expanded can be reduced (albeit at the expense of admissibility) and because the computational effort is reduced.

Another possibility is to modify the relative weights of $\hat{g}$ and $\hat{h}$ in the evaluation function. That is, we use $\hat{f} = \hat{g} + w\hat{h}$, where w is a positive number. Very large values of w overemphasize the heuristic component, whereas very small values of w give the search a predominantly breadth-first character. Experimental evidence suggests that search efficiency is often enhanced by allowing the value of w to vary inversely with the depth of a node in the search tree. At shallow depths, the search relies mainly on the heuristic component, whereas at greater depths, the search becomes increasingly breadth first, to ensure that some path to a goal will eventually be found.

We might think that search efficiency could be improved by conducting simultaneous searches from both the start node and a goal node. Such improvements can, typically, be achieved only for breadth–first searches. When a breadth–first search is used in both directions, we can be assured that the

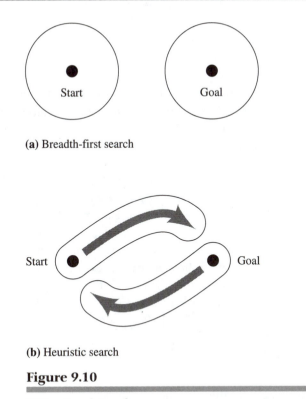

(a) Breadth-first search

(b) Heuristic search

Figure 9.10

Bidirectional Searches

search frontiers meet somewhere between start and goal (see Figure 9.10a), and termination conditions have been established so that the breadth–first bidirectional search is guaranteed to find an optimal path [Pohl 1971]. But if heuristic search is initiated at both start and goal nodes, the two search frontiers might not meet to produce an optimal path if the heuristic tends to focus the searches in inappropriate directions. (See Figure 9.10b.)

A useful measure of search efficiency is the *effective branching factor*, B. It describes how sharply a search process is focussed toward the goal. Suppose that search finds a path of length d and generates a total of N nodes. B is then equal to the number of successors of each node in that tree having the following properties:

- Each nonleaf node in the tree has the same number (B) of successors.
- The leaf nodes in the tree are all of depth d.
- The total number of nodes in the tree is N.

Therefore, B is related to path length d and to the total number of nodes generated, N, by the expressions

$$B + B^2 + \cdots + B^d = N$$

$$\frac{(B^d - 1)B}{(B - 1)} = N$$

Although B cannot be written explicitly as a function of d and N, a plot of B versus N for various values of d is given in Figure 9.11. A value of B near unity corresponds to a search that is highly focussed toward the goal, with very little branching in other directions. On the other hand, a "bushy" search graph would have a high B value.

To the extent that the effective branching factor is reasonably independent of path length, it can be used to give an estimate of how many nodes might be generated in searches of various lengths. For example, we can use Figure 9.11 to calculate that the use of the evaluation function $\hat{f}(n) = \hat{g}(n) + W(n)$ results in a B value equal to 1.2 for the Eight–puzzle problem illustrated in Figure 9.2. Suppose we wanted to estimate how many nodes would be generated using this same evaluation function in solving a more difficult Eight–puzzle problem, say, one requiring 30 steps. From Figure 9.11, we note that the 30–step puzzle would involve the generation of about 2000 nodes, assuming that the effective branching factor remained constant.

To summarize, there are three important factors influencing the efficiency of algorithm A*:

- The cost (or length) of the path found
- The number of nodes expanded in finding the path
- The computational effort required to compute $\hat{h}$

The selection of a suitable heuristic function permits us to balance these factors to maximize search efficiency.

All of the search methods discussed so far, including the heuristic ones, have $O(n)$ time complexity, where n is the number of nodes generated (assuming that the heuristic function can be computed in constant time). In particular, the complexity is $O(B^d)$ for breadth–first search when the effective branching factor is B, the arc costs are all equal, and goals are of depth d away from the start node. For uniform–cost search (that is, $\hat{h} \equiv 0$) and unequal arc costs, the complexity is $O(B^{C/c})$, where C is the cost of an optimal solution and c is the cost of the least costly arc [Korf 1992]. For many problems of practical interest, d (or C/c) is sufficiently large to make search (even heuristic search) for optimal solutions computationally infeasible. For example, if we are using search to compute the best next action (out of, say, four choices) when the goal being sought is 15 actions away, the search algorithm may have to expand as many as $4^{15} \approx 10^9$ nodes. Such lengthy calculations might not be practical in cases in which an agent must make a decision in a fraction of a second. Space complexity for A* is of the same order as time complexity because all nodes expanded have to be stored in a tree structure.

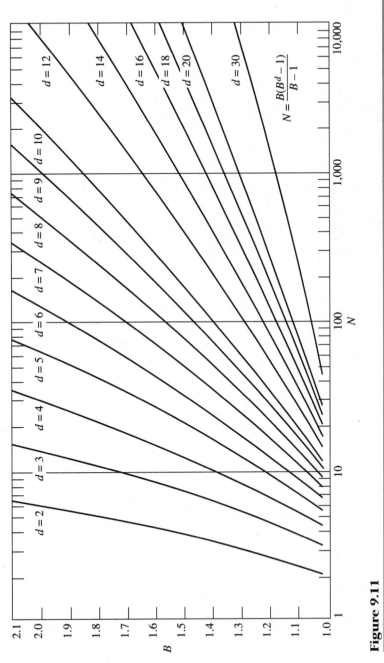

Figure 9.11

B Versus N for Various Values of d

Since agents will have time and memory bounds on their computational resources, it will be impossible to find optimal solutions for many tasks. Instead, it will be necessary to settle either for nonoptimal but acceptable solutions (called *satisficing* solutions) or for partial solutions. In the next chapter, I will present a variety of methods that can be used by agents with limited resources.

9.4   *Additional Readings and Discussion*

Heuristic search involves two kinds of computations. First, there is the *object-level* computation of actually expanding nodes and producing the path itself. Second, there is the *metalevel* computation of deciding which node to expand next. The object level is about physical actions in the world; the metalevel is about computational actions in the graph. Object–level/metalevel distinctions come up frequently in AI. They are thoroughly discussed in [Russell & Wefald 1991] and play a particularly important role in the abbreviated search methods to be discussed in the next chapter.

Sliding block puzzles have been used by many AI researchers as a testbed problem for heuristic search methods. An early paper by [Doran & Michie 1966] used the Eight–puzzle and initiated the use of evaluation functions in procedures for finding paths in graphs.

In 1990, Korf stated that while "IDA* can solve the Fifteen–puzzle, any larger puzzle [such as the Twenty–four puzzle] is intractable on current machines" [Korf 1990, p. 191]. Yet with a more powerful machine (a Sun Ultra Sparc workstation generating a million nodes per second) and with more powerful (automatically discovered) heuristics, [Korf & Taylor 1996] were able to find optimal solutions to randomly generated, solvable instances of the Twenty–four puzzle in times ranging between two and a quarter hours and a month. [Korf 1997] used IDA* to find optimal solutions to the $3 \times 3 \times 3$ Rubik's Cube puzzle.

Although puzzles have been useful for improving and testing search techniques, A* and related heuristic search procedures have been successfully applied to many practical problems.

For more on using relaxed models to discover heuristic functions, see [Mostow & Prieditis 1989, Prieditis 1993]. [Pohl 1973] experimented with varying the weight on the heuristic component of $\hat{f}$.

The classic book on heuristic search is [Pearl 1984]. [Kanal & Kumar 1988] is a collection of papers about search. The first paper in the latter book proposes a unification of search methods developed independently by AI and operations research people.

Exercises

9.1 In the "Four-Queens puzzle," we try to place four queens on a 4×4 chess board so that none can capture any other. (That is, only one queen can be on any row, column, or diagonal of the array.) Suppose we try to solve this puzzle using the following problem space: The *start node* is labeled by an empty 4×4 array; the *successor function* creates new 4×4 arrays containing one additional *legal* placement of a queen anywhere in the array; the *goal predicate* is satisfied if and only if there are four queens in the array (legally positioned).

1. Invent an *admissible* heuristic function for this problem based on the number of queen placements remaining to achieve the goal. (Note that *all* goal nodes are precisely four steps from the start node!)

2. Use your heuristic function in an A* search to a goal node. Draw the search tree consisting of all 4×4 arrays produced by the search and label each array by its value of g and $\hat{h}$. (Note that symmetry considerations mean we have to generate only three successors of the start node.)

9.2 This exercise assumes you have already completed Exercise 7.4 about the Tower–of–Hanoi puzzle. Refer to your solution to that exercise, or, if you have not already done it, do it now before continuing. Propose an admissible $\hat{h}$ function for this problem that is better than $\hat{h} \equiv 0$.

9.3 Algorithm A* does not terminate until a goal node is selected for expansion. However, a path to a goal node might be reached long before that node is selected for expansion. Why not terminate as soon as a goal node has been found? Illustrate your answer with an example.

9.4 The monotone condition on the heuristic function requires that $\hat{h}(n_i) \leq \hat{h}(n_j) + c(n_i, n_j)$ for all node-successor pairs (n_i, n_j), where $c(n_i, n_j)$ is the cost on the arc from n_i to n_j. It has been suggested that when the monotone condition is not satisfied, this fact can be discovered and $\hat{h}$ adjusted during search so that the condition is satisfied. The idea is that whenever a node n_i is expanded, with successor node n_j, we can increment $\hat{h}(n_j)$ by whatever amount is needed to satisfy the monotone condition. Construct an example to show that even with this scheme, when a node is expanded we have not necessarily found a least costly path to it.

9.5 Show that an admissible version of algorithm A* remains admissible if we remove from *OPEN* any node n for which $\hat{f}(n) > F$, where F is an upper bound on $f(n_0)$, and n_0 is the start node.

9.6 (Courtesy of Matt Ginsberg, Daphne Koller, and Yoav Shoham.) In this exercise, we consider the choice between two *admissible* heuristic functions, one of which is always "at least as accurate" as the other. More precisely, for a fixed goal, let $\hat{h}_1$ and $\hat{h}_2$ be two admissible heuristic functions such that $\hat{h}_1(n) \leq \hat{h}_2(n)$ for every node n in the search tree.

Now recall that the A* algorithm expands nodes according to their $\hat{f}$ values, but the order in which nodes of equal $\hat{f}$ value are expanded can vary, depending on the implementation of the priority queue. For a given heuristic function $\hat{h}$, we say that an ordering of the nodes in the search tree is $A^*_{\hat{h}}$-legal if expanding the nodes in that order is consistent with A* search using $\hat{h}$.

Let N denote the set of nodes expanded by an A* search using $\hat{h}_1$ (the "less accurate" heuristic function). Prove that there is always some search ordering that is $A^*_{\hat{h}_2}$-legal that expands only a (not necessarily strict) subset of the nodes in N. That is, prove that it is always *possible* that $\hat{h}_2$ leads to a smaller search space than $\hat{h}_1$. (Note that the question asks you to find *some* search ordering such that certain properties hold. Do you see why it is not possible, in general, to show that these properties hold for an *arbitrary* search ordering?)

Planning, Acting, and Learning

Now that we have explored several techniques for finding paths in graphs, it is time to show how these methods can be used by agents in realistic settings. I first revisit the assumptions made when I first considered graph-search planning methods in Chapter 7 and propose an agent architecture that tolerates these idealized assumptions. Next, I show how some of the search methods can be modified to lessen their time and space requirements—thus making them more usable in the proposed architecture. Finally, I show how heuristic functions and models of actions can be learned.

10.1 The Sense/Plan/Act Cycle

As mentioned in Chapter 7, the efficacy of search-based planning methods depends on several strong assumptions. Often, these assumptions are not met because

1. Perceptual processes might not always provide the necessary information about the state of the environment (because they are noisy or are insensitive to important properties). When two different environmental situations evoke the same sensory input, we have what is called *perceptual aliasing*.

2. Actions might not always have their modeled effects (because the models are not precise enough or because the effector system occasionally makes errors in executing actions).

3. There may be other physical processes in the world or other agents (as there might be, for example, in games with adversaries). These processes

might change the world in ways that would interfere with the agent's actions.

4. The existence of external effects causes another problem: during the time that it takes to construct a plan, the world may change in such a way that the plan is no longer relevant. This difficulty makes it pointless for an agent to spend too much time planning.

5. The agent might be required to act before it can complete a search to a goal state.

6. Even if the agent had sufficient time, its computational memory resources might not permit search to a goal state.

There are two main approaches for dealing with these difficulties while preserving the main features of search–based planning. In one, probabilistic methods are used to formalize perceptual, environmental, and effector uncertainties. In the other, we attempt to work around the difficulties with various additional assumptions and approximations.

A formal way of confronting the fact that actions have uncertain effects is to assume that for every action executable in a certain state, the resulting state is given by a known probability distribution. Finding appropriate actions under such circumstances is called a *Markov decision problem (MDP)* [Puterman 1994]. Dealing with the additional problem of imperfect perception can be formalized by assuming that the agent's sensory apparatus provides a probability distribution over the set of states that it might be in. Finding actions then is called a *partially observable Markov decision problem (POMDP)* [Lovejoy 1991, Monahan 1982, Cassandra, Kaelbling, & Littman 1994]. Discussing MDPs and POMDPs is beyond the scope of this book, but I touch on related techniques in Chapter 20 after my treatment of probabilistic inference.

Instead of pursuing the formal, probability–based methods here, I propose an architecture, called the *sense/plan/act* architecture, that gets around some of the aforementioned complications in many applications. The rationale for this architecture is that even if actions *occasionally* produce unanticipated effects and even if the agent *sometimes* cannot decide which world state it is in, these difficulties can be adequately dealt with by ensuring that the agent gets continuous feedback from its environment while it is executing its plan.

One way to ensure continuous feedback is to plan a sequence of actions, execute just the first action in this sequence, sense the resulting environmental situation, recalculate the start node, and then repeat the process. Agents that select actions in this manner are said to be *sense/plan/act* agents. For this method to be effective, however, the time taken to compute a plan must be less than the time allowed for each action. In Figure 10.1, I show an architecture for a sense/plan/act agent. In benign environments (those tolerant of a few missteps),

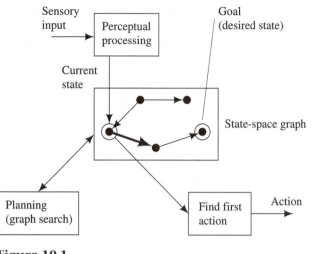

Figure 10.1

An Architecture for a Sense/Plan/Act Agent

errors in sensing and acting "average out" over a sequence of sense/plan/act cycles.

Environmental feedback in the sense/plan/act cycle allows resolution of some of the perceptual, environmental, and effector uncertainties. For feedback to be effective, however, we must assume that, on the average, sensing and acting are accurate. In many applications, this assumption is realistic. After all, it is the agent designer's task to provide sensory, perceptual, and effector modalities adequate to the task requirements. Often, the agent can enhance perceptual accuracy by comparing immediate sensory data with a stored model of the unfolding situation. (Recall that we saw a simple example of such filtering in the illustrative blackboard system of Chapter 5.)

10.2   *Approximate Search*

I next treat modifications to the search process that address the problem of limited computational and/or time resources at the price of producing plans that might be suboptimal or that might not always reliably lead to a goal state. Application of these techniques can then be incorporated in a sense/plan/act cycle even if the plan is not optimal (nor even correct). Qualitatively, so long as the first action has a tendency (on the average) to shorten the distance to the goal, multiple iterations of the sense/plan/act cycle will eventually achieve the goal.

As mentioned in the last chapter, relaxing the requirement of producing optimal plans often reduces the computational cost of finding a plan. This reduction can be done in either of two ways. First, we could search for a complete

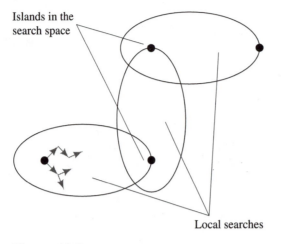

Islands in the
search space

Local searches

Figure 10.2

An Island–Driven Search

path to a goal node without requiring that it be optimal. Or we could search for
a partial path that does not take us all the way to a goal node. An A*–type search
can be used in both methods. In the first, we use a nonadmissible heuristic
function, and in the second, we quit searching before reaching the goal—using
either an admissible or nonadmissible heuristic function. Discontinuing search
before reaching the goal is an example of an *anytime algorithm* [Dean & Boddy
1988, Horvitz 1987]. Anytime algorithms are ones that can be stopped at any
time; the quality of the result generally improves with longer running times. In
the next few subsections, we elaborate on these and other approximate search
methods.

10.2.1   Island–Driven Search

In *island-driven search*, heuristic knowledge from the problem domain is used to
establish a sequence of "island nodes" in the search space through which it is
suspected that good paths pass. For example, in planning routes through difficult
terrain, such islands might correspond to mountain passes. Suppose n_0 is the start
node, n_g is the goal node, and $(n_1, n_2, \ldots, n_k)$ is a sequence of such islands. We
initiate a heuristic search with n_0 as the start node and with n_1 as the goal node
(using a heuristic function appropriate for that goal). When the search finds a
path to n_1, we start another search with n_1 as the start node and n_2 as the goal
node, and so on until we find a path to n_g. I show a schematic illustration of
island–driven search in Figure 10.2.

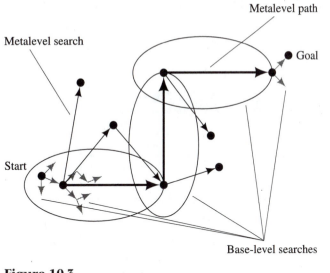

Metalevel path

Metalevel search

Goal

Start

Base-level searches

Figure 10.3

A Hierarchical Search

10.2.2   **Hierarchical Search**

Hierarchical search is much like island–driven search except that we do not have an explicit set of islands. We assume that we have certain "macro–operators" that can take large steps in an implicit search space of islands. A *start island* (near the start node) and these macro–operators form an implicit "metalevel" supergraph of islands. We search the supergraph first, with a *metalevel* search, until we produce a path of macro–operators that takes us from a node near the base–level start node to a node near the base–level goal node. If the macro–operators are already defined in terms of a sequence of base–level operators, the macro–operators are expanded into a path of base–level operators, and this path is then connected, by base–level searches, to the start and goal nodes. If the macro–operators are not defined in terms of the base–level operators, we must do base–level searches along the path of island nodes found by the metalevel search. The latter possibility is illustrated schematically in Figure 10.3.

As an example of hierarchical planning, consider the grid–space robot task of pushing a block to a given goal location. The situation is as illustrated in Figure 10.4. A pushable block is located in one of the cells as shown. The robot's goal is to push the block to the cell marked with a *G*. I assume that the robot can sense its eight surrounding cells and can determine whether an occupied surrounding cell contains an immovable barrier or a pushable block. As in Chapter 2, I assume that the robot can move in its column or row into an adjacent free cell or into an adjacent cell containing a pushable block, in which

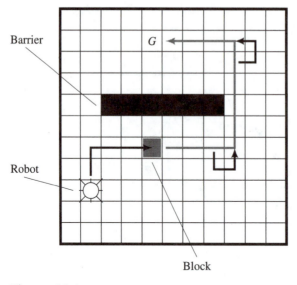

Barrier

Robot

Block

Figure 10.4

Pushing a Block

case the block moves one cell forward also (unless such motion is blocked by an immovable barrier).

Suppose the robot has an iconic model of its world, represented by an array similar to the cell array shown in Figure 10.4. Then, the robot could first make a metalevel plan of what the block's moves should be—assuming the block can move in the same way that the robot can move. The result of such a plan is shown by the gray arrow in Figure 10.4. Each step of the block's motion is then expanded into a base–level plan. The first one of the block's moves requires the robot to plan a path to a cell adjacent to the block and on the opposite side of the next target location for the block. The result of that episode of base–level planning is shown by a dark arrow in Figure 10.4. Subsequent base–level planning is trivial until the block must change direction. Then, the robot must plan a path to a cell opposite the block's direction of motion, and so on. The base–level plans to accomplish these changes in direction are also shown in Figure 10.4.[1]

In hierarchical planning, if there is likelihood of environmental changes during plan execution, it may be wise to expand only the first few steps of the metalevel plan. Expanding just the first metalevel step gives a base–level action to

---

1. An early AI paper on planning and execution involved a simulated robot and task much like that of Figure 10.4 [Nilsson & Raphael 1967].

execute, after which environmental feedback can be used to develop an updated metalevel plan.

10.2.3   Limited–Horizon Search

In some problems, it is computationally infeasible for any search method to find a path to the goal. In others, an action must be selected within a time limit that does not permit search all the way to a goal. In these, it may be useful to use the amount of time or computation available to find a path to a node thought to be on a good path to the goal even if that node is not a goal node itself. This substitute for a goal, let's call it node n^*, is the one having the smallest value of $\hat{f}$ among the nodes on the search frontier when search must be terminated.

Suppose the time available for search before an action must be selected allows search to a depth d. That is, all paths of length d or less can be searched. Nodes at that depth, denoted by $\mathcal{H}$, will be called *horizon nodes*. Then our search process will be to search to depth d and then select

$$n^* = \underset{n \in \mathcal{H}}{\operatorname{argmin}} \hat{f}(n)$$

as a surrogate for a goal node. I call this method *limited-horizon search*. [Korf 1990] studied this technique and calls it *minimin search*.[2] A sense/plan/act system would then take the first action on the path to n^*, sense the resulting state, and iterate by searching again and so on. We can expect that this first action toward a node having optimal heuristic merit has a good chance of being on a path to a goal. And, often an agent does not need to search all the way to a goal anyway; because of uncertainties, distant search may be irrelevant and provide no better information than does the heuristic function applied at the search horizon.

Limited–horizon search can be efficiently performed by a depth-first process to depth d. The use of a monotone $\hat{f}$ function to evaluate nodes permits great reductions in search effort. As soon as the first node, say, n_1, on the search horizon is reached, we can terminate search below any other node, n, with $\hat{f}(n) > \hat{f}(n_1)$. Node n cannot possibly have a descendant with an $\hat{f}$ value less than $\hat{f}(n_1)$, so there is no point in searching below it. (Under the monotone assumption, the $\hat{f}$ values of nodes along any path in the search tree are monotone nondecreasing.) $\hat{f}(n_1)$ is called an *alpha cut-off value*, and the process of terminating search below node n is an instance of a search process called *branch and bound*. Furthermore, whenever some other search–horizon node, say, n_2, is reached such that $\hat{f}(n_2) < \hat{f}(n_1)$, the alpha cut–off value can be lowered to $\hat{f}(n_2)$, which relaxes the condition for cut-offs. Alpha cut-off values can be lowered in this way whenever horizon nodes are

---

2. We might ask why not search to a given cost horizon rather than to a given depth horizon. Since the time required to search usually depends on depth and not cost, we use depth.

reached having $\hat{f}$ values smaller than the current alpha cut–off value. [Korf 1990] compares limited–horizon search with various other similar methods, including IDA* and versions of A* subject to limited time.

An extreme form of limited–horizon search uses a depth bound of 1. The immediate successors of the start node are evaluated, and the action leading to the successor with the lowest value of $\hat{f}$ is executed. These $\hat{f}$ values are analogous to the values of potential functions that I discussed in connection with robot navigation in Chapter 5, and, indeed, a potential function might well be an appropriate choice for $\hat{f}$ in robot navigation problems.

Formally, let $\sigma(n_0, a)$ be the description of the state the agent expects to reach by taking action a at node n_0. Applying the operator corresponding to action a at node n_0 produces that state description. Our policy for selecting an action at node n_0, then, is given by

$$a = \operatorname*{argmin}_{a} \hat{f}(\sigma(n_0, a)) = \operatorname*{argmin}_{a} [c(a) + \hat{h}(\sigma(n_0, a))]$$

where $c(a)$ is the cost of the action. I will use an equation similar to this later when I discuss methods for learning $\hat{f}(\sigma(n_0, a))$.

10.2.4 Cycles

In all of these cases where there are uncertainties and where an agent relies on approximate plans, use of the sense/plan/act cycle may produce repetitive cycles of behavior. That is, an agent may return to a previously visited environmental state and repeat the action it took there. Getting stuck in such cycles, of course, means that the agent will never reach a goal state. Korf has proposed a plan-execution algorithm called *Real-time* A* (RTA*) that builds an explicit graph of all states actually visited and adjusts the $\hat{h}$ values of the nodes in this graph in a way that biases against taking actions leading to states previously visited [Korf 1990].

10.2.5 Building Reactive Procedures

As mentioned at the beginning of Chapter 7, in a reactive machine, the designer has precalculated the appropriate goal–achieving action for every possible situation. Storing actions indexed to environmental states may require large amounts of memory. On the other hand, reactive agents can usually act more quickly than can planning agents. In some cases, it may be advantageous to precompute (*compile*) some frequently used plans *offline* and store them as reactive routines that produce appropriate actions quickly *online*.

For example, offline search could compute a *spanning tree* rooted at the goal of the state-space graph and containing paths from all (or, at least, many) of the nodes in the state space. A spanning tree can be produced by searching

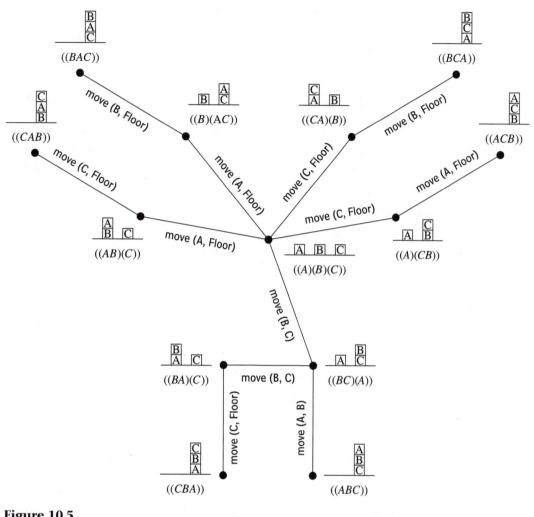

Figure 10.5

A Spanning Tree for a Block–Stacking Problem

"backward" from the goal. For example, a spanning tree for achieving the goal block *A* is on block *B* is on block *C* is shown in Figure 10.5. It shows paths to the goal from all of the other nodes.

Spanning trees and partial spanning trees can easily be converted to T-R programs, which are completely reactive. If a reactive program specifies an action for every possible state, it is called a *universal plan* [Schoppers 1987] or an *action policy*. I discuss action policies and methods for learning action policies toward the end of this chapter. Even if an action taken in a given state does not always result in the anticipated next state, the reactive machine is prepared to deal with whichever state does result.

10.3   *Learning Heuristic Functions*

Continuous feedback from the environment is one way to reduce uncertainties and to compensate for an agent's lack of knowledge about the effects of its actions. Also, useful information can be extracted both from the experience of searching and from the experience of acting in the world. I will discuss various ways in which an agent can learn to plan and to act more effectively.

10.3.1   **Explicit Graphs**

If the agent does not have a good heuristic function to estimate the cost to the goal, it is sometimes possible to learn such a function. I first explain a very simple learning procedure appropriate for the case in which it is possible to store an explicit list of all of the possible nodes.[3]

I assume first that the agent has a good model of the effects of its actions and that it also knows the costs of moving from any node to its successor nodes. We begin the learning process by initializing the $\hat{h}$ function to be identically 0 for all nodes, and then we start an A* search. After expanding node n_i to produce successors $S(n_i)$, we modify $\hat{h}(n_i)$ as follows:

$$\hat{h}(n_i) \leftarrow \min_{n_j \in S(n_i)} \left[\hat{h}(n_j) + c(n_i, n_j) \right]$$

where $c(n_i, n_j)$ is the cost of moving from n_i to n_j. The $\hat{h}$ values can be stored in a table of nodes (because there is a manageably small number of them). I assume also that if a goal node, say, n_g, is generated, we know that $\hat{h}(n_g) = 0$. Although this learning process does not help us reach a goal the first time we search any faster than would uniform–cost search, subsequent searches to the same goal (from possibly different starting states) will be accelerated by using the learned $\hat{h}$ function. After several searches, better and better estimates of the true h function will gradually propagate backward from goal nodes. (The learning algorithm LRTA* uses this same update rule for $\hat{h}$ [Korf 1990].)

If the agent does not have a model of the effects of its actions, it can learn them and also learn an $\hat{h}$ function at the same time by a similar process, although the learning will have to take place in the actual world rather than in a state–space model. (Of course, such learning could be hazardous!) I assume that the agent has

---

3. I discuss this special case simply to introduce some ideas that I later generalize; as I have already said, most problems of practical interest have search spaces too large to list all the nodes.

some means to distinguish the states that it actually visits and that it can name them and make an explicit graph or table to represent states and their estimated values, and the transitions caused by actions. I also assume that if the agent does not know the costs of its actions, it learns this cost upon taking them. The process starts with just a single node, representing the state in which the agent begins. It takes an action, perhaps a random one, and transits to another state. As it visits states, it names them and associates $\hat{h}$ values with them as follows:

$$\hat{h}(n_i) \leftarrow \left[\hat{h}(n_j) + c(n_i, n_j) \right]$$

where n_i is the node in which an action, say, a, is taken, n_j is the resulting node, $c(n_i, n_j)$ is the revealed cost of the action, $\hat{h}(n_j)$ is an estimate of the value of n_j, which is equal to 0 if n_j has never been visited before and is otherwise stored in the table.

Whenever the agent is about to take an action at a node, n, having successor nodes stored in the graph, it chooses an action according to the policy:

$$a = \operatorname*{argmin}_a \left[\hat{h}(\sigma(n, a)) + c(n_i, \sigma(n, a)) \right]$$

where $\sigma(n, a)$ is the description of the state reached from node n after taking action a.

This particular learning procedure begins with a random walk, eventually stumbles into a goal, and on subsequent trials propagates better $\hat{h}$ values backward—resulting in better paths. Because the action selected at node n is the one leading to a node estimated to be on a minimal-cost path from n to a goal, it is not necessary to evaluate all the successors of node n when updating $\hat{h}(n)$. As a model is gradually built up, it is possible to combine "learning in the world" with "learning and planning in the model." Such combinations have been explored by [Sutton 1990] in his DYNA system.

The technique can, however, result in learning nonoptimal paths because nodes on optimal ones might never be visited. Allowing occasional random actions (instead of those selected by the policy being learned) helps the agent learn new (perhaps better) paths to goals. Taking random actions is one way for an agent to deal with what is called "the exploration (of new paths) versus the exploitation (of already learned knowledge) tradeoff." There may be other ways also to ensure that all nodes are visited.

10.3.2 Implicit Graphs

Let's turn now to the case in which it is impractical to make an explicit graph or table of all the nodes and their transitions. As before, when we have a model of the effects of actions (that is, when we have operators that transform the description of a state into a description of a successor state), we can perform a search process guided by an evaluation function. Typically, the function may produce the same evaluation for several nodes, so applying the function to a state description is feasible, whereas storing all of the nodes and their values explicitly in a table might not be.

We can use methods similar to those described in Chapter 3 to learn the heuristic function while performing a search process. We first guess at a set of subfunctions that we think might be good components of a heuristic function. For example, in the Eight–puzzle we might use the functions $W(n) =$ the number of tiles in the wrong place, and $P(n) =$ the sum of the distances that each tile is from "home," and any other functions that might be related to how close a position is to the goal. We then write the heuristic function as a weighted linear combination of these:

$$\hat{h}(n) = w_1 W(n) + w_2 P(n) + \cdots$$

I mention two methods for learning the weights. In one, we set the weights initially to whatever values we think are best and conduct a search using $\hat{h}$ with these weight values. When we reach a goal node, n_g, we use the then final known value of $\hat{h}(n_g) = 0$ to back up $\hat{h}$ values for all nodes, n_i, along the path to the goal. Using these values as "training samples," we adjust the weights to minimize the sum of the squared errors between the training samples and the $\hat{h}$ function given by the weighted combination. The process must be performed iteratively over several searches.

Or we could use a method similar to the one I described earlier that adjusted $\hat{h}$ with every node expansion. After expanding node n_i to produce successor nodes $S(n_i)$, we adjust the weights so that

$$\hat{h}(n_i) \leftarrow \hat{h}(n_i) + \beta \left(\min_{n_j \in S(n_i)} \left[\hat{h}(n_j) + c(n_i, n_j) \right] - \hat{h}(n_i) \right)$$

or, rearranging,

$$\hat{h}(n_i) \leftarrow (1 - \beta)\hat{h}(n_i) + \beta \min_{n_j \in S(n_i)} \left[\hat{h}(n_j) + c(n_i, n_j) \right]$$

where $0 < \beta \leq 1$ is a learning rate parameter that controls how closely $\hat{h}(n_i)$ is made to approach $\min_{n_j \in S(n_i)} \left[\hat{h}(n_j) + c(n_i, n_j) \right]$. When $\beta = 0$, no change is made at all; when $\beta = 1$, we set $\hat{h}(n_i)$ equal to $\min_{n_j \in S(n_i)} \left[\hat{h}(n_j) + c(n_i, n_j) \right]$. Small values of β lead to very slow learning, whereas β near 1 may make learning erratic and nonconvergent.

This learning method is an instance of *temporal difference* learning, first formalized by [Sutton 1988]; the weight adjustment depends only on two temporally adjacent values of a function.[4] Sutton stated and proved several properties of the method relating to its convergence in various situations. The interesting point about the temporal difference method is that it can be applied during search before a goal is reached. (But the values of $\hat{h}$ that are being learned do not become relevant to the goal until the goal is reached.) This process, also, must be performed iteratively over several searches.

We note that this learning technique can also be applied even in situations in which we do not have models of the effects of actions. That is, the learning can take place in the actual world as discussed previously. Take a step (perhaps a random one or one chosen according to the emerging action policy), evaluate the $\hat{h}$'s before and after, note the cost of the step, and make the weight adjustments.

10.4   *Rewards Instead of Goals*

In discussing state–space search strategies, I have assumed that the agent had a single, short–term task that could be described by a goal condition. The goal was to change the world until its iconic model (in the form of a data structure) satisfied a given condition. In many problems of practical interest, the task cannot be so simply stated. Instead, the task may be an ongoing one. The user expresses his or her satisfaction and dissatisfaction with task performance by occasionally giving the agent positive and negative *rewards*. The task for the agent is to maximize the amount of reward it receives. (The special case of a simple goal–achieving task can be cast in this framework by rewarding the agent positively (just once) when it achieves the goal and negatively (by the amount of an action's cost) every time it takes an action.)

In this sort of task environment, we seek to describe an action policy that maximizes reward. One problem for ongoing, nonterminating tasks is that the future reward might be infinite, so it is difficult to decide how to maximize it. A way of proceeding is to discount future rewards by some factor. That is, the agent prefers rewards in the immediate future to those in the distant future. Our approach, then, assumes that the agent takes an action at every time step. (By "taking" an action, I mean either actually performing the action in the world or applying an operator in a graph–search model of the world.) Each action results in a change in the state description—either a change actually perceived by the agent or one computed by applying the operator in the model.

Let n denote a node in the state–space graph for the agent. Let π be a *policy* function on nodes whose value is the action prescribed by that policy at that node. Let $r(n_i, a)$ be the reward received by the agent when it takes an action, a, at n_i. If this action results in node n_j, then ordinarily we would have

4. Sutton credits [Samuel 1959] as the originator of the idea.

$r(n_i, a) = -c(n_i, n_j) + \rho(n_j)$, where $\rho(n_j)$ is the value of any special reward given for reaching node n_j. Some policies lead to larger discounted future rewards than others. We seek an *optimal policy*, π^*, that maximizes future discounted reward at every node.

Given a policy, π, we can impute a *value*, $V^\pi(n)$, for each node, n, in the state space; $V^\pi(n)$ is the total discounted reward that the agent will receive if it begins at n and follows policy π. Suppose we are at node n_i and take the action prescribed by $\pi(n_i)$, which results in node n_j. We can see that

$$V^\pi(n_i) = r[n_i, \pi(n_i)] + \gamma V^\pi(n_j)$$

where $0 < \gamma < 1$ is the *discount factor* that is used in computing the value at time t_i of a reward at time $t = t_{i+1}$, and $\pi(n_i)$ is the action prescribed by policy π at node n_i. For the optimal policy, π^*, we have

$$V^{\pi^*}(n_i) = \max_a \left(r[n_i, a] + \gamma V^{\pi^*}(n_j) \right)$$

That is, the value of n_i under the optimal policy is the amount the agent receives by taking that action at n_i that maximizes the sum of the immediate reward plus the discounted (by γ) value of n_j under the optimal policy. (Note that n_j is a function of the action, a, which also makes $V^{\pi^*}(n_j)$ a function of a.) If we knew the values of the nodes under an optimal policy (their so-called *optimal values*), we could write the optimal policy in the following interesting way:

$$\pi^*(n_i) = \underset{a}{\text{argmax}} \left(r[n_i, a] + \gamma V^{\pi^*}(n_j) \right)$$

The problem is that we typically don't know these values. But there is a learning procedure, called *value iteration*, that will (under certain circumstances) converge to the optimal values.

Value iteration works as follows: We begin by assigning, randomly, an *estimated value* $\hat{V}(n)$ to every node, n. Suppose at some step of the process we are at node n_i, and that the estimated value of node n_i is then $\hat{V}(n_i)$. We then select that action a that maximizes the sum of the immediate reward plus the estimated value of the successor node. (I assume here that we have operators that model the effects of actions and that can be applied to nodes to produce successor nodes.) Suppose this action a takes us to node n_j. Then we update the estimated value, $\hat{V}(n_i)$, of node n_i as follows:

$$\hat{V}(n_i) \leftarrow (1 - \beta)\hat{V}(n_i) + \beta \left[r(n_i, a) + \gamma \hat{V}(n_j) \right]$$

The estimated values of all other nodes are left unchanged.

We see that this adjustment moves the value of $\hat{V}(n_i)$ an increment (depending on β) closer to $\left[r(n_i, a) + \gamma \hat{V}(n_j) \right]$. To the extent that $\hat{V}(n_j)$ is a good estimate for $V^{\pi^*}(n_j)$, this adjustment helps to make $\hat{V}(n_i)$ a better estimate for $V^{\pi^*}(n_i)$.

Value iteration is usually presented for the more general case when actions have random effects and yield random rewards—both described by probability functions. Even then, providing that $0 < \beta < 1$ and that we visit each node infinitely often, value iteration will converge to the optimal values—expected values in the probabilistic case. (In deterministic domains, we can always use $\beta = 1$.) This result is somewhat surprising because we are exploring the space using (perhaps a bad) estimate of the optimal policy at the same time that we are trying to learn values of nodes under an optimal policy. For a full treatment of value iteration and related procedures, their relations to dynamic programming, and their convergence properties, see [Barto, Bradtke, & Singh 1995].

Learning action policies in settings in which rewards depend on a sequence of earlier actions is called *delayed-reinforcement learning*. Two problems arise when rewards are delayed. First, we must credit those state-action pairs most responsible for the reward. The task of doing so is called the *temporal credit assignment problem*. Value iteration is one method of propagating credit so that the appropriate actions are reinforced. Second, in state spaces too large for us to store the entire graph, we must aggregate states with similar $\hat{V}$ values. The task of doing so is called the *structural credit assignment problem*. Neural–network and other learning methods have been useful for that problem. Delayed–reinforcement learning is well reviewed in [Kaelbling, Littman, & Moore 1996].

10.5   *Additional Readings and Discussion*

Our sense/plan/act cycle is an instance of what Agre and Chapman call *interleaved planning* [Agre & Chapman 1990]. They contrast interleaved planning with their proposal for *improvisation*. In their words [Agre & Chapman 1990, p. 30]:

> Interleaved planning and improvisation differ in their understanding of trouble. In the world of interleaved planning, one assumes that the normal state of affairs is for things to go according to plan. Trouble is, so to speak, a marginal phenomenon. In the world of improvisation, one assumes that things are not likely to go according to plan. Quite the contrary, one expects to have to continually redecide what to do.

But, of course, isn't it the agent designer's job to see to it that the perceptual and motor systems are designed (with the task and environment in mind) so that "trouble" is, in fact, marginal? Plans in the form of T–R trees [Nilsson 1994] are quite robust in the face of marginal trouble. For more on interleaving planning and execution, see [Stentz 1995, Stentz & Hebert 1995, Nourbakhsh 1997].

Regarding search through islands see [Chakrabarti, Ghose, & DeSarkar 1986]. For models and analysis of hierarchical planning, see [Korf 1987, Bacchus & Yang 1992], respectively. [Stefik 1995, pp. 259–280] provides a very clear exposition of hierarchical planning.

In limited–horizon search, one must decide on the "horizon." Such a decision must take into account the tradeoff between the value of additional computation and the value of the action recommended by the computation already done. This tradeoff is influenced by the cost of delay in acting. Appraising the relative values of more computation and of immediate action is an instance of a metalevel computation. This subject is treated in detail in [Russell & Wefald 1991, Ch. 5]. Their DTA* algorithm implements some of their ideas on this subject.

[Lee & Mahajan 1988] describe methods for learning evaluation functions. Delayed–reinforcement and temporal difference learning methods are closely related to stochastic dynamic programming. See [Barto, Bradtke, & Singh 1995, Ross 1988]. For examples of robot systems that learn action policies based on rewards, see [Mahadevan & Connell 1992] and various chapters in [Connell & Mahadevan 1993b]. [Moore & Atkeson 1993] present efficient memory–based reinforcement methods for controlling physical systems. [Montague, et al. 1995] presents a model of bee foraging behavior based on reinforcement learning, and [Schultz, Dayan, & Montague 1997] describe how neural mechanisms in primates implement temporal difference learning mechanisms.

Exercises

10.1 (Courtesy of Matt Ginsberg.) Island–driven search is a technique where instead of finding a path directly to the goal, one first identifies an "island" that is a node more or less halfway between the initial node and the goal node. First we attempt to find an acceptable path to the goal that passes through this island node (by first finding a path from the start node to the island, and then finding one from the island to the goal); if no acceptable path through a halfway island can be found, we simply solve the original problem instead. Assume that search can only be done forward—that is, going toward the goal node.

1. Assume, for any value of d, that the time needed to search a tree with branching factor b and depth d is kb^d, that the time required to identify a suitable island is c, and that the probability that the island actually lies on an acceptable path to the goal is p. Find conditions on p and c such that the average time required by the island–driven approach will be less than the time required by ordinary breadth–first search.

2. Give an example of a search problem where island–driven search is likely to save time.

10.2 Consider a blocks–world problem in which there are N named blocks that can be in an arbitrary initial configuration and must be put in an arbitrary goal configuration. (Again, we ignore horizontal positions of the blocks and are concerned only with their vertical arrangements in stacks.) Suppose we use as an "island" the state in which all N blocks are on the floor. Discuss the implications of this approach in terms of search, memory, and time requirements and length of solution.

10.3 Explain how you would set up a hierarchical search procedure for the following graph. It is desired to find a path from any node in the graph to the node marked "Goal." (Although hierarchical search isn't required for such a small graph, this exercise will give you practice in thinking about hierarchical search in larger graphs where it would be helpful if not necessary.)

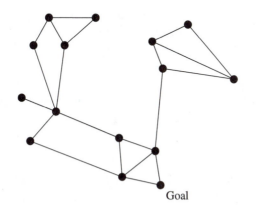

Goal

10.4 Imagine an agent confronted with a very large state space. Assume that the state–space graph has on the order of b^d nodes, where b is the average branching factor, and d is the average length of a path between two randomly chosen nodes in the state–space graph. We wish to compare two design strategies for designing an agent able to achieve an arbitrary goal state from an arbitrary initial state. One strategy would plan a path at run time using IDA*; that is, when given the goal and initial state, the agent would use IDA* to compute a path. The other strategy would precompute and store all possible paths, for all goal states and all start states. Compare these two strategies in terms of their time and space complexities. (You can use approximations appropriate for large values of d.)

10.5 You have a new job in a strange city and are staying with a friend in the country who drives you to a subway station in the city every morning from which you must take various trains to work. (The friend, who does deliveries in the city, drops you off at many different stations during your stay.) The stations of the subway system (of which there are a finite number) are laid out in a rectangular grid. One of the stations, let's call it Central, is the one you must reach to get to your job. You can always tell when (and if) you get to Central. At each station, you have your choice of four trains, north, east, south, and west. Each train is a local one and takes you only to an adjacent station in the grid where you might have to get off and reboard another train to continue. Some of the connections between adjacent stations are permanently out of service (decaying infrastructure), but it is known that there is still some path from any station in the grid to Central. Each time you visit a station, you must pay $1, and you receive $100 every day that you report for work. You do not have a route map, and you don't know anything about the locations of the various stations relative to Central. You decide to use value iteration to develop a policy for which train to take at each station. Value iteration seems appropriate because you can always see the name of your present station, which trains you can take from that station, and the names of the stations these trains reach.

1. Describe how value iteration would work for this problem. Is a temporal discount factor necessary? Why or why not? Prove that if you adjust the values of stations as you travel and that if you use these values to select trains, you will end up at Central on every trip. (Hint: Show that your algorithm adjusts values so that on no trial do you ever take an endless trip through some subset of the stations that does not include Central.)

2. If your learning algorithm does not guarantee producing values that eventually result in optimal (shortest–path) trips, explain why not and what might be done to guarantee optimality.

10.6 Consider the state–transition diagram shown here. There are two actions possible from the starting state, A. One, action a, leads to state B and yields an immediate reward of 0. The other, action b, leads to state C and produces an immediate reward of 1000. Once in state B, there is only one action possible. It produces a reward of +1 and leads back to B. Once in state C, there is also only one action possible. It produces a reward of −1 and leads back to C. What temporal discount factor would be required in order to prefer action a to action b?

11 Alternative Search Formulations and Applications

There are applications of search techniques beyond the problem of selecting actions for an agent. These applications include finding solutions to problems of assigning values to variables subject to constraints and solving optimization problems. Some specialized methods have been developed for these applications, and although they might not all seem immediately relevant to agent design, they are important AI techniques. I present some of them in this chapter.

11.1 Assignment Problems

The condition for a goal node in a graph–search problem might be defined by giving a specific data structure or state description that labels it, or it might be defined implicitly in terms of conditions or constraints on that data structure. In either case, when the problem is to find a sequence of actions for an agent, it isn't the data structure labeling the goal node itself that is of primary interest; rather, it is the sequence of steps that leads to the goal. Alternatively, when the goal node is defined not by a specific data structure but by conditions or constraints, it might be that the problem is to exhibit some data structure satisfying those conditions; the steps that produce it using graph–search methods might be irrelevant. We call this latter type of problem a *constraint-satisfaction* problem. A prominent member of this class involves assigning values to variables subject to constraints. These are called *assignment problems*, and they are the ones I shall consider now.

We can solve constraint–satisfaction problems by graph–search methods. A goal node is a node labeled by a data structure (or state description) that satisfies the constraints. Operators change one data structure into another. The start node is some initial data structure. A good example of an assignment problem is the

181

Figure 11.1

A Solution
to the Eight–
Queens
Problem

Eight-Queens problem. The problem is to place (assign) eight queens on a chess board in such a way that there is a queen in every row and column but with the additional constraint that only one queen can be in any single row, column, or diagonal. (That is, no queen can be placed so that it can capture any of the others, according to the rules of chess.) One solution to this problem is shown in Figure 11.1. We call this an assignment problem because it can be posed as a problem of assigning values from the set {row 1, row 2, . . . , row 8} to variables (position of queen in column 1, position of queen in column 2, . . . , position of queen in column 8).

In posing this problem as a graph–search problem, an obvious data structure would be an eight–by–eight array in which each cell contains one of two symbols (say, 1 or 0), representing queen (1) or empty (0). A goal state is defined implicitly by the condition that there must be eight queens all safe from capture. The operators linking state descriptions correspond to ways of transforming one array into another. For example, an operator could add a queen to an array that does not yet have eight queens, or it could move a queen to another cell. In assignment problems, since the path to the goal is not the important thing, we often have many choices about what the start state and the operators can be.

As another example of an assignment problem, one with a very large state space, consider the problem of inventing a crossword puzzle.[1] I show an array for a sample crossword puzzle in Figure 11.2. The problem is to fill in all of the blank squares in the array with letters such that all rows and columns have English words—according to the usual crossword puzzle rules. (I do not here consider the other half of the problem, namely, creating the hints to give to the person who is trying to solve our invented crossword puzzle.) In this problem, a state description is any array of letters and blank spaces (together with the blacked–out cells). A goal state is any such array that is a legitimate crossword puzzle solution. The operators linking state descriptions are any operations on an array of letters

---

1. Matt Ginsberg and students have tested various state–space search techniques on crossword puzzle generation problems [Ginsberg, et al. 1990].

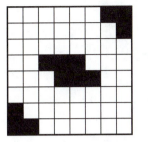

Figure 11.2

An Array for a Crossword Puzzle

and blanks that produce another array of letters and blanks. For example, an operator could add a word to an empty row or column, or it could change a letter to another letter.

11.2   *Constructive Methods*

We can use the search methods of the last chapters to solve assignment problems. The most straightforward approach is to attempt to construct the required assignment step by step—even though we are not particularly interested in the steps. We begin (the start node) with no assignments whatsoever. For the Eight-Queens problem, the corresponding data structure is an array containing all 0's. Each operator adds a queen to the array in such a way that the resulting array satisfies constraints among its queens. Since there must be a queen in every column, we can stipulate without loss of generality that the operator to be applied at a depth 0 node is the placement of a queen in the first column, and the operator to be applied at a depth 1 node is the placement of a queen in the second column, and so on. We call this approach a *constructive method* because the solution is constructed step by step. (Later, I will present a contrasting method.)

I illustrate in Figure 11.3 parts of search trees that might be produced using a constructive approach for the Eight-Queens problem and the crossword puzzle invention problem. (For better readability, I use an X to represent a queen's location rather than displaying an array of 1's and 0's.) Note in particular the operators used to generate a node from a previous node. For the crossword puzzle especially, it should be obvious that the state space is huge; there are thousands of other operators we could have applied at each of the nodes.

A computational technique called *constraint propagation* often helps markedly in reducing the size of the search space. It is used in combination with a constructive solution technique—assigning a value to each variable in turn. I describe this technique by showing how it is applied in a reduced version of the Eight-Queens problem. Consider the problem of placing four queens on a 4×4 chess board in such a way that no queen can capture any other. In the Four-Queens problem, we have four variables, q_1, q_2, q_3, q_4, representing the columns, one through four,

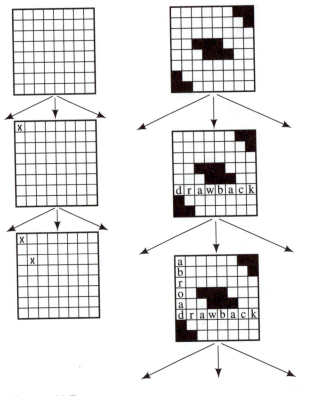

Figure 11.3

State Spaces for Constructive Formulations

respectively, in which a queen might be placed. Each of the variables can have one of four values, 1, 2, 3, or 4, corresponding to the row numbers. So, for example, when q_3 has value 2, a queen is placed in the second row of the third column. The Four–Queens problem places constraints on the values of these variables; thus, for example, if q_1 has value 1, q_2 cannot have value 1 or 2.

Constraints are represented in a directed graph called a *constraint graph*. Each node in this graph is labeled by a variable name together with a set of possible values for that variable. A directed *constraint arc*, (i, j), connects a pair of nodes i and j if the value of the variable labeling i is constrained by the value of the variable labeling j. I show an example of such a graph for the Four–Queens problem in Figure 11.4. In this problem, each variable constrains all of the others, so all of the nodes have arcs to all other nodes. We say that a directed arc, (i, j), is *consistent* if *each* value of the variable at the tail of the arc has at least one value of the variable at the head of the arc that violates no constraints. The arcs in Figure 11.4 are consistent because for each pair q_i and q_j $(i \neq j)$ and for each value of q_i there is a value of q_j that does not violate the constraint.

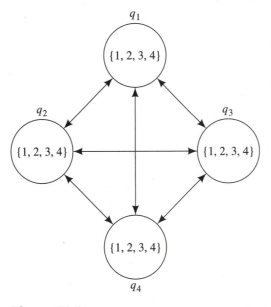

Figure 11.4

A Constraint Graph for the Four–Queens Problem

After assigning values to one or more of the variables, we can use the concept of arc consistency to rule out some of the values of other variables. The process of constraint propagation iterates over the arcs in the graph and eliminates values of variables at the tails of arcs in an attempt to enforce arc consistency. The process halts when no more values can be eliminated. I illustrate with an example. Suppose a depth–first search process begins by assigning the value 1 to the variable q_1. (That is, we place a queen in column 1, row 1.) Constraint propagation applied to this assignment then might proceed as follows:

1. Consider the arc (q_2, q_1): we eliminate $q_2 = 1$ and $q_2 = 2$ because the only remaining value of q_1 (the value we just assigned) is inconsistent with those values of q_2.

2. Consider the arc (q_3, q_1): we eliminate $q_3 = 1$ and $q_3 = 3$ because the value of q_1 is inconsistent with those values of q_3.

3. Consider the arc (q_4, q_1): we eliminate $q_4 = 1$ and $q_4 = 4$ because the value of q_1 is inconsistent with those values of q_4.

At this (incomplete) stage of constraint propagation, we are left with the graph shown in Figure 11.5. Subsequent steps of constraint propagation, as shown in the figure, eliminate all of the values of q_3, and thus we see that there is no solution

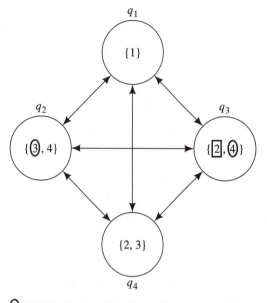

$\bigcirc$ Values eliminated by first making arc (q_2, q_3)
and then arc (q_3, q_2) consistent

$\square$ Value eliminated by next making arc (q_3, q_4) consistent

Figure 11.5

Constraint Graph with $q_1 = 1$

to the problem with $q_1 = 1$. No further search below the $q_1 = 1$ node in the search graph is necessary, and we can backtrack to creating the node $q_1 = 2$ instead.

Next, we do constraint propagation assuming $q_1 = 2$. The first few steps might proceed as follows:

1. Consider the arc (q_2, q_1): we eliminate $q_2 = 1$, $q_2 = 2$, and $q_2 = 3$.

2. Consider the arc (q_3, q_1): we eliminate $q_3 = 2$ and $q_3 = 4$.

3. Consider the arc (q_4, q_1): we eliminate $q_4 = 2$.

We are left with the graph shown in Figure 11.6. Continued constraint propagation eliminates all but one value of a variable for each node, leaving all arcs consistent. Thus, we see that before completing the search there is only one solution, and constraint propagation has found that solution for us.

Sometimes, as in this example, constraint propagation eliminates all values of one or more of the variables—permitting us to see that a search problem has no solution, given previous assignments of values to variables. Sometimes, it shows that there is only one consistent solution, given previous assignments. In these cases, constraint propagation eliminates further search. The basic idea

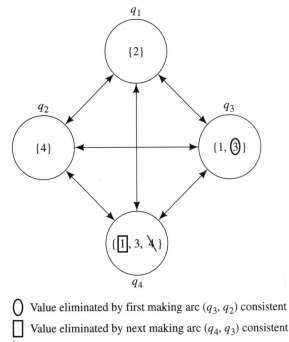

O   Value eliminated by first making arc (q_3, q_2) consistent

□   Value eliminated by next making arc (q_4, q_3) consistent

\   Value eliminated by next making arc (q_4, q_2) consistent

Figure 11.6

Constraint Graph with $q_1 = 2$

of constraint propagation has been extended to include more complex tests for consistency, but probably its most economical application involves the arc consistency check that I have just illustrated. Constraint propagation has been applied to a variety of interesting problems, including the problem of labeling lines with $+$, $-$, or $\rightarrow$ in visual scene analysis and to the propositional satisfiability problem considered later in the book. For an excellent survey of the method, its extensions, and its applications, see [Kumar 1992].

11.3   *Heuristic Repair*

There is another approach to setting up a problem for solution by graph–search methods. It is called the *repair approach* because it starts with a proposed solution, which most probably does not satisfy the constraints, and repairs it until it does. Thus, the initial node is labeled by a data structure that typically does not satisfy all of the constraints. The operators produce a new data structure that corresponds to a different proposed solution.

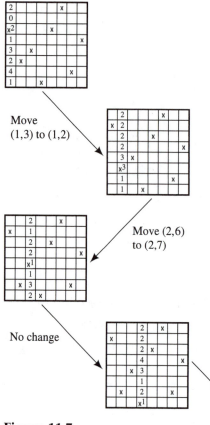

Figure 11.7

Repair Steps for the Eight–Queens Problem

For example, in the Eight–Queens problem, we might start with eight queens, one in each column, and in arbitrary, perhaps random, row positions. We repair a faulty solution by moving one of the queens to violate fewer constraints. In the so–called *min-conflicts* [Gu 1989, Minton, et al. 1992] version of repair, we consider each column in turn (starting, say, with the first) and label each cell in that column with the number of queens (outside of that column) that attack that cell. Then we move the queen in that column to the cell having the minimum number of attacking queens (the minimum number of conflicts). Ties are broken randomly. This operation produces a successor node labeled by (perhaps) a slightly repaired proposed solution. And so on through the columns. I illustrate part of a depth–first search for the Eight–Queens problem, using min–conflicts, in Figure 11.7. Again, queen locations are indicated by X's, and the numbers in the cells refer to the number of queens attacking that cell. Similar repair–based approaches

[Minton, et al. 1990] have been used to solve much larger problems, such as the Million-Queens problem.[2]

In applying the repair approach to the crossword puzzle invention problem, the start node can be any array that is completely filled with letters. We might repair a faulty solution by replacing some individual letter in an array with some other letter that, let us hope, is "on the way" toward making a row or column contain a word. The search space for the crossword puzzle problem is huge because there are thousands of other operators we could have applied at each of the nodes.

Whether we should use a constructive method or a repair method, and what to use for states and operators all can have dramatic effects on search difficulty.

11.4   *Function Optimization*

In some problems, instead of having an explicit goal condition, we may have some function, v, over data structures and we seek to find a structure having a maximum (or minimum) value of that function. If we think of the data structures as "points" in a space, this function can be thought of as a "landscape" over the space. One class of methods consists of those that traverse the landscape, looking for points of high elevation. Since we might not know the value of the global maximum, we might never know for sure if we have reached a point having maximal height.

Among the techniques for traversing a space are the *hill-climbing* methods, which traverse by moving from one point to that "adjacent" point having the highest elevation.[3] Hill-climbing methods typically terminate when there is no adjacent point having a higher elevation than the current point—thus, they can get stuck on local maxima.

We can use graph-searching methods to do hill climbing. Nodes are labeled by data structures, as usual. Operators correspond to the ways in which a given data structure can be changed to some adjacent one. Hill climbing follows a single path (much like depth-first search without backup), evaluating height as it goes, and never (well, hardly ever) descending to a lower point. Here is a simple hill-climbing algorithm for the problem of finding a node having a (locally) maximal value:

---

2. Although interesting as an exercise to illustrate constraint propagation and repair-based approaches, there happens to be a linear-time algorithm for the N-Queens problem [Abramson & Yung 1989].

3. When we are seeking to minimize a function, we should, strictly speaking, call them *descent methods*. But occasionally, I will use the generic phrase *hill climbing* to describe both activities. The distinction is unimportant in any case because we can always convert one problem into the other by multiplying the function we are optimizing by −1.

HILLCLIMB

1. Set the *current node*, n, to a randomly selected node, n_0.

2. Generate the successors of n (using operators defined for the problem), and select that successor, n_b, whose v value, $v(n_b) = v_b$, is highest among these. (Break ties arbitrarily.)

3. If $v_b < v(n)$, exit with n as the best node found so far.

4. Otherwise, set n to n_b, and go to step 2.

Note that this algorithm is very much like depth–first search, except that we always expand that successor having the highest value (and then only if its value is not less than that of its parent), and there is no provision for backup. The moves in hill–climbing search are irrevocable.

I illustrate hill climbing (actually hill descending in this case) with a problem of coloring the cells in a 3×3 grid. We are given some arbitrary configuration of red and blue grid cells and wish to find a coloring having a minimal number of pairs of adjacent cells with the same color. That is, we seek a node, n^*, in the state space for which, for all n, $v(n^*) \le v(n)$, where $v(n) =$ the number of pairs of adjacent cells in node n having the same color. For operators, we allow any cell to have its color changed from red to blue and vice versa. In Figure 11.8, I show part of the graph for this problem and the route taken by a hill–descending procedure.

In case a move does not result in a change in the value of v, we say that we are moving on a *plateau* in the search space. It is possible for a hill–climbing algorithm to wander endlessly on plateaus, revisiting previously visited nodes, without climbing into higher terrain. Such wandering can be limited by adding a counter that keeps track of the number of times the v value remains the same. At the cost of additional memory, we might ameliorate the plateau problem by refusing to move to any previously visited node having the same value as the current node.

Another difficulty is caused by "ridges" (or their inverse, "gullies") in the search space. In the case of hill climbing, it might be that no move exists that doesn't take us to nodes of lower height, but that two of the moves, executed serially, will increase the height. This problem is schematically illustrated in Figure 11.9. Each of the available moves takes us off the ridge to a lower elevation, but a sequence of two of them could move us higher up the ridge. The ridge problem can sometimes be avoided by combining two or more moves into "macro–moves" or by allowing a limited amount of "lookahead" search.

We can attack the problem of getting stuck on local maxima by performing several separate hill–climbing searches (either in parallel or in sequence), starting at different locations. Each of the searches may end up at different local maxima, and we can use the highest of these. The GP method discussed in Chapter 4 is

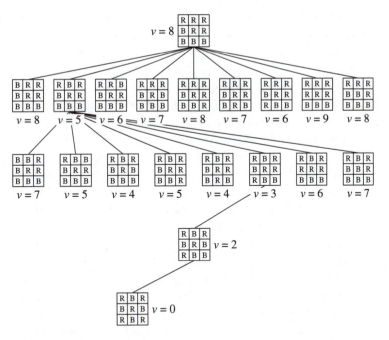

Figure 11.8

Solving the Two–Color Problem

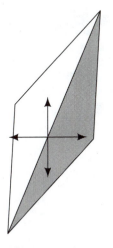

Figure 11.9

The Ridge Problem

a kind of stochastic hill–climbing method in which there are several "climbers" working in parallel and in which moves are made by creating offspring climbers. The function being optimized is the fitness function. The effectiveness of GA and GP methods can be compared with various versions of ordinary hill climbing [Juels & Wattenberg 1996, O'Reilly & Oppacher 1994].

A process known as *simulated annealing* [Kirkpatrick, Gelatt, & Vecchi 1983] is also useful for dealing with local extrema. There are different versions of the process; in one of these, we choose moves according to a probability distribution over the available moves. The distribution favors moves to nodes having lower elevation (hill descending again). We start the process with a distribution only negligibly biased toward these favored nodes, and gradually increase the bias until, late in the process, it is overwhelmingly probable that the move will be to a lower elevation node. The result is that at the beginning of the process, we are executing a random walk over the landscape. Eventually, as the process ensues, we start to descend into one of the valleys. If this valley is not very deep, it typically will neither be very broad, and soon a subsequent random move will jostle us out of it. It is less likely that we will move out of broad (and thus probably deep) valleys, and at the end of the process (with no random moves), we descend to its deepest point. The process gets its name by analogy with annealing in metallurgy, in which a material's temperature is gradually decreased allowing its crystalline structure to reach a minimal energy state. In simulated annealing, the parameter in the probability distribution that controls its width is often called the temperature.

Exercises

11.1 Refer to the image shown in Exercise 6.4 in Chapter 6. Explain how you would use a constraint graph and constraint propagation to find a consistent labeling for this image.

11.2 Use the method of heuristic repair to solve the problem of coloring the map shown here with four colors such that no two adjacent regions have the same color. Start with the colors shown.

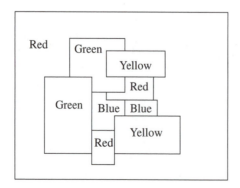

11.3 Use the min–conflicts method to solve the Four–Queens problem. Start with all of the queens on a main diagonal. Break ties randomly! (Working this problem out by hand may be tedious but is worth doing once.)

11.4 If you have not yet done Exercise 7.3 (the Missionary and Cannibals problem), do so now. Let the function f = the total number of people on the start side of the river. Can this problem be solved by a hill–descending method based on f? Why or why not?

12 Adversarial Search

Two-Agent Games

One of the challenges mentioned in Chapter 10 involved planning and acting in environments populated by other active agents. Lacking knowledge of how other agents might act, we can do little more than use a sense/plan/act architecture that does not plan too far into the unpredictable future. However, when knowledge permits, an agent can construct plans that explicitly consider the effects of the actions of other agents. Let's consider the special case of two agents. An idealized setting in which they can take each other's actions into account is one in which the actions of the agents are interleaved. First one agent acts, then the other, and so on.

For example, consider the grid–space world of Figure 12.1. Two robots, named "Black" and "White" can each move into an adjacent cell in their row or column. They move alternately (White moving first, say), and when it is their turn to move, they must move somewhere. Suppose the goal of White is to be in the same cell with Black. Black's goal is to prevent this from happening. White can plan by constructing a search tree in which, at alternate levels, Black's possible moves are considered also. I show part of such a search tree in Figure 12.2.

In order to select its best first action, White needs to analyze the tree to determine likely outcomes—taking into account that Black will act to prevent White from achieving its goal. In some conflict situations of this sort, it is possible that one agent can find a move such that no matter what the other does at any of its moves, the one will be able to achieve its goal. More commonly, because of computational and time limitations, neither agent will be able to find an action that guarantees its success. I shall be presenting limited–horizon search methods that are useful for finding heuristically reasonable actions in these cases. In any

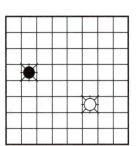

Figure 12.1

Two Robots in
Grid World

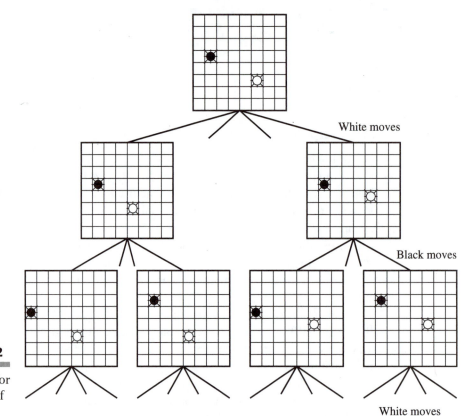

Figure 12.2

Search Tree for
the Moves of
Two Robots

case, after settling on a first move, the agent makes that move, senses what
the other agent does, and then repeats the planning process in sense/plan/act
fashion.

My grid–world example is an instance of what are called *two-agent, perfect-
information, zero-sum games*. In the versions I consider, two agents, called *players*,
move in turn until either one of them *wins* (and the other thereby *loses*), or the
result is a *draw*. Each player has a complete and perfect model of the environment

and of its own and the other's possible actions and their effects. (Although neither player has perfect knowledge of what the other will actually do in any situation.) Studying games of this sort gives us insight into some aspects of the more general problem of planning when there are multiple agents—even when the goals of the agents do not conflict.

You will recognize that many common games, including Chess, Checkers (Draughts), and Go, belong to this class. Indeed, computer programs have been written that play these games—in some cases at championship levels. Although the game of Tic-Tac-Toe (Noughts and Crosses) is not computationally interesting, its simplicity makes it quite useful for illustrating search techniques, and I will use it for that purpose. Some games (such as Backgammon) involve an element of chance, which makes them more difficult to analyze.

Iconic representations naturally suggest themselves in setting up state–space descriptions for many games—especially board games such as Chess. We used 8×8 arrays to represent the various positions of the Black and White robots in their 8×8 grid worlds.[1] Game moves are represented by operators that convert one state description into another. Game graphs are defined implicitly by a start node and the operators for each player. Search trees can be constructed just as we have done in previous chapters, although different techniques are used for selecting the first move. I turn to a discussion of these techniques next.

12.2   *The Minimax Procedure*

In my subsequent discussion of games, I name the two players *MAX* and *MIN*. Our task is to find a "best" move for *MAX*. We assume that *MAX* moves first, and that the two players move alternately thereafter. Thus, nodes at even–numbered depths correspond to positions in which it is *MAX*'s move next; these will be called *MAX* nodes. Nodes at odd–numbered depths correspond to positions in which it is *MIN*'s move next; these are the *MIN* nodes. (The top node of a game tree is of depth zero.) A *ply* of *ply-depth k* in a game tree consists of the nodes of depths $2k$ and $2k + 1$. The extent of searches in game trees is usually given in terms of ply depth—the amount of lookahead measured in terms of pairs of alternating moves for *MAX* and *MIN*.

As I have mentioned, complete search (to win, lose, or draw) of most game graphs is computationally infeasible. It has been estimated that the complete game graph for Chess has approximately 10^{40} nodes. It would take about 10^{22} centuries to generate the complete search graph for Chess, even assuming that a

---

1. However, in this case a better representation, which I leave to you to formulate, is based on whether the distance between the robots is even or odd when it is White's turn to move. Parity is preserved after a pair of moves!

successor could be generated in 1/3 of a nanosecond.[2] (The universe is estimated to be on the order of 10^8 centuries old.) Furthermore, heuristic search techniques do not reduce the effective branching factor sufficiently to be of much help. Therefore, for complex games, we must accept the fact that search to termination is impossible (except perhaps during the end game). Instead, we must use methods similar to the limited–horizon search process described in Chapter 10.

We can use either breadth–first, depth–first, or heuristic methods, except that the termination conditions must now be modified. Several artificial termination conditions can be specified based on such factors as a time limit, a storage–space limit, and the depth of the deepest node in the search tree. It is also usual in Chess, for example, not to terminate if any of the tip nodes represent "live" positions, that is, positions in which there is an immediate advantageous swap.

After search terminates, we must extract from the search tree an estimate of the best–first move. This estimate can be made by applying a *static evaluation function* to the leaf nodes of the search tree. The evaluation function measures the "worth" of a leaf node position. The measurement is based on various features thought to influence this worth; for example, in Checkers some useful features measure the relative piece advantage, control of the center, control of the center by kings, and so forth. It is customary in analyzing game trees to adopt the convention that game positions favorable to *MAX* cause the evaluation function to have a positive value, whereas positions favorable to *MIN* cause the evaluation function to have a negative value; values near zero correspond to game positions not particularly favorable to either *MAX* or *MIN*.

A good first move can be extracted by a procedure called the *minimax procedure*. (For simplicity, I explain this procedure and others depending on it as if the game graph were really just a game tree.) We assume that were *MAX* to choose among the tip nodes of a search tree, he would prefer that node having the largest evaluation. Since *MAX* can indeed choose that node if it is his turn to play, the *backed-up value* of a *MAX* node parent of *MIN* tip nodes is equal to the maximum of the static evaluations of the tip nodes. On the other hand, if *MIN* were to choose among tip nodes, he would presumably choose that node having the smallest evaluation (that is, the most negative). Since *MIN* can choose that node if it is his turn to play, the *MIN* node parent of *MAX* tip nodes is assigned a backed–up value equal to the minimum of the static evaluations of the tip nodes. After the parents of all tip nodes have been assigned backed–up values, we back up values another level, assuming that *MAX* would choose that successor *MIN* node with

---

2. In contrast, Schaeffer estimates that the complete game graph for Checkers has only about 10^{18} nodes [Schaeffer & Lake 1996]. Because *MAX* has only to show that one of its moves at every ply leads to a solution, a solution tree would thus have about the square root of this number or 10^9 nodes. Schaeffer and Lake think that flawless machine Checkers play is attainable "in the near future."

the largest backed–up value, whereas *MIN* would choose that successor *MAX* node with the smallest backed–up value.

We continue to back up values, level by level from the leaves, until, finally, the successors of the start node are assigned backed–up values. We are assuming it is *MAX*'s turn to move at the start, so *MAX* should choose as his first move the one corresponding to the successor having the largest backed–up value.

The validity of this whole procedure rests on the assumption that the backed–up values of the start node's successors are more reliable measures of the ultimate relative worth of these positions than are the values that would be obtained by directly applying the static evaluation function to these positions. The backed–up values are, after all, based on "looking ahead" in the game tree and therefore depend on features occurring nearer the end of the game, when presumably they are more relevant.

A simple example using the game of Tic–Tac–Toe illustrates the minimaxing method. (In Tic–Tac–Toe, players alternate putting marks in a 3×3 array. One marks crosses (X), and the other marks circles (O). The first to have a complete row, column, or diagonal filled in with his marks wins.) Let us suppose that *MAX* marks crosses and *MIN* marks circles and that it is *MAX*'s turn to play first. With a depth bound of 2, we conduct a breadth–first search until all of the nodes at level 2 are generated, and then we apply a static evaluation function to the positions at these nodes. Let our evaluation function, $e(p)$, of a position p be given simply by

If p is not a winning position for either player,

$e(p) =$ (number of complete rows, columns, or diagonals that are still open

for *MAX*) $-$ (number of complete rows, columns, or diagonals that are still

open for *MIN*)

If p is a win for *MAX*,

$e(p) = \infty$(I use ∞ here to denote a very large positive number)

If p is a win for *MIN*,

$e(p) = -\infty$

Thus, if p is

we have $e(p) = 6 - 4 = 2$.

We make use of symmetries in generating successor positions; thus the following game states are all considered identical:

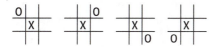

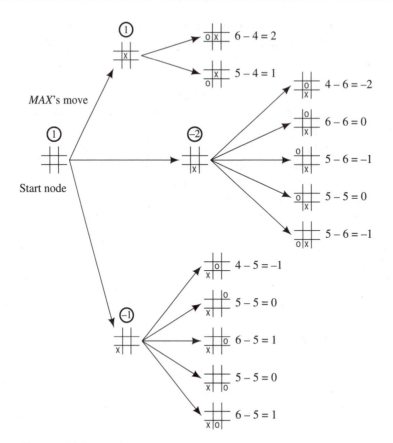

Figure 12.3

The First Stage of Search in Tic-Tac-Toe

(Early in the game, the branching factor of the Tic–Tac–Toe tree is kept small by symmetries; late in the game, it is kept small by the number of open spaces available.)

In Figure 12.3, I show the tree generated by a search to depth 2. Static evaluations are shown to the right of the tip nodes, and backed–up values are circled. Since

has the largest backed–up value, it is chosen as the first move. (Coincidentally, this would also be *MAX*'s best–first move if a complete search had been done.)

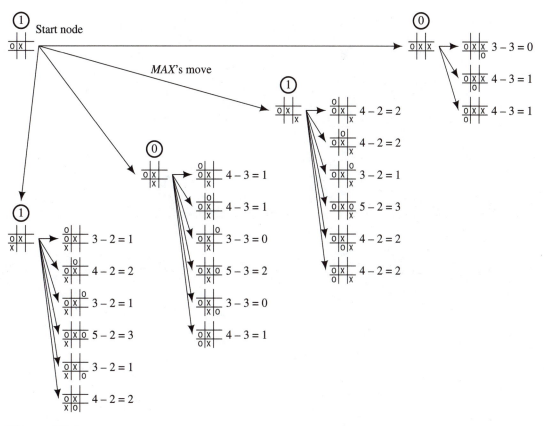

Figure 12.4

The Second Stage of Search in Tic-Tac-Toe

Now, following the sense/plan/act cycle, let us suppose that *MAX* makes this move and *MIN* replies by putting a circle in the square just to the left of the X (a bad move for *MIN*, who must not be using a good search strategy). Next *MAX* searches to depth 2 below the resulting configuration, yielding the search tree shown in Figure 12.4. There are now two possible "best" moves; suppose *MAX* makes the one indicated. Now *MIN* makes the move that avoids his immediate defeat, yielding

MAX searches again, yielding the tree shown in Figure 12.5.

Some of the tip nodes in this tree (for example, the one marked *A*) represent wins for *MIN* and thus have evaluations equal to $-\infty$. When these evaluations

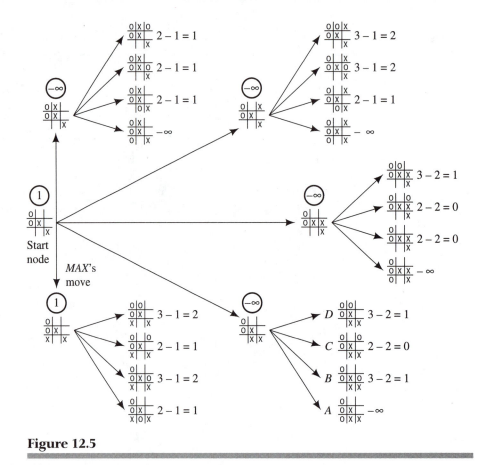

Figure 12.5

The Last Stage of Search in Tic-Tac-Toe

are backed up, we see that *MAX*'s best move is also the only one that avoids his immediate defeat. Now *MIN* can see that *MAX* must win on his next move, so *MIN* gracefully resigns.

12.3   *The Alpha-Beta Procedure*

The search procedure that I have just described separates completely the processes of search–tree generation and position evaluation. Only after tree generation is completed does position evaluation begin. It happens that this separation results in a grossly inefficient strategy. Remarkable reductions (amounting sometimes to many orders of magnitude) in the amount of search needed (to discover an equally good move) are possible if we perform tip-node evaluations and

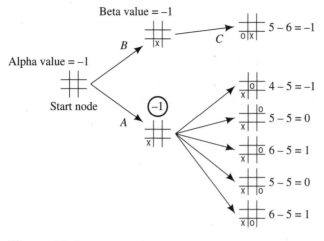

Figure 12.6

Part of the First Stage of Search in Tic–Tac–Toe

calculate backed–up values simultaneously with tree generation. The process is similar to alpha pruning discussed in Chapter 10.

Consider the search tree at the last stage of our Tic–Tac–Toe search (Figure 12.5). Suppose that a tip node is evaluated as soon as it is generated. Then after the node marked A is generated and evaluated, there is no point in generating (and evaluating) nodes B, C, and D; that is, since MIN has A available and MIN could prefer nothing to A, we know immediately that MIN will choose A. We can then assign A's parent the backed–up value of $-\infty$ and proceed with the search, having saved the search effort of generating and evaluating nodes B, C, and D. (Note that the savings in search effort would have been even greater if we were searching to greater depths; for then none of the descendants of nodes B, C, and D would have to be generated either.) It is important to observe that failing to generate nodes B, C, and D can in no way affect what will turn out to be MAX's best–first move.

In this example, the search savings depended on the fact that node A represented a win for MIN. The same kind of savings can be achieved, however, even when none of the positions in the search tree represents a win for either MAX or MIN.

Consider the first stage of the Tic–Tac–Toe tree shown earlier (Figure 12.3). I repeat part of this tree in Figure 12.6. Suppose that search had progressed in a depth–first manner and that whenever a tip node is generated, its static evaluation is computed. Also suppose that whenever a position can be given a backed–up value, this value is computed. Now consider the situation occurring at that stage of the depth–first search immediately after node A and all of its successors have been generated, but before node B is generated. Node A is now given the backed–up value of -1. At this point, we know that the backed–up value of the start node is bounded from below by -1. Depending on the backed–up values of the other successors of the start node, the final backed–up value of the start node may be greater than -1, but it cannot be less. We call this lower bound an *alpha value* for the start node.

Now let depth-first search proceed until node B and its first successor node, C, are generated. Node C is then given the static value of -1. Now we know that the backed–up value of node B is bounded from above by -1. Depending on the static values of the rest of node B's successors, the final backed–up value of node B can be less than -1, but it cannot be greater. We call this upper bound on node B a *beta value*. We note at this point, therefore, that the final backed–up value of node B can never exceed the alpha value of the start node, and therefore we can discontinue search below node B. We are guaranteed that node B will not turn out to be preferable to node A.

This reduction in search effort was achieved by keeping track of bounds on backed–up values. In general, as successors of a node are given backed–up values, the bounds on backed–up values can be revised. But we note that

- The alpha values of *MAX* nodes (including the start node) can never decrease.
- The beta values of *MIN* nodes can never increase.

Because of these constraints, we can state the following rules for discontinuing the search:

1. Search can be discontinued below any *MIN* node having a beta value less than or equal to the alpha value of any of its *MAX* node ancestors. The final backed–up value of this *MIN* node can then be set to its beta value. This value may not be the same as that obtained by full minimax search, but its use results in selecting the same best move.

2. Search can be discontinued below any *MAX* node having an alpha value greater than or equal to the beta value of any of its *MIN* node ancestors. The final backed–up value of this *MAX* node can then be set to its alpha value.

During search, alpha and beta values are computed as follows:

- The alpha value of a *MAX* node is set equal to the current largest final backed–up value of its successors.
- The beta value of a *MIN* node is set equal to the current smallest final backed–up value of its successors.

When search is discontinued under rule 1, we say that an *alpha cut-off* has occurred; when search is discontinued under rule 2, we say that a *beta cut-off* has occurred. The whole process of keeping track of alpha and beta values and making cut-offs when possible is usually called the *alpha-beta procedure*. The procedure terminates when all of the successors of the start node have been given final backed-up values, and the best first move is then the one creating that successor having the highest backed-up value. Employing this procedure always results in finding a move that is as good as the move that would have been found by the simple minimax method searching to the same depth. The only difference is that the alpha–beta procedure finds a best first move usually after much less search.

My verbal description of the alpha–beta procedure can be captured by a concise pseudocode recursive algorithm. The following version, which evaluates the minimax value of a node n relative to the cut-off values α and β, is adapted from [Pearl 1984, p. 234]:

$AB(n; \alpha, \beta)$

1. If n at depth bound, return $AB(n)$ = static evaluation of n. Otherwise, let $n_1, \ldots, n_k, \ldots, n_b$ be the successors of n (in order), set $k \leftarrow 1$ and, if n is a *MAX* node, go to step 2; else go to step 2'.

2. Set $\alpha \leftarrow \max[\alpha, AB(n_k; \alpha, \beta)]$.	2' Set $\beta \leftarrow \min[\beta, AB(n_k; \alpha, \beta)]$.
3. If $\alpha \geq \beta$, return β; else continue.	3' If $\beta \leq \alpha$, return α; else continue.
4. If $k = b$, return α; else proceed to n_{k+1}, i.e., set $k \leftarrow k + 1$ and go to step 2.	4' If $k = b$, return β; else proceed to n_{k+1}, i.e., set $k \leftarrow k + 1$ and go to step 2'.

We begin an alpha–beta search by calling $AB(s; -\infty, +\infty)$, where s is the start node. Throughout the algorithm, $\alpha < \beta$. The ordering of nodes in step 1 of the algorithm has an important effect on its efficiency, as we shall see.

An application of the alpha–beta procedure is illustrated in Figure 12.7. I show a search tree generated to a depth of 6. *MAX* nodes are depicted by a square, and *MIN* nodes are depicted by a circle. The tip nodes have the static values indicated. Now suppose we conduct a depth-first search employing the alpha–beta procedure. (My convention is to generate the bottom-most nodes first.) The subtree generated by the alpha–beta procedure is indicated by darkened branches. Those nodes cut off have X's drawn through them. Note that only 18 of the original 41 tip nodes had to be evaluated. (You can test your understanding of the procedure by attempting to duplicate the alpha–beta search on this example.)

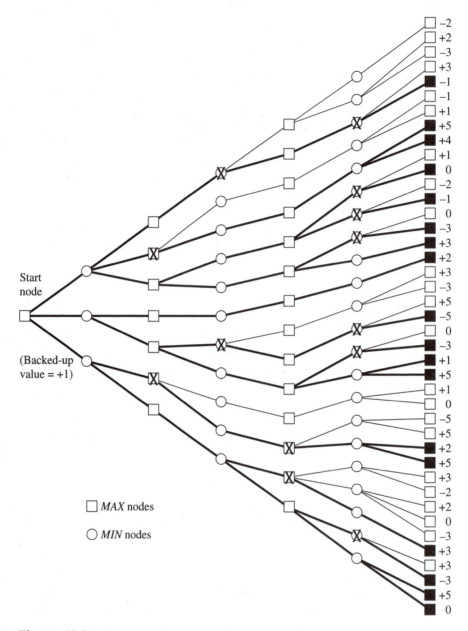

Figure 12.7

An Example of Alpha–Beta Search

12.4   *The Search Efficiency of the Alpha-Beta Procedure*

In order to perform alpha and beta cut–offs, at least some part of the search tree must be generated to maximum depth, because alpha and beta values must be based on the static values of tip nodes. Therefore, some type of a depth–first search is usually employed in using the alpha–beta procedure. Furthermore, the number of cut–offs that can be made during a search depends on the degree to which the early alpha and beta values approximate the final backed–up values.

Suppose a tree has depth d, and every node (except a tip node) has exactly b successors. Such a tree will have precisely b^d tip nodes. Suppose an alpha–beta procedure generated successors in the order of their true backed–up values—the lowest–valued successors first for *MIN* nodes and the highest–valued successors first for *MAX* nodes. (Of course, these backed–up values are not typically known at the time of successor generation, so this order could never really be achieved, except perhaps accidentally.)

It happens that this order maximizes the number of cut–offs that will occur and minimizes the number of tip nodes generated. Let us denote this minimal number of tip nodes by N_d. It can be shown [Slagle & Dixon 1969, Knuth & Moore 1975] that

$$N_d = \begin{cases} 2b^{d/2} - 1 & \text{for even } d \\ b^{(d+1)/2} + b^{(d-1)/2} - 1 & \text{for odd } d. \end{cases}$$

That is, the number of tip nodes of depth d that would be generated by optimal alpha–beta search is about the same as the number of tip nodes that would have been generated at depth $d/2$ without alpha–beta. Therefore, in the same time that search without alpha–beta would stop at a depth bound of $d/2$, alpha–beta search (with perfect ordering) can proceed to a depth of d. In other words, alpha–beta, with perfect ordering, reduces the effective branching factor from b to approximately $\sqrt{b}$.

Of course, perfect node ordering cannot be achieved. (If it could, we wouldn't need the search process at all.) In the worst case, alpha–beta search produces no cut–offs and thus leaves the effective branching factor unchanged. If the successor nodes are ordered randomly, Pearl has shown that alpha–beta search allows search depth to be increased by approximately 4/3; that is, the average branching factor is reduced to approximately $\sqrt[4]{b^3}$ [Pearl 1982b]. (See [Pearl 1984, Ch. 9] for a thorough analysis with historical commentary.) In practice, if good heuristics are used to order successor nodes, the alpha–beta procedure usually comes close to achieving the optimal reduction in the effective branching factor.

The most straightforward method for ordering successor nodes is simply to use the static evaluation function. Another technique for node ordering comes as a side effect of using a version of iterative deepening—first used in the Chess-playing program CHESS 4.5 [Slate & Atkin 1977]. The program first searched to a depth bound of one ply and then evaluated the best move; then it searched all over again to two ply and evaluated the best move; and so on. The main reason for these multiple, and seemingly wasteful, searches is that game–playing programs often have time constraints. Depending on the time resources available, search to deeper plys can be aborted at any time, and the move judged best by the search last completed can be made. The node-ordering side effect comes about because the successors judged to be best in the ply k search can be used to order nodes in the ply $k + 1$ search.

12.5   *Other Important Matters*

For most of the game (in most games), search must end before terminating positions are found (limited horizon), causing various difficulties. One difficulty is that search might end at a position in which *MAX* (or *MIN*) is able to make a great move. For this reason, most game–searching programs make sure that a position is *quiescent* before ending search at that position. A position is quiescent if its static value is not much different from what its backed-up value would be by looking a move or two ahead.

Even by insisting on quiescence before ending search along a certain branch, there can be situations in which disaster or success lurks just beyond the search horizon. There are situations in some games that inevitably lead to success for *MAX*, say, no matter what *MIN* does, but for which *MIN* is able to make quiescence-preserving stalling moves that push *MAX's* success beyond the search horizon. This so–called *horizon effect* is one of the primary difficulties facing game-playing programs.

Both the minimax method and its alpha–beta extension assume that the opposing player will always make its best move. There are occasions in which this assumption is inappropriate. Suppose, for example, that *MAX* is in a situation that appears to be losing—assuming that *MIN* will play optimally. Yet, there exists a move for *MAX* that gets it out of its difficulty if only *MIN* would make a mistake. The minimax strategy won't recommend such a move, yet (since the game appears lost anyway) there would seem to be little additional risk in gambling that *MIN* will err. Minimax would also be inappropriate if one player had some kind of model of the other player's strategy. Perhaps the other "player" is not really an opponent but simply another agent of change.

12.6   *Games of Chance*

Some games, such as Backgammon, involve an element of chance. For example, the moves that one is allowed to make might depend on the outcome of a throw of the dice. The game tree for a prototypical game of this type is shown schematically in Figure 12.8. (To make the tree somewhat simpler, I show only the six different

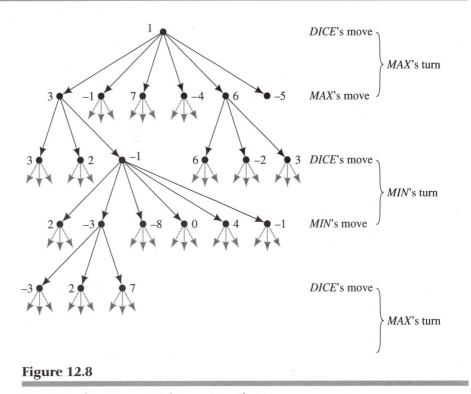

Figure 12.8

Game Tree for a Game Involving a Dice Throw

outcomes possible by throwing a single die.) *MAX*'s and *MIN*'s "turns" now each involve a throw of the die. We might imagine that at each dice throw, a fictitious third player, *DICE*, makes a move. That move is determined by chance. In the case of throwing a single die, the six outcomes are all equally probable, but the chance element could also involve an arbitrary probability distribution.

Values can be backed up in game trees involving chance moves also, except that when backing up values to nodes at which there is a chance move, we might back up the *expected* (average) values of the values of the successors instead of a maximum or minimum.[3] The numbers adjacent to the nodes in Figure 12.8 are presumed backed–up values. We back up the minimum value of the values of successors of nodes for which it is *MIN*'s move, the maximum value of the values of successors of nodes for which it is *MAX*'s move, and the expected value of the values of successors of nodes for which it is the *DICE*'s move. This modified backing–up procedure is sometimes called *expectimaxing*.

---

3. Of course, if we want to be very conservative about the outcome of a chance move, we might instead back up the worst value for *MAX* whenever it is *DICE*'s move.

Introducing a chance move often makes the game tree branch too much for effective searching. In such cases, it is extremely important to have a good static evaluation function so that search does not have to go very deep. If a sufficiently good static evaluation function were available, *MAX's* policy for choosing a move could look just at the positions one move ahead and make that move that maximizes the value of the static evaluation function of those positions. In the next section, we discuss techniques for learning action policies and for learning static evaluation functions in games having branching factors too large to permit search.

12.7 *Learning Evaluation Functions*

Some games (such as Go) allow so many moves at each stage that deep searches would seem not to be feasible.[4] Without any search, the best move would have to be selected based just on the static evaluation of the successors or by reacting to the immediate board position through various pattern recognition techniques. In Go, for example, effort has been devoted to finding ways to evaluate and to respond reactively to positions [Zobrist 1970, Reitman & Wilcox 1979, Kierulf, Chen, & Nievergelt 1990].

Sometimes, good static evaluation functions can be learned by neural networks. The game of Backgammon provides an example. A program called TD-GAMMON [Tesauro 1992, Tesauro 1995] learns to play Backgammon by training a layered, feedforward neural network. The structure of the neural net and its coding is as shown in Figure 12.9. The 198 inputs (which represent a Backgammon board situation) are fully connected to the hidden units, and the hidden units are fully connected to the output units. The hidden units and the output units are sigmoids. It is intended that the output units produce estimates, p_1, p_2, p_3, and p_4, of the probabilities of various outcomes of the game resulting from any given input board position. The overall value of a board position is then given by an estimated "payoff," $v = p_1 + 2p_2 - p_3 - 2p_4$. In using the network to play Backgammon, the dice are thrown and the boards permitted by all of the possible moves from the existing board and that dice roll are evaluated by the network. The board with the best value of v is selected, and the move that produces that board is made. (If it is White's move, the highest value of v is best; if it is Black's move, the smallest value of v is best.)

Temporal difference training of the network is accomplished during actual play using the network to play games against itself. When a move is made, the network weights are adjusted, using backpropagation, to make the predicted

---

4. Human Go players evidently perform searches over isolated subsets of the board, and it may be necessary and feasible for competent programs to do so also.

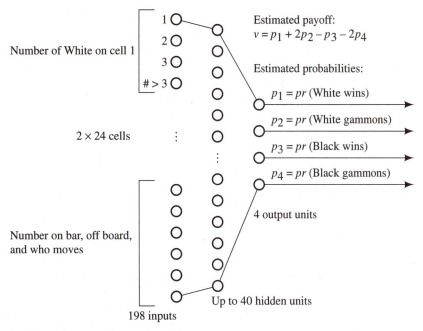

Hidden and output units are sigmoids
Learning rate: $c = 0.1$; initial weights chosen randomly between -0.5 and $+0.5$

Figure 12.9

The TD-GAMMON Network

payoff from the original position closer to that of the resulting position. For simplicity, I explain the method as if it used pure temporal difference learning. (A variant is actually used, but that variant need not concern us here.) If v_t is the network's estimate of the payoff at time t (before a move is made), and v_{t+1} is the estimate at time $t + 1$ (after a move is made), the standard temporal difference weight–adjustment rule is

$$\Delta \mathbf{W}_t = c(v_{t+1} - v_t)\frac{\partial v_t}{\partial \mathbf{W}}$$

where $\mathbf{W}_t$ is a vector of *all* weights in the network at time t, and $\frac{\partial v_t}{\partial \mathbf{W}}$ is the gradient of v_t in this weight space. (For a layered, feedforward network, such as that of TD-GAMMON, the weight changes for the weight vectors in each layer can be expressed in the manner described in Chapter 3.) The network is trained so that, for all t, its output, v_t, for an input before a move tends toward its output, v_{t+1}, for the input after a move (just as in value iteration). Experiments with this training method have been performed by having the network play many hundreds of thousands of games against itself. (Training runs have involved as many as a million and a half games.)

Performance of a well-trained network is at or near championship level. Based on 40 games played against a version of the program that uses some look-ahead search, Bill Robertie (a former Backgammon world champion) estimates that **TD-GAMMON 2.1** plays at a strong master level—extremely close (within a few hundredths of a point) to equaling the world's best human players [Tesauro 1995].

12.8 *Additional Readings and Discussion*

Just as puzzles have, games too have been important in refining and testing AI techniques. For example, [Russell & Wefald 1991, Ch. 4] propose and evaluate game–tree search algorithms (**MGSS*** and **MGSS2**) that use metalevel computations (involving the expected value of continued search) to prune the search tree in a way that is more efficient than alpha–beta. Berliner's **B*** algorithm uses interval bounds [Berliner 1979], which also permit more effective pruning. [Korf 1991] has extended the alpha–beta procedure to multiplayer games.

Instead of using numerical evaluation functions, some work on game playing has favored the use of pattern recognition techniques to decide whether one position is *better than* or *worse than* another position. This technique has been employed in programs that play Chess end games [Huberman 1968, Bratko & Michie 1980].

The most successful early work on game playing was that of Arthur Samuel who developed machine learning methods for the game of Checkers (Draughts) [Samuel 1959, Samuel 1967]. Samuel's Checker–playing programs played at near-championship level. Jonathan Schaeffer's **CHINOOK** program at the University of Alberta [Schaeffer, et al. 1992, Schaeffer 1997] is now regarded as the world Checkers champion. In 1997, the IBM program, **DEEP BLUE**, defeated the reigning world Chess champion, Garry Kasparov, in a championship match.

[Newborn 1996] is a book on computer Chess, recounting its history up through the 1996 defeat of **DEEP BLUE** by Garry Kasparov. For a review of this book plus commentary on the role of Chess as a research platform for AI, see [McCarthy 1997]. McCarthy thinks that Chess programs could perform better with less search if they used more humanlike reasoning methods. He thinks that Chess can again become a *"Drosophila"* for AI if researchers would use it to test knowledge–based reasoning methods.

[Michie 1966] coined the term *expectimax* and experimented with the technique.

[Lee & Mahajan 1988] have applied reinforcement learning methods to the game of Othello, and [Schraudolph, Dayan, & Sejnowski 1994] have applied temporal difference techniques to the game of Go.

For more on game search methods generally, see [Pearl 1984, Ch. 9].

Exercises

12.1 Why does search in game–playing programs always proceed forward from the current position rather than backward from the goal?

12.2 Consider the following game tree in which the static scores (in parentheses at the tip nodes) are all from the first player's point of view. Assume that the first player is the maximizing player.

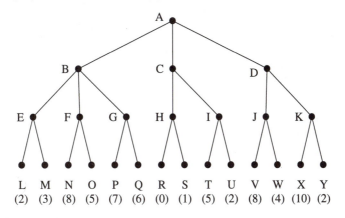

1. What move should the first player choose?
2. What nodes would not need to be examined using the alpha–beta algorithm—assuming that nodes are examined in left-to-right order?

12.3 (Courtesy of Matt Ginsberg.) Suppose that you are using alpha–beta pruning to determine the value of a move in a game tree, and that you have decided that a particular node, n, and its children can be pruned. If the game tree is in fact a graph and there is another path to the node n, are you still justified in pruning this node? Either prove that you are or construct an example that shows that you cannot.

12.4 Most game–playing programs do not save search results from one move to the next. Instead, they usually start completely over whenever it is the machine's turn to move. Why?

12.5 Comment (in one–half page or less) how you would modify the minimax strategy so that it could be used to select a move for one of the players in a three-person, perfect-information game. (A perfect-information game is one in which each player knows everything about each state of the game. Chess is a perfect-information game, but bridge is not.) Assume that the players, A, B, and C, play in turn. Assume that the game can end either in all players achieving a "draw" or by one of the three players achieving a "win." Also assume that the game tree cannot be searched to termination, but that evaluations of nonterminal positions must be backed up by some process analogous to the minimax strategy in order to select a move.

Part III
Knowledge Representation and Reasoning

The most formidable weapon against errors of every kind is reason.
—Thomas Paine, *The Age of Reason*

Why is this thus? What is the reason of this thusness?
—Artemus Ward

13 The Propositional Calculus

Using Constraints on Feature Values

I have discussed two rather different methods for modeling an agent's world: iconic based and feature based. Binary–valued features are *descriptions* of the world—what is true about it and what is not true about it. Iconic representations are *simulations* of certain aspects of the world. Although simulations are more direct and often therefore more efficient than descriptions, descriptions have a number of advantages of their own. The values of features are easy to communicate to other agents, whereas iconic models may not break up well into isolated pieces for incremental communication. Computing the values of features often requires less elaborate perceptual processing than would the construction or modification of an iconic model. And, in cases where the values of some features cannot be sensed directly, their values can sometimes be inferred from the values of other features using constraints imposed by the kind of world an agent finds itself in.

Furthermore, some information about an agent's environment is difficult or impossible to represent iconically. For example:

- General laws, such as "all blue boxes are pushable"
- Negative information, such as "block *A* is not on the floor" (without saying where block *A* is)
- Uncertain information, such as "either block *A* is on block *B* or block *A* is on block *C*"

Some of this difficult-to-represent information can be formulated as *constraints* on the values of features. These constraints, representing important knowledge

217

about the world an agent inhabits, can often be used to infer the values of features that cannot be sensed directly. Inferring information about an agent's *present* state (using computations based on constraints among features) can be contrasted with computing the *future* states resulting from an agent's actions (using the search methods discussed in Part II of this book). The first activity I will call "reasoning," and the second "projecting." For the next few chapters, I set aside the problem of projecting and concentrate on reasoning.

There are several applications involving reasoning about the values of features. To be sure, reasoning can enhance the effectiveness of agents (even reactive agents) as they decide upon actions. But there are many other applications as well. For example, it has proved possible to represent the functioning of various physical systems, including biological ones and electromechanical ones, by appropriate sets of features. Constraints among these features encode physical or other laws relevant to the organism or device. Reasoning can then be used, among other purposes, to diagnose malfunction in these systems; features associated with "causes" can be inferred from features associated with "symptoms," for example. This general approach is fundamental to an important class of AI applications called *expert systems*.

I begin my discussion of reasoning techniques with a motivating example. Consider a robot that is able to lift a block, if that block is liftable (that is, not too heavy), and if the robot's battery power source is adequate. If both of these conditions are satisfied, then when the robot tries to lift a block it is holding, its arm moves. We can represent these various conditions by binary–valued features:

x_1 (*BAT_OK*)

x_2 (*LIFTABLE*)

x_3 (*MOVES*)

I will use the mnemonic names of these features (given in parentheses) to aid the discussion. Assume that the robot can sense *BAT_OK* (by reading a gauge) and *MOVES* (by joint–angle sensors) but not *LIFTABLE*. Yet, the value of *LIFTABLE* may well be important for the robot to know for other tasks that it will have to perform. From my description, *we* know that if both *BAT_OK* and *LIFTABLE* have value 1, so will *MOVES*. Thus, if *MOVES* has value 0 when the robot attempts to move the block, then *we* know that either *BAT_OK* or *LIFTABLE* (or both) must have value 0. But if *BAT_OK* is sensed to have value 1, then it must be *LIFTABLE* that has value 0. Since we can reason thus, let's let the robot do so also. What is needed is a *language* in which both the constraints among features and the values of features can be expressed and *inference* mechanisms that are able to perform the required reasoning. The *propositional calculus*, a descendant of Boolean algebra, provides the necessary tools.

The constraint of my example would be written in the language of the propositional calculus as follows:

`BAT_OK ∧ LIFTABLE ⊃ MOVES`

where ∧ means "and," and ⊃ means "implies."

Mechanisms associated with this language can be used to derive consequences from statements in the language. Since logical languages are so important in artificial intelligence, I must treat them in some detail before returning to present yet more complex and intelligent agents based on the use of these languages.

First, some definitions. A *logic* involves

- A *language* (with a *syntax* for specifying what is a legal expression in the language)
- *Inference rules* for manipulating sentences in the language
- *Semantics* for associating elements of the language with elements of some subject matter

We will study two logical languages: the first and simpler of the two is called the *propositional calculus*; the second, and more useful one, is called the *first-order predicate calculus (FOPC)*. Many ideas important in first–order predicate calculus can be more simply introduced in the propositional calculus, so I will present that language first.

13.2   *The Language*

I will describe the elements of the propositional calculus formally. It's best for the moment not to attempt to associate meanings with elements of this language; think of what we are doing now as describing the rules of a meaningless game. Later, we'll talk about meaning. Here are the elements of the language:[1]

Atoms: the two distinguished atoms T and F and the countably infinite set of those strings of characters that begin with a capital letter, for example, P, Q, R, . . . , P1, P2, ON_A_B, and so on.

Connectives: ∨, ∧, ⊃, and ¬, called "or," "and," "implies," and "not," respectively. (Later, I give these connectives meanings related to their names; for now, they are meaningless symbols.)

---

1. To make it easier to distinguish logical expressions from other material in this book, I will adopt the following notational conventions: logical expressions will be set in so–called `typewriter font`, and symbols that stand for logical expressions will usually be set in lowercase Greek letters.

Syntax of *well-formed formulas (wffs)*, also called *sentences*:

- Any atom is a wff.

  Examples: P, R, P3

- If ω_1 and ω_2 are wffs, so are

  $\omega_1 \vee \omega_2$(called a *disjunction* of ω_1 and ω_2)

  $\omega_1 \wedge \omega_2$(called a *conjunction* of ω_1 and ω_2)

  $\omega_1 \supset \omega_2$(called an *implication*)

  $\neg \omega_1$(called a *negation* of ω_1)

  Atoms and atoms with a $\neg$ sign in front of them are called *literals*. In $\omega_1 \supset \omega_2$, ω_1 is called the *antecedent* of the implication, and ω_2 is called the *consequent* of the implication.

  Examples of wffs:

  $(P \wedge Q) \supset \neg P$

  $P \supset \neg P$

  $P \vee P \supset P$

  $(P \supset Q) \supset (\neg Q \supset \neg P)$

  $\neg \neg P$

- There are no other wffs.

  Example: $P \supset \neg \neg$ is not a wff.

Note the use of extra–linguistic separators, (and), in the preceding examples. They group wffs into (sub) wffs according to the recursive definitions. Some treatments of logic formalize separators as part of the language, but I will use them somewhat loosely and intuitively. Wffs can be recognized by using their definitions recursively. For example, I will show that $(P \wedge Q) \supset \neg R$ is a wff. First, note that since P and Q are wffs, so is $(P \wedge Q)$. And $\neg R$ is a wff because R is. Therefore, $(P \wedge Q) \supset \neg R$ is a wff.

13.3   *Rules of Inference*

We have a number of ways by which we can produce additional wffs from other ones. These are called *rules of inference*. A rule of inference typically has the form: γ can be *inferred* from α (or from α and β).[2] Here are some commonly used rules of inference:

---

2. I haven't yet connected the word *infer* to the meaning that you might be guessing; a rule of inference is simply a mechanical way of creating a new wff from others. Play along.

- The wff ω_2 can be inferred from the wffs ω_1 and $\omega_1 \supset \omega_2$ (this rule of inference is called *modus ponens*).
- The wff $\omega_1 \wedge \omega_2$ can be inferred from the two wffs ω_1 and ω_2 ($\wedge$ introduction).
- The wff $\omega_2 \wedge \omega_1$ can be inferred from the wff $\omega_1 \wedge \omega_2$ (commutativity of $\wedge$).
- The wff ω_1 can be inferred from the wff $\omega_1 \wedge \omega_2$ ($\wedge$ elimination).
- The wff $\omega_1 \vee \omega_2$ can be inferred either from the single wff ω_1 or from the single wff ω_2 ($\vee$ introduction).
- The wff ω_1 can be inferred from the wff $\neg(\neg\omega_1)$ ($\neg$ elimination).

13.4   *Definition of Proof*

The sequence of wffs $\{\omega_1, \omega_2, \dots, \omega_n\}$ is called a *proof* (or a *deduction*) of ω_n from a set of wffs Δ iff each ω_i in the sequence is either in Δ or can be inferred from a wff (or wffs) earlier in the sequence by using one of the rules of inference. If there is a proof of ω_n from Δ, we say that ω_n is a *theorem* of the set Δ. I use the following notation for expressing that ω_n can be proved from Δ:

$$\Delta \vdash \omega_n$$

The concept of proof and theoremhood is relative to a particular set of inference rules used. If we denote the set of inference rules by the letter $\mathcal{R}$, we sometimes then write the fact that ω_n can be proved from Δ using the inference rules in $\mathcal{R}$ by

$$\Delta \vdash_{\mathcal{R}} \omega_n$$

Example: Given a set, Δ, of wffs: $\{P, R, P \supset Q\}$, the following sequence is a proof of $Q \wedge R$ given the inference rules just presented:

$$\{P, P \supset Q, Q, R, Q \wedge R\}.$$

The concept of proof can be based on a partial order as well as on a sequence. This partial order can be represented by a tree structure. Each node in the proof tree is labeled by a wff and must correspond either to a wff in Δ or be inferable from its parents in the tree using one of the rules of inference. The labeled tree is a proof of the label of the root node. I show a sample proof tree in Figure 13.1.[3]

---

3. Note that a proof tree has parent-successor relations that are the reverse of those defined for trees in Chapter 7; the root node is at the *bottom* of the tree.

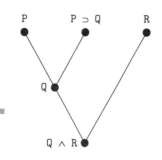

Figure 13.1

A Sample
Proof Tree

13.5   *Semantics*

13.5.1   Interpretations

Now it's time to talk about "meanings." *Semantics* has to do with associating elements of a logical language with elements of a domain of discourse. Such associations are what we mean by "meaning." For propositional logic, we associate atoms with *propositions* about the world. (Thus the name *propositional* logic.) So, for example, we might associate the atom BAT_OK with the proposition "The battery is charged." (We are not *compelled* to make the association suggested by a mnemonic atom string; we could make other ones instead.) An association of atoms with propositions is called an *interpretation*. In a given interpretation, the proposition associated with an atom is called the *denotation* of that atom.

Under a given interpretation, atoms have *values*—*True* or *False*. If atom α is associated with proposition P, then we say that α has value *True* just in case P is true of the world; otherwise, it has value *False*. The special atom T always has value *True*, and the special atom F always has value *False*. Since propositions about the world must either be true or false (an idealization we are willing to make here), we can specify an interpretation by assigning values directly to the atoms in a language—regardless of which proposition about the world each atom denotes.

If an agent's sensory apparatus for determining the truth or falsity of various propositions about the world is reliable, then when sensed feature x_1 has value 1, the corresponding proposition about the world will be true, and the associated propositional logic atom, perhaps X1, will have value *True*. For this reason, instead of representing sensed information for an agent by a value of 1 or 0 on a certain input "wire," we can represent it by a propositional calculus atom in an agent's memory structure that we call its *knowledge base*. The explicit occurrence of an atom, say, X1, in the knowledge base of an agent is intended to mean that the agent regards an associated proposition to be true in its world. We will soon see how an agent uses wffs in its knowledge base.

ω_1	ω_2	$\omega_1 \wedge \omega_2$	$\omega_1 \vee \omega_2$	$\neg\omega_1$	$\omega_1 \supset \omega_2$
True	True	True	True	False	True
True	False	False	True	False	False
False	True	False	True	True	True
False	False	False	False	True	True

Table 13.1

The Propositional Truth Table

13.5.2 The Propositional Truth Table

Given the values of atoms under some interpretation, we can use a *truth table* to compute a value for any wff under that same interpretation. The truth table establishes the semantics (meanings) of the propositional connectives. Let ω_1 and ω_2 be wffs; then the truth table rules are

- $(\omega_1 \wedge \omega_2)$ has value *True* if both ω_1 and ω_2 have value *True*; otherwise, it has value *False*.

- $(\omega_1 \vee \omega_2)$ has value *True* if one or both of ω_1 or ω_2 has value *True*; otherwise, it has value *False*.

- $\neg\omega_1$ has value *True* if ω_1 has value *False*; otherwise, it has value *False*.

- The semantics of $\supset$ is defined in terms of $\vee$ and $\neg$. Specifically, $(\omega_1 \supset \omega_2)$ is an alternative and equivalent form of $(\neg\omega_1 \vee \omega_2)$.

These are called truth table rules because they are usually presented in tabular form, as they are in Table 13.1.

We can use the truth table to compute the value of any wff given the values of the constituent atoms in the wff. As an example of the use of the truth table to compute the value of a wff, suppose P has value *False*, Q has value *False*, and R has value *True*. In this interpretation, what is the truth value of $[(P \supset Q) \supset R] \supset P$? Working from the "inside out," we first compute the value of $P \supset Q$ to be *True*; then we see that $(P \supset Q) \supset R$ is *True*. Finally, since P is *False*, the value of the entire expression must be *False*.

If an agent describes its world using n features (corresponding to propositions), and these features are represented in the agent's model of the world by a corresponding set of n atoms, then there are 2^n different ways its world can be—so far as the agent can discern—because there are 2^n ways in which the n atoms can have values of *True* and *False*. Each of the ways the world can be corresponds to an interpretation. Given values for the n atoms (an interpretation), the agent can use the truth table to find the values of any wffs. What about the reverse process? Suppose we are given the values of the wffs in a set of wffs. Do those values induce a unique interpretation? This question is important because often an agent is given a set of constraints among features (expressed as wffs that have value *True*). Can the agent then induce an assignment of values (an interpretation) to the atoms in its language and thus determine whether or not the corresponding propositions about the world are true or false? That is, do the formulas specify one of the 2^n ways the world can be? The answer is usually no. Instead, there may be many interpretations that give each wff in a set of wffs the value *True*. To explore this topic further, I next introduce the notion of models.

13.5.3   Satisfiability and Models

We say that an interpretation *satisfies* a wff if the wff is assigned the value *True* under that interpretation. An interpretation that satisfies a wff is called a *model* of that wff. An interpretation that satisfies each wff in a set of wffs is called a *model* of that set of wffs. Trivially, we can tell whether or not an interpretation satisfies any atom because an interpretation assigns a value to each atom. We can use the truth table to tell whether or not an interpretation satisfies a wff that comprises atoms.

In my block–lifting robot, I expressed a constraint among some features by the following wff:

BAT_OK ∧ LIFTABLE ⊃ MOVES

If this wff is to have value *True*, as we intend, then we must rule out all interpretations in which BAT_OK and LIFTABLE have value *True* and MOVES has value *False*. Each "constraint wff" tells us something about the way the world can be and thus rules out some of the possible models. (Each model corresponds to one of the ways the world can be.) In general, the more wffs we have that describe the world, the fewer models! This fact shouldn't be surprising; the more we know about the world, the less uncertainty there is about the way it could be.

It is possible that *no* interpretation satisfies a wff (or a set of wffs). In that case, the wff (or the set of wffs) is said to be *inconsistent* or *unsatisfiable*. Examples of unsatisfiable wffs are F and P ∧ ¬P (no interpretation makes these wffs *True*). An example of an unsatisfiable set of wffs is {P ∨ Q, P ∨ ¬Q, ¬P ∨ Q, ¬P ∨ ¬Q}. (Use the truth table to confirm that no interpretation makes *all* of these wffs *True*.)

13.5.4   Validity

A wff is said to be *valid* if it has value *True* under *all* interpretations of its constituent atoms. (Thus, a valid wff is vacuous; it tells us nothing about the way the world can be.) Here are some examples of valid wffs.

- P ⊃ P (which is the same as ¬P ∨ P)

- T

- ¬(P ∧ ¬P)

- Q ∨ T

- [(P ⊃ Q) ⊃ P] ⊃ P

- P ⊃ (Q ⊃ P)

Use of the truth table to determine the validity of a wff takes time exponential in the number of atoms because the wff must be evaluated for all combinations of the values of the atoms.

13.5.5   Equivalence

Two wffs are said to be *equivalent* if and only if their truth values are identical under *all* interpretations. I write equivalence with a ≡ sign. We can use the truth table to prove the following equivalences:

- DeMorgan's laws:

$$\neg(\omega_1 \lor \omega_2) \equiv \neg\omega_1 \land \neg\omega_2$$

$$\neg(\omega_1 \land \omega_2) \equiv \neg\omega_1 \lor \neg\omega_2$$

- Law of the contrapositive:

$$(\omega_1 \supset \omega_2) \equiv (\neg\omega_2 \supset \neg\omega_1)$$

- If ω_1 and ω_2 are equivalent, then the following formula is valid:

$$(\omega_1 \supset \omega_2) \land (\omega_2 \supset \omega_1)$$

Because of this fact, the notation $\omega_1 \equiv \omega_2$ is often used as an abbreviation for $(\omega_1 \supset \omega_2) \land (\omega_2 \supset \omega_1)$.

13.5.6   Entailment

If a wff ω has value *True* under all of those interpretations for which each of the wffs in a set Δ has value *True*, then we say that Δ *logically entails* ω and that ω *logically follows* from Δ and that ω is a *logical consequence* of Δ. I use the symbol ⊨ to denote logical entailment and write $\Delta \models \omega$. Here are some examples.

- $\{P\} \models P$

- $\{P, P \supset Q\} \models Q$

- $F \models \omega$ (where ω is *any* wff!)

- $P \land Q \models P$

In the last two examples, I abbreviate the notation slightly, as is often done in the case when Δ is a singleton.

Logical entailment is important in AI because it provides a very strong way of showing that if certain propositions are true about a world then some other proposition of interest (perhaps one that cannot be sensed) must also be true. For example, suppose we sense features that we associate with the formulas BAT_OK, and ¬MOVES, and that we represent some of our knowledge about the world by the formula BAT_OK ∧ LIFTABLE ⊃ MOVES. That is, we have three formulas, two of which describe a particular world situation and one of which describes general knowledge about the world. I leave it to you to establish by the truth table that ¬LIFTABLE is logically entailed by these three formulas. Since, by this entailment, ¬LIFTABLE has value *True* in *all* of the interpretations in which the three formulas have value *True*, it must *a fortiori* have value *True* in our *intended interpretation* (that is, the one we are associating with the robot's world). Therefore, the proposition that is part of our intended interpretation, namely, that "the block is not liftable," must be true!

Because entailment is such a powerful tool for determining the truth or falsity of propositions about the world, it is important for us to study how to represent information as wffs and how to produce entailed wffs efficiently. We can always do this using the truth table method, but we seek simpler methods. An attractive substitute for entailment is inference. Although they are fundamentally different concepts, they are linked by the concepts of soundness and completeness.

13.6   *Soundness and Completeness*

There are two important definitions that connect inference with entailment (now I finally give their intuitive meanings to the words *theorem* and *proof*):

1. If, for any set of wffs, Δ, and wff, ω, $\Delta \vdash_{\mathcal{R}} \omega$ implies $\Delta \models \omega$, we say that the set of inference rules, $\mathcal{R}$, is *sound*.

2. If, for any set of wffs, Δ, and wff, ω, it is the case that whenever $\Delta \models \omega$, there exists a proof of ω from Δ using the set of inference rules, $\mathcal{R}$, we say that $\mathcal{R}$ is *complete*.

I have not yet given a set of complete inference rules for the propositional calculus and will return to that matter in the next chapter.

When inference rules are sound and complete, we can determine whether one wff follows from a set of wffs by searching for a proof instead of by using the truth table. When the inference rules are sound, if we find a proof of ω from Δ, we know that ω logically follows from Δ. When the inference rules are complete, we know that we will eventually be able to confirm that ω follows from Δ (when it does so) by using a complete search procedure to search for a proof. Substituting proof methods for truth table methods usually gives great computational advantage in both the propositional calculus and the predicate calculus (which we will study later).

To determine whether or not a wff logically follows from a set of wffs or can be proved from a set of wffs is, in general, an NP–hard problem [Cook 1971]. (That is, its complexity cannot be proven to be less than exponential in the number of atoms.) Nevertheless, there are special cases that are tractable, and so it is important to understand the process of logical reasoning.

13.7   *The PSAT Problem*

Mostly, we will be attempting to establish that *all* the models of a set Δ are also models of some wff ω. We might occasionally, however, want to find at least one model of Δ; that is, we might want to show that the wffs in the set are each satisfiable by the same interpretation. Equivalently, we want a model for the formula that comprises the conjunction of all the wffs in Δ.

The problem of finding a model for a formula is known as the *propositional satisfiability (PSAT)* problem. In the next chapter, I show that any formula can be written as a conjunction of disjunctions of literals. A disjunction of literals is called a *clause*, and a formula written as a conjunction of clauses is said to be in *conjunctive normal form (CNF)*. Thus, it suffices to be able to solve the PSAT problem for CNF formulas. Many interesting problems, including ones involving constraint satisfaction, circuit synthesis, circuit diagnosis, and planning, can be encoded for solution as CNF PSAT problems ([Selman, Kautz, & Cohen 1994]).[4]

An exhaustive procedure for solving the CNF PSAT problem is to try systematically all of the ways to assign *True* and *False* to the atoms in the formula, checking each assignment to see if all of the clauses have value *True* under that assignment. If there are n atoms in the formula, there are 2^n different assignments, so for large n, the exhaustive procedure is computationally infeasible.

Interesting special cases of the PSAT problem are 2SAT and 3SAT. The *k*SAT problem is to find a model for a conjunction of clauses, the longest of which contains exactly k literals. 2SAT problems have polynomial complexity, whereas 3SAT ones are NP–complete. Thus, the general PSAT problem is NP–complete. But even though all known algorithms for solving a problem, like PSAT, take exponential time in the worst case, many such problems take only polynomial *expected* time. In fact, for many natural probability distributions, the PSAT problem only requires polynomial average time [Goldberg 1979, Purdom & Brown 1987].

---

4. Cook [Cook 1988] has pointed out that PSAT encodings are often only a logarithmic factor larger than their original source encodings.

GSAT is a nonexhaustive, greedy, hill–climbing type of search procedure [Selman, Levesque, & Mitchell 1992, Selman & Kautz 1993]. The procedure begins by selecting a random set of values for all of the atoms in the formula. This set of values is an interpretation. The number of clauses having value *True* under this interpretation is noted. Next, we go through the list of atoms and calculate, for each one, the increase in the number of clauses whose values would be *True* if the value of that atom were to be changed. We change the value of that atom giving the largest increase and continue. Of course, the largest increase may be 0 or negative, but GSAT makes the change in any case. Since the procedure may wander endlessly on a "plateau," it is terminated after some fixed number of changes. And since the procedure may terminate at a local maximum (an interpretation satisfying some but not all of the clauses), it may have to be restarted with another random interpretation to search for a higher maximum. GSAT has been able to find models for 2000 variable randomly generated 3SAT problems and has also been used to solve propositional encodings of large *N*–Queens problems. Random–walk variations (e.g., WALKSAT) on GSAT have been shown to improve its effectiveness [Selman, Kautz, & Cohen 1994, Selman, Kautz, & Cohen 1996].

13.8 *Other Important Topics*

13.8.1 Language Distinctions

The propositional calculus is a formal language that an artificial agent uses to describe its world. There is always a possibility of confusing the informal languages of mathematics and of English (which I am using in this book to talk *about* the propositional calculus) with the formal language *of* the propositional calculus itself. When we say, for example, that $\{P, P \supset Q\} \vdash Q$ we use the symbol $\vdash$. That symbol is *not* a symbol in the language of the propositional calculus; it is a symbol in our language used to talk about the propositional calculus. The *metalinguistic* symbols $\vdash$ and $\models$ should never be confused with the symbol $\supset$, for example.

13.8.2 Metatheorems

In addition to theorems *in* the propositional calculus (produced by chains of rules of inference), we will have theorems *about* the propositional calculus. (These are often called *metatheorems*.) Here are two important theorems about the propositional calculus.

- The deduction theorem: if $\{\omega_1, \omega_2, \ldots, \omega_n\} \models \omega$, then $(\omega_1 \wedge \omega_2 \wedge \ldots \wedge \omega_n) \supset \omega$ is valid, and vice versa.

• *Reductio ad absurdum*: if the set Δ has a model but $\Delta \cup \{\neg\omega\}$ does not (that is, there is no interpretation that satisfies all of the wffs in the combined set), then $\Delta \models \omega$.

13.8.3 Associative Laws

The binary connectives $\wedge$ and $\vee$ are associative. That is,

$$(\omega_1 \wedge \omega_2) \wedge \omega_3 \equiv \omega_1 \wedge (\omega_2 \wedge \omega_3)$$

$$(\omega_1 \vee \omega_2) \vee \omega_3 \equiv \omega_1 \vee (\omega_2 \vee \omega_3)$$

Thus, in these wffs, we can drop the parentheses and write

$$\omega_1 \wedge \omega_2 \wedge \omega_3$$

$$\omega_1 \vee \omega_2 \vee \omega_3$$

The first of these is called a *conjunction*, and the second is called a *disjunction*. The individual ω_i's in the first wff are called *conjuncts*, and in the second wff, *disjuncts*.

13.8.4 Distributive Laws

$$\omega_1 \wedge (\omega_2 \vee \omega_3) \equiv (\omega_1 \wedge \omega_2) \vee (\omega_1 \wedge \omega_3)$$

$$\omega_1 \vee (\omega_2 \wedge \omega_3) \equiv (\omega_1 \vee \omega_2) \wedge (\omega_1 \vee \omega_3)$$

Don't be misled by the apparent simplicity and obviousness of some of the material presented in this chapter; improper learning or remembering of these concepts will cause difficulties later!

Exercises

13.1 Show by means of a truth table that $\neg(P \wedge Q) \equiv (\neg P \vee \neg Q)$.

13.2 Prove that if Δ is inconsistent (that is, it has no model), then $\Delta \models \omega$, where ω can be any wff.

13.3 How would you use the truth table to prove that *modus ponens* is sound?

13.4 Consider the following seven clauses:

$$\neg A \vee \neg B \vee \neg C$$
$$\neg A \vee B$$
$$\neg A \vee C$$
$$\neg B \vee C$$
$$\neg B \vee A$$
$$\neg C \vee A$$
$$\neg C \vee B$$

The GSAT process for finding a model to satisfy a set of clauses sometimes ends in a local maximum. Show that there is an assignment of truth values for A, B, and c that is a local (but not a global) maximum of the number of clauses satisfied by that assignment.

13.5 (Courtesy of Bart Selman.) Show how the N–Queens problem can be represented as a PSAT problem. (Hint: Introduce one atom $q_{k,l}$ for each square (k, l) of the $N \times N$ board. If $q_{k,l}$ has value *True*, there is a queen on square (k, l); if it has value *False*, that square is empty. Now state the constraints of the problem in terms of these atoms.)

14 Resolution in the Propositional Calculus

14.1 *A New Rule of Inference: Resolution*

14.1.1 Clauses as wffs

In the last chapter, I mentioned several rules of inference, including *modus ponens*. Many of these can be combined into one rule, called *resolution*. The version of resolution that I will use in this book applies to a special format for wffs called *clauses*, which I now define.

First, recall that a *literal* is either an atom (in which case, it is called a *positive literal*) or the negation of an atom (in which case, it is called a *negative literal*). A *clause* is a set of literals. The set is an abbreviation for the disjunction of all the literals in the set. Thus, a clause is a special kind of wff. I usually write clauses as disjunctions, but some of my definitions involving resolution will be simpler when they are expressed using the set notation. As an example, the clause {P, Q, ¬R} (equivalent to P ∨ Q ∨ ¬R) is a wff. The empty clause {} (sometimes written as Nil) is equivalent to F (whose value is *False*).

14.1.2 Resolution on Clauses

The resolution rule for the propositional calculus can be stated as follows: from $\{\lambda\} \cup \Sigma_1$ and $\{\neg\lambda\} \cup \Sigma_2$ (where Σ_1 and Σ_2 are sets of literals and λ is an atom), we can infer $\Sigma_1 \cup \Sigma_2$, which is called the *resolvent* of the two clauses. The atom λ is the *atom resolved upon*, and the process is called *resolution*.

Here are some examples.

- Resolving R ∨ P and ¬P ∨ Q yields R ∨ Q. The two clauses being resolved can be rewritten as the implications ¬R ⊃ P and P ⊃ Q. A rule of inference called *chaining* applied to these implications yields $\neg R \supset Q$, which is equivalent to the resolvent $R \vee Q$. Thus we see that chaining is a special case of resolution.

- Resolving R and $\neg R \vee P$ yields P. Since the second clause is equivalent to $R \supset P$, we see that *modus ponens* is also a special case of resolution.

- Resolving $P \vee Q \vee R \vee S$ with $\neg P \vee Q \vee W$ on P yields $Q \vee R \vee S \vee W$. Note that only one instance of Q appears in the resolvent—which was, after all, defined to be a set!

- Resolving $P \vee Q \vee \neg R$ with $P \vee W \vee \neg Q \vee R$ on Q yields $P \vee \neg R \vee R \vee W$. Resolving them on R yields $P \vee Q \vee \neg Q \vee W$. In this case, since both $\neg R \vee R$ and $Q \vee \neg Q$ have value *True*, the value of each of these resolvents is *True*. In this example, we must resolve either on Q or on R—not on both simultaneously! That is, $P \vee W$ is not a resolvent of the two clauses!

Resolving λ, a positive literal, with $\neg \lambda$ produces the empty clause. From λ and $\neg \lambda$ we can infer F because λ and $\neg \lambda$ are contradictory. Any set of wffs containing λ and $\neg \lambda$ is unsatisfiable. On the other hand, a clause that contains an atom and its negation (such as $\lambda \vee \neg \lambda$) has value *True* regardless of the value of λ.

14.1.3   Soundness of Resolution

The resolution rule I have just presented is a sound rule of inference. That is, if the clauses $\{\lambda\} \cup \Sigma_1$ and $\{\neg \lambda\} \cup \Sigma_2$ both have value *True*, then their resolvent, namely, $\Sigma_1 \cup \Sigma_2$, does also. One way to prove that fact is to do "reasoning by cases." We know that the atom λ has either value *True* or value *False*. If (case 1) λ has value *True*, then $\neg \lambda$ has value *False*, and the clause Σ_2 must have value *True* in order for the clause $\{\neg \lambda\} \cup \Sigma_2$ to be *True*. If (case 2) λ has value *False*, then the clause Σ_1 must have value *True* in order for the clause $\{\lambda\} \cup \Sigma_1$ to have value *True*. Combining these two cases, we see that either Σ_1 or Σ_2 must have value *True*; hence $\Sigma_1 \cup \Sigma_2$ has value *True*. A similar argument can also be carried out using the truth table.

14.2   *Converting Arbitrary wffs to Conjunctions of Clauses*

Any wff in the propositional calculus can be converted to an equivalent conjunction of clauses. A wff written as a conjunction of clauses is said to be in *conjunctive normal form (CNF)*. (A wff written as a disjunction of conjunctions of literals is said to be in *disjunctive normal form (DNF)*.) I will use an example to illustrate the steps of the process of converting an arbitrary wff to CNF. The wff I use to illustrate this process is $\neg(P \supset Q) \vee (R \supset P)$.

1. Eliminate implication signs by using the equivalent form using $\vee$:

$\neg(\neg P \vee Q) \vee (\neg R \vee P)$

2. Reduce the scopes of ¬ signs by using DeMorgan's laws and by eliminating double ¬ signs:

$(P \wedge \neg Q) \vee (\neg R \vee P)$

3. Convert to CNF by using the associative and distributive laws. First,

$(P \vee \neg R \vee P) \wedge (\neg Q \vee \neg R \vee P)$

then

$(P \vee \neg R) \wedge (\neg Q \vee \neg R \vee P)$

A conjunction of clauses (that is, the CNF form of a wff) is usually expressed as a set of clauses (with conjunction of the clauses implied); thus,

$\{(P \vee \neg R), (\neg Q \vee \neg R \vee P)\}$

The following procedure might be useful in step 3 to convert wffs (or parts of wffs) from DNF form to CNF form. First, write the DNF wffs as a matrix whose row elements are the literals in each conjunct; we have implicit disjunction of the rows. For example, the DNF form $(P \wedge Q \wedge \neg R) \vee (S \wedge R \wedge \neg P) \vee (Q \wedge S \wedge P)$ can be written in matrix form as follows:

```
P  Q  ¬R
S  R  ¬P
Q  S  P
```

Now select a literal in each row and make a disjunction of these literals. In my example, one such selection might be $P \vee R \vee P$. Make all possible such selections. Each selection corresponds to a clause, and we take the conjunction of all these clauses as the CNF form of the original wff. We can simplify some of these clauses; for example, $P \vee R \vee P$ simplifies to $P \vee R$. We can eliminate some of the clauses; for example, $P \vee \neg P \vee Q$ can be eliminated because it trivially has value *True*. We can also eliminate clauses that are *subsumed* by one of the other clauses. (A clause, γ_1, *subsumes* a clause γ_2, if the literals in γ_1 are a subset of those in γ_2.) For example, $P \vee R$ subsumes both $P \vee R \vee Q$ and $P \vee R \vee S$.

14.3 *Resolution Refutations*

I have already shown that resolution is a sound rule of inference. That is, $\Delta \vdash_{res} \gamma$ implies $\Delta \models \gamma$, where γ is a clause. But resolution is not complete. For example, $P \wedge R \models P \vee R$, but we cannot infer $P \vee R$ using resolution on the set of clauses $\{P, R\}$ (because there is nothing that can be resolved). Therefore, we cannot use resolution directly to decide *all* logical entailments. However, we can show by resolution that the negation of P ∨ R is inconsistent with the set {P, R}, and thus, using proof by contradiction, establish that P ∧ R ⊨ P ∨ R.

To illustrate the process, the negation of P ∨ R is ¬P ∧ ¬R. Expressed as a (conjunctive) set of clauses, the negation of what we are trying to prove is {¬P, ¬R}. To show the inconsistency of these clauses with P ∧ R, we add P and R to that set to obtain {¬P, ¬R, P, R}. Resolving on members of this latter set produces the empty clause, which is a contradiction, and thus we have indirectly established P ∨ R from P ∧ R.

In general, a resolution refutation for proving an arbitrary wff, ω, from a set of wffs, Δ, proceeds as follows:

1. Convert the wffs in Δ to clause form—a (conjunctive) set of clauses.

2. Convert the negation of the wff to be proved, ω, to clause form.

3. Combine the clauses resulting from steps 1 and 2 into a single set, Γ.

4. Iteratively apply resolution to the clauses in Γ and add the results to Γ either until there are no more resolvents that can be added or until the empty clause is produced.

I state the following results without proof:[1]

- Completeness of resolution refutation: the empty clause will be produced by the resolution refutation procedure if $\Delta \models \omega$. Thus, we say that propositional resolution is *refutation complete.*

- Decidability of propositional calculus by resolution refutation: if Δ is a finite set of clauses and if $\Delta \not\models \omega$, then the resolution refutation procedure will terminate without producing the empty clause.

The reasoning we used in the block–lifting example of the last chapter can be performed using resolution refutation. We are given the set Δ of wffs:

1. BAT_OK

2. ¬MOVES

3. BAT_OK ∧ LIFTABLE ⊃ MOVES

The clause form of the third wff is

4. ¬BAT_OK ∨ ¬LIFTABLE ∨ MOVES

---

1. There are several proofs of the completeness of propositional resolution refutations; see [Genesereth & Nilsson 1987, p. 87] for one. (Propositional completeness also follows as a special case of the completeness of first–order resolution refutation, mentioned in Chapter 16.) Decidability follows from the fact that there are only a finite number of resolutions possible among a finite set of clauses.

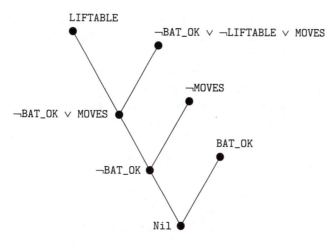

LIFTABLE

¬BAT_OK ∨ ¬LIFTABLE ∨ MOVES

¬MOVES

¬BAT_OK ∨ MOVES

BAT_OK

¬BAT_OK

Nil

Figure 14.1

A Resolution Refutation Tree

The negation of the wff to be proved yields another clause:

5. LIFTABLE

Now we perform resolutions to produce the following sequence of clauses:

6. ¬BAT_OK ∨ MOVES (from resolving 5 with 4)

7. ¬BAT_OK (from 6, 2)

8. Nil (from 6, 1)

We can also represent this refutation as a *refutation tree*, as in Figure 14.1.

14.4   *Resolution Refutation Search Strategies*

Although the resolution refutation procedure can easily be described as "perform resolutions until the empty clause is produced," there is the very important matter of which resolutions should be performed first. Also, it might be that some resolutions need not be performed at all. I take up these questions in this section.

14.4.1   **Ordering Strategies**

First of all, in what order should resolutions be performed? This question is analogous to questions about which node should be expanded next in state–space search. Various strategies, called *ordering strategies*, have been proposed. We can define, for example, *breadth-first* and *depth-first* strategies. But first, some definitions: let us call the original clauses (including the clause form of the negation of the wff to be proved) *0-th level resolvents*. An $(i + 1)$-th level resolvent is any resolvent of an *i*-th level resolvent and a *j*-th level resolvent with $j \leq i$. A breadth-first strategy is then one that generates first all of the first–level resolvents, then all of the second–level resolvents, and so on.

A depth-first strategy would produce first a first-level resolvent, then resolve that clause with some first-level or 0-th level clause to produce a second–level resolvent, and so on. With a depth bound, the standard backtracking strategy could be used. I will return to an application of depth–first resolution later in the book.

A popular strategy for partially ordering resolutions is the *unit-preference* strategy. In it, we prefer resolutions in which at least one clause consists of a single literal. Such a clause is called a *unit clause*. Note that the example illustrated in Figure 14.1 does not violate the unit–preference strategy (that is, no resolution in the refutation tree is between two nonunit clauses).

14.4.2   Refinement Strategies

Refinement strategies do not say anything about the *order* in which clauses are resolved; they permit only certain kinds of resolutions to take place at all. Some (but not all!) of these limitations leave resolution refutation complete.

Set of Support

A clause, γ_2, is a *descendant* of a clause, γ_1, if and only if (a) γ_2 is a resolvent of γ_1 and some other clause, or if (b) γ_2 is a resolvent of a descendant of γ_1 with some other clause. If γ_2 is a descendant of γ_1, then γ_1 is an *ancestor* of γ_2. Define the *set of support* to consist of those clauses that are either clauses coming from the negation of the theorem to be proved or descendants of those clauses.

The set–of–support strategy allows only those resolutions in which one of the clauses being resolved is in the set of support. Note that the resolution refutation of Figure 14.1 is one that adheres to the set–of–support limitation.

The set–of–support strategy is refutation complete [Chang & Lee 1973, p. 110]. That is, if we perform only set–of–support resolutions on an unsatisfiable set of clauses, the empty clause will eventually be produced.

Linear Input

The *linear-input* strategy allows only those resolutions in which at least one of the clauses being resolved is a member of the original set of clauses (including those coming from the negation of the wff to be proved). The resolution refutation of Figure 14.1 is one that adheres to the linear-input strategy also.

The linear–input strategy is not refutation complete, as can be seen by considering the following set of inconsistent clauses:

{P ∨ Q, P ∨ ¬Q, ¬P ∨ Q, ¬P ∨ ¬Q}

These clauses have no model, and thus there is a resolution refutation for them. I leave as an exercise the demonstration that there is no linear–input refutation for these clauses but that there is a resolution refutation for them.

Ancestry Filtering

The *ancestry-filtered* strategy allows only those resolutions in which at least one member of the clauses being resolved either is a member of the original set of clauses or is an ancestor of the other clause being resolved. The ancestry–filtered strategy is refutation complete [Luckham 1970].

14.5   *Horn Clauses*

There is a special type of clause that is important in AI and in other parts of computer science. A *Horn clause* is a clause that has at most one positive literal.
　　Here are some examples of Horn clauses.

P, ¬P ∨ Q, ¬P ∨ ¬Q ∨ R, ¬P ∨ ¬R

Clauses of this type were first investigated by the logician Alfred Horn [Horn 1951].
　　There are three types of Horn clauses.

- A single atom—often called a "fact."

- An implication—often called a "rule"—whose antecedent consists of a conjunction of positive literals and whose consequent consists of a single positive literal.

- A set of negative literals—written in implication form with an antecedent consisting of a conjunction of positive literals and an empty consequent. This form is obtained, for example, when one negates a wff to be proved consisting of a conjunction of positive literals. Such a clause is therefore often called a "goal."

Examples of these three types of Horn clauses are, respectively, P, $P \wedge Q \supset R$, and $P \wedge Q \supset$.
　　An important result about propositional Horn clauses is that there are linear–time deduction algorithms for them [Dowling & Gallier 1984]. Intuitively, the reason for the NP-hardness of inference with non-Horn clauses is that in attempting to prove a disjunction of positive literals, such as P ∨ Q, we have to consider

multiple cases—prove either P or Q. In Horn clauses, there are no disjunctions of positive literals.

Systems for proving goals from Horn clause rules and facts usually supply ordering information to the system by writing the facts and rules in a certain order, by writing the literals in the antecedent of each rule or goal in a certain order, and then by searching for a proof in depth–first fashion based on these orders. We'll study this procedure in more detail later after discussing the predicate calculus.

Exercises

14.1 Prove that the matrix procedure for converting from DNF to CNF preserves equivalence.

14.2 Heads, I win; tails, you lose. Express these statements (plus other statements you might need) in the propositional calculus, and then use resolution to prove that I win. (Alternatively, you can change the problem if you'd like to heads, you win; tails, I lose.)

14.3 The following wffs are instances of axioms that are sometimes used in the propositional calculus:

1. Implication introduction: $P \supset (Q \supset P)$
2. Implication distribution: $(P \supset (Q \supset R)) \supset ((P \supset Q) \supset (P \supset R))$
3. Contradiction realization: $(Q \supset \neg P) \supset ((Q \supset P) \supset \neg Q)$

Use resolution refutation to prove each of these formulas.

14.4 Consider the following unsatisfiable set of clauses:

$P \vee Q$

$P \vee \neg Q$

$\neg P \vee Q$

$\neg P \vee \neg Q$

1. Produce resolution refutations for each of the following strategies:
   (a) Set–of–support resolution (in which the set of support is the last clause in the preceding list of clauses)
   (b) Ancestry–filtered form resolution
   (c) A strategy that violates both set of support and ancestry filtering
2. Prove that there is no linear–input resolution refutation of this unsatisfiable set of clauses.

14.5 Convert the following propositional calculus wff into clauses:

$\neg[((P \vee \neg Q) \supset R) \supset (P \wedge R)]$

The Predicate Calculus

15.1 Motivation

The propositional calculus has several limitations. We can't, for example, express the fact that when we move block *B*, say, it is the same block that ON_B_C asserts is on block *C*. In the propositional calculus, atoms are strings that have no internal structure. In propositions about toy blocks, ON_A_B and ON_B_C are completely different with absolutely nothing in common. Even though I used mnemonic names for these atoms (to help us remember what I intend them to mean), I could just as well have used different proposition letters for them, say, P124 and Q23, respectively.

A more useful language would be one that could refer to *objects* in the world (such as blocks) as well as to *propositions* about the world. We need a language that has names for the objects about which we want to state propositions and names for the propositions we want to state. In our world of toy blocks (which I hereinafter call the "blocks world"), we might have had propositions such as ON_B_C ⊃ ¬CLEAR_C, where CLEAR_C is intended to mean that block *C* has nothing on it. To express a fact like this for each of several blocks would require several propositional formulas. It would be nice if we could simply say something like On(x, y) ⊃ ¬Clear(y), where *x* and *y* are variables that could refer to any blocks.

In this chapter, I present a language, called the *first-order predicate calculus*, which has these desired features. The predicate calculus has symbols called *object constants*, *relation constants*, and *function constants*, plus some other constructs that will be introduced later. These language entities will be used (when I discuss semantics) to refer to objects in the world and to propositions about the world.

15.2   *The Language and Its Syntax*

I first introduce a restricted version of the predicate calculus that I will later expand. Again, for now, resist the temptation to impute meanings to the constructs of the language. That way, you will be on the same footing as the computer programs that will have to manipulate these structures! All expressions in the language will be set in `typewriter font`. (There are many different typographical conventions for the predicate calculus used in books and papers. The one used here is not universal!)

Components

- We have an infinite set of *object constants*. These will be strings of alphanumeric characters (often mnemonic, but that helps only *us*, not the computer). My convention will be that object constants begin with either a capital letter or a numeral.

  Examples: `Aa`, `125`, `13B`, `Q`, `John`, `EiffelTower`

- And we will have an infinite set of *function constants* of all "arities."[1] These will be strings of alphanumeric characters beginning always with a lowercase letter and (for now) superscripted by their arity.

  Examples: $\texttt{fatherOf}^1$, $\texttt{distanceBetween}^2$, $\texttt{times}^2$

- We also have an infinite set of *relation constants* of all arities. These will be strings of alphanumeric characters beginning with a capital letter and (for now) superscripted by their arity. (I sometimes call a relation constant a *predicate*.)

  Examples: $\texttt{B17}^3$, $\texttt{Parent}^2$, $\texttt{Large}^1$, $\texttt{Clear}^1$, $\texttt{X11}^4$

- I also will use the propositional connectives $\vee$, $\wedge$, $\neg$, and $\supset$, and delimiters (,), [,], and separator ,.

Terms

- An object constant is a *term*.
- A function constant of arity *n*, followed by *n* terms in parentheses and separated by commas, is a term. This type of term is called a *functional expression*. In displaying such a term, I usually omit the arity superscript when its value is obvious from context. We might think of object constants as function constants of arity 0.

  Examples: `fatherOf(John, Bill)`, `times(4, plus(3, 6))`, `Sam`

---

1. The made-up word *arity* comes from the "ary" suffix in binary (arity = 2), tertiary (arity = 3), and so on.

wffs

- Atoms: a relation constant of arity n followed by n terms in parentheses and separated by commas is an *atom* (also called an *atomic formula*). A relation constant of arity 0 omits the parentheses. Again, I usually omit the arity superscript when its value is obvious from context.
    An atom is a wff.

    Examples: `Greaterthan(7, 2)`, `P(A, B, C, D)`, `Q`

- Propositional wffs: any expression formed out of predicate-calculus wffs in the same way that the propositional calculus forms wffs out of other wffs is a wff, called a *propositional wff*.

    Example: `[Greaterthan(7, 2) ∧ Lessthan(15, 4)] ∨ ¬Brother(John, Sam) ∨ P`

(Remember that the wffs used in these examples aren't supposed to mean anything!)

I will also use the extensions I made in the propositional calculus (conjunctions with more than two conjuncts, disjunctions with more than two disjuncts, clauses, (conjunctive) sets of clauses, etc.) as wffs in the predicate calculus. For now, these are the only terms and wffs we will consider; I will introduce others (which will allow the promised variables) shortly.

15.3 *Semantics*

15.3.1 Worlds

We now have a language that can be used to refer to objects in the world as well as to propositions. Here is what we can talk about now.

- The world can have an infinite number of *objects*, also called *individuals*, in it. These can be individuals that are rather concrete, like Block *A*, Mt. Whitney, Julius Caesar, and so on. Or they can be abstract entities like the number 7, π, the *set* of all integers, and so on. They can even be fictional or invented entities (about whose actual existence people might argue), like beauty, Santa Claus, a unicorn, honesty, and so on. As long as we are willing to give it a name and say something about it, we can think of it as an actual individual in a world we want to talk about.

- Functions on individuals. We can have an infinite number of functions of all arities that map n tuples of individuals into individuals. For example, there might be a function that maps a person into his or her father or one that maps the numbers 10 and 2 into the quotient 5.

- Relations over individuals. The individuals can participate in an arbitrary number of relations. These will each have arities. (A relation of arity 1 is called a *property*.) Thus, individuals might have properties such as heavy, big, blue, and so on, and they might participate in relations like bigger, in between, and so on. To specify an *n*–ary relation *extensionally*, we explicitly list *all* of the *n* tuples of individuals that participate in that relation.

15.3.2   Interpretations

An *interpretation* of an expression in the predicate calculus is an assignment that maps object constants into objects in the world, *n*–ary function constants into *n*–ary functions, and *n*–ary relation constants into *n*–ary relations. These assignments are called the *denotations* of their corresponding predicate–calculus expressions. The set of objects to which object constant assignments are made is called the *domain* of the interpretation.

Given an interpretation for its component parts, an atom has the value *True* just in case the denoted relation holds for those individuals denoted by its terms. If the relation doesn't hold, the atom has value *False*.

The values *True* and *False* of nonatomic wffs are determined by the same truth table used in the propositional calculus.

Example: Consider the blocks world again. It is a world in which there exist entities, **A**, **B**, **C**, and **Floor**.[2] We will eventually be creating an assignment that maps elements of the predicate calculus into these world objects. Since we cannot actually make the world objects themselves be the values of assignments, we imagine that the world is a mathematical structure, which (among other things) contains the mathematical objects **A**, **B**, **C**, and **Floor**. (Try not to be bothered by the statement "the world is a mathematical structure." Whatever the world *really* is, it won't matter for our purposes that we consider it to be a mathematical structure.)

We also imagine relations among these objects. For example, we might have the relations **On** and **Clear**. These relations can be defined extensionally by the *n* tuples of objects that participate in them. For example, suppose we have the configuration of blocks shown in Figure 15.1. In this world, the relation **On** is given by the pairs <**B**, **A**>, <**A**, **C**>, and <**C**, **Floor**>. The relation **Clear** is given by the singleton, <**B**>.

So, the individuals **A**, **B**, **C**, and **Floor**, and the relations **On** and **Clear** constitute the blocks world in this example. To describe that world in the predicate calculus, I employ the object constants A, B, C, and Fl, the binary relation constant On, and the unary relation constant Clear. I am using mnemonic symbols here for convenience; probably it would be better pedagogy to use the relation constants

---

2. I will sometimes use **boldface** notation for objects, functions, and relations in the world—as contrasted with typewriter notation for language elements of the predicate calculus—when I want to emphasize the distinction between language elements and what these elements denote.

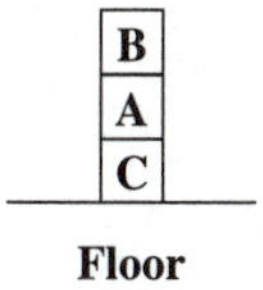

Floor

Figure 15.1

A Configuration of Blocks

Predicate Calculus	World
A	**A**
B	**B**
C	**C**
Fl	**Floor**
On	**On** $= \{< \mathbf{B}, \mathbf{A} >, < \mathbf{A}, \mathbf{C} >, < \mathbf{C}, \mathbf{Floor} >\}$
Clear	**Clear** $= \{< \mathbf{B} >\}$

Table 15.1

A Mapping between Predicate Calculus and the World

G0045, G123, . . . , and so on in order to emphasize the notion that the symbols used in our predicate–calculus language do not have any preassigned meanings.

Our intended interpretation (which is just one of many possible interpretations) for these predicate–calculus expressions is given in Table 15.1. We can use these assignments to determine the value of some predicate–calculus wffs:

On(A,B) is *False* because <A,B> is not in the relation **On**.

Clear(B) is *True* because <**B**> is in the relation **Clear**.

On(C,Fl) is *True* because <**C, Floor**> is in the relation **On**.

On(C, Fl) $\land$ ¬On(A, B) is *True* because both On(C,Fl) and ¬On(A, B) are *True*.

15.3.3 Models and Related Notions

Several semantic notions have the same definitions in the predicate calculus as they do in the propositional calculus. To review,

- An interpretation *satisfies* a wff if the wff has the value *True* under that interpretation.

- An interpretation that satisfies a wff is a *model* of that wff.

- Any wff that has the value *True* under *all* interpretations is *valid*.

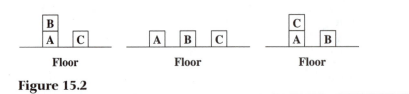

Figure 15.2

Three Blocks–World Situations

- Any wff that does not have a model is *inconsistent* or *unsatisfiable*.
- If a wff ω has value *True* under all of those interpretations for which each of the wffs in a set Δ has value *True*, then Δ *logically entails* ω ($\Delta \models \omega$).
- Two wffs are *equivalent* if and only if their truth values are identical under *all* interpretations (that is, if and only if the two wffs logically entail one another).

15.3.4   Knowledge

Predicate–calculus formulas can be used to represent knowledge that an agent has about the world. A set, Δ, of such formulas is called a *knowledge base* of the agent, and if the formula ω is included in Δ, we say (loosely) that the agent "knows" ω. (It would be more accurate to say that the agent "believes" ω.)

Let's examine more closely what might be meant when we say that a set of formulas embodies *knowledge* about the world. For example, do the following formulas embody knowledge about a possible blocks world?

1. $\texttt{On(A, Fl)} \supset \texttt{Clear(B)}$
2. $\texttt{Clear(B)} \wedge \texttt{Clear(C)} \supset \texttt{On(A, Fl)}$
3. $\texttt{Clear(B)} \vee \texttt{Clear(A)}$
4. $\texttt{Clear(B)}$
5. $\texttt{Clear(C)}$

Using the mnemonics as a hint, we can easily construct blocks–world interpretations that satisfy these formulas and thus are models of them. The situations we have in mind are illustrated pictorially in Figure 15.2. In all three of these, the model uses the same mapping of object constants to objects that was used in Table 15.1. The mappings between relation constants and relations in the world are different in the three models, however. In one, the relation constant $\texttt{On}$ is mapped to the relation $\mathbf{On} = \{< \mathbf{B}, \mathbf{A} >, < \mathbf{A}, \mathbf{Floor} >, < \mathbf{C}, \mathbf{Floor} >\}$, and the relation constant $\texttt{Clear}$ is mapped to the relation $\mathbf{Clear} = \{< \mathbf{C} > < \mathbf{B} >\}$. You can easily establish the models corresponding to the other two blocks–world situations.

There are also models of these formulas other than the ones suggested by the predicate–calculus mnenomics. For example, there is a model in which B and C are just different predicate–calculus names for the same object in the world, say, **B**. And there are models in which A, B, and C aren't assigned to blocks at all but to numbers, say.[3] Some of these alternative models might be ruled out by providing additional formulas. For example, we could rule out the models corresponding to two of the situations in Figure 15.2 by supplying the additional formula Clear(A), assuming again the assignment of object constants to objects given in Table 15.1. As I mentioned when discussing the propositional calculus, the more formulas we have, the fewer are their models. So, if we want to pin down the meanings of a set of formulas so that these formulas constitute "knowledge" about a particular world, we must have sufficient formulas so that their models not only include the world we have in mind but exclude worlds with which we do not want our world to be confused.

15.4 *Quantification*

Suppose we wanted to say that *every* object in the domain had a certain property (or participated in a certain relation). We could do this for finite domains by a conjunction such as Clear(B1) ∧ Clear(B2) ∧ Clear(B3) ∧ Clear(B4). But long conjunctions are cumbersome, and we can't even write down infinite ones, which might be needed if the domain were infinite.

Or suppose we wanted to say that at least one object in the domain had a certain property. For finite domains, such a statement could be made by a disjunction such as Clear(B1) ∨ Clear(B2) ∨ Clear(B3) ∨ Clear(B4). Again, there is a problem with large or infinite domains.

I introduce new syntactic entities for these purposes, namely, *variable symbols* and *quantifier symbols*. In addition to the syntactic entities previously introduced:

1. We have an infinite set of *variable symbols* consisting of strings beginning with lowercase letters near the end of the alphabet, such as p, q, r, s, t, ..., p1, p2, ..., and so on. (These will be distinguished from function constants by their use in context.) A variable symbol is a term (in addition to the terms I defined previously). Thus f(x, Bob, C17) is a ternary functional expression, for example.

2. We have the quantifier symbols, ∀ and ∃. ∀ is called a *universal quantifier*, and ∃ is called an *existential quantifier*.

---

3. There is a theorem by Löwenheim that states that all consistent sets of predicate–calculus wffs have a model whose domain is the integers [Löwenheim 1915].

3. If ω is a wff and ξ is a variable symbol, then both $(\forall\xi)\omega$ and $(\exists\xi)\omega$ are wffs. ξ is called the variable *quantified over*, and ω is said to be *within the scope of* the quantifier. Wffs of the form $(Q\xi)\omega$, where ξ is a variable symbol and Q is either $\forall$ or $\exists$ will most commonly (in our applications) be such that ω has the variable symbol ξ embedded somewhere within it as a term. If all variable symbols besides ξ in ω are quantified over in ω, then $(Q\xi)\omega$ is called a *closed wff* or *closed sentence*. In all of our applications, wffs will be closed.

Examples: $(\forall x)[P(x) \supset R(x)]$, $(\exists x)[P(x) \supset (\exists y)[R(x, y) \supset S(f(x))]]$

We would be able to show (after describing the semantics of quantifiers below) that $(\forall x)[(\forall y)\omega]$ is equivalent to $(\forall y)[(\forall x)\omega]$, so we could just as well group the universally quantified variables in a string in front of ω: $(\forall x, y)\omega$. In such a formula, ω is called the *matrix*. Similarly, for existential quantifiers. But mixtures of universal and existential quantifiers must retain their order! It is not the case that $(\forall x)[(\exists y)\omega]$ is equivalent to $(\exists y)[(\forall x)\omega]$.

We would also be able to show (after describing semantics below) that the variable of a quantifier is a kind of "dummy variable" and thus can be renamed without changing the value of the wff. Thus $(\forall x)\omega$ is equivalent to $(\forall y)\omega$ if all occurrences of x in ω are replaced by y. Similarly, for existential quantifiers.

Since quantifying over variable symbols gives the predicate calculus so much expressive power, you may ask whether or not we can quantify over relation and function symbols also. In the version of the predicate calculus we are using, such quantification is not allowed. For this reason, it is called the *first-order* predicate calculus. Second- and higher-order predicate calculi allow quantification over relation and function symbols, but at the expense of much more complex inference mechanisms.

15.5   *Semantics of Quantifiers*

15.5.1   **Universal Quantifiers**

$(\forall\xi)\omega(\xi)$ has the value *True* (under a given assignment of object constants, function constants, and relation constants to objects, functions, and relations) just in case $\omega(\xi)$ has the value *True* for *all* assignments of the variable symbol ξ to objects in the domain.

Example: Suppose we use the two interpretations for Clear and On suggested by the configurations in Figure 15.2. Under each of these interpretations, what is the truth value of $(\forall x)[On(x, C) \supset \neg Clear(C)]$? In these interpretations, the variable x can be assigned either to **A**, **B**, **C**, or **Floor**. We must investigate each of these assignments in turn for each of the interpretations. For example, with x assigned to **A**, if On(x, C) $\supset \neg$Clear(C) is to have value *True*, we would either have to have

<A,C> not in the relation **On** or <C> not in the relation **Clear**. In fact, in each interpretation, <C> is in the relation **Clear**, but <A, C> is not in the relation **On**, so the first assignment (of x to **A**) results in the value *True*. I leave it to you to investigate the remaining assignments.

15.5.2 Existential Quantifiers

$(\exists \xi)\omega(\xi)$ has the value *True* (under a given assignment to objects, functions, and relations) just in case $\omega(\xi)$ has the value *True* for *at least one* assignment of the variable symbol ξ to objects in the domain.

15.5.3 Useful Equivalences

The following equivalences, analogous to DeMorgan's laws, can be established given the semantics of the quantifiers:

$$\neg(\forall \xi)\omega(\xi) \equiv (\exists \xi)\neg\omega(\xi)$$

$$\neg(\exists \xi)\omega(\xi) \equiv (\forall \xi)\neg\omega(\xi)$$

And I have already mentioned

$$(\forall \xi)\omega(\xi) \equiv (\forall \eta)\omega(\eta)$$

15.5.4 Rules of Inference

The propositional–calculus rules of inference, suitably generalized, can also be used with the predicate calculus. These include *modus ponens*, $\wedge$ introduction and elimination, $\vee$ introduction, $\neg$ elimination, and resolution. I generalize the resolution rule in the next chapter. In addition to the propositional rules, two important ones are

- *Universal instantiation (UI)*. From $(\forall \xi)\omega(\xi)$, infer $\omega(\alpha)$, where $\omega(\xi)$ is any wff with variable ξ, α is any constant symbol, and $\omega(\alpha)$ is $\omega(\xi)$ with α substituted for ξ throughout ω.

  Example: From $(\forall x)P(x, f(x), B)$ infer $P(A, f(A), B)$.

- *Existential generalization (EG)*. From $\omega(\alpha)$, infer $(\exists \xi)\omega(\xi)$, where $\omega(\alpha)$ is a wff containing a constant symbol α, and $\omega(\xi)$ is a form with ξ replacing every occurrence of α throughout ω.

  Example: From $(\forall x)Q(A, g(A), x)$ infer $(\exists y)(\forall x)Q(y, g(y), x)$.

It is easy to show that both UI and EG are sound rules of inference.

15.6   *Predicate Calculus as a Language for Representing Knowledge*

15.6.1   Conceptualizations

The *big* problem for AI is *what* to say, not *how* to say it. The predicate calculus does no more than provide a uniform language in which knowledge about the world (after we have it!) can be expressed and reasoned about. The consequences of the knowledge thus represented can be explored through logical deduction methods to be described in the next chapter.

The first step in representing knowledge about a world is to *conceptualize* it in terms of its objects, functions, and relations. Conceptualization usually involves an act of invention on the part of the conceptualizer. There are often many choices about what kinds of objects we think might exist in our worlds. We are free to conceptualize the world in any way we wish; however, some conceptualizations will be more useful (not necessarily more "correct") than others.

Next, we invent predicate–calculus expressions whose intended meanings involve the objects, functions, and relations. Finally, we write wffs that are satisfied by the world as we have conceptualized it. These wffs will be satisfied by other interpretations as well; we need only to take care that they are not satisfied by interpretations that our state of knowledge about the world can preclude.

When designing agents that must reason about and interact with actual (rather than imagined) worlds, it is important that conceptualizations be *grounded*. That is, the truth values of at least some of the atoms used in a knowledge base must be evaluable through perceptual mechanisms connected to the world. Other atoms may be defined in terms of these primitive, perceptual ones, but the whole structure must rest on perception of some sort if the conclusions produced by logical methods are to have relevance to the world the robot inhabits. Mathematics, on the other hand, does not need to be grounded because mathematical statements need not be about the physical world.

The first serious proposal in AI to use the predicate calculus to represent knowledge about the world was by John McCarthy [McCarthy 1958]. A large project (the CYC project) to represent millions of commonsense facts about the world is described in [Guha & Lenat 1990, Lenat 1995, Lenat & Guha 1990]. For a more complete discussion of the role of logic in AI, see [Nilsson 1991]. For a textbook treatment of AI based on logic, see [Genesereth & Nilsson 1987].

15.6.2   Examples

I illustrate the process of conceptualizing knowledge about a world with some examples. Suppose we are designing an agent that delivers packages in an office building. Among other things, it will need to have a relation constant whose intended denotation is the property of something being a package. Let's use `Package(x)`. Most likely, it will need to have a relation constant whose intended denotation is that a certain object is in a certain room. Let's use Inroom(x,y). And, to handle my examples, it will need to have a relation constant whose intended denotation is that a certain object is smaller than another certain object. With these, we can express in the predicate calculus the following sample statements about the world of this robot:

- "All of the packages in room 27 are smaller than any of the packages in room 28."

$$(\forall x, y)\{[\text{Package}(x) \land \text{Package}(y) \land \text{Inroom}(x, 27) \land \text{Inroom}(y, 28)] \supset$$

$$\text{Smaller}(x, y)\}$$

- "Every package in room 27 is smaller than one of the packages in room 29."
  This statement is ambiguous as it stands (a common phenomenon when using everyday language). It could be represented by either of the following two formulas (which are not equivalent!):

$$(\exists y)(\forall x)\{[\text{Package}(x) \land \text{Package}(y) \land \text{Inroom}(x, 27) \land \text{Inroom}(y, 29)] \supset$$

$$\text{Smaller}(x, y)\}$$

$$(\forall x)(\exists y)\{[\text{Package}(x) \land \text{Package}(y) \land \text{Inroom}(x, 27) \land \text{Inroom}(y, 29)] \supset$$

$$\text{Smaller}(x, y)\}$$

Some knowledge about our robot's world may require us to conceptualize the notion of time. Consider, for example, the statement "Package A arrived before Package B." A reasonable conceptualization would have objects that are time intervals and ordering relations on the intervals. And we must have a way of stating the arrival time of an object. Let's use Arrived(x,z), where x denotes an arriving object, and z denotes the time interval during which it arrived. With these, we can write

$$(\exists z1, z2)[\text{Arrived}(A, z1) \land \text{Arrived}(B, z2) \land \text{Before}(z1, z2)]$$

I discuss a conceptualization for time intervals in more detail in Chapter 18. There are also other methods, some involving *temporal logics* [Emerson 1989, Shoham 1987], that have been used in computer science and AI to deal with time.

Inventing conceptualizations can often involve rather thorny questions. For example, it is difficult to decide how to deal with so-called mass nouns such as "milk" in the statement, "The package in room 28 contains one quart of milk." Is milk an object having the property, say, of being white? If so, what happens when we divide a quart into two pints? Does it become two objects (both of which are white), or does it remain as one? Many of these questions remain subjects for continuing research.

Later in the book, I will use conceptualizations that treat intangible things, such as situations and actions, as objects. I will also introduce extensions to the predicate calculus that will allow one agent to make statements about the knowledge of another agent, as in "Robot A knows that Package B is in room 28."

15.7 *Additional Readings and Discussion*

As previously mentioned, the use of logical sentences to represent knowledge and the use of logical inference procedures to do reasoning has been controversial in AI. See [McDermott & Doyle 1980] and the associated discussion for examples of the points made by both sides. Some of the controversy has to do with the mismatch between the precise semantics of logical languages due to [Tarski 1935] (see [Tarski 1956] for an English translation) and the more fluid and context-dependent ideas of meaning that seem to be required for representations of real–world (as opposed to mathematical) knowledge.

Tarskian semantics associates definite world individuals with object constants in the language. An alternative view emphasizes the need for so–called *indexical-functional* representations. In the words of Agre and Chapman [Agre & Chapman 1990, p. 21]:

> Whereas traditional representations posit a "semantic" correspondence between symbols in an agent's head and objectively individuated objects in the world, our theory describes a causal relationship between the agent and *indexically* and *functionally* individuated entities in the world. For example, one of the entities Pengi [described in [Agre & Chapman 1987]] works with is *the-bee-I-am-chasing*. This entity is individuated indexically in that it is defined in terms of its relationship to the agent ("I"). It is also individuated functionally in that it is defined in terms of one of the agent's ongoing projects (chasing a bee). Whereas in a traditional representation, the symbols BEE–34 and BEE–35 would always refer to the same two bees, different bees might be *the-bee-I-am-chasing* at different times.

Nevertheless, as we shall see in following chapters, researchers have been able to employ logical languages (with some extensions) to many AI representation and reasoning tasks.

[Enderton 1972, Pospesel 1976] are two books on logic—the first rather mathematical, and the second more informal. For a quite readable overview, which includes illustrative computer programs, see [Barwise & Etchemendy 1993].

Exercises

15.1 Give a model of the following formulas whose domain is the integers:

1. $On(A, Fl) \supset Clear(B)$

2. $Clear(B) \wedge Clear(C) \supset On(A, Fl)$

3. $Clear(B) \vee Clear(A)$

4. $Clear(B)$

5. $Clear(C)$

15.2 Show that the wff $(\exists x)\texttt{On}(x, A) \supset \neg\texttt{Clear}(A)$ has value *True* in each of the interpretations suggested by the configurations of Figure 15.2.

15.3 The following wffs have an obvious "blocks–world" interpretation:

On(C, A)

On(A, Fl)

On(B, Fl)

Clear(C)

Clear(B)

$(\forall x)[\texttt{Clear}(x) \supset \neg(\exists y)\texttt{On}(y, x)]$

Invent another interpretation (objects, relations, and a mapping) that satisfies the conjunction of these wffs.

15.4 For each of the following predicate–calculus expressions, say whether it can be a syntactically legal sentence (wff), and, if not, why not. For each *legal* sentence, say whether it is *valid* (necessarily true), *unsatisfiable* (necessarily false), or *contingent* (dependent on the interpretation). For each *contingent* sentence, give an interpretation for the symbols that makes the sentence true.

1. Won(Election, Clinton) $\wedge$ Won(Election, Bush)

2. $\neg$

3. $(\forall$ s$)$[Attends(s, (CS221 $\vee$ CS157))]

4. $(\forall$ x$)$ [Set(x) $\supset$ (Subset(x, x) $\vee$ $\neg$Subset(x, x))]

5. $(\forall$ x$)$ [P(x) $\vee$ Q(x)] $\supset \neg(\exists$ x$)$ [($\neg$P(x) $\vee$ Q(x))]

6. $(\forall$ x$)$[IsTrue(x)]

7. $(\exists$ x y z$)$[Equal(add(x, y), add(x, y, z))]

8. P(Igor) $\wedge$ Q(Bertha) $\wedge$ $(\forall$ x$)$ [$\neg$(P(x) $\vee$ Q(x))]

9. $(\neg(\exists x)) \supset$ NonExistent(x)

15.5 A steeple-building robot looks for two blocks that are clear and puts one of them on top of the other (if the block being moved can be located as being on some other block or on the floor). Write down a first-order predicate–calculus expression that might be used to determine whether or not there exist two such blocks.

15.6 A robot in grid world can move into a cell if that cell is one of the four adjacent cells and if that cell is free of obstacles. In that case, we say that the cell is *available*. Also, the grid world has no "tight spaces" (as defined in Chapter 2).

Invent predicate–calculus expressions that can be used to define when a cell is available and to describe the "no–tight–space" condition.

16 Resolution in the Predicate Calculus

Unification

I abbreviate wffs of the form $(\forall \xi_1, \xi_2, \ldots, \xi_n)(\lambda_1 \vee \lambda_2 \vee \ldots \vee \lambda_k)$ by $\lambda_1 \vee \lambda_2 \vee \ldots \vee \lambda_k$, where $\lambda_1, \lambda_2, \ldots, \lambda_k$ are literals that might contain occurrences of the variables $\xi_1, \xi_2, \ldots, \xi_n$. That is, I simply drop the universal quantifiers and assume universal quantification of any variables in the λ_i. (Later, I will show how any existentially quantified variables can be eliminated first.) Wffs in this abbreviated form are called *clauses*. Sometimes I write a clause using set notation $\{\lambda_1, \lambda_2, \ldots, \lambda_k\}$ and assume disjunction among the elements of the set.

If two clauses have matching but complementary literals, we can resolve them—just as in the propositional calculus. If we have a literal, $\lambda(\xi)$, in one clause (where ξ is a variable) and a complementary literal $\neg\lambda(\tau)$ in another clause, where τ is some term that does not contain ξ, we can substitute τ for ξ throughout the first clause and then do propositional resolution on the complementary literals to produce the *resolvent* of the two clauses.

Example: Consider the two clauses $P(f(y), A) \vee Q(B, C)$ and $\neg P(x, A) \vee R(x, C)$ $\vee S(A, B)$. Substituting $f(y)$ for the x in the second clause yields $\neg P(f(y), A)$ $\vee R(f(y), C) \vee S(A, B)$. Now the first literals in the two clauses are exactly complementary, so we can perform a resolution on this literal, $P(f(y), A)$, to yield the resolvent, $R(f(y), C) \vee S(A, B) \vee Q(B, C)$.

The appropriate substitution is computed by a process called *unification*. Unification is an extremely important process in AI. In order to describe it, I must first discuss the general topic of substitutions.

The terms of an expression can be variable symbols, object constants, or functional expressions, the latter consisting of function constants and terms. A *substitution instance* of an expression is obtained by substituting terms for variables in that expression. Thus, four substitution instances of P[x, f(y), B] are

    P[z, f(w), B]
    P[x, f(A), B]
    P[g(z), f(A), B]
    P[C, f(A), B]

The first instance is called an *alphabetic variant* of the original literal because we have merely substituted different variables for the variables appearing in P[x, f(y), B]. The last of the four instances shown is called a *ground instance*, since none of the terms in the literal contains variables. (A *ground term* is a term that contains no variables.)

We can represent any substitution by a set of ordered pairs: $s = \{\tau_1/\xi_1, \tau_2/\xi_2, \dots, \tau_n/\xi_n\}$. The pair τ_i/ξ_i means that term τ_i is substituted for every occurrence of the variable ξ_i throughout the scope of the substitution. Also, no variable can be replaced by a term containing that same variable. The substitutions used earlier in obtaining the four instances of P[x, f(y), B] are

$s1 = \{z/x, w/y\}$

$s2 = \{A/y\}$

$s3 = \{g(z)/x, A/y\}$

$s4 = \{C/x, A/y\}$

To denote a substitution instance of an expression, ω, using a substitution, s, I write ωs. Thus, P[z, f(w), B] = P[x, f(y), B]$s1$. The composition of two substitutions $s1$ and $s2$ is denoted by $s1s2$, which is that substitution obtained by first applying $s2$ to the terms of $s1$ and then adding any pairs of $s2$ having variables not occurring among the variables of $s1$. Thus,

$$\{g(x, y)/z\}\{A/x, B/y, C/w, D/z\} = \{g(A, B)/z, A/x, B/y, C/w\}$$

It can be shown that applying $s1$ and $s2$ successively to an expression ω is the same as applying $s1s2$ to ω; that is, $(\omega s1)s2 = \omega(s1s2)$. It can also be shown that the composition of substitutions is associative. That is, $(s1s2)s3 = s1(s2s3)$.

Example: Let ω be P(x, y), $s1$ be $\{f(y)/x\}$, and $s2$ be $\{A/y\}$. Then

$$(\omega s1)s2 = [P(f(y), y)]\{A/y\} = P(f(A), A)$$

and

$$\omega(s1s2) = [P(x, y)]\{f(A)/x, A/y\} = P(f(A), A)$$

Substitutions are not, in general, commutative; that is, it is not generally the case that $s1s2 = s2s1$. So, the order of applying substitutions makes a difference.

Example (using ω, $s1$, and $s2$ from the preceding example):

$\omega(s1s2) = P(f(A), A)$

$\omega(s2s1) = [P(x, y)]\{A/y, f(y)/x\} = P(f(y), A)$

When a substitution s is applied to every member of a set $\{\omega_i\}$ of expressions, I denote the set of substitution instances by $\{\omega_i\}s$. We say that a set $\{\omega_i\}$ of expressions is *unifiable* if there exists a substitution s such that $\omega_1 s = \omega_2 s = \omega_3 s = \ldots$. In such a case, s is said to be a *unifier* of $\{\omega_i\}$ since its use collapses the set to a singleton. For example, $s = \{A/x, B/y\}$ unifies $\{P[x, f(y), B], P[x, f(B), B]\}$, to yield $\{P[A, f(B), B]\}$. Although $s = \{A/x, B/y\}$ is a unifier of the set $\{P[x, f(y), B], P[x, f(B), B]\}$, in some sense it is not the simplest unifier. We note that we really did not have to substitute A for x to achieve unification. The most general (or simplest) unifier, *mgu*, g of $\{\omega_i\}$, has the property that if s is any unifier of $\{\omega_i\}$ yielding $\{\omega_i\}s$, then there exists a substitution s' such that $\{\omega_i\}s = \{\omega_i\}gs'$. Furthermore, the common instance produced by a most general unifier is unique except for alphabetic variants.

There are many algorithms that can be used to find the most general unifier of a finite set of unifiable expressions and that report failure when the set cannot be unified. The algorithm UNIFY, given here, is adapted from one given by [Chang & Lee 1973, p. 77]. It works on a set of *list-structured* expressions in which each literal and each term is written as a list. For example, the literal $\neg P(x, f(A, y))$ is written as $(\neg P \; x \; (f \; A \; y))$ in list–structured form. The expression $\neg P$ is the first top–level expression in our example list, and $(f \; A \; y)$ is the third top–level expression.

Basic to UNIFY is the idea of a *disagreement set*. The disagreement set of a nonempty set W of expressions is obtained by locating the first symbol (counting from the left) at which not all the expressions in W have exactly the same symbol, and then extracting from each expression in W the subexpression that begins with the symbol occupying that position. The set of these respective subexpressions is the disagreement set of W. For example, the disagreement set of the set of two lists $\{(\neg P \; x \; (f \; A \; y)), (\neg P \; x \; (f \; z \; B))\}$ is the set $\{A, z\}$. The disagreement set can be brought into agreement with the substitution A/z.

UNIFY(Γ) (Γ is a set of list–structured expressions.)

1. $k \leftarrow 0, \Gamma_k \leftarrow \Gamma, \sigma_k \leftarrow \epsilon$ (Initialization step; ϵ is the empty substitution.)

2. If Γ_k is a singleton, exit with σ_k, the mgu of Γ. Otherwise, continue.

3. $D_k \leftarrow$ the disagreement set of Γ_k.

4. If there exists elements v_k and t_k in D_k such that v_k is a variable that does not occur in t_k, continue. Otherwise, exit with failure; Γ is not unifiable.

5. $\sigma_{k+1} \leftarrow \sigma_k\{t_k/v_k\}, \Gamma_{k+1} \leftarrow \Gamma_k\{t_k/v_k\}$ (Note that $\Gamma_{k+1} = \Gamma_k\sigma_{k+1}$.)

6. $k \leftarrow k + 1$

7. Go to step 2.

[Chang & Lee 1973, p. 79] prove that UNIFY either finds a most general unifier of a set of unifiable expressions or reports failure when the expressions are not unifiable. The algorithm produces the mgu as a pair of list–structured expressions, but these can easily be converted back to the form used in first–order logic. There are several algorithms that perform unification, including one that runs in linear time [Paterson & Wegman 1978].

As examples, I list here the most general common substitution instances (those obtained by applying the mgu) for a few sets of literals. You might step through UNIFY for each of the sets of literals.

Sets of Literals	Most General Common Substitution Instances
$\{P(x), P(A)\}$	$P(A)$
$\{P[f(x), y, g(y)], P[f(x), z, g(x)]\}$	$P[f(x), x, g(x)]$
$\{P[f(x, g(A, y)), g(A, y)], P[f(x, z), z]\}$	$P[f(x, g(A, y)), g(A, y)]$

In step 4 of UNIFY, we check to see if a variable occurs in a term we are about to substitute for it. Such a substitution would lead to an infinite loop and is thus not allowed. As an example, suppose we are attempting to unify $P(x,x)$ with $P(f(z),z)$. UNIFY would first substitute $f(z)$ for x in these expressions, yielding $P(f(z),f(z))$ and $P(f(z),z)$. Without the *occur check*, it would then substitute $f(z)$ for z yielding $P(f(f(z)),f(f(z)))$ and $P(f(f(z)),f(z))$ and so on.

16.2   *Predicate-Calculus Resolution*

Suppose that γ_1 and γ_2 are two clauses (represented as sets of literals). If there is an atom ϕ in γ_1 and a literal $\neg\psi$ in γ_2 such that ϕ and ψ have a most general unifier, μ, then these two clauses have a resolvent, ρ. The resolvent is obtained by applying the substitution μ to the union of γ_1 and γ_2, leaving out the complementary literals. That is,

$$\rho = [(\gamma_1 - \{\phi\}) \cup (\gamma_2 - \{\neg\psi\})]\mu$$

Before two clauses are resolved, in order to avoid confusion about variables, we rename the variables in each clause so that none of the variables in one clause occurs in the other. For example, suppose we are resolving $P(x) \vee Q(f(x))$ against $R(g(x)) \vee \neg Q(f(A))$. We first rewrite the second clause, say, as $R(g(y)) \vee \neg Q(f(A))$ and then perform the resolution to obtain $P(A) \vee R(g(y))$. Renaming the variables is called *standardizing the variables apart*.

Here are some examples.

$\{P(x), Q(x, y)\}$ and $\{\neg P(A), R(B, z)\}$ resolve to produce $\{Q(A, y), R(B, z)\}$.

$\{P(x, x), Q(x), R(x)\}$ and $\{\neg P(A, z), \neg Q(B)\}$ resolve in two different ways to produce $\{Q(A), R(A), \neg Q(B)\}$ and $\{P(B, B), R(B), \neg P(A, z)\}$, respectively.

There is a slightly stronger definition of predicate–calculus resolution that is sometimes needed. For example, consider the two clauses {P(u), P(v)} and {¬P(x), ¬P(y)}. These clauses have ground instances equivalent to P(A) and ¬P(A), respectively (obtained with the substitution A/u, A/v, A/x, A/y). From these ground instances, we can infer the empty clause, so we ought to be able to infer it also from the original clauses, but we cannot do so using the resolution rule just given. The stronger rule is as follows.

Suppose that γ_1 and γ_2 are two clauses (again, represented as sets of literals). If there is a subset γ_1' of γ_1 and a subset γ_2' of γ_2 such that the literals of γ_1' can be unified with the negations of the literals of γ_2', with most general unifier, μ, then these two clauses have a resolvent, ρ. The resolvent is obtained by applying the substitution μ to the union of γ_1 and γ_2, leaving out the complementary subsets. That is,

$$\rho = [(\gamma_1 - \gamma_1') \cup (\gamma_2 - \gamma_2')]\mu$$

Using this definition of resolution, the two clauses {P(u), P(v)} and {¬P(x), ¬P(y)} resolve to produce the empty clause.

16.3 *Completeness and Soundness*

Predicate–calculus resolution is sound. That is, if ρ is the resolvent of two clauses ϕ and ψ, then $\{\phi, \psi\} \models \rho$. The proof of this fact is not much more difficult than the proof of soundness of propositional resolution. Just as in the propositional calculus, completeness of resolution is a more complicated matter. We cannot infer by resolution alone all the formulas that are logically entailed by a given set. For example, we cannot infer P(A) ∨ P(B) from P(A). In propositional resolution, we surmounted this difficulty by using resolution refutation, and we can do the same in the predicate calculus. To guarantee refutation completeness, however, we must use the stronger rule of resolution just given.

16.4 *Converting Arbitrary wffs to Clause Form*

Just as in the propositional calculus, any wff can be converted to clause form. The steps are as follows:

1. Eliminate implication signs (same as in propositional calculus).

2. Reduce scopes of negation signs (same as in propositional calculus).

3. Standardize variables. Since variables within the scopes of quantifiers are like "dummy variables," they can be renamed so that each quantifier has its own variable symbol.

   Example: $(\forall x)[\neg P(x) \vee (\exists x)Q(x)]$ would be rewritten as $(\forall x)[\neg P(x) \vee (\exists y)Q(y)]$.

4. Eliminate existential quantifiers.

Example: In $(\forall x)[(\exists y)\texttt{Height}(x, y)]$, the existential quantifier is within the scope of a universal quantifier, and thus the y that "exists" might depend on the value of x. For example, if the intended meaning of $(\forall x)[(\exists y)\texttt{Height}(x, y)]$ is "every person, x, has a height, y," then obviously height depends on the person. Let this dependence be explicitly defined by some unknown function, say, $\texttt{h}(x)$, which maps each value of x into the y that exists. Such a function is called a *Skolem function*.[1] If we use the Skolem function in place of the y that exists, we can eliminate the existential quantifier altogether and write $(\forall x)\texttt{Height}[x, \texttt{h}(x)]$.

The general rule for eliminating an existential quantifier from a wff is to replace each occurrence of its existentially quantified variable by a Skolem function whose arguments are those universally quantified variables that are bound by universal quantifiers whose scopes include the scope of the existential quantifier being eliminated. Function symbols used in Skolem functions must be "new" in the sense that they cannot be ones that already occur in any of the wffs to be used in a resolution refutation.

Thus, we can eliminate the $(\exists z)$ from

$$[(\forall w)Q(w)] \supset (\forall x)\{(\forall y)\{(\exists z)[P(x, y, z) \supset (\forall u)R(x, y, u, z)]\}\}$$

to yield

$$[(\forall w)Q(w)] \supset (\forall x)\{(\forall y)[P(x, y, g(x, y)) \supset (\forall u)R(x, y, u, g(x, y))]$$

and we can eliminate the $(\exists w)$ from

$$(\forall x)\{\neg P(x) \vee \{(\forall y)[\neg P(y) \vee P(f(x, y))] \wedge (\exists w)[Q(x, w) \wedge \neg P(w)]\}\}$$

to yield

$$*(\forall x)\{\neg P(x) \vee \{(\forall y)[\neg P(y) \vee P(f(x, y))] \wedge [Q(x, h(x)) \wedge \neg P(h(x))]\}\}$$

where $g(\texttt{x,y})$ and $h(\texttt{x})$ are Skolem functions.

If the existential quantifier being eliminated is not within the scope of any universal quantifiers, we use a Skolem function of no arguments, which is just a constant. Thus, $(\exists x)P(x)$ becomes $P(\texttt{Sk})$, where the constant symbol $\texttt{Sk}$ is used to refer to the entity that we know exists. Again, it is necessary that $\texttt{Sk}$ be a new constant symbol and not one used in other formulas to refer to known entities.

To eliminate all of the existentially quantified variables from a wff, we use the preceding procedure on each subformula in turn. Eliminating the

---

1. Skolem functions are named for the logician Thoralf Skolem [Skolem 1920].

existential quantifiers from a set of wffs produces what is called the *Skolem form* of the set of formulas.

It should be noted that the Skolem form of a wff is not *equivalent* to the original wff! The formula $(\exists x)P(x)$ is logically entailed by its Skolem form, $P(Sk)$, but not vice versa. As another example, note that $[P(A) \vee P(B)] \models (\exists x)P(x)$, but $[P(A) \vee P(B)] \not\models P(Sk)$. What *is* true is that a set of formulas, Δ, is satisfiable if and only if the Skolem form of Δ is. Or, more usefully for purposes of resolution refutations, Δ is unsatisfiable if and only if the Skolem form of Δ is unsatisfiable [Loveland 1978, pp. 41ff].

5. Convert to prenex form. At this stage, there are no remaining existential quantifiers, and each universal quantifier has its own variable symbol. We may now move all of the universal quantifiers to the front of the wff and let the scope of each quantifier include the entirety of the wff following it. The resulting wff is said to be in *prenex* form. A wff in prenex form consists of a string of quantifiers called a *prefix* followed by a quantifier-free formula called a *matrix*. The prenex form of the example wff marked with an * earlier is

$$(\forall x)(\forall y)\{\neg P(x) \vee \{[\neg P(y) \vee P(f(x, y))] \wedge [Q(x, h(x)) \wedge \neg P(h(x))]\}\}$$

6. Put the matrix in conjunctive normal form. Same as in propositional calculus. We may put any matrix into conjunctive normal form by repeatedly using one of the distributive rules, namely, by replacing expressions of the form $\omega_1 \vee (\omega_2 \wedge \omega_3)$ by $(\omega_1 \vee \omega_2) \wedge (\omega_1 \vee \omega_3)$.

When the matrix of the preceding example wff is put in conjunctive normal form, it becomes

$$(\forall x)(\forall y)\{[\neg P(x) \vee \neg P(y) \vee P(f(x, y))] \wedge [\neg P(x) \vee Q(x, h(x))] \wedge [\neg P(x)$$
$$\vee \neg P(h(x))]\}$$

7. Eliminate universal quantifiers. Since all of the variables in the wffs we use must be within the scope of a quantifier, we are assured that all the variables remaining at this step are universally quantified. Furthermore, the order of universal quantification is unimportant, so we may eliminate the explicit occurrence of universal quantifiers and assume, by convention, that all variables in the matrix are universally quantified. We are left now with just a matrix in conjunctive normal form.

8. Eliminate $\wedge$ symbols. We may now eliminate the explicit occurrence of $\wedge$ symbols by replacing expressions of the form $(\omega_1 \wedge \omega_2)$ with the set of wffs $\{\omega_1, \omega_2\}$. The result of repeated replacements is to obtain a finite set of wffs, each of which is a disjunction of literals. Any wff consisting solely of a disjunction of literals is called a clause. Our example wff is transformed into the following set of clauses:

$$\neg P(x) \lor \neg P(y) \lor P[f(x, y)]$$

$$\neg P(x) \lor Q[x, h(x)]$$

$$\neg P(x) \lor \neg P[h(x)]$$

9. Rename variables. Variable symbols may be renamed so that no variable symbol appears in more than one clause. We note that $(\forall x)[P(x) \land Q(x)]$ is equivalent to $[(\forall x)P(x) \land (\forall y)Q(y)]$. Our clauses are now

$$\neg P(x1) \lor \neg P(y) \lor P[f(x1, y)]$$

$$\neg P(x2) \lor Q[x2, h(x2)]$$

$$\neg P(x3) \lor \neg P[h(x3)]$$

The literals of a clause may contain variables, but these variables are always understood to be universally quantified.

16.5 Using Resolution to Prove Theorems

When resolution is used as a rule of inference in a theorem–proving system, the set of wffs from which we wish to prove a theorem is first converted into clauses. It can be shown that if the wff ω logically follows from a set of wffs, Δ, then it also logically follows from the set of clauses obtained by converting the wffs in Δ to clause form, and vice versa [Davis & Putnam 1960]. Therefore, for our purposes, clauses are a completely general form in which to express predicate–calculus wffs.

Resolution refutation can be shown to be both sound and complete [Robinson 1965]. (See also [Chang & Lee 1973, p. 85].) Thus, to prove a wff ω from Δ, we proceed just as we did in the propositional calculus. We negate ω, convert this negation to clause form, and add it to the clause form of Δ. Then we apply resolution until we deduce the empty clause. We can use any of the ordering and refinement strategies that we discussed in connection with resolution in the propositional calculus.

As an example, let's return to the package delivery robot mentioned in the last chapter. Suppose this robot knows that all of the packages in room 27 are smaller than any of the ones in room 28. That is,

1. $(\forall x, y)\{[\texttt{Package}(x) \land \texttt{Package}(y) \land \texttt{Inroom}(x, 27) \land \texttt{Inroom}(y, 28)] \supset \texttt{Smaller}(x, y)\}$

   Abbreviating the predicate symbols to make our formulas more compact and converting to clause form yields:

2. $\neg P(x) \lor \neg P(y) \lor \neg I(x, 27) \lor \neg I(y, 28) \lor S(x, y)$

   Suppose that the robot knows that package A is either in room 27 or in room 28 (but not which). It knows that package B is in room 27 and that package B is not smaller than package A.

3. $P(A)$

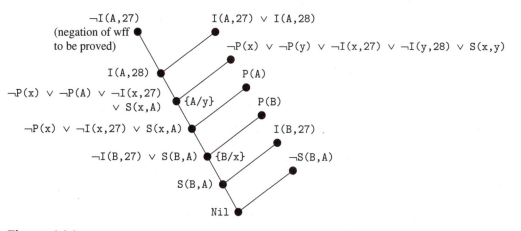

Figure 16.1

A Resolution Refutation

4. P(B)

5. I(A, 27) ∨ I(A, 28)

6. I(B,27)

7. ¬S(B, A)

Using resolution refutation, the robot can prove that package A is in room 27. A proof tree is shown in Figure 16.1. The negation of the wff to be proved is shown in the upper left; the wffs corresponding to what the robot knows explicitly are shown along the right-hand side of the figure. Substitutions used during the resolutions are also shown.

16.6   *Answer Extraction*

To use resolution to answer questions using knowledge about a domain represented by predicate-calculus wffs, we frequently have to do more than prove a theorem. For example, suppose we must prove a theorem of the form $(\exists \xi)\omega(\xi)$. We may also want to produce the ξ that we have proven exists. To do so, we must keep track of the substitutions made during the refutation process. We can keep track of the substitutions by using the device of an *answer literal*. We add a literal $\text{Ans}(\xi_1, \xi_2, \ldots)$ to each clause coming from the negation of the theorem to be proved and perform resolution until only an answer literal is left. The variables in the Ans literal are all of those variables that occur in the clause form of the negation of the theorem to be proved. The terms substituted during the proof for the variables in the Ans literal will then be instances of existentially quantified variables in the wff to be proved. The answer extraction process was invented by

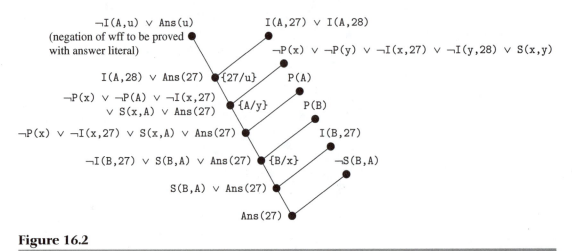

Figure 16.2

Answer Extraction

[Green 1969b]. It was later analyzed and extended by [Luckham & Nilsson 1971]. See also [Nilsson 1980, pp. 175ff].

I give an example of how the Ans literal is used in Figure 16.2. Now we prove the wff (∃u)I(A, u), which can be taken to be the way the robot asks itself "In which room is A?"

16.7 *The Equality Predicate*

The relation constants used in the formulas in a knowledge base usually have *intended* meanings (that is, relations), but these relations are circumscribed only by the set of models of the knowledge base and not at all (of course) by the particular symbols used for relation constants. The results of resolution refutations will be consistent with intended meanings only if the knowledge base suitably constrains the actual relations.

There are some important and commonly occurring relations, however, that we might want all knowledge bases to describe. An example is the equality relation, for which we might use a relation constant in either prefix form as in Equals(A,B) or in infix form as in A = B. Just because we include the formula Equals(A,B) in a knowledge base does not mean that from P(A) we will be able to conclude P(B). Nor would we be able to resolve Q(A,B) with ¬Q(B, A), for example. The knowledge base has no way of knowing what Equals means without additional formulas.

There are some well-known properties of equality that can be expressed in formulas, which we could add to the knowledge base. The equality relation is

- reflexive (∀x)Equals(x, x)
- symmetric (∀x, y)[Equals(x, y) ⊃ Equals(y, x)]

• transitive $(\forall x, y, z)[\text{Equals}(x, y) \land \text{Equals}(y, z) \supset \text{Equals}(x, z)]$

Even with these axioms we wouldn't be able to prove P(B) from P(A) and Equals(A,B). What is needed is to be able to substitute equal terms for equal terms in any expression. To sanction such substitutions, the knowledge base would additionally need to list all of the allowable substitutions explicitly (for each predicate constant and function constant)—an impractical requirement.

Several practical alternatives are possible. The strongest is called *paramodulation* [Wos & Robinson 1968], [Chang & Lee 1973, pp. 168–170]. Paramodulation is an equality–specific inference rule to be used in combination with resolution in cases where the knowledge base contains the equality predicate. The rule is defined as follows.

Suppose that γ_1 and γ_2 are two clauses (represented as sets of literals). If $\gamma_1 = \{\lambda(\tau) \cup \gamma_1'\}$ and $\gamma_2 = \{\text{Equals}(\alpha, \beta) \cup \gamma_2'\}$, where τ, α, and β are terms, where γ_1' and γ_2' are clauses, and where $\lambda(\tau)$ is a literal containing (possibly among other terms) the term τ, and if τ and α have a most general unifier σ, then infer the *binary paramodulant* of γ_1 and γ_2:

$$\pi = \{\lambda\sigma[(\beta\sigma)] \cup \gamma_1'\sigma \cup \gamma_2'\sigma\}$$

where $\lambda\sigma[(\beta\sigma)]$ denotes the result of replacing a single occurrence of $\tau\sigma$ in $\lambda\sigma$ by $\beta\sigma$. (The symmetry property of equality is handled by a paired rule that reverses the roles of α and β.)

In operation, the rule is not as complex as its formal definition makes it appear. As my first example (using a sledgehammer to crack a nut), we prove P(B) from P(A) and (A = B). (Here, I shift to infix notation for brevity.) For a refutation–style proof, we must deduce the empty clause from the clauses ¬P(B), P(A), and (A = B). Using paramodulation on the last two clauses, $\lambda(\tau)$ is P(A), τ is A, α is A, and β is B. Since A (in the role of τ) and A (in the role of α) unify trivially without a substitution, the binary paramodulant is P(B), which is the result of replacing an occurrence of τ (that is, A) with β (that is, B). Resolving this paramodulant with ¬P(B) yields the empty clause.

I leave it to you to work through the following example (taken from [Chang & Lee 1973, p. 170]):

The binary paramodulant of

P(g(f(x))) ∨ Q(x)

and

[f(g(B)) = A] ∨ R(g(C))

is

P(g(A)) ∨ Q(g(B)) ∨ R(g(C))

With a slight extension to the kinds of paramodulants allowed (beyond the binary ones), it can be shown that paramodulation combined with resolution refutation is complete for knowledge bases containing the equality predicate.

For problems that do not require substituting equals for equals, the power of paramodulation is not needed. In many cases, we can get by with a technique called *predicate evaluation*. If an external process is able to return a truth value for an equality predicate, we can replace that predicate (as it occurs in a formula) by T or F as appropriate. In resolution refutation, clauses containing the literal T can then be eliminated. The literal F in any clause can be eliminated (it can always be resolved away by an assumed omnipresent T).

Consider, for example, the problem (which might be faced by a delivery robot) of proving that if a package, say, A, is in a particular room, say, $R1$, then it cannot be in a different room, say, $R2$. The robot would have statements like the following in its knowledge base:

$(\forall x, y, u, v)[In(x, u) \wedge (u \neq v)] \supset \neg In(x, v)$

$In(A, R1)$

$\vdots$

It attempts to prove $\neg In(A, R2)$. Converting the first formula into clause form yields

$\neg In(x, u) \vee (u = v) \vee \neg In(x, v)$

The strategy postpones dealing with equality predicates until they contain only ground terms. Resolving the clause with the negation of the wff to be proved yields

$(R2 = v) \vee \neg In(A, v)$

Resolving this result with the given wff $In(A, R1)$ yields

$(R2 = R1)$

Now, we might imagine that the knowledge base actually contains the wff $\neg(R2 = R1)$. If it did, we could use it to produce the empty clause, completing the refutation. But in a large building with M rooms, we would need $\frac{M(M-1)}{2}$ such inequalities. And if the robot had to do any reasoning involving numbers, it might need an unmanageably large set of wffs, such as $\neg(3742 = 4861)$, and so on. Instead of having all of these wffs explicitly in the knowledge base, it would be better to provide a routine (that is, a program) that would be able to *evaluate* expressions of the form $(\alpha = \beta)$ for all (ground) α and β. In my example, the program would return F (or, equivalently, Nil) for the expression $(R2 = R1)$, and the refutation would be complete.

Several other commonly occurring relations (greater than, less than, ...) and functions (plus, times, divides, ...) could be evaluated directly rather than reasoned about with formulas. Evaluation of expressions is thus a powerful, efficiency–enhancing tool in automated reasoning systems.

16.8 *Additional Readings and Discussion*

Some people find the resolution inference rule nonintuitive and prefer, instead, so–called natural–deduction methods [Prawitz 1965]. These are called "natural" because inference is performed on sentences more or less "as is" without trans-formations into canonical forms. [Bledsoe 1977] discusses some of these nonres-olution methods.

Larry Wos and the late Woody Bledsoe have been leaders in applying resolu-tion and other inference methods to the task of proving theorems in mathematics. This work resulted in new resolution strategies, such as set of support [Wos, Car-son, & Robinson 1965] and unit preference. Examples of strong theorem–proving systems (some of which have solved open problems in mathematics) can be found in [Wos & Winker 1983, Boyer & Moore 1979, Stickel 1988, McCune 1992, McCune 1994, Wos 1993]. [Wos, et al. 1992] is a textbook treatment of computer theorem proving and its applications in problem solving.

Theorem proving has also been applied to the task of verifying and syn-thesizing computer programs given specifications. [Manna & Waldinger 1992] is a tutorial treatment of automatic program synthesis. [Manna & Waldinger 1985, Manna & Waldinger 1990] are book–length treatments of logic and programming. [Lowry & McCartney 1991] is a collection of articles on program synthesis.

Predicate evaluation is an instance of a more general process called *semantic attachment* in which data structures and programs are associated with (that is, attached to) elements of the predicate–calculus language. Attached structures and procedures can then be used to evaluate expressions in the language in a way that corresponds to their intended interpretations [Weyhrauch 1980, Myers 1994].

The *Journal of Automated Reasoning* covers both the theory and the application of theorem–proving techniques.

Exercises

16.1 Say whether or not the following pairs of expressions are unifiable, and show the most general unifier for each unifiable pair:

1. P(x, B, B) and P(A, y, z)

2. P(g(f(v)), g(u)) and P(x, x)

3. P(x, f(x)) and P(y, y)

4. P(y, y, B) and P(z, x, z)

5. $2 + 3 = x$ and $x = 3 + 3$

16.2 Explain why P(f(x, x), A) does not unify with P(f(y, f(y, A)), A).

16.3 Convert the following to clause form:

1. $((\exists x)[P(x)] \vee (\exists x)[Q(x)]) \supset (\exists x)[P(x) \vee Q(x)]$
2. $(\forall x)[P(x) \supset (\forall y)[(\forall z)[Q(x,y)] \supset \neg(\forall z)[R(y,x)]]]$
3. $(\forall x)[P(x)] \supset (\exists x)[(\forall z)[Q(x,z)] \vee (\forall z)[R(x,y,z)]]$
4. $(\forall x)[P(x) \supset Q(x,y)] \supset ((\exists y)[P(y)] \wedge (\exists z)[Q(y,z)])$

16.4 We are given the following paragraph:

Tony, Mike, and John belong to the Alpine Club. Every member of the Alpine Club is either a skier or a mountain climber or both. No mountain climber likes rain, and all skiers like snow. Mike dislikes whatever Tony likes and likes whatever Tony dislikes. Tony likes rain and snow.

Represent this information by predicate–calculus sentences in such a way that you can represent the question "Who is a member of the Alpine Club who is a mountain climber but not a skier?" as a predicate–calculus expression. Use resolution refutation with answer extraction to answer it.

16.5 Prove that $(\forall x)\lambda(x) \models \lambda(\tau)$, where τ is a ground term.

16.6 Show by a resolution refutation that the wff $(\exists x)P(x)$ logically follows from the wff $[P(A1) \vee P(A2)]$. Is there a resolution refutation that shows that the Skolemized form of $(\exists x)P(x)$, namely, $P(SK)$, logically follows from $[P(A1) \vee P(A2)]$?

16.7 Sam, Clyde, and Oscar are elephants. We know the following facts about them:

1. Sam is pink.
2. Clyde is gray and likes Oscar.
3. Oscar is either pink or gray (but not both) and likes Sam.

Use resolution refutation to prove that a gray elephant likes a pink elephant; that is, prove $(\exists x, y)[\text{Gray}(x) \wedge \text{Pink}(y) \wedge \text{Likes}(x, y)]$.

16.8 For each of the following formulas, either prove that it is valid or give a counterexample to its validity. (Hint: Don't rush into the resolution attempts immediately.)

1. $\{[(\exists x)P(x)] \supset Q(A)\} \supset \{(\forall x)[P(x) \supset Q(A)]\}$
2. $\{[(\forall x)P(x)] \supset Q(A)\} \supset \{(\exists x)[P(x) \supset Q(A)]\}$
3. $(\exists x)[P(x) \supset Q(A)] \supset (\forall x)[P(x) \supset Q(A)]$

16.9 Convert the following formula into one that has neither an existential quantifier nor a Skolem function.

$(\forall x, y)\{(\exists z)[\text{On}(x, z) \wedge \text{Above}(z, y)] \supset \text{Above}(x, y)\}$

16.10 Use resolution refutation on a set of clauses to prove that there is a green object if we are given:

- If pushable objects are blue, then nonpushable ones are green.
- All objects are either blue or green but not both.
- If there is a nonpushable object, then all pushable ones are blue.
- Object *O1* is pushable.
- Object *O2* is not pushable.

1. Convert these statements to expressions in first-order predicate calculus.
2. Convert the preceding predicate–calculus expressions to clause form.
3. Combine the preceding clause form expressions with the clause form of the negation of the statement to be proved, and then show the steps used in obtaining a resolution refutation.

16.11 The function cons(x,y) denotes the list formed by inserting the element x at the head of the list y. We denote the empty list by Nil; the list (2) by cons(2,Nil); the list (1,2) by cons(1,cons(2,Nil)); and so on. The formula Last(1,e) is intended to mean that e is the last element of the list 1. We have the following axioms:

- $(\forall\ u)$[Last(cons(u,Nil),u)]
- $(\forall\ x\ y\ z)$[Last(y,z) $\supset$ Last(cons(x,y),z)]

1. Prove the following theorem from these axioms by the method of resolution refutation:

    $(\exists v)$[Last(cons(2, cons(1, Nil)), v)]

2. Use answer extraction to find v, the last element of the list (2,1).

16.12 The following logic circuit has four wires, *W1*, *W2*, *W3*, and *W4*. It has an "and gate," *A*, and an "inverter," *B*. The input wires, *W1* and *W2*, can be either "on" or not. If the and gate, *A*, is functioning properly (*OK*), wire *W3* is "on" if and only if wires *W1* and *W2* both are "on." If the inverter, *B*, is functioning properly (*OK*), wire *W4* is "on" if and only if wire *W3* is not "on."

1. Use expressions like OK(A), ON(W1), and so on to describe the functioning of this circuit as defined.

2. Using the formulas describing the functioning of the circuit, and assuming that all components are functioning properly and that wires *W1* and *W2* are "on," use resolution to show that wire *W4* is not "on."

3. Again, using the formulas describing the functioning of the circuit, and given that wires *W1* and *W2* are "on," but that wire *W4* is also "on," use resolution to show that either the and gate or the inverter is not functioning properly.

17 Knowledge–Based Systems

17.1 Confronting the Real World

Now that we have studied the use of logic for representation and reasoning and illustrated its use with some rather simple examples, we ask whether it can be applied to "real–world" problems. AI research has found that applications such as medical diagnosis, tax consulting, and equipment design (to name just a few examples) typically require extensive knowledge of the subject at hand. This emphasis on the importance of knowledge in applications such as these prompts us to use the phrase *knowledge-based systems* to describe programs that reason over extensive knowledge bases. Do the methods I have described "scale up" sufficiently well for practical applications? What are some of the theoretical properties of reasoning methods that are relevant to this question? In this chapter, I deal with some of these questions and discuss some approaches that have proved useful for practical reasoning in realistic applications.

There are three major theoretical properties of logical reasoning systems, namely, soundness, completeness, and tractability. To be confident that an inferred conclusion is "true," we require soundness. To be confident that inference will eventually produce any true conclusion, we require completeness. To be confident that inference is feasible, we require tractability. Regarding the predicate calculus, we know that resolution refutation is sound and complete. Because it is complete, we know that if a wff ω is logically entailed by a set of wffs, Δ, resolution refutation can be used to show that it is. But if ω is *not* logically entailed by Δ, the resolution refutation procedure might never terminate. Thus, we cannot use resolution as a full *decision procedure*. Furthermore, it can be shown that there is no other method that will always tell us that a wff ω does not logically follow from a set of wffs Δ when it doesn't. Because of this fact, we say that the predicate calculus is *semi-decidable*. Semi–decidability, of course, makes the predicate calculus inherently intractable.

But the situation is worse. Even on problems for which resolution refutation terminates, the procedure is NP–hard—as is any sound and complete inference procedure for the first–order predicate calculus [Börger 1989]. So, although many reasoning problems can be formulated as problems of resolution refutation, the method is intractable for very large problems. This fact has led many to despair of using formal, logical methods for large–scale reasoning problems. (See, for example, [Schwartz 1987, McDermott 1987].) Yet, since humans themselves do complex reasoning, there must be heuristics and special formulations that permit tractable computations.

Researchers have explored various means to make reasoning more efficient. First, we could forego our insistence on the soundness of inference rules and use procedures that might occasionally (we hope rarely) "prove" an untrue formula. Second, we could forego our insistence on completeness and use procedures that are not guaranteed to find proofs of true formulas. Both of these modifications can be used to make reasoning more efficient. Third, we could use a language that is less expressive than the full predicate calculus. An example of a less expressive language, to be discussed next, is one that uses only Horn clauses. Reasoning is typically more efficient with Horn clauses, and they suffice for many applications.

17.2   *Reasoning Using Horn Clauses*

Earlier, I defined Horn clauses to be clauses that had at most one positive literal. If there is at least one negative literal and a single positive literal, the Horn clause can be written as an implication whose antecedent is a conjunction of positive literals and whose consequent is a single positive literal. Such a clause is called a *rule*. There may be no negative literals in the clause, in which case, we write it as an implication whose antecedent is empty and whose consequent is a single positive literal; such a clause is called a *fact*. Or there may be no positive literal in the clause, in which case, we write it as an implication whose consequent is empty and whose antecedent is a list of positive literals; such a clause is called a *goal*. Horn clauses form the basis of the programming language **PROLOG** [Colmerauer 1978, Clocksin & Mellish 1987, Sterling & Shapiro 1986, Bratko 1990]. In **PROLOG**, these clauses function as statements of the language and are written in the following formats:

- Rules: $\lambda_h :- \lambda_{b_1}, \ldots, \lambda_{b_n}$
  (which is a special way of writing the implication $\lambda_{b_1} \wedge \cdots \wedge \lambda_{b_n} \supset \lambda_h$), where each λ_i is a positive literal. The literal λ_h is called the *head* of the clause, and the ordered list of literals, $\lambda_{b_1}, \ldots, \lambda_{b_n}$, is called the *body*.

- Facts: $\lambda_h :-$

- Goals: $:- \lambda_{b_1}, \ldots, \lambda_{b_n}$

The literals in goals and in the bodies of rules are ordered lists, and this order plays an important role in the execution of a PROLOG program.

Inference over PROLOG clauses consists of attempting to "prove" a goal clause and is performed by executing a PROLOG program. Such a proof is achieved by resolutionlike operations performed on PROLOG facts, goals, and rules. Each resolution is performed between a goal and either a fact or a rule:

- A goal can resolve with a fact by unifying the fact with one of the literals in the goal. We call this literal the one resolved upon. The resolvent is a new goal consisting of a list of all of the substitution instances of the other literals in the original goal (i.e., those that were not resolved upon)—written in the same order as in the original goal. The substitution instances are obtained by applying the mgu of the unification to all of these other literals.

- A goal can resolve with a rule by unifying the head of the rule with one of the literals in the goal. The resolvent is a new goal formed by appending the list of substitution instances of all of the literals in the body of the rule to the *front* of the list of substitution instances of all of the other (nonresolved–upon) literals in the goal.

In PROLOG programs, the clauses are usually ordered in the following way: the first clause is the goal clause, then follow facts, and finally rules. In executing the program, the interpreter checks for resolutions with the goal by proceeding through the goal literals in order, examining each clause in order, performing the first possible resolution, and then starting over with the new goal clause. Proof of a goal clause succeeds when the new goal produced by a resolution is empty. That can happen only when a goal clause having a single literal resolves with a fact clause. (Thus, we put the facts first so as to succeed as soon as possible.) A goal clause fails (cannot be proved) if the interpreter has tried all resolutions for one of the goal literals and none results in new goals that can be proved. In that case, the interpreter backtracks to the previous goal clause and tries other resolutions on it. This process is readily seen to be equivalent to ordinary linear resolution on clauses using a depth–first, backtracking search procedure—with ordering of resolutions governed by the orderings of clauses and of literals within clauses. If the orders in which we select clauses to resolve and literals in these clauses to resolve upon are well chosen, a depth–first search using these orders can be an efficient way to find a proof. The PROLOG programmer specifies the order of resolutions for a depth–first search by writing the clauses in order and by writing the literals in each clause in order.

I illustrate PROLOG inference by some simple examples. The first does not involve variables and gives a high–level view of the process. Recall the block–lifting example used earlier to illustrate reasoning in the propositional calculus. A PROLOG program for proving that the arm moves, given that the block is liftable and the battery is charged, is shown here.

Figure 17.1

An AND/OR
Proof Tree

1. :- MOVES

2. BAT_OK :-

3. LIFTABLE :-

4. MOVES :- BAT_OK, LIFTABLE

The first resolution is between the goal clause and statement 4 yielding the new goal clause :- BAT_OK, LIFTABLE. The new goal clause resolves with statement 2 (resolving on the first literal in the new goal clause) yielding the new goal clause :- LIFTABLE. That resolves with statement 3, producing the empty goal clause, terminating the program successfully. In this case, no backtracking was necessary.

The proof we have just obtained can be displayed by the tree structure shown in Figure 17.1. The sets of nodes in gray boxes correspond to program statements (goals, rules, or facts). The nodes are labeled by literals in the program statements. There are two kinds of arcs, match arcs (indicated by double lines), and rule arcs (indicated by single lines). Rule arcs connect the body nodes of a rule with the head node of the same rule. Match arcs connect a body node of one rule (or a goal node) to an identically labeled head node of another rule (or to a fact). A goal node or a body node in such a tree is *proved* if it is connected by a match arc to a fact node or to a head node that has *all* of the nodes in its body proved. I use a circular symbol (⌣) joining rule arcs to emphasize that *all* of the body nodes must be proved in order for the head node to be proved. The tree in Figure 17.1 is an instance of what is called an AND/OR proof tree. In such a tree, body nodes are called *AND nodes* because they must all be proved. (If there had been alternative resolutions possible, the search for a proof tree could have generated additional nodes, called *OR nodes*, through alternative match arcs. We will see an example of an AND/OR tree with an embedded proof tree subsequently.)

As an example using variables,[1] we return to the blocks world. Suppose we want to use the concept of a block being *above* another block. Using the predicate calculus, we can define *above* in terms of *on* recursively by the following two formulas:

$(\forall x, y, z)[\text{On}(x, y) \supset \text{Above}(x, y)]$

$(\forall x, y)\{(\exists z)[\text{On}(x, z) \wedge \text{Above}(z, y)] \supset \text{Above}(x, y)\}$

With these definitions, the following **PROLOG** program can be used to prove that block A is above block C when A is on B and B is on C:

```
1) :- Above(A,C)

2) On(A,B) :-

3) On(B,C) :-

4) Above(x,y) :- On(x,y)

5) Above(x,y) :- On(x,z), Above(z,y)
```

The first possible resolution of the goal (with rule 4) produces the new goal :- On(A,C). That goal fails, so we backtrack to the original goal and try the next resolution (with rule 5) to produce an alternative new goal :- On(A,z), Above(z,C). Resolving on the first literal in this goal (with fact 2) produces the new goal :- Above(B,C). That goal resolves with rule 4 to produce :- On(B,C), which resolves with fact 3 to produce the empty goal, and the process terminates. The production of the goal :- Above(B,C) can be thought of as a recursive call to the same program.

The AND/OR tree illustrating the search performed by the **PROLOG** interpreter is shown in Figure 17.2. The nodes in the proof tree are indicated by bold ellipses, and the nodes in the part of the search that were aborted are indicated by shaded nodes. Some of the match arcs are labeled by substitutions (obtained when unifying body nodes with head nodes), and the boxed structures represent substitution instances of rules. In order that the tree represent a legal proof, substitutions must be *consistent*. Consistency here requires that the same term be substituted for the variable z throughout the proof tree. Of course, in **PROLOG** consistency is achieved by immediate substitution of terms for variables in creating a new goal. Note the use of instantiating variables apart in rule 4 of the proof tree.

---

1. **PROLOG** typographical conventions are the reverse of ours; in **PROLOG**, variables are capitalized, and constants are strings of lowercase alphanumerics. To facilitate comparison with FOPC, I adhere to my usual conventions.

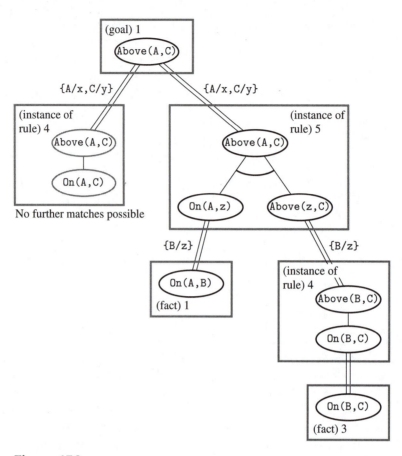

Figure 17.2

An AND/OR Tree

PROLOG is a general–purpose programming language that has proved useful in a variety of AI applications, especially in natural language processing [Pereira & Shieber 1987]. A textbook by [Shoham 1994] shows how PROLOG is used to implement several AI techniques. Logical languages related to PROLOG (such as DATALOG) are used to define "intensional relations" with which to augment the explicitly occurring (extensional relations) in a relational database. For a thorough treatment of the use of logical methods in databases, see [Ullman 1988, Ullman 1989]. [Minker 1997] is a readable survey article.

These elementary PROLOG programs illustrate how Horn clause rules can be used for reasoning problems. In PROLOG, reasoning proceeds "backward," beginning with the goal to be established, chaining through rules, and finally anchoring in facts. AI systems that perform this style of backward reasoning using goals, rules, and facts are said to perform *backward chaining. Forward chaining* is also possible. In that case, reasoning proceeds forward, beginning with facts, chaining through rules, and finally establishing the goal. Forward–chaining systems usually represent rules in standard implicational form, with an antecedent consisting of positive literals, and a consequent consisting of a positive literal. Just as PROLOG is a system based on backward chaining, there is a computer language, called OPS5 [Brownston, et al. 1985], that is based on forward chaining. Several practical and efficient reasoning systems have been written in OPS5.

In forward–chaining systems, a rule is applicable if each of the literals in its antecedent can be unified with a corresponding fact (using consistent substitutions). Since facts are ground atoms, variables occur in only one of a pair of expressions to be unified. This restricted form of unification is usually called *pattern matching*. Application of a rule (whose antecedent literals are matched consistently to facts) is achieved by adding the corresponding instance of the consequent of the rule to the list of facts. When more than one rule is applicable, some sort of external *conflict resolution* scheme is used to decide which rule will be applied. When there are large numbers of rules and facts, the number of unifications that must be tried becomes prohibitive. OPS5 uses a procedure called the RETE algorithm, which compiles the rules into a network used to guide facts efficiently through consistent matches with rules [Brownston, et al. 1985, Forgy 1982].

The process of forward chaining—facts triggering rules, which add new facts, and so on—is quite analogous to the workings of the blackboard systems I discussed in Chapter 5. In a specialized form, it also serves as a model of aspects of human cognitive processing. The facts correspond to what is called *working* or *short-term* memory. The rules correspond to *long-term* memory. In AI, the most fully developed systems based on this cognitive model are those based on the SOAR formalism [Laird, Newell, & Rosenbloom 1987, Rosenbloom, Laird, & Newell 1993].

17.3   *Maintenance in Dynamic Knowledge Bases*

Forward chaining makes manifest facts that were entailed by rules but that were not explicitly available in a knowledge base until they were deduced. Once available, these deduced facts might then be used to deduce additional facts, or they might evoke agent actions. Thus, forward–directed reasoning can be viewed as making changes to a knowledge base of facts. I elaborate on that view here.

Consider a knowledge base, KB, of propositional calculus atoms. Here, we call the atoms *premisses* instead of facts because we want to be able to reason about various "what–if" possibilities. For concreteness, let's consider an example in which the premisses are P and Q and the rules are $P \land Q \supset R$ and $P \lor R \supset S$. Note that the rules are implications with single–literal consequents, just as before, but now they are not restricted to being Horn rules.

P	Q	R	S
1	1	= P $\wedge$ Q	= P $\vee$ R

P	Q	R	S
1	1	1	1

P	Q	R	S
1	0	0	1

Figure 17.3

A Spreadline Reasoning System

A chain of forward reasoning using the rules allows us to add R and S as new atoms to KB. One way to think about this KB is that it is like a one–dimensional spreadsheet with one row and several columns. We might call it a "spreadline." We have a column for each of P, Q, R, and S. And we have a cell in each column for each of the values of these atoms. In each of P's and Q's value cells, we could enter either 1's (for *True*) or 0's (for *False*); in R's value cell, however, we would enter the formula P $\wedge$ Q, and in S's value cell we would enter the formula P $\vee$ R. These formulas are the antecedents of each of the rules. Some instances of spreadlines are illustrated in Figure 17.3. The one on top is a version that shows the formulas; the ones on the bottom show the deduced values of the cells for two examples. Just as in spreadsheets, any cell that has a formula in it, gets its value immediately calculated (by forward chaining) from the values of the components. And if the values of any components of a formula happen to change, the value of that formula is automatically changed as well.

We could extend the spreadline to contain any number of premisses and rules. Such a structure can be thought of as a kind of *dynamic knowledge base*. Reasoning processes are incorporated (using the formulas) in mechanisms external to the explicit values in the cells. Knowledge bases implemented in this manner are useful for a variety of purposes. Just like spreadsheets, they can be used to answer what–if questions. Someone (or an agent) might want to know how the values of various atoms would be changed if premisses were changed in a certain way. In AI, these spreadlines are called *reason maintenance* systems. They and other structures soon to be discussed are instances of what are generally called *truth maintenance systems (TMSs)*. The formulas entered in the values of rule cells are

P	Q	R	S
		= P ∧ Q	= P ∨ R

Instances of the KB

P	Q	R	S
1			1

P	Q	R	S
	1		

Figure 17.4

A KB with Missing Values

called *justifications*. They are usually expressed as disjunctions of conjunctions of atoms—disjunctive normal form. Various efficient procedures (such as the RETE algorithm [Forgy 1982]) have been devised to do the forward–chaining background computations to compute the values of all cells.

One interesting extension (beyond that of conventional spreadsheets) enables us to omit the values of certain premiss cells. Instead of having to label each of them as 1 or 0, we might not give them a value at all. If the values of premiss cells are missing, then so also might be the values of some of the rule cells. When a conventional spreadsheet confronts a formula having a component with a missing value, it might assume that value is 0, or it might warn the user about the missing value. Instead, when a dynamic knowledge base cannot compute the value of a formula (because of components having missing values), it reports the value of the formula as missing also—leaving the cell blank. I show an example in Figure 17.4; the formulas for R and S are the same as those in Figure 17.3. Note that in one case the value of S can be computed even though one of its components is missing.

In the vocabulary of TMSs, an atom whose value is neither 1 nor 0 is said to be OUT. I will use OUT as the value of OUT atoms instead of leaving their value cells empty. When a cell has a value of 1 or 0, it is IN. Note in particular that changing the value of a cell, say, P, from 1 to OUT is quite different from saying that P is *False*. Such a change just says that the KB no longer knows whether P is *True* (or *False*).

Allowing values of cells to be OUT permits an interesting generalization of rule types. We can have rules whose antecedents involve atoms that must be OUT instead of having a value of 1 or 0. I illustrate with an example. Suppose we can conclude U if R is *True* and S is OUT. We can write this in a form something like that of an implication:

$$R \wedge S^- \supset U$$

I superscript an atom by a minus sign ($^-$) if that atom has to be OUT. (The consequents in TMS implications never have superscripted signs. That is, when the antecedent is satisfied, the consequent is 1 and thus IN.)

TMSs should be thought of not as general–purpose reasoning systems (such as the ones we studied in Chapters 13 through 16), but as knowledge base maintenance systems that perform automatic updates when the truth values of certain atoms are changed. The use of IN's and OUT's permits an elementary sort of "nonmonotonic" or defeasible inference not sanctioned by ordinary reasoning systems. Ordinary logical inference is monotonic in the sense that when a new formula is added to a knowledge base, all of the deductions permitted before the formula was added are still valid. Adding new formulas never decreases the set of provable theorems. But if we make the deduction of an atom, say, ϕ, depend on some other atom being OUT, then when we add that other atom back IN, we will have to retract ϕ. In the example just given, if we find out that S has value *True*, then we have to retract U, which, of course, may lead to further retractions (or deductions).

Cycles among the rules present some difficulties, however. One is *mutual justification*. Consider the wffs P, P $\supset$ Q, Q $\supset$ R, R $\supset$ Q. If P has value *True*, so do Q and R. But if we don't know the value of P, we can't conclude anything about Q or R. But in dynamic knowledge base calculations, Q and R could justify themselves. Consider the stages of calculation illustrated in Figure 17.5. Initially, suppose P has value 1 leading to the starting KB in the figure. If P became OUT, the spreadline calculations could proceed as shown—resulting in Q and R justifying themselves without support from P. Additionally, when a formula has OUT's in it, the values of the atoms may either be indeterminate or overdetermined. In the first case, there may be more than one way that atoms could be IN or OUT; in the second, there may be no consistent values for them. (For more details, see [Shoham 1994, Ch. 5].)

Certain applications of a TMS system mandate that it would be inconsistent for all of the members of a certain subset of the atoms to be IN with value 1. These subsets are called *nogoods*. A *consistency maintenance system (CMS)* enforces these constraints by making some of the IN's OUT. Since consistency can often be maintained in several different ways, CMSs are nondeterministic.

Continuing with my use of spreadlines to frame my discussion of dynamic knowledge bases, there are applications in which the spreadline is used in a backward rather than a forward direction. That is, instead of starting with certain premises and using the formulas to update the values of all cells, we start with a particular cell's formula and ask which premiss values, together with certain other

Formulas

P	Q	R
	= P ∨ R	= Q

Starting KB

P	Q	R
1	1	1

Stages in calculation when P becomes OUT:

Stage 1: calculate new Q, using its formula and previous value of R

P	Q	R
OUT	1	1

Stage 2: calculate new R, given previous values of P and Q

P	Q	R
OUT	1	1

Figure 17.5

Mutual Justification

formulas called the *background theory*, will make the formula in that cell *True*. In these applications, the values of the cells are taken to be formulas—expressed in DNF form in terms of the premiss atoms. These formulas are called the *labels* of the cells. Knowledge bases that have these labels attached to atoms are called *assumption-based truth maintenance systems (ATMSs)*. The label of each atom consists of the various sets of premiss values (assumptions) that, together with the background theory, would make the atom have value *True*.

Consider, for example, the spreadline at the top of Figure 17.6. We reexpress the formulas in terms of the premisses and obtain the spreadline at the bottom of the figure to obtain the ATMS labels. Usually, set notation is used for the labels. A conjunction of atoms is represented by a set, and a disjunction of these conjunctions is represented by a list of multiple sets. In Figure 17.6, in order for U to have value *True*, for example, either P must be *True* (making V *True*) or R and Q must be *True* (making W True). In a minimal label for U we do not need to include

Premisses			Rules		
P	Q	R	S	W	U
			= P ∧ Q ∧ V	= R ∧ Q	= S ∨ W ∨ V

Background theory: P ⊃ V

ATMS labels

P	Q	R	S	W	U
P	Q	R	{P,Q}	{R,Q}	{P} {R,Q}

Figure 17.6

Conversion of a TMS to an ATMS

the set {P,Q} (making S *True*) because the occurrence of P in the label subsumes {P,Q}.

ATMSs can be used for a variety of purposes. One is to perform diagnosis. The formulas in Figure 17.6 might model the functioning of some electronic equipment, for example. If we observe that some aspect represented by U is not functioning (that is, U has value *False*), we can use the ATMS to determine that both P and R ∧ Q must have value *False*, for otherwise U would be *True*. Thus, we can determine that one of the two parts whose functionings are represented by R and Q must be faulty and that the part whose functioning is represented by P must be faulty also.

ATMSs sometimes have additional features and restrictions. Some of the premisses are taken as always having value *True* and thus are left out of the labels. (That is, these premisses are part of the background theory.) Also, labels might be modified by an assumption that some subsets of the premisses are nogoods, and thus cannot all have value *True*. For more details about TMSs, ATMSs, and their applications, see [de Kleer 1986a, de Kleer 1986b, de Kleer 1986c, Forbus & de Kleer 1993].

17.4   *Rule-Based Expert Systems*

One of the most successful applications of AI reasoning techniques using facts and rules has been in building *expert systems* that embody knowledge about a specialized field of human endeavor, such as medicine, engineering, or business. A survey of the many expert systems in use (circa 1988) is given in [Feigenbaum,

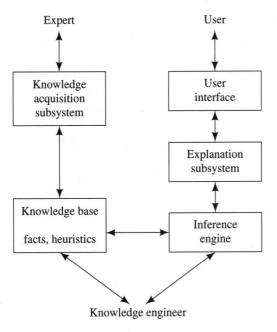

Figure 17.7

Basic Structure of an Expert System

McCorduck, & Nii 1988]. A textbook covering expert systems in engineering has been written by [Dym & Levitt 1991]. Strictly speaking, any program that functions as an expert can be called an expert system. The following definition is given in [Feigenbaum, McCorduck, & Nii 1988]:

> AI programs that achieve expert–level competence in solving problems by bringing to bear a body of knowledge are called knowledge–based systems or expert systems. Often, the term expert systems is reserved for programs whose knowledge base contains the knowledge used by human experts, in contrast to knowledge gathered from textbooks or nonexperts. More often than not, the two terms—expert system and knowledge–based system—are used synonymously.

In my treatment here, I will focus mainly on rule–based expert systems.

The basic structure of an expert system, in the context of its use, is shown in Figure 17.7 (adapted from [Feigenbaum, McCorduck, & Nii 1988]). The major parts of the system are the knowledge base and the inference engine. In terms of the reasoning systems discussed so far, the knowledge base consists of predicate-calculus facts and rules about the subject at hand. (Although it might also consist of knowledge represented in some syntactic variant of the predicate calculus.

We will see an example of such a variant in the next chapter.) The inference engine consists of all the processes that manipulate the knowledge base to deduce information requested by the user—resolution or forward or backward chaining, for example. (In some instances, the knowledge base and inference mechanisms might be tightly linked, as they are in TMSs, for example.) The user interface might consist of some kind of natural language processing system that allows the user to interact with the system in a limited form of natural language. (See Chapter 24.) Graphical user interfaces with menus are also used. The explanation subsystem analyzes the structure of the reasoning performed by the system and explains it to the user. (We will see a simple example of such explanations later.)

These four parts of the system are the parts that constitute the system as it is used in an application. In the construction of an expert system, a "knowledge engineer" (usually a computer scientist with AI training) works with an expert (or experts) in the field of application in order to represent the relevant knowledge of the expert in a form that can be entered into the knowledge base. This process is often aided by a knowledge acquisition subsystem that, among other things, checks the growing knowledge base for possible inconsistencies and incomplete information. These are then presented to the expert for resolution.

The process of building the system usually iterates through many cycles. At each step of the cycle, a prototype system is tested by the knowledge engineer and the expert to see if it makes the same kinds of inferences that the expert would make on typical problems that might be posed by a user. If the system responds differently than the expert would, the explanation subsystem is used to help the development team decide which information and inferences are responsible for the discrepancy. It may be that the expert needs to articulate certain information in more detail or provide additional information to cover the case at hand. This process continues until the development team is satisfied that the system operates appropriately. The process of crafting expert systems is one that requires experience and judgment. Various textbooks have been written on this subject; [Stefik 1995] is an excellent one. I attempt here only to give some of the fundamental ideas.

Rule–based expert systems are often based on reasoning with propositional logic Horn clauses (perhaps with some kind of additional mechanism for dealing with uncertainty). The knowledge base consists of rules gathered from experts. These systems have been applied in many settings. One could imagine a loan officer in a bank, for example, using such a system to help decide whether or not to grant a personal loan to an individual. A practical loan–approval system would take into account many factors, many more than we would want to consider in an illustrative example. But I can give an approximate idea of how such a system might work by describing a vastly oversimplified version. Suppose the following atoms are intended to denote the associated propositions:

- OK (The loan should be approved.)
- COLLAT (The collateral for the loan is satisfactory.)
- PYMT (The applicant is able to make the loan payments.)
- REP (The applicant has a good financial reputation.)
- APP (The appraisal on the collateral is sufficiently greater than the loan amount.)
- RATING (The applicant has a good credit rating.)
- INC (The applicant's income exceeds his/her expenses.)
- BAL (The applicant has an excellent balance sheet.)

Then, the following rules might be used to make a decision:

1. COLLAT $\wedge$ PYMT $\wedge$ REP $\supset$ OK
2. APP $\supset$ COLLAT
3. RATING $\supset$ REP
4. INC $\supset$ PYMT
5. BAL $\wedge$ REP $\supset$ OK

Suppose the loan officer wants to establish whether or not OK is true for a certain applicant. To prove OK, the inference engine searches for an AND/OR proof tree using either backward or forward chaining (or both). The AND/OR proof tree (if one exists) will have node OK as root node, and facts (determined to be true either by the user or listed in some database of facts) as the leaf nodes. The root and leaves will be connected (usually through intermediate nodes) through the rules.

Using the preceding rules in a backward–chaining fashion, the top part of the search tree for a proof of OK is shown in Figure 17.8. The user's goal, to establish OK, can be done either by proving *both* BAL and REP or by proving *each* of COLLAT, PYMT, and REP. These two alternative ways of proving OK are represented by the two OK nodes just under the root. Recall that these nodes are called *OR* nodes in an AND/OR tree. A node in an AND/OR tree that has OR–node successors can be proved by proving any one of those successors. Applying the other rules, as shown, results in other sets of nodes to be proved.

Let us assume for purposes of illustration that the truth (or falsity) of BAL, RATING, APP, and INC can be established either by querying a database or by having the reasoning system ask the loan–officer user directly. On the other hand, OK, PYMT, COLLAT, and REP denote concepts that are useful for the purposes of reasoning but ones about which neither the user nor a database has explicit information. (If the user already had knowledge of these concepts, he or she wouldn't need the expert system!) In full-scale expert systems, there may be

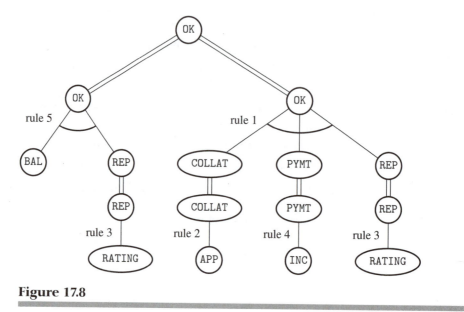

Figure 17.8

A Search Tree for a Proof

several alternative rules to be tried in linking the intermediate nodes with leaf nodes.

Queries by the system of the user or of a database can be interleaved with a search for a proof if the proof proceeds in depth–first fashion. If, for example, early in the search process the node BAL is found not to be true, search would then continue using rule 1. Proceeding through rules 1, 2, 3, and 4, the search process finally generates requests to find out about APP, INC, and RATING. If the truth of all of these nodes can be established (from the database or from the user), then we have a proof of OK. Of course, in realistic applications, the attempted proof trees will be both deeper and much broader.

Consulting systems attempt to answer a user's query by asking questions (of the user or of a database) about the truth of propositions that they might know about. Backward chaining through the rules is used to get to askable questions. If a user were to "volunteer" information, bottom–up, forward chaining through the rules could be used in an attempt to connect to the proof tree already built.

I can use this same example to describe how the system's reasoning can be explained to the user. The ability to give explanations for a conclusion is very important for acceptance of expert system advice. The proof tree is used to guide the explanation–generation process. Referring again to Figure 17.8, it is straightforward to see how the system's responses in the following dialog might be produced. (Each atom used by the reasoning system has some appropriate English sentence associated with it.)

User: Why do you believe that The loan should be approved?

System: Because The collateral for the loan is satisfactory, and The applicant is able to make the loan payments, and The applicant has a good financial reputation.

User: Why do you believe that The applicant has a good financial reputation?

System: Because the credit–rating service said that The applicant has a good credit rating.

User: Why did you ask me about whether or not The applicant's income exceeds his/her expenses?

System: Because I was trying to establish whether or not The applicant is able to make the loan payments.

User: Why are you trying to establish whether or not The applicant is able to make the loan payments?

System: Because that is one of the criteria in establishing whether or not The loan should be approved.

User: Why are you trying to establish whether or not The loan should be approved?

System: Because you asked me to.

In many applications, the system has access only to uncertain rules, and the user may also not be able to answer questions with certainty. For example, the following rule, suitably encoded in computer–understandable form, was used in the MYCIN system [Shortliffe 1976], which diagnosed bacterial infections:

```
Rule 300
If: 1)  The infection which requires therapy is meningitis, and
2) The patient does have evidence of serious skin or soft tissue
infection, and
3) Organisms were not seen on the stain of the culture, and
4) The type of the infection is bacterial
Then: There is evidence that the organism (other than those seen
on cultures or smears) which might be causing the infection is
staphylococcus-coag-pos (.75); streptococcus-group-a (.5).
```

Similarly, the following rule was used in the PROSPECTOR system [Duda, Gaschnig, & Hart 1979, Campbell, et al. 1982], which reasoned about ore deposits:

```
If there is a pre-intrusive, thorough-going fault system, then there
is (5, 0.7)  a regional environment favorable for a porphyry copper
deposit.
```

The numbers (.75 and .5 in MYCIN, and 5, 0.7 in PROSPECTOR) are ways to represent the certainty or strength of a rule. They are used by these systems in computing the certainty of conclusions. Techniques similar to those used by MYCIN and PROSPECTOR have been applied with good results. In Chapter 19, I introduce more sophisticated and well-founded techniques for dealing with uncertain information.

17.5   *Rule Learning*

Given the importance of rule–based systems and the human effort that is required to elicit good rules from experts, it is natural to ask whether or not expert-system rules could be learned automatically. There are two major types of learning, inductive and deductive. Both types can be used in learning rules. Neural–network learning, for example, is inductive because the functions learned are hypotheses about some underlying and unknown function. In successful learning, the hypotheses typically give correct outputs for most inputs, but they might also err. Inductive rule–learning methods create new rules about a domain—not derivable from any previous rules. I present methods for inductively learning rules in both the propositional and the predicate calculus.

Deductive rule learning enhances the efficiency of a system's performance by deducing additional rules from previously known domain rules and facts. The conclusions that the system can derive using these additional rules could also have been derived without them. But with the additional rules, the system might perform more efficiently. I will explain a technique called *explanation-based generalization (EBG)* for deducing additional rules.

17.5.1   Learning Propositional Calculus Rules

Several methods for inductive rule learning have been proposed; I describe one of them here.[2] I first describe the general idea for propositional Horn clause logic. Then, I show how a similar technique can be used to learn first–order logic Horn clause rules.

To frame my discussion, I use again my simple example of approving a bank loan. Instead of being given rules for this problem, suppose we are given a training set consisting of the values of attributes for a large number of individuals. To illustrate, consider the data given in Table 17.1 (I use 1 for *True* and 0 for *False*).[3] This table might be compiled, for example, from records of loan applications and the decisions made by human loan officers. Members of the training set for which the value of OK is 1 are called *positive instances*; members for which the value of OK

---

2. Rules can also be extracted from decision trees (see [Quinlan 1993, Ch. 5]) and from neural networks (see [Towell & Shavlik 1992, Towell, Shavlik, & Noordweier 1990]).

3. In real applications, of course, we would need much more data than that given here.

Individual	APP	RATING	INC	BAL	OK
1	1	0	0	1	0
2	0	0	1	0	0
3	1	1	0	1	1
4	0	1	1	1	1
5	0	1	1	0	0
6	1	1	1	0	1
7	1	1	1	1	1
8	1	0	1	0	0
9	1	1	0	0	0

Table 17.1

Bank Data

is 0 are called *negative instances*. From the training set, we desire to induce rules of the form

$$\alpha_1 \wedge \alpha_2 \wedge \ldots \alpha_n \supset \text{OK}$$

where the α_i are propositional atoms from the set {APP, RATING, INC, BAL}. If the antecedent of a rule has value *True* for an instance in the training set, we say that the rule *covers* that instance. We can change any existing rule to make it cover fewer instances by adding an atom to its antecedent. Such a change makes the rule more *specific*. Two rules can cover more instances than can one alone. Adding a rule makes the system using these rules more *general*. We seek a set of rules that covers all and only the positive instances in the training set.

Searching for a set of rules can be computationally difficult. I describe a "greedy" method, which I call *separate and conquer*.[4] We first attempt to find a single rule that covers *only* positive instances—even if it doesn't cover all the positive instances. We search for such a rule by starting with a rule that covers *all* instances (positive and negative), and we gradually make it more specific by adding atoms to its antecedent. Since a single rule might not cover all the positive instances, we gradually add rules (making them as specific as needed as we go) until the entire set of rules covers all and only the positive instances.

Here is how the method works for our example. We start with the provisional rule

$$\text{T} \supset \text{OK}$$

---

4. The method was originated by [Michalski 1969] and investigated in a series of programs based on Michalski's AQ algorithm.

which covers all instances. Now we must add an atom to make it cover fewer negative instances—working toward covering only positive ones. Which atom (from the set {APP, RATING, INC, BAL}) should we add? Several criteria have been used for making the selection. To keep my discussion simple, I will base our decision on an easy–to–calculate ratio:

$$r_\alpha = n_\alpha^+ / n_\alpha$$

where n_α is the total number of (positive and negative) instances covered by the (new) antecedent of the rule after the addition of α to the antecedent, and n_α^+ is the total number of positive instances covered by the (new) antecedent of the rule after the addition of α to the antecedent.

We select that α yielding the largest value of r_α. In our case, the values are

$r_{\text{APP}} = 3/6 = 0.5$

$r_{\text{RATING}} = 4/6 = 0.667$

$r_{\text{INC}} = 3/6 = 0.5$

$r_{\text{BAL}} = 3/4 = 0.75$

So, we select BAL, yielding the provisional rule

BAL ⊃ OK

This rule covers the positive instances 3, 4, and 7, but also covers the negative instance 1, so we must specialize it further. We use the same technique to select another atom. The calculations for the r_α's must now take into account the fact that we have already decided that the first component in the antecedent is BAL:

$r_{\text{APP}} = 2/3 = 0.667$

$r_{\text{RATING}} = 3/3 = 1.0$

$r_{\text{INC}} = 2/2 = 1.0$

Here we have a tie between RATING and INC. We might select RATING because r_{RATING} is based on a larger sample. (You should explore the consequences of selecting INC instead.)

The rule BAL ∧ RATING ⊃ OK covers only positive instances, so we do not need to add further atoms to the antecedent of this rule. But this rule does not cover all of the positive instances. Specifically, it does not cover positive instance 6. So, we must add another rule.

To learn the next rule, we first eliminate from the table all of the positive instances already covered by the first rule, to obtain the data shown in Table 17.2. We begin the process all over again with this reduced table, starting with the rule T ⊃ OK. This rule covers some negative instances, namely, 1, 2, 5, 8, and 9. To select an atom to add to the antecedent, we calculate

Individual	APP	RATING	INC	BAL	OK
1	1	0	0	1	0
2	0	0	1	0	0
5	0	1	1	0	0
6	1	1	1	0	1
8	1	0	1	0	0
9	1	1	0	0	0

Table 17.2

Reduced Data

$$r_{\text{APP}} = 1/4 = 0.25$$
$$r_{\text{RATING}} = 0/3 = 0.0$$
$$r_{\text{INC}} = 1/4 = 0.25$$
$$r_{\text{BAL}} = 0/1 = 0.0$$

Again, a tie. Let's arbitrarily select APP to give us the rule APP $\supset$ OK. This rule covers negative instances 1, 8, and 9, so we must add another atom to the antecedent. The r's are

$$r_{\text{RATING}} = 1/2 = 0.5$$
$$r_{\text{INC}} = 1/2 = 0.5$$
$$r_{\text{BAL}} = 0/1 = 0.0$$

We select RATING to give us the rule APP $\wedge$ RATING $\supset$ OK. This rule covers negative instance 9. Making this rule yet more specific (in the usual way) finally results in the rule APP $\wedge$ RATING $\wedge$ INC $\supset$ OK. These two rules, namely, BAL $\wedge$ RATING $\supset$ OK and APP $\wedge$ RATING $\wedge$ INC $\supset$ OK cover all and only the positive instances, so we are finished.

Since this process for finding rules employed greedy search, it should not be surprising that the learned rules can sometimes be simplified. For each rule, we can test to see if the rule can be discarded without changing the decisions made on the training set by the remaining set of rules. If there is no effect (or if there is little effect on accuracy when there is noise in the data), the rule can be eliminated. Similarly, for each atom in a rule, we can test to see if the atom can be removed with minimal effect. Indeed, if the data are noisy, we would want to modify the criterion that the learned rules should cover all and only the positive instances. Instead, we might permit each rule to cover "mainly" positive instances—permitting (as we must for noisy data) each rule to cover a small number of negative instances. Similarly, the set of rules learned might be permitted to fail to cover a "few" of the positive instances. These "pruning" operations and noise–tolerant modifications help minimize the risk of overfitting.

I can succinctly state this process for rule learning in pseudocode. I call it the *generic separate-and-conquer algorithm* (GSCA). In the algorithm,

> Ξ is the initial training set of instances of binary–valued features each labeled by the value of an atom, γ
>
> π is a set of rules to be learned
>
> ρ is one of the rules; it has γ as its consequent and (the conjunction of atoms) Γ as its antecedent
>
> α is an atom drawn from one of the features in Ξ

GSCA

1. Initialize $\Xi_{cur} \leftarrow \Xi$.

2. Initialize $\pi \leftarrow$ empty set of rules.

3. **repeat**   The outer loop adds rules until π covers all (or most) of the positive instances.

4. Initialize $\Gamma \leftarrow \text{T}$.

5. Initialize $\rho \leftarrow \Gamma \supset \gamma$.

6. **repeat**   The inner loop adds atoms to Γ until ρ covers only (or mainly) positive instances.

7. Select an atom α to add to Γ. This is a nondeterministic choice point that can be used for backtracking.

8. $\Gamma \leftarrow \Gamma \wedge \alpha$.

9. **until** ρ covers only (or mainly) positive instances in Ξ_{cur}.

10. $\pi \leftarrow \pi, \rho$. We add the rule ρ to the set of rules.

11. $\Xi_{cur} \leftarrow \Xi_{cur} - $ (the positive instances in Ξ_{cur} covered by π).

12. **until** π covers all (or most) of the positive instance in Ξ.

In the bank loan example, the rules learned are consistent with the rules originally given by the "expert" for this problem. With such a small training set, however, it is possible to learn idiosyncratic rules that might not accord with an expert's intuition about the problem. (For example, if we had broken ties differently, we would have learned different rules in this case.) Comparing the learned rules with the rules given us by the expert reveals that the learned rules do not mention any of the expert's nonmeasurable or nonaskable predicates (namely, COLLAT, PYMT, and REP); these are not represented by features in the data. Intermediate predicates simplify knowledge representation and reasoning by encapsulating commonly occurring groups of more primitive predicates. Learning these intermediate predicates is an important research problem. Some preliminary work has been done on the subject of "predicate invention." (See, for example, [Muggleton & Buntine 1988].) Even without producing rules involving intermediate predicates, rule learning can often be used to accelerate the process of building expert systems.

17.5.2 Learning First–Order Logic Rules

The rule–learning technique just described produces rules in propositional logic. Although many expert systems are based on propositional logic, more versatility is achieved by the use of rules with universally quantified variables. The subfield of *inductive logic programming (ILP)* concentrates on methods for inductive learning of Horn clauses in FOPC (and, thus, PROLOG programs). Several methods for learning Horn clauses have been developed—some with certain restrictions on the types of Horn clauses that can be produced. A full treatment of the subject is well beyond the scope of this book, but I will briefly outline a representative ILP technique using the separate–and–conquer approach. The method I describe is based on a system called FOIL [Quinlan 1990]. (For a full and readable treatment of the field, see [Lavrač & Džeroski 1994]. [Muggleton 1992] is a collection of ILP papers, and [Muggleton & De Raedt 1994] is a standard reference.)

To make my discussion conform to most of the ILP literature, I use notation that is closer to that of PROLOG, although to be consistent with my FOPC conventions, I continue to use uppercase letters for constants and lowercase ones for variable symbols. In ILP, our goal is to learn a program, π, consisting of Horn clauses, ρ, each of which is of the form $\rho :- \alpha_1, \alpha_2, \ldots, \alpha_i$, where the α_i are atomic formulas that unify with ground atomic facts. The idea is that π should evaluate to *True* when its variables are bound to some set of values known to be in the relation we are trying to learn; these are the positive instances, Ξ^+, of the *training set*. π should evaluate to *False* when its variables are bound to some set of values known not to be in the relation; these are the negative instances, Ξ^-. Just as in learning propositional rules, we want π to cover the positive instances and not cover the negative ones. The ground atomic facts with which the α are to unify are said to constitute *background knowledge*. We assume that they are given—as either subsidiary PROLOG programs, which can be run and evaluated, or explicitly in the form of a list of facts.

As an example, suppose a delivery robot navigating around in a building finds, through experience, that it is easy to go between certain pairs of locations and not so easy to go between certain other pairs. We show a partial map of such a building in Figure 17.9. In this building, the locations *A*, *B*, and *C* are *junctions*, and all of the other locations are *shops*.

We suppose that the robot has compiled a training set, Ξ, of pairs of locations—each pair labeled by whether or not it was easy to navigate the pair. We presume the robot has some information about properties of these locations

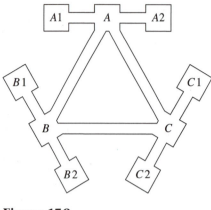

Figure 17.9

Map of Part of a Building

and about relations between these locations. Specifically, for any location it is known whether or not it is a junction, and for any pair of locations whether or not one member of the pair is a shop connected to a junction. These relations are denoted by expressions of the form Junction(x) and Shop(x,y). We want a learning program to learn a program, Easy(x,y) that covers the positive instances in Ξ but not the negative ones. Easy(x,y) can use the background subexpressions Junction(x) and Shop(x,y).

To make my example concrete, suppose the training set consists of the following positive instances of Easy (Ξ^+):

$\{< A, B >, < A, C >, < B, C >, < B, A >, < C, A >, < C, B >,$
$< A, A1 >, < A, A2 >, < A1, A >, < A2, A >, < B, B1 >, < B, B2 >,$
$< B1, B >, < B2, B >, < C, C1 >, < C, C2 >, < C1, C >, < C2, C >\}$

and the following negative instances of Easy (Ξ^-):

$\{< A, B1 >, < A, B2 >, < A, C1 >, < A, C2 >, < B, C1 >, < B, C2 >,$
$< B, A1 >, < B, A2 >, < C, A1 >, < C, A2 >, < C, B1 >, < C, B2 >,$
$< B1, A >, < B2, A >, < C1, A >, < C2, A >, < C1, B >, < C2, B >,$
$< A1, B >, < A2, B >, < A1, C >, < A2, C >, < B1, C >, < B2, C >\}$

We assume that the robot can evaluate Junction(x) and Shop(x,y) for any values of the variables. Specifically, for all of the locations named in Ξ, only the following give a value of *True* for Junction:

$\{A, B, C\}$

All other locations mentioned in Ξ give a value of *False for* Junction.

For all of the locations named in Ξ, only the following (ordered) pairs give a value of *True* for Shop:

$$\{< A1, A, >, < A2, A >, < B1, B >, < B2, B >, < C1, C >, < C2, C >\}$$

All other pairs of locations mentioned in Ξ give a value of *False* for Shop.

It happens that the following PROLOG program covers all of the positive instances of the training set and none of the negative ones:

```
Easy(x, y) :- Junction(x), Junction(y)
          :- Shop(x, y)
          :- Shop(y, x)
```

As with other learning problems, we want the induced program to generalize well; that is, if presented with arguments not represented in the training set (but for which we have values for the needed background relations), we would like the program to guess well. (Imagine that the building has repeated structure on other floors and wings not represented in the training set.)

The learning process to be explained uses a version of the GSCA algorithm. We start with a program having a single rule with no body, we add literals to the body until the rule covers only (or mainly) positive instances, and then we add additional rules in the same way until the program covers all (or most) and only (with few exceptions) positive instances. (The parenthetical loosenings apply to the case in which the data may be noisy.)

Typically, there are unlimited possible literals we might add to the body of a clause. Practical ILP systems restrict the literals in various ways. Typical allowed additions are

1. Literals used in the background knowledge.
2. Literals whose arguments are a subset of those in the head of the clause.
3. Literals that introduce a new distinct variable different from those in the head of the clause.
4. A literal that equates a variable in the head of the clause with another such variable or with a term mentioned in the background knowledge. (This possibility is equivalent to forming a specialization by making a substitution.)
5. A literal that is the same (except for its arguments) as that in the head of the clause. (This possibility admits recursive programs, which are disallowed in some systems and which I do not treat here.)

In my robot navigation example, the literals that we might consider adding to a clause are

```
Junction(x)

Junction(y)

Junction(z)

Shop(x,y)

Shop(y,x)

Shop(x,z)

Shop(z,y)

(x = y)
```

ILP systems that follow the approach I am discussing here (of specializing clauses by adding a literal) thus have well–defined methods of computing the possible literals to add to a clause. The matter of selecting which literal to add is more complicated; most systems use scoring methods similar to the one I used in the propositional logic rule–learning example.

I illustrate how the ILP version of GSCA works using my example of robot navigation. Knowing that the predicate Easy is a two–place predicate, the inner loop of our algorithm initializes the first clause to Easy(x,y) :-. This clause covers all the training instances (positive and negative), so we must add a literal to its (empty) body. For purposes of illustrating the algorithm and leaving aside the matter of how to select an atomic formula to add, suppose the algorithm adds Junction(x). The following positive instances in Ξ are covered by Easy(x,y) :- Junction(x):

$\{< A, B >, < A, C >, < B, C >, < B, A >, < C, A >, < C, B >,$

$< A, A1 >, < A, A2 >, < B, B1 >, < B, B2 >, < C, C1 >, < C, C2 >\}$

To compute this covering, we interpret the logic program Easy(x,y) :- Junction(x) for all pairs of cities in Ξ, using the cities given in the background relation Junction as ground facts. The following negative instances are also covered:

$\{< A, B1 >, < A, B2 >, < A, C1 >, < A, C2 >, < C, A1 >, < C, A2 >,$

$< C, B1 >, < C, B2 >, < B, A1 >, < B, A2 >, < B, C1 >, < B, C2 >\}$

Thus, another literal must be added. Suppose we next add Junction(y). The following positive instances are covered by Easy(x,y) :- Junction(x), Junction(y):

$\{< A, B >, < A, C >, < B, C >, < B, A >, < C, A >, < C, B >\}$

There are no longer any negative instances in Ξ covered so we terminate the first pass through the inner loop with the clause Easy(x,y) :- Junction(x), Junction(y).

But the program, π, consisting of just this clause does not cover the following positive instances:

$$\{< A, A1 >, < A, A2 >, < A1, A >, < A2, A >, < B, B1 >, < B, B2 >,$$
$$< B1, B >, < B2, B >, < C, C1 >, < C, C2 >, < C1, C >, < C2, C >\}$$

The positive instances that were covered by Easy(x,y) :- Junction(x), Junction(y) are removed from Ξ to form the Ξ_{cur} to be used in the next pass through the inner loop. Ξ_{cur} consists of all the negative instances in Ξ plus the positive instances (listed earlier) that are not yet covered. In order to attempt to cover them, the inner loop creates another clause, initially set to Easy(x,y) :- . This clause covers all the negative instances, and so we must add literals. Suppose we add the literal Shop(x,y). The clause Easy(x,y) :- Shop(x,y) covers no negative instances, so we are finished with another pass through the inner loop.

Easy(x,y) :- Shop(x,y) covers the following positive instances in Ξ_{cur}:

$$\{< A1, A >, < A2, A >, < B1, B >, < B2, B >, < C1, C >, < C2, C >\}$$

These instances are removed from Ξ_{cur} for the next pass through the inner loop. The program now contains two clauses:

Easy(x, y) :- Junction(x), Junction(y)

:- Shop(x, y)

This program is not yet adequate since it does not cover the following positive instances:

$$\{< A, A1 >, < A, A2 >, < B, B1 >, < B, B2 >, < C, C1 >, < C, C2 >\}$$

After the next pass through the inner loop, we add the clause Easy(x,y) :- Shop(y,x). Now the program covers all and only the positive instances, so the procedure terminates with

Easy(x, y) :- Junction(x), Junction(y)

:- Shop(x, y)

:- Shop(y, x)

This program can be applied (perhaps with good generalization) to other locations besides those named in Ξ—so long as we can evaluate the relations Junction and Shop for these other locations.

17.5.3 Explanation–Based Generalization

Now I turn to deductive learning and a method for deriving rules from previous rules and facts. I explain the method by way of a blocks–world example. Suppose our general knowledge about this world includes the following rules:

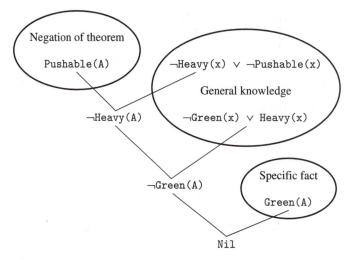

Figure 17.10

A Resolution Refutation Used in EBG

    Green(x) ⊃ Heavy(x)

    Heavy(x) ⊃ ¬Pushable(x)

Among the facts about this world is the following:

    Green(A)

Suppose we are asked to prove ¬Pushable(A). In this illustrative example, the proof is trivial, although it might be more complex in more realistic problems. I show the resolution refutation in Figure 17.10.

From the proof, we can construct an explanation for the conclusion. An *explanation* is the set of facts used in the proof. In this case, the explanation for ¬Pushable(A) is Green(A). Using the explanation, we could construct a new rule, namely,

    Green(A) ⊃ ¬Pushable(A)

But this rule would have limited utility because it applies only to block *A*. However, we notice that the proof can be generalized—A could have been anything, and the proof would still have worked. Generalizing the explanation by replacing the constant A by the variable x gives us Green(x). Following the structure of the proof for ¬Pushable(A), and without additional search, we see that with Green(x) in place of Green(A), we can prove ¬Pushable(x). The result of the process, which we call *explanation-based generalization (EBG)*, then, is the rule

    Green(x) ⊃ ¬Pushable(x)

This rule could have been established from the general rules alone, so we have really learned nothing new. But the EBG process guided us toward this rule based on our need to have established it for a specific case. For a more thorough discussion of EBG, see [Minton, et al. 1989].

In performing the EBG process, we assume that the general rule might be useful for other similar cases as well and is therefore worth deriving and saving. Of course, more rules might slow down the reasoning process by increasing the branching factor, so EBG must be used with care—possibly by keeping information about the *utility* of learned rules. Minton defines utility in terms of the average savings in search effort provided by the rule, how often the rule is used, and the cost of deciding whether or not the rule is applicable [Minton 1988, Minton 1990]. His PRODIGY system keeps only rules with high utility.

17.6   *Additional Readings and Discussion*

[Levesque & Brachman 1987] discuss the tradeoffs between expressibility of logical representations and the tractability of logical reasoning methods. [Levesque 1986] points out that the intractability of reasoning is due to the presence of disjunctions and negations in logical languages. He proposes to use *vivid* representations that dispense with these constructs. Representations using only Horn clauses (called *Horn theories*) are tractable if they do not contain function symbols. These restrictions are observed in a language called DATALOG used to augment the information in databases [Ullman 1989]. [Gogic, et al. 1995] provide comparisons of expressibility, tractability, and succinctness of various versions of propositional logic and its nonmonotonic extensions.

[Selman & Kautz 1991] propose the use of "approximate theories" to speed some inference procedures. These are Horn greatest-lower-bound (GLB) and Horn least-upper-bound (LUB) theories. If a formula does not follow from an LUB theory, it doesn't follow from the original theory. On the other hand, if it does follow from a GLB theory, it also follows from the original theory. [Kautz, Kearns, & Selman 1993] propose the use of characteristic models as a feasible way to perform inference in Horn theories.

In the next chapter, I will mention *terminological logics*—another way to obtain tractability by restricting the representation language.

As an alternative to restricting the language, we might use approximate inference methods—ones that might not be sound or complete. An example involves stochastic sampling of models [Khardon & Roth 1998].

The first proposal to use first-order logic (and resolution methods) as a programming language (and its interpreter) was due to [Green 1969a]. Independently, [Kowalski 1974] elaborated this idea and inspired the invention of PROLOG. Alain Colmerauer developed and wrote the first interpreter for PROLOG [Roussel 1975, Colmerauer 1973]. An efficient implementation is due to [Warren, Pereira, &

Pereira 1977]. The main journal for papers on this topic is the *Journal of Logic Programming*.

AND/OR graph structures are basic to problem–solving methods that reduce problems to alternative sets of subproblems (as in backward reasoning through rules). [Nilsson 1980, Ch. 3] presents an algorithm, AO*, for searching AND/OR graphs. It is based on earlier work by [Nilsson 1969, Martelli & Montanari 1973]. [Davis 1980] describes the use of metarules to control search over the AND/OR tree structures of rule–based expert systems. See also [Smith, Genesereth, & Ginsberg 1986, Smith 1989].

Determining minimal ATMS labels is NP–complete [Selman & Levesque 1990], even in the case of background theories consisting only of Horn clauses. However, [Kautz, Kearns, & Selman 1993] show that such labels can be computed in polynomial time if the computation is based on characteristic models. For other work on TMSs, see [Doyle 1979, de Kleer 1986a, de Kleer 1986b, de Kleer 1986c, Forbus & de Kleer 1993, Shoham 1994].

For an overview of the process of building expert systems, see [Bobrow, Mittal, & Stefik 1986]. [Stefik 1995] is a textbook dealing with many aspects of building knowledge–based systems. (It also contains much other material on AI.) Particularly useful is Stefik's annotated bibliography containing short paragraphs summarizing important papers in the field (Appendix A).

For an example of an expert system that configures Digital Equipment Corporation VAX–11/780 systems, see [McDermott 1982]. [Leonard–Barton 1987] presents the history of the development and use of an expert system at Digital Equipment Corporation. Ongoing work on applications is reported in the Proceedings of the Conferences on Innovative Applications of Artificial Intelligence (IAAI). Papers on expert systems regularly appear in *IEEE Expert*.

For more on predicate (concept) invention, see [Kautz & Selman 1992] and [Muggleton & Buntine 1988]. An impressive example of an application of ILP is in the prediction of protein secondary structure by the GOLEM system [Muggleton, King, & Sternberg 1992]. The Proceedings of the International Inductive Logic Programming Workshops contain current papers on that topic.

The Proceedings of the International Conferences on Knowledge Representation and Reasoning (KRR) contain papers describing ongoing research. [Brachman & Levesque 1985] is a collection of important papers on knowledge representation.

Exercises

17.1 The following questions pertain to PROLOG:

1. Explain why a PROLOG interpreter running a PROLOG program cannot be used to prove the negation of an atom.

2. Some reasoning systems (such as PROLOG) conclude $\neg\phi$ when they fail to prove the atom ϕ. This type of negation is known as *negation as failure*. Explain why we cannot, in general, logically conclude the literal $\neg P$ by failing to prove P.

17.2 The PROLOG interpreter, as described in this chapter, performs a prescribed resolution at each step. If all of the statements in a PROLOG program were converted to disjunctions of literals, describe a control strategy for a resolution refutation system that performs the same resolutions as does the PROLOG interpreter.

17.3 Tom claims to be a descendent of Paul Revere. Which would be the easier way to verify Tom's claim: by showing that Revere is one of Tom's ancestors (backward search) or by showing that Tom is one of Revere's descendants (forward search)? Why? Might there be exceptions to your answer?

17.4 In the circuit described in Exercise 16.12, suppose that *W1*, *W2*, and *W4* are "on." Describe how an ATMS system might be used to diagnose the possible faults in the circuit.

17.5 An inductive learning system observes that every time Q is true, one of the following formulas is also true:

P(A, B)

P(C, B)

P(D, B)

This learning system decides to create the rule

$(\forall x)(P(x, B) \supset Q)$

What is the rationale for this inductive generalization? Why didn't the system create the rule $(\forall x, y)(P(x, y) \supset Q)$?

17.6 An expert system is used to estimate whether or not people are good credit risks based on a number of factors that combine to produce a numeric score. To be judged a good credit risk, the score must be higher than some number, N. The designers of the expert system won't say what the value of N is, but we have learned that Pete is judged to be a good credit risk and that Joe's score is higher than Pete's. We can prove that Joe would be judged to be a good credit risk also by using the following domain rules:

$\forall(x, y, z)[\text{Greater}(x, y) \wedge \text{Greater}(y, z) \supset \text{Greater}(x, z)]$

$\forall(x)[C(x) \supset \text{Greater}(\text{score}(x), N)]$

$\forall(x)[\text{Greater}(\text{score}(x), N) \supset C(x)]$

and the following data:

    C(Pete)

    Greater(score(Joe), score(Pete))

First, use these axioms and data to prove that Joe is a good credit risk, and then use explanation–based generalization techniques on your proof to establish the rule

    $[\forall(x, y)\{[\text{Greater}(\text{score}(x), \text{score}(y)) \wedge C(y)] \supset C(x)\}$

18 Representing Commonsense Knowledge

The Commonsense World

18.1.1 What Is Commonsense Knowledge?

I have illustrated several AI techniques using puzzles and games and the grid world of locations, walls, doors, batteries, and blocks. We expanded our view slightly in the last chapter when I illustrated forward and backward reasoning with a very simple expert system for deciding about loan applications. Real expert systems, of course, have many more facts and rules than did my illustrative example, but even so they contain limited knowledge about quite circumscribed domains.

Much more extensive knowledge will be required for truly versatile, human-level AI systems. And these systems will need to know about many topics that have proved difficult to conceptualize formally. It is perhaps paradoxical that AI scientists find the very subjects that are easy for ten–year–old humans more refractory to AI methods than are subjects that experts must study for years. Physicists are able to describe detailed, exact physical phenomena by wave equations, relativity theory, and other mathematical constructs, but AI researchers still argue about the best way to represent the simple (but very useful) facts that a liquid fills the shape of a cup and will fall out if the cup is turned upside down. The highly theoretical characterizations invented by physicists and mathematicians seem easier to formalize than do ideas that, after all, enabled human beings to function pretty well even before Aristotle.

Consider just some of the things that a ten–year–old knows:

If you drop an object, it will fall. (Nowadays, a ten–year–old might also know that objects wouldn't "fall" if dropped in an orbiting satellite.)

301

People don't exist before they are born.

Fish live in water and will die if taken out.

People buy bread and milk in a grocery store.

People typically sleep at night.

Knowledge of this sort is usually called *commonsense knowledge*. Typically, knowledge about any subject is spread over a variety of levels—ranging from that possessed by the person-in-the-street to that of the specialist. But the most advanced scientific theories extant around 500 B.C., say, were little more than careful verbal formulations of people's everyday observations. To some the earth was flat, objects fell to the earth because that was "their natural place," and human diseases were caused by a variety of colorful "influences." When knowledge was scarce, little separated everyday, commonsense knowledge from advanced scientific knowledge. Commonsense knowledge was (and still is) adequate for many of the things that humans want to do. Scientific knowledge gradually separated itself from commonsense knowledge as people sought more precise descriptions of their world.

Even today, many of the things that we would want a robot to do could be based on medieval, if not prehistoric, science. Get under shelter when it is raining (no need for knowledge about low-pressure systems); take care not to spill the coffee out of its cup when stopping or turning abruptly (no need for advanced hydrodynamics); plug yourself in when the battery charge gets low (no need for electrochemical theory); pay the bills on time so that creditors do not take legal action (no need for complex psychological theories of the behavior of creditors).

I am not arguing here *against* advanced knowledge when such knowledge is required. Weather-forecasting systems need to know meteorology; systems controlling nuclear-power-plant heat exchangers need to know thermodynamics. It is just that for many tasks only the simple knowledge possessed by ten-year-olds is required. And deploying that knowledge (once we figure out how to represent it!) ought to be more tractable than using overly detailed scientific knowledge.

AI researchers have called knowledge about the commonsense world *naive* knowledge. Thus we attempt to construct theories about naive physics, naive economics, naive psychology, naive statistics, naive sociology, and so on. Although we have contrasted naive knowledge with expert knowledge, it should be stressed that these terms refer loosely to regions of a continuum. Different tasks require different levels of knowledge along this continuum. Taking physics as an example, a robot would need to know only simple properties of objects in order to stack blocks on a table. Commonsense physics for such a robot would have facts such as no two blocks can be in the same place, a block must be supported by the table or by another block, and so on. A robot that could hit billiard balls into the pockets of a pool table would need to know a bit more. For that task, a robot would have to know about rolling friction, inelastic collisions, transfer of momentum, and so on. We could obviously imagine tasks that would demand increasingly sophisticated knowledge until we approached the frontiers of modern science. So when we say that we are interested in formalizing commonsense knowledge, we do not have in mind a crisply defined region along this continuum. We are thinking vaguely of a rather broad region near the naive end of the spectrum.

18.1.2 Difficulties in Representing Commonsense Knowledge

What are some of the reasons that it has proved difficult to formalize commonsense knowledge? Probably one reason is its sheer bulk. Much expert knowledge can be compartmentalized in such a way that a few hundred or a few thousand facts are sufficient to build useful expert systems. How many will be needed by a system capable of general human–level intelligence? No one knows for sure. Doug Lenat, who is bravely leading an effort to build a large knowledge base of such facts, called CYC, thinks that between one and ten million will be needed [Guha & Lenat 1990, Lenat & Guha 1990, Lenat 1995]. In 1990, the CYC authors said:

> Perhaps the hardest truth to face, one that AI has been trying to wriggle out of for 34 years, is that there is probably no elegant, effortless way to obtain this immense knowledge base. Rather, the bulk of the effort must (at least initially) be manual entry of assertion after assertion. [Guha & Lenat 1990, p. 33]

Another difficulty is that commonsense knowledge seems not to have well-defined frontiers that enable us to get a grip on parts of it independently of the other parts. Conceptualizations of the commonsense world would probably involve many entities, functions, and relations that would crop up diffusely throughout the conceptualization. Thus, as we attempt to develop a conceptualization, we wouldn't know whether we had "gotten it right" until we had nearly finished the entire, exceedingly large job.

Another roadblock for formalizing commonsense knowledge is that knowledge about some topics just doesn't seem to be easily captured by declarative sentences. Describing shapes and other complex physical objects by sentences is difficult. For example, can a human face be described in words so that it can be recognized by another person who hasn't seen it before? How do we use words to capture a tree, a mountain view, a tropical sunset? If something cannot be described in English or some other natural language, there is good reason to believe that we will not find a conceptualization of it that can be described in logic either.

Related to the difficulty of capturing knowledge in a declarative sentence is the difficulty that many sentences we might use for describing the world are only approximations. In particular, universal sentences (that is, those of the form "All *x*'s are *y*'s") are seldom valid unless they are merely definitions. Various modifications to ordinary logic have been proposed to deal with the fact that much knowledge is approximate. I touch on one approach later in this chapter and present another, based on probability theory, in Chapters 19 and 20.

Besides the difficulty caused by interdependent knowledge, it isn't always obvious how we ought to conceptualize some subjects. Should we think of time, for example, as the set of real numbers (that is, as a continuum of *instants*), or as just the integers, or as intervals of the real line, or as something else? Whereas we might want to imagine *the past* as a single *time line*, how are we to imagine *the future*? Even though we might not want to admit that there is more than one future (*Qué será, será*), we are all used to imagining *alternative* futures that our actions can affect. How do we conceptualize the world so that a statement like, "If I hadn't gone to law school, I wouldn't have met you," makes sense? What kind of entity do we want an *intention* to be so that our conceptualization can handle statements like "I didn't intend to arrive late"?

18.1.3   The Importance of Commonsense Knowledge

Granted that building machines with commonsense is difficult—why is it important? Won't most of the useful applications of AI be in expert systems, where knowledge is less difficult to formalize? There are several answers to this question. First, I would argue that machines with commonsense will find many commercially valuable applications. Few would argue about the value of a "household robot." Such a machine could be given the tasks of keeping the house neat, doing the laundry, preparing and serving meals, performing routine household maintenance (such as replacing burned-out light bulbs), doing the dishes, and so on. But think of the knowledge such a robot would have to have! Enough to be able to answer questions like, where do burned-out light bulbs go? how do you pick up a plate? a glass? where do all of the things go that come out of the dishwasher? how do you tell that the vacuum cleaner needs emptying? how long does lettuce ordinarily keep in the refrigerator? and so on and on.

I could argue also that commonsense knowledge is what is needed in order to make expert systems more useful. Expert systems perform well only within their very tightly circumscribed areas of expertise. General commonsense knowledge would at least enable them to recognize when the user wants information outside of that area. It would also allow the system to predict more accurately when its knowledge is relevant to the task at hand and when it isn't.

The structure of commonsense knowledge might also be important in expanding the knowledge of an expert system. We are all familiar with the use of analogies and metaphors in our own reasoning. Spatial metaphors are particularly common. For example, we say quantum electrodynamics is *beyond* our *limit* of knowledge; cleanliness is *next to* godliness; Mary's salary is *above* John's; and so on. There is ample reason to suspect that metaphors are more than simply linguistic coincidences. The foundations of our conceptualizations of a good many subjects may, in fact, be based on spatial and other commonsense ideas. Thus, an expert system possessing a basic commonsense conceptualization of the world might already be well equipped to expand its knowledge base with little augmentation or revision.

Finally, commonsense knowledge is undoubtedly required in order to understand natural language—a subject I take up in Chapter 24.

18.1.4   Research Areas

Even though we do not yet have systems with commonsense (with the possible exception of CYC—a work in progress), AI researchers have attacked the problem of representing commonsense knowledge on several fronts:

1. Objects and materials. The world consists of objects. Some, such as blocks in the grid world, are discrete, solid things that are relatively easy to talk about and describe. Some objects are hierarchical, in the sense that they consist of parts (other objects) put together in a certain fashion. There are also fluids and gases and collections, such as piles of sand, bags of flour, and galaxies. A notable effort at describing materials and their properties (especially liquids) is that of [Hayes 1978, Hayes 1985a, Hayes 1985b].

2. Space. The physical world has spatial extent. Objects exist in space and are located in space relative to other objects. Thus, we must have ways to talk about things being inside, above, and next to other things, for example. We must also be able to describe how large things are, what their shapes are, and so on. An early AI effort at formalizing various notions about space is that of [Kautz 1985]. For papers on spatial reasoning in various robotics tasks, see [Chen 1990].

3. Physical properties. AI systems should also be able to reason about such physical properties as mass, temperature, volume, pressure, radiation level, wavelength, and any relations among them.

4. Physical processes and events. Objects fall, balls are thrown, grass grows, glasses are filled and emptied, candles burn, hot objects cool. In physics, many such processes are described by differential equations, and we could use these equations in AI. Often, however, we do not need the exact (and expensive) solutions provided by physics. Instead, AI researchers have developed a *qualitative physics* in which general trends can be inferred without the need for exact calculation [Weld & de Kleer 1990].

5. Time. Processes (including computation) occur in time, and computer scientists and AI researchers have developed various techniques for describing and reasoning about time. Special *temporal logics* [Emerson 1989] used in the analysis of computer programs have certain important aspects of time built into them. AI people have tended to handle time in two other ways (but see [Shoham 1987] for a discussion of the use of temporal logics in AI). First, explicit mention of time can be ignored altogether by referring instead to *situations*, which are "snapshots" of the world at unspecified times. Situations are linked by actions that transform one situation into another. I deal with this approach in Chapter 21. Second, time and time intervals can be included among the entities that are explicitly reasoned about. As an example of the formalization of a concept needed for commonsense reasoning, I describe this approach to formalizing time in the next section of this chapter.

18.2   *Time*

How are we to think about time? Is it like the "real line" of numbers extending both into the infinite past and infinite future? Or is it like the countable integers, beginning with 0 at the "big bang" and ticking in discrete time units? Some early societies thought time was circular—proceeding in cycles of endless repetition. We need to decide on what picture we will use before we can state useful facts about time.

The picture most often used in AI was formalized by James Allen [Allen 1983, Allen 1984]. (See also [Allen 1991a] for a discussion of the many ways to represent time.) In this picture, time is something that events and processes occur *in*. (In a perfectly static world, with nothing at all going on, there would be no need for time; in fact, it would be hard even to see how time could be defined in such a world.) These "containers" for events and processes are called *intervals*. Time intervals are like intervals on the real number line. In this conceptualization then, time intervals are among the entities that "exist."

To describe time intervals, we need to give them names, and we will use predicate–calculus object constants, such as $I1, I2, \ldots$, to denote them. To say that some event or process, denoted by E, occupied (fully) the interval I, we would write $Occurs(E,I)$. (I leave it to you to think about how to formalize the notions of events and processes; for present purposes, they too are entities that "exist.")

Time intervals have beginning and ending *time points*. Time points are thought of as real numbers. The beginning of an interval is given by a function, denoted by $start$; the end of an interval is given by a function denoted by end. A basic fact about intervals is

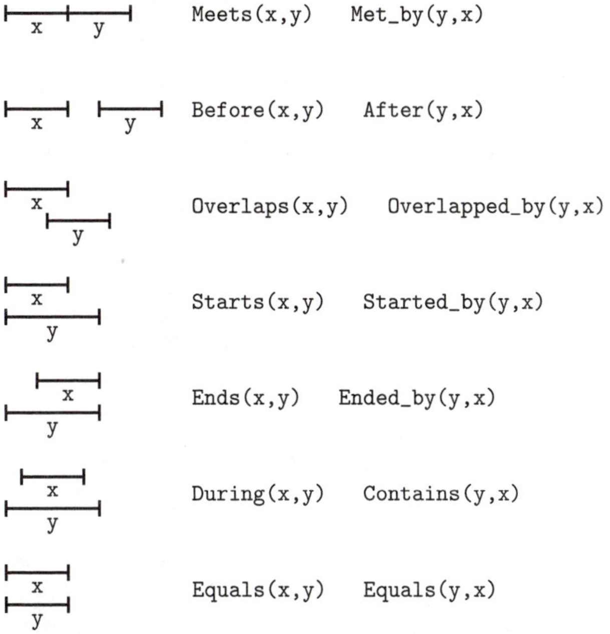

Figure 18.1

Relations between Intervals

$$(\forall x)[\text{start}(x) \leq \text{end}(x)]$$

(When the beginning and end of an interval are the same, the interval collapses to the degenerate case.)

We define a basic relation between intervals as follows:

$$(\forall x, y)[\text{Meets}(x, y) \equiv (\text{end}(x) = \text{start}(y)]$$

(Two intervals *meet* if the end of the first is the same as the start of the second.) We can define six other relations between intervals either in terms of Meets or in terms of the start and end times of the intervals. These are denoted by Before, Overlaps, Starts, Ends, During, and Equals. We also have the inverses Met_by, After, Overlapped_by, Started_by, Ended_by, and Contains. (Equals is its own inverse.) For example,

$$(\forall x, y)\{\text{Before}(x, y) \equiv (\exists z)[\text{Meets}(x, z) \wedge \text{Meets}(z, y)]\}$$

$$(\forall x, y)\{\text{Before}(x, y) \equiv [(\text{end}(x) < \text{start}(y)]\}$$

I show a graphical illustration of these relations in Figure 18.1 and leave it to you to complete the definitions I began with Before.

The interval relations can be used to express some commonsense facts about events in time. For example, to say that the event of water flowing out of a faucet is preceded by turning a valve counterclockwise and followed by turning a valve clockwise, we might write

$$(\forall y)\{\texttt{Occurs}(\texttt{Flow}, y)$$

$$\supset (\exists x, z)[\texttt{Occurs}(\texttt{Turn\_ccw}, x) \wedge \texttt{Occurs}(\texttt{Turn\_cw}, z) \wedge \texttt{Overlaps}(x, y)$$

$$\wedge \texttt{Overlaps}(y, z)]\}$$

There are also some basic axioms expressing such things like the transitivity of `Before`. This particular formalization of time has been applied to a variety of temporal reasoning problems.

18.3   *Knowledge Representation by Networks*

18.3.1   **Taxonomic Knowledge**

Often, the entities of both commonsense and expert domains can be arranged in hierarchical structures that organize and simplify reasoning. In CYC's representation of commonsense knowledge, for example, the most fundamental entity is denoted by the object constant `Thing`. In CYC, there are several kinds of *things*: objects in the world, mathematical objects, events and processes, and so on. These are arranged in a taxonomy or hierarchy that implicitly encodes facts of the forms "X is a P, all P's are Q's, all Q's are R's," and so forth. (See [Guha & Lenat 1990] for a discussion of CYC's hierarchy.) Taxonomic hierarchies can be encoded either in networks or in data structures called *frames*. I discuss the network representation first, using information about office machines as an illustrative example.

Suppose we want to represent the following facts: Snoopy is a laser printer, all laser printers are printers, all printers are machines, plus some related information. As predicate–calculus statements, we might have

`Laser_printer(Snoopy)`

$(\forall x)[\texttt{Laser\_printer}(x) \supset \texttt{Printer}(x)]$

$(\forall x)[\texttt{Printer}(x) \supset \texttt{Office\_machine}(x)]$

The `Laser_printer`, `Printer`, and `Office_machine` predicates represent categories in a taxonomy. One important type of reasoning using taxonomic knowledge involves transitivity of categories. For example, given the preceding facts, we can deduce $(\forall x)[\texttt{Laser\_printer}(x) \supset \texttt{Office\_machine}(x)]$ and `Office_machine(Snoopy)`.

The members of each taxonomic category might all have certain properties, such as the energy source of all office machines is an electric wall outlet. These properties can be expressed by a function and an equality predicate:

$(\forall x)[\texttt{Office\_machine}(x) \supset [\texttt{energy\_source}(x) = \texttt{wall\_outlet}]]$

Note that the members of subcategories typically *inherit* the properties common to their supercategories:

$$(\forall x)[\texttt{Laser\_printer}(x) \supset [\texttt{energy\_source}(x) = \texttt{wall\_outlet}]]$$

These common kinds of inferences about entities in a taxonomic hierarchy are facilitated by a graphical representation called a *semantic network.*

18.3.2   Semantic Networks

Semantic networks are graph structures that encode taxonomic knowledge of objects and their properties. Here, I discuss a simple version of them that incorporates the main ideas. There are two kinds of nodes:

- Nodes labeled by relation constants corresponding to either taxonomic categories or properties
- Nodes labeled by object constants corresponding to objects in the domain

There are three kinds of arcs connecting the nodes:

- Subset arcs (sometimes called *isa links*)
- Set membership arcs (sometimes called *instance links*)
- Function arcs

I show an example of such a network having these various kinds of nodes and arcs in Figure 18.2.

Reasoning about properties and set membership is easier and more efficient in a semantic network than it would be using unguided resolution on the corresponding wffs.[1] To determine whether or not an object, represented by node *A*, is a member of some set, represented by node *B*, we follow the arcs up from *A* to see if we encounter node *B*. Referring to Figure 18.2, it is easy to determine, for example, that R2D2 is an office machine. To determine the value of some property of an object represented by node *A*, we follow the arcs up from *A* to look for a node having this same property. For example, to determine the energy source for Snoopy, we follow the arcs from `Snoopy` up to the `Office_machines` node and see that the answer, `Wall_outlet`, is represented there.

18.3.3   Nonmonotonic Reasoning in Semantic Networks

As already mentioned, reasoning in ordinary logic is *monotonic* because adding axioms to a logical system does not diminish the set of theorems that can be

---

1. Although a modification of the unification procedure that takes into account "type information" on variables, along with other heuristics, results in resolution systems that are essentially as efficient [Stickel 1985].

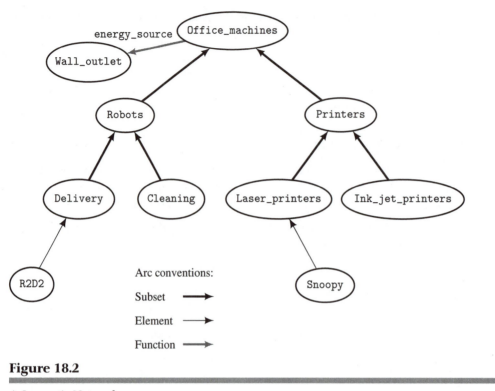

Figure 18.2

A Semantic Network

proved. That is, if Δ' is a superset of Δ, then for any ω for which $\Delta \vdash \omega$, it is also the case that $\Delta' \vdash \omega$. But there are many examples of commonsense reasoning by humans that seem to be nonmonotonic. We often make default inferences—ones that barring knowledge to the contrary, we are willing to assume are true. But, if new, contradictory knowledge arrives, we then must retract the default inference. There are many systems and logical mechanisms that have been proposed for capturing this nonmonotonic phenomenon—I already described how TMSs do so. Other formalisms are default logic [Reiter 1980], autoepistemic logic [Moore 1985a], nonmonotonic logic [McDermott & Doyle 1980], and circumscription [McCarthy 1980, McCarthy 1986].

Here, I describe a simple (albeit not fully adequate) mechanism for nonmonotonic reasoning called *cancellation of inheritance*. The mechanism is best explained using semantic networks. Suppose we want to say that the energy source of office machines, by default, is an electric wall outlet, but that, as an exception to this rule, the energy source of a robot is a battery. We could express that knowledge by adding another function arc to the semantic network, as shown in Figure 18.3.

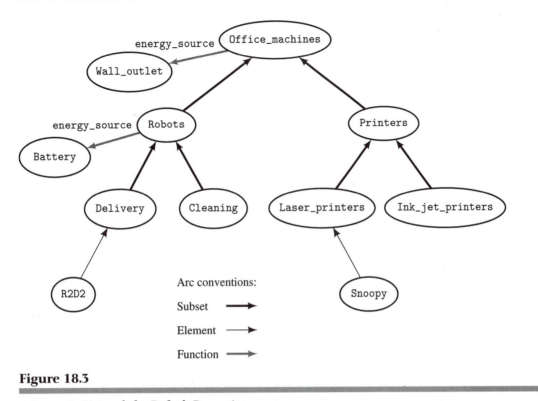

Figure 18.3

A Semantic Network for Default Reasoning

It would seem that the property inheritance mechanism in the new network would lead to a contradiction. Although property inheritance allows us
to conclude (correctly) that the energy source of printers is a wall outlet, it also
contradicts the explicitly represented fact that the energy source of robots is a
battery (assuming that batteries and wall outlets are different). We are protected
from this contradiction by the way in which the network is used. Information
about the most specific categories (ordered according to the subset or instance
arcs) takes precedence over less specific categories. So, in the case in which we
want to inquire about the energy source of R2D2, we first locate the node labeled
R2D2 in the network and inquire whether or not that node has an energy_source
function arc. If it does, we accept the answer given by the node at the head of that
arc as final. If it does not, we follow arcs up the hierarchy until we come to the
first node that has an energy_source function arc. We then use the node at the
head of that arc to answer the query. Information associated with nodes high in
the taxonomic hierarchy is general, default information—subject to cancellation
by more specific information associated with nodes lower in the hierarchy.

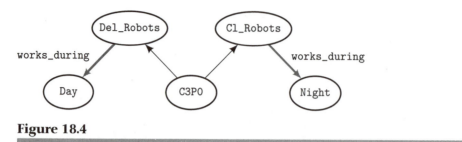

Figure 18.4

Conflicting Defaults

There are various difficulties associated with the property inheritance mechanism. One problem is that properties inherited from different parent nodes might conflict. The subnetwork shown in Figure 18.4 illustrates this problem. C3PO is both a delivery robot and a cleaning robot; does it work the night shift or the day shift? In cases of conflict, no conclusion can be drawn. In more sophisticated nonmonotonic systems, default knowledge is prioritized so that one default can take precedence over another in cases of multiple inheritance.

18.3.4   Frames

Taxonomic knowledge can also be encoded in a data structure called a *frame*. A frame has a name and a set of attribute–value pairs. The frame name corresponds to a node in a semantic network. The attributes correspond to the names of arcs associated with this node, and the values correspond to nodes at the other ends of these arcs. The attribute–value pairs are usually called *slots*, the attributes are called *slot names*, and the values are called *slot fillers*. I show an example in Figure 18.5. Note that we can also represent what is sometimes called *metaknowledge* in these representations; the date that the frame was created and the creator of the frame, for example, are knowledge about the frame, not about printers.

Semantic networks and frames do have difficulties, however, in expressing certain kinds of knowledge. For example, it is difficult (but not impossible [Hendrix 1979]) to express disjunctions (and thus implications), negations, and general, nontaxonomic knowledge. These problems have led to hybrid systems, such as KRYPTON [Brachman, Gilbert, & Levesque 1985]. CLASSIC is another hybrid system [Borgida, et al. 1989]. These use what are called *terminological logics*—employing hierarchical structures to represent entities, classes, and properties and logical expressions for other information.

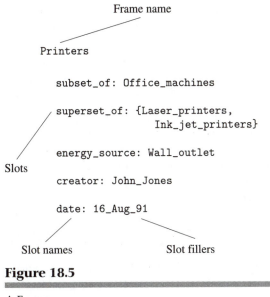

Frame name

Printers

    subset_of: Office_machines

    superset_of: {Laser_printers,
                  Ink_jet_printers}

    energy_source: Wall_outlet

Slots

    creator: John_Jones

    date: 16_Aug_91

Slot names   Slot fillers

Figure 18.5

A Frame

Additional Readings and Discussion

For more on commonsense representation and reasoning methods, see [Davis 1990, Hobbs & Moore 1985]. Regarding CYC, there are five reviews of [Lenat & Guha 1990] in *Artificial Intelligence*, 61(1): 41–104, 1993.

[Sowa 1991] is an edited collection of papers on and related to semantic networks. The property inheritance mechanism, developed by AI researchers for efficient reasoning in semantic networks, has been incorporated as a basic feature of class hierarchies in object-oriented programming languages. For an experimental comparison of various terminological–logic systems, see [Heinsohn, et al. 1992].

Cancellation of inheritance in semantic networks is a nonmonotonic reasoning technique. I have already cited the more sophisticated mechanisms of default logic and circumscription. For a review, see [Brewka, Dix, & Konolige 1997]. Another nonmonotonic reasoning convention is known as the *closed-world assumption* (*CWA*). The CWA augments a knowledge base, Δ, of predicate–calculus formulas by including with Δ the negations of all of the ground atoms that cannot be deduced from Δ. This process is nonmonotonic because if an atom α is added to Δ, the literal $\neg\alpha$ added by CWA must then be retracted. For a collection of papers on nonmonotonic reasoning, see [Ginsberg 1987].

Some of the work on knowledge representation concentrates on languages and formalisms that allow different knowledge-intensive programs to share information. Examples are the *knowledge interchange format* (KIF) [Genesereth &

Fikes 1992] and KQML [Finin, Labrou, & Mayfield 1997]. These systems depend on establishing common conceptualizations of knowledge called *ontologies*. [Gruber 1997] describes principles for their design.

Human commonsense representation and reasoning seem to involve many mechanisms that are quite different from the logical ones studied in this book. The use of analogies and metaphors seems to be fundamental. Analogical reasoning has been studied by several researchers in AI and psychology, including [Gentner 1983]. [Lakoff 1987, Lakoff & Johnson 1980] are books about the role of analogies in human thinking and language. Case–based reasoning is another reasoning method that exploits analogies and similarities with previously solved problems [Kolodner 1993]. (See also the special issue on case–based reasoning of *Machine Learning*, 10(3): 1–5, 1993.)

Exercises

18.1 It is commonplace to assume that *knowledge* can be encoded by predicate-calculus formulas constituting a *knowledge base*. Consider, for example, the following formulas that are alleged to encode some of the knowledge about personnel and organization of the ACME Company:

$$\vdots$$

Salary(Joe, 20000)

Dept(Joe, Sales)

Boss_of(Joe, Henry)

$(\forall x, y)[[Dept(x, Sales) \land Salary(x, y)] \supset (y \geq 20000)]$

$$\vdots$$

Any account of what it means for these formulas to encode knowledge would have to apply also, of course, in the case in which all of the mnemonic predicate constants (e.g., Salary) and object constants (e.g., Henry) were replaced by less suggestive "gensym" constants. In what technical sense can it be said that the formulas (with the gensym constants, say) encode *knowledge* about the ACME Company?

18.2 (Courtesy of Daphne Koller.) Consider the following argument:

Wellington heard about Napoleon's death. Therefore, Napoleon could not have heard about Wellington's death.

Provide a formal first–order logic derivation of this argument. (Hint: When doing knowledge representation, it is often a good idea to start out with a provisional vocabulary and a provisional set of axioms, and modify them as you see what's required for the proof.)

1. List a set of relation constants, function constants, and object constants needed for a first-order logic representation of the knowledge in this domain. Your domain elements should be *people*, *times*, and *events* (such as a person's death). (Hint: It is often easier to use functions in cases where they make sense. It's OK for a function not to be defined over the entire space (e.g., an event may have a time but a person may not), so long as it's always used consistently.)

2. Using this vocabulary, write down the basic facts as well as any commonsense axioms used in this argument.

3. Using a formal logical proof, prove the conclusion from the facts you wrote down.

18.3 Suppose that we had to prove that a bird named *Tweety* is located in a zoo. If we had a knowledge base, our goal would be something like

Bird(x) ∧ Name(x, Tweety) ∧ Located_in(x, y) ∧ Zoo(y)

Suppose that we know 500 birds, five things named *Tweety*, 10^{10} object/location pairs, and 100 zoos. Further, each object has a unique location and each location has about 1000 objects.

1. In solving this problem by proving each conjunct in order (taking due account of the substitutions made in solving the conjuncts), what is the optimal ordering of conjuncts? (For a given problem, the *optimal* ordering of conjuncts is the order that generates the smallest search space or, in other words, gives the least number of possible solutions that need to be checked.)

2. One popular heuristic is to order conjuncts according to which has the smallest number of answers (at the time it is attempted). This heuristic is sometimes called *cheapest first*. What is the order of the conjuncts using this heuristic?

3. Prove that the *cheapest-first* heuristic is always optimal, or modify the example to create a counterexample.

18.4 Construct an example to show that the closed–world assumption (CWA) applied to a set of formulas can lead to an inconsistency.

18.5

1. Express as predicate-calculus wffs the information in the semantic network shown here. Take care that the wffs are written in such a way that they explicitly state the inheritance cancellation information that is implicit in the inheritance hierarchy.

2. Can you prove that Fido has four legs from your predicate–calculus wffs? If not, what information would you need to add in order to complete the proof?

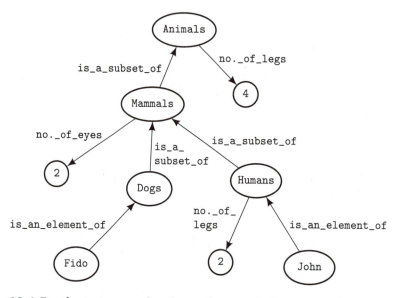

18.6 For the two examples shown here, pick the most appropriate knowledge representation system and encode the statements of the examples in the selected representation. Use your representation and a reasoning system appropriate to it to answer the question in each example. Explain in some detail how the reasoning system arrives at the answer—showing resolution refutations, for example, if a reasoning system based on resolution is used. Use diagrams if they are helpful in your explanations.

1. Typically, birds fly. Ostriches are birds. Oliver is an ostrich. Ostriches do not fly.

   Q. Does Oliver fly?

2. Seymore is an elephant and John's friend. All elephants are gray or a friend of Bert. No friend of Bert is a friend of John.

   Q. Is Seymore gray?

19 Reasoning with Uncertain Information

An agent often has only uncertain information about its task and about its environment. The techniques I have described so far had limited abilities for representing and reasoning about uncertain knowledge. A statement such as $P \lor Q$ allows us to express uncertainty about which of P or Q is true, but I have not yet described how we might represent *how certain* we are about either P or Q.

In ordinary logic, we can deduce Q from P and $P \supset Q$. That is, if an agent knows $P \supset Q$, and it subsequently learns P, it can infer Q also. Are there analogous inference processes when information is uncertain? Various formalisms have been employed to represent and reason about uncertain information. I have already alluded to ones used by MYCIN and PROSPECTOR. The formalism that is most well developed (and, some would argue, most appropriate) is based on probabilities. I begin the chapter with a brief review of the fundamentals of probability theory.

19.1 Review of Probability Theory

19.1.1 Fundamental Ideas

Assume we have a collection of *random variables*, $V_1, V_2, \ldots, V_k$. When we want to talk about the value of V_i without saying what this value is, we use the symbol v_i. In our applications, the random variables stand for features of a domain of interest. The values of the random variables can be of different types. If the variables stand for propositions, their values are either *True* or *False* (or, possibly, 1 or 0); if the variables stand for physical measurements (such as height, weight, speed, etc.), the values are numeric; if the variables stand for categories (such as color, letters of the alphabet, etc.), the values are categorical. For example, the result of a coin toss might be represented by the single variable, C, whose value, c, could be either of the categorical values H (heads) or T (tails). If we are talking about the results of flipping a coin k times, we would need k variables, $(C_1, \ldots, C_k)$, each one of which could have value H or T.

We denote the *joint probability* that the values of $V_1, V_2, \ldots, V_k$ are $v_1, v_2, \ldots, v_k$, respectively, by the expression $p(V_1 = v_1, V_2 = v_2, \ldots, V_k = v_k)$. An expression of the form $p(V_1, V_2, \ldots, V_k)$ is called a *joint probability function* over the variables $V_1, \ldots, V_k$. It maps the set of variables into a real number between 0 and 1. Substituting specific values for the variables in $p(V_1, V_2, \ldots, V_k)$ gives us an expression of the form $p(v_1, v_2, \ldots, v_k)$—an abbreviation for $p(V_1 = v_1, V_2 = v_2, \ldots, V_k = v_k)$. Thus, for a fair coin toss, we might have $p(H) = 1/2$. If we flipped a fair coin five times, we might have $p(H, T, T, H, T) = 1/32$. $p(H, T, T, H, T)$ is the joint probability of the first toss resulting in heads, the second toss resulting in tails, the third toss resulting in tails, the fourth toss resulting in heads, and the fifth toss resulting in tails.

Probability functions must satisfy certain properties; among these are

(a) $0 \le p(V_1, V_2, \ldots, V_k) \le 1$

for any assignment of values to the variables, and

(b) $\sum p(V_1, V_2, \ldots, V_k) = 1$

where the summation is over all values of the variables. Thus, in our coin–flipping example, $p(H) = 1/2$ is consistent with property (a), whereas $p(H) = 1/2$ together with property (b) constrains $p(T)$ to be $1/2$. I will not have much to say here about how to assign probabilities to the values of random variables. Just as the truth or falsity of various propositions denoted by wffs in the propositional calculus is based on the subjective judgment of experts in the domain of application (or by perceptual processing of sensory data), so are the probability values of random variables dependent on expert judgment or on perceptual processing. Our main concern instead will be how to perform calculations that will tell us the probabilities of certain variables of interest.

In the applications that I consider in this chapter, the variables correspond to propositions about a domain. These propositions may be either true or false. The corresponding propositional variables will thus have values *True* or *False*. We may be uncertain about the truth of one or more of these propositions; this uncertainty is represented by the probability of the value(s) of the corresponding variable(s). Thus, the techniques to be described in this chapter can be considered as probabilistic alternatives for the methods discussed in Chapters 13 and 14 for representation and reasoning using propositional logic. (Developing probabilistic alternatives for first–order logic remains a frontier research problem; see, for example, [Nilsson 1986, Glesner & Koller 1995].)

It will be helpful to frame my presentation of important concepts with a specific example. I will use the same one used earlier to illustrate reasoning in the propositional calculus. Recall the propositional atoms BAT_OK, MOVES, and LIFTABLE, which are intended to mean, respectively, the battery is fully charged, the arm moves (when holding the block), and the block is liftable. To these, we add the atom GAUGE, which is intended to mean that the gauge indicating the status of the battery says that the battery is fully charged. To make my diagrams and formulas somewhat less cumbersome, I will rename these atoms by the single letters B, M, L, and G. Now, let us suppose that we are unsure about whether these atoms are *True* or *False*. Before any sensor readings are taken, we have a priori probabilities on various combinations of these values. That is, for example, we think it quite unlikely that M is *False* when the others are all *True*.

Because there are 4 binary–valued variables, there are 16 joint probabilities over these variables, each of the form $p(B = b, M = m, L = l, G = g)$, where b, m, l, and g are *True* or *False*. An agent designer might specify these 16 values, subject to the constraints that each is between 0 and 1 and that they all sum to 1. As an example, I list some of these joint probabilities in the following table:

(B,M,L,G)	Joint probability
(*True, True, True, True*)	0.5686
(*True, True, True, False*)	0.0299
(*True, True, False, True*)	0.0135
(*True, True, False, False*)	0.0007
. . .	

(Of course, a designer would be unlikely to specify the probabilities with the degree of precision given in the table. I do so to make these values consistent with other related probabilities for this example given later in the chapter.)

When we know the values of all of the joint probabilities for a set of random variables, we can compute what is called the *marginal probability* of one of these random variables. For example, the marginal probability $p(B = b)$ is defined to be the sum of all of those 8 of the 16 joint probabilities for which $B = b$:

$$p(B = b) = \sum_{B=b} p(B, M, L, G)$$

Using this formula, the marginal probability $p(B = True) = 0.95$, which is the sum of the 8 joint probabilities in which the value of B is *True*.

Lower order joint probabilities can also be computed by summing appropriately over the full joint probabilities. For example, the joint probability $p(B = b, M = m)$ is the sum of all of those 4 full joint probabilities for which $B = b$ and $M = m$:

$$p(B = b, M = m) = \sum_{B=b, M=m} p(B, M, L, G)$$

It follows that when lower order joint probabilities are known, we can use them also to calculate marginal and other lower order joint probabilities. Thus, for example,

$$p(B = b) = \sum_{B=b} p(B, M)$$

and

$$p(B = b, M = m) = \sum_{B=b, M=m} p(B, M, L)$$

When dealing with propositional variables (ones having values *True* or *False*), I often employ a shorthand notation. Instead of having to write $p(B = True, M = False)$, for example, I will sometimes write $p(B, \neg M)$—assuming that unnegated variables have been instantiated to *True* and negated ones have been instantiated to *False*. This abbreviated notation will be used only when context makes it clear that I am denoting a probability value for an instantiation of variables rather than a probability function over the variables.

Thus, given the full joint probability function (say, as a table) for a collection of random variables, we can in principle compute all of the marginal probabilities and all of the lower order joint probabilities. However, when we have a large collection of random variables, the task of specifying all of the joint probabilities, let alone computing the lower order probabilities, becomes intractable. Fortunately, in most applications, the joint probabilities satisfy certain special conditions that enable their specification and computations over them to become feasible. These conditions will be described later in the chapter.

19.1.2 Conditional Probabilities

We want to be able to use information about the values of some variables to obtain probabilities for the values of others. For example, if the block–lifting robot senses that its arm does not move, it might want to calculate the probability that (given that fact) the battery is charged. Such calculations are called *probabilistic inference* in analogy with logical inference methods. Before explaining how probabilistic inferences can be performed, I must first define what are called *conditional probabilities*.

The conditional probability function of V_i given V_j is denoted by $p(V_i|V_j)$. For any values of the variables V_i and V_j, it is given by

$$p(V_i|V_j) = \frac{p(V_i, V_j)}{p(V_j)}$$

where $p(V_i, V_j)$ is the joint probability of V_i and V_j, and $p(V_j)$ is the marginal probability of V_j. From this expression, we see that we can also write a joint probability in terms of a conditional probability:

$$p(V_i, V_j) = p(V_i|V_j)p(V_j)$$

Returning to our block–lifting example, we can calculate the probability that the battery is charged given that the arm does not move:

$$p(\text{B} = \textit{True}|\text{M} = \textit{False}) = \frac{p(\text{B} = \textit{True}, \text{M} = \textit{False})}{p(\text{M} = \textit{False})}$$

Both the numerator and denominator of this expression can be calculated by appropriate sums of joint probabilities, as explained earlier.

Conditional probabilities are easily understood under a *frequency* interpretation of probabilities. In such an interpretation, $p(\text{M} = \textit{False})$, for example, is the ratio of the number of times the arm does not move to the total number of attempts (in some imagined experiment carried out an infinite number of times). Thus, the probability that the battery is charged given that the arm does not move is the number of times the arm does not move *and* the battery is charged divided by the number of times the arm does not move. A conditional probability is thus a normalized version of a joint probability.

Venn[1] diagrams, such as the one in Figure 19.1, are helpful to illustrate joint and conditional probabilities (for a small number of variables). In that diagram, I show two overlapping elliptical regions, one denoting occasions in which the arm does not move (M = *False*) and one denoting occasions in which the battery is charged (B = *True*). The areas of each of these regions are proportional to the corresponding (marginal) probabilities, shown using shorthand notation in the figure. The area outside of both ellipses corresponds to the occasions in which the arm does move and the battery is not charged ($p(\text{M} = \textit{True}, \text{B} = \textit{False})$).

Note especially the three separate disjoint parts of the ellipses, namely, those corresponding to the joint occurrences of the arm not moving and the battery not being charged, the arm not moving and the battery being charged, and the arm moving and the battery being charged. The areas of each of these disjoint regions are proportional to the corresponding joint probabilities, as shown in the diagram. The way in which we calculate a marginal probability from joint probabilities is obvious from the diagram: $p(\text{B}) = p(\text{B}, \text{M}) + p(\text{B}, \neg\text{M})$.

We can also have joint conditional probabilities of several variables conditioned on several other variables. For example, (using shorthand notation)

$$p(\neg\text{G}, \text{B}|\neg\text{M}, \text{L}) = \frac{p(\neg\text{G}, \text{B}, \neg\text{M}, \text{L})}{p(\neg\text{M}, \text{L})}$$

---

1. John Venn was an English logician [Venn 1880].

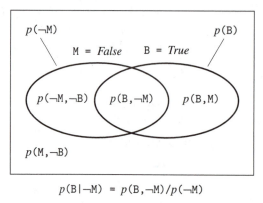

$$p(B|\neg M) = p(B,\neg M)/p(\neg M)$$

Figure 19.1

A Venn Diagram

In calculating any conditional probability, the joint and marginal probabilities that occur in the computation can be calculated from any full set of joint probabilities that contain all of the needed variables, as described earlier.

We can also express a joint probability in terms of a *chain* of conditional probabilities. For example,

$$p(B, L, G, M) = p(B|L, G, M)p(L|G, M)p(G|M)p(M)$$

The general form for this *chain rule* is

$$p(V_1, V_2, \ldots, V_k) = \prod_{i=1}^{k} p(V_i|V_{i-1}, \ldots, V_1)$$

The chain rule expression depends on the way in which we choose to order the V_i. Different possible orders give different expressions, but they all have the same value for the same set of variable values.

Since the way in which we order variables in a joint probability function is unimportant (so long as we keep track of which is which), we can write

$$p(V_i, V_j) = p(V_i|V_j)p(V_j) = p(V_j|V_i)p(V_i) = p(V_j, V_i)$$

Note then that

$$p(V_i|V_j) = \frac{p(V_j|V_i)p(V_i)}{p(V_j)}$$

This last equation is very important. It is called *Bayes' rule*.[2]

---

2. Bayes' rule was first formulated by Reverend Thomas Bayes [Bayes 1763].

I mention one final notational convention. When we have joint probabilities of a collection of variables or probabilities conditioned on a collection of variables, it will be convenient to use set notation. Thus, $p(\mathcal{V})$ will sometimes be used as an abbreviation for $p(V_1, \ldots, V_k)$, where $\mathcal{V} = \{V_1, \ldots, V_k\}$. Similarly, we might use the abbreviation $p(\mathcal{V}|\mathcal{V}_j)$, where $\mathcal{V}_j$ is also a set of variables. If the variables $(V_1, \ldots, V_k)$ have values $v_1, \ldots, v_k$, respectively, we denote that fact by the expression $\mathcal{V} = \mathbf{v}$, where now $\mathcal{V}$ and $\mathbf{v}$ are ordered lists.

19.2   *Probabilistic Inference*

19.2.1   A General Method

The general setting for probabilistic inference is that we have a set, $\mathcal{V}$, of propositional variables $V_1, \ldots, V_k$, and we are given, as *evidence*, that the variables in a subset, $\mathcal{E}$, of $\mathcal{V}$, have certain definite values, $\mathcal{E} = \mathbf{e}$ (of *True* or *False*). In agent applications, the "given" variables would typically have values determined by perceptual processes. We desire to calculate the conditional probability, $p(V_i = v_i|\mathcal{E} = \mathbf{e})$, that some variable, V_i, has value v_i, given the evidence. We call this process *probabilistic inference*.

Since V_i has value *True* or *False*, there are two conditional probabilities in which we might be interested, namely, $p(V_i = True|\mathcal{E} = \mathbf{e})$ and $p(V_i = False|\mathcal{E} = \mathbf{e})$. Of course, we need only calculate one of these because $p(V_i = True|\mathcal{E} = \mathbf{e}) + p(V_i = False|\mathcal{E} = \mathbf{e}) = 1$, regardless of the value of $\mathcal{E}$. I illustrate by describing a "brute-force" method for calculating $p(V_i = True|\mathcal{E} = \mathbf{e})$. Using the definition for conditional probability, we have

$$p(V_i = True|\mathcal{E} = \mathbf{e}) = \frac{p(V_i = True, \mathcal{E} = \mathbf{e})}{p(\mathcal{E} = \mathbf{e})}$$

$p(V_i = True, \mathcal{E} = \mathbf{e})$ is obtained by using our rule for calculating lower order joint probabilities from given higher order ones:

$$p(V_i = True, \mathcal{E} = \mathbf{e}) = \sum_{V_i=True, \mathcal{E}=\mathbf{e}} p(V_1, \ldots, V_k)$$

where the V_i, $i = 1, \ldots, k$ constitute our collection of propositional variables. That is, we sum over all values of the joint probability for which $V_i = True$ and for which the evidence variables have their given values. The calculation of $p(\mathcal{E} = \mathbf{e})$ can be done in a similar manner, although as my next example illustrates, it need not be explicitly calculated.

As an example, suppose we have joint probabilities given by

$p(P, Q, R) = 0.3$

$p(P, Q, \neg R) = 0.2$

$p(P, \neg Q, R) = 0.2$

$$p(P, \neg Q, \neg R) = 0.1$$

$$p(\neg P, Q, R) = 0.05$$

$$p(\neg P, Q, \neg R) = 0.1$$

$$p(\neg P, \neg Q, R) = 0.05$$

$$p(\neg P, \neg Q, \neg R) = 0.0$$

We are given $\neg R$ as evidence and wish to calculate $p(Q|\neg R)$. Using the procedure just given, we calculate

$$p(Q|\neg R) = \frac{p(Q, \neg R)}{p(\neg R)} = \frac{[p(P, Q, \neg R) + p(\neg P, Q, \neg R)]}{p(\neg R)}$$

$$= \frac{(0.2 + 0.1)}{p(\neg R)} = \frac{0.3}{p(\neg R)}$$

Now we can either calculate the marginal $p(\neg R)$ directly or (as is usually done) calculate $p(\neg Q|\neg R)$ by the same method just used—avoiding the calculation of $p(\neg R)$ by taking advantage of the fact that $p(Q|\neg R) + p(\neg Q|\neg R) = 1$. I proceed with the latter method:

$$p(\neg Q|\neg R) = \frac{p(\neg Q, \neg R)}{p(\neg R)} = \frac{[p(P, \neg Q, \neg R) + p(\neg P, \neg Q, \neg R)]}{p(\neg R)}$$

$$= \frac{(0.1 + 0.0)}{p(\neg R)} = \frac{0.1}{p(\neg R)}$$

Since these two quantities must sum to one, we have that $p(Q|\neg R) = 0.75$.

In general, probabilistic inference using this method is intractable because, to perform it in cases in which we have k variables, we need an explicit list of all of the 2^k values of the joint probability, $p(V_1, V_2, \ldots, V_k)$. For many problems of interest, we couldn't write down such a list even if we knew it (which we generally do not).

In view of this intractability, we might ask, "how do humans reason so effectively with uncertain information?" Pearl [Pearl 1986, Pearl 1988, Pearl 1990] surmised that we do it by formulating our knowledge of a domain in a special manner that greatly simplifies the computation of the conditional probabilities of certain variables given evidence about them. These efficient knowledge formulations involve what are called *conditional independencies* among various of the variables—a subject to which I now turn.

19.2.2   Conditional Independence

We say that a variable, V, is *conditionally independent* of a set of variables, $\mathcal{V}_i$, given a set $\mathcal{V}_j$, if $p(V|\mathcal{V}_i, \mathcal{V}_j) = p(V|\mathcal{V}_j)$ and use the notation $I(V, \mathcal{V}_i|\mathcal{V}_j)$ to state this fact. The intuition behind conditional independence is that if $I(V, \mathcal{V}_i|\mathcal{V}_j)$, then $\mathcal{V}_i$ tells us nothing more about V than we already knew by knowing $\mathcal{V}_j$. As far as V is concerned, if we know V_j we can ignore V_i. In our block–lifting example, it seems reasonable that if we already know (by some other means) that the battery is charged ($B = True$), then insofar as we are concerned about the arm moving (M), we don't need explicit knowledge about G (the gauge indicates that the battery is charged). That is, $p(M|B, G) = p(M|B)$.

If a single variable, V_i, is conditionally independent of another variable, V_j, given a set $\mathcal{V}$, we have (by definition) $p(V_i|V_j, \mathcal{V}) = p(V_i|\mathcal{V})$. By the definition of conditional probability, we have $p(V_i|V_j, \mathcal{V})p(V_j|\mathcal{V}) = p(V_i, V_j|\mathcal{V})$. Combining these two results yields

$$p(V_i, V_j|\mathcal{V}) = p(V_i|\mathcal{V})p(V_j|\mathcal{V})$$

for the case in which $I(V_i, V_j|\mathcal{V})$. Note that V_i and V_j appear symmetrically. Thus, saying that V_i is conditionally independent of V_j, given $\mathcal{V}$, is also to say that V_j is conditionally independent of V_i, given $\mathcal{V}$. It suffices to say that V_i and V_j are conditionally independent given $\mathcal{V}$. This same result applies to sets, namely, if $\mathcal{V}_i$ and $\mathcal{V}_j$ are conditionally independent given $\mathcal{V}$ (that is, $I(\mathcal{V}_i, \mathcal{V}_j|\mathcal{V})$), then $p(\mathcal{V}_i, \mathcal{V}_j|\mathcal{V}) = p(\mathcal{V}_i|\mathcal{V})p(\mathcal{V}_j|\mathcal{V})$. If $\mathcal{V}$ is empty, we simply say that $\mathcal{V}_i$ and $\mathcal{V}_j$ are independent.

As a generalization of pairwise independence, we say that the variables $V_1, \ldots V_k$ are *mutually conditionally independent*, given a set $\mathcal{V}$ if each of the variables is conditionally independent of all of the others, given $\mathcal{V}$. Since

$$p(V_1, V_2, \ldots, V_k|\mathcal{V}) = \prod_{i=1}^{k} p(V_i|V_{i-1}, \ldots, V_1, \mathcal{V})$$

and, since each V_i is conditionally independent of the others given $\mathcal{V}$, we have

$$p(V_1, V_2, \ldots, V_k|\mathcal{V}) = \prod_{i=1}^{k} p(V_i|\mathcal{V})$$

When $\mathcal{V}$ is empty, we have

$$p(V_1, V_2, \ldots, V_k) = p(V_1)p(V_2) \cdots p(V_k)$$

and say that the variables are *unconditionally independent*.

Conditional independencies can be conveniently represented in structures called *Bayes networks* (also called *belief networks*). These structures are very useful for probabilistic inference. The conditional independencies represented in Bayes networks can lead to great economies in probabilistic inference computations.

19.3 Bayes Networks

A Bayes network is a directed, acyclic graph (DAG) whose nodes are labeled by random variables. A Bayes network stipulates that each node, V_i, in the graph is conditionally independent of any subset of the nodes that are not descendants of V_i given the parents of V_i. That is, let $\mathcal{A}(V_i)$ be *any* set of nodes in the graph that are *not* descendants of V_i, and let $\mathcal{P}(V_i)$ be the immediate parents of V_i in the graph. The graph is simply a way of stating that, for all V_i in the graph, $I(V_i, \mathcal{A}(V_i) | \mathcal{P}(V_i))$, which means that $p(V_i | \mathcal{A}(V_i), \mathcal{P}(V_i)) = p(V_i | \mathcal{P}(V_i))$.

Let $V_1, V_2, \ldots, V_k$ be the nodes in a Bayes network. Given the conditional independence assumptions made by the network, we can write down the joint probability of all of the nodes in the network as follows:

$$p(V_1, V_2, \ldots, V_k) = \prod_{i=1}^{k} p(V_i | \mathcal{P}(V_i))$$

This expression can be derived in a straightforward manner by applying the conditional independencies to the chain rule expression for the joint probability of all of the variables using any chain rule order consistent with the partial order implied by the Bayes network DAG.

Bayes networks are sometimes called *causal networks* because the arcs connecting the nodes can be thought of as representing direct causal relationships. Human experts are often able to relate causes and effects in such a way that reveals inherent conditional independencies representable by the resulting Bayes net. Structuring Bayes networks using intuitive notions of causality usually results in networks for which the implied conditional independence assumptions are appropriate. In the words of one researcher [Heckerman 1996, p. 14]: ". . . to construct a Bayesian network for a given set of variables, we draw arcs from cause variables to immediate effects. In almost all cases, doing so results in a Bayesian network [whose conditional–independence implications are accurate]."

I illustrate the construction of a Bayes network using our block–lifting example. We start with what we imagine to be "first causes" for this domain, namely, the variables corresponding to the propositions "the battery is charged" (B) and "the block is liftable" (L). B and L have a causal influence on M ("the arm moves"), and B has a causal influence on G ("the gauge indicates that the battery is charged"). Thus, we would draw the Bayes network for this problem as shown in Figure 19.2. Note that, among other things, the network states that $p(M|G, B, L) = p(M|B, L)$. If there were another node in the network, say, U (meaning the block is up), it would not be the case that $p(M|G, B, L, U) = p(M|B, L)$ because U would be a descendant of M. (The block being up influences the probability that the arm moves. How else did the block get up?) The expression for the joint probability function for all of the nodes in the network is given in the figure.

We see that in order to calculate the value of joint probabilities given by the Bayes network, we need to know the conditional probability functions of each node in the network conditioned just on its parents, as shown in Figure 19.2. For nodes without parents, the probabilities are not conditioned on other nodes;

Prior probabilities associated with
each node having no parents

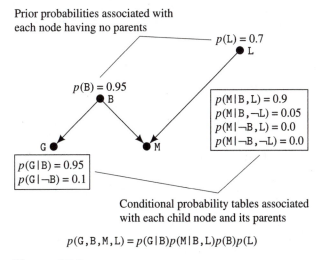

$p(L) = 0.7$

$p(B) = 0.95$

$p(M|B,L) = 0.9$
$p(M|B,\neg L) = 0.05$
$p(M|\neg B,L) = 0.0$
$p(M|\neg B,\neg L) = 0.0$

$p(G|B) = 0.95$
$p(G|\neg B) = 0.1$

Conditional probability tables associated
with each child node and its parents

$$p(G,B,M,L) = p(G|B)p(M|B,L)p(B)p(L)$$

Figure 19.2

A Bayes Network

these are called the *prior probabilities* of these variables. Therefore, a complete specification of the probabilities for a set of random variables involves a Bayes network for these variables along with *conditional probability tables (CPTs)* for each node in the network.

The Bayes network formula for the joint probability function for our block–lifting example should be compared with a similar one (assuming no conditional independencies) obtained by using the chain rule:

$$p(G, M, B, L) = p(G|B, M, L)p(M|B, L)p(B|L)p(L)$$

Note that the Bayes network formula is simpler. Without the conditional independencies stipulated by the Bayes network, the specification of a joint probability for all four variables of this example involved specifying 16 separate joint probabilities (actually just 15 are needed because they must sum to 1). As is evident from Figure 19.2, the assumptions made by the Bayes network require us to specify only 8 probabilities. When there are several conditional independencies among the variables in the domain, the joint probability expression calculated from the Bayes network requires the specification of many fewer probabilities than would be required without these independencies. This reduction can sometimes make otherwise intractable problems feasible.

![gray bar]

19.4 *Patterns of Inference in Bayes Networks*

There are three important patterns of inference in Bayes networks. To explain these, I continue with our example.

- Causal or top–down inference. Suppose we want to calculate $p(M|L)$, the probability that the arm moves given that the block is liftable. Since the block being liftable is one of the causes of the arm being able to move, we say that this calculation is an example of *causal reasoning*. L is called the *evidence* used in the inference, and M is called the *query node*. Here is how we perform the inference in this case: first, we expand $p(M|L)$ (a marginal) into the sum of two joint probabilities (because we want to mention the other parent, B, of M):

$$p(M|L) = p(M, B|L) + p(M, \neg B|L)$$

  Next, we want M to be conditioned on this other parent as well as on L, so we use a form of the chain rule to write

$$p(M|L) = p(M|B, L)p(B|L) + p(M|\neg B, L)p(\neg B|L)$$

  But $p(B|L) = p(B)$ (from the structure of the network; note that B has no parents). Similarly, $p(\neg B|L) = p(\neg B)$.

  Therefore, $p(M|L) = p(M|B, L)p(B) + p(M|\neg B, L)p(\neg B)$. Since all of these quantities are given along with the network, we can compute

$$p(M|L) = 0.855.$$

  The operations that we performed in this example are worth noting because they can be generalized to more complex versions of causal reasoning, as we shall see later. The main operations are as follows:

  (a) Rewrite the desired conditional probability of the query node, V, given the evidence, in terms of the joint probability of V and all of its parents (*that are not evidence*), given the evidence.

  (b) Reexpress this joint probability back to the probability of V conditioned on all of the parents.

- Diagnostic or bottom–up inference. Now let's calculate $p(\neg L|\neg M)$, the probability that the block is not liftable given that the arm does not move. Here the roles of query and evidence are reversed from what they were in the last example. Since we are using an effect (or symptom) to infer a cause, we call this type of reasoning *diagnostic reasoning*.

$$p(\neg L|\neg M) = \frac{p(\neg M|\neg L)p(\neg L)}{p(\neg M)} \text{(Bayes' rule)}$$

Now we calculate $p(\neg M|\neg L) = 0.9525$ (using causal reasoning) and compute $p(\neg L|\neg M) = \frac{0.9525 \times 0.3}{p(\neg M)} = \frac{0.28575}{p(\neg M)}$. Similarly, $p(L|\neg M) = \frac{p(\neg M|L)p(L)}{p(\neg M)} = \frac{0.0595 \times 0.7}{p(\neg M)} = \frac{0.03665}{p(\neg M)}$. Since these two expressions must sum to 1, $p(\neg L|\neg M) = 0.88632$.

The calculations used in this simple example of diagnostic reasoning can also be generalized. The main step is the use of Bayes' rule to convert the problem into one of causal reasoning.

- Explaining away. If our only evidence is $\neg M$ (the arm does not move), we can compute the probability that the block is not liftable, $\neg L$, as we just did. But if we are also given $\neg B$ (the battery is not charged), then $\neg L$ ought to become less certain. In this case, we say that $\neg B$ *explains* $\neg M$, making $\neg L$ less certain. This type of inference uses a top–down or causal reasoning step embedded in a bottom–up or diagnostic one.

$$p(\neg L|\neg B, \neg M) = \frac{p(\neg M, \neg B|\neg L)p(\neg L)}{p(\neg B, \neg M)} \text{(Bayes' rule)}$$

$$= \frac{p(\neg M|\neg B, \neg L)p(\neg B|\neg L)p(\neg L)}{p(\neg B, \neg M)} \text{(def. of conditional probability)}$$

$$= \frac{p(\neg M|\neg B, \neg L)p(\neg B)p(\neg L)}{p(\neg B, \neg M)} \text{(structure of the Bayes network)}$$

From this expression, using the probabilities given in the network and solving for $p(\neg B, \neg M)$ in the usual way, we compute $p(\neg L|\neg B, \neg M) = 0.030$, which is, as expected, much less than $p(\neg L|\neg M)$ computed earlier. Again, note the use of Bayes' rule, an important step in the process of explaining away.

19.5 *Uncertain Evidence*

The expression $p(V|\mathcal{E})$, where V is a query node, does not give us the appropriate probability when the evidence, $\mathcal{E}$, itself is uncertain. In Bayes network calculations, in order for evidence nodes to be "given," we must be certain about the truth or falsity of the propositions they represent. We can achieve that requirement by arranging to have each so–called evidence node (the ones about which we are uncertain) have a child node, about which we can be certain. So, in the last example we considered (explaining away), suppose the robot is not certain that its arm did not move; it might have a somewhat unreliable joint–angle sensor. In that case, the evidence could be provided by a node M', representing the proposition "the arm sensor says that the arm moved." We can be certain that that proposition is either true or false, depending on its reading. The Bayes network would then be used to calculate $p(\neg L|\neg B, \neg M')$ instead of $p(\neg L|\neg B, \neg M)$. Of course, the network will need the values of $p(M'|M)$ and $p(M'|\neg M)$, which describe the reliability of the sensor.

Note that the network in Figure 19.2 already provides for the fact that we may be uncertain about whether or not the battery is charged. Node B has a child node, G, and we expressed how reliable the gauge is by the probabilities $p(G|B)$ and $p(G|\neg B)$.) I leave it to you (perhaps after reading further) to compute $p(\neg L|\neg G, \neg M')$.

Even with the simplifications given by a Bayes network, the brute-force method we have just used for calculating various conditional probabilities of interest from a joint probability is, in general, intractable for large networks. Its worst–case time complexity is exponential in the number of propositional variables. Fortunately, there are several shortcut methods for calculating conditional probabilities for networks of special forms. I consider some of these methods next after first presenting another result about conditional independencies in Bayes networks.

19.6   *D-Separation*

It happens that a Bayes network implies more conditional independencies than just those involving the parents of a node. For example, in Figure 19.2, $p(M|G, B) = p(M|B)$; that is, M is conditionally independent of G given B (even though we are not given both of M's parents). Intuitively, in the network of Figure 19.2, knowledge of (the effect) G can influence knowledge about (a cause) B, which influences knowledge about (another effect) M. But if we are given the cause, B, there is nothing more that G can tell us about M. In this case, we say that B *d-separates* (direction–dependent separation) G and M.

Other conditional independencies of this sort exist in Bayes networks. I state them here and refer you to [Pearl 1988, pp. 117–122] for the proofs.

Two nodes V_i and V_j are conditionally independent given a set of nodes $\mathcal{E}$ (that is, $I(V_i, V_j|\mathcal{E})$) if for every *undirected* path in the Bayes network between V_i and V_j, there is some node, V_b, on the path having one of the following three properties (see Figure 19.3):

1. V_b is in $\mathcal{E}$, and both arcs on the path lead out of V_b.

2. V_b is in $\mathcal{E}$, and one arc on the path leads in to V_b and one arc leads out.

3. Neither V_b nor any descendant of V_b is in $\mathcal{E}$, and both arcs on the path lead in to V_b.

When any one of these conditions holds for a path, we say that V_b *blocks* the path, given $\mathcal{E}$. Note that the paths referred to in this result are undirected paths, that is, paths that ignore arc directions. If *all* paths between V_i and V_j are blocked, then we say that $\mathcal{E}$ *d-separates* V_i and V_j (direction–dependent separation) and conclude that V_i and V_j are conditionally independent given $\mathcal{E}$. Additional

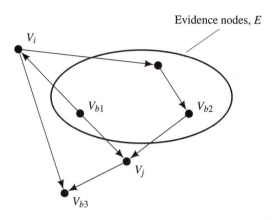

V_i is independent of V_j given the evidence nodes because all three paths between them are blocked. The blocking nodes are

(a) V_{b1} is an evidence node, and both arcs lead out of V_{b1}.

(b) V_{b2} is an evidence node, and one arc leads into V_{b2} and one arc leads out.

(c) V_{b3} is not an evidence node, nor are any of its descendants, and both arcs lead into V_{b3}.

Figure 19.3

Conditional Independence via Blocking Nodes

examples of conditional independence due to d–separation in Figure 19.2 are as follows:

- $I(\text{G, L}|\text{B})$ because, by rule 1, B blocks the (only) path between G and L, given B. By rule 3, M also blocks this path, given B, because M is not a member of the set of evidence

- $I(\text{G, L})$ and $I(\text{B, L})$ because, by rule 3, M blocks the (only) path between G and L and between B and L, given the empty set of evidence. (M is not a member of the empty set of evidence.)

Note, however, that B and L are not conditionally independent given M because although M is on a path between B and L, both arcs on this path lead into M and M is in the set of evidence—so M does not block the path in this case.

The concept of d–separation can also be applied to sets. Two sets of nodes, $\mathcal{V}_i$ and $\mathcal{V}_j$, are conditionally independent, given $\mathcal{E}$ if they are d–separated by $\mathcal{E}$. They are d–separated by $\mathcal{E}$ if *every* undirected path between all nodes in $\mathcal{V}_i$ and all nodes in $\mathcal{V}_j$ is blocked, given $\mathcal{E}$.

Even using d–separation, probabilistic inference in Bayes networks is, in general, NP–hard [Cooper 1990]. Some simplifications can be made, however, for an important class of networks called *polytrees*. A polytree is a DAG for which there is just one path, along arcs in either direction, between any two nodes in the DAG. The network in Figure 19.2, for example, is a polytree. I will illustrate how probabilistic inference in polytrees is performed by an extended symbolic example. (The method to be illustrated is based on an algorithm suggested by [Russell & Norvig 1995, pp. 447ff].)

19.7   *Probabilistic Inference in Polytrees*

The network shown in Figure 19.4 is a typical example of a polytree. In this network, we will want to calculate the probability of Q given some of the other nodes. Note that some of the nodes are connected to Q only through Q's parents. We will say that these nodes are *above* Q. The other nodes are connected to Q only through Q's immediate successors (its *children*). We will say that these nodes are *below* Q. Also note that there is no path (except for the one through Q connecting a node above Q with a node below it—for otherwise the network would not be a polytree). These definitions and connection property apply to every node in a polytree! Our examples will be of three types:

1. All evidence nodes are above Q. As a typical example of this type, we will calculate $p(Q|P5, P4)$.

2. All evidence nodes are below Q. As a typical example of this type, we will calculate $p(Q|P12, P13, P14, P11)$.

3. There are evidence nodes both above and below Q.

19.7.1   Evidence Above

Let's calculate $p(Q|P5, P4)$ where all of the evidence nodes are above Q. Our calculation is a trace of the execution of a "bottom–up" recursive algorithm that calculates the probability of each of the ancestors of Q, given the evidence, until either we reach the evidence or the evidence is below that ancestor. The algorithm proceeds as follows:

First, we "involve the parents" (of Q):

$$p(Q|P5, P4) = \sum_{P6,P7} p(Q, P6, P7|P5, P4)$$

(The special notation used to index this summation means we add four versions of $p(Q, P6, P7|P5, P4)$—the original, one substituting ¬P6 for P6, one substituting ¬P7 for P7, and one with both substitutions.)

Next, we make the parents of Q part of the evidence by using the definition of conditional independence to write

$$p(Q, P6, P7|P5, P4) = p(Q|P6, P7, P5, P4)p(P6, P7|P5, P4)$$

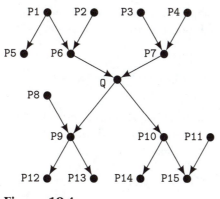

Figure 19.4

A Typical Polytree

Substitution yields

$$p(Q|P5, P4) = \sum_{P6,P7} p(Q|P6, P7, P5, P4)p(P6, P7|P5, P4)$$

Now, because a node is conditionally independent of nondescendants given its parents,

$$p(Q|P5, P4) = \sum_{P6,P7} p(Q|P6, P7)p(P6, P7|P5, P4)$$

Then, d–separation allows us to split the parents:

$$p(Q|P5, P4) = \sum_{P6,P7} p(Q|P6, P7)p(P6|P5, P4)p(P7|P5, P4)$$

And, finally d–separation allows us to ignore evidence above one parent in calculating the probability of the other:

$$p(Q|P5, P4) = \sum_{P6,P7} p(Q|P6, P7)p(P6|P5)p(P7|P4)$$

It is very important to note that the terms being summed are (a) the probabilities of the query node, given the various values of its parents (which probabilities are given along with the Bayes network), and (b) the probabilities of each of the parents given just that part of the evidence above that parent (a recursive call to the very algorithm we are executing). These results follow directly from the fact that we are working with a polytree.

This same procedure is applied recursively until finally either we reach nodes having an evidence node as a parent or we reach nodes having no parents (nodes that are not themselves evidence nodes). We have the first of these two cases in calculating $p(P7|P4)$; the evidence node, P4, is one of the parents of the query node, P7. In that case, the step of "involving the parents" is simpler because one of them is already involved. Because $p(\text{P7}, \text{P3}|\text{P4}) = p(\text{P7}|\text{P3}, \text{P4})p(\text{P3}|\text{P4})$, we can write

$$p(\text{P7}|\text{P4}) = \sum_{\text{P3}} p(\text{P7}|\text{P3}, \text{P4})p(\text{P3}|\text{P4}) = \sum_{\text{P3}} p(\text{P7}|\text{P3}, \text{P4})p(\text{P3})$$

(The last step follows because $I(\text{P3}, \text{P4})$.) All of the terms in this sum are given by the Bayes net, so the procedure ends along this branch for this example.

In calculating $p(\text{P6}|\text{P5})$, we obtain

$$p(\text{P6}|\text{P5}) = \sum_{\text{P1},\text{P2}} p(\text{P6}|\text{P1}, \text{P2})p(\text{P1}|\text{P5})p(\text{P2})$$

Here, we must next calculate $p(\text{P1}|\text{P5})$, and we note that the evidence node is no longer "above" the query node; it is "below." We can no longer use this recursive procedure, but must use the "evidence–below" procedure—yet to be described. In this example, we simply use Bayes' rule to obtain $p(\text{P1}|\text{P5}) = \frac{p(\text{P5}|\text{P1})p(\text{P1})}{p(\text{P5})}$. Now all of the quantities needed to calculate $p(\text{P6}|\text{P5})$ are given by the Bayes network. We can assemble all of these results (performing all of the summations) to get a final answer for $p(\text{Q}|\text{P5}, \text{P4})$.

19.7.2   Evidence Below

Next, let's calculate $p(\text{Q}|\text{P12}, \text{P13}, \text{P14}, \text{P11})$ where all of the evidence nodes are below Q. Again, our calculation is a trace of the execution of a recursive algorithm. It proceeds as follows: at the top level, we use Bayes' rule to write

$$p(\text{Q}|\text{P12}, \text{P13}, \text{P14}, \text{P11}) = \frac{p(\text{P12}, \text{P13}, \text{P14}, \text{P11}|\text{Q})p(\text{Q})}{p(\text{P12}, \text{P13}, \text{P14}, \text{P11})}$$

$$= kp(\text{P12}, \text{P13}, \text{P14}, \text{P11}|\text{Q})p(\text{Q})$$

where $k = \frac{1}{p(\text{P12},\text{P13},\text{P14},\text{P11})}$ is a normalizing factor to be calculated later in the same way as we did in our earlier examples. By d–separation, $I(\{\text{P12}, \text{P13}\}, \{\text{P14}, \text{P11}\}|\text{Q})$, yielding

$$p(\text{Q}|\text{P12}, \text{P13}, \text{P14}, \text{P11}) = kp(\text{P12}, \text{P13}|\text{Q})p(\text{P14}, \text{P11}|\text{Q})p(\text{Q})$$

Note that we have split the set {P12, P13, P14, P11} into two subsets corresponding to the two children of Q. Each of the terms $p(\text{P12}, \text{P13}|\text{Q})$ and $p(\text{P14}, \text{P11}|\text{Q})$ involves a case of calculating the probability of a set of query nodes given a single evidence node above them. Thus, we can use something like the previous algorithm. Because there is only a single evidence node, it is convenient to use a *top-down* recursive algorithm instead of a *bottom-up* one as before.

I illustrate how the top–down version proceeds by calculating $p(P12, P13|Q)$ first. The key step is to involve that single child, P9, of Q that is above the set of query nodes, {P12,P13}. Note first that $p(P12, P13, P9|Q) = p(P12, P13|P9, Q)p(P9|Q)$ by the definition of conditional independence. Then,

$$p(P12, P13|Q) = \sum_{P9} p(P12, P13|P9, Q)p(P9|Q)$$

Now, by d–separation, $I(\{P12, P13\}, Q|P9)$, so

$$p(P12, P13|Q) = \sum_{P9} p(P12, P13|P9)p(P9|Q)$$

Of the terms in this sum, $p(P9|Q)$ is calculated by involving all of the parents of P9:

$$p(P9|Q) = \sum_{P8} p(P9|P8, Q)p(P8)$$

$p(P9|P8, Q)$ is given by the network. The other term, $p(P12, P13|P9)$, is a recursive call to the same top–down procedure that calculates the probability of a set of query nodes given a single evidence node above them. In this case, the recursive call terminates after one step because the children of P9 are the evidence nodes. Because P12 and P13 are independent given P9, we have $p(P12, P13|P9) = p(P12|P9)p(P13|P9)$. Both of these probabilities are given by the network.

Applying the top–down procedure to $p(P14, P11|Q)$ yields

$$p(P14, P11|Q) = \sum_{P10} p(P14, P11|P10)p(P10|Q)$$

and then

$$p(P14, P11|Q) = \sum_{P10} p(P14|P10), p(P11|P10)p(P10|Q)$$

because $I(P14, P11|P10)$. Only the middle term of this product is not given directly by the network. We use the top–down procedure again to calculate that term:

$$p(P11|P10) = \sum_{P15} p(P11|P15, P10)p(P15|P10)$$

Here

$$p(P15|P10) = \sum_{P11} p(P15|P10, P11)p(P11) \text{ (Why?)},$$

but in $p(P11|P15, P10)$, the query node P11 is above the evidence nodes, so we have to apply the top level of this procedure (using Bayes' rule) again:

$$p(P11|P15, P10) = \frac{p(P15, P10|P11)p(P11)}{p(P15, P10)} = k_1 p(P15, P10|P11)p(P11)$$

where $k_1 = \frac{1}{p(\text{P15,P10})}$ and $p(\text{P11})$ is given directly by the network; the algorithm terminates with

$$p(\text{P15, P10}|\text{P11}) = p(\text{P15}|\text{P10, P11})p(\text{P10}|\text{P11}) = p(\text{P15}|\text{P10, P11})p(\text{P10})$$

because P10 and P11 are independent.

Now, all of the results can be collected, and the sums and k and k_1 can be computed, to obtain a final answer for $p(\text{Q}|\text{P12, P13, P14, P11})$.

The complexity of both the evidence–above and evidence–below algorithms is linear in the number of nodes in the network (for polytrees).

19.7.3   Evidence Above and Below

If there is evidence both above and below Q, as in

$$p(\text{Q}|\{\text{P5, P4}\}, \{\text{P12, P13, P14, P11}\})$$

we separate the evidence into above, $\mathcal{E}^+$, and below, $\mathcal{E}^-$, portions and use a version of Bayes' rule to write

$$p(\text{Q}|\mathcal{E}^+, \mathcal{E}^-) = \frac{p(\mathcal{E}^-|\text{Q}, \mathcal{E}^+)p(\text{Q}|\mathcal{E}^+)}{p(\mathcal{E}^-|\mathcal{E}^+)}.$$

As usual, we treat $\frac{1}{p(\mathcal{E}^-|\mathcal{E}^+)} = k_2$ as a normalizing factor and write

$$p(\text{Q}|\mathcal{E}^+, \mathcal{E}^-) = k_2 p(\mathcal{E}^-|\text{Q}, \mathcal{E}^+)p(\text{Q}|\mathcal{E}^+)$$

Note that Q d–separates $\mathcal{E}^-$ from $\mathcal{E}^+$, so

$$p(\text{Q}|\mathcal{E}^+, \mathcal{E}^-) = k_2 p(\mathcal{E}^-|\text{Q})p(\text{Q}|\mathcal{E}^+)$$

Note that we calculated the first probability in this product already as part of the top–down procedure for calculating $p(\text{Q}|\mathcal{E}^-)$. The second probability was calculated directly by the bottom–up procedure.

19.7.4   A Numerical Example

I demonstrate the use of some of these methods numerically with the smaller, abstract polytree shown in Figure 19.5. We want to calculate $p(\text{Q}|\text{U})$.

As usual for diagnostic reasoning, we first apply Bayes' rule to obtain

$$p(\text{Q}|\text{U}) = kp(\text{U}|\text{Q})p(\text{Q}), \text{ where } k = \frac{1}{p(\text{U})}.$$

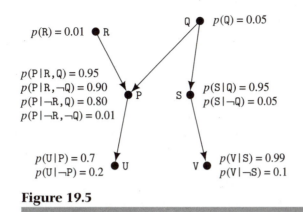

$p(R) = 0.01$ R

$p(P|R,Q) = 0.95$
$p(P|R,\neg Q) = 0.90$
$p(P|\neg R,Q) = 0.80$
$p(P|\neg R,\neg Q) = 0.01$

P

S $p(S|Q) = 0.95$
     $p(S|\neg Q) = 0.05$

Q $p(Q) = 0.05$

$p(U|P) = 0.7$
$p(U|\neg P) = 0.2$ U

V $p(V|S) = 0.99$
     $p(V|\neg S) = 0.1$

Figure 19.5

A Small Polytree

The top-down algorithm successively calculates

$$p(U|Q) = \sum_P p(U|P)p(P|Q)$$

$$p(P|Q) = \sum_R p(P|R, Q)p(R)$$

$$= p(P|R, Q)p(R) + p(P|\neg R, Q)p(\neg R)$$

$$= 0.95 \times 0.01 + 0.8 \times 0.99 = 0.80, \text{ thus}$$

$$p(\neg P|Q) = 0.20$$

$$p(U|Q) = p(U|P) \times 0.8 + p(U|\neg P) \times 0.2$$

$$= 0.7 \times 0.8 + 0.2 \times 0.2 = 0.60, \text{ thus}$$

$$p(Q|U) = k \times 0.6 \times 0.05 = k \times 0.03$$

$$p(\neg Q|U) = kp(U|\neg Q)p(\neg Q)$$

$$p(U|\neg Q) = \sum_P p(U|P)p(P|\neg Q)$$

$$p(P|\neg Q) = \sum_R p(P|R, \neg Q)p(R)$$

$$= p(P|R, \neg Q)p(R) + p(P|\neg R, \neg Q)p(\neg R)$$

$$= 0.90 \times 0.01 + 0.01 \times 0.99 = 0.019, \text{ thus}$$

$$p(\neg P|\neg Q) = 0.98$$

$$p(U|\neg Q) = p(U|P) \times 0.019 + p(U|\neg P) \times 0.98$$

$$= 0.7 \times 0.019 + 0.2 \times 0.98 = 0.21, \text{ thus}$$

$$p(\neg Q|U) = k \times 0.21 \times 0.95 = k \times 0.20$$

Thus, $k = 4.35$, and finally

$$p(\mathbb{Q}|\mathbb{U}) = 4.35 \times 0.03 = 0.13$$

Calculations like those of this example can be organized to avoid repeating subcalculations. One method of doing so is called *bucket elimination* [Dechter 1996].

When the network is not a polytree, the recursive procedures just described will not terminate because of the multiple paths between nodes. Other techniques have been proposed for dealing with these more complicated networks. Among them is a Monte Carlo method (called *logic sampling* [Henrion 1988]). In that technique, the marginal probabilities of the parentless nodes are used to assign random values (such as *True* or *False*) to those nodes. Using those values, the CPTs of their descendants are used to assign random values to these descendants, and so on down the network. Finally, every node in the network has a value. This process is repeated many times, and we keep track of all the values assigned to the nodes. In the limit of an infinite number of trials, the node values will be consistent with the joint probability for the nodes stipulated by the network and its CPTs. After a large number of trials, we can estimate $p(\mathbb{Q}|\mathbb{E})$, say, by dividing the number of times $\mathbb{Q}$ and $\mathbb{E}$ were assigned value *True* and dividing by the number of times $\mathbb{E}$ had value *True*. Clearly, the same method can be used to calculate the joint probability of a set of query nodes given a set of evidence nodes.

Another method, called *clustering* [Lauritzen & Spiegelhalter 1988], groups nodes in the network into "supernodes" in such a way that the graph of supernodes is a polytree. The possible values of the supernodes are all the combinations of values of their component nodes. The polytree algorithm can then be used, but now there are many CPTs for each of the supernodes—giving the conditional probabilities for all of the values of the supernodes, conditioned on all of the values of the parent nodes (which may themselves be supernodes).

19.8   *Additional Readings and Discussion*

There are several textbooks on probability that can be consulted to supplement my brief review; [Feller 1968] is one.

Some researchers think that nonmonotonic reasoning can best be handled by probabilistic methods. See, for example, [Goldszmidt, Morris, & Pearl 1990].

In AI, work on probabilistic inference using Bayes networks began with [Pearl 1982a, Kim & Pearl 1983] who developed "message–passing" algorithms for trees and polytree networks, respectively. The polytree method described in this chapter is based on that of [Russell & Norvig 1995, pp. 447ff]. My treatment of Bayes nets was limited to discrete–valued variables. Some work has also been done with continuous random variables; see [Shachter & Kenley 1989]. [Wellman 1990] has investigated "qualitative" networks.

I have already cited the book on probabilistic inference by [Pearl 1984]. [Neapolitan 1990] is a textbook on the use of probabilistic methods in expert systems. [Henrion 1990] is an introductory article about probabilistic inference in Bayes nets. [Jensen 1996] is a textbook on Bayes networks, featuring the HUGIN system. [Neal 1991] investigates the connections between Bayes networks and neural networks. A special issue on "Uncertainty in AI" of the *Communications of the ACM* was guest edited by David Heckerman, Michael Wellman, and Abe Mamdani (vol. 38, no. 3, March 1995).

Bayes networks are being used in many expert–system applications. A typical example is PATHFINDER, which assists pathologists with the diagnosis of lymph node diseases [Heckerman 1991, Heckerman & Nathwani 1992]. Another is CPCS-BN for internal medicine [Pradhan, et al. 1994], which has 448 nodes and 908 arcs and compares favorably with the world's leading diagnosticians in internal medicine.

There are several alternatives to Bayes networks for reasoning with uncertain information. The MYCIN expert system for medical diagnosis and treatment recommendations used *certainty factors* [Shortliffe 1976, Buchanan & Shortliffe 1984]. [Duda, Hart, & Nilsson 1976] used *sufficiency* and *necessity* indices in their PROSPECTOR expert system for aiding mineral exploration.

Other methods are based on fuzzy logic and "possibility theory" [Zadeh 1975, Zadeh 1978, Elkan 1993] and Dempster–Shafer rules of combination [Dempster 1968, Shafer 1979]. [Nilsson 1986] develops a "probabilistic logic" and provides citations to related work in probability theory and multivalued logics. My view now is that probabilistic inference in Bayes networks dominates these other methods for most expert–system applications, but the subject remains controversial.

Human behavior, when confronted with uncertainties, can be quite inconsistent [Tversky & Kahneman 1982] and thus might not provide useful models for engineering.

[Shafer & Pearl 1990] is a collection of papers on uncertain reasoning. Proceedings of the annual conferences on Uncertainty in Artificial Intelligence (UAI) contain descriptions of ongoing research. The *International Journal of Approximate Reasoning*, as well as some of the other AI journals and AI conference proceedings, publishes important papers.

Exercises

19.1 Suppose that colored balls are distributed in three indistinguishable boxes, *B*1, *B*2, and *B*3, as follows:

	B1	**B2**	**B3**
Red	2	4	3
White	3	2	4
Blue	6	3	3

A box is selected at random from which a ball is selected at random. The ball is red. What are the probabilities of the box selected being B1, B2, or B3? Explain your reasoning.

19.2 Consider the belief network shown here.

$p(P)$ (P)

$p(Q|P)$
$p(Q|\neg P)$

(Q)

1. Derive an expression for the probability of $P \supset Q$.

2. When are $p(P \supset Q)$ and $p(Q|P)$ equal?

3. Assume the conditional probability table for the network is not known. Instead, all that is known are the values of $p(P)$ and of $p(P \supset Q)$. What can be said about the value of $p(Q)$?

19.3 An admissions committee for a college is trying to determine the probability that an admitted candidate is really qualified. The relevant probabilities are given in the Bayes network shown here. Calculate $p(A|D)$.

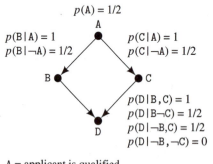

$p(A) = 1/2$

A

$p(B|A) = 1$
$p(B|\neg A) = 1/2$

$p(C|A) = 1$
$p(C|\neg A) = 1/2$

B   C

$p(D|B,C) = 1$
$p(D|B\neg C) = 1/2$
$p(D|\neg B,C) = 1/2$
$p(D|\neg B,\neg C) = 0$

D

A = applicant is qualified
B = applicant has high grade point average
C = applicant has excellent recommendations
D = applicant is admitted

$p(A|D) = ?$

19.4 (Courtesy of Judea Pearl, a resident of earthquake country.) The belief network shown here formalizes the following situation: you have a new burglar alarm installed at home. It is fairly reliable at detecting a burglary, but also responds on occasion to minor earthquakes. You also have two neighbors, John and Mary, who have promised to call you at work when they hear the alarm. John quite reliably calls when he hears the alarm, but sometimes confuses the telephone ringing with the alarm and calls then too. Mary, on the other hand, likes rather loud music and sometimes misses the alarm altogether.

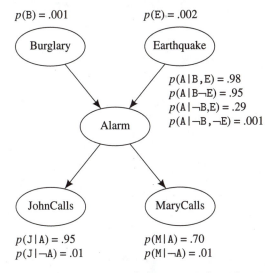

$p(B) = .001$

$p(E) = .002$

Burglary

Earthquake

$p(A\,|\,B,E) = .98$
$p(A\,|\,B\lnot E) = .95$
$p(A\,|\,\lnot B,E) = .29$
$p(A\,|\,\lnot B,\lnot E) = .001$

Alarm

JohnCalls

MaryCalls

$p(J\,|\,A) = .95$
$p(J\,|\,\lnot A) = .01$

$p(M\,|\,A) = .70$
$p(M\,|\,\lnot A) = .01$

To exercise your ability to work with joint probabilities as defined by belief networks, calculate the joint probability that neither John nor Mary calls and that there is both an earthquake and a burglary. That is, calculate $p(\lnot J, \lnot M, B, E)$.

19.5 In a galaxy far, far away, 90% of the taxicabs are green and 10% are blue. An accident involving a taxicab occurs; we presume that the accident rate for green taxicabs is the same as that for blue taxicabs. A court considers the accident, and a newspaper reporter who was at the scene says, "The cab involved was blue." This reporter is usually reliable; in fact, his statements are correct 80% of the time. That is, if the taxicab involved in the accident was in fact blue (or green), the probability that our witness would say "blue" (or "green") is 0.8. What is the probability that the taxicab involved in the accident was blue, given the reporter's statement?

19.6 Orville, the robot juggler, drops balls quite often when its battery is low. In previous tests, it has been determined that the probability that it will drop a ball when its battery is low is 0.9. Whereas when its battery is not low, the probability that it drops a ball is only 0.01. The battery was recharged not so long ago, and our best guess (before looking at Orville's latest juggling record) is that the odds that the battery is low are 10 to 1 against. A robot observer, with a somewhat unreliable vision system, reports that Orville dropped a ball. The reliability of the observer is given by the following probabilities:

p(observer says that Orville drops | Orville does drop) = 0.9

p(observer says that Orville drops | Orville doesn't drop) = 0.2

Draw the Bayes network, and calculate the probability that the battery is low given the observer's report.

20 Learning and Acting with Bayes Nets

20.1 Learning Bayes Nets

The problem of learning a Bayes network is the problem of finding a network that *best matches* (according to some scoring metric) a *training set* of data, Ξ, where Ξ is a set of instances of values for all (or at least some) of the variables. By "finding a network," we mean finding both the structure of the DAG and the conditional probability tables (CPTs) associated with each node in the DAG.

20.1.1 Known Network Structure

If we knew the structure of the network, we have only to find the CPTs. Let's describe that case first. Often human experts can come up with the appropriate structure for a problem domain but not the CPTs. And learning the CPTs is still needed in the case in which we must also learn network structure. There is an easy and a harder setting for learning the CPTs. In the easy case, there is no missing data. That is, each member of the training set Ξ has a value for *every* variable represented in the network. In more realistic settings, however, it is often the case that the values of some of the variables are missing for some of the training records; missing data makes learning the CPTs somewhat harder.

No Missing Data

I begin by assuming no missing data. Here, if we have an ample number of training samples, we have only to compute sample statistics for each node and its parents. Suppose we want the CPTs for some node V_i given its parents $\mathcal{P}(V_i)$. Following my earlier convention, we denote the value of V_i by v_i. There are as many tables for the node V_i as there are different values for V_i (less one). In the

343

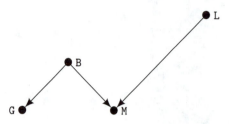

G	M	B	L	**Number of instances**
True	*True*	*True*	*True*	54
True	*True*	*True*	*False*	1
True	*False*	*True*	*True*	7
True	*False*	*True*	*False*	27
False	*True*	*True*	*True*	3
False	*False*	*True*	*False*	2
False	*False*	*False*	*True*	4
False	*False*	*False*	*False*	2
				100

Figure 20.1

A Network and Some Sample Values

Boolean case, which I again assume, there is just one CPT for each node. Let V_i have k_i parent nodes. Then, there are 2^{k_i} entries (rows) in the table because each parent can have one of two possible values. Let's denote the variables associated with the parents of V_i by the vector variable $\mathbf{P}_i$ and the values of these variables by the vector of values $\mathbf{p}_i$. The sample statistic $\hat{p}(V_i = v_i | \mathbf{P}_i = \mathbf{p}_i)$ is given by the number of samples in Ξ having $V_i = v_i$ *and* $\mathbf{P}_i = \mathbf{p}_i$ divided by the number of samples having $\mathbf{P}_i = \mathbf{p}_i$. To learn CPTs, we simply use these sample statistics for the real thing for all of the nodes in the network.

An example might make this calculation more clear. Consider a Bayes network with the same structure as that of Figure 19.2, which I repeat as Figure 20.1 without the CPTs. Suppose we observe 100 sets of values of G, M, B, L, as shown in the figure. (Note that some combinations do not appear, and some combinations appear more frequently than do others.) To calculate the sample probability $\hat{p}(B = True)$, for example, we simply calculate the fraction of times that B has value *True* among all of the samples and obtain $\hat{p}(B = True) = 0.94$. Similarly, $\hat{p}(L = True) = 0.68$. For the nodes B and L, these probabilities are all that are needed for their CPTs.

We calculate the rows of the CPT for node M in a manner illustrated by the following typical calculation: to calculate $\hat{p}(M = True | B = True, L = False)$ (which we write as $\hat{p}(M|B, \neg L)$ in my shorthand notation), we count the number of times that M has value *True*, B has value *True*, and L has value *False* and divide that number by the number of times that B has value *True* and L has value *False*. This gives us

$\hat{p}(M|B, \neg L) = 0.03$. We make similar calculations for the CPT for node G. You might want to calculate the complete set of sample statistics and compare them with the CPTs given in Figure 19.2.

Notice that some of the sample statistics in my example are based on very small samples—leading to possibly inaccurate estimates of the corresponding underlying probabilities. In general, the exponentially large number of parameters of a CPT may overwhelm the ability of the training set to produce good estimates for these parameters. Mitigating this problem is the possibility that many of the parameters will have the same (or close to the same) value. Techniques for using this redundancy to reduce the number of parameters that must be estimated in a CPT have been explored by [Friedman & Goldszmidt 1996a].

It is also the case that before samples are observed, we may have prior probabilities for the entries in the CPTs. Bayesian updating of the CPTs, given a training set, gives appropriate weight to the prior probabilities, although the procedure is somewhat complex (see [Heckerman, Geiger, & Chickering 1995]). When there is a very large training set, the effect of the priors is greatly diminished.

Missing Data

In gathering training data to be used by a learning process, it frequently happens that some data are missing. Sometimes, data meant to be captured are inadvertently missing, and sometimes the fact that data are missing is important in itself. I will deal with the former case here. A simple, convergent process of iteratively computing sample statistics has been shown to be effective [Lauritzen 1991]. I give the main idea of the method using the example just presented. Suppose, instead of the data shown in Figure 20.1, we have the following data:

G	M	B	L	**Number of instances**
True	True	True	True	54
True	True	True	False	1
*	*	True	True	7
True	False	True	False	27
False	True	*	True	3
False	False	True	False	2
False	False	False	True	4
False	False	False	False	2

The occurrence of an asterisk (*) indicates that the value of the variable associated with that position is missing for that group of variable values. The question is, how do we deal with these missing values in attempting to estimate the CPTs for this network? Let's consider first the three samples in which G = *False*, M = *True*, L = *True*, and the values of B are missing. Each of these three samples could either have had B = *True* or B = *False*; we don't know which. But, for these samples, we do know the values of G, M, and L. Thus, although we don't know the value of B, we could compute the probability, $p(B|\neg G, M, L)$, of B given the values of G, M, and L. This probability could be computed using probabilistic inference methods previously explained—working on the network structure (Figure 20.1) and the CPTs of the network, if we had these CPTs. (Of course, we don't have them yet, but I will discuss that difficulty shortly.) Thus, for purposes of computing sample statistics for estimating the network's CPTs, each of these three samples could be replaced by two *weighted* samples—one in which B = *True*, weighted by $p(B|\neg G, M, L)$, and one in which B = *False*, weighted by $p(\neg B|\neg G, M, L) = 1 - p(B|\neg G, M, L)$. (Note from Figure 20.1, by the way, that $p(B|\neg G, M, L) = p(B|\neg G, M)$ because B is conditionally independent of L, given G and M.)

We employ the same process for the seven samples in which B = *True*, L = *True*, and the values of G and M are missing. Each of these samples is replaced by four weighted samples corresponding to the combinations (G, M); (G, ¬M); (¬G, M); and (¬G, ¬M), and weighted, respectively, by the probabilities $p(G, M|B, L)$, $p(G, \neg M|B, L)$, $p(\neg G, M|B, L)$, and $p(\neg G, \neg M|B, L)$. Again, we could use the network structure and CPTs to compute these probabilities. (One can see the danger here of an exponential explosion of samples when the number of missing values in any one sample is large.)

Now, we can use the weighted samples (in which missing values have been filled in—in all possible ways) together with the rest of the samples (which didn't have missing values) for frequency counts from which to compute estimates of the CPTs. This process is the same as I described in the case in which there were no missing values, except that now some of the counts will not be whole numbers (because of the weights). But as previously mentioned, in order to compute the weights by probabilistic inference, we need the CPTs, which we don't yet have. A method called *expectation maximization (EM)* [Dempster, Laird, & Rubin 1977] can be used to zero in on a set of CPTs. First, we select random values for the parameters in the CPTs for the entire network. We use these random values to compute the needed weights (the conditional probabilities of the values of the missing data given the values of the observed data). We use the weights in turn to estimate new CPTs. We interate this process until the CPTs converge, which they are guaranteed to do. In most problems, convergence is rapid.

Applying the EM method is best left to computer programs for performing probabilistic inference and for doing the frequency counts. Even my small example with missing values would require quite tedious calculations.

20.1.2 Learning Network Structure

If the network structure is not known, we must then attempt to find that structure, as well as its associated CPTs, that best fits the training data. In order to do so, we need a metric by which to score candidate networks, and we need to specify a procedure for searching among possible structures. I deal with both of these matters in this subsection.

The Scoring Metric

Several measures might be used to score competing networks. One is based on *description length*. The idea is this: suppose we wanted to transmit the training set, Ξ, to someone. To do so, we would encode the values of the variables into a string of bits, say, and send the bits. How many bits would we need? That is, what is the length of the message? Efficient codes take advantage of the statistical properties of the data to be sent, and it is these statistical properties that we are attempting to model in the Bayes network. If we found an appropriate Bayes network, we could use a Huffman code based on it to encode the data to be transmitted. From information theory [Cover & Thomas 1991], the best encoding of a set of data, Ξ, distributed according to the joint probabilities given by a Bayes network $\mathcal{B}$ requires $L(\Xi, \mathcal{B})$ bits:

$$L(\Xi, \mathcal{B}) = -\log p[\Xi]$$

where $p[\Xi]$ is the probability (according to the joint distribution stipulated by $\mathcal{B}$) of the particular data being sent. Given some particular data Ξ, we might try to find that network, say, $\mathcal{B}_0$, that minimizes $L(\Xi, \mathcal{B})$. Before settling on this approach, let us calculate $\log p[\Xi]$. Suppose the data, Ξ, consists of m samples: $\mathbf{v}_1, \ldots, \mathbf{v}_m$, where each $\mathbf{v}_i$ is an n-dimensional vector of values of the n variables. $p[\Xi]$ is then the joint probability $p[\mathbf{v}_1, \ldots, \mathbf{v}_m]$. Assuming that each datum is provided independently according to the probability distribution specified by $\mathcal{B}$, we have

$$p(\Xi) = \prod_{i=1}^{m} p(\mathbf{v}_i)$$

and

$$-\log p(\Xi) = -\sum_{i=1}^{m} \log p(\mathbf{v}_i)$$

where each $p(\mathbf{v}_i)$ (itself the joint probability that the variables have the values specified by $\mathbf{v}_i$) is computed from the Bayes net, $\mathcal{B}$. These computations, though tedious, could certainly be used to score various trial Bayes networks. Each network, of course, consists not only of the network graph structure but must also include the CPTs. It can be shown that, given a network structure and a training set, Ξ, the CPTs that minimize $L(\Xi, \mathcal{B})$ are just those that are obtained from the sample statistics computed from Ξ [Friedman & Goldszmidt 1996a].

But $L(\Xi, \mathcal{B})$ alone is not a very good metric because its use favors large networks with many arcs. Such a network would be overly specialized to Ξ; that is, it would *overfit* the data. The appropriate adjustment to the scoring metric can be made by realizing that in order to transmit Ξ to someone using an efficient code based on $\mathcal{B}$, we must also transmit a description of $\mathcal{B}$ so that the receiver will be able to decode the message. Thus, we must add a term to $L(\Xi, \mathcal{B})$, and that term is the length of the message needed to transmit $\mathcal{B}$. Roughly speaking, the number of bits required to transmit $\mathcal{B}$ is $\frac{|\mathcal{B}|\log m}{2}$, where $|\mathcal{B}|$ is the number of parameters in $\mathcal{B}$, and $\frac{\log m}{2}$ is generally considered to be the number of bits that are appropriate to represent each numeric parameter. The adjusted scoring metric, $L'(\Xi, \mathcal{B})$, is therefore

$$L'(\Xi, \mathcal{B}) = -\sum_{i=1}^{m} \log p(\mathbf{v}_i) + \frac{|\mathcal{B}|\log m}{2}$$

Now, we search for a network giving a minimum description length for encoding both the data and the network. Using both factors allows us to make a proper tradeoff for sending both the data and the network.

As an example, we calculate $L'(\Xi, \mathcal{B})$ for the network shown in Figure 19.2 for sending the data shown in Figure 20.1. First, we calculate $L(\Xi, \mathcal{B})$, the number of bits required to send the data of Figure 20.1—assuming that the data is drawn from a probability distribution given by the Bayes net of Figure 19.2. The probability of the first entry in the table of Figure 20.1 is

$$p(\text{first entry}) = p(G|B)p(M|B, L)p(B)p(L)$$

$$= 0.95 \times 0.9 \times 0.95 \times 0.7 = 0.569$$

Taking the negative logarithm (to the base 2) yields

$$-\log p(\text{first entry}) = 0.814$$

There are 54 of these "first entries" in the data, so the contribution to $L(\Xi, \mathcal{B})$ of the 54 first entries is $54 \times 0.814 = 43.9$. The data in the other entries in the table contribute totals of 6.16, 27.9, 52.92, 16.33, 12.32, 24.83, and 12.32, respectively. Summing these contributions yields

$$L(\Xi, \mathcal{B}) = 196.68 \text{ bits}$$

Next, we calculate $\frac{|\mathcal{B}|\log 100}{2}$, the number of bits required to send the network of Figure 19.2. There are eight parameters in this network, so

$$\frac{|\mathcal{B}|\log 100}{2} = 4 \times 6.64 = 26.58 \text{ bits}$$

Thus the scoring metric for this network is

$$L'(\Xi, \mathcal{B}) = 196.68 + 26.58 = 223.26 \text{ bits}$$

Other networks could be evaluated in a similar fashion. Presumably, the one in Figure 19.2 is near optimal.

Searching Network Space

The set of all possible Bayes nets is, of course, so large that we could not even contemplate any kind of exhaustive search to find one that minimizes $L'(\Xi, \mathcal{B})$. What is possible is a kind of hill–descending or "greedy" search in which we start with a given network (such as one with no arcs, which assumes independence among all of the variables), evaluate $L'(\Xi, \mathcal{B})$ for that network, and then make small changes to it to see if these changes produce networks that decrease $L'(\Xi, \mathcal{B})$. The small changes can be adding or deleting an arc, or reversing an arc direction. Every time a change is made we use the sample statistics derived from Ξ to compute CPTs for the changed network. These CPTs are then used to compute the $-\sum_{i=1}^{m} \log p(\mathbf{v}_i)$ component of $L'(\Xi, \mathcal{B})$. The number of parameters in the new network is used to compute the $\frac{|\mathcal{B}| \log m}{2}$ component. These computations are simplified by the fact that the computation of description length is *decomposable* into computations over each CPT in the network. When the scoring metric is decomposable, the total metric is the sum of the local metrics [Friedman & Goldszmidt 1996a]. So, when an arc is added, deleted, or reversed, we need compute only changes in the sample statistics and $p(V_i | \mathcal{P}(V_i))$ for the nodes, V_i, involved in the change. The other $p(V_i | \mathcal{P}(V_i))$ remain the same. Decomposable measures other than description length have also been used to score how well a network fits the data (see [Heckerman, Geiger, & Chickering 1995]).

Bayes network learning methods have been used to learn network structure and the CPTs for some nontrivial problems. As an example, consider the networks in Figure 20.2. Three networks are shown. The first is a network encoding relationships among 37 variables for a problem involving an alarm system used in ventilator management in a hospital intensive–care unit. This known network was used to generate a size–10,000 training set of random values for the 37 nodes. Using this random sample, and starting with the second network (the one without any dependencies), the third network was learned using methods similar to those just described. (For details, see [Spirtes & Meek 1995].) Note the very close similarity in structure—only one arc is missing.

Sometimes network structure can be simplified substantially by adding nodes to the network that represent variables whose values are not given in the training set, Ξ. Such nodes are called *hidden nodes*. As a simple example, consider the two Bayes nets shown in Figure 20.3. The network on the left has more parameters than the one with the hidden node, H, on the right; its description–length score will be worse if the one on the right also does as well or better at fitting the data (as it will if it is a better representation of the underlying causal relationships among the variables). Since we cannot measure the hidden variable, its existence has to be invented by the search process. To do so, greedy search must add to its list of possible changes the addition of a new node (see [Heckerman 1996]). The value of the corresponding variable is, of course, "missing data," and the

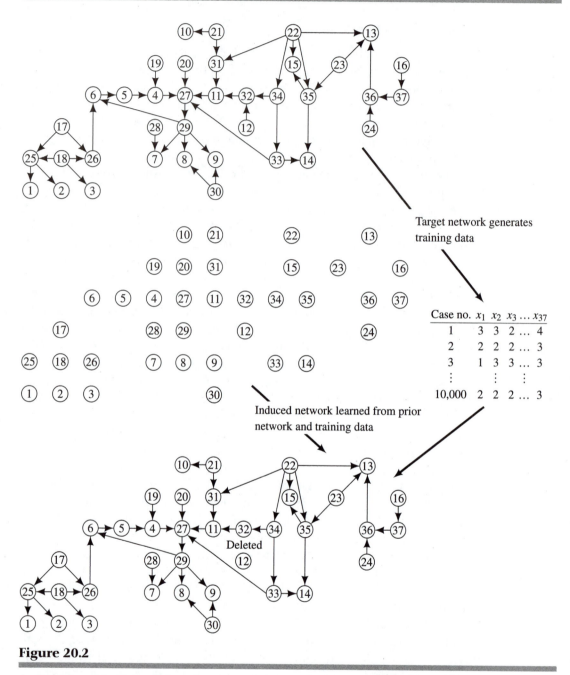

Target network generates training data

Induced network learned from prior network and training data

Case no.	x_1	x_2	x_3	...	x_{37}
1	3	3	2	...	4
2	2	2	2	...	3
3	1	3	3	...	3
⋮		⋮		⋮	
10,000	2	2	2	...	3

Figure 20.2

An Experiment in Network Learning

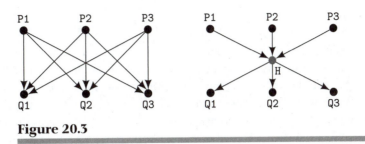

Figure 20.3

Two Networks—One with a Hidden Variable

probabilities associated with this variable must be adduced by the EM method as described earlier.[1]

Probabilistic Inference and Action

20.2.1   The General Setting

There are many applications of probabilistic inference. A prominent one is in expert systems for making best guesses based on general knowledge applied to specific data. Diagnosis of disease states given symptoms is an example. Here, I describe how probabilistic inference using Bayes networks can be employed by an agent that must decide on a best next action given sensory information and a scoring metric on environmental states. (My treatment is based on that of [Russell & Norvig 1995, Ch. 17] following a method described by [Dean & Wellman 1991, Ch. 7].)

The problem I examine is a generalization of the one we attacked in Chapter 10. Recall that there I described an agent that used a sense/plan/act cycle. The planning phase computed a best next action to be taken in the current environmental situation by looking ahead toward the goal—sometimes only up to a limited horizon. The act phase executed the first action recommended by the planner, and the sense phase attempted to discern the resulting environmental situation for the next cycle. In Chapter 10, I also generalized the notion of a "goal" to a schedule of "rewards" that were given (or taken) in certain environmental states. The rewards, in turn, induced a "value" for each state in terms of the total discounted future reward that would be realized by an agent that acted so as to maximize its reward. I keep this generalized notion of goal here, attributing a *utility* to each environmental state.

---

1. Inventing hidden nodes in learning Bayes networks is analogous to inventing new atoms in learning propositional rules or to inventing new relation constants (predicates) in learning logic programs.

Previously, my architecture for sense/plan/act agents adopted a somewhat inconsistent set of assumptions about the environment and about the reliability of sensing and acting. I assumed that an agent could accurately determine its current state through sensing and that it could accurately predict the effects of all of its actions. Yet, in case these assumptions were unjustified (and they typically are unjustified), our agent took a single action and immediately used its sensors to find out which environmental state actually resulted. I rationalized this approach by saying that even if the action taken didn't always have its predicted effect, and even if the sensors were sometimes in error, the sensors (on average) would keep the agent informed about its progress through state space, and repeated planning would reorient the agent toward the goal (or rewards) as needed.

Now, having tools that allow us to deal more appropriately with uncertainty, I can explicitly adopt more realistic assumptions. Rather than knowing which state it is in, our new agent knows only the probabilities that it is in various states. And instead of sensors that give exact knowledge of environmental state, our agent's sensors can at best sharpen these probabilities. The effects of actions are known only loosely: an action taken in a given state might lead to any one of a set of new states—with a probability associated with each. Through planning and sensing, we want our agent to select that action that maximizes its expected utility. The computations required by an agent able to deal with this problem in its full generality are excessive, and again approximations and further limiting assumptions are forced upon us. I discuss these next in the context of a specific example.

20.2.2   An Extended Example

Since working with the kinds of assumptions already discussed greatly increases computational difficulty, my example uses a trivial agent and environment so as not to obscure the main ideas. Consider a robot that exists in the one–dimensional grid of five cells shown in Figure 20.4. Environmental state involves only the robot's location; we represent it by a state variable E that has five possible values $\{-2, -1, 0, 1, 2\}$. Each location has a utility, U, for the robot. The middle cell has a utility of 0; it and the other utility values are as shown in the figure. Let's suppose, to start the process, that the robot knows (precisely) that it is in the cell marked 0 at time $t = 0$. That is, $E_0 = 0$.

The action taken by the robot at the i–th time step is denoted by the symbol A_i. It can attempt to move one cell to the left ($A_i = L$) or one cell to the right ($A_i = R$). In either case, a move has its intended effect with a probability of 0.5; with a probability of 0.25, each action has no effect; and with a probability of 0.25, an action causes the robot to move to the adjacent cell in the opposite direction from that intended. Thus, after a few moves, the robot has only probabilistic knowledge of its actual position.

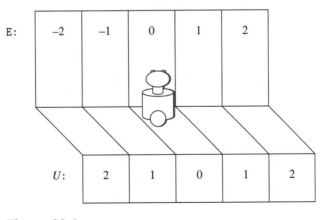

Figure 20.4

A Robot Confined to Five Cells

The robot senses its location at the i-th time step via a sensory signal, S_i. But we assume that the sensor is somewhat unreliable. Given that E_i has a certain value, the probability that S_i has that same value is 0.9. The probability that it instead has each of the other values is 0.025.

The problem for this robot, in the face of its various handicaps, is to make moves that maximize the expected value of its utility some number of moves ahead. The decision techniques used to select the robot's next action are most simply explained if we maximize expected utility just one move ahead. Let's suppose that the robot has attempted to move right at time $t = 0$; that is, $A_0 = R$. The resulting environmental state is given by E_1. To continue its sense/plan/act cycle, it senses its location by observing, say, $S_1 = 1$. What move should it make next? Indeed, after making that move, how should it continue to select moves based on sensory data, inferences it makes about its present location, and the effects of its actions?

Probabilistic inference using a special type of belief network, called a *dynamic decision network*, can be used to select utility-maximizing actions. I show the network appropriate for this problem in Figure 20.5. This network allows the robot to make inferences iteratively as actions are taken and as newly sensed information becomes available. After being given the values $E_0 = 0$, $A_0 = R$, and $S_1 = 1$, we can use ordinary probabilistic inference to calculate the expected utility value, U_2, that would result first from $A_1 = R$ and then from $A_1 = L$. The robot then selects that action that gives the larger value. (Action selection in this case is based on looking ahead just one move. Further lookahead would involve calculating more distant utilities for alternative action sequences.) I use differently shaped nodes in dynamic decision networks to indicate different assumptions

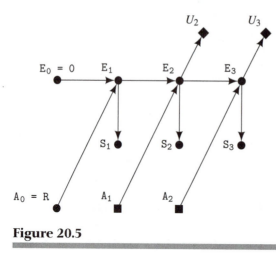

Figure 20.5

A Dynamic Decision Network

about those nodes. Box–shaped nodes (■) indicate variables whose values are still under the complete control of the agent. These are called *decision nodes*. In a dynamic decision network, they become ordinary belief–network nodes (with known values) after an agent has taken its decision. Diamond–shaped nodes (♦) indicate variables that are values of utilities. Expected values of utility variables are functions of the probabilities of the various values of their parents.

Notice by the structure of the network that the environment is Markovian. That is, what can be known (without sensing) about environmental state at time $t + 1$ is completely determined (probabilistically) by the environmental state and action at time t. Most agent environments can be assumed to be Markovian in this sense (or additional variables can be introduced to make them so). Note also that the structure of the network embodies the assumption that what is sensed at time t is conditionally independent of everything that goes before, given the environment at time t.

After moving the time frontier a step forward by taking the planned action at time $t = 1$ (planned through the process of maximizing expected utility, U_2), and after sensing what can be sensed, S_2, about the next state, E_2, the whole process repeats with another sense/plan/act cycle. It will be instructive to carry out some of the calculations.

First, we need to calculate the two expected utilities, given what is known at time $t = 0$ and assuming the two different possibilities for A_1:

$$Ex[U_2 \mid E_0 = 0, A_0 = R, S_1 = 1, A_1 = R]$$

and

$$Ex[U_2 \mid E_0 = 0, A_0 = R, S_1 = 1, A_1 = L]$$

To compute these expected values, we need to calculate $p(E_2 \mid E_0 = 0, A_0 = R, S_1 = 1, A_1)$ for the various values of E_2 for each of the two values of A_1. The form of these calculations will be repeated in subsequent steps, but for concreteness, I do it for the step in question. The form is also the same for each of the values of A_1, so I do it for just $A_1 = R$. We use the polytree algorithm explained in the last chapter to calculate $p(E_2 \mid E_0 = 0, A_0 = R, S_1 = 1, A_1 = R)$.

First, we "involve the parent not already given" to obtain

$$p(E_2 \mid E_0 = 0, A_0 = R, S_1 = 1, A_1 = R)$$

$$= \sum_{E_1} p(E_2 \mid E_0 = 0, A_0 = R, S_1 = 1, A_1 = R, E_1) p(E_1 \mid E_0 = 0, A_0 = R, S_1 = 1, A_1 = R)$$

This equation can be simplified by taking into account conditional independencies:

$$p(E_2 \mid E_0 = 0, A_0 = R, S_1 = 1, A_1 = R)$$

$$= \sum_{E_1} p(E_2 \mid A_1 = R, E_1) \, p(E_1 \mid E_0 = 0, A_0 = R, S_1 = 1)$$

In decision networks used for robot action selection, the first term in the preceding sum is called the *action model* of the Markov process. For a given immediately prior state and action, it gives the probabilities of the various possible subsequent situations. Following the polytree algorithm, the second term in the sum is then rewritten using Bayes' rule:

$$p(E_1 \mid E_0 = 0, A_0 = R, S_1 = 1) = kp(S_1 = 1 \mid E_0 = 0, A_0 = R, E_1) p(E_1 \mid E_0 = 0, A_0 = R)$$

where k is a normalizing factor chosen (later) to make probabilities sum to 1. Again using conditional independencies, we obtain

$$p(E_1 \mid E_0 = 0, A_0 = R, S_1 = 1) = kp(S_1 = 1 \mid E_1) p(E_1 \mid E_0 = 0, A_0 = R)$$

The first term in the preceding product is called the *sensor model*. For any environmental situation, it gives the probability that the sensor will have various values. (A completely reliable and maximally informative sensor would concentrate all of the probability on one sensor value for each environmental state.) The second term is again an action model.

Collecting our results yields

$$p(E_2 \mid E_0 = 0, A_0 = R, S_1 = 1, A_1 = R)$$

$$= k \sum_{E_1} p(E_2 \mid A_1 = R, E_1) \, p(S_1 = 1 \mid E_1) p(E_1 \mid E_0 = 0, A_0 = R)$$

To evaluate this expression (for the various values of E_2), we use the probability assumptions we have made about the effects of actions and the reliability of the sensor. To demonstrate, let's just calculate $p(E_2 = 1 \mid E_0 = 0, A_0 = R, S_1 = 1, A_1 = R)$. The calculations involve the following probabilities, which would be entries in the CPTs for the network in Figure 20.5. (We must sum over all values of E_1.)

$$p(E_2 = 1 \mid A_1 = R, E_1 = 0) = 0.5$$

$$p(E_2 = 1 \mid A_1 = R, E_1 = 1) = 0.25$$

$$p(E_2 = 1 \mid A_1 = R, E_1 = 2) = 0.25$$

$$p(E_2 = 1 \mid A_1 = R, E_1 = -1) \text{ and } p(E_2 = 1 \mid A_1 = R, E_1 = -2) \text{ are both } 0$$

$$p(S_1 = 1 \mid E_1 = -2) = 0.025$$

$$p(S_1 = 1 \mid E_1 = -1) = 0.025$$

$$p(S_1 = 1 \mid E_1 = 0) = 0.025$$

$$p(S_1 = 1 \mid E_1 = 1) = 0.9$$

$$p(S_1 = 1 \mid E_1 = 2) = 0.025$$

$$p(E_1 = -1 \mid E_0 = 0, A_0 = R) = 0.25$$

$$p(E_1 = 0 \mid E_0 = 0, A_0 = R) = 0.25$$

$$p(E_1 = 1 \mid E_0 = 0, A_0 = R) = 0.5$$

$$p(E_1 = -2 \mid E_0 = 0, A_0 = R) \text{ and } p(E_1 = 2 \mid E_0 = 0, A_0 = R) \text{ are both } 0$$

Performing the summation yields

$$p(E_2 = 1 \mid E_0 = 0, A_0 = R, S_1 = 1, A_1 = R)$$

$$= k \times [(0.5 \times 0.025 \times 0.25) + (0.25 \times 0.9 \times 0.5)]$$

$$= k \times 0.14375$$

We perform similar calculations to obtain $p(E_2 \mid E_0 = 0, A_0 = R, S_1 = 1, A_1 = R)$ for other values of E_2. Since the sum of all of these is 1, we can solve for k. Using these probabilities for E_2, we calculate the expected value of U_2 given that $A_1 = R$. We repeat the process to calculate the expected value of U_2 given that $A_1 = L$ and select that action that yields the larger value. (From the structure of the problem, we know it will be $A_1 = R$, but, of course, I used this example just to illustrate the method—not to be surprised.)

20.2.3 Generalizing the Example

Analysis of the equation for $p(E_2 \mid E_0 = 0, A_0 = R, S_1 = 1, A_1 = R)$ allows us to extend it to subsequent time steps. This equation is being evaluated at time $t = 1$ just as $S_1 = 1$ has been sensed and before action $A_1 = R$ has been taken. The other "given" values are in the past. Thus we could instead write $p(E_2 \mid < \textit{values before } t = 1 >, S_1 = 1, A_1 = R)$. Similarly, the expression $p(E_1 \mid E_0 = 0, A_0 = R)$ in the summation could be written as $p(E_1 \mid < \textit{values before } t = 1 >)$. With these changes, we have

$$p(E_2 \mid < \textit{values before } t = 1 >, S_1 = 1, A_1)$$

$$= k \sum_{E_1} p(E_2 \mid A_1, E_1)\, p(S_1 = 1 \mid E_1) p(E_1 \mid < \textit{values before } t = 1 >)$$

This way of writing the equation suggests the following generalization:

$$p(E_{i+1} \mid < \textit{values before } t = i >, S_i = s_i, A_i)$$

$$= k \sum_{E_i} p(E_{i+1} \mid A_i, E_i) p(S_i = s_i \mid E_i) p(E_i \mid < \textit{values before } t = i >)$$

To make decisions about actions, we use this equation in the following way as we proceed in time. To calculate the action, A_i, to be taken at time $t = i$:

1. From the last time step, $(i - 1)$ (and after sensing $S_{i-1} = s_{i-1}$), we have already calculated $p(E_i \mid < \textit{values before } t = i >)$ for all values of E_i.

2. At time $t = i$, we sense $S_i = s_i$ and use the sensor model to calculate $p(S_i = s_i \mid E_i)$ for all values of E_i.

3. From the action model, we calculate $p(E_{i+1} \mid A_i, E_i)$ for all values of E_i and A_i.

4. For each value of A_i, and for a particular value of E_{i+1}, we sum the product $p(E_{i+1} \mid A_i, E_i)p(S_i = s_i \mid E_i)p(E_i \mid < \textit{values before } t = i >)$ over all values of E_i and multiply by a constant, k, to yield values proportional to $p(E_{i+1} \mid < \textit{values before } t = i >, S_i = s_i, A_i)$.

5. We repeat the preceding step for all the other values of E_{i+1} and calculate the constant k to get the actual values of $p(E_{i+1} \mid < \textit{values before } t = i >, S_i = s_i, A_i)$ for each value of E_{i+1} and A_i.

6. Using these probability values, we calculate the expected value of U_{i+1} for each value of A_i and select that A_i that maximizes that expected value.

7. We take the action selected in the previous step, advance i by 1, and iterate.

And that is the essence of using a dynamic decision network to select actions. The method extends beyond this trivial example. The way actions affect the environment and the way the environment affects sensory stimuli are well modeled in general by a network similar to that of Figure 20.5. Instead of having a single environmental variable, E_i, at each time step, we might have a vector of values $\mathbf{E}_i = (E_{i1}, \ldots, E_{in})$. Similarly, instead of having a single sensory variable, S_i, we might have a vector of values $\mathbf{S}_i = (S_{i1}, \ldots, S_{im})$. The dynamic decision network at each time step would, of course, have to be extended to include nodes for all of these variables and their dependencies, but the general form of the calculations is the same as in my simple example. Although the networks internal to a given time step might be complex, the Markov assumption simplifies the dependencies between time steps.

Looking ahead more than one step involves propagating probabilities up to the point where an expected utility is to be calculated. Obviously, such an extension rapidly becomes impractical. But it also could become not very useful because the probability distribution on E_i might become quite diffuse. Thus, the compromise involving the somewhat inconsistent assumptions I made before presenting this probabilistic extension remains a reasonable alternative.

20.3   *Additional Readings and Discussion*

Learning Bayes nets is an active field of research with important new papers appearing annually. [Neal 1991] describes methods for learning Bayes nets using neural networks. The technique I described for evaluating proposed Bayes net structures used the concept of minimum description length [Rissanen 1984]. [Friedman 1997] describes a technique for learning Bayes networks when both the structure of the network is unknown and when there is missing data. Early work on learning Bayes networks was done by [Cooper & Herskovitz 1992].

[Forbes, et al. 1995] propose a system for driving an autonomous vehicle using dynamic decision networks.

The evaluation of utilities in stochastic situations constitutes the subject matter of *decision theory*. For a treatment of the use of decision theory in AI, see [Horvitz, Breese, & Henrion 1988]. The theory of Markov decision problems (MDPs) [Puterman 1994] and of partially observable Markov decision problems (POMDPs) [Cassandra, Kaelbling, & Littman 1994] provide the basic theoretical models of the effects of actions in stochastic situations.

Exercises

20.1 Consider a Bayes network with the following structure:

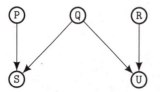

Suppose that we can control the "causal variables," P, Q, and R. That is, we can arrange experiments in which these variables take on any combinations of values (*True* or *False*) that we desire and then observe the resulting values for S and U. What combinations of these variables would be needed in order to learn the CPTs for S and U? Can we learn the prior probabilities for P, Q, and R from such an experiment?

20.2 Count the number of parameters needed for each of the networks shown in Figure 20.3.

20.3 A Bayes network has the known structure shown in the figure. (Note that this structure implies that the X_i are conditionally independent given C.) Given a training set of values of X_1, X_2, X_3, each paired with a value for C, show how sample statistics can be employed to compute an estimate of $p(C \mid X_1, X_2, X_3)$.

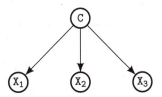

20.4 Using the assumptions and results of the previous exercise, suppose C represents the name of one of two actions that should be taken by a robot when its binary-valued sensory inputs have the values given by X_1, X_2, X_3. Suppose the policy for choosing an action is choose $C = 1$ if $p(C = 1 \mid X_1, X_2, X_3) \geq p(C = 2 \mid X_1, X_2, X_3)$. Show that such a policy can be implemented by a TLU whose inputs are X_1, X_2, X_3. Interpret your result as a method of training the TLU. (In this problem, the belief network does not have a causal interpretation; that is, the action that should be taken is not a "cause" of the sensory inputs.)

20.5 A robot lives in a 5×5 grid as shown. The numbers in the grid represent relative temperature values. Suppose the robot begins in one of the cells with temperature = 2. It doesn't know which of the possible temperature = 2 cells it begins in, but it does have a map of the grid that indicates the temperature values of each cell.

4	5	6	7	8
3	4	5	6	7
2	3	4	5	6
1	2	3	4	5
0	1	2	3	4

Assume that the robot can accurately sense the temperature value of the cell it occupies. It is capable of four actions, namely, those denoted by north, east, south, and west, and must choose among them in order to maximize its expected temperature. A strong wind is blowing from a southwesterly direction. Ordinarily, each of the actions would move the robot one cell in the indicated direction, but with the wind the actions have the following effects whenever the robot is in a cell with temperature = 2:

south $\rightarrow$ no effect

west $\rightarrow$ no effect

north $\rightarrow$ moves one cell north with probability = 0.5

north $\rightarrow$ moves two cells north with probability = 0.25

north $\rightarrow$ moves one cell east with probability $= 0.25$

east $\rightarrow$ moves one cell east with probability $= 0.5$

east $\rightarrow$ moves two cells east with probability $= 0.5$

1. Draw a dynamic decision network corresponding to one action step. Show the relevant entries in the CPT(s).

2. Calculate the expected temperature, $Ex[T1 \mid A_0]$, for each of the four actions.

3. Now suppose that the robot is not sure of its temperature at time $t = t_0$. Instead, it senses a signal $S_0 = 2$, which informs it about its temperature. The sensory model for S_0 includes

    $p(S_0 = 2 \mid T_0 = 2) = 0.9$

    $p(S_0 = 2 \mid T_0 = 3) = 0.3$

    $p(S_0 = 2 \mid T_0 = i) = 0$ for all values of i different from 2 or 3

    Draw a one–step dynamic decision network for this case.

4. Assuming that the actions have the same effects when taken in a cell with temperature $= 3$ that they do when taken in a cell with temperature $= 2$, what is the expected temperature resulting from each of the four actions in this case?

Part IV

Planning Methods Based on Logic

Failing to plan is planning to fail.
—Effie Jones

Deliberate often—decide once.
—Latin proverb

21 The Situation Calculus

21.1 Reasoning about States and Actions

In Chapter 7, I introduced the notion of state spaces and how they could be searched to compute plans of actions to achieve goals. There, I talked about searching either iconic- or feature–based state spaces. Now, with richer languages to describe features and the constraints among them, we can investigate feature–based planning methods much more thoroughly.

The fact that we can leave out properties of world states that are irrelevant to the problem at hand or that are not known is one of the powerful aspects of using a feature–based approach. This aspect is particularly important in describing the goal condition that we want the agent to achieve by its actions. Starting from the configuration in Figure 21.1, we might want the agent to develop a plan for getting some block on block B (without caring which block is on block B or where block B is). This goal can be described simply by the formula $(\exists x)\mathtt{On}(x, B)$. In general, a goal condition can be described by any wff in the predicate calculus, and we can determine if a goal is satisfied in a world state described by formulas by attempting to prove the goal wff from those formulas.

In this and the next chapter, I present techniques for finding a set of actions to achieve a state described by a goal wff. Here, I use the apparatus of the predicate calculus to reason directly about states and actions. As in all predicate–calculus reasoning, search is still necessary, but now search is over a space of logical expressions rather than over a space of models of world states. In the next chapter, I describe an alternative method in which operators are used to change state descriptions, and search will be over a space of state descriptions.

The *situation calculus* [McCarthy & Hayes 1969, Green 1969a] is a predicate-calculus formalization of states, actions, and the effects of actions on states. We

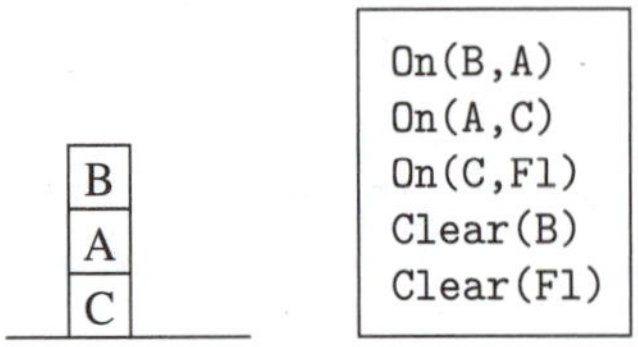

```
          On(B,A)
          On(A,C)
  B       On(C,Fl)
  A       Clear(B)
  C       Clear(Fl)
```

Figure 21.1

A Configuration of Blocks

represent our knowledge about states and actions as formulas in the first–order predicate calculus and then use a deduction system to ask questions such as "Does there exist a state such that it satisfies certain (goal) properties, and if so, how can the present state be transformed into that state by actions?" The answer to such a query constitutes a plan for achieving the desired state. Although the situation calculus figured prominently in some early AI planning systems, it has now largely been supplanted by the methods to be discussed in the next chapter. The formalism remains important, however, for exposing and helping to clarify conceptual problems involving the effects of actions.

I introduce the situation calculus by way of a blocks–world example. Suppose we identify the state shown in Figure 21.1 as *S0*. Using first–order predicate calculus, we might describe *S0* by the following formula:

$$On(B, A) \wedge On(A, C) \wedge On(C, Fl) \wedge Clear(B) \wedge \cdots$$

In order to describe this state and other states in the situation calculus, we *reify*[1] states; that is, we include them in our conceptualization of the world as entities that exist. We might have any number of such states; they can be denoted by constant symbols (such as $S0, S1, S2, \ldots$), by variables, or by functional expressions. We change our atomic wffs to include a term denoting the state in which the intended relation holds. A corresponding change is made to our intended interpretation of these atomic wffs—they now denote relations over states and are called *fluents*. We make a statement about what is true in state *S0* by the formula

$$On(B, A, S0) \wedge On(A, C, S0) \wedge On(C, Fl, S0) \wedge Clear(B, S0)$$

We might also have propositions true of all states. For example,

$$(\forall x, y, s)[On(x, y, s) \wedge \neg(y = Fl) \supset \neg Clear(y, s)]$$

---

1. The verb *reify* means to regard something abstract as a material or concrete thing.

and

$$(\forall s)\text{Clear}(\text{Fl}, s)$$

(The intended meaning of Clear(x, s) is that x is available to have something put on it.) With these general axioms, we can prove various statements about *S0*; for example, we can prove ¬Clear(A, S0) and Clear(Fl, S0).

To represent actions and their effects, we use the following steps:

1. Reify the actions (that is, we imagine that there is such a *thing* as an action). Thus, actions can be denoted by constant symbols, by variables, or by functional expressions. In situation calculus formulations, an action is regarded as a function of the entities involved in the action. In my example, actions are functions of blocks. For instance, let's consider the action of moving a block from one place to another. We use the expression move(B, A, Fl) to denote the action of moving *B* from *A* to the floor.[2] (Think of an action as an "object" given by the value of the function.)

   In general, we can represent a family of move actions by the *schema*, move(x, y, z), where x, y, and z are *schema variables*. Instantiations of these variables by constant symbols produce expressions denoting actual instances of the actions.

2. Next, imagine a function constant, do, that denotes a function that maps actions and states into states. If α denotes an action and σ denotes a state, then do(α, σ) denotes a function that maps the state–action pair into the state obtained by performing the action denoted by α in the state denoted by σ.

3. Express the effects of actions by wffs. In some formulations, there are two such wffs for each action–fluent pair. (For now, we ignore pairs in which the action has no effect on the fluent.) For the pair {On, move}, these wffs are

   $$[\text{On}(x, y, s) \wedge \text{Clear}(x, s) \wedge \text{Clear}(z, s) \wedge (x \neq z)$$

   $$\supset \text{On}(x, z, \text{do}(\text{move}(x, y, z), s))]$$

   and

   $$[\text{On}(x, y, s) \wedge \text{Clear}(x, s) \wedge \text{Clear}(z, s) \wedge (x \neq z)$$

   $$\supset \neg\text{On}(x, y, \text{do}(\text{move}(x, y, z), s))]$$

   where we assume that all variables mentioned in a formula are universally quantified. The first of these formulas is called the *positive effect axiom*.

---

2. Note that, in contrast with the move operator used previously, our expression here for moving a block includes the place from which that block was moved.

It describes how an action makes a fluent true. The second is called a *negative effect axiom*. It describes how an action makes a fluent false. In this example, the antecedent of an effect axiom describes the *preconditions* that must be satisfied in order to apply the action. The consequent describes how the fluent is changed after applying the action.

Even though we have defined Clear in terms of On, we can also write effect axioms for the {Clear, move} pair; of course, they must be consistent with the definition and with the effect axioms for {On, move}. The effect axioms for {Clear, move} are

$$[On(x, y, s) \wedge Clear(x, s) \wedge Clear(z, s) \wedge (x \neq z) \wedge (y \neq z)$$

$$\supset Clear(y, do(move(x, y, z), s))]$$

and

$$[On(x, y, s) \wedge Clear(x, s) \wedge Clear(z, s) \wedge (x \neq z) \wedge (z \neq Fl)$$

$$\supset \neg Clear(z, do(move(x, y, z), s))]$$

In this example, the antecedents consist of two parts. One part expresses the *preconditions* under which the action can be executed; the other part expresses the condition under which the action, if executed, will have the effect expressed in the consequent of the axiom. In the positive effect axiom, this second part is $(y \neq z)$. (Even if $y = z$, the action can be executed—moving the block from a position back to the same position, but it won't have the effect claimed in the consequent.) In the negative effect axiom, this second part is $(z \neq Fl)$. (Since we assume the floor is always clear, no action can make it not clear.)

To illustrate how effect axioms might be used, consider the blocks–world situation shown at the top of Figure 21.2. This situation satisfies the preconditions of the effects axioms using the substitution {B/x, A/y, S0/s, Fl/z}. Therefore, we can apply the action denoted by move(B,A,Fl) and infer the consequents, namely,

On(B, Fl, do(move(B, A, Fl), S0)),

¬On(B, A, do(move(B, A, Fl), S0)), and

Clear(A, do(move(B, A, Fl), S0))

Each of these expressions has do(move(B, A, Fl), S0)) as its postaction state term. (For brevity, we might denote this postaction state as S1.) In Figure 21.2, I show the state resulting after applying the action and the formulas describing that state. (Besides the formulas inferred from the effect axioms, there are other formulas also true of S1; I will describe shortly how these other formulas can be inferred.)

It is important to realize that, even after an action, all of the formulas that we had before performing the inference permitted by the action are still true! (After moving *B* to the floor, it is still the case that *B* was on *A* in state *S0*. Likewise, before moving *B* to the floor, it is the case that *B* is on the floor in the state denoted by do(move(B, A, F1), S0).) Formulas in the situation calculus are "stateless" in the sense that they are *always* true (of the states they talk about).

21.2 *Some Difficulties*

21.2.1 Frame Axioms

As is evident in Figure 21.2, not all of the statements true about state do(move(B, A, F1), S0) can be inferred by the effects axioms. For example, after the move, it is obvious that some of the facts that were true of the state before the move, such as that *C* was on the floor and that *B* was clear, are also true of the state after the move. Actions typically have only "local" effects and thus leave many fluents unchanged. In order to make inferences about these constancies, we need a pair of what are called *frame axioms* for each action and for each fluent that doesn't

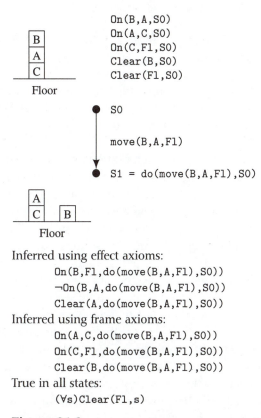

```
                      On(B,A,S0)
    ┌───┐             On(A,C,S0)
    │ B │             On(C,F1,S0)
    ├───┤             Clear(B,S0)
    │ A │             Clear(F1,S0)
    ├───┤
    │ C │
  ──┴───┴──
    Floor
                  ●   S0
                  │
                  │   move(B,A,F1)
                  │
                  ▼
                  ●   S1 = do(move(B,A,F1),S0)
    ┌───┐
    │ A │
    ├───┤  ┌───┐
    │ C │  │ B │
  ──┴───┴──┴───┴──
    Floor
```

Inferred using effect axioms:
      On(B,F1,do(move(B,A,F1),S0))
      ¬On(B,A,do(move(B,A,F1),S0))
      Clear(A,do(move(B,A,F1),S0))
Inferred using frame axioms:
      On(A,C,do(move(B,A,F1),S0))
      On(C,F1,do(move(B,A,F1),S0))
      Clear(B,do(move(B,A,F1),S0))
True in all states:
      $(\forall s)$Clear(F1,s)

Figure 21.2

Mapping a State–Action Pair into a State

change as a result of the action. For example, the frame axioms for the pair {move, On} are

$$[On(x, y, s) \wedge (x \neq u)] \supset On(x, y, do(move(u, v, z), s))$$

and

$$\left(\neg On(x, y, s) \wedge [(x \neq u) \vee (y \neq z)]\right) \supset \neg On(x, y, do(move(u, v, z), s))$$

(If a block is on a second block before an action, then it is still on the second block after the action if that action did not remove it from the second block. If a block is not on a second block before an action, then it is still not on the second block after the action if that action did not place it on the second block.)

In analogy with effect axioms, the first of the frame axioms is called a *positive frame axiom*; the second is called a *negative frame axiom*.

The frame axioms for the pair {move, Clear} are

$$Clear(u, s) \wedge (u \neq z) \supset Clear(u, do(move(x, y, z), s))$$

$$\neg Clear(u, s) \wedge (u \neq y) \supset \neg Clear(u, do(move(x, y, z), s))$$

(If a block is clear before an action, it is still clear after the action if that action did not place another block on top of it. If a block is not clear before an action, it is still not clear after the action if that action did not remove another block from it.)

Frame axioms are used to prove that a property of a state remains true if the state is changed by an action that doesn't affect that property. One of the {move, Clear} frame axioms, for example, can be used to infer Clear(B, do(move(B, A, Fl), S0)) in Figure 21.2. Since, typically, we will have a pair of frame axioms for every combination of fluent and action, it becomes unmanageably difficult in realistic problems to represent how actions change the world in this formulation of the situation calculus.

Several authors have explored how the number of frame axioms can be reduced and how they can be automatically derived from the effect axioms. I won't discuss these techniques here, but they involve the assumption that the *only* changes that can be made to a fluent are the ones that are explicitly specified by the effect axioms. (You might refer to [Pednault 1986, Schubert 1990, Reiter 1991, Elkan 1992].) Even if the number of frame axioms can be reduced, using them to make inferences about what fluents do not change over a sequence of several actions is computationally cumbersome. The various difficulties associated with dealing with fluents that are not affected by actions have come to be called the *frame problem*. In the next chapter, I discuss one approach toward circumventing some aspects of the frame problem.

21.2.2 Qualifications

The antecedent of the transition formula describing an action such as move gives the preconditions for a rather idealized case. Suppose we wanted to be more precise by making sure that the object to be moved is not too heavy. Then we would have to add another conjunct, ¬Too_heavy(x, s) to the precondition. This cautious concern can be pursued indefinitely, leading to adding other qualifications such as ¬Glued_down(x, s), ¬Armbroken(s), . . . , with the obvious intended interpretations. The difficulty of specifying all of the important qualifications has come to be called the *qualification problem*. Attempts have been made to confront the qualification problem using nonmonotonic reasoning. The idea is that the effects axioms allow default conclusions that can be withdrawn if further qualifications should be added. (See, for example, [Dean & Wellman 1991, pp. 63ff].) These attempts have not been entirely successful.

21.2.3 Ramifications

There is yet another problem. In complex domains, we often deduce statements about objects based on general knowledge of the domain. For example, a robot might reason that a package that it is carrying is in a room if the robot itself is in that room. Rather than use effects and frame axioms to reason about the location of the package, we might prefer to reason about the location of the robot and then use our general knowledge to reason about the location of the package. For example, suppose in situation S0 we have the fact In(PA, R1), where PA denotes some package and R1 denotes some room. Using its effects axioms, after moving into some different room (denoted, say, by R2), the robot can conclude that it (the robot) is indeed there in the new situation. It can even infer that the package is there in the new situation. But how do we now prevent the frame axioms from concluding that the package isn't still in the room denoted by R1 in the new situation? Keeping track of which derived formulas survive subsequent state transitions is known as the *ramification problem*. Various mechanisms (related to truth maintenance procedures) have been proposed for dealing with the ramification problem.

21.3 *Generating Plans*

Let us temporarily ignore the frame, qualification, and ramification problems and show how the situation calculus could, in principle, be used to plan a sequence of actions using reasoning methods. To generate a plan that achieves some goal, $\gamma(s)$, we attempt to prove $(\exists s)\gamma(s)$ and use the answer predicate to extract the state as a function of the nested actions that produce it.

For example, suppose we want a plan that gets block B on the floor from the initial state, *S0*, given in Figure 21.1. To compute this plan, we must prove

(∃s)On(B, F1, s). We will prove by resolution refutation that the negation of (∃s)On(B, F1, s), namely, (∀s)¬On(B, F1, s), together with the formulas that describe *S0* and the effects of *move* are inconsistent. We will use an answer predicate to capture the substitutions made during the proof. Our formulas for this problem are

¬On(B, F1, s) ∨ Ans(s)

On(B, A, S0)

On(A, C, S0)

On(C, F1, S0)

Clear(B, S0)

Clear(F1, S0)

[On(x, y, s) ∧ Clear(x, s) ∧ Clear(z, s) ∧ (x ≠ z)

⊃ On(x, z, do(move(x, y, z), s))]

The last formula is the positive effect axiom for {On, move}. It must be converted to clause form before we can perform a resolution refutation. As we do the refutation, we leave the equality predicate, $(x \neq z)$ (which is a way of writing $\neg(x = z)$), alone until all of its variables are bound. Then, as discussed previously, we assume that we have an infinite supply of axioms like $(A = A)$, $\neg(A = B)$, and so on to use in resolutions against them. I leave it to you to verify that a resolution refutation produces Ans(do(move(B, A, F1), S0)).

If several actions are required to achieve a goal, the action functions would be nested. For example, we would get Ans(do(move(A, C, B), do(move(B, A, F1), S0))) if the problem were to get block *A* on block *B* from the initial state shown in Figure 21.1. But you will note, if you try to work out this problem with the appropriate effects and frame axioms, that the proof effort is much too large for such a simple plan. Most attempts to use the situation calculus to generate plans have been thwarted by this aspect of the frame problem.

21.4 *Additional Readings and Discussion*

The qualification problem was first pointed out by [McCarthy 1977]. There have been various attempts to handle the frame and qualification problems using nonmonotonic reasoning methods. [Hanks & McDermott 1986] discovered that nonmonotonic conclusions can be ambiguous about which fluents change and which stay the same. Later work by [Baker 1991] and [Shoham 1988] addressed this problem. (See [Kartha 1994] for comments about Baker's approach.) Another nonmonotonic approach to the frame problem uses a "successor–state axiom" to limit and describe all of the changes that can be made to any fluent by any action [Reiter 1991]. [Shanahan 1997] is a book about the frame problem.

Although most current research on agent planning uses the alternatives described in the next chapter, the situation calculus and the associated language GOLOG (alGOl in LOGic) [Levesque, et al. 1997] are the basis for robotics research in the Cognitive Robotics Group at University of Toronto [Scherl & Levesque 1993].

Exercises

21.1 Imagine a robot, R, in a room with two boxes, B1 and B2. In the initial state, the robot is at place PR, B1 is at place P1, and B2 is at place P2. In this problem, it is possible for all three entities (R, B1, and B2) to be at the same place. In fact, we want B1 and B2 to be at place P3. The robot has two actions, denoted by goto(x) and push(y,w,z). The action denoted by goto(x) moves the robot from wherever it is to the place denoted by x; it has no preconditions. Its *only* effect is that the robot will be at x after executing the action. The action denoted by push(y,w,z) moves the robot and the box denoted by y to the place denoted by z. It can be executed only if the robot and the box are both at the same place, say, w. Its effects are that the robot and the object y will both be at place z.

1. Express the initial state and the goal condition as wffs in the situation calculus. Put the initial–state formula and the negation of the goal formula in clause form.

2. Express the preconditions and effects of the two actions as wffs in the situation calculus. Convert these wffs to clause form.

3. Write down *all* the frame axioms, and convert them to clause form.

4. Outline a general strategy for the steps that would be required to derive a plan to achieve the goal from the initial state. You do not actually have to produce a proof; simply explain in words how you would proceed.

21.2 Imagine a room with a robot, a table, a book, and three distinguished places in the room, namely, the center, an alcove, and a doorway. The robot is at the doorway, the book is on the table, and the table is in the center. The robot can move between any of the places in the room (even if something is already there). The robot can push the table from one place to another if and only if the robot is at the same place as the table.

1. Describe this initial situation in the situation calculus.

2. Write formulas in the situation calculus that describe the effect of the robot moving.

3. Write formulas in the situation calculus that describe the effect of the robot pushing the table.

4. Write the frame axioms needed to show that the locations of the book and table do not change when the robot moves.

5. Write the frame axioms needed to show the effect on the location of the book of the robot pushing the table.

6. Express the situation in which the book is on the table and the table is in the alcove in terms of the initial situation and the action operations.

21.3 Set up a situation calculus formulation of the Tower–of–Hanoi puzzle. (See Exercise 7.4.) That is,

1. Specify the formulas describing the initial situation, *S0*.

2. Propose a "law–of–motion" formula that describes the effects of a move. Also, write down at least one frame axiom pair associated with the effects of a move.

3. Write down the formula that specifies the goal.

21.4 Consider the following "blocks–world" problem: there are two blocks (named *A* and *B*) and three locations (named *L1*, *L2*, and *L3*). The intended meaning of the formula At(x, y, s) is that block *x* is in place *y* in state *s*. The intended meaning of the formula Empty(z, s) is that place *z* is empty in state *s*. We have a single action: move(x, y, z) denotes the act of moving block *x* from location *y* to location *z*. We assume that move has as a precondition that the place a block is being moved to must be empty. Do the following:

1. Write the operator description and frame axioms for move.

2. Describe an initial state in which *A* is at location *L1* and *B* is at location *L3*.

3. Describe the goal of getting *A* to location *L2* while leaving *B* at location *L3*.

4. Use resolution, with the Ans predicate, to generate an action sequence that when executed in the initial state results in satisfying the goal just described. Make any assumptions about things not being equal, for example, (B ≠ A), that you might need in the proof.

22 Planning

22.1 STRIPS *Planning Systems*

22.1.1 Describing States and Goals

An appealing way to attack the frame problem involves blending our state–space and situation–calculus approaches. This blend involves imagining that the predicate–calculus formulas describing a set of world states are themselves a kind of "state"—much as I did in Chapter 7 when I discussed feature–based state spaces. In the blocks world, for example, the world states in which block *B* is on top of block *A* on top of block *C* on the floor (as in Figure 22.1) are described by

```
On(B, A)
On(A, C)
On(C, Fl)
Clear(B)
Clear(Fl)
```

These formulas describe a set of world states because they are satisfied by all of those states in which the relations intended by the formulas are true. If there were other blocks and if the blocks had other properties, color, for example, the states being described would include all of those in which there were these other blocks and in which blocks have all possible colors, and so on.

In the first family of planning methods to be described in this chapter, we think of the formulas describing a set of world states as a data structure that can be changed in ways corresponding to agent actions. I will be describing methods to search the space of these data structures in order to find one that describes

373

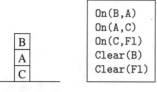

```
On(B,A)
On(A,C)
On(C,Fl)
Clear(B)
Clear(Fl)
```

Figure 22.1

A State Description

the set of world states satisfying a goal. In a state–space search over these data structures, the data structures are states of the planning process. To distinguish between planning states and world states, I will usually refer to the former as *state descriptions*.

To avoid various technical difficulties, which need not concern us here, I restrict both the before- and after–action state descriptions to conjunctions (or sets) of ground literals. I allow one exception to this restriction, namely, state descriptions can contain arbitrary formulas true in all states—such as $On(x, y) \supset (y = Fl) \vee \neg Clear(y)$. I restrict goals to (possibly existentially quantified) conjunctions of literals. In what follows, I write goal wffs of the form $(\exists x1, x2, \ldots, xn)\gamma(x1, x2, \ldots, xn)$ simply as $\gamma(x1, x2, \ldots, xn)$—assuming existential quantification of all of the variables. Although these restrictions can be lifted in various ways, several interesting planning problems can be posed and solved even with them in place.

Given a goal wff, γ, our search methods attempt to find a sequence of actions that produces a world state described by some state description, S, such that $S \models \gamma$. We say then that the state description *satisfies* the goal. For our restricted state and goal wffs, $S \models \gamma$ when there exists a substitution, σ, such that $\gamma\sigma$ is a conjunction of ground literals each of which appears in S. Whether or not $S \models \gamma$ can be established by attempting to unify the first literal in γ with a literal in S, applying the unifying substitution to the rest of the literals in γ and continuing for all of the literals in γ. (This process is the same as that used by the **PROLOG** interpreter when it checks to see if the body of a clause can be unified away with facts.)

We can search a space of state descriptions either in a forward direction, from start to goal, or in a backward direction, from goal back to start. Some authors refer to planning methods using forward search as *progression planning* and methods using backward search as *regression planning*. I begin with forward search.

22.1.2   Forward Search Methods

To do forward search over the space of state descriptions, we will need *operators* corresponding to actions—operators that change a before–action state description into an after–action state description. The search completes successfully when it produces a state description, S, such that $S \models \gamma$ for the goal wff γ. Our operators are based on those of a system called STRIPS [Fikes & Nilsson 1971, Fikes, Hart, & Nilsson 1972]. A STRIPS operator consists of three parts:

1. A set, PC, of ground literals called the *preconditions* of the operator. An action corresponding to an operator can be executed in a state only if all of the literals in PC are also in the before–action state description.

2. A set, D, of ground literals called the *delete list*.

3. A set, A, of ground literals called the *add list*.

To produce the after–action state description, we first delete from the before–action state description any literals in D and then add all of the literals in A. All literals not mentioned in D carry over to the after–action state description. This carryover is called the STRIPS *assumption* and is one method of attacking the frame problem.

STRIPS operators are usually defined by schemas that correspond to action schemas. An operator schema, called a STRIPS *rule*, has free variables, and it is the ground instances of these rules that correspond to actual operators. Here is an example of a STRIPS rule with free variables x, y, and z:

move(x, y, z)

    PC: On(x, y) $\wedge$ Clear(x) $\wedge$ Clear(z)

    D: Clear(z), On(x, y)

    A: On(x, z), Clear(y), Clear(Fl)

(I include the formula Clear(Fl) explicitly in the add list because if z is Fl, Clear(Fl) would be deleted, and we want it always to be true.) An example of an instance of this STRIPS rule for the action of moving block B from A to the *Floor* is shown in Figure 22.2.

Note that the precondition of a STRIPS rule itself is in the form of a goal, namely, a conjunction of literals. This is not a coincidence and will be exploited. When interpreted as a goal wff, the free variables in PC are assumed to be existentially quantified. An instance of a STRIPS rule can be applied to a state description, S, if a ground instance of the PC (considered as a goal) is satisfied by the state description. As mentioned earlier, such an instance can be found by unifying, in turn, each of the literals in the PC with a literal in the state description—applying the unifying substitution to the remaining literals in the PC. The applicable operator instance is then obtained by applying the resulting substitution to all of the elements of the STRIPS rule. Rules must be written in such a way that applying such a substitution always results in a ground instance of the rule. That is, there can be no free variables in D or A that do not occur in PC. Figure 22.2 is an illustration of the application of a STRIPS operator.

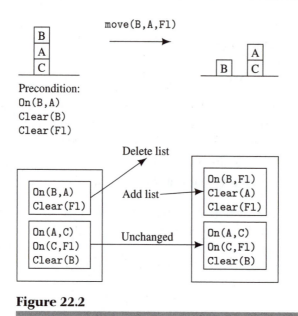

Figure 22.2

A STRIPS Operator

In the forward search method, we generate new state descriptions by applying instances of STRIPS rules until a state description is produced that satisfies the goal wff. I show part of a search graph generated by forward search in Figure 22.3. Since most of the literals in a state description are not changed by STRIPS operators, we can economize in implementations of forward search by keeping track of just the changes. (We could use A* search by using some appropriate $\hat{h}$ that estimates cost to a goal state and some appropriate $\hat{g}$ that reflects the costs of actions.) Note that, in contrast with the situation calculus, we do not have to prove that actions leave some relations unchanged. The STRIPS assumption takes care of that.

Without heuristics about which instances of which rules to apply, forward search is impractical in realistic applications in which the state descriptions and the number of rules are large. One method of making forward search more efficient is to identify islands in the search space toward which to focus search on its way to a goal state description. In the next subsection, I describe a method for identifying and exploiting islands.

22.1.3   Recursive STRIPS

When a goal condition consists of a conjunction of literals, as I am assuming here, we can focus forward search by a *divide-and-conquer* heuristic. First, achieve one of the conjuncts, then another, and so on. A state description in which one of the conjuncts is satisfied represents an island in the search space. We work first toward that island, applying operators that produce a state description in which

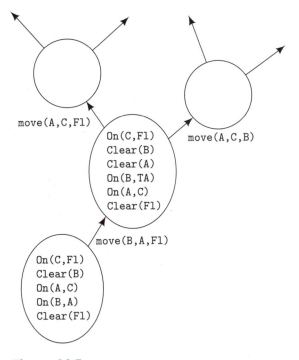

Figure 22.3

Forward Search

the corresponding conjunct is satisfied. Then, we work toward another island, and so on. Of course, it is possible that in achieving subsequent conjuncts we might disachieve earlier ones.

A system called the *General Problem Solver* (GPS) [Newell, Shaw, & Simon 1959, Newell & Simon 1963], developed early in the history of AI, exploited search–space islands in this manner. The operators for achieving these islands were identified by a process called "means–ends analysis." As applied to planning systems using STRIPS rules, this technique involves selecting an instance of one of the conjuncts in the goal condition and selecting an instance of a STRIPS rule that will achieve it. Then, we create as a subgoal the precondition needed for applying that rule, and we work toward that subgoal recursively in the same island–identifying way until it is satisfied; then we apply the operator to create the island state description and go on to identify another island, and so on. This procedure is the basis for a recursive program we call STRIPS. Here is how STRIPS solves a conjunctive goal formula, γ:

> STRIPS(γ). The procedure uses a global data structure $\mathcal{S}$ consisting of a set of ground literals. This data structure is initially set to the initial state description and is changed by and during the procedure.

1. **repeat** The main loop of STRIPS is iterative and continues until a state description is produced that satisfies the goal, γ. The termination test in step 9 produces a substitution, σ (possibly empty), such that some conjuncts (possibly none) of $\gamma\sigma$ appear in $\mathcal{S}$. There can be several substitutions tried in performing the test, so the test is a possible backtracking point.

2. $g \leftarrow$ an element of $\gamma\sigma$ such that $\mathcal{S} \not\models g$. Another selection and therefore a backtracking point. In "means–ends–analysis" terms, g is regarded as a "difference" that must be "reduced" to achieve the goal.

3. $f \leftarrow$ a STRIPS rule whose add list contains a literal, λ, that unifies with g with mgu s. Since there may be several such rules, this is another backtracking point. f is an operator that is "relevant" to reducing the difference.

4. $f' \leftarrow fs$. The instance of f using substitution s. Note that f' is not necessarily a ground instance, and therefore its precondition may contain variables.

5. $p \leftarrow$ precondition formula of f' (instantiated with the substitution s).

6. STRIPS(p). A recursive call to produce a state description that satisfies the subgoal. This call will typically change $\mathcal{S}$.

7. $f'' \leftarrow$ a ground instance of f' applicable in $\mathcal{S}$.

8. $\mathcal{S} \leftarrow$ result of applying f'' to $\mathcal{S}$. Note that $\mathcal{S}$ always consists of a conjunction of ground literals.

9. **until** $\mathcal{S} \models \gamma$.

Note that in step 9, we are always testing against the entire goal γ. If one of the conjuncts of γ is disachieved in the process of achieving another, either the first will have to be reachieved before the process can terminate or the process will backtrack to try a path that does not disachieve the first.

Although not explicitly mentioned in my description of the algorithm, the sequence of goal–achieving operators that constitutes a plan can be extracted from a trace of a successful execution of the algorithm. These in turn correspond to the actions that the agent can execute, either "ballistically" (in situations where that is appropriate) or in a sense/plan/act cycle.

The following example illustrates how the algorithm works. Suppose initially we have the situation depicted in Figure 21.1 and we attempt to achieve the goal On(A, Fl) $\wedge$ On(B, Fl) $\wedge$ On(C, B). The goal test in step 9 does not find any conjuncts satisfied by the initial state description. Suppose STRIPS selects On(A,Fl) as g. The rule instance move(A,x,Fl) has On(A,Fl) on its add list, so we call STRIPS recursively to achieve that rule's precondition, namely, Clear(A) $\wedge$ Clear(Fl) $\wedge$ On(A, x). The test in step 9 in the recursive call produces the substitution C/x, which leaves all but `Clear(A)` satisfied by the intial state. This literal is selected, and the rule instance `move(y,A,u)` is selected to achieve it.

We call STRIPS recursively again to achieve the rule's precondition, namely, `Clear(y) ∧ Clear(u) ∧ On(y, A)`. The test in step 9 of this second recursive call produces the substitution `B/y`, `Fl/u`, which makes each literal in the precondition one that appears in the initial state. So, we can pop out of this second recursive call to apply an operator, namely, `move(B,A,Fl)`, which changes the initial state to

    On(B,Fl)

    On(A,C)

    On(C,Fl)

    Clear(A)

    Clear(B)

    Clear(Fl)

Now, back in the first recursive call, we perform again the step 9 test (namely, `Clear(A) ∧ Clear(Fl) ∧ On(A, x)`). This test is satisfied by our changed state description with the substitution `C/x`, so we can pop out of the first recursive call to apply the operator `move(A,C,Fl)` to produce a third state description:

    On(B,Fl)

    On(A,Fl)

    On(C,Fl)

    Clear(A)

    Clear(B)

    Clear(C)

    Clear(Fl)

Now we perform the step 9 test in the main program again. The only conjunct in the original goal that does not appear in the new state description is `On(C,B)`. Recurring again from the main program, we note that the precondition of `move(C,Fl,B)` is already satisfied, so we can apply it to produce a state description that satisfies the main goal, and the process terminates.

22.1.4 Plans with Run–Time Conditionals

We can generalize slightly the kinds of formulas allowed in state descriptions if we are able to refine those state descriptions during plan execution by perceptual processes. Consider what it means to allow disjunctions of literals in a state description formula. To be specific, suppose we had the wff On(B, A) ∨ On(B, C) in a state description. This wff is intended to mean that either B is on A or it is on C, but the system does not know which at the time the plan is being generated.

The applicability of some STRIPS operators to such a state description and/or the effects of these operators might not depend on which of On(B, A) or On(B, C) is satisfied. For those operators, it does not matter that there is a disjunction in the state description; the disjunction would simply pass on through to the after–action state description.

But certain operators might have one of On(B, A) or On(B, C) as a precondition, for example. In order to execute the actions corresponding to such operators, the system would have to know which of the disjuncts is satisfied at the time the action is executed (that is, at run time). Perhaps perceptual processes could make that determination. If so, a *run-time conditional* can be inserted into the plan at the point of application of such an operator. In constructing the plan subsequent to a run-time conditional, the planning process splits into as many branches as there are disjuncts that might satisfy operator preconditions. Each branch maintains a separate line of state descriptions and operators. In my example, one branch would assume that On(B, A) is (or will be) true of the world when the subsequent actions are to be executed, and the other would assume that On(B, C) is (or will be) true of the world. Each of these branches is called a *context*. At planning time, the system might not know which state description describes the actual state of the world at the time the context splits, but one of them certainly does. Alternative plan completions are constructed for each context. Then, at run time when the system encounters a split into two or more contexts, perceptual processes determine which of the disjuncts is true, and execution proceeds along the appropriate path. In complex problems, there may be several branching contexts.

Sometimes it just happens as a result of previous actions that a perceptual process is able to determine which disjunct is true in the world at the time that information is needed. More typically, the system must plan to obtain that information by using operators corresponding to information–gathering actions. In my example, in order to determine which of On(B, A) or On(B, C) is true, the system might have to execute actions that can read the lettering on the blocks. Such actions can be described by STRIPS operators whose effects include a formal way of specifying "know which." The run–time conditionals would then have these know which's as preconditions.

22.1.5 The Sussman Anomaly

Consider applying recursive STRIPS to the blocks–world problem shown in Figure 22.4. The goal condition is On(A, B) ∧ On(B, C). STRIPS has to achieve one of the conjuncts first. Suppose it selects On(A, B). It moves *C* off *A*, suppose to the *Floor*. Then it moves *A* to *B*. But in achieving the other conjunct, On(B, C), it will undo On(A, B) and will have to reachieve it. Suppose instead it selects On(B, C) first. It moves *B* on *C*, but in achieving the other conjunct, On(A, B), it will undo On(B, C) and will have to reachieve it. Neither option results in a plan having a minimal

Figure 22.4

The Sussman Anomaly

number of operators. This particular blocks–world problem is called the *Sussman anomaly* after the person who posed it [Sussman 1975].

The difficulty that recursive STRIPS has with this problem is that it narrowly focuses on one conjunct at a time in a sort of depth–first fashion. If the forward search used a breadth–first strategy, it would find the shortest plan. But as I have pointed out, breadth–first forward search is computationally infeasible in realistic settings.

One alternative is to attempt a breadth–first, backward–directed search; perhaps it would be computationally more efficient than forward search since there are typically many fewer conjuncts in the goal wff than there are ground literals in the initial state description. I discuss backward search next.

22.1.6   **Backward Search Methods**

We can search backward from a goal state using the STRIPS rules. To do so, we must *regress* goal wffs through STRIPS rules to produce *subgoal* wffs. The *regression* of a formula γ through a STRIPS rule α is the weakest formula γ' such that if γ' is satisfied by a state description before applying an instance of α (and γ' satisfies the precondition of that instance of α), then γ will be satisfied by the state description after applying that instance of α. (A formula ϕ_1 is *weaker* than a formula ϕ_2 if $\phi_2 \models \phi_1$. Thus, P $\vee$ Q is weaker than P, and P is weaker than P $\wedge$ Q, for example.)

Regression computations are straightforward if we start with a goal that is a conjunction of ground literals and regress only through STRIPS operators (ground instances of STRIPS rules). In that case, all of the regressions will also be conjunctions of ground literals. I show an example in Figure 22.5 in which we use the process to search backward from a goal description. The problem here is to achieve A on B on C on the *Floor* from a state in which B is on A, A is on C, and C is on the *Floor*. In this problem, we regress the goal condition, On(C, Fl) $\wedge$ On(B, C) $\wedge$ On(A, B), through any operator that achieves one of the conjuncts in the goal. Let's regress through move(A, Fl, B) to produce a subgoal wff. The operator achieves one of the conjuncts, namely, On(A, B), so On(A, B) needn't be in the subgoal. But any preconditions of the operator not already in the goal description must be in the subgoal. In this case, these are Clear(B), Clear(A), and On(A, Fl). The other two conjuncts in the goal wff, namely, On(C, Fl) and On(B, C),

Goal

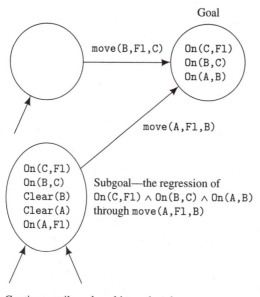

move(B,Fl,C)

On(C,Fl)
On(B,C)
On(A,B)

move(A,Fl,B)

On(C,Fl)
On(B,C)
Clear(B)
Clear(A)
On(A,Fl)

Subgoal—the regression of
On(C,Fl) ∧ On(B,C) ∧ On(A,B)
through move(A,Fl,B)

Continue until a subgoal is produced
that is satisfied by current world state

Figure 22.5

Regressing a Conjunction through a STRIPS Operator

are neither added nor destroyed by the operator, so they simply pass through the operator to appear in the subgoal. As shown in Figure 22.5, another alternative in our backward search would be to regress the goal wff through move(B, Fl, C). Backward search proceeds (perhaps using something akin to A*) until a subgoal is produced that is satisfied by the current state description.

It is interesting to note what happens if a set of literals is regressed through an operator having one of those literals on its delete list. There is no way an operator can achieve a literal λ if that literal is deleted by the operator! Thus, the regression of any conjunction containing λ through an operator that deletes λ is F. Of course, search need not be pursued backward from a state description containing F—such a state is impossible to achieve.

It is often advisable to regress a goal through a rule that is not completely instantiated—that is, through one still containing some schema variables. In Figure 22.5, we considered using move(A, Fl, B) as one way to achieve On(A, B). Why did we decide to move *A* from the *Floor*? Well, we had to move it from somewhere. But why should we have committed to moving it from the *Floor*? Perhaps there would be a better plan that moved it from somewhere else instead. One way to delay this decision is to leave the "from place" in the move operator temporarily unspecified. Doing so is an instance of what is called *least commitment planning*. We leave the "from place" unspecified by regressing the goal through

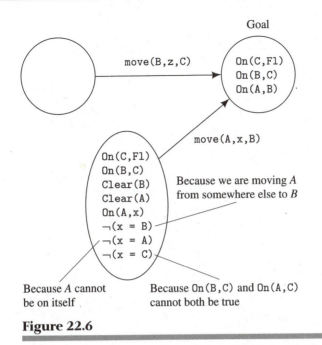

Figure 22.6

Regressing a Conjunction through a STRIPS Rule Containing a Variable

the partially instantiated operator move(A, x, B). In Figure 22.6, I show the result of this regression. The result is much like that obtained earlier except that now one of the preconditions, On(A, x), has a variable. Interpreted as a subgoal, this literal can be satisfied if it unifies with a ground literal in a state description. Backward search through a space of subgoals containing variables must now allow for additional operators that instantiate the variables—either with other variables or with constants. One heuristic is to delay instantiation until the literals containing them can be unified with literals in the initial state description.

Sometimes various reasoning processes can be used to place constraints on the variables. In the example illustrated in Figure 22.6, the variable x in On(A, x) cannot be equal to A, for it is block A that we are moving. Neither can x be equal to B because we are moving A from somewhere else to B. Also, x cannot be C, but the reason is a bit more subtle. If x were C, we would have On(A, C) as one of the conjuncts in the subgoal. But, then, On(B, C) in the goal could not regress to On(B, C) in the subgoal because both block B and block A cannot simultaneously be on C. (Note that the subgoals used in recursive calls of STRIPS are different from the subgoals created by regression!)

The full procedure for regressing goals and subgoals through STRIPS rules that are not fully instantiated is rather complex—it is explained in a bit more detail in [Nilsson 1980, pp. 288ff]. I show a small example of backward search in Figure 22.7. In this case, the variables are instantiated to F1 by reasoning that their constraints

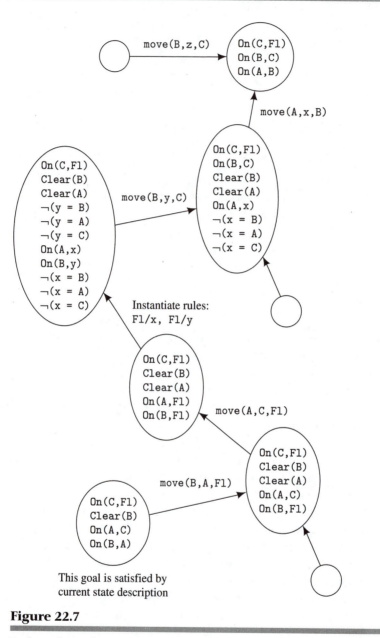

Figure 22.7

Backward Search

rule out the only possible alternative instantiations. Search terminates when a subgoal is produced that is satisfied by the initial state description. The sequence of rules that links the main goal with the subgoal satisfied by the initial state can then be read off and instantiated to operators of a goal–achieving plan by performing the instantiations discovered in the search. A more complex example is given in [Nilsson 1980, pp. 292–296].

Backward search using regression, although possibly more efficient than forward search, is complicated by the occurrence of variables. In small blocks-world problems, variables can be instantiated without too much difficulty, but it is doubtful whether the method is computationally feasible in much larger problems without using domain–specific heuristics.

In breadth–first forward or backward search, no commitment is made to achieving goal conjuncts in any particular order. The Sussman anomaly is an example of a problem in which it is best to interleave the steps needed in solving each of the conjuncts. Delaying commitment about the order of the steps in the final plan is another instance of least–commitment planning and can best be achieved by searching in a space of plans instead of searching in spaces of formulas. In "plan spaces," the steps in a plan can be partially ordered. I discuss this planning strategy, called *partial-order planning (POP)*, in the next section. (Plans with partially ordered steps are sometimes called *nonlinear plans.*)

22.2   *Plan Spaces and Partial-Order Planning*

Two different approaches to plan generation are illustrated in Figure 22.8. When searching (forward, say) in a space of formulas, STRIPS rules are applied to sets of formulas to produce successor sets of formulas, and so on until a state description is produced that satisfies the goal formula. But when searching in a space of plans, the successor operators are not STRIPS rules, but are instead operators that transform incomplete, uninstantiated or otherwise inadequate plans into more highly articulated plans, and so on until an executable plan is produced that transforms the initial state description into one that satisfies the goal condition. The operators in plan–space search transform plans into other plans by various means. These include (a) adding steps to the plan, (b) reordering the steps already in the plan, (c) changing a partially ordered plan into a fully ordered one, (d) changing a plan schema (with uninstantiated variables) into some instance of that schema. Examples of some of these plan–transforming operators are shown in Figure 22.9.

Let's illustrate plan–space search methods as applied to the Sussman anomaly (Figure 22.4). My description is based roughly on the systematic, nonlinear planning (SNLP) technique of [McAllester & Rosenblitt 1991] and on NONLIN [Tate 1977]. The basic components of a plan are STRIPS rules. These are represented by graph structures having two types of nodes; oval nodes are labeled with the

State-space search:

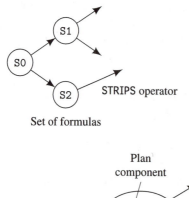

Set of formulas

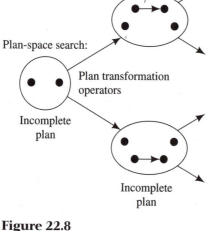

Figure 22.8

State–Space Versus Plan–Space Search

names of STRIPS rules, and box nodes are labeled with precondition and effect literals of those rules. Such a graph structure is shown in Figure 22.10. Note that the boxes at the top of the graph are effects, and the boxes at the bottom are preconditions.

We represent both the goal wff and the literals of the initial state by fictitious rule graphs called finish and start. The rule finish has as its preconditions the overall goal; its effect is taken to be Nil. The operator start has as its effects all of the literals that are in the initial state description; its precondition is taken to be T. I illustrate these two graphs for the Sussman anomaly in Figure 22.11.

The initial plan structure (before we have applied any plan-transformation operators) consists of just the (unconnected) start and finish rules as shown in

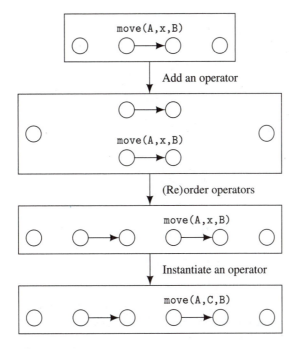

Figure 22.9

Some Plan–Transforming Operators

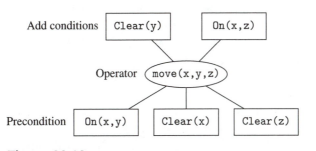

Figure 22.10

Graphical Representation of a STRIPS Rule

Figure 22.11. It is, of course, quite incomplete. (I will define what it means for a plan to be complete later.)

Search for a plan now begins by applying one of the plan-transformation operators to the initial plan structure. Least-commitment planners use a variety of methods to select plan-transformation operators. One transformation that might

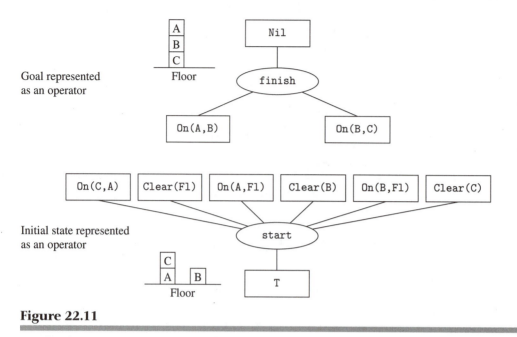

Figure 22.11

Graphical Representations of `finish` and `start` Rules

be selected at this stage would extend the initial plan structure by adding a rule
to achieve one of the conjuncts of the goal. Suppose we decide to achieve On(A, B)
by adding the rule instance move(A, y, B). We add the graph structure for this
instance to the initial plan structure. Since we have decided that the addition of
this rule is supposed to achieve On(A, B), we link that effect box of the rule with
the corresponding precondition box of the `finish` rule. The result is shown in
Figure 22.12. Note that we have not yet made a commitment about from which
place *A* is being moved.

Several plan transformations are possible at this stage. We could instantiate
y to F1 and put in a link between On(A, F1) of the instantiated move operator
precondition and the On(A, F1) that is true in the initial state. We could also put
in a link between the two Clear(B)'s. Or we could attempt to establish the Clear(A)
precondition of move(A, y, B). This condition could be established by inserting the
rule instance move(u, A, v)—move something (an instance of u) that is on *A* to
somewhere else (an instance of v). Then we could instantiate u to C and v to F1
and establish corresponding links to formulas in the initial state. The result of
this series of plan–alteration steps would produce the plan structure shown in
Figure 22.13.

At this stage, we see that the preconditions of the two move operators are
satisfied at the time the operators are to be applied. There is an implied ordering of

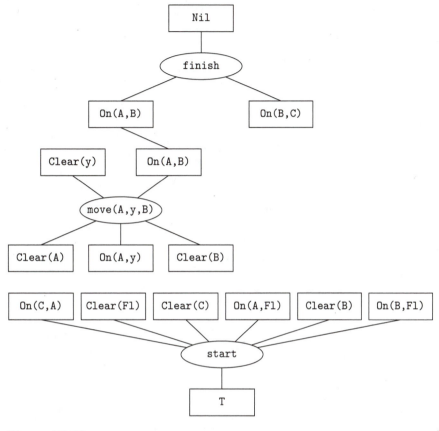

Figure 22.12

The Next Plan Structure

the two move operators in the graph structure representing the as–yet incomplete plan. Later in my description of the planning process, I will want to refer to these two occurrences of move operators. For this reason, I have labeled them by a and b in Figure 22.13. I represent explicitly the fact that b must come before a, by the notation $b < a$, where $<$ represents "before." Note the two boxes, On(C, F1) and Clear(F1), that are "products" of the move operators but are not "consumed" by subsequent operators. These cause no harm in the plan so long as they do not contradict conditions that must be true later in the plan.

Suppose next we consider how to achieve the other main goal conjunct On(B, C). This condition can be achieved by the rule instance move(B, z, C)—that is, by moving B from somewhere to C. So we can add this step into the plan structure. Suppose then that we instantiate z to F1 so that we can connect to initial conditions. The resulting plan structure is shown in Figure 22.14.

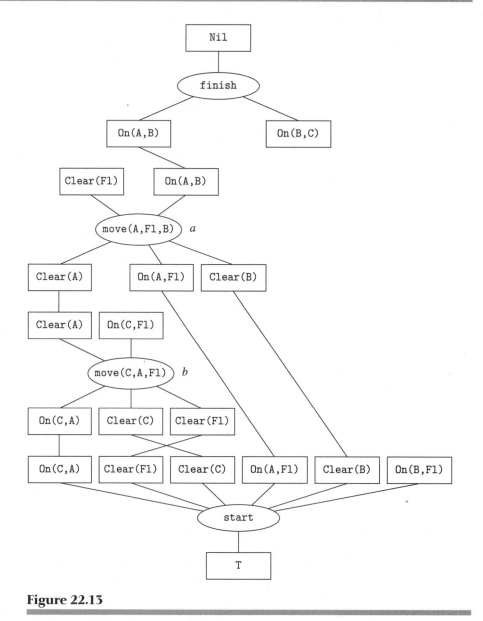

Figure 22.13

A Subsequent Plan Structure

Now we have a plan structure involving operators *a*, *b*, and *c*, that are only partially ordered. So far, we have made no commitment about where *c* is to occur in the ordering of plan steps. In partially ordered plans, we need to consider problems caused by the fact that one operator, if executed at the wrong time, may undo preconditions needed by another operator. Such possibilities are

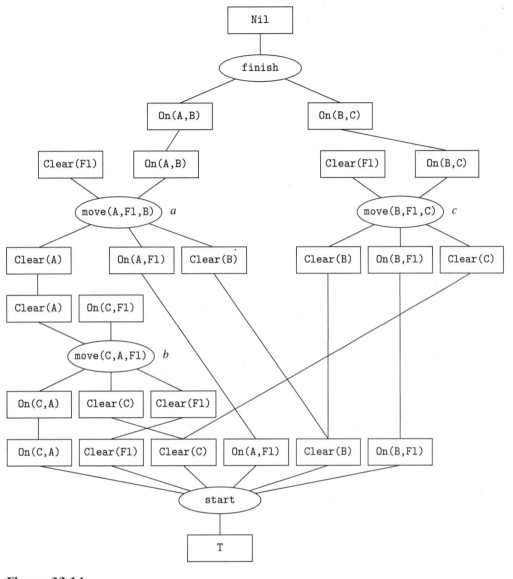

Figure 22.14

A Later Stage of the Plan Structure

represented by *threat arcs* in plan–structure graphs. Consider the graph structure shown in Figure 22.15. The heavy, gray arcs are threat arcs. Threat arcs are drawn from operator (oval) nodes to those precondition (boxed) nodes that (a) are on the delete list of the operator, and (b) are not descendants of the operator node. Thus, in Figure 22.15, the operator move(A, F1, B) deletes Clear(B),

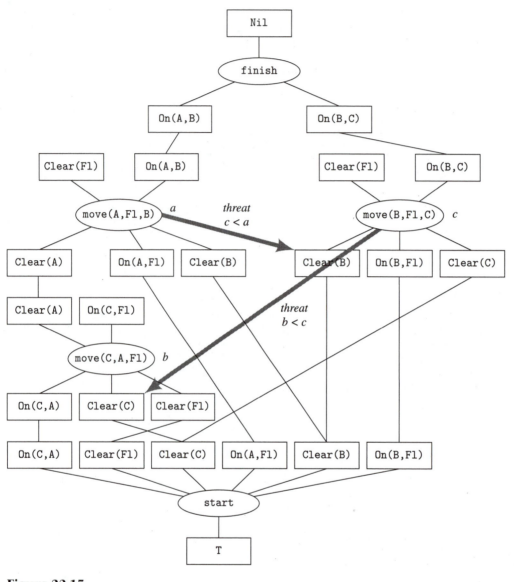

Figure 22.15

Putting in the Threat Arcs

a precondition of move(B, F1, C). In this sense, move(A, F1, B) *threatens* move(B, F1, C) because if the former were to be executed first, we would not be able to execute the latter. Threat arcs must be *discharged* by placing constraints on the ordering of operators. A plan is not complete until we can find a consistent set of ordering constraints that discharges all threat arcs. In my example, such a set of consistent ordering constraints is $(c < a, b < c)$. And, of course, the graph structure itself implies the constraint $(b < a)$—which is consistent with the other ordering constraints. Thus, our plan structure of Figure 22.15 has resulted in the total order: $(b < c < a)$. The plan is complete because all threat arcs are discharged, and all conditions required by the operators (including the `finish` operator) are satisfied at the time the operator is applied. The final plan is then {move(C, A, F1), move(B, F1, C), move(A, F1, B)}.

22.3 *Hierarchical Planning*

22.3.1 ABSTRIPS

I have already mentioned hierarchical search procedures in Chapter 10. Several investigators have developed hierarchical planners based on STRIPS rules. One, the ABSTRIPS system [Sacerdoti 1974], assigns *criticality numbers* to each conjunct in each precondition of a STRIPS rule. The easier it is to achieve a conjunct (all other things being equal), the lower is its criticality number. In ABSTRIPS, planning proceeds in levels using these criticality numbers:

1. Assume all preconditions of criticality less than some threshold value are already true, and develop a plan based on that assumption. Here we are essentially postponing the achievement of all but the hardest conjuncts.

2. Lower the criticality threshold by 1, and using the plan developed in step 1 as a guide, develop a plan that assumes that preconditions of criticality lower than the threshold are true.

3. And so on.

I illustrate the ABSTRIPS idea with an example—this time using a robot that must travel from one room to another. I define the initial situation, the goal, and the rules to be used in Figure 22.16. The rule goto(r1, d, r2) models the action schema of taking the robot from room *r1*, through door *d*, to room *r2*. The rule open(d) opens door *d*. Criticality numbers are shown circled above the corresponding literal in the preconditions of these rules. In particular, we assume that it is a relatively easy detail to open a door compared to going through a door; open(d) has a criticality value of 1.

First, we construct an abstract plan (using any of the planning methods I have discussed so far)—assuming that all preconditions of criticality 1 are already satisfied. The plan that achieves In(R3) at this level of abstraction is {goto(R1, D1, R2), goto(R2, D2, R3)}. Next, we construct a more detailed plan to achieve first the preconditions of the first operator in the abstract plan, then apply that operator, and then achieve the preconditions of the second operator in the abstract plan, and so on. The preconditions of these operators can be regarded as islands in the search space—islands found by the first-level, abstract planning

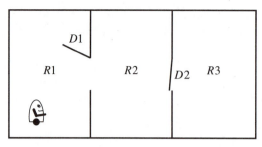

Initial state: In(R1)∧ Open(D1)∧Closed(D2)

Goal: In(R3)

STRIPS rules:

goto(r1,d,r2)

      ②   ①   ②

PC: In(r1)∧ Open(d)∧ Connects(r1,d,r2)
D: In(r1)
A: In(r2)

open(d)

      ①

PC: Closed(d)
D: Closed(d)
A: Open(d)

Figure 22.16

A Planning Problem for ABSTRIPS

process. But now, when achieving these preconditions, we lower the criticality threshold by 1 to require that we achieve all of the preconditions of criticality 1 also. The result is to produce the plan {goto(R1, D1, R2), open(D2), goto(R2, D2, R3)}. In general, we could have more than two criticality values; then the planning process would descend through several levels of abstraction.

The plan–development process used by ABSTRIPS is what is called *length first*. That is, we develop a complete plan at each level of abstraction before descending to a more detailed level to develop a complete plan there. There are alternatives to length–first plan development. We could, for example, develop a complete plan at the top level to identify a sequence of islands in the search space. These islands would be the preconditions of the various first–level operators. Then, we could develop the first part of a plan at the next level that is complete just to the first island. And so on until we have a complete plan at the lowest level to the

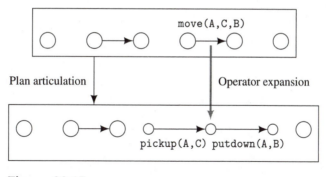

Figure 22.17

Articulating a Plan

first island for that level. We presume that at the lowest level of detail, the first operator in the plan corresponds to an action that can be executed in the initial state. This *depth-first* planning process would be appropriate in situations in which we use a sense/plan/act cycle. After executing the first action and perceiving the resulting state, we repeat the process by replanning—perhaps using some of the more abstract levels of the previous plan as a guide.

Hierarchical planning is an instance of the technique I described in Chapter 9 in which a simplified or relaxed version of a problem is solved first in order to obtain values for a heuristic function to be used in the actual problem. Each level of an abstract planning process can be regarded as a simplified version of the level below. ([Pearl 1984, pp. 131–132] mentions the relationship between his simplified-model proposal and ABSTRIPS.)

22.3.2 Combining Hierarchical and Partial-Order Planning

The planning systems, NOAH, SIPE, and O-PLAN [Sacerdoti 1977, Wilkins 1988, Currie & Tate 1991], combine partial-order, plan-space planning with hierarchical planning. Besides the plan-space operators that I have already mentioned (instantiating variables, adding STRIPS rules, etc.), these systems include operators that articulate abstract plans into ones at a lower level of detail. These articulations can be likened to the plan-space operators considered earlier. For example, our move rule used in the blocks world might be composed of the sequence of more primitive rules pickup and putdown. These lower-level rules would typically have more detailed preconditions that would require the insertion of other lower-level rules to make the plan complete at that level. (See Figure 22.17.) This process would continue until all operators (or at least the first operator) corresponded to primitive actions that could be executed.

22.4   *Learning Plans*

Just as we used EBG in Chapter 17 to learn new rules for a reasoning system, we can use it also to learn new STRIPS rules consisting of a sequence of already existing STRIPS rules. These learned rules can then be used for creating more complex plans. Of course, we are faced with the same utility problem that I mentioned earlier. A learned rule might not be worth saving unless it is used often, saves planning effort, and is not expensive to use. I explain the technique for learning new rules by an illustrative example.

Consider the problem of changing the configuration of blocks, as shown in Figure 22.18. Initially, block *A* is on block *B*, which is on block *C*, and we want both *A* and *B* to be on the floor. Any of the planning methods so far discussed would create the plan {move(A,B,Fl), move(B,C,Fl)}. Is this plan worth saving in the form of a new STRIPS rule? It might be if our agent often had to solve this specific problem. The plan would have even more utility if it could be generalized so that it moved the top two blocks (whatever their names) from a stack of blocks to the same target place. Since the construction of the plan did not depend on the names of the blocks, it would appear that an EBG–like process could produce a plan schema with variable symbols in place of the object constants A, B, and C. But since this two–step plan does depend on the target place being the floor, the object constant Fl cannot be generalized.

The plan–generalization process uses information about the preconditions and effects of the operators in the plan. A convenient way to represent this information is in the form of a *triangle table* [Fikes, Hart, & Nilsson 1972]. I show the table for the block–unstacking problem in Figure 22.19. Each column of the table is headed by one of the operators in the plan—in the order in which these operators occur in the plan. Just as in partial–order planning, it is convenient to imagine fictitious start and finish operators. The table displays the preconditions for each operator and what each operator achieves. The cells below each operator contain certain literals (possibly repeated) that are added by the operator. The cells to the left of each operator contain literals that are preconditions of the operator. We index cells in the table by their row position, i, starting with row 1 at the top of the table, and by their column position, j, starting with column 1 at the left of the table. Specifically, cell (i, j) (for $i \geq j$) contains literals that are added by operator i that are needed as preconditions of operator $j + 1$ and that survive the application of operators between i and $j + 1$. So, the *start* operator has cells below it that contain literals that are present in the initial state description and are either needed by subsequent operators or satisfy conjuncts in the goal condition. The *finish* operator has cells to its left that contain literals that satisfy the goal condition.

The next step in the plan–generalization procedure replaces *all* object constants in the triangle table by variable symbols. Each occurrence of an object

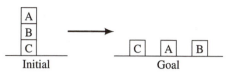

Figure 22.18

Unstacking Two Blocks

```
start

┌─────────────────┐
│ Clear(F1)       │
│ On(A,B)         │
│ Clear(A)          move(A,B,F1)
├─────────────────┼──────────────┐
│ Clear(F1)       │ Clear(B)     │
│ On(B,C)         │              │
│                 │               move(B,C,F1)
├─────────────────┼──────────────┼──────────────┐
│                 │              │              │
│                 │ On(A,F1)     │ On(B,F1)      finish
└─────────────────┴──────────────┴──────────────┘
```

Figure 22.19

A Triangle Table for Block Unstacking

constant is replaced by its own variable symbol. The process then attempts to find the most general instance of the resulting plan schema such that the pre–conditions of all rules are met at the time a rule instance is to be applied. The preconditions of each rule, starting with the first, are checked, and substitutions are made if needed to satisfy the preconditions. For this problem, the resulting triangle–table schema is shown in Figure 22.20.

The generalized plan schema, in triangle–table form, is called a *MACROP* (for macro–operator). It can be used as a STRIPS rule for creating longer plans. The conjunction of the literals in column 1 are the preconditions of the MACROP, and the literals in row 3 are literals on the add list. (Analysis of the delete lists of the individual rules is needed to compute the delete list.) The generalization process itself and the use of triangle tables for monitoring the execution of plans are discussed in [Fikes, Hart, & Nilsson 1972].

In addition to learning MACROPS, attempts at constructing specific plans can also produce control–strategy information that might reduce future planning

start

Clear(F1) On(x,y) Clear(x)	move(x,y,F1)		
Clear(F1) On(y,z)	Clear(y)		
		move(y,z,F1)	
	On(x,F1)	On(y,F1)	finish

Figure 22.20

A Triangle–Table Schema for Block Unstacking

effort. For example, in our last problem, in attempting to achieve the conjunction On(A, F1) ∧ On(B, F1), it is important to achieve the conjunct On(A,F1) first. (Achieving On(B,F1) first might move A to the top of another block in order to make B clear, and then A would have to be moved again to the floor.) Minton's PRODIGY system was able to learn control information of this sort using EBG [Minton 1988]. (For an alternative approach based on partial evaluation, see [Etzioni 1993].)

Another type of learning useful in planning is to learn the effects of the rules themselves. An agent might have available a large number of actions but might not know the effects of these actions or under what conditions they can be executed. Some results on the difficult but important problem of learning *action models* have been achieved by [Shen 1994, Gil 1992, Wang 1995, Benson 1997]. [Benson 1997] uses a teleo–reactive (T-R) program representation in which to represent the plans constructed using the learned operators. As mentioned in Chapter 2, the T-R representation gives added robustness to plan execution.

22.5   *Additional Readings and Discussion*

[Lifschitz 1986] notes that the original descriptions of STRIPS lacked the precision and restrictions needed to prevent unsound or nonsensical formulations. He discusses restrictions on the language used by STRIPS that are needed to avoid these problems. (I adhere to these restrictions in the present formulation.) [Pednault 1986, Pednault 1989] present a version of STRIPS that both avoids the problems mentioned by Lifschitz and is able to formulate multiagent plans using rules with conditional effects. [Bylander 1994] shows that planning with propositional

STRIPS operators is intractable in the worst case. (See [Bylander 1993] for average case analysis.) [Erol, Nau, & Subrahmanian 1992] present a thorough analysis of the complexity of STRIPS-type planning systems.

[Gupta & Nau 1992] prove that in blocks-world problems in which world states and goals are described by conjunctions of ground atoms, finding an optimal (shortest) plan is, in general, NP-hard. (Nevertheless, [Chapman 1989] shows that a simple reactive system can quickly perform block-stacking tasks if it is equipped with appropriate sensory predicates.)

The use of regression of goals through STRIPS rules, a process required for backward-directed search, was introduced by [Waldinger 1975].

[Blum & Furst 1995] translate planning problems posed in terms of STRIPS rules into structures called *planning graphs* for solution by path-finding methods. [Kautz & Selman 1996, Kautz, McAllester, & Selman 1996] propose methods for converting planning graphs to propositional logic PSAT problems for solution by WALKSAT. They also propose new techniques for direct encoding of planning problems as PSAT problems. See also [Ernst, Millstein, & Weld 1997]. This work is very important because it may result in scalable planning methods that exploit efficient stochastic and hill-climbing search techniques.

Sacerdoti's NOAH system [Sacerdoti 1975, Sacerdoti 1977] and Tate's INTER-PLAN [Tate 1977] were the first partial-order planners. Chapman's TWEAK system [Chapman 1987] was the first formalization of a partial-order planner and introduced several important concepts. He showed that the problem of finding a partial-order plan to achieve a conjunction of atomic goal conditions was NP-hard—under certain reasonable formulations.

McAllester and Rosenblitt's SNLP formulation of a partial-order planner was implemented by [Soderland & Weld 1991]. This implementation was followed by UCPOP [Penberthy & Weld 1992]. [Ephrati, Pollack, & Milshtein 1996] used an A*-type search to select plan-space operators. A comparison of partial-order and total-order planners is given in [Minton, Bresina, & Drummond 1994]. For a survey of least-commitment and partial-order planning methods, see [Weld 1994].

[Christensen 1990, Knoblock 1990] developed methods for automatically learning operator hierarchies. [Tenenberg 1991] studied abstractions needed by hierarchical planners. [Erol, Hendler, & Nau 1994] is another hierarchical, partial-order planner.

[Dean & Wellman 1991] is a book that nicely integrates AI planning and temporal reasoning methods with modern control theory. Approaching this middle ground from the other direction is the work on discrete event systems by [Ramadge & Wonham 1989]. For additional discussion of temporal reasoning and its role in planning, see [Allen, et al. 1990]. [Zweben & Fox 1994] present the application of various planning and search methods to the problem of scheduling. [Wilkins, et al. 1995] extends planning methods to applications involving uncertainty.

Many of the important papers in planning are contained in the collection by [Allen, et al. 1990]. Papers on learning and planning are in [Minton 1993]. A book entitled *Practical Planning* describes the SIPE system and its applications [Wilkins 1988].

Papers on planning regularly appear in the major AI journals and conference proceedings. There is also an International Conference on AI Planning Systems (AIPS). For a sampling of recent applications of planning and scheduling techniques, see [Tate 1996].

Exercises

22.1 (Courtesy of Daphne Koller and Yoav Shoham.) Consider the problem of devising a plan for a kitchen–cleaning robot.

1. Write a set of STRIPS-style operators that might be used. When you describe the operators, take into account the following considerations:
   (a) Cleaning the stove or the refrigerator will get the floor dirty.
   (b) The stove must be clean before covering the drip pans with tin foil.
   (c) Cleaning the refrigerator generates garbage and messes up the counters.
   (d) Washing the counters or the floor gets the sink dirty.

2. Write a description of an initial state of a kitchen that has a dirty stove, refrigerator, counters, and floor. (The sink is clean, and the garbage has been taken out.) Also write a description of the goal state where everything is clean, there is no trash, and the stove drip pans have been covered with tin foil.

22.2 Invent a parameterized STRIPS rule, move(x, y), that gives the preconditions and effects for a move (of the blank spot) from position x to position y in the Eight–puzzle.

22.3 Explain how recursive STRIPS would solve the Sussman anomaly.

22.4 Explain how backward search using regressions based on STRIPS rules would solve the Sussman anomaly.

22.5 Set up a STRIPS formulation of the Tower–of–Hanoi puzzle. (See Exercises 5.3, 7.4, and 9.2.) That is,

1. Specify the STRIPS rule that describes the effects of a move, and specify the goal condition.

2. Write down the axioms describing the initial state, and show how this rule is applied to produce one of the successor states. (Don't forget to include formulas that are true in all states and may be needed to prove preconditions and the goal condition.)

22.6 An expendable Martian robot plans a one-way trip to a Martian mountain 20 kilometers from its base camp. (It need not return to base camp.) The robot can travel exactly 10 kilometers on a pellet of fuel. It can also carry a pellet of fuel as freight. Base camp is named *B*, the mountain is named *M*, and a staging site (10 kilometers from base camp and from the mountain) is named *S*. There are three pellets of fuel, *P1*, *P2*, and *P3*, at *B*, and the robot is initially unfueled. The robot has four actions:

1. goto(x, y), where x is the initial place (one of B, M, or S), and y is the destination place (one of B, M, or S). The robot must have a pellet of fuel in its fuel hopper in order to execute this action, and it can only go between B and S and between S and M on one pellet of fuel.

2. pickup(u, x), where u is a pellet of fuel located at place x. The effect of this action is that the robot is carrying u as freight.

3. putdown(u, x), where u is a pellet of fuel deposited at place x. The robot has to be carrying u in order to execute putdown.

4. refuel(u, x), where u is a pellet of fuel at place x that is put in the robot's fuel hopper.

   (Assume that it takes no fuel to execute the pickup, putdown, and refuel actions.)

We use the following predicate forms (with obvious intended meanings):

Atrobot(x), where x is one of the places, B, M, or S.

At(r, x), where x is one of the places, B, M, or S, and r is one of the fuel pellets. (We do not consider a pellet that is on board the robot to be at x even if the robot is at x.)

Carrying(u) states that the robot is carrying fuel pellet u (as freight).

Fueled states that the robot has a pellet of fuel (ready to burn) in its fuel hopper.

Cango(x, y) gives the range of the robot on one pellet of fuel. It states that the robot can go from x to y (if it is fueled).

We want to set up this problem so that a STRIPS-type problem solver can produce a plan to get the robot to the mountain.

1. What is the initial state description and the goal condition?

2. What are the operators and their descriptions (preconditions, delete list, add list) needed to solve this problem? To make the problem a bit simpler, you do not need to include predicates like Place(x) or Pellet(x) in your formulas.

3. Give a solution plan to the preceding problem that a STRIPS system (working forward from initial state to goal) might produce. Write your solution in the following format:

Literals in the initial state, S0
First Operator
Literals in the subsequent state, S1
Second Operator
etc. until a state satisfying the goal is reached

22.7 Invent an "iconic" data structure form (not predicate–calculus formulas) to represent the possible states for the Martian robot and the fuel pellets of the previous exercise. What is the data structure for the initial state?

To show that you understand how to construct and use operators for this problem, show the data structures for the states produced by applying the operators refuel(P1, B) and pickup(P1, B) to the start node.

22.8 Suppose our Martian robot has sensors that enable it to determine the truth or falsity of the following predicates:

Atfuelpellet(S)

Atfuelpellet(B)

Fueled

Carrying

Atrobot(B)

Atrobot(S)

Atrobot(M)

which have the obvious intended meanings.

The robot has the following actions:

refuel fuels the robot with a fuel pellet (if there is a fuel pellet at the robot's location).

pickup loads a pellet as freight onto the robot (if there is a fuel pellet at the robot's location).

putdown unloads a pellet at the robot's current location.

goto(x) gets the robot to place x (if it is fueled and if x is within 10 kilometers).

Design a production system (of the type described in Chapter 2) that will execute the appropriate action for all combinations of sensory inputs.

22.9 (Courtesy of Daphne Koller and Yoav Shoham.) Consider using a partial-order planning system (as described in this chapter) for planning the development and release of a software product. Assume that in this domain there exist the following four STRIPS operators:

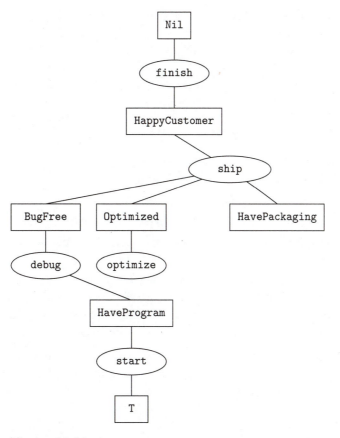

Figure 22.21

The Partial Plan for Exercise 22.9

Operator	Preconditions	Add list	Delete list
optimize	HaveProgram	Optimized	BugFree
debug	HaveProgram	BugFree	
ship	HaveProgram BugFree Optimized HavePackaging	HappyCustomer	
designPackaging	HaveProgram	HavePackaging	

The planning problem is to get from a state in which `HaveProgram` is true to one in which `HappyCustomer` is true. As we know, partial-order planning methods will add the following two "dummy" operators:

Operator	Preconditions	Add list	Delete list
start	T	HaveProgram	Nil
finish	HappyCustomer	Nil	HappyCustomer

Suppose we start with the partial plan shown in Figure 22.21. The partial plan currently contains no ordering constraints other than those implied by the partial order of the partial plan.

1. What are the existing threat arc(s) in this partial plan, if any?

2. List the preconditions of any operator in this partial plan that are not supported by a causal link.

3. Show one possible plan that the partial–order planning process might produce (that is, extend the figure shown with additional operators, and list the ordering constraints). You need not show all of the steps taken to produce the plan—showing the completed plan is sufficient.

22.10 Describe how the ABSTRIPS system could be used to produce an "anytime" plan. Comment briefly on why you would expect the quality or reliability of the plan to improve with time spent planning.

Part V

Communication and Integration

Human intelligence [is characterized as] intrinsically social—a capacity that . . . emerged in order to enable early humans to negotiate the difficulties of living in groups and coordinate individuals' activities with those of other group members.

—Attributed to Merlyn Donald by Catherine Snow in a book review in *Science*, p. 1611, vol. 275, 14 March 1997.

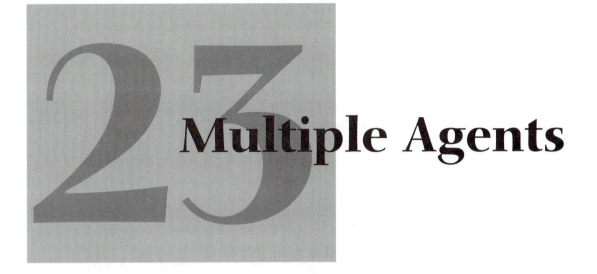

Multiple Agents

Interacting Agents

Except for our study of games in Chapter 12, our concern so far has been with a single agent reacting, planning, reasoning, and learning in an environment more or less compatible with its abilities and goals. I assumed that the pertinent effects of any other agents or processes could be either mitigated by appropriate agent reactions or ignored. Now I begin to consider how the actions of other agents can be anticipated in each agent's own planning, and, indeed, how an agent can even affect the actions of other agents in the service of its own goals. To predict what another agent will do, we will need methods for one agent to *model* another; to affect what another agent will do, we will need methods for one agent to *communicate* with another. These are subjects I take up in this and the next chapter.

I shall adopt an "agent–centric" view in which we identify with the structure and goals of a single agent (which I call *our* agent) acting in an environment containing *other* agents and/or processes. In contrast with most of my earlier assumptions, the effects on our agent of the actions of the other agents and processes can be quite profound; they can be helpful, neutral, or even inimical to the goals of our agent. My treatment can be specialized to include the case in which several agents coordinate their activities to achieve common goals— so–called *distributed artificial intelligence (DAI)*.

Before launching into the central topics of this and the next chapter, I point out that the simplest kind of agent interaction requires neither models of the other agents nor explicit communication. Our agent may simply react to the environmental effects of the other agents as they occur and are perceived. A kind of implicit, but unintended, communication among the agents can occur through these environmental effects. For example, another agent may change the environmental configuration of blocks in such a way that our agent can now perform an action that it could not perform before. Such an action on the part of the other agent accomplishes both its world–changing goal and signals to our agent that the world is now ready for our agent to act. Or another agent may emit some kind of audio signal that our agent can perceive. As far as the other agent is concerned, its "squeak" may simply be a built–in reaction to a perceived environmental situation. But the squeak, perceived by our agent, might evoke a reaction that an external observer might interpret as a response to a communication intended and planned by the other agent. The designer of a group of agents can arrange for coordination among them by such a system of reactive signaling and responding—just as the designer of a distributed system arranges for coordinating the behavior of its components.

Just as the reactive machines considered in Chapters 2 through 6 were capable of surprisingly complex individual behaviors, so is this implicit sort of communication capable of supporting rather complex interactions. Some of the group behavior of animals, such as schooling, flocking, and nest building seems to be of this sort. (See, for example, [Mataric 1996, Theraulaz & Bonabeau 1995].)

23.2 *Models of Other Agents*

23.2.1 **Varieties of Models**

If our agent is to take into account the activity of other agents and processes as it makes and executes its own plans, it will need to have models that can be used to predict how those other agents and processes will behave. Since agents and processes are physical phenomena, we could use the languages of engineering and physics to describe their operation. The behavior of physical agents such as robots can be described by using models at various levels of detail ranging from electromechanical diagrams of their components to the computer programs that control them. The behavior of physical processes can often be described by differential equations.

A significant body of research in AI has considered the problem of modeling physical processes; this work is usually called *naive physics* or *qualitative physics* [Weld & de Kleer 1990]. Qualitative physics seeks to replace exact calculations required to solve the differential equations underlying various physical phenomena with more approximate AI–style reasoning methods operating on qualitative models of process dynamics. I will not be discussing this style of modeling here, however, preferring to concentrate instead on higher-level models of other agents. (In fact, many physical processes could be modeled as if they were reactive agents—governed perhaps by T–R programs.[1])

Even though agents are themselves physical processes and could be modeled like any other engineered device, we shall find it convenient to use specialized techniques to model agents. The spectrum of increasingly complex agents that we have studied in this book suggests a variety of ways to model other agents. Our agent might assume, for example, that another agent is a T–R program that evaluates conditions and selects actions. Whatever the form of the other agent's program, our agent's model of it need not be as complex as the real thing, so long as the model can give reasonably useful predictions of the other agent's behavior in various circumstances. Or our agent might assume that the other agent creates plans using a set of STRIPS rules and executes these plans to achieve its goals. In any case, it is often useful to presume that the other agent maintains and uses an internal environmental model of its own in order to select actions. An agent's model, along with its apparatus for using that model to select actions, is called a *cognitive structure*. Often, the cognitive structure also includes an agent's goals and intentions. (I take intentions to be the actions that the agent has decided to execute, when it is appropriate to do so given its plan.) Our agent has the task of modeling the presumed cognitive structures of other agents in sufficient detail and accuracy so that it can reason with these descriptions to predict what other agents will do.

The part of an agent's cognitive structure that I will focus on here is its model of its environment and of the cognitive structures of other agents. We have studied two kinds of models used by agents, iconic and feature based. Recall that an iconic model of the environment attempts to *simulate* relevant aspects of the environment; a feature–based model attempts to *describe* the environment—perhaps by formulas in the predicate calculus. We have this choice again as we consider how our agent might model another agent. Actually, we now have four choices. Our agent can use either an iconic or a feature–based model of the other agent's cognitive structure. And the other agent itself might be presumed to be using either an iconic or feature–based model. The four possibilities are shown in Table 23.1, along with the type of modeling strategy each provokes. I will be discussing three of these modeling strategies in the next few subsections. (It turns out that when our agent uses a feature–based modeling strategy, it isn't too relevant whether the other agent is presumed to use a feature–based or an iconic model. For present purposes, when our agent uses a feature–based strategy, it will presume that the other agent does also.)

---

1. Some primitive peoples carried this view to an extreme—seeing purposeful agents causing such physical phenomena as lightning, hurricanes, eclipses, and earthquakes.

Our agent	Other agent	Modeling strategy
iconic	iconic	simulation
iconic	feature based	simulated database
feature based	iconic	descriptive
feature based	feature based	intentional

Table 23.1

Modeling Strategies

23.2.2 Simulation Strategies

In Chapter 12, we have already seen a simple example of an agent using an iconic model of another agent's (presumed) iconic model. The process of computing the likely game positions that an opponent will present our agent with when it is the opponent's turn to play uses an iconic model of what is presumed to be the opponent's iconic model of the effects of its actions. Iconic models are often useful but suffer from an important limitation already mentioned, namely, they have difficulty representing ignorance or uncertainty. This difficulty also plagues the simulated database approach, as we shall see in the next subsection.

23.2.3 Simulated Databases

The most obvious way for our agent to model another agent's formulas (which describe for the other agent the other agent's world) would seem to be for our agent to build a hypothetical database of formulas presumed to be the same formulas that our agent thinks actually populate that other agent's world model. That is, our agent could simply attempt to duplicate what it thinks the other agent's model to be. So, for example, if our agent thinks that the other agent has the formula On(A,B) in its world model, our agent could have an "other-agent" database containing the formula On(A,B) in it. Having that formula in the database modeling the other agent in no way precludes our agent from having the formula On(A,C) in its own model of the world. Also, of course, our agent might not know anything about the vocabulary in which the other agent describes its world. For example, the other agent might actually represent the same proposition that our agent represents by the string On(A,B) by the string $#4(QW,V) instead. So long as the agents do not have to communicate by sending these untranslated formulas to each other, this vocabulary difference need not concern us.

This particular approach might be feasible for some relatively simple types of reasoning about the other agent. But it has the same deficiencies as do all iconic models. An example of the most obvious one is that it is difficult for our agent to represent the fact that either the other agent has On(A, B) in its model or it has On(A, C) in its model. Note that putting On(A, B) ∨ On(A, C) in the simulated database would represent something different. In one case, it is our agent that is uncertain; in the other, it is the other agent that is uncertain. For our agent to represent its own uncertainty, it would have to have two model databases—one for each case. If, furthermore, there were additional uncertainties of this type, the number of different model databases would have to increase exponentially with the number of uncertainties to handle all of the combinations.

To give a related difficulty for this method, suppose our agent doesn't know whether or not the other agent has On(A, B) in its world model. We cannot simply omit the formula On(A,B) from the model database because doing so would imply that the other agent doesn't have this formula in its world model (and it might). Again, the problem is one of distinguishing between our agent's lack of knowledge and that of the other agent.

23.2.4 The Intentional Stance

To be able to make these distinctions, our agent needs some sort of language (perhaps a variant of the predicate calculus) that is capable of *describing* another agent's *knowledge* and *beliefs* about the world rather than simulating them. When our agent describes another agent's knowledge and beliefs, it is taking what Dennett calls an *intentional stance* toward the other agent [Dennett 1971]. We humans often adopt an intentional stance toward the machines that we use. For example, we might say "This computer *knows* that this year is a leap year." (See also, [McCarthy 1979a].)

Three possibilities have been suggested for constructing intentional–stance models of another agent. First, we could *reify* the other agent's beliefs (just as we reified actions in the situation calculus). [McCarthy 1979b] proposes such an approach. That is, we could give names to these beliefs and use a relation constant, Bel, intended to denote a relation between an agent and (one of) its beliefs. But we would need to connect these names (of the other agent's beliefs) with similar beliefs of our agent (denoted by logical formulas), and an appropriate connection mechanism has proved problematical.

Second, our agent could assume that the other agent actually represents its beliefs about the world by predicate–calculus formulas in its database of facts describing the world. Then our agent could use a relation constant, Bel, which this time denotes a relation between another agent and a string that exists in that other agent's database. For example, our agent might use the formula Bel(Sam, 'On(A,B)') to denote the proposition that an agent named Sam has the string named 'On(A,B)' (denoting the formula On(A,B)) in its database of world knowledge. Such an approach involves relations between agents and formulas and has thus been called a *metalinguistic* approach [Perlis 1985; Perlis 1988; Konolige 1982; Kowalski & Kim 1991; and Genesereth & Nilsson 1987, Ch. 10].

Third, we could use an elaboration of the predicate calculus involving what are called *modal operators.* Such operators can be used to construct formulas denoting propositions about who knows or believes what from simpler ones that denote the actual knowledge or beliefs themselves. I explain this elaboration in the next section.

23.3   *A Modal Logic of Knowledge*

23.3.1   **Modal Operators**

We are familiar with the use of the connectives $\wedge$ and $\vee$ in propositional and first-order logic. We can think of these connectives as *operators* that construct more complex formulas from simpler components. When these operators construct a new formula, the truth value of that new formula depends on the truth values of the operands as well as on the special properties of the operator. Here, we want to construct a formula whose intended meaning is that a certain agent knows a certain proposition. The components consist of a term denoting the agent and a formula denoting a proposition that that agent knows. To accomplish this construction, I introduce the *modal operator* **K**. For example, to say that Sam (the name of an agent) knows that block A is on block B, we would write

    K(Sam, On(A, B))

The sentence formed by combining **K** with the term Sam and the formula On(A,B) yields a new formula, the intended meaning of which is "Sam knows that block A is on block B." (Occasionally, throughout this chapter, I will use the abbreviation $\mathbf{K}_\alpha(\phi)$ for $\mathbf{K}(\alpha,\phi)$, where α denotes an agent, and ϕ is a formula.)

Note that I have begun using "knows" instead of "believes." Philosophers have long argued about the distinction between knowledge and belief. One distinction is that whereas an agent can believe a false proposition, it cannot *know* anything that is false. It happens that defining and using a logic of knowledge is somewhat simpler than defining and using an appropriate logic of belief. Therefore, in this section, I limit my discussion to knowledge—taking it to be a useful idealization that can be adjusted in various ways to make it appropriate for dealing with beliefs.

The language that uses the operator **K** is called a modal first-order language. The syntax for formulas in this language is as follows:

1. All of the wffs of ordinary first-order predicate calculus are also wffs of the modal language.

2. If ϕ is a closed wff of the modal language (one with no unquantified, free variables), and if α is a ground term, then $\mathbf{K}(\alpha,\phi)$ is a wff of the modal language.

3. As usual, if ϕ and ψ are wffs, then so are any expressions that can be constructed from ϕ and ψ by the usual propositional connectives.

As examples, the following are wffs:

- **K**[Agent1, **K**(Agent2, On(A,B))], which is intended to mean that Agent1 knows that Agent2 knows that A is on B.

- **K**(Agent1, On(A, B)) $\vee$ **K**(Agent1, On(A, C)), which is intended to mean that either Agent1 knows that A is on B or it knows that A is on C.

- **K**[Agent1, On(A, B) $\vee$ On(A, C)], which is intended to mean that Agent1 knows that either A is on B or that A is on C.

- **K**(Agent1, On(A, B)) $\vee$ **K**(Agent1, ¬On(A, B)), which is intended to mean that Agent1 knows whether or not A is on B.

- ¬**K**(Agent1, On(A, B)), which is intended to mean that Agent1 does not know that A is on B.

Note that, according to our syntax, the expression $(\exists x)$**K**(Agent1, On(x, B)) is not a legal wff. The expression On(x, B) is not closed inside the modal operator; it contains a free variable that is quantified outside of the modal operator. Some versions of modal logic allow this type of "quantifying in," but it presents difficulties that are beyond the scope of my treatment here.

23.3.2   Knowledge Axioms

The operators $\wedge$ and $\vee$ have *compositional semantics*—meaning that the truth value of a formula constructed from component formulas using these operators depends on the operator and on the truth values of the component formulas. The semantics of **K**, however, are not compositional. The truth value of **K**(Agent1, On(A,B)), for example, cannot necessarily be determined from the properties of **K**, the denotation of Agent1, and the truth value of On(A,B). Of course, if On(A,B) has value F, so should all the instances of $\mathbf{K}_\alpha$(On(A, B)) for any value of α (because an agent cannot know anything that is false). But even if On(A,B) has value *True*, no instance of $\mathbf{K}_\alpha$(On(A, B)) need have value *True* (because the agent denoted by α might not know the proposition denoted by On(A,B)). Similarly, even if two formulas, ϕ and ψ, are equivalent, it is not necessarily the case that if $\mathbf{K}_\alpha(\phi)$ has value *True*, so will $\mathbf{K}_\alpha(\psi)$ for any value of α. (The agent denoted by α might not know that those formulas are equivalent.[2]) The semantics of modal formulas must respect these observations.

An elegant semantics for statements in this modal language involves *possible worlds*. (For an alternative approach, see [Konolige 1986].) Although I will not discuss the possible-worlds account here, it amounts (roughly) to saying that

---

2. The **K** operator is therefore said to be *referentially opaque*.

an agent *knows* a proposition just when that proposition is true in all of the worlds that are possibilities for that agent. Conversely, an agent doesn't know a proposition if (for all that agent knows) there are some worlds in which the proposition is true and some in which it is false. Refer to [Fagin, et al. 1995] for a thorough discussion of logics of knowledge. Even without delving into the semantics of a logic of knowledge, I can nevertheless propose some schemes to allow our agent to reason about another agent's beliefs. These schemes will use axioms stating the special properties of knowledge along with a new inference rule and *modus ponens*.

Some commonly accepted axiom schemas are

$$[\mathbf{K}_\alpha(\phi) \wedge \mathbf{K}_\alpha(\phi \supset \psi)] \supset \mathbf{K}_\alpha(\psi) \tag{23.1}$$

which is intended to mean that if an agent knows ϕ, and if it knows $\phi \supset \psi$, then that agent also knows ψ (because we assume that it can and does perform *modus ponens*). This axiom schema is sometimes written in the equivalent form:

$$\mathbf{K}_\alpha(\phi \supset \psi) \supset [\mathbf{K}_\alpha(\phi) \supset \mathbf{K}_\alpha(\psi)] \tag{23.2}$$

This axiom is called the *distribution axiom* because it sanctions distributing the **K** operator over implications.

Another axiom schema that seems appropriate, called the *knowledge axiom*, states that an agent cannot possibly *know* something that is false:

$$\mathbf{K}_\alpha(\phi) \supset \phi \tag{23.3}$$

The knowledge axiom implies that an agent does not know contradictions: $\neg\mathbf{K}(\alpha, \text{F})$.

As a third property of knowledge, it seems reasonable to assume that if an agent knows something, it knows that it knows it. This property is expressed by the *positive-introspection axiom*:

$$\mathbf{K}_\alpha(\phi) \supset \mathbf{K}_\alpha(\mathbf{K}_\alpha(\phi)) \tag{23.4}$$

In some axiomatizations of knowledge, we also state that, if an agent does not know something, it knows that it does not know it—the *negative-introspection axiom*:

$$\neg\mathbf{K}_\alpha(\phi) \supset \mathbf{K}_\alpha(\neg\mathbf{K}_\alpha(\phi)) \tag{23.5}$$

The next property we might want is that any agent knows all these axioms (as well as all valid formulas). We can express this property by adding to our logic another rule of inference. This rule, called *epistemic necessitation*, allows us (that is, our agent) to infer $\mathbf{K}_\alpha(\phi)$ if ϕ is a valid formula. We can write this rule of inference as

$$\text{from } \vdash \phi \text{ infer } \mathbf{K}_\alpha(\phi) \tag{23.6}$$

Since *modus ponens* is the only inference rule needed in propositional logic, axiom 23.2 and rule 23.6 enable us to conclude that an agent knows *all* the propositional consequences of its knowledge; that is, it is *logically omniscient*. We can express this fact as an inference rule as follows:

from $\phi \vdash \psi$ and from $\mathbf{K}_\alpha(\phi)$ infer $\mathbf{K}_\alpha(\psi)$ (23.7)

An equivalent formulation of this rule is

from $\vdash (\phi \supset \psi)$ infer $\mathbf{K}_\alpha(\phi) \supset \mathbf{K}_\alpha(\psi)$ (23.8)

Logical omniscience seems unrealistic for finite agents, who, after all, cannot derive *all* the consequences of whatever they might know explicitly. If an agent cannot derive a proposition (even though it follows from other propositions it knows), can it really be said that it *knows* that proposition? Does someone who knows the axioms of number theory *know all* of the theorems? It depends on what we take *know* to mean. We might have, for example, a *Platonic* view of knowledge in which, by definition, an agent *knows* all the consequences of its knowledge—even though it might not necessarily explicitly *believe* them. Even though logical omniscience does seem too strong, it is useful as an approximation since intelligent agents will do *some* reasoning.

From logical omniscience (rule 23.7), we can derive

$$\mathbf{K}(\alpha, (\phi \wedge \psi)) \equiv \mathbf{K}(\alpha, \phi) \wedge \mathbf{K}(\alpha, \psi)$$ (23.9)

That is, the **K** operator *distributes* over conjunctions. However, it does not distribute over disjunctions because (as I have already argued, for example) it is not the case that $\mathbf{K}(\alpha, (\phi \vee \psi)) \supset \mathbf{K}(\alpha, \phi) \vee \mathbf{K}(\alpha, \psi)$.

I have already noted that our agent can represent that another agent knows whether or not ϕ, without our agent knowing whether or not ϕ. It uses the expression $\mathbf{K}(\alpha, \phi) \vee \mathbf{K}(\alpha, \neg\phi)$.

23.3.3 Reasoning about Other Agents' Knowledge

Our agent can carry out proofs of some statements about the knowledge of other agents using only the axioms of knowledge, epistemic necessitation, and its own reasoning abilities (*modus ponens*, resolution). I illustrate this process with the so-called Wise–Man puzzle. Suppose there are three wise men who are told by their king that at least one of them has a white spot on his forehead; actually, all three have white spots on their foreheads. I assume that each wise man can see the others' foreheads but not his own, and thus each knows whether the others have white spots. There are various versions of this puzzle, but suppose our agent is told that the first wise man says, "I do not know whether I have a white spot," and that the second wise man then says, "I also do not know whether I have a white spot." I can formulate this puzzle in our logic of knowledge to show that our agent can then prove that the third wise man then knows that he has a white spot.

I show how the reasoning goes by considering the simpler, two–wise–man version of this puzzle. We give the wise men names A and B. The information that we will need is contained in the following assumptions derived from the statement of the puzzle:

1. A and B know that each can see the other's forehead. Thus, for example,

1a. If A does not have a white spot, B will know that A does not have a white spot,

1b. A knows (1a).

2. A and B each know that at least one of them has a white spot, and they each know that the other knows that. In particular,

2a. A knows that B knows that either A or B has a white spot.

3. B says that he does not know whether he has a white spot, and A thereby knows that B does not know.

Statements (1b), (2a), and (3) are written as the first three lines, respectively, of the following proof of $\mathbf{K}(\texttt{A},\texttt{White(A)})$:

1. $\mathbf{K_A}\left[\neg\texttt{White(A)} \supset \mathbf{K_B}(\neg\texttt{White(A)})\right]$
   (given)

2. $\mathbf{K_A}\left[\mathbf{K_B}(\neg\texttt{White(A)} \supset \texttt{White(B)})\right]$
   (given)

3. $\mathbf{K_A}(\neg\mathbf{K_B}(\texttt{White(B)}))$
   (given)

4. $\neg\texttt{White(A)} \supset \mathbf{K_B}(\neg\texttt{White(A)})$
   (1. and axiom 23.3)

5. $\mathbf{K_B}\left[\neg\texttt{White(A)} \supset \texttt{White(B)}\right]$
   (2. and axiom 23.3)

6. $\mathbf{K_B}(\neg\texttt{White(A)}) \supset \mathbf{K_B}(\texttt{White(B)})$
   (5. and axiom 23.2)

7. $\neg\texttt{White(A)} \supset \mathbf{K_B}(\texttt{White(B)})$
   (resolution on the clause forms of 4. and 6.)

8. $\neg\mathbf{K_B}(\texttt{White(B)}) \supset \texttt{White(A)}$
   (contrapositive of 7.)

9. $\mathbf{K_A}\left[\neg\mathbf{K_B}(\texttt{White(B)}) \supset \texttt{White(A)}\right]$
   (1.–5., 8., rule 23.7)

10. $\mathbf{K_A}(\neg\mathbf{K_B}(\texttt{White(B)})) \supset \mathbf{K_A}(\texttt{White(A)})$
    (axiom 23.2)

11. $\mathbf{K}_A(\texttt{White(A)})$

   (*modus ponens* using 3. and 10.)

To derive line 9 in the proof, we use rule 23.7 to justify stating that A believes a consequence of a proof (line 8) from premises (lines 4 and 5) when it believes those premises (lines 1 and 2).

   In the three–wise–man version, there is another level of nested reasoning, but the basic strategy is the same. In fact, we can solve the k–wise–man puzzle (for arbitrary k) assuming that each of the first $(k-1)$ wise men claims that he does not know whether or not he has a white spot.

   Various combinations of axioms 23.2 through 23.5, with the axioms of ordinary propositional logic, the ordinary inference rules, and rule 23.6, constitute what we will call the *modal logics of knowledge*. Logicians have given special names to various modal–logic systems—each having somewhat different axiom schemes. For a fixed agent A, axioms 23.2 through 23.5 are the axioms of a system of modal logic called $S5$. If we left out axiom 23.5, we would have the system $S4$. If we left out axioms 23.4 and 23.5, we would have *system T*. If we left out axioms 23.3, 23.4, and 23.5, we would have *system K*.

23.3.4 Predicting Actions of Other Agents

In order to predict what another agent, $A1$, might do, our agent must have a model of $A1$. If $A1$ is not too complex, then one possibility is for our agent to assume that $A1$'s actions are controlled by a T–R program. (Perhaps our agent used a learning procedure to induce a T–R program that accounts acceptably well for $A1$'s past actions.) Suppose the conditions in that program are γ_i, for $i = 1, \ldots, k$. Now to predict $A1$'s future actions, our agent needs to be able to reason about how $A1$ will evaluate these conditions. We will see in the next chapter that it is often appropriate for our agent to take an intentional stance toward $A1$ and attempt to establish whether or not $\mathbf{K}_{A1}(\gamma_i)$ for $i = 1, \ldots, k$.

23.4 *Additional Readings and Discussion*

[Shoham 1993] has incorporated the idea of reasoning about the goals and plans of other agents into his high–level approach to distributed systems that uses what he calls "agent–oriented programming."

   Minsky's *Society of Mind* [Minsky 1986] proposes that even agents that we think of as unitary (such as ourselves) are, in reality, made up of hundreds of simpler agents acting in a heterarchy. (For reviews of this book and a response by Minsky, see *Artificial Intelligence*, vol. 59, 1991.)

   A modal logic of knowledge was first proposed by [Hintikka 1962]. Possible-worlds semantics for modal logics was invented by [Kripke 1963]. [Moore 1985b] axiomatized the possible-worlds semantics entirely within first-order logic and used this formalization to investigate the interactions between knowledge and action. Logics of knowledge are called *epistemic logics*. There are also logics of belief (*doxastic logics*), of obligation (*deontic logics*), and of other modalities. Specialized ways of handling belief (as opposed to knowledge) have been investigated by [Levesque 1984b, Fagin & Halpern 1985, Konolige 1986]. [Cohen & Levesque 1990] use a modal logic to investigate the relationship between intention and commitment.

[Moore 1985a, Moore 1993] point out that the metalevel activity of reasoning about one's own knowledge, *autoepistemic reasoning*, is a form of nonmonotonic reasoning.

Many important DAI papers are collected in [Bond & Gasser 1988], and current research is reported in the Proceedings of the International Conferences on Multi-Agent Systems. Work on reasoning about knowledge is reported in the Proceedings of the Workshops on Theoretical Aspects of Reasoning about Knowledge (TARK).

Exercises

23.1 Prove that one cannot know both P and ¬P using instances of the knowledge axioms.

23.2 The formula schema $\neg\mathbf{K}_\alpha\neg(\mathbf{K}_\alpha(\phi)) \supset \phi$ is known as the *Brouwer axiom*. Prove it (using resolution refutation and the knowledge axioms).

23.3 Suppose we are given the following sentences:

1. $\mathbf{K}_J(\mathbf{K}_S(P) \vee \mathbf{K}_S(Q))$
   (John knows that Sam knows P or that Sam knows Q.)
2. $\mathbf{K}_J(\mathbf{K}_S(P \supset R))$
   (John knows that Sam knows P ⊃ R.)
3. $\mathbf{K}_J(\mathbf{K}_S(\neg R))$
   (John knows that Sam knows ¬R.)

Prove $\mathbf{K}_J(\mathbf{K}_S(Q))$.

23.4 Various axiom schemas for knowledge were given on page 414ff. Examine each of these, and discuss whether or not they would also be appropriate for *belief* and under what conditions. For example, would the following axiom schema be appropriate?

$$[\mathbf{B}_\alpha(\phi) \wedge \mathbf{B}_\alpha(\phi \supset \psi)] \supset \mathbf{B}_\alpha(\psi)$$

Propose any other axioms that you think would be appropriate for belief (as contrasted with knowledge). Can belief be defined in terms of knowledge (or vice versa)?

23.5 I stated on page 413 that an expression like $(\exists x)\mathbf{K}(\text{Agent1}, \text{On}(x, B))$ is not a legal wff. Yet, how else would we say that Agent1 knows of a certain object that it is on B (without our knowing what object that was)? (Note that the intended meaning of the expression $\mathbf{K}(\text{Agent1}, (\exists x)\text{On}(x, B))$ is that Agent1 knows that some object is on B but that Agent1 might not know what object that was.) Describe some of the difficulties of admitting an expression like $(\exists x)\mathbf{K}(\text{Agent1}, \text{On}(x, B))$ as a wff.

24 Communication among Agents

Speech Acts

There are two classes of methods by which our agent can intentionally influence the actions of another agent. Suppose our agent knows how the other agent will react to perceived changes in its environment. Then, our agent can act to make whatever environmental changes it predicts will evoke desired behavior. For example, our agent could put a block in front of another agent that our agent knows reactively stacks blocks.

Or our agent can attempt to change the other agent's goals, knowledge (or beliefs), or action–selection mechanisms. It could do that most straightforwardly by "writing" directly on these elements of the other agent's cognitive structure. This method might be used, for example, by a human user (our "agent") to control an agent possessing this kind of interface channel. More interestingly, our agent could communicate with the other agent in such a way as to cause the other agent to make changes in its beliefs and/or goals (which may eventually cause the other agent to take the desired actions). The communication medium will depend on the other agent's sensory and perceptual apparatus. Possibilities include, for example, "writing" (based on the other agent's visual abilities), "sounds" (based on the other agent's aural abilities), or "radio" (based on the other agent's electromagnetic reception abilities). When an agent takes such an action, intended to affect another agent's cognitive structure, we say that it has engaged in a *communicative act*.

Communicative acts among humans often involve spoken language (using the medium of acoustic waves). Thus, language theorists have come to call all types of communicative acts *speech acts*. They call the human or agent taking the action the *speaker* and the human or agent at whom the act is directed the *hearer*.

These terms are used whether or not speech itself is actually used. According to the philosopher John Searle [Searle 1969], who was the first to develop the underlying theory, there are several categories of speech acts: *representatives* (those that state a proposition), *directives* (that request or command), *commissives* (that promise or threaten), *expressives* (that thank or apologize), and *declarations* (that actually change the state of the world, such as "I now pronounce you husband and wife").

Speech acts can have various physical manifestations; they can be a sequence of physical motions (as in sign language), a string of symbols (as in text), an acoustic disturbance (squeals, speech), or flashing lights. The manifestation of a speech act is called an *utterance*—regardless of its form. As noted by Searle, the utterance must both express the propositional content and the type of the speech act that it manifests. For example, if written English text is the medium, then the utterance put block A on block B expresses both its nature as a request and its propositional content, namely, On(A,B). (Such an utterance would be intended by the speaker to change the goal structure of the hearer.)

Speech acts are presumed to have an effect on the hearer's knowledge. If our agent, say, *A*1, commits a *representative* speech act informing a hearer, *A*2, that a proposition denoted by ϕ is true, then *A*1 can assume that the effect of this speech act is that *A*2 *knows* that *A*1 *intended* to *inform* *A*2 that ϕ. I have not described how *A*2 might represent knowledge of this intention nor how *A*1 might represent the knowledge that *A*2 knows about the intention. Representations of goals and intentions to inform involve a bit more apparatus than I am prepared to present in this book. Fortunately, I can finesse the problem by talking instead about what effect *A*1 intends such a speech act to have on *A*2; *A*1 wants the effect of its speech act to be that *A*2 believes ϕ. The effect on the hearer intended by the speaker is called the *perlocutionary* effect of the speech act—as contrasted with its *illocutionary* effect, which is the effect the speech act actually has. Of course, the realization of the perlocutionary effect is entirely under the control of the hearer and can be presumed only if either the hearer is extremely credulous or the hearer believes the speaker to be trustworthy. Returning to my example, I can simplify our discussion by assuming that *A*1 presumes its act (informing *A*2 that ϕ) has its perlocutionary effect. We assume that *A*1 represents that effect on *A*2 by the formula $\mathbf{K}(A2, \phi)$.

When humans use language, the perlocutionary (intended) effect of a sentence that appears to be of one type is sometimes actually of another. For example, in the sentence You left the refrigerator door open, the speaker is actually intending to request the hearer to close the refrigerator. Speech acts whose perlocutionary effects are different from what they appear to be are called *indirect speech acts*. A speaker using an indirect speech act presumes that a hearer can infer the speaker's goal from the context of the situation and will use that goal to decide on the perlocutionary effect of the speech act. Thus, Do you have the time? is an indirect (and thus presumably more polite) way of asking the hearer to tell the speaker the time and not a request for whether or not the hearer knows the time.

24.1.1   Planning Speech Acts

We can treat speech acts just like other agent actions. Our agent can use a plan–generating system to make plans comprising speech acts and other actions. To do so, it needs a model of the effects of these actions. Consider, for example, $\text{Tell}(\alpha, \phi)$, a representative–type speech act in which our agent informs agent α that ϕ is true. We could model the effects of that action by the STRIPS rule:

$\text{Tell}(\alpha, \phi)$

$\quad PC : \text{Next\_to}(\alpha) \wedge \phi \wedge \neg\mathbf{K}(\alpha, \phi)$

$\quad D : \neg\mathbf{K}(\alpha, \phi)$

$\quad A : \mathbf{K}(\alpha, \phi)$

The precondition $\text{Next\_to}(\alpha)$ ensures that our agent is sufficiently close to agent α to enable reliable communication; the precondition ϕ is imposed to ensure that our agent actually believes ϕ before it can inform another agent of that fact; and the precondition $\neg\mathbf{K}(\alpha, \phi)$ ensures that our agent does not communicate redundant information. We assume that the action has its perlocutionary effect, namely, that α knows ϕ. Suppose our agent has the blocks–world goal On(B, F1) in a situation in which $\text{On(A, B)} \wedge \text{On(B, C)} \wedge \text{On(C, F1)}$. Further suppose that our agent knows that whenever agent $A1$ knows that block B is clear and on block C, agent $A1$ reactively moves block B to the floor. Using the usual blocks–world STRIPS rules and the preceding rule for Tell, our agent constructs the plan $\{\text{Move(A, B, F1)}, \text{Tell(A1, Clear(B)} \wedge \text{On(B, C))}\}$.

24.1.2   Implementing Speech Acts

The implementation or physical manifestation of a speech act is the utterance, and I must now discuss how a communicative act, like $\text{Tell}(\alpha, \phi)$, is actually transmitted as an utterance from a speaker to a hearer. I consider two possibilities: (a) direct transmission of a logical formula from speaker to hearer, and (b) transmission by the speaker of some string of symbols that the hearer then translates into its cognitive structure (perhaps into a logical formula).[1]

If the speaker and hearer share the same kind of feature–based model of the world, using logical formulas composed of identical symbols, then a speech act can be implemented by transmitting a logical formula (plus information about what type of speech act is being sent). In that case, for example, the speech act

---

1. Symbol strings are just one example of what might be transmitted; humans also use diagrams, pictures, and other media to transmit information to other humans.

Tell(A1, Clear(B) ∧ On(B, C)) could be implemented by having our agent send $A1$ the formula Clear(B) ∧ On(B, C) along with an indication that a representative-type speech act is being sent. Notice that doing so presumes that the formula Clear(B) ∧ On(B, C) means the same thing to $A1$ that it does to our agent. (Recall that the phrase "means the same thing" implies that the logical models for our agent and for $A1$ of that formula along with all the other formulas in their databases are substantially the same.) Even in cases where we are building and programming all of the agents (ours and the other agents), the assumption of identical knowledge–representation vocabularies is very strong—implausible in interesting situations. Even when the knowledge–representation vocabularies and models of two agents start out identical, if the agents encounter any new objects, for example, there is little likelihood that they will give them the same internal names. If the agents are able to invent new predicates, defined in terms of more primitive ones, even equivalent new predicates may have different symbols. And just because our agent takes an intentional stance toward another agent, it may not be the case that the other agent encodes its model of the world using logical formulas.

Given these limitations, how is communication among agents possible? One answer involves the second of the two alternatives mentioned earlier: using an agreed–upon, common communication language. Through design, usage, and instruction, communicating agents learn how strings of symbols transmitted in this common language change the cognitive structures of other agents. Taking an intentional stance, our agent can predict, for example, that if it transmits to agent $A1$ the string[2] block B is on block C and block B is clear, the (perlocutionary) effect on $A1$'s cognitive structure can be described by the formula **K**(A1, On(B, C) ∧ Clear(B)) in our agent's knowledge base (regardless of how $A1$ actually represents that knowledge). In this example, our agent executes the speech act Tell(A1, On(B, C) ∧ Clear(B)) by sending the utterance block B is on block C and block B is clear. The hearer translates the utterance into whatever internal form it uses to represent this knowledge. Of course, since presumably we are designing these agents, we can make any selection we would like for a common communication language. We might invent an English–like language, as in the example, if our agents also needed to communicate with humans in something like English.

The use of languages based on symbol strings presupposes solutions to two problems: how to generate a symbol string given a speech act, and how to translate a symbol string into an effect on cognitive structure. Although I have motivated the use of symbol strings as a communication medium among artificial agents, machine generation and understanding of *natural* languages—languages that humans speak and write, such as English, French, and Chinese—are of inde-

---

2. My convention is to use sans serif font for communicative symbol strings.

pendent interest. Also, both the generation and understanding of symbol strings for communication have been mainly studied in the context of natural languages. For these reasons, my treatment of communication among agents via strings will focus on utterances of English–like sentences. Natural language processing, generation and understanding, is extremely difficult, and only limited progress has so far been achieved. Human–level competence no doubt presupposes solutions to a number of AI problems, as we shall see in the next section. Nevertheless, some applications are already possible. I give a brief summary of some of the major techniques used by language understanding systems in the next section. (I omit a discussion of language generation. Anyone interested might see [Appelt 1985, Sadek, et al. 1996] for treatments of the use of planning and reasoning to generate natural language sentences, [McKeown & Swartout 1987] for a review of techniques, and [McDonald & Bolc 1988] for a textbook on the subject. Several commercial computer interface systems have some limited abilities to generate text and speech.)

24.2 *Understanding Language Strings*

I next consider how a string of symbols, transmitted by a speaker who intends the string to convey a certain proposition, can be translated by a hearer into a formula denoting (we hope) the same proposition. Some (but not all!) of the information needed by this translation process is embedded in the syntactic properties of the string. For example, an English speaker would intend the string block B is on block C to be translated as On(B,C) and not as On(C,B). These syntactic properties are most conveniently described by grammars that not only delimit which strings are legal sentences of the language but also define the structure of sentences. My examples illustrating these ideas will use a simple "proto-English" that simultaneously serves as an example of a not–too–improbable agent language and as a first step toward an introduction to the technology of natural language understanding.

24.2.1 Phrase–Structure Grammars

Phrase–structure grammars define how the basic components of symbol strings, the symbols themselves, can be aggregated into *phrases*, and how these phrases can themselves be aggregated finally into *sentences*. The way in which a sentence is broken down into its component phrases, terminating in the symbols of the string, defines the *structure* of a sentence. This structure is key to translating the sentence into a logical formula. The components of the language are *terminal symbols* and *nonterminals*. The highest–level nonterminal is the sentence, represented by the symbol *S*. Each nonterminal can be defined as a sequence of other symbols, either nonterminal ones or terminal ones or both. In so–called *context-free* grammars, the definition of a nonterminal symbol is independent of the symbols surrounding it in a string. I illustrate with a sample context–free grammar appropriate for limited communication about the blocks world.

A sentence, *S*, is defined to be a noun phrase (*NP*) followed by a verb phrase (*VP*). This definition is denoted by the rule

$$S \leftarrow NP \, VP$$

We might also want to allow a sentence to be composed, recursively, of a sentence followed by a conjunction (*Conj*) followed by another sentence:

$$S \leftarrow S \, Conj \, S$$

These two rules can be written in the shorthand notation (called *Backus-Naur form* (*BNF*)):

$$S \leftarrow NP \, VP \mid S \, Conj \, S$$

where the | is read as "or."

Now we must define the nonterminal symbols, *NP*, *VP*, and *Conj*, that we have just introduced. Some of these nonterminals will be defined in terms of additional nonterminals, and so on until all definitions bottom out in terminal symbols. A conjunction is defined to be either the terminal symbol and or the terminal symbol or:

$$Conj \leftarrow \text{and} \mid \text{or}$$

A noun phrase is defined to be either a noun (*N*) or an adjective (*Adj*) followed by a noun:

$$NP \leftarrow N \mid Adj \, N$$

For our simple three–block world, a noun is one of the terminal symbols A, B, C, or floor (the commonly agreed–upon names of the entities in the blocks world). We also allow the terminal nouns block A, block B, and block C.[3] These definitions can be denoted by the rule

$$N \leftarrow \text{A} \mid \text{B} \mid \text{C} \mid \text{block A} \mid \text{block B} \mid \text{block C} \mid \text{floor}$$

We have the following definition for an adjective:

$$Adj \leftarrow \text{clear} \mid \text{empty} \mid \text{occupied}$$

---

3. Technically, the combination block with A is called a *noun-noun combination*. We simplify the discussion by treating them simply as additional nouns.

S ← *NP VP* | *S Conj S*
Conj ← and | or
NP ← *N* | *Adj N*
N ← A | B | C | block A | block B | block C | floor
Adj ← clear | empty | occupied
VP ← is *Adj* | is *PP*
PP ← *Prep NP*
Prep ← on | above | below

Table 24.1

A Grammar for Blocks–World Communication

A verb phrase is defined as follows:

VP ← is *Adj* | is *PP*

Finally, prepositional phrases (*PP*) and prepositions (*Prep*) are defined

PP ← *Prep NP*

Prep ← on | above | below

For convenience, I collect all of these rules together in Table 24.1. In natural language processing systems, the terminal symbols are all of the individual words in the language. These are stored in a database called a *lexicon*.

The structure of sentences that are allowed by grammar rules such as these can conveniently be displayed as trees. For example, the structure of the sentence block B is on block C and block B is clear is shown in Figure 24.1. In a completed structure, each nonleaf node is labeled by a nonterminal symbol and has descendants given by one of the grammar rules. Each leaf node is labeled by a terminal symbol. Nodes labeled by nonterminal symbols are box shaped; nodes labeled by terminal symbols are circular.

Using the grammar, we can determine that the following strings are legal sentences:[4]

block C is occupied

A is on C

B is on occupied C

occupied B is on clear C

---

4. For simplicity, I ignore here matters of capitalization and punctuation, although grammars incorporating these features could be written.

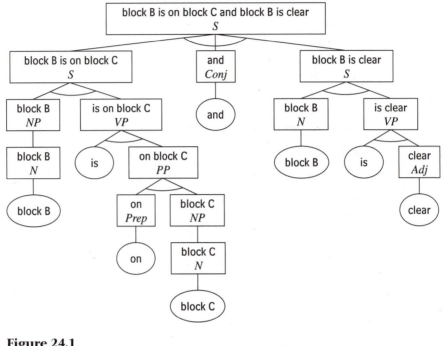

Figure 24.1

The Structure of a Sentence

Deciding whether or not an arbitrary string of symbols is a legal sentence is called *parsing* the string, and the parsing process is called *syntactic analysis*. Various parsing algorithms exist. In a *top-down* algorithm, grammar rules are applied (in a "backward" direction) to the nonterminal symbol *S*, rewriting it in terms of its component phrases, until a set of terminals is produced that match the given string. You will recognize that this process searches through a space of AND/OR trees until it finds a solution tree. (The tree shown in Figure 24.1 is such a solution tree.) In a *bottom-up* algorithm, substrings of the string being analyzed are replaced by nonterminal symbols, and these nonterminal symbols are themselves replaced by other nonterminal symbols (all according to the grammar rules), until the single nonterminal symbol, *S*, is produced. For search efficiency, this process usually proceeds in left-to-right fashion along the string. You will recognize that this process can be implemented by a depth–first, backtracking search.

24.2.2 Semantic Analysis

Recall that the purpose of transmitting a string of symbols is that it be translated by a hearer into a logical formula. I have already mentioned that the grammatical structure of the string reveals much about its intended meaning. I describe here a method by which a translation into a logical formula is a side effect of the parsing process itself. This added benefit is achieved by associating components of logical formulas with each phrase of a sentence. Each rule in the phrase-structure grammar specifies how the formula component associated with a given phrase is composed from the formula components associated with the constituent subphrases. For example, the rule

$PP \leftarrow Prep\ NP$

must specify the semantic association for *PP* in terms of the semantic associations for *Prep* and *NP*. These semantic associations are indicated by expressing each nonterminal symbol as a functional expression, taking the semantic association as the argument; for example, *PP(sem)*.

At the conclusion of parsing, the formula associated with the nonterminal symbol *S* is then taken to be the *meaning* of the string. With these associations, the grammar is called an *augmented phrase-structure grammar*, and the parsing process accomplishes what is called a *semantic analysis* (as well as the usual syntactic analysis).

I illustrate this process by augmenting our sample phrase-structure grammar and carrying out a semantic analysis for the sample sentence already parsed. I begin by associating logical constructs with each of the terminal symbols. Let's start with those terminal symbols that the grammar rules classify as nouns. Intuitively, nouns should be associated with object constants in the predicate calculus. For our sample grammar, this association is accomplished by writing the rule $N \leftarrow$ A | B | C | block A | block B | block C | floor as follows:

A $\rightarrow$ *Noun*(E(A))

B $\rightarrow$ *Noun*(E(B))

C $\rightarrow$ *Noun*(E(C))

block A $\rightarrow$ *Noun*(Block(A))

block B $\rightarrow$ *Noun*(Block(B))

block C $\rightarrow$ *Noun*(Block(C))

floor $\rightarrow$ *Noun*(Floor(Fl))

The first of these rules, for example, states that the semantic component to be associated with the noun "A" is the atom, E(A). (The intended meaning of E(A) is that the object denoted by A is an "entity.") In parsing, the rule states that an occurrence of the terminal symbol A in a symbol string can be rewritten as *Noun*(E(A)). (Note carefully the use of typographic conventions in these rules: sans serif font for terminal symbols in the proto-English communication language, *italic* font for the names of nonterminal symbols in our grammar, and typewriter font for predicate-calculus expressions.) We write the rule in left-to-right fashion (with a right–going arrow) because the rules are meant to be applied "bottom up"—replacing terminal symbols by the formula on the right–hand side of the arrow.

If we perform the replacements indicated by some of these rules in our sample sentence, we obtain the following partially analyzed sentence:

Noun(Block(B)) is on *Noun*(Block(C)) and *Noun*(Block(B)) is clear

Next, let's write augmented rules for the terminals and and or:

and → *Conj*(∧)

or → *Conj*(∨)

Applying the rule for and yields

Noun(Block(B)) is on *Noun*(Block(C)) *Conj*(∧) *Noun*(Block(B)) is clear

The formula components associated with the other terminal symbols are not quite so straightforward. The adjectives, clear, empty, and occupied, all state a property of some object, so they should introduce predicate–calculus atoms using appropriate relation constants and object constants. But at the time we replace these adjectives, we might not know about which object they are stating a property. Thus, the adjective, clear, for example, would have a rule something like

clear → *Adj*(Clear(x))

The expression Clear(x) is to be interpreted as a predicate–calculus *form* that needs to be *applied* to some object constant in order to produce a predicate–calculus formula. As is done elsewhere in computer science, we use what are called *lambda expressions* to define such forms. Thus, a more precise statement of the adjective rule for clear is

clear → *Adj*(λx Clear(x))

Here we see that the "meaning" of a phrase is sometimes expressed as something that operates on the meaning of another phrase. If we were to apply the form to the object constant B, for example, we would get

(λx Clear(x))B = Clear(B)

Applying the rule for clear to our partially interpreted sentence yields

Noun(Block(B)) is on *Noun*(Block(C)) *Conj*(∧) *Noun*(Block(B)) is *Adj*(λx Clear(x))

(We would have similar rules for the other adjectives.)

Before giving rules involving the other terminal symbols, let's move to a nonterminal—noun phrases. First, a noun is a noun phrase (with no change in semantics):

$Noun(\phi(\sigma)) \rightarrow NP(\phi(\sigma))$

where $\phi(\sigma)$ is any unary atom (with schema variable σ). Applying this rule yields

$NP(\texttt{Block(B)})$ is on $NP(\texttt{Block(C)})$ $Conj(\wedge)$ $NP(\texttt{Block(B)})$ is $Adj(\lambda x Clear(x))$

A noun phrase is also an adjective followed by a noun phrase. We don't need that rule to parse our sample sentence, so I give it later in a summary table.

In our sample grammar, we have only one verb, namely, is. It is always used either with an adjective or with a prepositional phrase. When used with an adjective, we have the rule

is $Adj(\lambda x \; \phi(x)) \rightarrow VP(\lambda x \; \phi(x))$

where, in this rule, ϕ is any unary relation constant denoting the property associated with the adjective. (The word is in this simple language adds no additional semantic content.)

Before giving the other rule for a verb phrase, I show how a noun phrase is combined with a verb phrase to produce a sentence:

$NP(\phi(\sigma))VP(\lambda x \; \psi(x)) \rightarrow S((\lambda x \; \psi(x) \wedge \phi(\sigma))\sigma)$

where, here, ψ is any relation constant (in our grammar it can be of any arity) whose single lambda variable, x, is bound when the lambda expression is applied. Here we have our first instance of combining the semantics of two constituent phrases. The combination is achieved by applying a lambda expression derived from the verb phrase to the object constant contributed by the noun phrase. This application can be done before parsing takes place to yield the condensed rule

$NP(\phi(\sigma))VP(\lambda x \; \psi(x)) \rightarrow S(\psi(\sigma) \wedge \phi(\sigma))$

Applying these rules yields, successively,

$NP(\texttt{Block(B)})$ is on $NP(\texttt{Block(C)})$ $Conj(\wedge)$ $NP(\texttt{Block(B)})$ $VP(\lambda x Clear(x))$

$NP(\texttt{Block(B)})$ is on $NP(\texttt{Block(C)})$ $Conj(\wedge)$ $S(\texttt{Clear(B)} \wedge \texttt{Block(B)})$

Next, we deal with prepositions and prepositional phrases:

on $\rightarrow Prep(\lambda xy \; On(x, y))$

(Note that on introduces a two–place predicate. The lambda notation keeps track of which variable is which.)

$Prep(\lambda xy \; \psi(x, y))NP(\phi(\sigma)) \rightarrow PP(\lambda x \; (\lambda y \; \psi(x, y) \wedge \phi(\sigma))\sigma)$

which can be reduced to

$$Prep(\lambda xy \ \psi(x, y))NP(\phi(\sigma)) \rightarrow PP(\lambda x \ \psi(x, \sigma) \wedge \phi(\sigma))$$

where ψ is any of the two–place relation constants associated with our prepositions.

The other rule for a verb phrase is

is $PP(\lambda x \ \psi(x, \sigma)) \rightarrow VP(\lambda x \ \psi(x, \sigma))$

(Note that, here, ψ is a binary relation constant with one schema variable σ and one lambda variable, x, to be bound later.) We can apply these rules, together with our earlier rule for S to yield, successively,

$NP(\texttt{Block(B)})$ is $Prep(\lambda xy \ \texttt{On}(x, y)) \ NP(\texttt{Block(C)}) \ Conj(\wedge) \ S(\texttt{Clear(B)} \wedge \texttt{Block(B)})$

$NP(\texttt{Block(B)})$ is $PP(\lambda x \ \texttt{On}(x, \texttt{C})) \wedge (\texttt{Block(C)}) \ Conj(\wedge) \ S(\texttt{Clear(B)} \wedge \texttt{Block(B)})$

$NP(\texttt{Block(B)}) \ VP(\lambda x \ \texttt{On}(x, \texttt{C})) \wedge (\texttt{Block(C)}) \ Conj(\wedge) \ S(\texttt{Clear(B)} \wedge \texttt{Block(B)})$

$S(\texttt{Block(B)} \wedge \texttt{Block(C)} \wedge \texttt{On(B, C)}) \ Conj(\wedge) \ S(\texttt{Clear(B)} \wedge \texttt{Block(B)})$

Finally, we have the rule that conjoins two sentences:

$S(\gamma_1)Conj(\wedge)S(\gamma_2) \rightarrow S(\gamma_1 \wedge \gamma_2)$

Applying this rule, rearranging, and simplifying yields

$S(\texttt{On(B, C)} \wedge \texttt{Clear(B)} \wedge \texttt{Block(B)} \wedge \texttt{Block(C)})$

The semantic parse tree, showing all stages of semantic analysis of this sentence, is shown in Figure 24.2. For clarity, the predicate–calculus formulas are shown adjacent to their corresponding nodes (rather than as arguments of the associated nonterminals). Note how the semantic structure associated with phrases is composed from the semantic structures of subphrases. We say that augmented grammars of this kind have *compositional semantics*. For reference, all of the rules of this grammar are collected in Table 24.2.

24.2.3   **Expanding the Grammar**

Although the grammar shown in Table 24.2 is capable of translating many blocks-world sentences into logical formulas, I constructed it only to illustrate the general idea of this style of semantic analysis. I could add several obvious additional rules without undue complication. For example, I could add other rules for more adjectives (red, heavy, . . .), more prepositions (next to, between, . . .), and more nouns for additional blocks and for agents. The only verb in this language, is, did not play an important role. I could add knows, which would involve translation into a modal form using **K**. Translating other verbs, as in the sentence Sam moves block A from block C to block B, would obligate us to decide how to conceptualize such

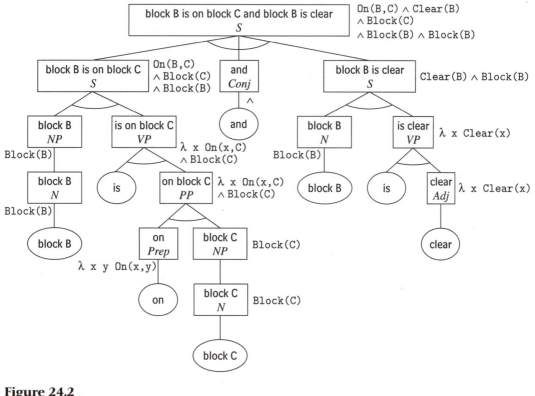

Figure 24.2

A Semantic Parse Tree

actions and how to describe them by logical formulas. Adding tensed verbs (for example, moved) would require translation into a formula capable of describing temporal events.

Sentences containing articles, such as the and a, usually involve translation into quantified formulas. For example, block A is on a block should be translated into $(\exists x)On(A, x)$. English sentences involving words like every, all, and some are often ambiguous regarding quantifier scope. For example, the sentence all blocks are on a block could be translated either as $(\forall x)(\exists y)On(x, y)$ or as $(\exists y)(\forall x)On(x, y)$. Resolving such ambiguities often can be done only by referring to other sources of knowledge—knowledge not contained in the sentence itself. I discuss some of the issues surrounding ambiguities and their resolution in more detail later. Semantic analysis often postpones the resolution of ambiguities by translating first into a special language of *quasi-logical form* [Russell & Norvig 1995, pp. 676ff], which is capable of retaining certain ambiguities rather than translating directly into a formula of first–order logic, which generally does not accommodate ambiguity.

$A \rightarrow Noun(\text{E(A)})$

$B \rightarrow Noun(\text{E(B)})$

$C \rightarrow Noun(\text{E(C)})$

block $A \rightarrow Noun(\text{Block(A)})$

block $B \rightarrow Noun(\text{Block(B)})$

block $C \rightarrow Noun(\text{Block(C)})$

floor $\rightarrow Noun(\text{Floor(Fl)})$

and $\rightarrow Conj(\wedge)$

or $\rightarrow Conj(\vee)$

clear $\rightarrow Adj(\lambda x\ \text{Clear}(x))$

empty $\rightarrow Adj(\lambda x\ \text{Clear}(x))$

occupied $\rightarrow Adj(\lambda x\ \neg\text{Clear}(x))$

on $\rightarrow Prep(\lambda xy\ \text{On}(x, y))$

above $\rightarrow Prep(\lambda xy\ \text{On}(x, y))$

below $\rightarrow Prep(\lambda xy\ \text{On}(y, x))$

is $Adj(\lambda x\ \phi(x)) \rightarrow VP(\lambda x\ \phi(x))$

is $PP(\lambda x\ \psi(x, \sigma)) \rightarrow VP(\lambda x\ \psi(x, \sigma))$

$Prep(\lambda xy\ \psi(x, y))NP(\phi(\sigma)) \rightarrow PP(\lambda x\ \psi(x, \sigma) \wedge \phi(\sigma))$

$Noun(\phi(\sigma)) \rightarrow NP(\phi(\sigma))$

$Adj(\lambda x\ \phi(x))NP(\psi(\sigma)) \rightarrow NP(\phi(\sigma) \wedge \psi(\sigma))$

$NP(\phi(\sigma))VP(\lambda x\ \psi(x)) \rightarrow S(\psi(\sigma) \wedge \phi(\sigma))$

$S(\gamma_1)Conj(\wedge)S(\gamma_2) \rightarrow S(\gamma_1 \wedge \gamma_2)$

Table 24.2

An Augmented Phrase-Structure Grammar

Translation of the quasi-logical form into logic is then done in a separate phase that is able to use additional knowledge to resolve remaining ambiguities.

Sentences in natural languages usually cannot be adequately defined by context-free languages. For example, consider the sentence block A and block B are on block C. A grammar with the context-free rule $S \leftarrow NP\ VP$ that accepted this sentence might also accept block A and block B is on block C because is on block C would be accepted as a legal *VP*. Enforcing singular–plural agreement between subject and verb would either require additional context-free rules defining singular (plural) noun phrases and singular (plural) verb phrases, or it would require some kind of context-sensitive device. Interestingly, the same augmentation technique that allowed associating semantic forms with phrases can also be used to enforce a variety of these context-sensitive restrictions, including those involving number (singular, plural), person (first, second, or third), tense, verb type (transitive or intransitive), and case (subjective, objective). To enforce singular–plural agreement, for example, we add an extra argument, n

(for number), to the appropriate phrase names. Our rule for a sentence would then become $S(n) \leftarrow NP(n) \, VP(n)$, where for simplicity I have omitted the arguments specifying the semantic forms. When this rule is applied, the bindings for the variable n, namely, either s (singular) or p (plural) would have to agree. The binding for n in $VP(n)$ would, in turn, be determined by which of the following rules was used at the bottom of the parse tree: are $\rightarrow Verb(p)$ or is $\rightarrow Verb(s)$. The binding for n in $NP(n)$ would be similarly determined. Grammars that use this mechanism are called *unification grammars* because of the role that unification of terms plays in enforcing agreements among the variables.

24.3   *Efficient Communication*

Substantial efficiency of communication can often be achieved by relying on the hearer to use its own knowledge to help determine the meaning of an utterance. "A word to the wise is sufficient." If a speaker knows that a hearer can figure out what the speaker means, the speaker can send shorter, less self–contained messages. One of the main reasons why it is so difficult for computers to understand natural languages is that understanding requires many sources of knowledge, including knowledge about the context in which communication occurs, and general "commonsense" knowledge shared by the speaker and hearer. In the next subsections, I will briefly touch on these subjects.

24.3.1   Use of Context

If the hearer and speaker share the same context (that is, they both know the situation in which each is speaking and hearing an utterance), then that context can be used as a source of knowledge in determining the meaning of an utterance. Use of context allows the language to have pronouns (such as he and it) and *indexicals* (such as here, now, I, and you). The context can include previous communications, the current environmental situation, or both. For example, consider the utterance block A is clear and it is on block B. The hearer processes the phrase it is on block B in the context of having already heard and understood the phrase block A is clear. In this context, the hearer can assume that it refers to the block already mentioned, namely, block A.[5] The use of the word it in my sample sentence (instead of repeating the words block A) amounts only to a small savings, but lots of similar economies add up to worthwhile increases in efficiency. Of course, to gain this efficiency, the speaker must know that the hearer will be able to (and will) figure out the referent.

---

5. Linguists use the term *anaphora* to describe phrases (including pronouns) that refer to things that have already been mentioned. In general, determining the meaning of anaphoric items is extremely complex; my example is a very special and simple case.

Figure 24.3

Pointing Establishes the Meaning of an Indexical

When a speaker uses the indexical I, a hearer in the same context knows to which person (or machine) the word I refers. For example, if robot R1 says I know that block A is on block B, then a hearer who knows the identity of robot R1 as it is speaking can interpret the utterance as meaning **K**(R1, On(A,B)). Sometimes indexicals like this are used in association with pointing actions. For example, in Figure 24.3, we see a robot pointing to a block and saying this is block B. The hearing robot, seeing the speaking robot pointing to a block, interprets the utterance as implying On(A,B). The speaker makes the utterance because it wants the hearer to know On(A,B) and realizes that the hearer cannot see the label on block *B* but can see the label on block *A* and can see that *A* is on the block pointed to. Again, perhaps a small savings but a contribution to efficient communication.

24.3.2   Use of Knowledge to Resolve Ambiguities

Even if it were possible to design an agent communication language in which propositions could be transmitted and understood in isolation without ambiguity, such unambiguous communication would require unmanageably large vocabularies and overly complex phrasings. People who use natural languages can usually discern the intended meanings of otherwise ambiguous words and phrases by using various sources of knowledge. This ability allows us humans to be more efficient in our use of language and would perhaps confer similar benefits on communicating agents.

Computational linguists have classified several types of ambiguity occurring in natural language utterances. I describe these types using examples from the blocks world and from similar situations in which robots communicate among themselves (and with humans). (The language and semantics used in these examples would be somewhat more complex than that defined in Table 24.2.)

Lexical Ambiguity

The same word can have several different meanings, and the resulting ambiguity is called *lexical*. The sentence robot R1 is <u>hot</u> could mean that R1 is very good at accomplishing its tasks, or it could mean that R1 is overheated. Resolving the ambiguity would require additional knowledge about R1 and the situation in which the sentence occurs.

Syntactic Ambiguity

Sometimes sentences can be parsed in more than one way; that is, phrases can be put together differently. The sentence I saw R1 in room 37 might imply that either (or both) the speaker doing the seeing and R1 were in room 37. If the hearer already knows the referred-to location of either the speaker or R1, the ambiguity can be resolved. (The classic example of this sort is I saw the Grand Canyon flying to New York. The ambiguity in that case is resolved by the commonsense knowledge that people fly but canyons don't.) Different parses can be due to lexical ambiguities; in the sentence clear block A and B and C are on the floor, clear could be either a verb or an adjective. Another classic example of this sort is time flies like an arrow.

Referential Ambiguity

The use of pronouns and other anaphora can cause ambiguity. Processes for resolving such *referential* ambiguity can involve complex reasoning on the part of both the speaker and the hearer. In the sentence block A is on block B and <u>it</u> is not clear, the speaker probably intended that it refer to block *A* instead of to block *B*. The speaker might reasonably assume that the hearer would use commonsense knowledge to deduce ¬Clear(B) from the phrase block A is on block B and therefore would also conclude that it in the phrase it is not clear refers to block *A* (because speakers do not usually send redundant information).

Pragmatic Ambiguity

The processes for using knowledge of context and other knowledge for resolving ambiguities is usually called *pragmatic analysis* (to contrast these processes with syntactic and semantic analyses). But, of course, if a hearer's commonsense knowledge and knowledge about context is uncertain, even pragmatic analysis can fail to resolve all ambiguities. In the sentence R1 is in the room with R2, the meaning of the phrase the room would be ambiguous if the hearer thought that R2 was either in room 37 or room 38, but didn't know which.

24.4 Natural Language Processing

My example of agent communication in the blocks world displays just a small fraction of what would be needed in a system that could understand sentences spoken (or written) by a human. The subject of natural language processing (NLP) is an immense field with many potential applications, including translation from one language into another, retrieval of information from databases, human/computer interaction, and automatic dictation. Language–competent computer systems would be able to understand and generate written and spoken sentences either as text (that is, strings of sentences) or in interactive conversation. The field is far from being able to achieve these goals, although there are research systems and some commercial products with limited capabilities.

NLP has been described as "AI–hard" (in analogy with NP–hard). That is, to produce a system as competent with language as a human is would require solving "the AI problem." Much of the difficulty lies in resolving pragmatic ambiguities, which seems to require reasoning over a large commonsense knowledge base. Of course, there are also major issues involved in building lexicons, grammars, and parsing systems adequate to handle natural languages.

Almost any sentence taken from text or conversation can be used to illustrate the problems. Let's see what a language–understanding system needs to do in order to analyze a sentence taken from conversation. (I touch on just a few of the problems!) Consider the following piece of conversation between a professor and a graduate student:

P: Well, I'll need to see your printout.

S: I can't unlock the door to the small computer room to get it.

P: Here's the key.

How would a computer system analyze the student's sentence? Many NLP systems are organized as a sequence of steps. First, the sentence is translated into a logical form, using a grammar with semantic composition rules and a lexicon. Here are just some of the problems illustrated by the sentence at this level of processing:

- The lexicon may contain roots of words, such as lock, with their various meanings. It also needs to have information about how prefixes and suffixes can be attached to roots and how these attachments affect meaning (*morphological analysis*).

- The grammar and semantic analysis needs to be able to handle a much wider variety of parts of speech than did our simple blocks–world grammar. Adverbs, such as quickly, change the meaning of the verb they modify. Consider, for example, an adjective, such as small, whose meaning might vary depending on what noun the adjective modifies. A small room might be bigger than a large computer.

- The phrase the small computer room might mean the small room in which there are computers or the room in which small computers are kept. In order to postpone resolving this ambiguity until later, the system might produce either a logical form that retains the ambiguity or two different logical forms.

- The system needs to be able to find the referents to I and to it. I is probably easily determined to refer to the speaker. At this level of analysis, it could refer to the door, the room, or something (yet to be determined) mentioned in previous discourse. Again, resolving the ambiguity should probably be postponed.

- Interpreting the word can't, a contraction of cannot, requires the ability to handle negations. In this case, the system also needs to be able to note that can might mean either physically able to or permitted to.

After the alternative logical forms are produced, the system reasons with general world knowledge to resolve some of the ambiguities. Here, it can be decided that it must refer to something in previous discourse because it is unlikely that the speaker would be trying to "get" a door or a room. Also, can probably means physically able to because unlocking a door requires a key and keys are things that people often do not have.

The system also uses world knowledge specific to the present environment to decipher the phrase small computer room. Suppose the system knows that all of the rooms designated as computer rooms contain small computers, and that just one of these rooms is a small one, room 246, say. Thus small computer room must refer to room 246.

Final analysis of this sentence requires knowledge of the discourse and the ability to reason about the intentions of the speaker. The professor asked for a printout, so it must refer to that. The chain of reasoning here is rather complex. The request for a printout sets up a goal for the student, and it can be presumed that the student makes a plan to achieve that goal. Construction of the plan falters when the student realizes he doesn't have a key to the room containing the printout. The sentence is about the reason the student cannot achieve the goal, and the system must interpret it as such. Further, the system needs to decide whether the student's utterance is an attempt to negotiate a change in goal ("Let's not even bother about my trying to get the printout because I don't have a key and maybe you (the professor) don't really need the printout") or is (indirectly) a request for the key to a specific room (which key the student knows the professor has) so that the student can produce an executable plan to achieve the goal. The indirect request for the key also contains the reason why the key is needed—a reason the student assumes the professor would need to have in order to be persuaded to give the student the key.

Methods for performing all of this reasoning, and for representing the knowledge being reasoned about, are still frontier research topics for artificial intelligence. Thus, computer understanding of discourse like that of our example is, indeed, AI-hard. The problem is further complicated by the fact that these difficult aspects of language understanding must probably be combined with some reactive-type processes. For example, the student in the preceding situation might have simply uttered the ungrammatical Key? instead of the longer sentence. The professor would probably have responded by handing over the key to the appropriate computer room—very little parsing as such would have been needed! But such a response would have required the professor to decide which key to hand over, and it is unclear whether complex reasoning would be needed to make that decision or simply context-dependent reactive processes.

Natural language processing, including speech and text generation and understanding, is a field that overlaps and depends upon AI but also has its own traditions and techniques. I have only brushed lightly against part of the subject here. Those interested in more details might begin with [Russell & Norvig 1995, Ch. 22 and 23] and [Allen 1995, Grosz, Sparck Jones, & Webber 1986]. (Also see the special issue devoted to NLP of the journal *Artificial Intelligence*, vol. 63, nos. 1–2, October 1993.)

24.5 *Additional Readings and Discussion*

[Cohen & Perrault 1979] describe how speech acts can be planned using AI planning systems. In order that a speech act achieves its perlocutionary effect (that is, its speaker-intended effect), a hearer must sometimes be able to guess at the overall plan of the speaker by observing a sequence of the speaker's actions. [Kautz 1991] reviews this problem and presents a formal theory of plan recognition and its implementation.

The foundational work on language syntax and parsing is that of [Chomsky 1965]. My treatment of syntactic and semantic processing of word strings is loosely based on definite clause grammars originally developed by [Pereira & Warren 1980]. There are many other grammar formalisms, including the augmented transition networks (ATNs) of [Woods 1970]. A typical large grammar for English is that used in SRI International's TEAM system TEAM [Grosz, et al. 1987].

[Magerman 1993] describes statistical methods for learning grammars, and [Charniak 1993] generalizes the notion of a grammar to one that has probabilities associated with the rules.

[Grosz, Sparck Jones, & Webber 1986] and [Waibel & Lee 1990] are collections of important papers on natural language processing and on speech recognition, respectively.

Contrasting with language-understanding approaches, vector-based comparisons between the word-frequency statistics of text documents can often be used to classify documents into meaningful categories based on content [Masand, Linoff, & Waltz 1992, Stanfill & Waltz 1986].

Exercises

24.1 Can you think of a situation in which it would be helpful for an agent to utter a `tell` speech act in which the propositional content of the act is known by the uttering agent not to be true?

24.2 Use the grammar given on page 434 (Table 24.2) (the semantic one) to produce a semantic analysis of the sentence

block B is on floor or block B is on C

24.3 How would you modify the grammar on page 434 (Table 24.2) to include the word not so that not could be used with adjectives (as in not clear) or with prepositions (as in not on) ?

24.4 Discuss in two or three short paragraphs the major similarities in the problems of natural language understanding and scene analysis.

24.5 Robot *A* has the vocabulary and semantic grammar shown on page 434 (Table 24.2). Explain how robot *A* might set up block situations and make utterances in such a way that a perceptive robot *B* could induce the appropriate grammar. (Hint: Start by having robot *A* point to block *B* and simultaneously uttering B, etc.) What do you have to assume about robot *B*'s abilities?

25 Agent Architectures

I have followed an agent–oriented presentation of the subject matter of artificial intelligence. Although mainly adhering to the agent theme, I have also stressed that the technologies used to build intelligent agents also find other applications: in image classification and analysis, in expert consulting and reasoning systems, in scheduling and planning, and in natural language processing systems, to name just a few. Often, I have assumed that the agents under discussion were robots, but many of the ideas apply to nonphysical agents as well. In this final chapter, I speculate about how the various AI techniques might be integrated in intelligent agent architectures.

But first we must ask, can anything at all be said about intelligent agent architectures in general? Just as there are millions of species of animals, occupying millions of different niches, I expect that, similarly, there will be many, many species of artificial agents—performing the countless tasks that we humans will want them to do. The exact forms of their architectures will depend on their tasks and on the environments in which they perform these tasks. For example, some will work in time–stressed situations in which reactions to unpredictable and changing environmental states must be fast and unequivocal. Others will have the time and the knowledge to predict the effects of future courses of action so that more rational choices can be made.

Some of these agents will be more complex and intelligent than others, of course. So perhaps we can focus our discussion of agent architectures on those agents that require all of the abilities discussed in this book: built-in reactions; iconic and feature–based memory structures; search techniques; reasoning, planning, and communicating. Can we hope that there will be an ideal architecture for agents that possess what might be called "human-level" intelligence?

Probably not. Even humans are born with or trained into a large number of different styles. Some think in pictures, some in symbols, some in sounds; some are impetuous, some deliberate; some want details, some the big picture; some adapt easily to new situations, some are rigid; and on and on. Although we all run on pretty much the same "wetware," our cognitive architectures might be quite different.

Given my belief that there is probably not a single, ideal, intelligent agent architecture, I will proceed by discussing some "reference" ones with which I am most familiar and which I think are at least illustrative of the range of possibilities. You should understand, though, that several others have been proposed and used.

25.1   *Three-Level Architectures*

One of the first integrated intelligent agent systems was a collection of computer programs and hardware known as "Shakey the Robot" [Nilsson 1984b]. Shakey already used many of the techniques described in this book—although in forms more primitive than their modern counterparts. The hardware consisted of a mobile cart, about the size of a small refrigerator, with touch-sensitive "feelers," a television camera, and an optical range-finder—all controlled by a computer over a two-way radio/video link (see Figure 25.1). The cart was capable of rolling around an environment consisting of large boxes in rooms separated by walls and connected by doorways; it could push the boxes from one place to another in its world. Its suite of programs consisted of those needed for visual scene analysis (it could recognize boxes, doorways, and room corners), for planning (using STRIPS, it could plan sequences of actions to achieve goals), and for converting its plans into intermediate-level and low-level actions in its world. Shakey's architecture is shown in Figure 25.2.

Shakey's design can be viewed as an early example of what has come to be called a *three-level architecture*. The levels correspond to different paths from sensory signals to motor commands. In Figure 25.2, I have highlighted these paths as follows: low level by a gray arrow, intermediate level by broken gray arrows, and high level by broken dark arrows. The low-level actions (*LLAs*) use a short and fast path from sensory signals to effectors. Important "reflexes" are handled by this pathway—such as stop when touch sensors detect a close object. Servo control of motors for achieving set point targets for shaft angles and so on are also handled by the low-level mechanisms.

The intermediate level combines the LLAs into more complex behaviors—ones whose realization depends on the situation (as sensed and modeled) at the time of execution. As an example, one intermediate-level action (*ILA*) is gothrudoor—a routine that gets Shakey through a named doorway. It comprises appropriate

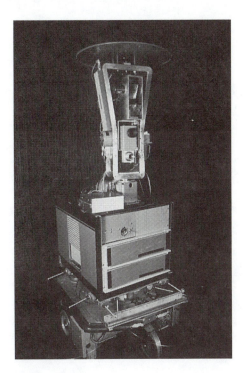

Figure 25.1

Shakey the Robot

roll-forwards and turns, guided by touch detectors and by information in an internal model, until it concludes that Shakey is completely through the doorway. Shakey's ILAs are coded in a form very similar to the T–R programs mentioned in Chapter 2.

The high–level path involves a STRIPS planner. A goal, expressed as a predicate–calculus wff, is given to the executive system that supervises the construction of a plan by STRIPS. The completed plan is expressed as a sequence of ILAs, which, along with their preconditions and effects, are represented by a triangle table. The triangle table is executed much like a T–R program. Triangle-table–form plans are also stored for possible future use in a plan library (after being generalized, as discussed in Chapter 22).

More recently, the three–level architecture has been used in a variety of robot systems. Usually some type of servo control of primitive actions is used at the lowest level. Many different AI subsystems are used at the intermediate and high levels, ranging from blackboard systems, dynamic Bayes belief networks, fuzzy logic, and plan–space planners. As a typical example, refer to [Connell 1992].

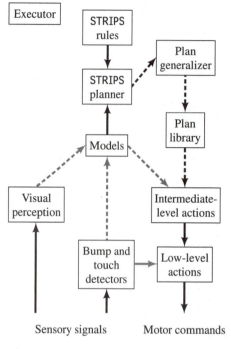

Figure 25.2

Shakey Architecture

25.2 *Goal Arbitration*

A three–level architecture is one way to deal with the problem of combining the ability to react quickly with the ability to plan sequences of actions to achieve complex goals. In most agent architectures, reflex actions take precedence over planning. The need for acting reflexively is just one instance of the general case in which an agent needs to attend to several (sometimes competing) goals simultaneously. Agents will often have several goals that they are attempting to achieve. Some are given to them by their users (with different priorities), and some (such as the need for safety, refueling, and self–maintenance) are built in. Each member of a set of goals has a certain "urgency" that depends on the priority of the goal at that time and on the relative cost of achieving it from the present situation.[1] Some goals are best handled by low–level routines, some can be achieved by stored ILAs, and some will require planning. Since goal urgency

---

1. These priorities and costs can be accommodated by a reward schedule similar to that discussed in Chapter 10.

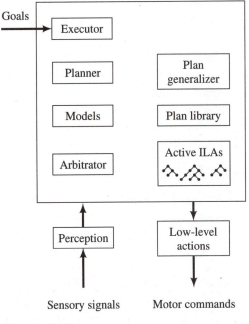

Figure 25.3

Combining Planning and Reacting

will change as the agent acts and finds itself in new, sometimes unexpected, situations, the agent architecture must be able to arbitrate among competing ILAs and planning.

[Benson & Nilsson 1995] proposed an agent architecture that integrated abilities to react, to learn, and to plan. Those aspects of the architecture relevant to arbitration are shown in Figure 25.3. Goals and their priorities are given to the system through the Executor and remain active until rescinded by the user. The system has a number of ILAs, stored as T–R programs and matched to specific goals, stored in its Plan library. If any of the active goals can be accomplished by the T–R programs already stored in the Plan library, those T–R programs become Active ILAs. Goals for which there are no existing T–R programs cause the Planner to attempt to generate new T–R programs—either by extending appropriate T–R programs already in the Plan library or by starting anew. Any new T–R programs generated by the Planner to achieve an active goal become Active ILAs. Permanent, built–in goals have prebuilt T–R programs that are always Active ILAs.

The actions actually performed by the agent are actions called for by one of the Active ILAs. The task of the Arbitrator is to select at each moment which T–R program is currently "in charge" of the agent. This selection is made using a simple type of cost–benefit calculation that takes into account the priority of the goals and the estimated cost of achieving them. (For details, see [Benson & Nilsson 1995].) Maintaining safety and avoiding danger always have high priority and thus would always be selected in any situation in which immediate action (reflexes) would be appropriate. The Arbitration module works concurrently with the Planner so that the agent can act (if appropriate) while planning. Even lower-priority goals would be pursued in situations in which they could be achieved with lower estimated cost than could expensive higher-priority goals.[2]

25.3   *The Triple-Tower Architecture*

In the three-level architecture, the higher levels use more abstract perceptual predicates and more complex actions than do the lower ones. Whereas reflex actions are typically evoked by primitive sensory signals, the coordination of higher-level actions requires more elaborate perceptual processing. Hierarchies or "towers" of perceptual and action processing have been proposed by [Albus 1991]. The perceptual processing tower starts with the primitive sensory signals and proceeds layer by layer to more refined and abstract representations of what is being sensed. The action tower composes more and more complex sequences of primitive actions. Connections between the perceptual tower and the action tower can occur at all levels of the hierarchies. The lowest-level connections correspond to simple reflexes, whereas connections at the higher levels correspond to the evocation of complex actions by the perceptual predicates specialized for those actions.

To account explicitly for the internal representations required by agents, I would suggest adding a third or "model" tower, as shown in Figure 25.4. Sensory precepts that give the agent its representation of the world are stored in a hierarchy of models—each level containing information used by whatever planning and action-evocation processes are appropriate for that level. At intermediate levels, for example, there might be models (such as potential functions or topological state spaces) appropriate for route planning. At higher levels, logical reasoning, planning, and communication would require declarative representations, such as those based on logic or semantic networks.

Although something like the triple-tower architecture has intuitive appeal, it serves only as a rough, still almost vacuous, suggestion that begs for elaboration. I believe that further progress requires more experimental work directed at integrating component AI technologies (such as those discussed in this book) in perceiving and acting agents.

---

2. This particular agent architecture also accommodated learning models of actions (which the Planner could use). For details on the learning component, see [Benson 1997].

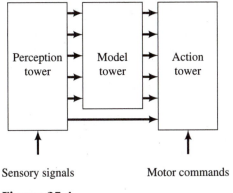

Sensory signals   Motor commands

Figure 25.4

The Triple-Tower Architecture

 ## 25.4 *Bootstrapping*

"Human–level" artificial intelligence will no doubt require much more refined perceptual and action repertoires than those of contemporary robots and agents. The most notable lack is the commonsense knowledge that must populate the higher levels of the model tower. Most AI researchers agree that this knowledge must somehow be encoded in our agents before they can perform even the routine tasks that humans find easy. The CYC project is a direct effort by a group of researchers to encode the knowledge they think is required. Since the early days of AI, some researchers have thought that this knowledge could be obtained the "easy way" by automatic learning programs, by self–organizing systems, by simulated evolution, or by some such shortcut. Even the handcrafting CYC researchers hope that after CYC reaches a certain critical stage, the system will be able to learn more knowledge on its own—by reading text, by conversing with humans, and by being taught. Humans learn much of the knowledge they use by a process of "bootstrapping" from previously obtained knowledge—first, as infants, from built-in tendencies, and later, through the various Piagetian stages, from previously acquired skills and concepts, and then, as adults, through practice, reading, and communicating. It now seems to me that the amount of knowledge that will be required by AI agents to exhibit human-level intelligence is so large, that a similar, yet-to-be-discovered bootstrapping process will be required. Probably this process will involve techniques similar to some of the automatic learning procedures I have described in several parts of the book. My guess is that we must find a way to have an agent itself add additional floors to its triple towers after its designers appropriately craft the lower stories.

25.5   *Additional Readings and Discussion*

[Whitehead, Karlsson, & Tenenberg 1993] developed a system that was able to learn how to achieve each of several goals and could arbitrate among them when they were all active.

In noting the multiplicity of different block diagrams for agent architectures, Stan Rosenschein used to say "Boxes, boxes, we've all got boxes." In addition to the architectural schemes mentioned in this chapter, I cite a few more (realizing that I'm leaving out many others): [Laird, et al. 1991, Hayes–Roth 1995, Gat 1992, Wilkins, et al. 1995, Bates, Loyall, & Reilly 1992, Firby & Kahn 1995].

In all of these, a critical question is whether to refine a plan or to act on the plan in hand (which might be a plan that was compiled when time was not critical, such as at design time). As mentioned earlier in the book, metalevel architectures (as described, for example, by [Russell & Wefald 1991, Ch. 2]) can be used to make such a decision. In any case, the nature of the computational time-space tradeoff seems to be such that most agent actions ought to be reactive, with planning and learning used to extend the fringes of what an agent already knows how to do.

In this book, I have tried to cover most of the currently known AI techniques that I think will be required to achieve human–level AI. It's a large collection, but it must get larger before we get close to our goal. We will continue, I think, to draw on ideas from psychology, neurophysiology, control theory, signal processing, and economics as well as from computer science as we make progress. To those readers who choose to join this odyssey, my advice is to be eclectic, imaginative, and humble as we confront the large gap between the modest abilities of existing AI systems and the exquisite complexity of animal and human intelligence. But our humility need not and should not weaken our goals nor blunt our daring.

Exercises

25.1 Isaac Asimov's three laws of robotics are

1. A robot may not injure a human being, or, through inaction, allow a human being to come to harm.

2. A robot must obey the orders given it by human beings except where such orders would conflict with the First Law.

3. A robot must protect its own existence as long as such protection does not conflict with the First or Second Law.

Describe as many difficulties as you can think of regarding building these laws into autonomous agents—both physical agents and software agents. What AI abilities would be required?

25.2 Do you think the AI techniques, conceptual apparatus, and theory presently available and surveyed in this book are adequate to support the construction of machines we could truly call "intelligent"? Why? If you think present AI knowledge is inadequate, answer at least one of the following questions, giving evidence for your answer:

1. Are substantial increments of new theory and ideas needed, and if so, in what areas?

2. Do we merely need larger and faster (and perhaps more parallel) computers?

3. Has AI research been pursuing inappropriate paths, and are wholly new approaches needed? If so, where should AI research concentrate attention?

4. Are the long-term goals of AI impossible in principle?

25.3 Now that you have surveyed many of the important ideas in AI, return to Chapter 1 and do Exercise 1.5, commenting on the appropriateness and prospects of strong AI versus weak AI. (There are no "right" answers, but there are some well-reasoned ones.)

Bibliography

[Abramson & Yung 1989] Abramson, B., and Yung, M., "Divide and Conquer under Global Constraints: A Solution to the N–Queens Problem," *Journal of Parallel and Distributed Computing*, 6:649–662, 1989.

[Agre & Chapman 1987] Agre, P., and Chapman, D., "Pengi: An Implementation of a Theory of Activity," *Proceedings of the Sixth National Conference on Artificial Intelligence (AAAI-87)*, pp. 268–272, Menlo Park, CA: AAAI Press, 1987.

[Agre & Chapman 1990] Agre, P., and Chapman, D., "What Are Plans For?" *Robotics and Autonomous Systems*, 6:17–34, 1990. Also in [Maes 1990a].

[Albus 1991] Albus, J. S., "Outline for a Theory of Intelligence," *IEEE Systems, Man, and Cybernetics*, 21(3):473–509, May/June 1991.

[Allen 1983] Allen, J., "Maintaining Knowledge about Temporal Intervals," *Communications of the ACM*, 26(11):832–843, 1983. (Reprinted in Weld, D., and de Kleer, J. (eds.), *Readings in Qualitative Reasoning about Physical Systems*, San Francisco: Morgan Kaufmann, 1990.)

[Allen 1984] Allen, J., "Towards a General Theory of Action and Time," *Artificial Intelligence*, 23:123–154, 1984.

[Allen 1991a] Allen, J., "Time and Time Again: The Many Ways to Represent Time," *International Journal of Intelligent Systems*, 6:341–355, 1991.

[Allen 1991b] Allen, J., "Temporal Reasoning and Planning," in Allen, J., Kautz, H., Pelavin, R., and Tenenberg, J. (eds.), *Reasoning About Plans*, Ch. 1, San Francisco: Morgan Kaufmann, 1991.

[Allen 1995] Allen, J., *Natural Language Understanding*, Menlo Park, CA: Benjamin/Cummings, 1995.

[Allen, et al. 1990]   Allen, J., Hendler, J., and Tate, A. (eds.), *Readings in Planning*, San Francisco: Morgan Kaufmann, 1990.

[Almeida 1987]   Almeida, L. B., "A Learning Rule for Asynchronous Perceptrons with Feedback in a Combinatorial Environment," in M. Caudill and C. Butler (eds.), *IEEE First International Conference on Neural Networks*, San Diego, 1987, vol. II, pp. 609–618, New York: IEEE, 1987.

[Aloimonos 1993]   Aloimonos, Y. (ed.), *Active Perception*, Hillsdale, NJ: Lawerence Erlbaum Associates, 1993.

[Anderson & Donath 1990]   Anderson, T., and Donath, M., "Animal Behavior as a Paradigm for Developing Robot Autonomy," *Robotics and Autonomous Systems*, 6:145–168, 1990. Also in [Maes 1990a].

[Andre 1995]   Andre, D., "The Automatic Programming of Agents That Learn Mental Models and Create Simple Plans of Action," in *Proceedings of the Fourteenth International Joint Conference on Artificial Intelligence (IJCAI-95)*, pp. 741–747, San Francisco: Morgan Kaufmann, 1995.

[Appelt 1985]   Appelt, D., "Planning English Referring Expressions," *Artificial Intelligence*, 26(1):1–33, 1985. (Also in Grosz, B., Jones, K., and Webber, B. (eds.), *Readings in Natural Language Processing*, pp. 501–517, San Francisco: Morgan Kaufmann, 1986.)

[Bacchus & Yang 1992]   Bacchus, F., and Yang, Q., "The Expected Value of Hierarchical Problem-Solving," in *Proceedings of the Tenth National Conference on Artificial Intelligence (AAAI-92)*, pp. 369–374, Menlo Park, CA: AAAI Press, 1992.

[Baker 1991]   Baker, A., "Nonmonotonic Reasoning in the Framework of Situation Calculus," *Artificial Intelligence*, 49:5–23, 1991.

[Ballard 1991]   Ballard, D. H., "Animate Vision," *Artificial Intelligence*, 48(1):57–86, 1991.

[Ballard & Brown 1982]   Ballard, D. H., and Brown, C. M., *Computer Vision*, Englewood Cliffs, NJ: Prentice Hall, 1982.

[Barr & Feigenbaum 1981]   Barr, A., and Feigenbaum, E. (eds.), *The Handbook of Artificial Intelligence, Volume 1*, Reading, MA: Addison-Wesley, 1981. (See the following two entries and [Cohen & Feigenbaum 1982] for the other three volumes.)

[Barr & Feigenbaum 1982]   Barr, A., and Feigenbaum, E. (eds.), *The Handbook of Artificial Intelligence, Volume 2*, Reading, MA: Addison-Wesley, 1982.

[Barr, Cohen, & Feigenbaum 1989]   Barr, A., Cohen, P. R., and Feigenbaum, E. (eds.), *The Handbook of Artificial Intelligence, Volume 4*, Reading, MA: Addison-Wesley, 1989.

[Barto, Bradtke, & Singh 1995]   Barto, A., Bradtke, S., and Singh, S., "Learning to Act Using Real-Time Dynamic Programming," *Artificial Intelligence*, 72(1,2):81–138, January 1995.

[Barwise & Etchemendy 1993]   Barwise, J., and Etchemendy, J., *The Language of First-Order Logic: Including the Macintosh Program Tarski's World 4.0*, Center for the Study of Language and Information (CSLI), Stanford, California, third revised and expanded edition, 1993.

[Bates 1994]   Bates, J., "The Role of Emotion in Believable Agents," *Communications of the ACM*, 37(7):122–125, 1994.

[Bates, Loyall, & Reilly 1992]   Bates, J., Loyall, A. B., and Reilly, W. S., "Integrating Reactivity, Goals, and Emotion in a Broad Agent," Technical Report CMU–CS–92–142, School of Computer Science, Carnegie Mellon University, Pittsburgh, PA, May 1992. (Also appeared in the *Proceedings of the Fourteenth Annual Conference of the Cognitive Science Society*, Bloomington, Indiana, July 1992.)

[Bayes 1763]   Bayes, T., "An Essay Towards Solving a Problem in the Doctrine of Chances," *Phil. Trans.*, 3:370–418, 1763. Reproduced in Deming, W. (ed.), *Two Papers by Bayes*, New York: Hafner, 1963.

[Beer 1995]   Beer, R., "A Dynamical Systems Perspective on Agent–Environment Interaction," *Artificial Intelligence*, 72(1–2):173–215, 1995.

[Beer, Chiel, & Sterling 1990]   Beer, R., Chiel, H., and Sterling, L., "A Biological Perspective on Autonomous Agent Design," *Robotics and Autonomous Systems*, 6:169–186, 1990. Also in [Maes 1990a].

[Benson 1997]   Benson, S., *Learning Action Models for Reactive Autonomous Agents*, Stanford University Computer Science Department Ph.D. dissertation, Report No. STAN–CS–TR–97–1589, Stanford, CA 94305, 1997.

[Benson & Nilsson 1995]   Benson, S., and Nilsson, N., "Reacting, Planning and Learning in an Autonomous Agent," in Furukawa, K., Michie, D., and Muggleton, S. (eds.), *Machine Intelligence 14*, Oxford: The Clarendon Press, 1995.

[Berliner 1979]   Berliner, H., "The B* Tree–Search Algorithm: A Best–First Proof Procedure," *Artificial Intelligence*, 12(1):23–40, 1979.

[Bhanu & Lee 1994]   Bhanu, B., and Lee, S., *Genetic Learning for Adaptive Image Segmentation*, Boston: Kluwer Academic Publishers, 1994.

[Binford 1982]   Binford, T. O., "Survey of Model–Based Image Analysis Systems," *The International Journal of Robotics Research*, 1(1):18–64, 1982.

[Binford 1987]   Binford, T. O., "Generalized Cylinder Representation," in Shapiro, S. C. (ed.), *Encyclopedia of Artificial Intelligence*, pp. 321–323, New York: John Wiley & Sons, 1987. (This article is based on an unpublished 1971 paper by Binford entitled "Visual Perception by Computer.")

[Bledsoe 1977]   Bledsoe, W., "Non–Resolution Theorem Proving," *Artificial Intelligence*, 9(1):1–35, 1977.

[Blum & Furst 1995]   Blum, A., and Furst, M., "Fast Planning through Planning Graph Analysis," in *Proceedings of the Fourteenth International Joint Conference on Artificial Intelligence (IJCAI-95)*, pp. 1636–1642, San Francisco: Morgan Kaufmann, 1995.

[Blumberg 1996]   Blumberg, B., *Old Tricks, New Dogs: Ethology and Interactive Creatures*, Ph.D. Dissertation, MIT Media Lab, Massachusetts Institute of Technology, 1996.

[Bobrow 1968]   Bobrow, D., "Natural Language Input for a Computer Problem Solving System," in Minsky, M. (ed.), *Semantic Information Processing*, pp. 133–215, Cambridge, MA: MIT Press, 1968.

[Bobrow, Mittal, & Stefik 1986]   Bobrow, D., Mittal, S., and Stefik, M., "Expert Systems: Perils and Promise," *Communications of the ACM*, 29(9):880–894, 1986.

[Bond & Gasser 1988]   Bond, A., and Gasser, L. (eds.), *Readings in Distributed Artificial Intelligence*, San Francisco: Morgan Kaufmann, 1988.

[Boole 1854]   Boole, G., *An Investigation of the Laws of Thought on Which Are Founded the Mathematical Theories of Logic and Probabilities*, New York: Dover Publications, 1854.

[Börger 1989]   Börger, E., *Computability, Complexity, Logic*, Amsterdam: North–Holland, 1989.

[Borgida, et al. 1989]   Borgida, A., Brachman, R., McGuinness, D., and Resnick, A., "CLASSIC: A Structural Data Model for Objects," *SIGMOD Record*, 18(2):58–67, 1989.

[Boyer & Moore 1979]   Boyer, R., and Moore, J., *A Computational Logic*, New York: Academic Press, 1979.

[Brachman & Levesque 1985]   Brachman, R., and Levesque, H. (eds.), *Readings in Knowledge Representation*, San Francisco: Morgan Kaufmann, 1985.

[Brachman, Gilbert, & Levesque 1985]   Brachman, R., Gilbert, V., and Levesque, H., "An Essential Hybrid Reasoning System: Knowledge and Symbol Level Accounts of KRYPTON," in *Proceedings of the Ninth International Joint Conference on Artificial Intelligence (IJCAI-85)*, pp. 532–539, San Francisco: Morgan Kaufmann, 1985.

[Brain, et al. 1962]   Brain, A. E., et al., "Graphical Data Processing Research Study and Experimental Investigation," Report No. 8 (pp. 9–13) and No. 9 (pp. 3–10), Contract DA 36–039 SC–78343, SRI International, Menlo Park, CA, June 1962 and September 1962.

[Braitenberg 1984]   Braitenberg, V., *Vehicles: Experiments in Synthetic Psychology*, Cambridge, MA: MIT Press, 1984.

[Bratko 1990]   Bratko, I., *PROLOG Programming for Artificial Intelligence*, second edition, Reading, MA: Addison–Wesley, 1990.

[Bratko & Michie 1980]   Bratko, I., and Michie, D., "An Advice Program for a Complex Chess Programming Task," *Computer Journal*, 23(4):353–359, 1980.

[Brave 1996]   Brave, S., "The Evolution of Memory and Mental Models Using Genetic Programming," in Koza, J., et al. (eds.), *Genetic Programming 1996: Proceedings of the First Annual Conference*, pp. 261–266, Stanford University, July 28–31, 1996, Cambridge, MA: MIT Press, 1996.

[Breiman, et al. 1984]   Breiman, L., Friedman, J., Olshen, R., and Stone, C., *Classification and Regression Trees*, Belmont, CA: Wadsworth, 1984.

[Brewka, Dix, & Konolige 1997]   Brewka, G., Dix, J., and Konolige, K., *Nonmonotonic Reasoning: An Overview*, CSLI Lecture Notes, No. 73, Center for the Study of Language and Information, Stanford, CA: Stanford University, 1997.

[Brooks 1981]   Brooks, R., "Symbolic Reasoning among 3-D Models and 2-D Images," *Artificial Intelligence*, 17:285–348, 1981.

[Brooks 1986]   Brooks, R. A., "A Robust Layered Control System for a Mobile Robot," *IEEE Journal of Robotics and Automation*, RA-2(1):14–23, March 1986.

[Brooks 1990]   Brooks, R., "Elephants Don't Play Chess," *Robotics and Autonomous Systems*, 6:3–15, 1990. Also in [Maes 1990].

[Brooks 1991a]   Brooks, R. A., "Intelligence without Representation," *Artificial Intelligence*, 47(1/3):139–159, January 1991.

[Brooks 1991b]   Brooks, R. A., "Intelligence Without Reason," in *Proceedings of the Twelfth International Joint Conference on Artificial Intelligence (IJCAI-91)*, pp. 569–595, San Francisco: Morgan Kaufmann, 1991.

[Brooks & Mataric 1993]   Brooks, R., and Mataric, M., "Real Robots, Real Learning Problems," in Connell, J., and Mahadevan, S. (eds.), *Robot Learning*, Ch. 8, Boston: Kluwer Academic Publishers, 1993.

[Brownston, et al. 1985]   Brownston, L., Farrell, R., Kant, E., and Martin, N., *Programming Expert Systems in OPS5*, Reading, MA: Addison-Wesley, 1985.

[Bryson & Ho 1969]   Bryson, A., and Ho, Y.-C., *Applied Optimal Control*, New York: Blaisdell, 1969.

[Buchanan & Shortliffe 1984]   Buchanan, B., and Shortliffe, E. (eds.), *Rule-Based Expert Systems: The MYCIN Experiments of the Stanford Heuristic Programming Project*, Reading, MA: Addison-Wesley, 1984.

[Bylander 1993]   Bylander, T., "An Average Case Analysis of Planning," in *Proceedings of the Eleventh National Conference on Artificial Intelligence (AAAI-93)*, pp. 480–485, Menlo Park, CA: AAAI Press, 1993.

[Bylander 1994]   Bylander, T., "The Computational Complexity of Propositional STRIPS Planning," *Artificial Intelligence*, 69(1/2):165–204, 1994.

[Campbell, et al. 1982]   Campbell, A. N., Hollister, V., Duda, R., and Hart, P., "Recognition of a Hidden Mineral Deposit by an Artificial Intelligence Program," *Science*, 217(4563):927–929, 1982.

[Canny 1986]   Canny, J., "A Computational Approach to Edge Detection," *IEEE Trans. on Pattern Analysis and Machine Intelligence*, PAMI-8(6):679–698, November 1986.

[Carbonell, et al. 1992]   Carbonell, J., Blythe, J., Etzioni, O., Gil, Y., Kahn, D., Knoblock, C., Minton, S., Perez, A., Reilly, S., Veloso, M., and Wang, X., "PRODIGY 4.0: The Manual and Tutorial," Carnegie–Mellon University Computer Science Tech. Report CMU–CS–92–1560, Pittsburg, PA, 1992.

[Cassandra, Kaelbling, & Littman 1994]   Cassandra, A., Kaelbling, L., and Littman, M., "Acting Optimally in Partially Observable Stochastic Domains," in *Proceedings of the Twelfth National Conference on Artificial Intelligence (AAAI-94)*, pp. 1023–1028, Menlo Park, CA: AAAI Press, 1994.

[Chakrabarti, Ghose, & DeSarkar 1986]   Chakrabarti, P., Ghose, S., and DeSarkar, S., "Heuristic Search through Islands," *Artificial Intelligence*, 29(3):339–347, 1986.

[Chang & Lee 1973]   Chang, C.-L., and Lee, R., *Symbolic Logic and Mechanical Theorem Proving*, Boston: Academic Press, 1973.

[Chapman 1987]   Chapman, D., "Planning for Conjunctive Goals," *Artificial Intelligence*, 32(3):333–377, 1987.

[Chapman 1989]   Chapman, D., "Penguins Can Make Cake," *AI Magazine*, 10(4):45–50, 1989.

[Charniak 1993]   Charniak, E., *Statistical Language Learning*, Cambridge, MA: MIT Press, 1993.

[Chauvin & Rumelhart 1995]   Chauvin, Y., and Rumelhart, D., *Backpropagation: Theory, Architectures, and Applications*, Hillsdale, NJ: Lawrence Erlbaum, 1995.

[Chen 1990]   Chen, S., (ed.), *Advances in Spatial Reasoning*, Norwood, NJ: Ablex Publishing, 1990.

[Chomsky 1965]   Chomsky, N., *Aspects of the Theory of Syntax*, Cambridge, MA: MIT Press, 1965.

[Christensen 1990]   Christensen, J., "A Hierarchical Planner That Generates Its Own Hierarchies," in *Proceedings of the Eighth National Conference on Artificial Intelligence (AAAI-90)*, pp. 1004–1009, Menlo Park, CA: AAAI Press, 1990.

[Churchland, Ramachandran, & Sejnowski 1994]   Churchland, P. S., Ramachandran, V. S., and Sejnowski, T. J., "A Critique of Pure Vision," in Koch, C., and Davis, J. (eds.), *Large-Scale Neuronal Theories of the Brain*, pp. 23–60, Cambridge, MA: MIT Press, 1994.

[Clocksin & Mellish 1987]   Clocksin, W., and Mellish, C., *Programming in PROLOG* (third edition), New York: Springer-Verlag, 1987.

[Clowes 1971]   Clowes, M., "On Seeing Things," *Artificial Intelligence*, 2:79–116, 1971.

[Cohen & Feigenbaum 1982]   Cohen, P. R., and Feigenbaum, E. (eds.), *The Handbook of Artificial Intelligence, Volume 3*, Reading, MA: Addison-Wesley, 1982.

[Cohen & Levesque 1990]   Cohen, P., and Levesque, H., "Intention Is Choice with Commitment," *Artificial Intelligence*, 42(2–3):213–361, 1990.

[Cohen & Perrault 1979]   Cohen, P., and Perrault, C. R., "Elements of a Plan-Based Theory of Speech Acts," *Cognitive Science*, 3:177–212, 1979.

[Colmerauer 1973]   Colmerauer, A., et al., "Un Système de Communication Homme–Machine en Français," Research Report, Université Aix–Marseille II, Groupe d'Intelligence Artificielle, France, 1973.

[Colmerauer 1978]   Colmerauer, A., "Metamorphosis Grammars," in Bolc, L. (ed.), *Natural Language Communication with Computers*," Berlin: Springer-Verlag. (This article is an English translation of a 1975 technical report written in French.)

[Connell 1990]   Connell, J. H., "A Colony Architecture Applied to Robot Navigation," *Technical Report 1151*, MIT AI Lab, MIT, Cambridge, MA, June 1990.

[Connell 1992]   Connell, J. H., "SSS: A Hybrid Architecture Applied to Robot Navigation," in *Proc. 1992 IEEE International Conf. on Robotics and Automation*, pp. 2719–2724, 1992.

[Connell & Mahadevan 1993a]   Connell, J., and Mahadevan, S., "Rapid Task Learning for Real Robots," in Connell, J., and Mahadevan, S. (eds.), *Robot Learning*, Ch. 5, Boston: Kluwer Academic Publishers, 1993.

[Connell & Mahadevan 1993b]   Connell, J., and Mahadevan, S. (eds.), *Robot Learning*, Boston: Kluwer Academic Publishers, 1993.

[Cook 1971]   Cook, S., "The Complexity of Theorem–Proving Procedures," in *Proc. of the 3rd Annual ACM Symposium on Theory of Computing*, pp. 151–158, New York: Association for Computing Machinery, 1971.

[Cook 1988]   Cook, S., "Short Propositional Formulas Represent Nondeterministic Computations," *Information Processing Letters*, 26(5):269–270, 1988.

[Cooper 1990]   Cooper, G., "Computational Complexity of Probabilistic Inference Using Bayesian Belief Networks (Research Note)," *Artificial Intelligence*, 42(2/3):393–405, 1990.

[Cooper & Herskovitz 1992]   Cooper, G., and Herskovitz, E., "A Bayesian Method for the Induction of Probabilistic Networks from Data," *Machine Learning*, 9:309–347, 1992.

[Cormen, Leiserson, & Rivest 1990]   Cormen, T., Leiserson, C., and Rivest, R., *Introduction to Algorithms*, Cambridge, MA, and New York: MIT Press and McGraw-Hill, 1990.

[Cover & Thomas 1991]   Cover, T., and Thomas, A., *Elements of Information Theory*, New York: John Wiley & Sons, 1991.

[Currie & Tate 1991]   Currie, K., and Tate, A., "O–PLAN: The Open Planning Architecture," *Artificial Intelligence*, 52(1):49–86, 1991.

[Davis 1990]   Davis, E., *Representations of Commonsense Knowledge*, San Francisco: Morgan Kaufmann, 1990.

[Davis & Putnam 1960]   Davis, M., and Putnam, H., "A Computing Procedure for Quantification Theory," *Journ. Assoc. of Comp. Mach.*, 7(3):201–215, 1960.

[Davis 1980]   Davis, R., "Meta–Rules: Reasoning about Control," *Artificial Intelligence*, 15(3):179–222, 1980.

[de Kleer 1986a]   de Kleer, J., "An Assumption–Based TMS," *Artificial Intelligence*, 28(2):127–162, 1986.

[de Kleer 1986b]   de Kleer, J., "Extending the ATMS," *Artificial Intelligence*, 28(2):163–196, 1986.

[de Kleer 1986c]   de Kleer, J., "Problem Solving with the ATMS," *Artificial Intelligence*, 28(2):197–224, 1986.

[Dean & Boddy 1988]   Dean, T., and Boddy, M., "An Analysis of Time–Dependent Planning," in *Proceedings of the Seventh National Conference on Artificial Intelligence (AAAI-88)*, pp. 49–54, Menlo Park, CA: AAAI Press, 1988.

[Dean & Wellman 1991]   Dean, T., and Wellman, M., *Planning and Control*, San Francisco: Morgan Kaufmann, 1991.

[Dean, Basye, & Kaelbling 1993]   Dean, T., Basye, K., and Kaelbling, L., "Uncertainty in Graph–Based Map Learning," in Connell, J., and Mahadevan, S. (eds.), *Robot Learning*, Ch. 7, Boston: Kluwer Academic Publishers, 1993.

[Dechter 1996]   Dechter, R., "Bucket Elimination: A Unifying Framework for Probabilistic Inference," in *Proceedings of the Twelfth Conference on Uncertainty in AI*, pp. 211–219, San Francisco: Morgan Kaufmann, 1996.

[Dempster 1968]   Dempster, A. P., "A Generalization of Bayesian Inference," *Journal of the Royal Statistical Society, Series B*, 30:205–247, 1968.

[Dempster, Laird, & Rubin 1977]   Dempster, A., Laird, N., and Rubin, D., "Maximum Likelihood from Incomplete Data via the EM Algorithm," *Journal of the Royal Statistical Society, Series B*, 39:1–38, 1977.

[Dennett 1971]   Dennett, D., "Intentional Systems," *The Journal of Philosophy*, 68(4):87–106, 1971.

[Dennett 1995]   Dennett, D., *Darwin's Dangerous Idea*, New York: Simon & Schuster, 1995.

[Deutsch 1960]   Deutsch, J. A., *The Structural Basis of Behavior*, Chicago: The University of Chicago Press, 1960.

[Dietterich 1990]   Dietterich, T., "Machine Learning," in Traub, J., et al. (eds.), *Annual Review of Computer Science*, 4:255–306, 1990.

[Dietterich & Bakiri 1991]   Dietterich, T., and Bakiri, G., "Error–Correcting Output Codes: A General Method for Improving Multiclass Inductive Learning Programs," in *Proceedings of the Ninth National Conference on Artificial Intelligence (AAAI-91)*, pp. 572–577, Menlo Park, CA: AAAI Press, 1991.

[Dietterich & Bakiri 1995]   Dietterich, T., and Bakiri, G., "Solving Multiclass Learning Problems via Error–Correcting Output Codes," *Journal of Artificial Intelligence Research*, 2:263–286, 1995.

[Dijkstra 1959]   Dijkstra, E., "A Note on Two Problems in Connection with Graphs," *Numerische Mathematik*, (1):269–271, 1959.

[Doran & Michie 1966]   Doran, J., and Michie, D., "Experiments with the Graph Traverser Program," *Proc. Royal Society of London*, vol. 294 (series A), pp. 235–259, 1966.

[Dowling & Gallier 1984]   Dowling, W., and Gallier, J., "Linear–Time Algorithms for Testing the Satisfiability of Propositional Horn Formulas," *Journal of Logic Programming*, (3):267–284, 1984.

[Doyle 1979]   Doyle, J., "A Truth Maintenance System," *Artificial Intelligence*, 12(3):231–272, 1979. (Reprinted in Webber, B., and Nilsson, N. (eds.), *Readings in Artificial Intelligence*, San Francisco: Morgan Kaufmann, 1981.)

[Dreyfus 1979]   Dreyfus, H., *What Computers Can't Do: The Limits of Artificial Intelligence*, revised edition, New York: Harper and Row, 1979.

[Dreyfus 1992]   Dreyfus, H., *What Computers Still Can't Do: A Critique of Artificial Reason*, Cambridge, MA: MIT Press, 1992.

[Dreyfus & Dreyfus 1986]   Dreyfus, H., and Dreyfus, S., *Mind over Machine: The Power of Human Intuition and Expertise in the Era of the Computer*, (with T. Athanasiou), Oxford: Blackwell, 1986.

[Duda, Hart, & Nilsson 1976]   Duda, R. O., Hart, P. E., and Nilsson, N., "Subjective Bayesian Methods for Rule–Based Inference Systems," *Proc. AFIPS Nat. Computer Conference*, vol. 47:1075–1082, 1976. (Reprinted in Webber, B., and Nilsson, N. (eds.), *Readings in Artificial Intelligence*, San Francisco: Morgan Kaufmann, 1981.)

[Duda, Hart, & Stork 1998]   Duda, R. O., Hart, P. E., and Stork, D., *Pattern Classification*, second edition, New York: John Wiley & Sons, 1998.

[Duda, Gaschnig, & Hart 1979]   Duda, R., Gaschnig, J., and Hart, P., "Model Design in the PROSPECTOR Consultant System for Mineral Exploration," in Michie, D. (ed.), *Expert Systems in the Microelectronic Age*, pp. 153–167, Edinburgh: Edinburgh University Press, 1979. (Reprinted in Webber, B., and Nilsson, N. (eds.), *Readings in Artificial Intelligence*, pp. 337ff, San Francisco: Morgan Kaufmann, 1981.)

[Dym & Levitt 1991]   Dym, C., and Levitt, R., *Knowledge-Based Systems in Engineering*, New York: McGraw–Hill, 1991.

[Elkan 1992]   Elkan, C., "Reasoning about Action in First–Order Logic," in *Proc. of the Ninth Biennial Conf. of the Canadian Society for Computational Studies of Intelligence*, pp. 221–227, San Francisco, Morgan Kaufmann, 1992.

[Elkan 1993]   Elkan, C., "The Paradoxical Success of Fuzzy Logic," in *Proceedings of the Eleventh National Conference on Artificial Intelligence (AAAI-93)*, pp. 698–703, Menlo Park, CA: AAAI Press, 1993.

[Elman 1990]   Elman, J., "Finding Structure in Time," *Cognitive Science*, 14:179–211, 1990.

[Emerson 1989]   Emerson, E., "Temporal and Modal Logic," in van Leeuwen, J. (ed.), *Handbook of Theoretical Computer Science*, pp. 995–1072, Amsterdam: North-Holland, 1989.

[Enderton 1972]   Enderton, H., *A Mathematical Introduction to Logic*, New York: Academic Press, 1972.

[Ephrati, Pollack, & Milshtein 1996]   Ephrati, E., Pollack, M., and Milshtein, M., "A Cost–Directed Planner: Preliminary Report," in *Proceedings of the Thirteenth National Conference on Artificial Intelligence (AAAI-96)*, pp. 1194–1201, Menlo Park, CA: AAAI Press, 1996.

[Erman, et al. 1980]   Erman, L., Hayes–Roth, F., Lesser, V., and Reddy, R., "The Hearsay–II Speech–Understanding System: Integrating Knowledge to Resolve Uncertainty," *Computing Surveys*, 12:213–253, 1980.

[Ernst, Millstein, & Weld 1997]   Ernst, M., Millstein, T., and Weld, D., "Automatic SAT–Compilation of Planning Problems," in *Proceedings of the Fifteenth International Conference on Artificial Intelligence (IJCAI-97)*, pp. 1169–1176, San Francisco: Morgan Kaufmann, 1997.

[Erol, Nau, & Subrahmanian 1992]   Erol, K., Nau, D., and Subrahmanian, V., "On the Complexity of Domain–Independent Planning," in *Proceedings of the Tenth National Conference on Artificial Intelligence (AAAI-92)*, pp. 381–386, Menlo Park, CA: AAAI Press, 1992.

[Erol, Hendler, & Nau 1994]   Erol, K., Hendler, J., and Nau, D., "HTN Planning: Complexity and Expressivity," in *Proceedings of the Twelfth National Conference on Artificial Intelligence (AAAI-94)*, pp. 1123–1128, Menlo Park, CA: AAAI Press, 1994.

[Etzioni 1993]   Etzioni, O., "Acquiring Search–Control Knowledge via Static Analysis," *Artificial Intelligence*, 62(2):255–301, 1993.

[Etzioni & Weld 1994]   Etzioni, O., and Weld, D., "A Softbot–Based Interface to the Internet," *Communications of the ACM*, 37(7):72–76, July 1994.

[Evans 1968]   Evans, T. G., "A Program for the Solution of a Class of Geometric–Analogy Intelligence–Test Questions," in Minsky, M. (ed.), *Semantic Information Processing*, pp. 271–353, Cambridge, MA: MIT Press, 1968.

[Fagin & Halpern 1985]   Fagin, R., and Halpern, J., "Belief, Awareness, and Limited Reasoning," in *Proceedings of the Ninth International Joint Conference on Artificial Intelligence (IJCAI-85)*, pp. 491–501, San Francisco: Morgan Kaufmann, 1985.

[Fagin, et al. 1995]   Fagin, R., Halpern, J., Moses, Y., and Vardi, M., *Reasoning about Knowledge*, Cambridge, MA: MIT Press, 1995.

[Faugeras 1993]   Faugeras, O., *Three-Dimensional Computer Vison: A Geometric Viewpoint*, Cambridge, MA: MIT Press, 1993.

[Feigenbaum & Feldman 1963]   Feigenbaum, E., and Feldman, J. (eds.), *Computers and Thought*. New York: McGraw–Hill, 1963.

[Feigenbaum, Buchanan, & Lederberg 1971]   Feigenbaum, E., Buchanan, B., and Lederberg, J., "On Generality and Problem Solving: A Case Study Using the DENDRAL Program," in Meltzer, B., and Michie, D. (eds.), *Machine Intelligence 6*, pp. 165–190, Edinburgh: Edinburgh University Press, 1971.

[Feigenbaum, McCorduck, & Nii 1988]   Feigenbaum, E., McCorduck, P., and Nii, H. P., *The Rise of the Expert Company: How Visionary Companies Are Using Artificial Intelligence to Achieve Higher Productivity and Profits*, New York: Times Books, 1988.

[Feller 1968]   Feller, W., *An Introduction to Probability Theory and Applications*, vol. 1, New York: John Wiley & Sons, 1968.

[Fikes & Nilsson 1971]   Fikes, R., and Nilsson, N., "STRIPS: A New Approach to the Application of Theorem Proving to Problem Solving," *Artificial Intelligence*, 2(3/4):189–208, 1971.

[Fikes, Hart, & Nilsson 1972]   Fikes, R., Hart, P., and Nilsson, N., "Learning and Executing Generalized Robot Plans," *Artificial Intelligence*, 3(4):251–288, 1972.

[Finin, Labrou, & Mayfield 1997]   Finin, T., Labrou, Y., and Mayfield, J., "KQML as an Agent Communication Language," in Bradshaw, J. (ed.), *Software Agents*, Cambridge, MA: MIT Press, 1997.

[Firby & Kahn 1995]   Firby, R. J., and Kahn, R., "An Architecture for Vision and Action," in *Proceedings of the Fourteenth International Joint Conference on Artificial Intelligence (IJCAI-95)*, pp. 72–79, San Francisco: Morgan Kaufmann, 1995.

[Fischler & Firschein 1987]   Fischler, M. A., and Firschein, O. (eds.), *Readings in Computer Vision: Issues, Problems, Principles, and Paradigms*, San Francisco: Morgan Kaufmann, 1987.

[Fleischmann, et al. 1995]   Fleischmann, R., et al., "Whole-Genome Random Sequencing and Assembly of *Haemophilus influenzae Rd*," *Science*, 269:496–512, July 28, 1995.

[Forbes, et al. 1995]   Forbes, J., Huang, T., Kanazawa, K., and Russell, S., "The BATmobile: Towards a Bayesian Automatic Taxi," in *Proceedings of the Fourteenth International Joint Conference on Artificial Intelligence (IJCAI-95)*, pp. 1878–1885, San Francisco: Morgan Kaufmann, 1995.

[Forbus & de Kleer 1993]   Forbus, K., and de Kleer, J., *Building Problem Solvers*, Cambridge, MA: MIT Press, 1993.

[Forgy 1982]   Forgy, C., "RETE: A Fast Algorithm for the Many Pattern/Many Object Pattern Match Problem," *Artificial Intelligence*, 19(1):17–37, 1982.

[Frege 1879]   Frege, G., "Begriffsschrift, a Formula Language Modelled upon That of Arithmetic, for Pure Thought," (1879), in van Heijenoort, J. (ed.), *From Frege to Gödel: A Source Book in Mathematical Logic, 1879–1931*, pp. 1–82, Cambridge, MA: Harvard University Press, 1967.

[Friedman 1997]   Friedman, N., "Learning Belief Networks in the Presence of Missing Values and Hidden Variables," *Proceedings of the Fourteenth International Conference on Machine Learning (ICML '97)*, San Francisco: Morgan Kaufmann, 1997.

[Friedman & Goldszmidt 1996a]   Friedman, N., and Goldszmidt, M., "Learning Bayesian Networks with Local Structure," in *Proceedings of the Twelfth Conference on Uncertainty in Artificial Intelligence*, pp. 252–262, San Francisco: Morgan Kaufmann, 1996.

[Friedman & Goldszmidt 1996b]   Friedman, N., and Goldszmidt, M., "Building Classifiers Using Bayesian Networks," *Proceedings of the Thirteenth National Conference on Artificial Intelligence (AAAI-96)*, pp. 1277–1284, Menlo Park, CA: AAAI Press, 1996.

[Fu 1994]   Fu, L. M., *Neural Networks in Computer Intelligence*, New York: McGraw–Hill, 1994.

[Galton 1987]   Galton, A., *Temporal Logics and Their Applications*, London: Academic Press, 1987.

[Gardner 1982]   Gardner, M., *Logic Machines and Diagrams* (second edition). Chicago: The University of Chicago Press, 1982.

[Garey & Johnson 1979]   Garey, M., and Johnson, D., *Computers and Intractability*, New York: W. H. Freeman, 1979.

[Gaschnig 1979]   Gaschnig, J., "Performance Measurement and Analysis of Certain Search Algorithms," Carnegie–Mellon University Computer Science Tech. Report CMU-CS-79-124, Pittsburg, PA, 1979.

[Gaschnig 1979]   Gaschnig, J., "A Problem–Similarity Approach to Devising Heuristics: First Results," in *Proceedings of the Sixth International Joint Conference on Artificial Intelligence (IJCAI-79)*, pp. 301–307, San Francisco: Morgan Kaufmann, 1979. (Reprinted in Webber, B., and Nilsson, N. (eds.), *Readings in Artificial Intelligence*, pp. 23–29, San Francisco: Morgan Kaufmann, 1981.)

[Gat 1992]   Gat, E., "Integrating Planning and Reacting in a Heterogeneous Asynchronous Architecture for Controlling Real–World Mobile Robots," in *Proceedings of the Tenth National Conference on Artificial Intelligence (AAAI-92)*, pp. 809–815, Menlo Park, CA: AAAI Press, 1992.

[Gelernter 1959]   Gelernter, H., "Realization of a Geometry Theorem–Proving Machine," *Proc. Intern. Conf. Inform Proc.*, UNESCO House, Paris, pp. 273–282, 1959. (Reprinted in Feigenbaum, E., and Feldman, J. (eds.), *Computers and Thought*, pp. 134–152, New York: McGraw–Hill, 1963.)

[Genesereth & Nilsson 1987]   Genesereth, M., and Nilsson, N., *Logical Foundations of Artificial Intelligence*, San Francisco: Morgan Kaufmann, 1987.

[Genesereth & Fikes 1992]   Genesereth, M., and Fikes, R. (eds.), *Knowledge Interchange Format, Version 3.0 Reference Manual*, Computer Science Department, Stanford University, Technical Report Logic–92–1, June 1992.

[Gentner 1983]   Gentner, D., "Structure Mapping: A Theoretical Framework for Analogy," *Cognitive Science*, 7:155–170, 1983.

[Gibson 1950]   Gibson, J. J., *The Perception of the Visual World*, Boston: Houghton Mifflin, 1950.

[Gibson 1979]   Gibson, J. J., *The Ecological Approach to Visual Perception*, Boston: Houghton Mifflin, 1979.

[Gil 1992]   Gil, Y., *Acquiring Domain Knowledge for Planning by Experimentation*, Ph.D. dissertation, School of Computer Science, Carnegie–Mellon University, 1992.

[Ginsberg 1987]   Ginsberg, M. (ed.), *Readings in Nonmonotonic Reasoning*, San Francisco: Morgan Kaufmann, 1987.

[Ginsberg 1993]   Ginsberg, M., "Dynamic Backtracking," *Journal of Artificial Intelligence Research*, 1:25–46, 1993.

[Ginsberg 1996]   Ginsberg, M., "Do Computers Need Commonsense?" in *Proceedings of the Fifth International Conference on Principles of Knowledge Representation and Reasoning (KR-96)*, pp. 620–626, San Francisco: Morgan Kaufmann, 1996.

[Ginsberg, et al. 1990]   Ginsberg, M., Frank, M., Halpin, M., and Torrance, M., "Search Lessons Learned from Crossword Puzzles," in *Proceedings of the Eighth National Conference on Artificial Intelligence (AAAI-90)*, pp. 210–215, Menlo Park, CA: AAAI Press, 1990.

[Ginsberg & Harvey 1992]   Ginsberg, M. L., and Harvey. W. D., "Iterative Broadening," *Artificial Intelligence*, 55(2/3):367–383, 1992.

[Glesner & Koller 1995]   Glesner, S., and Koller, D., "Constructing Flexible Dynamic Belief Networks from First–Order Probabilistic Knowledge Bases," *Proceedings of the European Conference on Symbolic and Quantitative Approaches to Reasoning and Uncertainty (ECSQARU)*, Fribourg, Switzerland, July 1995, in Froidevaux, C., and Kohlas, J. (eds.), *Lecture Notes in Artificial Intelligence*, pp. 217–226, Berlin: Springer–Verlag, 1995.

[Gogic, et al. 1995]   Gogic, G., Kautz, H., Papadimitriou, C., and Selman, B., "The Comparative Linguistics of Knowledge Representations," in *Proceedings of the Fourteenth International Joint Conference on Artificial Intelligence (IJCAI-95)*, pp. 862–869, San Francisco: Morgan Kaufmann, 1995.

[Goldberg 1979]   Goldberg, A., "On the Complexity of the Satisfiability Problem," Courant Computer Science Report No. 16, New York University, NY, 1979.

[Goldberg 1989]   Goldberg, D., *Genetic Algorithms in Search, Optimization, and Machine Learning*, Reading, MA: Addison–Wesley, 1989.

[Goldszmidt, Morris, & Pearl 1990]   Goldszmidt, M., Morris, P., and Pearl, J., "A Maximum Entropy Approach to Nonmonotonic Reasoning," in *Proceedings of the Eighth National Conference on Artificial Intelligence (AAAI-90)*, pp. 646–652, Menlo Park, CA: AAAI Press, 1990.

[Green 1969a]   Green, C., "Application of Theorem Proving to Problem Solving," in *Proceedings of the First International Joint Conference on Artificial Intelligence (IJCAI-69)*, pp. 741–747, San Francisco: Morgan Kaufmann, 1969.

[Green 1969b]   Green, C., "Theorem–Proving by Resolution as a Basis for Question–Answering Systems," in Meltzer, B., and Michie, D. (eds.), *Machine Intelligence 4*, pp. 183–205, Edinburgh: Edinburgh University Press, 1969.

[Gregory 1966]   Gregory, R., *Eye and Brain: The Psychology of Seeing*, New York: McGraw–Hill, 1966.

[Grimson 1990]   Grimson, W. E. L., *Object Recognition by Computer: The Role of Geometric Constraints*, Cambridge, MA: MIT Press, 1990.

[Grosz, Sparck Jones, & Webber 1986]   Grosz, B., Sparck Jones, K., and Webber, B. (eds.), *Readings in Natural Language Processing*, San Francisco: Morgan Kaufmann, 1986.

[Grosz, et al. 1987]   Grosz, B., Appelt, D., Martin, P., and Pereira, F., "Team: An Experiment in the Design of Transportable Natural-Language Interfaces," *Artificial Intelligence*, 32(2):173–244, 1987.

[Gruber 1997]   Gruber, T., "Toward Principles for the Design of Ontologies Used for Knowledge Sharing," in Guarino, N., and Poli, R. (eds.), *Formal Ontology in Conceptual Analysis and Knowledge Representation*, Amsterdam: Kluwer Academic Publishers, 1997. (Original paper presented at the International Workshop on Formal Ontology, March 1993, Stanford Knowledge Systems Laboratory Report KSL-93–04.)

[Gu 1989]   Gu, J., *Parallel Algorithms and Architectures for Very Fast AI Search*, Ph.D. thesis, University of Utah, 1989.

[Guha & Lenat 1990]   Guha, R. V., and Lenat, D., "Cyc: A Midterm Report," *AI Magazine*, pp. 33–59, Fall 1990.

[Gupta & Nau 1992]   Gupta, N., and Nau, D., "On the Complexity of Blocks-World Planning," *Artificial Intelligence*, 56(2/3):223–254, 1992.

[Guzman 1968]   Guzman, A., "Decomposition of a Visual Scene into Three-Dimensional Bodies," *Proc. Fall Joint Computer Conference*, vol. 33, pp. 291–304, 1968.

[Hanks & McDermott 1986]   Hanks, S., and McDermott, D., "Default Reasoning, Nonmonotonic Logics, and the Frame Problem," in *Proceedings of the Fifth National Conference on Artificial Intelligence (AAAI-86)*, pp. 328–333, Menlo Park, CA: AAAI Press, 1986. (Reprinted in Ginsberg, M. (ed.), *Readings in Nonmonotonic Reasoning*, pp. 390–395, San Francisco: Morgan Kaufmann, 1987.)

[Harnad 1990]   Harnad, S., "The Symbol Grounding Problem," *Physica D*, 42(1–3):335–346, 1990.

[Hart, Nilsson, & Raphael 1968]   Hart, P., Nilsson, N., and Raphael, B., "A Formal Basis for the Heuristic Determination of Minimum Cost Paths," *IEEE Trans. Syst. Science and Cybernetics*, SSC-4(2):100–107, 1968.

[Hart, Nilsson, & Raphael 1972]   Hart, P., Nilsson, N., and Raphael, B., "Correction to 'A Formal Basis for the Heuristic Determination of Minimum Cost Paths,' " *SIGART Newsletter*, no. 37, pp. 28–29, December 1972.

[Harvey 1994]   Harvey, W. D., *Nonsystematic Backtracking Search*, Ph.D. dissertation, Department of Computer Science, Stanford University, December 1994.

[Haussler 1988]   Haussler, D., "Quantifying Inductive Bias: AI Learning Algorithms and Valiant's Learning Framework," *Artificial Intelligence*, 36:177–221, 1988. (Reprinted in Shavlik, J., and Dietterich, T. (eds.), *Readings in Machine Learning*, pp. 96–107, San Francisco: Morgan Kaufmann, 1990.)

[Haussler 1990] Haussler, D., "Probably Approximately Correct Learning," *Proceedings of the Eighth National Conference on Artificial Intelligence (AAAI-90)*, pp. 1101–1108, Menlo Park, CA: AAAI Press, 1990.

[Hayes 1978] Hayes, P. J., "The Naive Physics Manifesto," in Michie, D. (ed.), *Expert Systems in the Microelectronic Age*, Edinburgh: Edinburgh University Press, 1978.

[Hayes 1985a] Hayes, P. J., "The Second Naive Physics Manifesto," in Hobbs, J., and Moore, R. (eds.), *Formal Theories of the Commonsense World*, Ch. 1, pp. 1–36, Norwood, NJ: Ablex, 1985.

[Hayes 1985b] Hayes, P. J., "Naive Physics I: Ontology for Liquids," in Hobbs, J., and Moore, R. (eds.), *Formal Theories of the Commonsense World*, Ch. 3, pp. 71–107, Norwood, NJ: Ablex, 1985.

[Hayes & Ford 1995] Hayes, P., and Ford, K., "Turing Test Considered Harmful," in *Proceedings of the Fourteenth International Joint Conference on Artificial Intelligence (IJCAI-95)*, pp. 972–977, San Francisco: Morgan Kaufmann, 1995.

[Hayes–Roth 1985] Hayes–Roth, B., "A Blackboard Architecture for Control," *Artificial Intelligence*, 26(3):251–321, 1985.

[Hayes–Roth 1995] Hayes–Roth, B., "An Architecture for Adaptive Intelligent Systems," *Artificial Intelligence*, 72(1/2):329–365, 1995.

[Hayes–Roth, et al. 1992] Hayes–Roth, B., Washington, R., Ash, D., Hewett, R., Collinot, A., Vina, A., Seiver, A., "Guardian: An Intelligent Agent for ICU Monitoring," *J. AI in Medicine*, 4:165–185, 1992.

[Haykin 1994] Haykin, S., *Neural Networks: A Comprehensive Foundation*, New York: Macmillan College Publishing, 1994.

[Hebert, et al. 1997] Hebert, M., et al., "Mobility for Unmanned Ground Vehicles," in Firschein, O., and Strat, T. (eds.), *Reconnaissance, Surveillance, and Target Acquisition for the Unmanned Ground Vehicle: Providing the Surveillance "Eyes" for an Autonomous Vehicle*, San Francisco: Morgan Kaufmann, 1997.

[Heckerman 1991] Heckerman, D., *Probabilistic Similarity Networks*, Cambridge, MA: MIT Press, 1991.

[Heckerman 1996] Heckerman, D., "A Tutorial on Learning with Bayesian Networks," Microsoft Research Technical Report, MSR–TR–95–06, Redmond, WA, March 1995 (revised November 1996).

[Heckerman & Nathwani 1992] Heckerman, D., and Nathwani, B., "An Evaluation of the Diagnostic Accuracy of Pathfinder," *SIAM Journal on Computing*, 25:56–74, 1992.

[Heckerman, Geiger, & Chickering 1995] Heckerman, D., Geiger, D., and Chickering, D., "Learning Bayesian Networks: The Combination of Knowledge and Statistical Data," *Machine Learning*, 20:3, 197–243, 1995.

[Heinsohn, et al. 1992]   Heinsohn, J., Kudenko, D., Nebel, B., and Profitlich, H.-J., "An Empirical Analysis of Terminological Representation Systems," *Proceedings of the Tenth National Conference on Artificial Intelligence (AAAI-92)*, pp. 767–773, Menlo Park, CA: AAAI Press, 1992.

[Hendrix 1979]   Hendrix, G., "Encoding Knowledge in Partitioned Networks," in Findler, N. (ed.), *Associative Networks*, pp. 51–92, New York: Academic Press, 1979.

[Henrion 1988]   Henrion, M., "Propagation of Uncertainty in Bayesian Networks by Probabilistic Logic Sampling," in Lemmer, J., and Kanal, L. (eds.), *Uncertainty in Artificial Intelligence*, 2:149–163, New York: Elsevier/North-Holland, 1988.

[Henrion 1990]   Henrion, M., "An Introduction to Algorithms for Inference in Belief Nets," in Henrion, M., Shachter, R., Kanal, L., and Lemmer, J. (eds.), *Uncertainty in Artificial Intelligence*, 5, Amsterdam: North Holland, 1990.

[Hertz, Krogh, & Palmer 1991]   Hertz, J., Krogh, A., and Palmer, R., *Introduction to the Theory of Neural Computation*, Reading, MA: Addison-Wesley, 1991.

[Hintikka 1962]   Hintikka, J., *Knowledge and Belief*, Ithaca, NY: Cornell University Press, 1962.

[Hobbs & Moore 1985]   Hobbs, J., and Moore, R., (eds.), *Formal Theories of the Commonsense World*, Norwood, NJ: Ablex, 1985.

[Holland 1975]   Holland, J., *Adaptation in Natural and Artificial Systems*, Ann Arbor: The University of Michigan Press, 1975. (Second edition printed in 1992 by MIT Press, Cambridge, MA.)

[Holland 1986]   Holland, J. H., "Escaping Brittleness: The Possibilities of General-Purpose Learning Algorithms Applied to Parallel Rule-Based Systems," in Michalski, R., Carbonell, J., and Mitchell, T. (eds.), *Machine Learning: An Artificial Intelligence Approach, Volume 2*, Ch. 20, San Francisco: Morgan Kaufmann, 1986.

[Horn 1951]   Horn, A., "On Sentences Which Are True of Direct Unions of Algebras," *Jour. of Symbolic Logic*, 16:14–21, 1951.

[Horn 1986]   Horn, B. K. P., *Robot Vision*, Cambridge, MA: MIT Press, 1986.

[Horowitz & Pavlidis 1976]   Horowitz, S., and Pavlidis, T., "Picture Segmentation by a Tree Traversal Algorithm," *Jour. Assoc. Comp. Mach.*, 23(2):368–388, April 1976.

[Horswill 1993]   Horswill, I., "Polly: A Vision-Based Artificial Agent," in *Proceedings of the Eleventh National Conference on Artificial Intelligence (AAAI-93)*, pp. 824–829, Menlo Park, CA: AAAI Press, 1993.

[Horvitz 1987]   Horvitz, E., "Reasoning about Beliefs and Actions under Computational Resource Constraints," in *Proc. of the 1987 Workshop on Uncertainty in Artificial Intelligence*, pp. 429–444, 1987. (Also in Kanal, L., et al. (eds.), *Uncertainty in Artificial Intelligence 3*, pp. 301–324, New York: Elsevier, 1989.)

[Horvitz, Breese, & Henrion 1988] Horvitz, E., Breese, J., and Henrion, M., "Decision Theory in Expert Systems and Artificial Intelligence," *International Journal of Approximate Reasoning*, 2:247–302, 1988.

[Hubel 1988] Hubel, D., *Eye, Brain, and Vision*, New York: W. H. Freeman, 1988.

[Hubel & Wiesel 1968] Hubel, D., and Wiesel, T., "Receptive Fields and Functional Architecture of Monkey Striate Cortex," *Journal of Physiology (London)*, 195(1):215–243, March 1968.

[Huberman 1968] Huberman, B. J., *A Program to Play Chess End Games*, Stanford University Computer Science Department Report CS 106, August 19, 1968.

[Hueckel 1973] Hueckel, M., "A Local Visual Operator Which Recognizes Edges and Lines," *Journal of the Assoc. for Comp. Machinery*, 20(4):634–647, October 1973.

[Huffman 1971] Huffman, D., "Impossible Objects as Nonsense Sentences," in *Machine Intelligence 6*, Meltzer, B., and Michie, D. (eds.), pp. 295–323, New York: American Elsevier, 1971.

[Jain, Kasturi, & Schunck 1995] Jain, R., Kasturi, R., and Schunck, B., *Machine Vision*, New York: McGraw–Hill, 1995.

[Jensen 1996] Jensen, F., *An Introduction to Bayesian Networks*, New York: Springer–Verlag, 1996.

[Johnson–Laird 1988] Johnson–Laird, P., *The Computer and the Mind: An Introduction to Cognitive Science*, Cambridge, MA: Harvard University Press, 1988.

[Jordan & Rumelhart 1992] Jordan, M., and Rumelhart, D., "Forward Models: Supervised Learning with a Distal Teacher," *Cognitive Science*, 16:307–354, 1992.

[Juels & Wattenberg 1996] Juels, A., and Wattenberg, M., "Stochastic Hillclimbing as a Baseline Method for the Evaluation of Genetic Algorithms," in *Neural Information Processing Systems 8*, Cambridge, MA: MIT Press, 1996.

[Julesz 1971] Julesz, B., *Foundations of Cyclopean Perception*, Chicago: The University of Chicago Press, 1971.

[Kaelbling & Rosenschein 1990] Kaelbling, L., and Rosenschein, S., "Action and Planning in Embedded Agents," *Robotics and Autonomous Systems*, 6:35–48, 1990. Also in [Maes 1990].

[Kaelbling, Littman, & Moore 1996] Kaelbling, L. P., Littman, M. L., and Moore, A. W., "Reinforcement Learning: A Survey," *Journal of Artificial Intelligence Research*, 4:237–285, 1996.

[Kanal & Kumar 1988] Kanal, L., and Kumar, V. (eds.), *Search in Artificial Intelligence*, Berlin: Springer–Verlag, 1988.

[Karmarkar 1984] Karmarkar, N., "A New Polynomial–Time Algorithm for Linear Programming," *Combinatorica*, 4(4):373–395, 1984.

[Kartha 1994] Kartha, G. N., "Two Counterexamples Related to Baker's Approach to the Frame Problem," *Artificial Intelligence*, 69(1–2):379–391, 1994.

[Kautz 1985]   Kautz, H., "Formalizing Spatial Concepts and Spatial Language," in *Commonsense Summer: Final Report*, Center for the Study of Language and Information (CSLI) Technical Report CSLI-85-35, Stanford University, Stanford, CA, 1985.

[Kautz 1991]   Kautz, H., "A Formal Theory of Plan Recognition and Its Implementation," in Allen, J., Kautz, H., Pelavin, R., and Tenenberg, J. (eds.), *Reasoning About Plans*, Ch. 2, San Francisco: Morgan Kaufmann, 1991.

[Kautz & Selman 1992]   Kautz, H., and Selman, B., "Forming Concepts for Fast Inference," in *Proceedings of the Tenth National Conference on Artificial Intelligence (AAAI-92)*, pp. 787–793, Menlo Park, CA: AAAI Press, 1992.

[Kautz & Selman 1996]   Kautz, H., and Selman, B., "Pushing the Envelope: Planning, Propositional Logic, and Stochastic Search," in *Proceedings of the Thirteenth National Conference on Artificial Intelligence (AAAI-96)*, pp. 1194–1201, Menlo Park, CA: AAAI Press, 1996.

[Kautz, Kearns, & Selman 1993]   Kautz, H., Kearns, M., and Selman, B., "Reasoning with Characteristic Models," *Proceedings of the Eleventh National Conference on Artificial Intelligence (AAAI-93)*, pp. 34–39, Menlo Park, CA: AAAI Press, 1993.

[Kautz, McAllester, & Selman 1996]   Kautz, H., McAllester, D., and Selman, B., "Encoding Plans in Propositional Logic," in *Proceedings of the Fifth International Conference on Principles of Knowledge Representation and Reasoning (KR-96)*, pp. 374–384, San Francisco: Morgan Kaufmann, 1996.

[Kearns & Vazirani 1994]   Kearns, M., and Vazirani, U., *An Introduction to Computational Learning Theory*, Cambridge, MA: MIT Press, 1994.

[Khardon & Roth 1998]   Khardon, R., and Roth, D., "Learning to Reason," *Journal of the ACM*, to appear, 1998.

[Kierulf, Chen, & Nievergelt 1990]   Kierulf, A., Chen, K., and Nievergelt, J., "Smart Game Board and Go Explorer: A Study in Software and Knowledge Engineering," *Comm. of the ACM*, 33(2):152–167, 1990.

[Kim & Pearl 1983]   Kim, J., and Pearl, J., "A Computational Model for Combined Causal and Diagnostic Reasoning in Inference Systems," in *Proceedings of the Eighth International Joint Conference on Artificial Intelligence (IJCAI-83)*, pp. 190–193, San Francisco: Morgan Kaufmann, 1983.

[Kirkpatrick, Gelatt, & Vecchi 1983]   Kirkpatrick, S., Gelatt, C., and Vecchi, M., "Optimization by Simulated Annealing," *Science*, 220:671–680, 1983.

[Kirsh 1991]   Kirsh, D., "Today the Earwig, Tomorrow Man?" *Artificial Intelligence*, 47(1–3):161–184, 1991.

[Knuth & Moore 1975]   Knuth, D. E., and Moore, R. W., "An Analysis of Alpha–Beta Pruning," *Artificial Intelligence*, 6(4), 293–326, 1975.

[Knoblock 1990]   Knoblock, C. A., "Learning Abstraction Hierarchies for Problem Solving," in *Proceedings of the Eighth National Conference on Artificial Intelligence (AAAI-90)*, pp. 923–928, Menlo Park, CA: AAAI Press, 1990.

[Koenderink 1984]   Koenderink, J., "The Structure of Images," *Biological Cybernetics*, 50:363–370, 1984.

[Kolodner 1993]   Kolodner, J., *Case-Based Reasoning*, San Francisco: Morgan Kaufmann, 1993.

[Konolige 1982]   Konolige, K., "A First-Order Formalization of Knowledge and Action for a Multi-Agent Planning System," in Hayes, J., Michie, D., and Pao, Y. (eds.), *Machine Intelligence 10*, Chichester, England: Ellis Horwood, Ltd., 1982.

[Konolige 1986]   Konolige, K., *A Deduction Model of Belief*, London: Pitman, 1986.

[Korf 1985]   Korf, R., "Depth-First Iterative Deepening: An Optimal Admissible Tree Search Algorithm," *Artificial Intelligence*, 27:97–109, 1985.

[Korf 1987]   Korf, R., "Planning as Search: A Quantitative Approach," *Artificial Intelligence*, 33(1):65–88, 1987.

[Korf 1990]   Korf, R., "Real-Time Heuristic Search," *Artificial Intelligence*, 42, 1990.

[Korf 1991]   Korf, R., "Multi-Player Alpha-Beta Pruning," *Artificial Intelligence*, 48:99–111, 1991.

[Korf 1992]   Korf, R., "Search," in Shapiro, S. (ed.), *Encyclopedia of Artificial Intelligence, Second Edition*, pp. 1460–1467, New York: John Wiley & Sons, 1992.

[Korf 1993]   Korf, R., "Linear-Space Best-First Search," *Artificial Intelligence*, 62, 41–78, 1993.

[Korf 1996]   Korf, R., "Space-Efficient Search Algorithms," *ACM Computing Surveys*, 27(3):337–339, 1996.

[Korf 1997]   Korf, R., "Finding Optimal Solutions to Rubik's Cube Using Pattern Databases," in *Proceedings of the Fourteenth National Conference on Artificial Intelligence (AAAI-97)*, pp. 700–705, Menlo Park, CA: AAAI Press, 1997.

[Korf & Taylor 1996]   Korf, R., and Taylor, L., "Finding Optimal Solutions to the Twenty-Four Puzzle," in *Proceedings of the Thirteenth National Conference on Artificial Intelligence (AAAI-96)*, pp. 1202–1207, Menlo Park, CA: AAAI Press, 1996.

[Kowalski 1974]   Kowalski, R., "Predicate Logic as a Programming Language," in *Proceedings of the IFIP-74 Congress*, pp. 569–574, Amsterdam: Elsevier/North-Holland, 1974.

[Kowalski & Kim 1991]   Kowalski, R., and Kim, J.-S., "A Metalogic Programming Approach to Multi-Agent Belief," in Lifschitz, V. (ed.), *Artificial Intelligence and Mathematical Theory of Computation: Papers in Honor of John McCarthy*, pp. 231–246, Boston: Academic Press, 1991.

[Koza 1992]   Koza, J., *Genetic Programming: On the Programming of Computers by Means of Natural Selection*, Cambridge, MA: MIT Press, 1992.

[Koza 1994]   Koza, J., *Genetic Programming II: Automatic Discovery of Reusable Programs*, Cambridge, MA: MIT Press, 1994.

[Koza, et al. 1996]   Koza, J., Bennett, F., III, Andre, D., and Keane, M., "Automated WYSIWYG Design of Both the Topology and Component Values of Analog Electrical Circuits Using Genetic Programming," in Koza, John R., Goldberg, David E., Fogel, David B., and Riolo, Rick L. (eds.), *Genetic Programming 1996: Proceedings of the First Annual Conference*, Stanford University, July 28–31, 1996, Cambridge, MA: MIT Press.

[Kripke 1963]   Kripke, S., "Semantical Considerations on Modal Logic," *Acta Philosophica Fennica*, 16:83–94, 1963.

[Kuipers, et al. 1993]   Kuipers, B., Froom, R., Lee, W-Y., Pierce, D., "The Semantic Hierarchy in Robot Learning," in Connell, J., and Mahadevan, S. (eds.), *Robot Learning*, Ch. 6, Boston: Kluwer Academic Publishers, 1993.

[Kuipers & Byun 1991]   Kuipers, B., and Byun, Y-T., "A Robot Exploration and Mapping Strategy Based on a Semantic Hierarchy of Spatial Representations," *Robotics and Autonomous Systems*, 8:47–63, 1991.

[Kumar & Kanal 1988]   Kumar, V., and Kanal, L., "The CDP: A Unifying Formulation for Heuristic Search, Dynamic Programming, and Branch-and-Bound," in Kanal, L., and Kumar, V. (eds.), *Search in Artificial Intelligence*, Ch. 1, pp. 1–27, Berlin: Springer-Verlag, 1988.

[Kumar 1992]   Kumar, V., "Algorithms for Constraint-Satisfaction Problems: A Survey," *Artificial Intelligence Magazine*, 13(1):32–44, Spring 1992.

[Laird, Newell, & Rosenbloom 1987]   Laird, J., Newell, A., and Rosenbloom, P., "SOAR: An Architecture for General Intelligence," *Artificial Intelligence*, 33(1):1–64, 1987.

[Laird, et al. 1991]   Laird, J., Yager, E., Hucka, M., and Tuck, C., "Robo-Soar: An Integration of External Interaction, Planning, and Learning Using SOAR," *Robotics and Autonomous Systems*, 8:113–129, 1991.

[Lakoff 1987]   Lakoff, G., *Women, Fire, and Dangerous Things: What Categories Reveal about the Mind*, Chicago: The University of Chicago Press, 1987.

[Lakoff & Johnson 1980]   Lakoff, G., and Johnson, M., *Metaphors We Live By*, Chicago: The University of Chicago Press, 1980.

[Langley 1996]   Langley, P., *Elements of Machine Learning*, San Francisco: Morgan Kaufmann, 1996.

[Latombe 1991]   Latombe, J.-C., *Robot Motion Planning*, Dordrecht: Kluwer Academic Publishers, 1991.

[Lauritzen 1991]   Lauritzen, S., "The EM Algorithm for Graphical Association Models with Missing Data," Tech. Report TR–91–05, Dept. of Statistics, Aalborg University, Denmark, 1991.

[Lauritzen & Spiegelhalter 1988]   Lauritzen, S., and Spiegelhalter, D., "Local Computations with Probabilities on Graphical Structures and Their Application to Expert Systems," *Journal of the Royal Statistical Society*, B 50(2):157–224, 1988.

[Lavrač & Džeroski 1994]   Lavrač, N., and Džeroski, S., *Inductive Logic Programming*, Chichester, England: Ellis Horwood, 1994.

[LeCun, et al. 1989]   LeCun, Y., Boser, B., Denker, J., Henderson, D., Howard, R., Hubbard, W., and Jackel, L., "Backpropagation Applied to Handwritten Zip Code Recognition," *Neural Computation*, 1(4), 1989.

[Lee & Mahajan 1988]   Lee, K.-F., and Mahajan, S., "A Pattern Classification Approach to Evaluation Function Learning," *Artificial Intelligence*, 36(1):1–26, 1988.

[Lenat 1995]   Lenat, D., "CYC: A Large-Scale Investment in Knowledge Infrastructure," *Comm. ACM*, 38(11):33–38, November 1995.

[Lenat & Guha 1990]   Lenat, D., and Guha, R., *Building Large Knowledge Bases*, Reading, MA: Addison-Wesley, 1990.

[Leonard-Barton 1987]   Leonard-Barton, D., "The Case for Integrative Innovation: An Expert System at Digital," *Sloan Management Review*, pp. 7–19, Fall 1987.

[Letvinn, et al. 1959]   Letvinn, J., Maturana, H., McCulloch, W., and Pitts, W., "What the Frog's Eye Tells the Frog's Brain," *Proc. IRE*, 47:1940–1951, 1959.

[Levesque 1984a]   Levesque, H., "Foundations of a Functional Approach to Knowledge Representation," *Artificial Intelligence*, 23(2):155–212, 1984.

[Levesque 1984b]   Levesque, H., "A Logic of Implicit and Explicit Belief," in *Proceedings of the Fourth National Conference on Artificial Intelligence (AAAI-84)*, pp. 198–202, Menlo Park, CA: AAAI Press, 1984.

[Levesque 1986]   Levesque, H., "Making Believers Out of Computers," *Artificial Intelligence*, 30(1):81–108, 1986.

[Levesque & Brachman 1987]   Levesque, H., and Brachman, R., "Expressiveness and Tractability in Knowledge Representation and Reasoning," *Computational Intelligence*, 3(2):78–93, 1987.

[Levesque, et al. 1997]   Levesque, H., Reiter, R., Lesprance, Y., Lin, F., and Scherl, R., "GOLOG: A Logic Programming Language for Dynamic Domains," *Journal of Logic Programming*, Special Issue on Reasoning about Action and Change, 31(1–3):59–83, 1997.

[Lifschitz 1986]   Lifschitz, V., "On the Semantics of STRIPS," in Georgeff, M., and Lansky, A. (eds.), *Reasoning about Actions and Plans: Proceedings of the 1986 Workshop*, Timberline, Oregon, pp. 1–9, San Francisco: Morgan Kaufmann, 1986. (Also in Allen, J., Hendler, J., and Tate, A. (eds.), *Readings in Planning*, pp. 523–530, San Francisco: Morgan Kaufmann, 1990.)

[Lindsay, et al. 1980]   Lindsay, R., Buchanan, B., Feigenbaum, E., and Lederberg, J., *Applications of Artificial Intelligence for Organic Chemistry: The DENDRAL Project*, New York: McGraw-Hill, 1980.

[Lovejoy 1991]   Lovejoy, W., "A Survey of Algorithmic Methods for Partially Observed Markov Decision Processes," *Annals of Operations Research*, 28(1–4):47–66, 1991.

[Loveland 1978]   Loveland, D. W., *Automated Theorem Proving: A Logical Basis*, New York: North–Holland, 1978.

[Löwenheim 1915]   Löwenheim, L., "Über Möglichkeiten im Relativekalkül," *Mathematische Annalen*, 76:447–470, 1915. (English translation appears in van Heijenoort, J. (ed.), *From Frege to Gödel: A Source Book in Mathematical Logic, 1879–1931*, Cambridge, MA: Harvard University Press, 1967.)

[Lowry & McCartney 1991]   Lowry, M., and McCartney, R., *Automating Software Design*, Cambridge, MA: MIT Press, 1991.

[Lucas 1961]   Lucas, J. R., "Minds, Machines, and Gödel," *Philosophy*, 36:112–127, 1961. (Also in Anderson, A. R. (ed.), *Minds and Machines*, pp. 43–59, Englewood Cliffs, NJ: Prentice Hall, 1964.)

[Luckham 1970]   Luckham, D., "Refinement Theorems in Resolution Theory," *Proc. IRIA 1968 Symp. on Automatic Demonstration*, Springer–Verlag Lecture Notes in Mathematics, No. 125, pp. 163–190, 1970.

[Luckham & Nilsson 1971]   Luckham, D. C., and Nilsson, N., "Extracting Information from Resolution Proof Trees," *Artificial Intelligence*, 2(1): 27–54, 1971.

[Maes 1990a]   Maes, P. (ed.), *Designing Autonomous Agents: Theory and Practice from Biology to Engineering and Back*, Cambridge, MA: MIT Press, 1990.

[Maes 1990b]   Maes, P., "Guest Editorial," *Robotics and Autonomous Systems*, 6:1–2, 1990. Also in [Maes 1990a].

[Magerman 1993]   Magerman, D., *Natural Language Parsing as Statistical Pattern Recognition*, Ph.D. thesis, Department of Computer Science, Stanford University, 1993.

[Mahadevan 1992]   Mahadevan, S., "Enhancing Transfer in Reinforcement Learning by Building Stochastic Models of Robot Actions," in *Proceedings of the Ninth International Workshop on Machine Learning (ML92)*, pp. 290–299, San Francisco: Morgan Kaufmann, 1992.

[Mahadevan & Connell 1992]   Mahadevan, S., and Connell, J., "Automatic Programming of Behavior–Based Robots Using Reinforcement Learning," *Artificial Intelligence*, 55(1–2):311–365, 1992.

[Manna & Waldinger 1985]   Manna, Z., and Waldinger, R., *The Logical Basis for Computer Programming, Volume 1: Deductive Reasoning*, Reading, MA: Addison–Wesley, 1985.

[Manna & Waldinger 1990]   Manna, Z., and Waldinger, R., *The Logical Basis for Computer Programming, Volume 2: Deductive Systems*, Reading, MA: Addison–Wesley, 1990.

[Manna & Waldinger 1992]   Manna, Z., and Waldinger, R., "Fundamentals of Deductive Program Synthesis," *IEEE Transactions on Software Engineering*, 18(8):674–704, 1992.

[Marr 1982]   Marr, D., *Vision: A Computational Investigation into the Human Representation and Processing of Visual Information*, New York: W. H. Freeman, 1982.

[Marr & Hildreth 1980]   Marr, D., and Hildreth, E., "Theory of Edge Detection," *Proc. Royal Soc. of London, Series B*, Vol. 207, pp. 187–217, 1980.

[Marr & Poggio 1979]   Marr, D., and Poggio, T., "A Computational Theory of Human Stereo Vision," *Proceedings of the Royal Society London, B*, 204:301–328, 1979.

[Martelli & Montanari 1973]   Martelli, A., and Montanari, U., "Additive AND/OR Graphs," in *Proceedings of the Third International Joint Conference on Artificial Intelligence (IJCAI-73)*, pp. 1–11, San Francisco: Morgan Kaufmann, 1973.

[Masand, Linoff, & Waltz 1992]   Masand, B., Linoff, G., and Waltz, D., "Classifying News Stories Using Memory Based Reasoning," in *Proceedings of ACM/SIGIR*, pp. 59–65, 1992.

[Mataric 1990]   Mataric, M., "A Distributed Model for Mobile Robot Environment Learning and Navigation," *Technical Report No. AIM-TR-1228*, MIT AI Lab, MIT, Cambridge, MA, 1990.

[Mataric 1996]   Mataric, M., "Designing and Understanding Adaptive Group Behavior," *Adaptive Behavior*, 4(1):51–80, 1996.

[Mataric 1997]   Mataric, M., "Studying the Role of Embodiment in Cognition," *Cybernetics and Systems*, 28(6):457–470, (Special Issue on Epistemological Aspects of Embodied AI), July 1997.

[Mauldin 1994]   Mauldin, M. L., "Chatterbots, Tinymuds, and the Turing Test: Entering the Loebner Prize Competition," in *Proceedings of the Twelfth National Conference on Artificial Intelligence (AAAI-94)*, pp. 16–21, Menlo Park, CA: AAAI Press, 1994.

[McAdams & Shapiro 1995]   McAdams, H., and Shapiro, L., "Circuit Simulation of Genetic Networks," *Science*, 269:650–656, August 4, 1995.

[McAllester & Rosenblitt 1991]   McAllester, D., and Rosenblitt, D., "Systematic Nonlinear Planning," in *Proceedings of the Ninth National Conference on Artificial Intelligence (AAAI-91)*, pp. 634–639, Menlo Park, CA: AAAI Press, 1991.

[McCarthy 1958]   McCarthy, J., "Programs with Common Sense," *Mechanisation of Thought Processes, Proceedings of the Symposium of the National Physics Laboratory*, Vol. I, pp. 77–84, London: Her Majesty's Stationary Office, 1958. (Also in Minsky, M. (ed.), *Semantic Information Processing*, pp. 403–410, Cambridge, MA: MIT Press, 1968, and Brachman, R., and Levesque, H. (eds.), *Readings in Knowledge Representation*, pp. 299–307, San Francisco: Morgan Kaufmann, 1985.)

[McCarthy 1977]   McCarthy, J., "Epistemological Problems in Artificial Intelligence," in *Proceedings of the Fifth International Joint Conference on Artificial Intelligence (IJCAI-77)*, pp. 1038–1044, San Francisco: Morgan Kaufmann, 1977.

[McCarthy 1979a]   McCarthy, J., "Ascribing Mental Qualities to Machines," in Ringle, M. (ed.), *Philosophical Perspectives in Artificial Intelligence*, pp. 161–195, Atlantic Highlands, NJ: Humanities Press, 1979.

[McCarthy 1979b]   McCarthy, J., "First-Order Theories of Individual Concepts and Propositions," in Hayes, J., Michie, D., and Mikulich, L. (eds.), *Machine Intelligence 9*, pp. 129–147, Chichester, England: Ellis Horwood, Ltd., 1979.

[McCarthy 1980]   McCarthy, J., "Circumscription: A Form of Non-monotonic Reasoning," *Artificial Intelligence*, 13(1–2):27–39, 1980.

[McCarthy 1986]   McCarthy, J., "Applications of Circumscription to Formalizing Commonsense Knowledge," *Artificial Intelligence*, 28(1):89–116, 1986.

[McCarthy 1997]   McCarthy, J., "AI as Sport," (a Review of [Newborn 1996]), *Science*, 276:1518–1519, June 6, 1997.

[McCarthy & Hayes 1969]   McCarthy, J. and Hayes, P., "Some Philosophical Problems from the Standpoint of Artificial Intelligence," in Meltzer, B., and Michie, D. (eds.), *Machine Intelligence 4*, Edinburgh: Edinburgh University Press, 1969.

[McClelland & Rumelhart 1981]   McClelland, J., and Rumelhart, D., "An Interactive Activation Model of Context Effects in Letter Perception, Part I: An Account of Basic Findings," *Psychological Review*, 88:375–407, 1981.

[McClelland & Rumelhart 1982]   McClelland, J., and Rumelhart, D., "An Interactive Activation Model of Context Effects in Letter Perception, Part II: The Contextual Enhancement Effect and Some Tests and Extensions of the Model," *Psychological Review*, 89:60–84, 1982.

[McCorduck 1979]   McCorduck, P., *Machines Who Think*, San Francisco: W. H. Freeman, 1979.

[McCulloch & Pitts 1943]   McCulloch, W., and Pitts, W., "A Logical Calculus of the Ideas Immanent in Nervous Activity," *Bulletin of Math. Biophysics*, 5:115–133, 1943.

[McCune 1992]   McCune, W., "Automated Discovery of New Axiomatizations of the Left Group and Right Group Calculi," *Automated Reasoning*, 9(1):1–24, 1992.

[McCune 1994]   McCune, W., *OTTER 3.0 Reference Manual and Guide*, Technical Report ANL-94/6, Argonne National Laboratory, Argonne, IL, 1994.

[McDermott 1987]   McDermott, D., "A Critique of Pure Reason," *Computational Intelligence*, 3(3):151–237, 1987.

[McDermott & Doyle 1980]   McDermott, D., and Doyle, J., "Non-monotonic Logic I," *Artificial Intelligence*, 13(1–2):41–72, 1980.

[McDermott 1982]   McDermott, J., "R1: A Rule-Based Configurer of Computer Systems," *Artificial Intelligence*, 19(1):39–88, 1982.

[McDonald & Bolc 1988]   McDonald, D., and Bolc, L., *Natural Language Generation Systems*, New York: Springer-Verlag, 1988.

[McFarland 1987]   McFarland, D. (ed.), *The Oxford Companion to Animal Behavior*, Oxford: Oxford University Press, 1987.

[McFarland & Bösser 1993]   McFarland, D., and Bösser, T., *Intelligent Behavior in Animals and Robots*, Cambridge, MA: MIT Press, 1993.

[McKeown & Swartout 1987]   McKeown, K., and Swartout, W., "Language Generation and Explanation," in *Annual Review of Computer Science*, vol. 2, Palo Alto, CA: Annual Reviews, 1987.

[Mérõ 1984]   Mérõ, L., "A Heuristic Search Algorithm with Modifiable Estimate," *Artificial Intelligence*, 23:13–27, 1984.

[Michalewicz 1992]   Michalewicz, Z., *Genetic Algorithms + Data Structures = Evolution Programs*, Berlin: Springer-Verlag, 1992.

[Michalski 1969]   Michalski, R., "On the Quasi-Minimal Solution of the General Covering Problem," *Proc. of the Fifth International Symposium on Information Processing (FCIP 69)*, Vol. A3, pp. 125–128, (Switching Circuits), Bled, Yugoslavia, 1969.

[Michie 1966]   Michie, D., "Game-Playing and Game-Learning Automata," in Fox, L. (ed.), *Advances in Programming and Non-numerical Computation*, pp. 183–200, New York: Pergamon, 1966.

[Miller, Pople, & Myers 1982]   Miller, R., Pople, H., and Myers, J., "INTERNIST-1: An Experimental Computer-Based Diagnostic Consultant for General Internal Medicine," *New England Journal of Medicine*, 307:468–476, 1982.

[Minker 1997]   Minker, J., "Logic and Databases: Past, Present, and Future," *AI Magazine*, 18(3):21–47, Fall 1997.

[Minnix, McVey, & Iñigo 1991]   Minnix, J., McVey, E., and Iñigo, R., "Multistage Self-Organizing Neural Network with Biologically Inspired Preprocessing Features for Rotation and Scale Invariant Pattern Recognition," *Proc. of the IEEE*, pp. 1605–1610, 1991.

[Minsky 1967]   Minsky, M., *Computation: Finite and Infinite Machines*, Englewood Cliffs, NJ: Prentice Hall, 1967.

[Minsky 1986]   Minsky, M., *Society of Mind*, New York: Simon & Schuster, 1986.

[Minton 1988]   Minton, S., *Learning Search Control Knowledge: An Explanation-Based Approach*, Boston: Kluwer Academic Publishers, 1988.

[Minton 1990]   Minton, S., "Quantitative Results Concerning the Utility of Explanation-Based Learning," *Artificial Intelligence*, 42(2–3):363–391, 1990.

[Minton 1993]   Minton, S. (ed.), *Machine Learning Methods for Planning*, San Francisco: Morgan Kaufmann, 1993.

[Minton, et al. 1989]   Minton, S., Carbonell, J., Knoblock, C., Kuokka, D., Etzioni, O., and Gil, Y., "Explanation-Based Learning: A Problem Solving Perspective," *Artificial Intelligence*, 40(1–3):63–118, 1989.

[Minton, et al. 1990]   Minton, S., Johnston, M., Phillips, A., and Laird, P., "Solving Large–Scale Constraint–Satisfaction and Scheduling Problems Using a Heuristic Repair Method," in *Proceedings of the Eighth National Conference on Artificial Intelligence (AAAI-90)*, pp. 17–24, Menlo Park, CA: AAAI Press, 1990.

[Minton, et al. 1992]   Minton, S., Johnston, M., Philips, A., and Laird, P., "Minimizing Conflicts: A Heuristic Repair Method for Constraint Satisfaction and Scheduling Problems," *Artificial Intelligence*, 58(1–3):161–205, 1992.

[Minton, Bresina, & Drummond 1994]   Minton, S., Bresina, J., and Drummond, M., "Total–Order and Partial–Order Planning: A Comparative Analysis," *Journal of Artificial Intelligence Research*, 2:227–262, 1994.

[Mitchell, M. 1996]   Mitchell, M., *An Introduction to Genetic Algorithms*, Cambridge, MA: MIT Press, 1996.

[Mitchell, T. 1997]   Mitchell, T., *Machine Learning*, New York: McGraw-Hill, 1997.

[Monahan 1982]   Monahan, G., "A Survey of Partially Observable Markov Decision Processes: Theory, Models, and Algorithms," *Management Science*, 28:1–16, January 1982.

[Montague, et al. 1995]   Montague, P., Dayan, P., Person, C., and Sejnowski, T., "Bee Foraging in Uncertain Environments Using Predictive Hebbian Learning," *Nature* 377:725–728, 1995.

[Moore 1959]   Moore, E. F., "The Shortest Path through a Maze," in *Proceedings of an International Symposium on the Theory of Switching, Part II*, pp. 285–292, Cambridge, MA: Harvard University Press, 1959.

[Moore 1985a]   Moore, R., "Semantical Considerations on Nonmonotonic Logic," *Artificial Intelligence*, 25(1):75–94, 1985.

[Moore 1985b]   Moore, R., "A Formal Theory of Knowledge and Action," in Hobbs, J., and Moore, R. (eds.), *Formal Theories of the Commonsense World*, pp. 319–358, Norwood, NJ: Ablex, 1985.

[Moore 1993]   Moore, R., "Autoepistemic Logic Revisited," *Artificial Intelligence*, 59(1–2):27–30, 1993.

[Moore & Atkeson 1993]   Moore, A., and Atkeson, C., "Prioritized Sweeping–Reinforcement Learning with Less Data and Less Time," *Machine Learning*, 13:103–130, 1993.

[Mostow & Prieditis 1989]   Mostow, J., and Prieditis, A., "Discovering Admissible Heuristics by Abstracting and Optimizing: A Transformational Approach," in *Proceedings of the Eleventh International Joint Conference on Artificial Intelligence (IJCAI-89)*, pp. 701–707, San Francisco: Morgan Kaufmann, 1989.

[Muggleton 1992]   Muggleton, S., *Inductive Logic Programming*, New York: Academic Press, 1992.

[Muggleton & Buntine 1988]   Muggleton, S., and Buntine, W., "Machine Invention of First-Order Predicates by Inverting Resolution," in Laird, J. (ed.), in *Proceedings of the*

Fifth International Conference on Machine Learning, pp. 339ff, San Francisco: Morgan Kaufmann, 1988.

[Muggleton, King, & Sternberg 1992]   Muggleton, S., King, R., and Sternberg, J., "Protein Secondary Structure Prediction Using Logic–Based Machine Learning," *Protein Engineering*, 5(7):647–657, 1992.

[Muggleton & De Raedt 1994]   Muggleton, S., and De Raedt, L., "Inductive Logic Programming: Theory and Methods," *Journal of Logic Programming*, 19,20:629–679, 1994.

[Myers 1994]   Myers, K., "Hybrid Reasoning Using Universal Attachment," *Artificial Intelligence*, (67)2:329–375, 1994.

[Nalwa 1993]   Nalwa, V. S., *A Guided Tour of Computer Vision*, Reading, MA: Addison–Wesley, 1993.

[Nalwa & Binford 1986]   Nalwa, V., and Binford, T., "On Detecting Edges," *IEEE Trans on Pattern Analysis and Machine Intelligence*, PAMI–8(6):699–714, November 1986.

[Nalwa & Pauchon 1987]   Nalwa, V., and Pauchon, E., "Edgel Aggregation and Edge Description," *Computer Vision, Graphics, and Image Processing*, 40:79–94, 1987.

[Neal 1991]   Neal, R., "Connectionist Learning of Belief Networks," *Artificial Intelligence*, 56:71–113, 1991.

[Neapolitan 1990]   Neapolitan, R., *Probabilistic Reasoning in Expert Systems: Theory and Algorithms*, New York: John Wiley & Sons, 1990.

[Newborn 1996]   Newborn, M., *Computer Chess Comes of Age*, New York: Springer–Verlag, 1996.

[Newell 1964]   Newell, A., "The Possibility of Planning Languages in Man–Computer Communication," in *Communication Processes*, Proceedings of a Symposium held in Washington, 1963, New York: Pergamon, 1964.

[Newell 1973]   Newell, A., "Production Systems: Models of Control Structures," in Chase, W. (ed.), *Visual Information Processing*, New York: Academic Press, 1973.

[Newell 1982]   Newell, A., "The Knowledge Level," *Artificial Intelligence*, 18(1):87–127, 1982.

[Newell 1991]   Newell, A., *Unified Theories of Cognition*, Cambridge, MA: Harvard University Press, 1991.

[Newell, Shaw, & Simon 1957]   Newell, A., Shaw, J., and Simon, H., "Empirical Explorations of the Logic Theory Machine," *Proc. West. Joint Computer Conf.*, vol. 15, pp. 218–239, 1957. (Reprinted in Feigenbaum, E., and Feldman, J. (eds.), *Computers and Thought*, pp. 109–133, New York: McGraw–Hill, 1963.)

[Newell, Shaw, & Simon 1958]   Newell, A., Shaw, J. C., and Simon, H. A., "Chess–Playing Programs and the Problem of Complexity," *IBM Jour. R & D*, 2:320–355, 1958. (Reprinted in Feigenbaum, E., and Feldman, J. (eds.), *Computers and Thought*, pp. 109–133, New York: McGraw–Hill, 1963.)

[Newell, Shaw, & Simon 1959]   Newell, A., Shaw, J. C., and Simon, H. A., "Report on a General Problem-Solving Program for a Computer," *Computers and Automation*, 8(7):10–16, 1959.

[Newell & Simon 1963]   Newell, A., and Simon, H., "GPS, A Program That Simulates Human Thought," in Feigenbaum, E., and Feldman, J. (eds.) *Computers and Thought*, pp. 279–293, New York: McGraw-Hill, 1963.

[Newell & Simon 1972]   Newell, A., and Simon, H., *Human Problem Solving*, Englewood Cliffs, NJ: Prentice Hall, 1972.

[Newell & Simon 1976]   Newell, A., and Simon, H. A., "Computer Science as Empirical Inquiry: Symbols and Search," *Communications of the Association for Computing Machinery*, 19(3):113–126, 1976.

[Nii 1986a]   Nii, H. P., "Blackboard Systems: The Blackboard Model of Problem Solving and the Evolution of Blackboard Architectures," *The AI Magazine*, 7(2):38–64, Summer 1986.

[Nii 1986b]   Nii, H. P., "Blackboard Systems (Part Two): Blackboard Application Systems, Blackboard Systems from a Knowledge Engineering Perspective," *The AI Magazine*, 7(3):82–106, 1986.

[Nilsson 1965]   Nilsson, N., *The Mathematical Foundations of Learning Machines*, San Francisco: Morgan Kaufmann, 1990. (This book is a reprint of Nilsson, N., *Learning Machines: Foundations of Trainable Pattern-Classifying Systems*, New York: McGraw-Hill, 1965.)

[Nilsson 1969]   Nilsson, N., "Searching Problem-Solving and Game-Playing Trees for Minimal Cost Solutions," in Morrell, A. (ed.), *Information Processing 68*, vol. 2, pp. 1556–1562, Amsterdam: North-Holland, 1969.

[Nilsson 1980]   Nilsson, N., *Principles of Artificial Intelligence*, San Francisco: Morgan Kaufmann, 1980.

[Nilsson 1984a]   Nilsson, N., "Artificial Intelligence, Employment, and Income," *The AI Magazine*, 5(2):5–14, Summer 1984.

[Nilsson 1984b]   Nilsson, N., *Shakey the Robot*, Technical Note 323, SRI International, Menlo Park, CA, 1984.

[Nilsson 1986]   Nilsson, N., "Probabilistic Logic," *Artificial Intelligence*, 28(1):71–87, 1986.

[Nilsson 1991]   Nilsson, N., "Logic and Artificial Intelligence," *Artificial Intelligence*, 47:31–56, 1991.

[Nilsson 1994]   Nilsson, N., "Teleo-Reactive Programs for Agent Control," *Journal of Artificial Intelligence Research*, 1, pp. 139–158, January 1994.

[Nilsson & Raphael 1967]   Nilsson, N., and Raphael, B., "Preliminary Design of an Intelligent Robot," in Tou, J. T. (ed.), *Computer and Information Sciences-II*, pp. 235–259, New York: Academic Press, 1967.

[Norvig 1992]   Norvig, P., *Paradigms of Artificial Intelligence Programming: Case Studies in Common LISP*, San Francisco: Morgan Kaufmann, 1992.

[Nourbakhsh 1997]   Nourbakhsh, I., *Interleaving Planning and Execution for Autonomous Robots*, Boston: Kluwer Academic Publishers, 1997.

[O'Reilly & Oppacher 1994]   O'Reilly, U.-M., and Oppacher, F., "Program Search with a Hierarchical Variable Length Representation: Genetic Programming, Simulated Annealing and Hill Climbing," in Davidor, Y., Schwefel, H., and Manner, R. (eds.), *Lecture Notes in Computer Science, No. 866*, Berlin: Springer–Verlag, 1994.

[Paterson & Wegman 1978]   Paterson, M. and Wegman, M., "Linear Unification," *Journal of Computer and System Science*, 16:158–167, 1978.

[Pearl 1982a]   Pearl, J., "Reverend Bayes on Inference Engines: A Distributed Hierarchical Approach," in *Proceedings of the Second National Conference on Artificial Intelligence (AAAI-82)*, pp. 133–136, Menlo Park, CA: AAAI Press, 1982.

[Pearl 1982b]   Pearl, J., "A Solution for the Branching Factor of the Alpha–Beta Pruning Algorithm and its Optimality," *Comm. ACM*, 25(8):559–564, 1982.

[Pearl 1984]   Pearl, J., *Heuristics: Intelligent Search Strategies for Computer Problem Solving*, Reading, MA: Addison–Wesley, 1984.

[Pearl 1986]   Pearl, J., "Fusion, Propagation, and Structuring in Belief Networks," *Artificial Intelligence*, 29:241–288, 1986.

[Pearl 1988]   Pearl, J., *Probabilistic Reasoning in Intelligent Systems: Networks of Plausible Inference*, San Francisco: Morgan Kaufmann, 1988.

[Pearl 1990]   Pearl, J., "Reasoning under Uncertainty," *Annual Review of Computer Science*, vol. 4, 1989–1990, pp. 37–72, Palo Alto, CA: Annual Reviews, 1990.

[Pednault 1986]   Pednault, E., "Formulating Multiagent, Dynamic–World Problems in the Classical Planning Framework," in Georgeff, M., and Lansky, A. (eds.), *Reasoning about Actions and Plans: Proceedings of the 1986 Workshop*, Timberline, Oregon, pp. 47–82, San Francisco: Morgan Kaufmann, 1986. (Also in Allen, J., Hendler, J., and Tate, A. (eds.), *Readings in Planning*, pp. 675–710, San Francisco: Morgan Kaufmann, 1990.)

[Pednault 1989]   Pednault, E., "ADL: Exploring the Middle Ground between STRIPS and the Situation Calculus," in Brachman, R., Levesque, H., and Reiter, R. (eds.), *Proceedings of the First International Conference on Principles of Knowledge Representation and Reasoning (KR-89)*, pp. 324–332, San Francisco: Morgan Kaufmann, 1989.

[Penberthy & Weld 1992]   Penberthy, J., and Weld, D., "UCPOP: A Sound, Complete Partial–Order Planner for ADL," in *Proceedings of the Third International Conference on Principles of Knowledge Representation and Reasoning (KR-92)*, pp. 103–113, San Francisco: Morgan Kaufmann, 1992.

[Penrose 1989]   Penrose, R., *The Emperor's New Mind: Concerning Computers, Minds, and the Laws of Physics*, Oxford: Oxford University Press, 1989.

[Penrose 1994]   Penrose, R., *Shadows of the Mind: Search for the Missing Science of Consciousness*, Oxford: Oxford University Press, 1994.

[Pereira & Shieber 1987]   Pereira, F., and Shieber, S., *PROLOG and Natural Language Analysis*, CSLI Lecture Notes, No. 10, Center for the Study of Language and Information, Stanford University, Stanford, CA, 1987.

[Pereira & Warren 1980]   Pereira, F., and Warren, D., "Definite Clause Grammars for Language Analysis: A Survey of the Formalism and a Comparison with Augmented Transition Networks," *Artificial Intelligence*, 13:231–278, 1980.

[Perlis 1985]   Perlis, D., "Languages with Self-Reference, I: Foundations," *Artificial Intelligence*, 25:301–332, 1985.

[Perlis 1988]   Perlis, D., "Languages with Self-Reference, II: Knowledge, Belief, and Modality," *Artificial Intelligence*, 34:179–212, 1988.

[Perona & Malik 1990]   Perona, P., and Malik, J., "Scale-Space and Edge Detection Using Anisotropic Diffusion," *IEEE Transactions on Pattern Analysis and Machine Intelligence*, PAMI-12:7:629–639, July 1990.

[Pineda 1987]   Pineda, F. J., "Generalization of Back-Propagation to Recurrent Neural Networks," *Physical Review Letters*, 59:2229–2232, 1987.

[Pingle 1969]   Pingle, K., "Visual Perception by a Computer," in *Automatic Interpretation and Classification of Images*, Grasselli, A. (ed.), pp. 277–284, New York: Academic Press, 1969.

[Pohl 1971]   Pohl, I., "Bi-directional Search," in *Machine Intelligence 6*, Meltzer, B., and Michie, D. (eds.), pp. 127–140, Edinburgh: Edinburgh University Press, 1971.

[Pohl 1973]   Pohl, I., "The Avoidance of (Relative) Catastrophe, Heuristic Competence, Genuine Dynamic Weighting and Computational Issues in Heuristic Problem Solving," in *Proceedings of the Third International Joint Conference on Artificial Intelligence (IJCAI-73)*, pp. 20–23, San Francisco: Morgan Kaufmann, 1973.

[Pollack & Ringuette 1990]   Pollack, M. E., and Ringuette, M., "Introducing the Tileworld: Experimentally Evaluating Agent Architectures," in *Proceedings of the Eighth National Conference on Artificial Intelligence (AAAI-90)*, pp. 183–189, Menlo Park, CA: AAAI Press, 1990.

[Pomerleau 1991]   Pomerleau, D., "Rapidly Adapting Artificial Neural Networks for Autonomous Navigation," in Lippmann, P., et al. (eds.), *Advances in Neural Information Processing Systems, 3*, pp. 429–435, San Francisco: Morgan Kaufmann, 1991.

[Pomerleau 1993]   Pomerleau, D., *Neural Network Perception for Mobile Robot Guidance*, Boston: Kluwer Academic Publishers, 1993.

[Port & van Gelder 1995]   Port, R., and van Gelder, T., *Mind as Motion: Explorations in the Dynamics of Cognition*, Cambridge, MA: Bradford Books/MIT Press, 1995.

[Pospesel 1976]   Pospesel, H., *Introduction to Logic: Predicate Logic*, Englewood Cliffs, NJ: Prentice Hall, 1976.

[Powers 1995]   Powers, R., *Galatea 2.2*, New York: Farrar, Straus & Giroux, 1995.

[Powley, Ferguson, & Korf 1993]   Powley, C., Ferguson, C., and Korf, R., "Depth–First Heuristic Search on a SIMD Machine," *Artificial Intelligence*, 60:199–242, 1993.

[Pradhan, et al. 1994]   Pradhan, M., Provan, G., Middleton, B., and Henrion, M., "Knowledge Engineering for Large Belief Networks," in *Proceedings of the Tenth Conference on Uncertainty in Artificial Intelligence*, pp. 484–490, San Francisco: Morgan Kaufmann, 1994.

[Prawitz 1965]   Prawitz, D., *Natural Deduction: A Proof Theoretical Study*, Stockholm: Almquist and Wiksell, 1965.

[Prieditis 1993]   Prieditis, A, "Machine Discovery of Effective Admissible Heuristics," *Machine Learning*, 12(1–3):117–141, 1993.

[Purdom & Brown 1987]   Purdom, P. W., Jr., and Brown, C., "Polynomial Average–Time Satisfiability Problems," *Information Science*, 41:23–42, 1987.

[Puterman 1994]   Puterman, M., *Markov Decision Processes—Discrete Stochastic Dynamic Programming*, New York: John Wiley & Sons, 1994.

[Quinlan 1979]   Quinlan, J., "Discovering Rules from Large Collections of Examples: A Case Study," in Michie, D. (ed.), *Expert Systems in the Microelectronic Age*, Edinburgh: Edinburgh University Press, 1979.

[Quinlan 1990]   Quinlan, J. R., "Learning Logical Definitions from Relations," *Machine Learning*, 5(3):239–266, 1990.

[Quinlan 1993]   Quinlan, J. R., *C4.5: Programs for Machine Learning*, San Francisco: Morgan Kaufmann, 1993.

[Ramadge & Wonham 1989]   Ramadge, P., and Wonham, M., "The Control of Discrete Event Systems," *Proc. of the IEEE*, 77(1):81–93, 1989.

[Reichardt 1965]   Reichardt, W., "On the Theory of Lateral Nervous Inhibition in the Complex Eye of Limulus," *Progress in Brain Research*, 17:64–73, 1965

[Reiter 1980]   Reiter, R., "A Logic for Default Reasoning," *Artificial Intelligence*, 13(1–2):81–132, 1980.

[Reiter 1991]   Reiter, R., "The Frame Problem in the Situation Calculus: A Simple Solution (Sometimes) and a Completeness Result for Goal Regression," in Lifschitz, V. (ed.), *Artificial Intelligence and Mathematical Theory of Computation: Papers in Honor of John McCarthy*, pp. 359–380, New York: Academic Press, 1991.

[Reitman & Wilcox 1979]   Reitman, W., and Wilcox, B., "The Structure and Performance of the INTERIM.2 Go Program," in *Proceedings of the Sixth International Joint Conference on Artificial Intelligence (IJCAI-79)*, pp. 711–719, San Francisco: Morgan Kaufmann, 1979.

[Resnick 1993]   Resnick, M., "Behavior Construction Kits," *Communications of the ACM*, 36(7):64–71, July 1993.

[Rich & Knight 1991]   Rich, E., and Knight, K., *Artificial Intelligence* (second edition), New York: McGraw-Hill, 1991.

[Rissanen 1984]   Rissanen, J., "Universal Coding, Information, Prediction, and Estimation," *IEEE Transactions on Information Theory*, IT-30(4):629–636, 1984.

[Rivest 1987]   Rivest, R., "Learning Decision Lists," *Machine Learning*, 2, 229–246, 1987.

[Rivest & Schapire 1993]   Rivest, R., and Schapire, R., "Inference of Finite Automata Using Homing Sequences," *Information and Computation*, 103(2):299–347, 1993.

[Roberts 1963]   Roberts, L., *Machine Perception of Three-Dimensional Solids*, Tech. Report 315, MIT Lincoln Laboratory, Ph.D. dissertation, Massachusetts Institute of Technology, 1963.

[Robinson 1965]   Robinson, J. A., "A Machine-Oriented Logic Based on the Resolution Principle," *Journal of the Association for Computing Machinery*, 12(1):23–41, 1965.

[Rohwer & Forrest 1987]   Rohwer, R., and Forrest, B., "Training Time-Dependence in Neural Networks," in Caudill, M., and Butler, C. (eds.), *IEEE First International Conference on Neural Networks*, San Diego, 1987, vol. II, pp. 701–708, New York: IEEE, 1987.

[Rosenblatt 1962]   Rosenblatt, F., *Principles of Neurodynamics*, Washington, DC: Spartan Books, 1962.

[Rosenschein & Kaelbling 1995]   Rosenschein, S., and Kaelbling, L., "A Situated View of Representation and Control," *Artificial Intelligence*, 73:149–173, 1995.

[Rosenbloom, Laird, & Newell 1993]   Rosenbloom, P., Laird, J., and Newell, A., (eds.), *The Soar Papers: Research on Integrated Intelligence*, vols. 1 and 2, Cambridge, MA: MIT Press, 1993.

[Ross 1988]   Ross, S., *A First Course in Probability*, third edition, London: Macmillan, 1988.

[Roussel 1975]   Roussel, P., "PROLOG: Manual de Reference et d'Utilization," Technical Report, Université Aix-Marseille II, Groupe d'Intelligence Artificielle, France, 1975.

[Rumelhart, et al. 1986]   Rumelhart, D. E., Hinton, G. E., and Williams, R. J., "Learning Internal Representations by Error Propagation," in Rumelhart, D. E., and McClelland, J. L. (eds.), *Parallel Distributed Processing*, Vol 1., pp. 318–362, 1986.

[Russell 1997]   Russell, S., "Rationality and Intelligence," *Artificial Intelligence*, (94)1:57–77, 1997.

[Russell & Norvig 1995]   Russell, S., and Norvig, P., *Artificial Intelligence: A Modern Approach*, Englewood Cliffs, NJ: Prentice Hall, 1995. (Revised edition to appear in 1998.)

[Russell & Wefald 1991]   Russell, S., and Wefald, E., *Do the Right Thing*, Cambridge, MA: MIT Press, 1991.

[Sacerdoti 1974]   Sacerdoti, E., "Planning in a Hierarchy of Abstraction Spaces," *Artificial Intelligence*, 5(2):115–135, 1974. (Reprinted in Allen, J., Hendler, J., and Tate, A. (eds.), *Readings in Planning*, pp. 98–108, San Francisco: Morgan Kaufmann, 1990.)

[Sacerdoti 1975]   Sacerdoti, E., "The Non-linear Nature of Plans," in *Proceedings of the Fourth International Joint Conference on Artificial Intelligence (IJCAI-75)*, pp. 206–214, San

Francisco: Morgan Kaufmann, 1975. (Reprinted in Allen, J., Hendler, J., and Tate, A. (eds.), *Readings in Planning*, pp. 162–170, San Francisco: Morgan Kaufmann, 1990.)

[Sacerdoti 1977] Sacerdoti, E., *A Structure for Plans and Behavior*, New York: American Elsevier, 1977.

[Sadek, et al. 1996] Sadek, M., Ferrieux, A., Cozannet, A., Bretier, P., Panaget, F., and Simonin, J., "Effective Human–Computer Cooperative Spoken Dialogue: The AGS Demonstrator," in *Proc. ICSLP'96 International Conf. on Spoken Language Processing*, pp. 546–549, Philadelphia, PA, October 3–6, 1996.

[Samuel 1959] Samuel, A. L., "Some Studies in Machine Learning Using the Game of Checkers," *IBM Jour. R & D*, 3:211–229, 1959. (Reprinted in Feigenbaum, E., and Feldman, J. (eds.), *Computers and Thought*, pp. 71–105, New York: McGraw–Hill, 1963.)

[Samuel 1967] Samuel, A. L., "Some Studies in Machine Learning Using the Game of Checkers II—Recent Progress," *IBM Jour. R & D*, 11(6), 601–617, 1967.

[Schaeffer 1997] Schaeffer, J., *One Jump Ahead: Challenging Human Supremacy in Checkers*, New York: Springer-Verlag, 1997.

[Schaeffer, et al. 1992] Schaeffer, J., Culberson, J., Treloar, N., Knight, B., Lu, P., and Szafron, D., "A World Championship Caliber Checkers Program," *Artificial Intelligence*, 53(2–3):273–289, 1992.

[Schaeffer & Lake 1996] Schaeffer, J. and Lake, R., "Solving the Game of Checkers," in Nowakowski, R. J. (ed.), *Games of No Chance*, pp. 119–133, Cambridge: Cambridge University Press, 1996.

[Scherl & Levesque 1993] Scherl, R., and Levesque, H., "The Frame Problem and Knowledge Producing Actions," in *Proceedings of the Eleventh National Conference on Artificial Intelligence (AAAI-93)*, pp. 689–695, Menlo Park, CA: AAAI Press, 1993.

[Schoppers 1987] Schoppers, M. J., "Universal Plans for Reactive Robots in Unpredictable Domains," in *Proceedings of the Tenth International Joint Conference on Artificial Intelligence (IJCAI-87)*, pp. 1039–1046, San Francisco: Morgan Kaufmann, 1987.

[Schraudolph, Dayan, & Sejnowski 1994] Schraudolph, N., Dayan, P., and Sejnowski, T., "Temporal Difference Position Evaluation in the Game of GO," in Cowan, J., et al. (eds.), *Advances in Neural Information Processing Systems, 6*, pp. 817–824, San Francisco: Morgan Kaufmann, 1994.

[Schubert 1990] Schubert, L., "Monotonic Solution of the Frame Problem in the Situation Calculus: An Efficient Method for Worlds with Fully Specified Actions," in Kyberg, H., Loui, R., and Carlson, G. (eds.), *Knowledge Representation and Defeasible Reasoning*, pp. 23–67, Boston: Kluwer Academic Publishers, 1990.

[Schultz, Dayan, & Montague 1997] Schultz, W., Dayan, P., and Montague, P. R., "A Neural Substrate for Prediction and Reward," *Science*, 275:1593–1599, March 14, 1997.

[Schwartz 1987]   Schwartz, J., "The Limits of Artificial Intelligence," in the *Encyclopedia of Artificial Intelligence*, New York: John Wiley & Sons, 1987.

[Searle 1969]   Searle, J., *Speech Acts: An Essay in the Philosophy of Language*, Cambridge: Cambridge University Press, 1969.

[Searle 1980]   Searle, J., "Minds, Brains, and Programs," *The Behavioral and Brain Sciences*, 3:417–457, 1980 (with open peer commentary). (Reprinted in Hofstadter, D. R., and Dennett, D. C. (eds.), *The Mind's Eye: Fantasies and Reflections on Self and Soul*, pp. 351–373, New York: Basic Books, 1981.)

[Searle 1992]   Searle, J., *The Rediscovery of the Mind*, Cambridge, MA: MIT Press, 1992.

[Sejnowski & Rosenberg 1987]   Sejnowski, T., and Rosenberg, C., "Parallel Networks That Learn to Pronounce English Text," *Complex Systems*, 1:145–168, 1987.

[Selman & Kautz 1991]   Selman, B., and Kautz, H., "Knowledge Compilation Using Horn Approximations," in *Proceedings of the Ninth National Conference on Artificial Intelligence (AAAI-91)*, pp. 904–909, Menlo Park, CA: AAAI Press, 1991.

[Selman & Kautz 1993]   Selman, B., and Kautz, H., "An Empirical Study of Greedy Local Search for Satisfiability Testing," in *Proceedings of the Eleventh National Conference on Artificial Intelligence (AAAI-93)*, pp. 46–51, Menlo Park, CA: AAAI Press, 1993.

[Selman, Kautz, & Cohen 1994]   Selman, B., Kautz, H., and Cohen, B., "Noise Strategies for Improving Local Search," in *Proceedings of the Twelfth National Conference on Artificial Intelligence (AAAI-94)*, pp. 337–343, Menlo Park, CA: AAAI Press, 1994.

[Selman, Kautz, & Cohen 1996]   Selman, B., Kautz, H., and Cohen, B., "Local Search Strategies for Satisfiability Testing," in Du, D., Gu, J., and Pardalos, P. (eds.), *Satisfiability Problem: Theory and Applications*, Vol. 35, Dimacs Series in Discrete Mathematics and Theoretical Computer Science, Providence, RI: American Mathematical Society, 1996.

[Selman & Levesque 1990]   Selman, B., and Levesque, H., "Abductive and Default Reasoning: A Computational Core," in *Proceedings of the Eighth National Conference on Artificial Intelligence (AAAI-90)*, pp. 343–348, Menlo Park, CA: AAAI Press, 1990.

[Selman, Levesque, & Mitchell 1992]   Selman, B., Levesque, H., and Mitchell, D., "A New Method for Solving Hard Satisfiability Problems," in *Proceedings of the Tenth National Conference on Artificial Intelligence (AAAI-92)*, pp. 440–446, Menlo Park, CA: AAAI Press, 1992.

[Shachter & Kenley 1989]   Shachter, R., and Kenley, C., "Gaussian Influence Diagrams," *Management Science*, 35:527–550, 1989.

[Shafer 1979]   Shafer, G., *A Mathematical Theory of Evidence*, Princeton, NJ: Princeton University Press, 1979.

[Shafer & Pearl 1990]   Shafer, G., and Pearl, J. (eds.), *Readings in Uncertain Reasoning*, San Francisco: Morgan Kaufmann, 1990.

[Shanahan 1997]   Shanahan, M., *Solving the Frame Problem: A Mathematical Investigation of the Commonsense Law of Inertia*, Cambridge, MA: MIT Press, 1997.

[Shannon 1950]   Shannon, C., "Programming a Computer for Playing Chess,"*Philosophical Magazine* (Series 7), vol. 41, pp. 256–275, 1950.

[Shannon & McCarthy 1956]   Shannon, C., and McCarthy, J. (eds.), *Automata Studies, Annals of Mathematical Studies*, 34, Princeton, NJ: Princeton University Press, 1956.

[Shapiro 1992]   Shapiro, S., *Encyclopedia of Artificial Intelligence*, Vols. 1 and 2 (second edition), New York: John Wiley & Sons, 1992.

[Shavlik & Dietterich 1990]   Shavlik, J., and Dietterich, T. (eds.), *Readings in Machine Learning*, San Francisco: Morgan Kaufmann, 1990.

[Shen 1994]   Shen, W.-M., *Autonomous Learning from the Environment*, San Francisco: W. H. Freeman, 1994.

[Shirai 1987]   Shirai, Y., *Three-Dimensional Computer Vision*, Berlin: Springer-Verlag, 1987.

[Shoham 1987]   Shoham, Y., "Temporal Logics in AI: Semantical and Ontological Considerations," *Artificial Intelligence*, 33(1):89–104, 1987.

[Shoham 1988]   Shoham, Y., *Reasoning about Change: Time and Causation from the Standpoint of Artificial Intelligence*, Cambridge, MA: MIT Press, 1988.

[Shoham 1993]   Shoham, Y., "Agent-Oriented Programming," *Artificial Intelligence*, 60:51–92, 1993.

[Shoham 1994]   Shoham, Y., *AI Programming in PROLOG*, San Francisco: Morgan Kaufmann, 1994.

[Shoham 1996]   Shoham, Y., "The Open Scientific Borders of AI, and the Case of Economics," *ACM Computing Surveys*, 28(4):11ff, December 1996.

[Shortliffe 1976]   Shortliffe, E. H., *Computer-Based Medical Consultations: MYCIN*, New York: Elsevier, 1976.

[Shrobe 1988]   Shrobe, H. (ed.), *Exploring Artificial Intelligence: Survey Talks from the National Conference on Artificial Intelligence*, San Francisco: Morgan Kaufmann, 1988.

[Skolem 1920]   Skolem, T., "Logisch-kombinatorische Untersuchungen über die Erfüllbarkeit oder Beweisbarkeit Mathematischer Sätze Nebst einem Theoreme über die Dichte Mengen," *Videnskapsselskapets Skrifter, I, Matematisk-naturvidenskabelig Klasse*, 4, 1920.

[Slate & Atkin 1977]   Slate, D., and Atkin, L., "Chess 4.5—The Northwestern University Chess Program," in Fry, P. (ed.), *Chess Skill in Man and Machine*, pp. 82–118, New York: Springer-Verlag, 1977.

[Slagle 1963]   Slagle, J. R., "A Heuristic Program That Solves Symbolic Integration Problems in Freshman Calculus," *Jour. Assoc. of Comp. Mach.*, 10:507–520, 1963. (Also in Feigenbaum, E., and Feldman, J. (eds.), *Computers and Thought*, pp. 191–203, New York: McGraw-Hill, 1963.)

[Slagle & Dixon 1969]   Slagle, J., and Dixon J., "Experiments with Some Programs that Search Game Trees," *Jour. Assoc. Comp. Mach.*, 16:2:189–207, 1969.

[Smith 1989]   Smith, D. E., "Controlling Backward Inference," *Artificial Intelligence*, 39(2):145–208, 1989.

[Smith, Genesereth, & Ginsberg 1986]   Smith, D. E., Genesereth, M., and Ginsberg, M., "Controlling Recursive Inference," *Artificial Intelligence*, 30(3):343–389, 1986.

[Soderland & Weld 1991]   Soderland, S., and Weld, D., "Evaluating Nonlinear Planning," Technical Report TR-91-02-03, University of Washington Department of Computer Science and Engineering, Seattle, WA, 1991.

[Sowa 1991]   Sowa, J. (ed.), *Principles of Semantic Networks*, San Francisco: Morgan Kaufmann, 1991.

[Spirtes & Meek 1995]   Spirtes, P., and Meek, C., "Learning Bayesian Networks with Discrete Variables from Data," in *Proceedings of First International Conference on Knowledge Discovery and Data Mining*, San Francisco: Morgan Kaufmann, 1995.

[Stallman & Sussman 1977]   Stallman, R., and Sussman, G., "Forward Reasoning and Dependency-Directed Backtracking in a System for Computer-Aided Circuit Analysis," *Artificial Intelligence*, 9(2):135–196, 1977.

[Stanfill & Waltz 1986]   Stanfill, C., and Waltz, D., "Toward Memory-Based Reasoning," *Communications of the ACM*, 29(12):1213–1228, 1986.

[Stefik 1995]   Stefik, M., *Introduction to Knowledge Systems*, San Francisco: Morgan Kaufmann, 1995.

[Stentz 1995]   Stentz, A., "The Focussed D* Algorithm for Real-Time Replanning," in *Proceedings of the Fourteenth International Joint Conference on Artificial Intelligence (IJCAI-95)*, pp. 1652–1659, San Francisco: Morgan Kaufmann, 1995.

[Stentz & Hebert 1995]   Stentz, A., and Hebert, M., "A Complete Navigation System for Goal Acquisition in Unknown Environments," *Autonomous Robots*, 2(2):127–147, 1995.

[Sterling & Shapiro 1986]   Sterling, L., and Shapiro, E., *The Art of PROLOG*, Cambridge, MA: MIT Press, 1986.

[Stickel 1985]   Stickel, M., "Automated Deduction by Theory Resolution," *Journal of Automated Reasoning*, 1(4):333–355, 1985.

[Stickel 1988]   Stickel, M., "A PROLOG Technology Theorem Prover: Implementation by an Extended PROLOG Compiler," *Journal of Automated Reasoning*, 4:353–380, 1988.

[Stickel & Tyson 1985]   Stickel, M., and Tyson, M., "An Analysis of Consecutively Bounded Depth-First Search with Applications in Automated Deduction," in *Proceedings of the Ninth International Joint Conference on Artificial Intelligence (IJCAI-85)*, pp. 1073–1075, San Francisco: Morgan Kaufmann, 1985.

[Strat 1992]   Strat, T., *Natural Object Recognition*, Berlin: Springer-Verlag, 1992.

[Sussman 1975]   Sussman, G., *A Computer Model of Skill Acquisition*, Amsterdam: Elsevier/North-Holland, 1975.

[Sutton 1988]   Sutton, R., "Learning to Predict by the Methods of Temporal Differences," *Machine Learning*, 3:9–44, 1988.

[Sutton 1990]   Sutton, R., "Integrated Architectures for Learning, Planning, and Reacting Based on Approximating Dynamic Programming," in *Proceedings of the Seventh International Conference on Machine Learning*, pp. 216–224, San Francisco: Morgan Kaufmann, 1990.

[Tarski 1935]   Tarski, A., "Die Wahrheitsbegriff in den Formalisierten Sprachen," *Studia Philosophica*, 1:261–405, 1935.

[Tarski 1956]   Tarski, A., *Logic, Semantics, Metamathematics: Papers from 1923 to 1938*, Oxford: Oxford University Press, 1956.

[Tate 1977]   Tate, A., "Generating Project Networks," in *Proceedings of the Fifth International Joint Conference on Artificial Intelligence (IJCAI-77)*, pp. 888–893, San Francisco: Morgan Kaufmann, 1977. (Reprinted in Allen, J., Hendler, J., and Tate, A. (eds.), *Readings in Planning*, pp. 291–296, San Francisco: Morgan Kaufmann, 1990.)

[Tate 1996]   Tate, A. (ed.), *Advanced Planning Technology, The Technological Achievements of the ARPA/Rome Laboratory Planning Initiative*, Menlo Park, CA: AAAI Press, May 1996.

[Teller 1994]   Teller, A., "The Evolution of Mental Models," in Kinnear, K., Jr. (ed.), *Advances in Genetic Programming*, Ch. 9, Cambridge, MA: MIT Press, 1994.

[Tenenberg 1991]   Tenenberg, J., "Abstraction in Planning," in Allen, J., Kautz, H., Pelavin, R., and Tenenberg, J. (eds.), *Reasoning about Plans*, Ch. 4, San Francisco: Morgan Kaufmann, 1991.

[Tesauro 1992]   Tesauro, G., "Practical Issues in Temporal Difference Learning," *Machine Learning*, 8, nos. 3/4:257–277, 1992.

[Tesauro 1995]   Tesauro, G., "Temporal-Difference Learning and TD–Gammon," *Comm. ACM*, 38(3):58–68, March 1995.

[Theraulaz & Bonabeau 1995]   Theraulaz, G., and Bonabeau, E., "Coordination in Distributed Building," *Science*, 269:686–688, August 4, 1995.

[Thorpe, et al. 1992]   Thorpe, C., Hebert, M., Kanade, T., and Shafer, S., "The New Generation System for the CMU Navlab," in Masaki, I. (ed.), *Vision-Based Vehicle Guidance*, pp. 30–82, Berlin: Springer–Verlag, 1992.

[Towell & Shavlik 1992]   Towell, G., and Shavlik, J., "Interpretation of Artificial Neural Networks: Mapping Knowledge-Based Neural Networks into Rules," in Moody, J., Hanson, S., and Lippmann, R. (eds.), *Advances in Neural Information Processing Systems, 4*, pp. 977–984, San Francisco: Morgan Kaufmann, 1992.

[Towell, Shavlik, & Noordweier 1990]   Towell, G., Shavlik, J., and Noordweier, M., "Refinement of Approximate Domain Theories by Knowledge-Based Artificial Neural Networks," in *Proceedings of the Eighth National Conference on Artificial Intelligence (AAAI-90)*, pp. 861–866, Menlo Park, CA: AAAI Press, 1990.

[Tracy & Bouthoorn 1997]   Tracy, K., and Bouthoorn, P., *Object-Oriented Artificial Intelligence Using C++*, New York: Computer Science Press, 1997.

[Trappl 1986]   Trappl, R., *Impacts of Artificial Intelligence: Scientific, Technological, Military, Economic, Societal, Cultural, and Political*, New York: North–Holland, 1986.

[Turing 1950]   Turing, A. M., "Computing Machinery and Intelligence," *Mind*, 59:433–460, 1950. (Reprinted in Feigenbaum, E., and Feldman, J. (eds.), *Computers and Thought*, pp. 11–35, New York: McGraw–Hill, 1963.)

[Tversky & Kahneman 1982]   Tversky, A., and Kahneman, D., "Causal Schemata in Judgements under Uncertainty," in Kahneman, D., Slovic, P., and Tversky, A. (eds.), *Judgements under Uncertainty: Heuristics and Biases*, Cambridge: Cambridge University Press, 1982.

[Ullman 1988]   Ullman, J. D., *Principles of Database and Knowledge-Base Systems, Vol. I: Classical Database Systems*, New York: Computer Science Press, 1988.

[Ullman 1989]   Ullman, J. D., *Principles of Database and Knowledge-Base Systems, Vol. II: The New Technologies*, New York: Computer Science Press, 1989.

[Unger 1989]   Unger, S., *The Essence of Logic Circuits*, Englewood Cliffs, NJ: Prentice Hall, 1989.

[Venn 1880]   Venn, J., "On the Diagrammatic and Mechanical Representation of Propositions and Reasonings," *Phil. Mag.*, pp. 123ff, 1880.

[Waibel & Lee 1990]   Waibel, A., and Lee, K.-F. (eds.), *Readings in Speech Recognition*, San Francisco: Morgan Kaufmann, 1990.

[Waibel, et al. 1988]   Waibel, A., Hanazawa, T., Hinton, G., Shikano, K., and Lang, K., "Phoneme Recognition: Neural Networks versus Hidden Markov Models," in *Proc. of the International Conf. on Acoustics, Speech and Signal Processing*, New York, 1988.

[Waldinger 1975]   Waldinger, R., "Achieving Several Goals Simultaneously," in Elcock, E., and Michie, D. (eds.), *Machine Intelligence 8*, pp. 94–138, Chichester, England: Ellis Horwood, 1975.

[Walter 1953]   Walter, G., *The Living Brain*, New York: Norton and Company, 1953.

[Waltz 1975]   Waltz, D., "Understanding Line Drawings of Scenes with Shadows," in Winston, P. (ed.), *The Psychology of Computer Vision*, pp. 19–91, New York: McGraw–Hill, 1975.

[Wang 1995]   Wang, X., "Learning by Observation and Practice: An Incremental Approach for Planning Operator Acquisition," in *Proceedings of the Twelfth International Conference on Machine Learning*, pp. 549–557, San Francisco: Morgan Kaufmann, 1995.

[Warren, Pereira, & Pereira 1977]   Warren, D., Pereira, L., and Pereira, F., "PROLOG: The Language and Its Implementation Compared with LISP," *SIGPLAN Notices*, 12(8):109–115, 1977.

[Weiss & Kulikowski 1991]   Weiss, S., and Kulikowski, C., *Computer Systems That Learn*, San Francisco: Morgan Kaufmann, 1991.

[Weizenbaum 1965] Weizenbaum, J., "ELIZA—A Computer Program for the Study of Natural Language Communication between Man and Machine," *Communications of the Association for Computing Machinery*, 9(1):36–45, 1965.

[Weizenbaum 1976] Weizenbaum, J., *Computer Power and Human Reason: From Judgment to Calculation*, New York: W. H. Freeman, 1976.

[Weld 1994] Weld, D., "An Introduction to Least Commitment Planning," *AI Magazine*, 15(4):27–61, 1994.

[Weld & de Kleer 1990] Weld, D., and de Kleer, J., *Readings in Qualitative Reasoning about Physical Systems*, San Francisco: Morgan Kaufmann, 1990.

[Wellman 1990] Wellman, M., "Fundamental Concepts of Qualitative Probabilistic Networks," *Artificial Intelligence*, 44:257–303, 1990.

[Wellman 1996] Wellman, M., "Market-Oriented Programming: Some Early Lessons," in Clearwater, S. (ed.), *Market-Based Control—A Paradigm for Distributed Resource Allocation*, Singapore: World Scientific, 1996.

[Werbos 1974] Werbos, P., *Beyond Regression: New Tools for Prediction and Analysis in the Behavioral Sciences*, Ph.D. Thesis, Harvard University, 1974.

[Weyhrauch 1980] Weyhrauch, R., "Prolegomena to a Theory of Mechanized Formal Reasoning," *Artificial Intelligence*, 13(1–2):133–170, 1980.

[Whitehead, Karlsson, & Tenenberg 1993] Whitehead, S., Karlsson, J., and Tenenberg, J., "Learning Multiple Goal Behavior via Task Decomposition and Dynamic Policy Merging," in Connell, J., and Mahadevan, S. (eds.), *Robot Learning*, Ch. 3, Boston: Kluwer Academic Publishers, 1993.

[Widrow & Hoff 1960] Widrow, B., and Hoff, M. E., "Adaptive Switching Circuits," *1960 IRE WESCON Convention Record*, pp. 96–104, New York, 1960.

[Widrow 1962] Widrow, B., "Generalization and Information Storage in Networks of Adaline 'Neurons,'" in Yovitz, M., Jacobi, G., and Goldstein, G. (eds.), *Self-Organizing Systems 1962*, pp. 435–461, Washington, DC: Spartan Books, 1962.

[Wiener 1948] Wiener, N., *Cybernetics: Control and Communication in the Animal and in the Machine*, New York: John Wiley & Sons, 1948.

[Wilkins 1988] Wilkins, D. E., *Practical Planning: Extending the Classical AI Planning Paradigm*, San Francisco: Morgan Kaufmann, 1988.

[Wilkins, et al. 1995] Wilkins, D. E., Myers, K., Lowrance, J., and Wesley, L., "Planning and Reacting in Uncertain and Dynamic Domains," *Journal of Experimental and Theoretical Artificial Intelligence*, 7(1):197–227, 1995.

[Wilson 1991] Wilson, S., "The Animat Path to AI," in Meyer, J. A., and Wilson, S. (eds.), *From Animals to Animats; Proceedings of the First International Conference on the Simulation of Adaptive Behavior*, Cambridge, MA: MIT Press/Bradford Books, 1991.

[Winograd 1972]   Winograd, T., *Understanding Natural Language*, New York: Academic Press, 1972.

[Winograd & Flores 1986]   Winograd, T., and Flores, F., *Understanding Computers and Cognition: A New Foundation for Design*, Norwood, NJ: Ablex, 1986. (Four reviews and a response appear in *Artificial Intelligence*, 31(2): 213–261, 1987.)

[Wooldridge 1968]   Wooldridge, D., *Mechanical Man: The Physical Basis of Intelligent Life*, New York: McGraw–Hill, 1968.

[Woods 1970]   Woods, W., "Transition Network Grammars for Natural Language Analysis," *Communications of the Association for Computing Machinery*, 13(10):591–606, 1970.

[Woods 1973]   Woods, W., "Progress in Natural Language Understanding: An Application to Lunar Geology," in *AFIPS Conf. Proc.*, vol. 42, pp. 441–450, 1973.

[Wos 1993]   Wos, L., "Automated Reasoning Answers Open Questions," *Notices of the AMS*, 5(1):15–26, January 1993.

[Wos, Carson, & Robinson 1965]   Wos, L., Carson, D., and Robinson, G., "Efficiency and Completeness of the Set-of-Support Strategy in Theorem Proving," *Journal of the Association for Computing Machinery*, 12:536–541, 1965.

[Wos & Robinson 1968]   Wos, L., and Robinson, G., "Paramodulation and Set of Support," in *Proc. of the IRIA Symposium on Automatic Demonstration*, pp. 276–310, Berlin: Springer-Verlag, 1968.

[Wos & Winker 1983]   Wos, L., and Winker, S., "Open Questions Solved with the Assistance of AURA," in Bledsoe, W., and Loveland, D. (eds.), *Automated Theorem Proving: After 25 Years: Proceedings of the Special Session of the 89th Annual Meeting of the American Mathematical Society*, pp. 71–88, Denver, Colorado: American Mathematical Society, 1983.

[Wos, et al. 1992]   Wos, L., Overbeek, R., Lusk, E., and Boyle, J., *Automated Reasoning: Introduction and Applications*, second edition, New York: McGraw–Hill, 1992.

[Zadeh 1975]   Zadeh, L., "Fuzzy Logic and Approximate Reasoning," *Synthese* 30, pp. 407–428, 1975.

[Zadeh 1978]   Zadeh, L., "Fuzzy Sets as a Basis for a Theory of Possibility," *Fuzzy Sets and Systems*, 1:3–28, 1978.

[Zhu, Wu, & Mumford 1998]   Zhu, S. C., Wu, Y., and Mumford, D., "FRAME: Filters, Random Fields, and Maximum Entropy Towards a Unified Theory for Texture Modeling," *Int'l Journal of Computer Vision*, to appear.

[Zobrist 1970]   Zobrist, A., *Feature Extraction and Representation for Pattern Recognition and the Game of Go*, Ph.D. Dissertation, University of Wisconsin, 1970.

[Zweben & Fox 1994]   Zweben, M., and Fox, M. (eds.), *Intelligent Scheduling*, San Francisco: Morgan Kaufmann, 1994.

Index

Page numbers in *italic* are references to the bibliography.

▬ Symbols

λ (atom, literal), 231
∧ and ∨ (binary connectives), 229
∧ (conjunction), 220, 229
⊢ (derives), 221
∨ (disjunction), 220, 229
¬ elimination, 221
≡ (equivalence), 225, 244
∃ (existential quantifier), 245
⊃ (implication), 220
∧ introduction, 221
⊨ (logical entailment), 225, 244
⊢ and ⊨ (metalinguistic symbols), 228
K (modal operator), 412
¬ (negation), 220
Ξ⁻ (negative instances of training set), 291
Ξ⁺ (positive instances of training set), 291
ℜ (set of inference rules), 226
Γ and Δ (set of wffs), 221
∀ (universal quantifier), 245

▬ A

A*
admissibility of, 145–150
iterative-deepening (IDA*), 153–154
Abramson, B., 189, *453*
abstractions (for hierarchical planners), 399
ABSTRIPS, 393–394
action and perception, 21–27
action and perception components, 23
action computation phase, 23

action functions, 27–33
action model learning, 398
action models in a Markov process, 355
action part of a production rule, 27
action policy, 171, 175
actions
local effects of, 367
operators corresponding to, 374
activation (sigmoid input), 46
Adaline (adaptive linear element), 38
add list, 123, 375
admissibility of **A***, 145–150
admissible algorithm, 148
admissible heuristic functions, 161
adversarial (game tree) search, 195–213
advice-taker system, 6, 8
agent architectures, 23, 72, 164–165, 443–451
agent-centric view, 407
agent-oriented programming, 417
agents, 11
communication among, 407, 421–441
with deduction and reasoning, 13
evolutionary sequence of, 11, 15
with goals and plans, 13
interacting, 407–408
with knowledge about the world, 244–245, 248–249
knowledge base, 222, 244
logically omniscient, 415
modeling other, 407–412
multiple, 407–419
positive and negative rewards for, 175–177
predicting actions of other, 417

agents *(cont.)*
  reasoning about other agents' knowledge,
    415–417
  sense/plan/act, 164–165
  stimulus-response, 21–35
  that plan, 117–127, 352–358, 363–404
Agre, P., 177, 250, *453*
AI Magazine, 16
Albus, James, 1, 448, *453*
algorithm A*, 142–154
  efficiency of, 158
ALIVE system, 34
Allen, James, 306, 399, 440, *453*, *454*
Almeida, L. B., 55, *454*
Aloimonos, Y., 103, *454*
alpha cut-off value, 169, 204–205
alpha-beta procedure, 202–208
alphabetic variant, 254
alternative futures, 304
ALVINN network, 87
ALVINN system, 87–88, 110
ambiguities
  lexical, 436–437
  use of knowledge to resolve, 436–437
American Association for AI (AAAI), 16
analogical representations, 75
analogies (in human reasoning), 314
anaphora, 435
ancestor of a clause, 236
ancestor of a node (graph), 124
ancestry-filtered strategy, 237
and function, 25
AND gates, 31
AND nodes, 272
Anderson, T., 14, *454*
AND/OR tree, 272–274, 283, 298
Andre, David, 65, 69, *454*, *472*
animal models, utility theory in, 15
animat approach, 7, 10, 14
anisotropic diffusion, 100
answer extraction, 261–262
answer literal, 261
antecedent of an implication, 220
anytime algorithm, 166
AO* algorithm, 298
Appelt, D., 425, *454*, *466*
approximate search, 165–172
approximate theories, 297
AQ algorithm, 287
arbitration among goals, 446–448, 450
arcs, 124–125, 272, 309
Aristotle, 8
arities, 240
Ars Magna, 8

artificial ant problem, 81
artificial intelligence (AI)
  approaches to, 6–7
  brief history of, 8–11
  defined, 1
  important journals and conferences on, 16
  published proceedings on, 16
  weak vs. strong, 17
  what it is, 1–6
artificial potential field, 76
Ash, D., *467*
Asimov's three laws of robotics, 450
assignment problems, 181–183
associative laws (propositional calculus), 229
assumption-based truth maintenance
  systems (ATMSs), 279–280, 298
Atkeson, C., 178, *478*
Atkin, L., 207, *487*
ATNs, 440
atoms (atomic formulas), 241
  Boolean, 26
  denotation of, 222
  in predicate calculus, 241
  in propositional calculus, 219
  resolved upon, 231
  True or *False* values of, 222–223
attachment, semantic, 265
attribute noise, 51
attribute-value pairs called slots, 312
augmented phrase-structure grammar, 429,
  434
augmented transition networks (ATNs), 440
augmented vectors, 39
autoepistemic logic/reasoning, 310, 418
autonomous systems, 13
autonomy, 13
averaging
  combining edge enhancement with, 96
  in image processing, 91–93
averaging window, 91
axiom schemas for modal logic, 414

━━ **B**

B* search, 212
Bacchus, F., 177, *454*
Backgammon, 208, 210–212
background knowledge in ILP, 291
background theory in ATMSs, 279
backing up $\hat{f}$ values, 154
backing up (minimax), 198
backjumping, 136
backprop
  algorithm, 49

method, 45–51
network trained by, 50
backtracking search, 133–135
Backus–Naur form (BNF), 426
backward chaining, 275
backward reasoning, 274
backward search in planning
methods, 381–385
using regression, 381–385
Bacteriophage E6, 2–3
bacterium haemophilus influenzae, 3
Baker, A., 370, *454*
Bakiri, G., 45, *460*
Ballard, D. H., 102, 103, 107, 111, *454*
band crossings, 97
bank loan example, 286–290
Barr, A., 17, *454*
Barto, A., 178, *454*
Barwise, J., 250, *455*
Basye, K., 80, *460*
Bates, J., 34, 450, *455*
Bayes, Rev. Thomas, 322, *455*
Bayes networks (Bayes nets), 325–358
description length of, 347
known network structure (CPT learning),
343–346
learning, 343–351
learning and acting with, 343–360
learning network structure, 346–351
missing data, 345–346
no missing data, 343–345
patterns of inference in, 328–329
scoring metric, 347–348
searching network space, 349
Bayes' rule, 322
Beer, R., 7, 14, *455*
Begriffsschrift, 8
behavior modules, 32
behavior–based approach, 14
belief networks, 325
belief vs. knowledge, 244, 412, 418
beliefs, reifying, 411
Bennett, F., III, *472*
Benson, S., 398, 447, 448, *455*
Berliner, H., 212, *455*
best–first (heuristic) search, 139–162
best–first search (recursive), 154–155
beta cut–off, 205
beta value (node), 204
Bhanu, B., 111, *455*
bidirectional searches, 157
binary paramodulant, 263
Binford, T., 97, 106, *455*, *479*
biological evolution, 59

blackboard architecture, 77
blackboard systems, 77–79
blade (in scene analysis), 103
Bledsoe, Woody, 265, *455*
blocking a path, 330
blocking nodes, 331
blocks world, 11, 118, 242
Blum, A., 399, *456*
Blumberg, B., 34, *456*
Blythe, J., *458*
Bobrow, D., 9, 298, *456*
Boddy, M., 166, *460*
body of a clause, 270
Bolc, L., 425, *476*
boldface notation in this book, 242
Bonabeau, E., 408, *489*
Bond, A., 418, *456*
Boole, George, 8, *456*
Boolean algebra, 25–26
Boolean functions
classes and forms of, 26–27
as electronic circuits, 29
bootstrapping, 449
Börger, E., 270, *456*
Borgida, A., 312, *456*
Boser, B., *473*
Bösser, T., 15, *477*
bottom–up design, 7
bottom–up parsing algorithms (grammars),
428
bottom–up research, 14
boundary–following robot, 21, 60–68
bounded rationality, 15
Bouthoorn, P., *490*
Boyer, R., 265, *456*
Boyle, J., *492*
Brachman, R., 297, 298, 312, *456*, *473*
Bradtke, S., 178, *454*
Brain, A. E., 45, *456*
Braitenberg, V., 21, *456*
branch and bound search process, 169
branching factor (graph tree), 124
Bratko, I., 212, 270, *456*
Brave, S., 69, *456*
breadth–first search, 121, 131–133
bidirectional, 157, 385
strategies (in resolution), 235
Breese, J., 358, *469*
Breiman, L., 55, *457*
Bresina, J., 399, *478*
Bretier, P., *485*
Brewka, G., 313, *457*
Brooks, Rodney, 7, 32, 33, 34, 107, *457*
Brown, C. M., 102, 107, 111, 227, *483*, *454*

Brownston, L., 275, *457*
brute-force search methods, 14
Bryson, A., 41, *457*
Buchanan, B., 10, 339, *457, 462, 473*
bucket elimination (in probabilistic inference), 338
building reactive procedures, 170–172
Buntine, W., 291, 298, *478*
Bylander, T., 398, 399, *457*
Byun, Y.-T., 80, *472*

▰▰ C

calculus philosophicus, 8
Campbell, A. N., 10, 285, *457*
cancellation of inheritance, 310
Canny, J., *457*
Canny operator, 97
Carbonell, J., *458, 477*
Carson, D., 265, *492*
cascade network, 56–57
case-based reasoning, 314
Cassandra, A., 164, 358, *458*
categorical features, 23, 38, 317
causal networks, 326
causal reasoning, 328
causal (top-down) inference, 328
causes and symptoms, 218
certainty factors, 339
C4.5, 55
chain of conditional probabilities, 322
chain rule
    in calculus, 40, 47
    for joint probability function, 322
chaining (inference rule), 232
Chakrabarti, P., 177, *458*
Chang, C.-L., 236, 255, 256, 260, 263, *458*
Chapman, D., 177, 250, 399, *453, 458*
character recognition, 54, 85
Charniak, E., 440, *458*
Chauvin, Y., 50, *458*
cheapest-first heuristic, 315
checkers-playing programs, 8, 198, 212
Chen, K., 210, *470*
Chen, S., 305, *458*
CHESS 4.5, 207
chess-playing programs, 8, 10, 197, 212
Chickering, D., 345, 349, *467*
Chiel, H., 14, *455*
child (of a graph node), 124
child program, 64
CHINOOK, 212
Chomsky, N., 9, 440, *458*
Christensen, J., 399, *458*

chronological backtracking, 133
Church, Alonzo, 9
Churchland, P. S., 110, *458*
circumscription, 310, 313
CLASSIC system, 312
classical AI, 6
classification noise, 51
classifier systems, 60
clauses
    ancestors of, 236
    in Boolean functions, 26
    converting arbitrary wffs to, 232–233, 257–260
    descendants of, 236
    as disjunctions of literals, 227, 231
    head and body, 270
    resolution on, 231–232, 256–257
    resolvent of two, 231, 253, 256–257
    rules, facts, and goals, 270
    sets of literals, 231
    subsuming other clauses, 233
    as wffs, 231
Clocksin, W., 270, *458*
closed wff, 246
closed-world assumption (CWA), 313
Clowes, M., 105, *458*
clustering (of Bayes net nodes), 338
CNF PSAT problems, 227
cognitive science, 9, 14
cognitive structure, 409
cognology, 8
Cohen, B., 227, 228, *486*
Cohen, Paul, 17, *454, 458*
Cohen, Phil, 418, 440, *458*
coin-flipping example, 238, 318
Collinot, A., *467*
Colmerauer, Alain, 270, 297, *459*
commissives (speech acts), 422
commonsense knowledge
    difficulties in representing, 303–304
    importance of, 304–305
    objects and materials, 305
    physical processes and events, 305
    physical properties, 305
    representing, 301–316
    research areas, 305–306
    space, 305
    time, 306
    what it is, 301–303
commonsense world, 301–306
communication, 407, 421–441
    efficient, 435–437
    and integration, 405–451
    use of context in, 435–436

communicative act, 421
commutativity of ∧, 221
complement of a variable, 25
completeness (predicate calculus), 257
completeness (propositional calculus),
    226–227
complex information processing, 8
complexity analysis, 15
    of STRIPS, 399
compositional semantics, 413, 432
computation vs. memory, 117–118
Computational Learning Theory (COLT), 55
computer vision, 85–113
concept writing, 8
conceptualizations, 248–249
    grounded, 248
    inventing, 249
    of knowledge, 248–249
condition part of a production rule, 27
conditional independence, 324–325
    via blocking nodes, 331
    due to d–separation, 331
conditional probabilities, 320–323
conditional probability tables (CPTs), 327
    learning of, 343
conferences, major AI, 16
conflict resolution, 78, 275
Confucius, 115
conjunct, 229
conjunction (∧), 220, 229
conjunction (*Conj*), 426
conjunction of clauses, 27, 232–233, 259
conjunction of literals (in Boolean functions),
    26
conjunctions, regressing, 382–383
conjunctive normal form (CNF), 27, 227, 232,
    259
connectives (propositional calculus), 219
Connell, J., 32, 33, 123, 178, 445, *459*, 474
consequent of an implication, 220
consistency condition, 150–153
consistency maintenance system (CMS), 278
consistent substitutions, 273
constraint arc, 184
constraint graphs, 184–185, 186–187
constraint propagation, 183
constraint satisfaction problem, 104, 181
constraints on feature values, 217–219
constructive formulations, state spaces for,
    184
constructive methods, 183–187
consulting systems, 284
context, in communication, 435–436
context, in planning, 380

context–free grammars, 425–426
context units in neural nets, 73
contradiction (proof by), 234
contrapositive, law of, 225
convolution, 91
Cook, Stephen, 9, 227, *459*
Cooper, G., 358, *459*
Copernicus, 16
Cormen, T., 125, *459*
correspondence problem in stereo vision,
    110
costs of arcs (graph), 124
Cover, T., 347, *459*
Cozannet, A., *485*
CPCS-BN, 339
credit assignment problems, 177
criticality numbers, 393
cross validation, 53–54
crossover operation, 64
crossword puzzle, array for, 183
Culberson, J., *485*
Currie, K., 395, *459*
curve fitting, 52
CYC project, 10, 248, 303, 305, 308, 313, 449
cycles in search, 170

━━━ **D**

Darwin, 16
DATALOG, 274, 297
Davis, E., 260, 298, 313, *459*
Davis, M., *459*
Davis, R., *459*
Dayan, P., 178, 212, 478, *485*, 486
de Kleer, J., 280, 298, 305, 408, *460*, *463*, 491
De Raedt, L., 291, *479*
Dean, T., 80, 166, 351, 369, 399, *460*
Dechter, R., 338, *460*
decision lists, 34
decision nodes, 354
decision procedure, 269
decision theory, 358
decision tree, 55
declarations (speech acts), 422
deduction or proof, 221
deduction theorem (propositional calculus),
    228
deductive rule learning, 286, 295–297
DEEP BLUE, 10, 212
default information, 311
default logic, 310
definite–clause grammar, 440
delayed–reinforcement learning, 177
delete list, 123, 375

Delta rule, 41
DeMorgan's laws, 26–27, 225, 247
Dempster, A., 339, 346, *460*
Dempster-Shafer rules, 339
DENDRAL, 10
Denker, J., *473*
Dennett, D., 15, 411, *460*
denotation of an atom, 222
denotations (in predicate calculus), 242
deontic logics, 418
dependency-directed backtracking, 136
depth bound, 133
depth calculation from a single image, 109
depth information (image), 108–110
depth of root node (graph), 124
depth-first planning process, 395
depth-first strategies, 235
derives (⊢), 221
DeSarkar, S., 177, *458*
descendant of a clause, 236
descendant of a node (graph), 124
descent methods, 189
describing states and goals, 373–374
describing the environment, 12, 409
Deutsch, J. A., 34, *460*
diagnostic (bottom-up) inference, 328
diagnostic reasoning, 328
Dietterich, T., 45, 55, *460*, *487*
difficult-to-represent information, 217
Dijkstra, E., 133, *460*
directed acyclic graph (DAG), 325
directed graph, 124
directed tree, 124
directives (speech acts), 422
disagreement set, 255
discharged threat arcs, 392
discontinuities in a scene, 88–89
discount factor (γ), 175–176
disjunct, 229
disjunction (∨), 220, 229
disjunction of literals (in Boolean functions),
      26
disjunction of terms (in Boolean functions),
      26
disjunctive normal form (DNF), 26, 232
distributed artificial intelligence (DAI), 407,
      418
distribution axiom, 414
distributive laws, 26, 229–230
divide-and-conquer heuristic, 376
Dix, J., 313, *457*
Dixon, J., 207, *488*
domain of an interpretation, 242
Donald, Merlyn, 405

Donath, M., 14, *454*
Doran, J., 160, *461*
dot product unit (DPU), 57
Dowling, W., 237, *461*
doxastic logics, 418
Doyle, J., 250, 298, 310, *461*, *476*
Dreyfus, H., 15, *461*
Dreyfus, S., 15, *461*
Drummond, M., 399, *478*
d-separation, 330–332
Duda, R., 10, 53, 54, 285, 339, *457*, *461*
dummy variable, 246
durative procedure, 28
Dym, C., 281, *461*
DYNA, 173
dynamic backtracking, 136
dynamic decision network, 353–354, 358
dynamic knowledge bases, 275–280
dynamic programming, 178
dynamical system, 7, 55
Džeroski, S., 291, *473*

E

Earthquake alarm example, 340–341
edge enhancement (in image processing),
      93–97
edge (graph), 124
edge (image), 93
effective branching factor, 157
efficient communication, 435–437
Eight-puzzle, 129–130, 131–133, 139, 142, 146,
      158, 174, 183, 400
Eight-Queens problem, 182–183, 188
elevator problem, 80
ELIZA program, 5
Elkan, C., 339, 368, *461*
Elman, J., 73, *461*
Elman networks, 73–74
embodiment, 2, 4
emergent behavior, 7
Emerson, E., 249, 306, *461*
Encyclopedia of AI, 17
Enderton, H., 250, *462*
Engineering Applications of AI (EAAI), 16
entailment, 225
environment, representation of, 71–73
Ephrati, E., 399, *462*
epipolar line, 110
epistemic logics, 418
epistemic necessitation, 414
equality predicate, 262–265
equipotential curves, 77
equivalent wffs, 225, 244, 247

Erman, L., *462*
Ernst, M., 399, *462*
Erol, K., 399, *462*
error function, 39
error-correction procedure, 43
Etchemendy, J., 250, *455*
ethological models, 14, 34, 80
Etzioni, O., 398, *458*, *462*, *477*
evaluation functions, 139–141, 198
    discovery of, 155–156
    learning of, 172–175, 210–212
Evans, T. G., 9, *462*
even-parity function, 45
evidence
    in inference, 328
evidence above and below (polytrees),
    332–336
evidence nodes (polytrees), 329, 332
evolution, 59
evolutionary computation, 59–60
evolutionary search processes, 60
existential generalization (EG), 247
existential quantifier (∃), 245, 247
expanding a node, 122, 131
expectation maximization (EM), 346
expectimaxing, 209, 212
expert systems, 10, 218, 280, 291, 339
    basic structure of, 281
    rule-based, 280–286
explaining away, 329
explanation (facts used in a proof), 296
explanation-based generalization (EBG), 286,
    295–297
explicit graphs, 172–173
Exploring AI, 17
expressibility/tractability tradeoff, 297
expressives (speech acts), 422
extensionally specified *n*-ary relations, 242

━━━ **F**

$\hat{f}$ values, 139, 154
fact (atom), 237
fact clause, 270
Fagin, R., 414, 418, *462*
Farmer, Sam, 19
Farrell, R., *457*
father program, 64
Faugeras, O., 111, *462*
feature values, constraints on, 217–219
feature vectors, 71–73
feature-based model, 12
feature-based representation, 74
feature-based state spaces, 122–123

feature-based vs. iconic models, 12, 74–75,
    409
feedforward networks, 44
Feigenbaum, E., 9, 10, 17, 280, 281, *454*, *458*,
    462 463, *473*
Feldman, J., 9, *462*
Feller, W., 338, *463*
Ferguson, C., *483*
Ferrieux, A., *485*
Fifteen-puzzle, 129
Fikes, R., 122, 314, 375, 396, 397, *463*
Finin, T., 314, *463*
Firby, R. J., 450, *463*
Firschein, O., 111, *463*
first-order logic rules, learning, 291–295
first-order predicate calculus (FOPC), 219,
    239, 246
Fischler, M. A., 111, *463*
fitness as a function of generation number,
    68
fitness of a program, 63
fixed increment error-correction procedure,
    56
Fleischmann, R., 3, *463*
flocking behavior, 408
Flores, F., 2, *492*
fluents, 364
FOIL, 291
folds (disjoint subsets), 53
folds (in scene analysis), 103
Forbes, J., 358, *463*
Forbus, K., 280, 298, *463*
Ford, K., 14, *467*
Forgy, C., 275, 277, *463*
Forrest, B., 55, *484*
forward chaining, 275
forward search methods, 374–377
Four-Queens problem, 160–161, 184–185, 193
Fox, M., 399, *492*
frame axioms, 367–368
frame problem, 368
frames, 308, 312–313
Frank, M., *465*
Frege, Gottlieb, 8, *463*
frequency interpretation of probabilities, 321
Friedman, J., *457*
Friedman, N., 345, 347, 349, 358, *463*, *464*
Froom, R., *472*
Fu, L. M., *464*
function constants, 239–240
function optimization, 60, 189–192
functional expressions (in predicate calculus),
    240
functional programs, 60

functionally individuated entities, 250
Furst, M., 399, *456*
future states (agent), 218
fuzzy hyperplane, 42
fuzzy logic, 339

▬ G

$\hat{g}$ function, 156
Gallier, J., 237, *461*
Galton, A., *464*
game playing, 10, 195–213
game tree
    for a game of chance, 209
    looking ahead in, 199
    ply of ply-depth k in, 197
games of chance, 197, 208–210
gap filler, 79
Gardner, Martin, 8, *464*
Garey, M., 15, *464*
Gaschnig, J., 10, 136, 155, 285, *461*, *464*
Gasser, L., 418, *456*
Gat, E., 450, *464*
Gaussian smoothing function, 92–93
Geiger, D., 345, 349, *467*
Gelatt, C., 192, *470*
Gelernter, H., 8, *464*
General Problem Solver (GPS), 9, 377
general vs. specific rules, 287
general viewpoint (in scene analysis), 104
generalization, network, 51–54
generalization accuracy, 51, 53
generalized cylinders, 106–107
generalized Delta procedure, 41–42
generalized Delta vs. Widrow–Hoff, 42
generic separate-and-conquer algorithm
    (GSCA), 290
Genesereth, M., 34, 80, 234, 248, 298, 313, 412,
    464, *488*
genetic algorithms (GAs), 60
genetic programming (GP), 60–68
Gentner, D., 314, *464*
Ghose, S., 177, *458*
Gibson, J. J., 110, *464*
Gil, Y., 398, *458*, *464*, *477*
Gilbert, V., 312, *456*
Ginsberg, Matt, 14, 136, 161, 178, 182, 213,
    298, 313, *465*, *488*
Glesner, S., 318, *465*
global consistency of heuristic functions, 150
Go game, 210
goal arbitration, 446–448, 450
goal clause, 270–271
goal condition, 28, 131, 363, 369, 374

goal descriptions, 373–374
goal node, 120, 125
goal predicate, 161
goal set, 125
goal-achieving production systems, 28
goals, 175–177, 237, 351
Gödel, Kurt, 9
Gogic, G., 297, *465*
Goldberg, A., 227, *465*
Goldberg, D., 60, *465*
Goldszmidt, M., 338, 345, 347, 349, *463*, *464*,
    465
GOLEM system, 298
GOLOG (alGOl in LOGic), 371
good-old-fashioned-AI (GOFAI), 6
GP (genetic programming) process, 62–65
gradient descent methods, 39–40, 189
grammar
    for blocks-world communication, 427
    expanding, 432–435
graph, 124
graph notation, 124–125
GRAPHSEARCH, 141–155
graph-search planning, 120–121
graph-searching algorithm, 141–155
greedy methods, 228, 287, 349
Green, Cordell, 8, 262, 297, 363, *465*
Gregory, R., 111, *465*
grid-world robot, 11, 21–23, 61
Grimson, W. E. L., 106, *465*
Grosz, B., 440, *466*
ground instance, 254
ground term, 254
grounded conceptualizations, 248
Gruber, T., 314, *466*
GSAT, 228
GSCA algorithm, 290, 293–294
Gu, J., 188, *466*
Guha, R., 10, 248, 303, 308, 313, *466*, *473*
Gupta, N., 399, *466*
Guzman, A., 105, *466*

▬ H

$\hat{h}$ function, 156
haemophilus influenzae bacterium, 3
Halpern, J., 418, *462*
Halpin, M., *465*
Hanazawa, T., *490*
Handbook of AI, The, 17
Hanks, S., 370, *466*
Harnad, S., 2, *466*
Hart, P., 10, 53, 54, 122, 146, 148, 151, 285, 339,
    375, 396, 397, *457*, *461*, *463*, *466*

Harvey, W. D., *465*, *466*
Haugeland, John, 6
Haussler, D., 38, *466*, *467*
Hayes, P., 14, 305, 363, *467*, *476*
Hayes-Roth, B., 77, 450, *467*
Hayes-Roth, F., *462*
Haykin, S., 55, *467*
head of a clause, 270
Hebert, M., 110, 177, *467*, *488*, *489*
Heckerman, David, 326, 339, 345, 349, *467*
Heinsohn, J, 313, *468*
Henderson, D., *473*
Hendler, J., 399, *454*, *462*
Hendrix, G., 312, *468*
Henrion, M., 338, 339, 358, *468*, *469*, *483*
Herskovitz, E., 358, *459*
Hertz, J., 55, *468*
heuristic functions
    discovery of, 155–156
    global consistency of, 150
    learning, 172–175, 210–212
    and search efficiency, 155–160
heuristic processes, 131
heuristic programming, 8
heuristic repair, 187–189
heuristic search, 139–162
    bidirectional, 157
    notation, 143
Hewett, R., *467*
Hexmoor, Henry, 1
hidden nodes, 349
hidden units, 45
hierarchical planning, 167–168, 177, 393–395
hierarchical search, 167–169
hierarchies, taxonomic, 308–309
Hildreth, E., 97, *475*
HILLCLIMB, 190–192
hill-climbing methods, 39–40, 189
hill-climbing searches, 190–192
Hintikka, J., 417, *468*
Hinton, G., *484*, *490*
history of AI, 8–11
Ho, Y-C., 41, *457*
Hobbs, J., 313, *468*
Hoff, M. E., 9, *491*
Holland, John, 60, *468*
Hollister, V., *457*
homogeneous region (image), 99
horizon effect, 208
horizon nodes, 169
horizontal architecture, 32
Horn, Alfred, 103, 111, 237, *468*
Horn, B. K. P., *468*

Horn clauses, 237–238, 270–275
    greatest-lower-bound (GLB) theories, 297
    least-upper-bound (LUB) theories, 297
    methods for learning, 291
    types of, 237
Horn theories, 297
Horowitz, S., 99, *468*
Horswill, I., 110, *468*
Horvitz, E., 166, 358, *468*, *469*
household robot, 304
Howard, R., *473*
Huang, T., *463*
Hubbard, W., *473*
Hubel, D., 10, 110, 111, *469*
Huberman, B. J., 212, *469*
Hucka, M., *472*
Hueckel, M., 97, *469*
Hueckel operator, 97
Huffman, D., 105, *469*
HUGIN system, 339
human-level intelligence, 1, 15, 443, 450
hyperplane, 30, 38–39
hysteretic agents, 80

▬ **I**

iconic representations, 12, 74–77
iconic vs. feature-based models, 12, 74–75, 409
IDA*, 153
ID3, 55
illocutionary effect (speech acts), 422
ILP systems, 291, 294
image attributes, 101–102
image depth information, 108–110
image edges, 88
image intensity, taking derivatives of, 95
image intensity array, 91
image junctions, labeling by type, 106
image processing, 91–102
    averaging, 91–93
    edge enhancement, 93–95
    region finding, 97–101
image regions, 88, 99–101
image shading, 102
image smoothing, 92–96
image texture, 101–102
implication (⊃), 220
implication (rule), 237
implicit graphs, 173–175
implicit state-space graph components, 130–131
inconsistent set of wffs, 224
inconsistent wff, 244

indexical–functional representations, 250
indexically individuated entities, 250
indirect speech acts, 422
individuals (in predicate calculus), 241
    functions on, 241
    relations over, 241–242
induction, mathematical, 146
inductive logic programming (ILP), 291
inductive rule learning, 286
inference, patterns of, 328–329
inference rules (predicate calculus), 247
inference rules (propositional calculus),
    219–221
informedness (of A*), 148–149
inheritance
    cancellation of, 310
    property, 311
    of subcategories, 309
Iñigo, R., 14, 477
intelligent behavior, defining, 15
intended interpretation, 226, 243
intention, 304, 409, 421–422
intentional stance, 411–412
interacting agents, 407–408
interleaved planning, 177
intermediate–level action (ILA), 444, 447
International Conference on Machine
    Learning (ICML), 55
International Joint Conferences on AI (IJCAI),
    16
INTERPLAN, 399
interpretation
    domain of, 242
    of a line drawing, 103
    in predicate calculus, 242–243
    in propositional calculus, 222
    satisfying a wff, 243
intervals, time, 306–307
isa links, 309
island–driven search, 166, 177
isotropic heat diffusion, 93, 100
iterative broadening, 136
iterative–deepening A* (IDA*), 153–154
iterative–deepening search, 135–136

J

Jackel, L., 473
Jain, R., 111, *469*
Jensen, F., 339, *469*
Johnson, D., 15, *464*
Johnson, M., 314, *472, 478*
Johnson–Laird, P., 14, *469*
joint probabilities, 318–320, 323–324, 326

joint probability function, 318
Jones, Effie, 361
Jordan, M., 123, *469*
journals, AI, 16
Juels, A., 192, *469*
Julesz, B., 110, *469*
JULIA program, 5
justifications, 277

K

Kaelbling, L., 7, 33, 80, 164, 177, 358, *458, 460,*
    469, 484
Kahn, D., 450, *458*
Kahn, R., *463*
Kahneman, D., 339, *490*
Kanade, T., *489*
Kanal, L., 160, *469, 472*
Kanazawa, K., *463*
Kant, E., *457*
Karlsson, J., 450, *491*
Karmarkar, N., 55, *469*
Karp, Richard, 9
Kartha, G. N., 370, *470*
Kasparov, Garry, 10, 212
Kasturi, R., 111, *469*
Katz, Edward, 31
Kautz, H., 227, 228, 297, 298, 305, 399, 440, *465,*
    470, 486
KB (knowledge base), 222, 244, 276–277, 314
k–clause CNF expression, 27
Keane, M., *472*
Kearns, M., 38, 297, 298, *470*
Kenley, C., 339, *486*
Khardon, R., 297, *470*
Kierulf, A., 210, *470*
KIF, 313
Kim, J–S., 338, 412, *470, 471*
King, R., 298, *479*
Kirkpatrick, S., 192, *470*
Kirsh, D., 32, *470*
k–layer network of sigmoid units, 46
Kleene, Stephen, 9
Knight, B., *485*
Knight, K., *484*
Knoblock, C., 399, *458, 471, 477*
knowledge
    vs. belief, 244, 412, 418
    conceptualizing, 248–249
    in predicate calculus, 244–245, 248–249
    representation by semantic networks,
        308–313
    to resolve ambiguities, 436–437
knowledge axioms, 413–415

knowledge base, 222, 244, 276–277, 314
knowledge engineer, 282
knowledge interchange format (KIF), 313
knowledge level, 6
knowledge sources (KSs), 77
knowledge-based systems, 6, 269–300
Knuth, D. E., 207, 470
Koenderink, J., 93, 471
Koller, Daphne, 161, 314, 318, 400, 402, 465
Kolodner, J., 314, 471
Konolige, K., 313, 412, 413, 418, 457, 471
Korf, R., 135, 153, 154, 158, 160, 169, 170, 172,
    177, 212, 471, 483
Kowalski, R., 297, 412, 471
Koza, J., 11, 60, 69, 471, 472
KQML system, 314
Kripke, S., 417, 472
Krogh, A., 55, 468
KRYPTON, 312
kSAT problem, 227
k-term DNF expression, 27
Kudenko, D., 468
Kuipers, B., 80, 472
Kulikowski, C., 55, 490
Kumar, V., 160, 187, 469, 472
Kuokka, D., 477

━━ **L**

labels of cells (in TMSs), 279
labels of lines, 104
labels (or classes) of vectors, 37
Labrou, Y., 314, 463
Laird, J., 275, 450, 472, 484
Laird, N., 346, 460
Laird, P., 478
Lake, R., 198, 485
Lakoff, G., 2, 314, 472
lambda expressions, 430
lambda notation, 431
Lang, K., 490
Langley, P., 55, 472
language and syntax (in predicate calculus),
    240–241
language generation, 425
language (in propositional calculus), 219–220,
    228
language strings, 425–435
language understanding, 425–440
Laplacian, 96
Laplacian filtering, 96–98
lateral inhibition, 111
Latombe, J-C., 77, 472
Lauritzen, S., 338, 345, 472

Lavrač, N., 291, 473
law of the contrapositive, 225
layered feedforward network, 45
leaf nodes (graph), 124–125
learning, neural nets, 37–57
learning, two major types of, 286
learning Bayes nets, 343–351
learning Bayes network structure, 346–351
learning control information, 397
learning evaluation functions, 172–175,
    210–212
learning first-order logic rules, 291–295
learning heuristic functions, 172–175
learning plans, 396–398
learning process, supervised, 38
learning propositional calculus rules, 286–291
learning rate parameter, 41
learning rules, 286–297
least commitment planning, 382, 385
leave-one-out cross validation, 54
LeCun, Y., 54, 473
Lederberg, J., 10, 462, 473
Lee, K-F., 178, 212, 440, 473, 490
Lee, R., 236, 255, 256, 260, 263, 458
Lee, S., 111, 455
Lee, W-Y., 472
legal wffs (in predicate calculus), 241, 251
legal wffs (in propositional calculus), 220
LEGO robots, 33
Leibniz, Gottfried, 8
Leiserson, C., 125, 459
Lenat, Doug, 10, 248, 303, 308, 466, 473
length-first plan-development process, 394
Leonard-Barton, D., 298, 473
Lesprance, Y., 473
Lesser, V., 462
Letvinn, J., 10, 110, 473
Levesque, H., 228, 297, 298, 312, 371, 418, 456,
    458, 473, 485, 486
Levitt, R., 281, 461
Lewis, Albert, 19
lexical ambiguity, 436–437
lexicon, 427
Lifschitz, V., 398, 473
limited-horizon search, 169–170
Lin, F., 473
Lindsay, R., 10, 473
line drawing, 103
linear programming, 55
linear-input strategy, 236–237
linearly separable functions, 29
line-labeling scene analysis, 104
Linoff, G., 440, 475
literals, 26, 220, 231

Littman, M., 164, 177, 358, *458*, *469*
Llull, Ramon, 8
local effects of actions, 367
Loebner, Hugh, 5
Loebner Prize competition, 5
logic
   definition, 219
   planning methods based on, 361–404
logic sampling (Bayes net), 338
Logic Theorist, 8
logical consequence, 225
logical entailment (⊨), 225–226, 244
logically omniscient agent, 415
long-term memory, 275
looking ahead in a game tree, 199
Lovejoy, W., 164, *474*
Loveland, D., 259, *474*
low-level actions (LLAs), 444
Löwenheim, L., 245, *474*
Lowrance, J., *491*
Lowry, M., 265, *474*
Loyall, A. B., 450, *455*
Lucas, J. R., 9, *474*
Luckham, D., 262, *474*
LUNAR system, 10
Lusk, E., *492*

▬ **M**

Machina speculatrix, 21
machine evolution, 59–70
machine intelligence, 8
machine learning, 37
Machine Learning journal, 55
machines
   biological and computational, 2
   reactive, 19–113
   thinking, 2
MACROP (macro-operator), 397
Maes, P., 7, *474*
Magerman, D., 440, *474*
Mahadevan, S., 123, 178, *459*, *474*
Mahajan, S., 178, 212, *473*
maintenance in dynamic knowledge bases,
   275–280
Malik, J., 100, *482*
Mamdani, Abe, 339
Manna, Z., 265, *474*
many-to-one nature of imaging process, 86
map learning, 80
maplike iconic representation, 76
mapping a state–action pair into a state, 367
marginal probability, 319
marker propagation in graph searching, 121

Markov assumption, 357
Markov decision problem (MDP), 164, 358
Markov process, 355
Markovian environment, 354
Marr, D., 10, 97, 110, 111, *475*
Marr–Hildreth operator, 97–98
Martelli, A., 298, *475*
Martian robot, 401–402
Martin, N., *457*
Martin, P., *466*
Masand, B., 440, *475*
Mataric, M., 2, 32, 34, 408, *457*, *475*
match arcs, 272
mathematical induction, 146
matrix of a wff, 246, 259
Maturana, H., *473*
Mauldin, M. L., 5, *475*
Mayfield, J., 314, *463*
McAdams, H., 3, *475*
McAllester, D., 385, 399, *470*, *475*
McCarthy, John, 6, 8, 212, 248, 310, 363, 370,
   411, *475*, *476*, *487*
McCartney, R., 265, *474*
McClelland, J., 14, *476*
McCorduck, P., 10, 281, *463*, *476*
McCulloch, Warren, 9, *473*, *476*
McCulloch–Pitts neurons, 9
McCune, W., 265, *476*
McDermott, D., 250, 270, 310, 370, *466*, *476*
McDermott, J., 10, 298, *476*
McDonald, D., 425, *476*
McFarland, D., 15, 34, *477*
McGuinness, D., *456*
McKeown, K., 425, *477*
McVey, E., 14, *477*
meaning of a phrase (semantics), 430
meaning of a string (semantics), 429
meanings (semantics), 222, 241, 246
means–ends analysis, 377
Meek, C., 349, *488*
Mellish, C., 270, *458*
memory
   vs. computation, 117–118
   long– and short–term, 275
   state machine, 71
Mérõ, L., 153, *477*
message–passing algorithms, 338
metaknowledge, 312, 398
metalevel computation, 160
metalevel search, 167
metalinguistic approach, 412
metalinguistic symbols (⊢ and ⊨), 228
metatheorems (propositional calculus),
   228–229

mgu (most general unifier), 255
Michalewicz, Z., 60, 477
Michalski, R., 287, 477
Michie, D., 160, 212, *456*, *461*, 477
Middleton, B., *483*
Miller, R., 10, 477
Million-Queens problem, 189
Millstein, T., 399, *462*
Milshtein, M., 399, *462*
min-conflicts heuristic, 188
minimal cost between two nodes (graph), 124
minimax procedure, 197–202
minimin search, 169
minimum description length, 347–348, 358
minimum spanning tree, 126
Minker, J., 274, 477
Minnix, J., 14, 477
Minsky, M., 9, 417, 477
Minton S., 188, 189, 297, 398, 400, *458*, 477, 478
missing data, 345–346
"Missionary and Cannibals" problem,
    126–127, 193
Mitchell, D., 228, *486*
Mitchell, M., 60, *478*
Mitchell, T., 55, *478*
Mittal, S., 298, *456*
modal logics of knowledge, 412–417
modal operator (**K**), 412–413
model tower, 448
model-based vision, 106–108
modeling physical processes, 408
modeling strategies, 410
models
    iconic vs. feature-based, 74–75, 409
    meaning of in this book, 12
    of other agents, 407–412
    varieties of, 408–409
    of a wff or set of wffs, 224, 243
modus ponens, 221, 232
Monahan, G., 164, *478*
monomial, 26, 30
monotone condition, 150–153
monotonic inference, 278, 309
Montague, P., 178, *478*, *486*
Montanari, U., 298, *475*
Moore, A., 177, 178, *469*, *478*
Moore, E. F., 121, *478*
Moore, J, 265, *456*
Moore, R. C., 310, 313, 317, 417, 418, *468*, *478*
Moore, R. W., 207, *470*
more informed (in A*), 148
morphological analysis, 438
Morris, P., 338, *465*
Moses, Y., *462*

most fit individual in a generation, 66–68
Mostow, J., 160, *478*
mother program, 64
Muggleton, S., 291, 298, *478*, *479*
multiple agents, 407–419
Mumford, D., 102, *492*
mutation operator, 64
mutual justification, 278–279
mutually conditional independence, 325
MYCIN expert system, 285, 317, 339
Myers, J., 10, 477
Myers, K., 265, *479*, *491*

N

naive knowledge, 302
naive physics, 302, 408
Nalwa, V. S., 10, 97, 101, 103, 105, 107, 111, *479*
Nalwa-Binford operator, 97
n-ary relations, 242
Nathwani, B., 339, *467*
natural language processing (NLP), 437–440
natural languages, 424
natural-deduction methods, 265
Nau, D., 399, *462*, *466*
Neal, R., 339, 358, *479*
Neapolitan, R., 339, *479*
Nebel, B., *468*
necessity indices, 339
negation (¬), 220
negation as failure, 299
negation of a Boolean variable, 25
negative effect axiom, 366
negative frame axiom, 368
negative instances, 287
negative literals, 231, 237
negative-introspection axiom, 414
network, neural. *See* neural networks.
network generalization, 51
network learning experiment (Bayes), 350
network of TISA units, 31
network of TLUs, 29, 45
network space (Bayes), searching, 349
network structure (Bayes), learning, 346–351
networks of logical gates, 9
networks (semantic), 308–313
Neural Information Processing Systems
    (NIPS) conferences, 54
neural networks (neural nets), 7, 10, 30, 37–57,
    73, 86–87, 123, 210, 339, 358
Newborn, M., 212, *479*
Newell, Allen, 4, 6, 8, 9, 14, 80, 155, 275, 377,
    472, 479, 480, 484
Nievergelt, J., 210, *470*

Nii, H. P., 77, 281, *463*, *480*
Nilsson, N., 9, 16, 28, 34, 43, 80, 122, 146, 148, 151, 168, 177, 234, 248, 262, 298, 318, 339, 375, 396, 397, 412, 444, 447, 448, *455*, *461*, *463*, *466*, *474*, *480*
NOAH system, 395, 399
nodes
   explained, 124–125
   kinds of (in semantic nets), 309
   ordering (for alpha–beta search), 207
nogoods, 278
noise, performance limited by, 51
noise-tolerant modifications, 290
NONLIN, 385
nonlinear plans, 385
nonmonotonic inference, 278, 309, 338
nonmonotonic logic, 310
nonmonotonic reasoning in semantic networks, 309–312
nonterminals (grammars), 425
Noordweier, M., 286, *489*
Norvig, P., 11, 41, 332, 338, 351, 433, 440, *481*, *484*
notational conventions (fonts) in this book, xxii, 219, 242, 273
no-tight-space condition, 21, 72, 251
noun phrase (NP), 426, 431
noun–noun combination, 426
Nourbakhsh, I., 177, *481*
NP-hard problems, 227, 237, 270, 331, 399
N-Queens problem, 189, 228, 230

O

object constants, 239–240
object-level computation, 160
objects, 239, 241
Occam, William of, 52
Occam's Razor principle, 52
occlude, 103
occur check, 256
Olshen, R., *457*
ontologies, 314
operators, 131
operators corresponding to actions, 374
operators (schema instances), 118
O-PLAN system, 395
Oppacher, F., 192, *481*
OPS5, 275
optimal ordering of conjuncts, 315
optimal path (graph nodes), 124
optimistic estimator, 146
or function, 25
OR nodes, 273, 283

ordering strategies (in resolution search), 235–236
ordering successor nodes (for alpha–beta search), 207
ordinary logic, monotonic, 278, 309
O'Reilly, U-M., 192, *481*
out-of-sample-set error rate, 53
Overbeek, R., *492*
overfitting data, 52
   avoiding, 53
   minimizing risk of (in GSCA), 290

P

Paine, Thomas, 215
Palmer, R., 55, *468*
Panaget, F., *485*
Papadimitriou, C., *465*
paramodulation, 263
parent (of a graph node), 124
parent programs, 64
parents (in Bayes nets), 326, 332, 334
parsing a string (grammars), 428
partial-order planning (POP), 385–393, 395
partially observable Markov decision problems (POMDPs), 164, 358
Paterson, M., 256, *481*
path of length k (graph), 124
PATHFINDER, 339
pattern matching, 275
Pauchon, E., 103, *479*
Pavlidis, T., 99, *468*
PC AI magazine, 16
Pearl, Judea, 150, 155, 156, 160, 207, 212, 338, 339, 340, *465*, *470*, *481*, *487*
Pednault, E., 368, 398, *481*
Penberthy, J., 399, *481*
Penrose, R., 9, *481*, *482*
perception, 24
   and action, 21–27
   and action components, 23
perceptrons, 9, 38
perceptual aliasing, 163
perceptual processing phase, 23
Pereira, F., 274, 298, 440, *466*, *482*, *490*
Pereira, L., 297, *490*
Perez, A., *458*
Perlis, D., 412, *482*
perlocutionary effect, 422
Perona, P., 100, *482*
Perrault, C. R., 440, *458*
Person, C., *478*
perspective projection, 85
Phillips, A., *478*

phrase–structure grammars, 425–428
phrases (grammars), 425
physical grounding hypothesis, 7
physical symbol system hypothesis, 4, *6*
Pierce, D., 472
Pineda, F. J., 55, *482*
Pingle, K., 97, *482*
Pitts, Walter, 9, *473*, *476*
pixel, 91
plan of this book, 11–13
plan recognition, 440
plan spaces, 385–393
plan transformations, 388–391
plan–generalization process, 396
planning, 373–404
    agents that plan, 117–127
    combining with reacting, 447
    hierarchical and partial-order, 395
    graphs, 399
    methods based on logic, 361–404
    speech acts, 423
    in state–space graphs, 120
plans
    articulating, 395
    learning, 396–398
    with run–time conditionals, 379–380
plan–space vs. state–space search, 386
plan–transforming operators, 387
plateau (in a search space), 190, 228
Platonic view of knowledge, 415
ply of ply–depth k in a game tree, 197
Poggio, T., 110, *475*
Pohl, I., 160, *482*
pointing (accompanying an indexical), 436
Pollack, M., 399, 462, *482*
polynomial expected time (for PSAT
    problems), 227
polytrees, 331–338
Pomerleau, D., 87, *482*
Pople, H., 10, *477*
Port, R., 7, *482*
positive effect axiom, 365
positive frame axiom, 368
positive instances, 286
positive literal, 231
positive–introspection axiom, 414
Pospesel, H., 250, *483*
possibility theory, 339
possible worlds, 413
Post, Emil, 9
Powers, R., 14, *483*
Powley, C., *483*
Pradhan, M., 339, *483*
pragmatic analysis, 437

Prawitz, D., 265, *483*
precondition list, 122
preconditions, 366, 375
predicate calculus, 8, 239–251
    completeness and soundness, 257
    language and syntax, 240–241
    representing agent knowledge, 244–245,
        248–249
    resolution in, 253–268
    rules of inference, 247
    semantics, 241–245, 246–247
    and the world, 243
predicate evaluation, 264
predicate invention, 291, 298, 351
predicates (relation constants), 240
predicting a feature vector with a neural
    network, 123
predicting actions of other agents, 417
predicting consequences of actions, 117–118
prefix (in prenex form wff), 259
prenex form, wff in, 259
Prieditis, A., 160, *478*, *483*
primal sketch, 97
prior probabilities, 327
probabilistic inference, 320, 323–325
    and action, 351–358
    conditional independence, 324–325
    general method, 323–324
    in polytrees, 332–338
probabilistic logic, 339
probability function properties, 318
probability theory
    fundamental ideas, 317–320
    review, 317–323
probably approximately correct learning
    (PAC), 38
PRODIGY system, 297, 398
production rules (productions), 27
production systems, 27–29, 77–78, 80
Profitlich, H-J., *468*
program
    expressed as a tree, 61
    fitness of, 63
    representation in GP, 60
    verification and synthesis, 265
progression planning, 374
projecting, 121, 218
PROLOG, 270–275, 297–299, 374
proof
    or deduction, 221
    search tree for, 284
proof tree, 222, 284
properties
    inheritance of, 309, 311

properties (*cont.*)
  in predicate calculus, 241
propositional calculus, 217–230
  associative laws, 229
  definition of proof, 221
  definitions, 219
  language, 219–220
  language distinctions, 228
  metatheorems, 228–229
  resolution in, 231–238
  rule learning, 286–291
  rules of inference, 220–221
  semantics, 222–226
  soundness and completeness, 226–227
propositional satisfiability (PSAT) problem, 227–228
propositional truth table, 223–224
propositional wffs (in FOPC), 241
propositions, 222, 239
PROSPECTOR expert system, 285, 317, 339
proto-English, 425
Provan, G., *483*
proved node, 272
proving a goal clause, 271
proving theorems using resolution, 234, 260–261
pruning operations, 290
PSAT problem, 227–228
psychological models, 14, 80, 314
published proceedings on AI, 16
Purdom, P. W., Jr., 227, *483*
purposive vision, 103, 110
Puterman, M., 164, 358, *483*
Putnam, H., 260, *459*

■ **Q**

QA3, 8
qualification problem, 369
qualitative Bayes networks, 339
qualitative physics, 305, 408
quantification, 245–247
quantifier semantics, 246–247
quantifier symbols, 245
quasi-logical form, 433
query node, 328
quiescent position (in game-search programs), 208
Quinlan, Ross, 55, 286, 291, *483*

■ **R**

Ramachandran, V. S., 110, *458*
Ramadge, P., 399, *483*

ramification problem, 369
random variables, 317
range image, 102
Raphael, B., 146, 148, 151, 168, *466*, *480*
ratiocinator, 8
RBFS, 154
reacting combined with planning, 447
reactive agents, 11–12
reactive machines, 19–113
reactive procedures, building, 170–172
real-time A* (RTA*), 170
real-world problems, 269–270
reason maintenance systems, 276
reasoning, 218
  by cases, 232
  about other agents' knowledge, 415–417
  about states and actions, 363–367
  with uncertain information, 317–342
reasoning agents, 13
recurrent networks, 44, 55, 73
recursive best-first search, 154–155
recursive STRIPS, 376–377, 379
Reddy, R., *462*
reductio ad absurdum, 229
referential ambiguity, 437
refinement strategies (in resolution), 236–237
refutation complete resolution, 234, 257
region finding (in image processing), 97–101
regions, image, 88, 99–101
regressing a conjunction, 382–383
regression, 381
regression planning, 374
Reichardt, W., 111, *483*
reifying
  actions, 365
  beliefs, 411
  states, 364
Reilly, W. S., 450, 455, 458
Reiter, R., 310, 368, 370, 473, *483*
Reitman, W., 210, *483*
relation constants, 239–240, 262
relaxation method for solving linear equalities, 41
relaxed problem, 155–156
repair approach, 187
repair steps for Eight-Queens problem, 188
representative speech act, 422
representing action functions, 27–33
representing commonsense knowledge, 301–316
representing the environment by feature vectors, 71–73
reproduction, 59
Resnick, A., *456*

Resnick, M., 33, *484*
resolution
    on clauses, 231–232
    a new rule of inference, 231–232
    in predicate calculus, 253–268
    in propositional calculus, 231–238
    soundness of, 232, 257
    using to prove theorems, 260–261
resolution refutation, 233–235, 260–261
    completeness of, 233, 257
    ordering strategies, 235–236
    refinement strategies, 236–237
    search strategies, 235–237
    tree, 235
    used in EBG, 296
resolvent of two clauses, 231, 253
RETE algorithm, 275, 277
rewards instead of goals, 175–177
Rich, E., *484*
Richards, Charles, 93
ridge problem, 191
Ringuette, M., 11, *482*
Rissanen, J., 358, *484*
Rivest, R., 34, 80, 125, *459*, *484*
Robertie, Bill, 212
Roberts, Larry, 10, *484*
Roberts cross, 112
Robinson, G., 263, 265, *492*
Robinson, J. A., 260, *484*
robot vision, 85–113
Rohwer, R., 55, *484*
root node (graph), 124–125
Rosenberg, C., 14, 54, *486*
Rosenblatt, Frank, 9, 38, *484*
Rosenblitt, D., 385, 399, *475*
Rosenbloom, P., 275, *472*, *484*
Rosenschein, Stan, 7, 33, 450, *469*, *484*
Ross, S., 178, *484*
Roth, D., 297, *470*
Roussel, P., 297, *484*
Rubik's Cube, 160
Rubin, D., 346, *460*
rule arcs, 272
rule clause, 270
rule learning, 286–297
rule-based expert systems, 280–286
rules
    general vs. specific, 287
    implication, 237
rules of inference
    in predicate calculus, 247
    in propositional calculus, 220–221
    resolution, 231–232, 256–257

Rumelhart, D., 14, 41, 50, 123, *458*, *469*, 476, *484*
run-time conditional, 379–380
Russell, S., 11, 13, 15, 41, 178, 212, 332, 338, 351, 433, 440, 450, *463*, *484*

S

Sacerdoti, E., 393, 395, 399, *484*, *485*
Sadek, M., 425, *485*
Samuel, Arthur, 8, 175, 212, *485*
satisfiability of interpretations, 224
satisficing solutions, 160
satisfying interpretation of a wff, 224, 243
scene analysis, 89–91, 102–108
    general viewpoint, 104
    interpreting lines and curves, 103–106
    line-labeling, 104
    model-based vision, 106–108
scene discontinuities, 88–89
Schaeffer, Jonathan, 198, 212, *485*
Schapire, R., 80, *484*
schema, 118, 365, 375
Scherl, R., 371, *473*, *485*
Schoppers, M. J., 171, *485*
Schraudolph, N., 212, *485*
Schubert, L., 368, *485*
Schultz, W., 178, *486*
Schunck, B., 111, *469*
Schwartz, J., 270, *486*
scoring metric, 347–348
search algorithms, relationships among, 149
search efficiency
    of alpha-beta procedure, 207–208
    heuristic functions and, 155–160
search graphs and trees, 145
search in state spaces, 115–213
search strategies, resolution refutation, 235–237
search tree (AND/OR) for a proof, 284
searches
    alternative formulations, 181–193
    of explicit state spaces, 121–122
    heuristic, 139–162
    of network space (Bayes), 349
    uninformed, 129–138
Searle, John, 3, 4, 422, *486*
Seiver, A., *467*
Sejnowski, T., 14, 54, 110, 212, *458*, *478*, *485*, *486*
selective survival, 59
Selman, Bart, 227, 228, 230, 297, 298, 399, *465*, *470*, *486*
semantic analysis, 428–432

semantic attachment, 265
semantic networks, 309
   for default reasoning, 311
   nonmonotonic reasoning in, 309–312
semantic parse tree, 433
semantics (predicate calculus), 241, 246–247
semantics (propositional calculus), 219,
   222–226
semi–decidability, 270
sense/plan/act agents, 164–165
sense/plan/act architecture, 164–165
sense/plan/act cycle, 163–165
sensor model, 355
sensory filter, 79
sentence structure (grammars), 425, 428
sentences (grammars), 425
sentences (wffs). *See* wffs.
separate and conquer, 287
set of expressions, unifiable, 255
set of inference rules ($\mathcal{R}$), 226
set of negative literals (goal), 237
set of wffs (Δ, Γ), 221, 244
   inconsistent or unsatisfiable, 224, 244
   model of, 224, 243
set–of–support strategy, 236
Shachter, R., 339, *486*
Shafer, G., 339, *486*
Shafer, S., *489*
Shakey the Robot, 444–446
Shanahan, M., 370, 487
Shannon, Claude, 8, 487
Shapiro, E., 270, *488*
Shapiro, L., 3, *475*
Shapiro, S., 17, 471, 487
Shavlik, J., 55, 286, 487, *489*
Shaw, J. C., 8, 9, 155, 377, *479*, *480*
Shen, W–M., 398, 487
Shieber, S., 274, *482*
Shikano, K., *490*
Shirai, Y., 106, 487
Shoham, Yoav, 15, 161, 249, 274, 278, 298, 306,
   370, 400, 402, 417, 487
Shortliffe, E., 10, 285, 339, *457*, 487
short–term memory, 275
Shrobe, H., 17, 487
SIGART, 16
sigmoid function, 41–42
sigmoid units, k–layer network of, 46
signal processing, 4
Simon, Herbert, 4, 6, 8, 9, 14, 155, 377, *479*, *480*
Simonin, J., *485*
simulated annealing, 192
simulated databases, 410–411

simulating the environment (iconic model),
   12, 75, 409
simulation, 12
Singh, S., 178, *454*
SIPE system, 395, 400
situated automata, 7
situation calculus, 363–372
   difficulties, 367–369
   frame problem, 368
   generating plans, 369–370
   qualifications, 369
   ramifications, 369
Skolem, Thoralf, 258, 487
Skolem form of a set of formulas, 259
Skolem form of a wff, 259
Skolem function, 258
Slagle, J., 9, 207, 487, *488*
Slate, D., 207, 487
slot fillers, 312
slot names, 312
slots (attribute–value pairs), 312
Smith, D. E., 298, *488*
smoothing function, 92
smoothing operation, 92–93
smoothing with a Gaussian filter, 94, 96
Snow, Catherine, 405
SOAR formalism, 275
Sobel, Irwin, 97
Sobel operator, 97
social implications, 16
Soderland, S., 399, *488*
softbots, 11
sombrero function in Laplacian filtering,
   96–97
soundness
   of predicate–calculus resolution, 257
   of propositional calculus, 226–227, 232
Sowa, J., 313, *488*
space, representation of, 305
spanning trees, 125–126, 170–171
Sparck Jones, K., 440, *466*
spatial metaphors, 305
speaker and hearer, 421
specific rules vs. general rules, 287
speech acts, 421–425
   categories of, 422
   implementing, 423–425
   indirect, 422
   planning, 423
speech recognition, 54, 440
Spiegelhalter, D., 338, *472*
Spirtes, P., 349, *488*
split–and–merge method, 99–101
spreadline (as TMS and ATMS), 276–280

S-R agents, 21–35
Stallman, R., 136, *488*
standardizing variables apart, 256
Stanfill, C., 440, *488*
start island (hierarchical search), 167
start node, 119, 130
state descriptions, 130, 373–374
state machine memory, 71
state machines, 71–83
state spaces, 119, 363
    for constructive formulations, 184
    feature-based, 122–123
    formulating, 129–130
    implicit, 130
    search in, 115–213
    searching explicit, 121–122
states
    mapping a state–action pair, 367
    reifying, 364
state–space graph components (implicit),
    130–131
state–space graphs, 118–121
state–space vs. plan–space search, 386
static evaluation function, 198
statistical methods (grammars), 440
steering an automobile example, 86–88
Stefik, M., 177, 282, 298, *456*, *488*
Stentz, A., 177, *488*
stereo vision, 108–110
Sterling, L., 14, 270, *455*, *488*
Sternberg, J., 298, *479*
Stickel, M., 135, 265, 309, *488*
stimulus–response (S–R) agents, 21–35
Stone, C., 457
Stork, D., 53, 54, *461*
Strat, T., 111, *488*
STRIPS, 122, 373–385
    assumption, 375
    operator, 123, 375
    operator preconditions, 122, 375
    planner (in Shakey), 445
    planning systems, 373–385
    plans with run–time conditionals, 379–380
    recursive, 376–379
    rule, 375, 385, 423
strong AI, 17, 451
structural credit assignment problem, 177
structure of a sentence (grammars), 425, 428
subcategories and inheritance, 309
subgoal wffs, 381
Subrahmanian, V., 399, *462*
substitution instance of an expression, 254
substitution (s), 255
subsuming a clause, 233

subsumption architecture, 32–33
subsumption modules, 33
subsymbolic approaches to AI, 7
subsymbolic processing, 4
successor function, 131, 161
successor (of a graph node), 124
successors (children), 332
successor–state axiom, 370
sufficiency indices, 339
supercategories, and inheritance, 309
supernodes, 338
supervised learning process, 38
surface reflectivity, 102
Sussman, G., 136, 380, 381, *488*
Sussman anomaly, 380–381, 385
Sutton, R., 173, 174, 175, *489*
Swartout, W., 425, 477
syllogisms, 8
symbol grounding, 7
symbol level, 6
symbol strings (in communication), 423
symbol-processing approaches to AI, 6
symptoms and causes, 218
syntactic ambiguity, 437
syntactic analysis (grammars), 428
systematic nonlinear planning (SNLP), 385

T

tabula rasa systems, 13
Tarski, A., 250, *489*
Tarskian semantics, 250
task-oriented (purposive) vision, 103
Tate, A., 385, 395, 399, 400, *454*, *459*, *489*
taxonomic hierarchies, 308–309
taxonomic knowledge, 308–309
Taylor, L., 160, *471*
TD-GAMMON network, 210–212
TEAM system, 440
teleo-reactive (T–R) programs, 28, 398, 445,
    447
Teller, A., 69, *489*
temporal credit assignment problem, 177
temporal difference learning, 174, 210
temporal logics, 249, 306
Tenenberg, J., 399, 450, *489*, *491*
terminal symbols (grammars), 425
terminological logics, 297, 312
terms (in Boolean functions), 26
terms (in predicate calculus), 240
Tesauro, G., 210, *489*
texels, 101
theorem (in logic), 221
theorem proving, 234, 260–261

Theraulaz, G., 408, *489*
things, kinds of, 308
thinking, 2, 4
Thomas, A., 347, *459*
Thorpe, C., 110, *489*
threat arcs in plan-structure graphs, 391–392
three-level architectures, 444–446
3SAT problem, 227–228
threshold logic units (TLUs), 29–30, 38–44
threshold weight, 39
Tic-Tac-Toe, 199–203
tight spaces, 21, 72, 251
time, 249, 306
time intervals
    describing, 306–307
    that meet, 307
time points, 306
tip nodes (graph), 124–125
TISA units, 31–32
TLU geometry, 38–39
TLUs, 29–30, 38–44
top-down algorithms (grammars), 428
top-down design, 6
top-down research, 14
Torrance, M., *465*
tournament selection process, 63
Towell, G., 286, *489*
Tower-of-Hanoi puzzle, 81, 127, 372, 400
toy agents, 11
toy problems, 9–10
T-R programs, 28, 398, 445, 447
tractability/expressibility tradeoff, 297
tractable computations, 15, 237, 269, 297
Tracy, K., *490*
training set, 37, 44, 53, 286, 291
Trappl, R., 16, *490*
tree notation, 125
Treloar, N., *485*
triangle tables, 396–398, 445
triangulation in stereo vision, 108–109
trihedral vertex polyhedra, 103, 105
triple-tower architecture, 448–449
tropisms, 34
tropistic agents, 34
True or *False* atoms, 222–223
truth maintenance systems (TMSs), 276, 298
truth table
    propositional, 223–224
    rules, 223
Tuck, C., *472*
Turing, Alan, 2, 4, 5, 9, *490*
Turing test, 2, 4–5, 14
Tversky, A., 339, *490*
TWEAK system, 399

Twenty-four puzzle, 160
two-agent games, 195–197
two-agent perfect-information zero-sum
    games, 196
two-color problem, 191
2SAT problem, 227
typewriter font (in this book), 219, 242
Tyson, M., 135, *488*

U

UCPOP, 399
Ullman, J. D., 274, 297, *490*
uncertain evidence, 329–330
uncertain information, 317–342
unconditional independence, 325
undirected graphs, 124
undirected path, 330
undirected tree (graph), 124
Unger, S., 34, *490*
unifiable set of expressions, 255
unification, 253–256
unification grammars, 435
unifier of a set of expressions, 255
uniform-cost search, 133, 149, 158
UNIFY algorithm, 255–256
uninformed search, 129–138
unit clause, 236
unit-preference strategy, 236
universal instantiation (UI), 247
universal plan, 171
universal quantifier (∀), 245–247
unsatisfiable wffs, 224, 232, 244, 251
useful equivalences, 229, 247
utility of learned rules, 297
utility theory in animal models, 15
utterance, 422

V

valid wff, 224–225, 243, 251
validation set, 53
value iteration, 176–177
van Gelder, T., 7, *482*
Vardi, M., *462*
variable
    Boolean, 25
    conditionally independent, 324–325
    quantified over, 246
    random, 317
    standardized apart, 256
variable symbol, 245
Vazirani, U., 38, *470*
Vecchi, M., 192, *470*

vector labels (or classes), 37
Veloso, M., *458*
Venn, John, 321, *490*
Venn diagrams, 321–322
verb phrase (VP), 426, 431
vertical architecture, 32
Vina, A., *467*
virus (E6 Bacteriophage), 2–3
vision, robot, 85–113
visual processing stages, 89
visual texture, 101–102
vivid representations, 297

W

Waibel, A., 54, 440, *490*
Waldinger, R., 265, 399, 474, *490*
WALKSAT, 228, 399
wall–following robot, 21, 60–68
Walter, Grey, 21, *490*
Waltz, D., 105, 440, *475*, *488*, *490*
Wang, X., 398, *458*, *490*
Ward, Artemus, 215
Warren, D., 297, 440, *482*, *490*
Washington, R., *467*
wasp problem, 82
water–jug puzzle, 137
Wattenberg, M., 192, *469*
weak AI, 17, 451
Webber, B., 440, *466*
Wefald, E., 13, 15, 178, 212, 450, *484*
Wegman, M., 256, *481*
weight changes, computing in a layered
        neural net, 48–50
weight space, 40
weighted samples (Bayes nets), 346
Weiss, S., 55, *490*
Weizenbaum, Joseph, 5, 16, *491*
Weld, D., 11, 305, 399, 408, 462, *481*, *488*, *491*
well–formed formulas (wffs), 220, 241, 246
Wellman, Michael, 15, 339, 351, 369, 399, *460*,
        491
Werbos, P., 41, *491*
Wesley, L., *491*
Weyhrauch, R., 265, *491*
wffs, 220, 241, 246
    clauses as, 231, 253

closed, 246
equivalent, 225, 244
inconsistent or unsatisfiable, 224, 244
interpretation that satisfies, 224, 243
model of, 224, 243
model of a set of, 224
in prenex form, 259
within the scope of a quantifier, 246
Skolem form of, 259
validity of, 224–225, 243
White, T. H., 115
Whitehead, S., 450, *491*
Widrow, B., 9, 38, *491*
Widrow–Hoff procedure, 41
Widrow–Hoff vs. generalized Delta, 42
Wiener, N., 9, *491*
Wiesel, T., 110, *469*
Wilcox, B., 210, *483*
Wilkins, D. E., 395, 399, 400, 450, *491*
Williams, R. J., *484*
Wilson, S., 7, *491*
Winker, S., 265, *492*
Winograd, T., 2, 10, *492*
wise–man puzzle, 415–418
Wonham, M., 399, *483*
Woods, W., 10, 440, *492*
Wooldridge, D., *492*
working (short–term) memory, 275
worlds (in predicate calculus), 241–242
worst–case results, 15
Wos, Larry, 263, 265, *492*
Wu, Y., 102, *492*

Y

Yager, E., *472*
Yang, Q., 177, *454*
Yung, M., 189, *453*

Z

Zadeh, L., 339, *492*
zero–crossings, 94, 96–97
0–th level resolvents, 236
Zhu, S. C., 102, *492*
Zobrist, A., 210, *492*
Zweben, M., 399, *492*